GUIDE TO RECORDINGS

		Text Page	Unit I CD	6-CD Set	Full Downloads	Brief Downloads
Global Perspectives	Balinese gamelan, *Bopong*	201	---	3:35	108	---
Beethoven	Symphony No. 5 in C Minor, Op. 67, I	209	---	3:1–9	45	17
Beethoven	Symphony No. 5, II	209	---	3:10–11	46	18
Beethoven	Symphony No. 5, III	209	---	3:12–13	47	19
Beethoven	Symphony No. 5, IV	209	---	3:14–15	48	20
Beethoven	Piano Sonata in E, Op. 109, I	216	---	2:42–45	49	---
Schubert	"Erlkönig"	234	---	3:16	50	21
R. Schumann	*Dichterliebe*, "Im wunderschönen Monat Mai"	238	---	3:17	51	22
R. Schumann	*Dichterliebe*, "Die alten, bösen Lieder"	238	---	3:18	52	---
C. Schumann	"Der Mond kommt still gegangen"	241	---	3:19	53	23
Schubert	Moment Musical No. 2 in A-flat	243	---	3:20–23	54	---
R. Schumann	*Carnaval*, "Eusebius"	244	---	3:24	55	24
R. Schumann	*Carnaval*, "Florestan"	244	---	3:25	56	25
Chopin	Nocturne in F-sharp, Op. 15, No. 2	245	---	3:26	57	26
Berlioz	*Fantastic* Symphony, V	249	---	3:27–33	58	27
Verdi	*Rigoletto*, from Act III, "La donna è mobile" and "Bella figlia dell'amore"	259	---	4:1–6	59–60	28–29
Wagner	*The Valkyrie*, Act I, scene i	269	---	4:7–12	61	30
Puccini	*Madame Butterfly*, from Act II, "Un bel dì"	275	---	4:13	62	31
Tchaikovsky	Overture-Fantasy, *Romeo and Juliet*	279	---	4:14–25	63	32
Musorgsky	*Pictures at an Exhibition*, "Promenade [1]"	284	---	4:26	64	33
Musorgsky	*Pictures at an Exhibition*, "Gnomus"	284	---	4:27	65	---
Musorgsky	*Pictures at an Exhibition*, "Promenade [2]"	284	---	4:28	66	---
Musorgsky	*Pictures at an Exhibition*, "The Great Gate at Kiev"	284	---	4:29	67	34
Brahms	Violin Concerto in D, Op. 77, III	289	---	4:30–35	68	---
Mahler	Symphony No. 1, III (Funeral March)	293	---	4:36–43	69	35
Global Perspectives	Beijing opera, *The Prince Who Changed into a Cat*	299	---	4:44	109	---
Debussy	*Clouds*, from Three Nocturnes	313	---	5:1–6	70	36
Stravinsky	*The Rite of Spring*, from Part I, "The Adoration of the Earth"	317	---	5:7–13	71	37
Schoenberg	*Pierrot lunaire*, No. 8, "Night"	321	---	5:14	72	---
Schoenberg	*Pierrot lunaire*, No. 18, "The Moonfleck"	321	---	5:15	73	38
Berg	*Wozzeck*, Act III, scenes iii and iv	324	---	5:16–20	74–75	---
Ives	Second Orchestral Set, II, "The Rockstrewn Hills Join in the People's Outdoor Meeting"	331	---	5:21–22	76	39
Ravel	Piano Concerto in G, I	337	---	5:23–27	77	---
Bartók	Music for Strings, Percussion, and Celesta, II	341	---	5:28–34	78	---
Crawford	Prelude for Piano No. 6 (Andante Mystico)	345	---	5:35	79	---
Still	*Afro-American* Symphony, IV	348	---	5:36–40	80	---
Copland	*Appalachian Spring*, Sections 1, 2, and 5	350	---	5:41–43	81–83	40–42
Copland	*Appalachian Spring*, Section 6	350	---	5:44	84	---
Prokofiev	*Alexander Nevsky* Cantata, "The Battle on Ice" (excerpts)	354	---	6:1–2	85–86	---
Webern	Five Orchestral Pieces, IV	362	---	6:3	87	43
Varèse	*Poème électronique* (excerpt)	364	---	6:4	88	---
Ligeti	*Lux aeterna*	366	---	6:5–8	89	---
Reich	*Music for 18 Musicians* (excerpt)	369	---	6:9–10	90–91	44–45
Crumb	*Voices from a Forgotten World* (*American Songbook*, Volume 5), "The House of the Rising Sun" and "Hallelujah, I'm a Bum!"	374	---	6:11–12	92–93	---
León	*Indígena*	375	---	6:13–16	94	---
Thomas	"If You Ever Been Down" Blues	387	---	6:17	95	46
Ellington/Tizol	"Conga Brava"	391	---	6:18	96	47
Parker and Davis	"Out of Nowhere"	395	---	6:19	97	48
Davis	*Bitches Brew* (excerpt)	396	---	6:20	98	---
Global Perspectives	Yoruba drumming, "Ako"	397	---	6:23	110	51
Bernstein	*West Side Story*, Cha-cha, meeting scene, and "Cool"	399	---	6:21–22	99–100	---
Global Perspectives	South African popular song, "Anoku Gonda"	411	---	6:24	111	---

LISTEN

Eighth
EDITION

JOSEPH KERMAN
University of California, Berkeley

GARY TOMLINSON
Yale University

with
VIVIAN KERMAN

BEDFORD / ST. MARTIN'S
Boston ◆ New York

For Bedford/St. Martin's

Vice President, Editorial, Macmillan Higher Education Humanities: Edwin Hill
Editorial Director for English and Music: Karen Henry
Senior Developmental Editor: Caroline Thompson
Senior Production Editor: Deborah Baker
Senior Production Supervisor: Jennifer Wetzel
Executive Marketing Manager: Sandi McGuire
Editorial Assistant: Brenna Cleeland
Copy Editor: Barbara Jatkola
Indexer: Leoni McVey
Photo Researcher: Susan Doheny
Director of Rights and Permissions: Hilary Newman
Senior Art Director: Anna Palchik
Text Design: Marsha Cohen
Cover Design: William Boardman
Cover Art: Dance 2, 2000 (oil on board), Bayo Iribhogbe. Private Collection/Bridgeman Images.
Composition: CodeMantra
Printing and Binding: RR Donnelley

Manufactured in the United States of America.
9 8 7 6 5 4
f e d c b a

For information, write: Bedford/St. Martin's, 75 Arlington Street, Boston, MA 02116   (617-399-4000)

ISBN: 978-1-4576-6985-9
ISBN: 978-1-4576-9698-5 (loose-leaf edition)

TO THE MEMORY OF
Joseph and Vivian Kerman

About the Authors

Joseph Kerman was a leading musicologist, music critic, and music educator from the 1950s into the 2000s. He conceived *Listen* together with his wife, Vivian Kerman, and was its original author. From his first book, *Opera as Drama* (1956), to his last, *Opera and the Morbidity of Music* (2008), including studies of Bach, Beethoven, William Byrd, concertos, and more, Kerman reshaped our understanding and appreciation of Western classical music. He was long a professor at the University of California, Berkeley, where he served two terms as chair of the Music Department.

Gary Tomlinson did the same at the University of Pennsylvania before he moved to Yale University in 2011, where he is now the John Hay Whitney Professor and Director of the Whitney Humanities Center. A former MacArthur Fellow, he has authored books on Claudio Monteverdi, Renaissance musical culture, opera, and the singing rituals of the Aztecs and Incas. His latest book, *A Million Years of Music*, describes the evolutionary emergence of music.

Teaching was the heart and soul of Kerman's musical career, and it remains such in Tomlinson's. Between them, their wide-ranging course offerings have encompassed harmony and ear-training, opera, world music, popular music, interdisciplinary studies, seminars in music history, criticism, anthropology, and — many times over — Introduction to Music for non-majors.

Tomlinson and Kerman worked together on five editions of *Listen*. Joseph Kerman died early in 2014, just shy of his ninetieth birthday, as this edition went to press.

Brief Contents

⊙ Music for the Listening Exercises is on the Unit I CD bound into this book
▤ and in LaunchPad for *Listen* at **macmillanhighered.com/listen8e**.
Interactive versions of the Listening Charts can also be found in LaunchPad.
See the inside back cover for details.

■ Listening Exercises

■ Listening Charts

Contents

UNIT I

Fundamentals / 2

CHAPTER 8

The Early Baroque Period 79

CHAPTER 11 Baroque Vocal Music 135

CHAPTER 12 Music and the Enlightenment 150

PRELUDE

UNIT
IV

The Nineteenth Century / 202

CHAPTER 15

Beethoven   204

CHAPTER 16

PRELUDE

Music after Beethoven: Romanticism   218

CHAPTER 17

The Early Romantics   233

CHAPTER 18

Romantic Opera   256

UNIT
V

The Twentieth Century and Beyond / 300

CHAPTER 23

The Late Twentieth Century 358

CHAPTER 24 Music in America: Jazz and Beyond 381

Preface
To the Instructor

When Joseph and Vivian Kerman launched the first edition of *Listen* back in 1972, they no doubt hoped—but could not have expected—that it would still be reaching students over forty years later. The staying power of the book is a tribute to many things and many people, but above all it commemorates their initial vision and their continued efforts across several decades in revising and improving it. Joe himself came to regard *Listen* as far and away the most important contribution of his career, a judgment that sets a high bar, given *Opera as Drama*, *The Beethoven Quartets*, *Contemplating Music*, and the rest. But who would gainsay that judgment, in the light of the hundreds of thousands of undergraduates whose lives have been touched and even transformed in courses employing *Listen*?

The Kermans' vision was at first almost unique: to focus the attention of non-major undergraduates on close, analytic listening to great music at the same time as they came to understand its place in a historical chronology of styles and in a broader story of Western culture. *Listen* fulfills this vision in a fashion still unsurpassed, and we continue to revise and improve the book in ways that respond to the changing landscape of teaching introductory courses to the Western musical tradition.

New to This Edition

The changes in *Listen*, Eighth Edition, answer to the desires, viewpoints, and indeed criticisms we have solicited from users and non-users alike. Particularly important have been users' views on the teaching effectiveness of individual works. Of course we have retained the basic elements that have always distinguished *Listen*: the stimulating prose, the high-quality recordings, the unmatched Listening Charts, the clear laying-out of musical basics in Unit I, and the broad context outlined in Prelude chapters for each new historical phase. To these we have added new features, new repertory, and a clean, updated new design.

New Features

Each historical unit begins with an arresting two-page spread designed to orient the student quickly and effectively. On the left is a very short description of the materials introduced in the unit, on the right a time line of the works students will encounter, tabulating composers' names, titles of works, and chronological order of composition. In between is an artwork characteristic of the period at hand, with a caption explaining what makes it so.

Each chapter ends with a new bullet list of Goals for Review: checklists of the listening skills and key concepts students should particularly attend to as they study.

New Repertory

As in every new edition, we have sought to improve the coverage of the musical repertories at the heart of our enterprise. We have added a movement from Vivaldi's *The Four Seasons*, always a favorite with students and teachers alike. The coverage of the Classical symphony now exemplifies variations, rondo, and minuet forms with movements from three of Haydn's *London* symphonies. A Beethoven piano sonata movement shows features of his late style.

For the twentieth and twenty-first centuries, the rethinking has been extensive. For the early part of the period, the coverage of modernism is more inclusive and varied, with the addition of new works by Ruth Crawford and William Grant Still. For the most recent years, *Listen* adds new selections by Tania León, George Crumb, and John Adams.

All told, the new works are as follows:

- Vivaldi, Violin Concerto in E, *La Primavera* (Spring), Op. 8, No. 1, I (Allegro)
- Haydn, Symphony No. 94 in G ("The Surprise"), II (Andante)
- Haydn, Symphony No. 99 in E-flat, III (Allegretto)
- Haydn, Symphony No. 101 in D ("The Clock"), IV (Finale. Vivace)
- Beethoven, Piano Sonata in E, Op. 109, I (Vivace)
- Ruth Crawford, Prelude for Piano No. 6 (Andante Mystico)
- William Grant Still, *Afro-American* Symphony, IV (Lento, con risoluzione)
- George Crumb, "The House of the Rising Sun" and "Hallelujah, I'm a Bum!" from *Voices from a Forgotten World* (*American Songbook*, Volume 5)
- Tania Léon, *Indígena*
- John Adams, *Doctor Atomic*

New Design

The publishers of *Listen*, no less than the authors, have always worked hard to make this textbook attractive to look at; we all take pride in the book's design and appearance. But the real point of a good design is to make it both easy and inviting to find your way around in a book. Of necessity there is a lot of diverse material here, lots of bits and pieces—the main text, boxes and charts of different kinds, music, marginalia. The new design introduced in this edition enhances the flow of the text and emphasizes important information to make student reading a more effective learning experience. In general, the design gives a clean, updated "look."

Students these days, perhaps more than ever before, are used to getting information quickly and clearly. *Listen*, Eighth Edition makes this possible without sacrificing the nuance of subject matter and presentation for which the book has always been praised.

New Formats

Listen has always moved forward with new technological developments that are essential to the teaching of music appreciation. For this edition, we offer the full and brief sets of the *Listen* recordings in a convenient downloadable format; the full set is also available on six high-quality CDs. Streaming recordings and an interactive e-book are available in LaunchPad, a new, fully customizable course space. See page xxvii for details.

Distinctive Features of *Listen*

In the midst of many changes, what have not changed are our basic coverage and organization, which have proved solid over many editions. For new users, we draw attention to the following strong features that we believe set *Listen* apart.

Fundamentals

The Fundamentals unit develops basic musical concepts in a logical, orderly sequence. It begins with rhythm and meter and continues with pitch, dynamics, and tone color, pausing to consider the musical instruments students will be listening to. Next comes melody, and only then are the more challenging issues of harmony, tonality, and modality raised. The introduction to music notation, not necessary for this unit or the book as a whole, is found in an appendix. This presentation, we feel, allows instructors to pick and choose issues they want to highlight more easily without losing the logic of the presentation.

Eight Listening Exercises that work with music on the Unit I CD (bound into the back of the book) illustrate rhythm, melody, texture, modality, and so on, and culminate in the encyclopedic *Young Person's Guide to the Orchestra* by Benjamin Britten. We show students how to listen to this work as an informal summary of fundamentals at the end of the unit.

Flexible Coverage

The main emphasis of *Listen* is on the common-practice repertory, with a careful selection of more modern material and a generous unit on pre-eighteenth-century music. After Unit I, the historical scheme goes from "early music"—in effect, everything before Bach and Handel, when the standard repertory begins—to the three great periods of Western classical music: the eighteenth and nineteenth centuries, and the twentieth century to the present. Units III, IV, and V, each containing several chapters, cover these periods. Unit II, "Early Music: An Overview," is independent of the rest of the text; nothing later in the book depends on having studied it, so if your course plan begins with Bach and Handel in Unit III, students will not need to skip back for explanations of continuo texture, recitative, fugue, and so on.

Cultural Background

The Baroque and Classical eras and the nineteenth and twentieth centuries are introduced by what we call "Prelude" chapters. Each summarizes features of the culture of the time, emphasizing those that stand in close relation to music. The Prelude chapters also contain concise accounts of the musical styles of the eras, so that these chapters furnish background of two kinds—cultural and stylistic—for listening to specific pieces of music in the chapters that follow.

Biography boxes segregate material on the lives of the major composers from discussions of their music—again, making the book easier to read and easier to work from. The boxes include portraits, concise lists of works that can serve for study or reference, and, under the heading "Encore," suggestions for further listening. Time lines in Appendix A locate composers at a glance in relation to other important historical figures and events.

Non-Western Music

The seven Global Perspectives segments of *Listen* are positioned so as to elaborate on the European and American topics discussed around them. The Global Perspectives segment on sacred chant, for example, comes at the end of the Middle Ages chapter, where Gregorian chant has been discussed; African ostinato forms are exemplified after the early Baroque chapter; and a brief look at complex instrumental forms in Japanese and Indonesian traditions follows the eighteenth-century unit, with its examination of sonata form and other formal types in the Classical symphony.

We believe these materials broaden the coverage of *Listen* in a meaningful way, but we certainly do not offer them as a token survey of world musics. If they are a token of anything, it is the authors' belief that music making worldwide shows certain common tendencies in which the European classical tradition has shared.

Listening Charts

One of the strongest features of *Listen*, instructors have always told us, is the format for Listening Charts. The charts for instrumental works all fit onto one page, visible at a glance, with concise descriptions and identifications. Off at the side, brief music tags can easily be consulted by those who read music—and just as easily ignored by those who don't. To see how these charts work, turn to the section "How to Use This Book" on pages xxxiv–xxxvii. Interactive versions of the Listening Charts can be found in LaunchPad for *Listen* at **macmillanhighered.com/listen8e**. Guides for songs, operas, and other vocal works offer texts in original languages and parallel translations; they are set in "Listen" boxes throughout the book.

In the end, this text owes its success less to "features" than to two basic attributes, which the authors have been grateful to hear about many times from many instructors over the history of the book. *Listen* is distinctive in its writing style and, related to that, in the sense it conveys of personal involvement with the music that is treated. The tone is lively and alert, authoritative but not stiff and not without humor. We sound (because we are) engaged with music and we work to engage the student.

The excitement and joy that the experience of music can provide—this, more than historical or analytical data about music—is what most instructors want to pass on to their students. Our efforts are rewarded when students tell us years later that music they studied has become a part of their lives. This is what teaching is about (which is why technology will never replace live instructors), and this is what we have always tried to do in *Listen*.

Acknowledgments

We express our gratitude to the many practiced "music appreesh" instructors who have reviewed this book and its supplements and given us the benefit of their advice for this revision. Their criticisms and suggestions have significantly improved the text, as have the market surveys in which an even larger number of instructors generously participated. In addition to users of previous editions who over the years have given us suggestions, we wish to thank

Lois Ash, Delaware State University; Jeanne Belfy, Boise State University; Roxanne Classen, MacEwan University; Cathryn Clayton, University of Utah; Bruce Cook, Diablo Valley College; Lara Saville Dahl, Georgia State University; Chris Davis, North Greenville University; Melissa Derechailo, Wayne State College; Leanne Dodge, Columbia University; Jennifer Duerden, Brigham Young University–Hawaii; Tracey Ford, Joliet Junior College; Janine Gaboury, Michigan State University; Gary Gackstatter, St. Louis Community College–Meramec; Scott Gleason, Fordham University; John Glennon, Ivy Tech Community College; David Gramit, University of Alberta; Rolf Groesbeck, University of Arkansas at Little Rock; Ross Hagen, Utah Valley University; Barry Hause, East Central Community College; Sharon A. Hickox, University of Nevada, Reno; Todd Jones, University of Kentucky; Karl Kolbeck, Wayne State College; Julianne Lindberg, University of Nevada, Reno; Robin Liston, Baker University; John McClusky, University of Kentucky; Ginny Nixon, Concordia University; Matthew Parker, Trident Technical College; Todd Quinlan, Blinn College; Katie Roberts, Brigham Young University; Catherine Roche-Wallace, University of Louisiana, Lafayette; Ruth Spencer, City College of New York; George Sprengelmeyer, Quinnipiac University; Yiorgos Vassilandonakis, College of Charleston; and Steven Voigt, James Madison University.

The production of a major textbook is a complex, year-long process drawing on professionals from many areas. The main contributors to *Listen* are listed on the back of the title page, and we are truly grateful to all of them. Our first, special thanks go to the team that has worked in the trenches with the authors to turn this book and its ancillaries into realities and make them better in countless ways. Senior Editor Caroline Thompson, Senior Production Editor Deborah Baker, Art Director Anna Palchik, Designer Marsha Cohen, Editorial Assistant Brenna Cleeland, and picture and permissions consultants Martha Friedman, Kalina Ingham, Susan Doheny, and Margaret Gorenstein—the project would have been unmanageable without the expertise and hard work of all of them. Carrie Thompson's efforts in particular often assumed larger-than-life, even operatic proportions. Tom Laskey of Sony Music, responsible for recordings acquisitions and production, kept his head through the conniptions of the recording industry (even while authors around him did not). The cover was designed by Billy Boardman. Karen Henry, Editorial Director for English and Music, is a longtime supporter of and coworker on *Listen*; Edwin Hill, Vice President, Editorial, is a new and welcome supporter of the project.

We are delighted that Professor Mark Harbold has again undertaken the *Instructor's Resource Manual* for the present edition, and we are grateful and fortunate indeed that Davitt Moroney agreed to perform a work specially for the CD set: He recorded the Frescobaldi Canzona, Balletto, and Corrente on the seventeenth-century Spanish organ by Greg Harrold at the University of California, Berkeley, in meantone tuning.

The high quality of *Listen* is a tribute to the expertise, dedication, tenacity, and artistry of all of these people. We are indebted to them all.

G. T.
(for J. K. also)
Branford, CT, July 2014

Resources for *Listen,* Eighth Edition

Bedford/St. Martin's offers resources and format choices that help you and your students get the most out of your book and course. To learn more about or to order any of the following products, contact your Macmillan sales representative, e-mail sales support (sales_support@bfwpub.com), or visit the Web site at **macmillanhighered.com/catalog/listen**.

LaunchPad for *Listen,* Eighth Edition: Where Students Learn

LaunchPad provides engaging content and new ways to enhance your course. Get an **interactive e-book** combined with **unique, book-specific materials** in a fully customizable course space; then assign and mix our resources with yours.

- **The complete *Listen* recordings** are included in LaunchPad in a streaming format, integrated with the e-book. LaunchPad makes all of the music for the course available in one place, so there's no need to purchase discs or downloads. Music for the Listening Exercises in Unit I is included in addition to all the recordings from the 6-CD set.

- **Interactive Listening Charts** provide the book's 29 Listening Charts in a multimedia format, making it even easier for students to listen as they read the brief explanatory notes. Students can play back main sections of the charts with a single mouse click in order to study and compare specific events in the music.

- **Pre-built units**—including chapter text, streaming music, listening quizzes, reading quizzes, and more—are **easy to adapt and assign** by adding your own materials and mixing them with our high-quality multimedia content and ready-made assessment options.

- LaunchPad also provides access to a **gradebook** that provides a clear window on the performance of your whole class, individual students, and even individual assignments.

- A **streamlined interface** helps students focus on what's due, and social commenting tools let them **engage**, make connections, and learn from each other. Use LaunchPad on its own or integrate it with your school's learning management system so that your class is always on the same page.

To get the most out of your course, order LaunchPad for *Listen* packaged with the print book for a reasonable additional charge. (LaunchPad for *Listen* can also be purchased on its own.) An activation code is required.

- To order LaunchPad for *Listen* on its own, use ISBN 978-1-4576-9894-1.

- To order LaunchPad for *Listen* packaged with the paperback edition, use ISBN 978-1-319-02398-0.

- To order LaunchPad for *Listen* packaged with the loose-leaf edition, use ISBN 978-1-319-02400-0.

Select Value Packages

Add value to your text by packaging one of the following resources with *Listen,* Eighth Edition. To learn more about package options for any of the following products, contact your Macmillan sales representative or visit **macmillanhighered.com/catalog/listen**.

The 6-CD set for *Listen* includes all of the recordings discussed in the text in a high-quality format that students can keep. To order the 6-CD set packaged with the paperback text, use ISBN 978-1-319-02397-3.

Access cards for music downloads make the *Listen* recordings available in a less expensive digital format that's easy for students to load onto their iPods and other devices. Choose the full set of downloads, which includes all of the music from the 6-CD set, or the brief set of downloads, a selection of core listening that replaces the former 3-CD set.

- To order the full set of downloads packaged with the paperback text, use ISBN 978-1-319-02402-4.

- To order the brief set of downloads packaged with the paperback text, use ISBN 978-1-319-02404-8.

Save Money with the Loose-Leaf Edition of *Listen*

The loose-leaf edition does not have a traditional binding; its pages are loose and three-hole punched to provide flexibility and a low price to students. To order the loose-leaf edition on its own, use ISBN 1-4576-9698-3 or 978-1-4576-9698-5. To package the loose-leaf edition with CDs or downloads, visit **macmillanhighered .com/catalog/listen** or contact your Macmillan sales representative.

Instructor Resources

macmillanhighered.com/catalog/listen
You have a lot to do in your course. Bedford/St. Martin's wants to make it easy for you to find the support you need—and to get it quickly. All of the following resources are available for download from the Bedford/St. Martin's online catalog at the URL above.

The Instructor's Resource Manual, prepared by Mark Harbold of Elmhurst College, is the most comprehensive teaching guide to accompany any music appreciation textbook. In addition to chapter overviews and suggested teaching objectives, the instructor's manual includes detailed suggestions for lectures, demonstrations, class discussions, and further listening. The manual is provided as a PDF file.

Additional Listening Charts and **Additional Texts and Translations** make it easy to add works not discussed in this edition of *Listen* to your course.

The Index of Terms and Musical Examples suggests examples from the *Listen* recordings to illustrate key terms and concepts from the book.

PowerPoint Presentations outline the main points of each chapter and contain selected visuals from the book. You can download, edit, and customize the slides to create your own presentations.

The Test Bank contains more than 1,800 multiple choice and essay questions designed to assess students' comprehension and listening skills. The Test Bank is available for download in Microsoft Word format or in a computerized test bank format that offers additional editing and customization features. Answer keys are included.

DVDs of complete performances of works discussed in this edition are available to qualified adopters. For information, contact your Macmillan sales representative.

Introduction
To the Student

Music matters to us. It may not carry us through our moment-to-moment interactions with one another, the way language does, or frame our ideas in words. It may not carry us from one place to another, refrigerate and cook our food, or enable us to search the Internet, as our advanced technologies do. It may even be less important to our immediate comfort, as an old joke has it, than indoor plumbing. Yet it *matters* to us, and matters deeply.

Every reader of this book comes to it having grown up surrounded by music of one type or another—usually, these days, of many types. Most readers have counted musical experiences among the important formative moments of their lives. And in fact it is hard for us to think of major events without music: a ceremony, a parade, a holiday, a party. Music saturates human societies—all of them, without exception.

Perhaps you have wondered just *why* music matters so much. If so, you're not alone. Philosophers, psychologists, musicologists, and many others have been asking the same question in a line stretching all the way back to Plato, 2,500 years ago, and probably farther than that. The answers are not easy to come by, but in general they involve the ways in which music seizes us, commands our attention, changes our outlook, arouses our emotions, even transforms us—in short, the ways music *moves* us.

Music in ceremony: The University of Maryland band marches in the presidential inauguration. *Katherine Frey/The Washington Post via Getty Images.*

It is the basic premise of this book that these experiences can be deepened by careful study devoted to the music at hand. We can extend music's transformative powers by thinking about how it is put together, how it relates to other music and other arts, and when and where it was made, and then, above all, by taking this knowledge and *listening* carefully again and again. We did not choose our title, after all, by accident: *Listen!*

Classical Music — and Other Kinds

Listen cannot survey all types of music; to do so would require not one book but very many indeed. The particular tradition of music to which we devote our attention is what has come to be known as *classical music;* but this term, if it is unavoidable, is also vague and in need of some preliminary explanation.

Classical or *classic* is ordinarily used to describe something old and established, and valued on that account. Think of the classical antiquity of Greece and Rome, classic literature, classic movies, or classic rock from the 1960s and 1970s. *Classical music,* in the way we use the term, refers to a tradition extending over more than a thousand years, practiced mainly (until recently) in Europe, and cultivated especially by privileged levels of society. Sometimes this tradition goes under other names: Western music, music of the Western tradition, or even simply art music—though this should not be taken to imply that other kinds of music are not art.

The *classical* in classical music has come to contrast this tradition with another kind of music, *popular music,* especially the multiple branches of popular music that evolved across the twentieth century from African American roots. This development, which embraces everything from spirituals to jazz and the blues, from ragtime to hip-hop, and from Elvis and the Beatles to Beyoncé and the latest winner of *The Voice,* has been so important in recent decades that it has threatened to cast classical music completely into the shadows. It is not the central focus of *Listen,* but it is a major force in music, and we take stock of it in a chapter at the end of the book.

We also take up other kinds of music for comparison. All through this book we make sidelong glances toward musical traditions from around the world, from outside the Western classical heritage: Chinese, Native American, African, and more. The Global Perspectives inserts in which these non-Western traditions are raised do not attempt to do justice to the great richness of these traditions. Instead, they aim to point up broad similarities between them and Western traditions—similarities of musical technique or of the social uses of music, or sometimes of both together.

Classical Music and History

The classical tradition, as we said above, has extended over a thousand years. Across this long span of time, the tradition has evolved and been transformed many times over; but it has also endured. It has provided many, many generations of listeners with pleasure, joy, inspiration, and solace, and it can do the same for us.

It is also true, however, that the classical music most performed and listened to today comes from a period of European history shorter than a millennium. It stems especially from the eighteenth and nineteenth centuries, the period from around 1700 to 1900, beginning with Vivaldi, Bach, and Handel, including Haydn, Mozart, and Beethoven, and concluding with Mahler, Debussy, and Stravinsky. This central historical period of classical music, together with its outgrowths across the twentieth century and into our own time, forms the main coverage of *Listen*. This coverage is a historical one in that it is arranged in chronological order, with careful attention paid to the sequence of musical styles and to the influence of each on successive ones.

At the same time, we do not ignore the earlier centuries of the millennium of classical music. These, from about 1000 C.E. up to 1700 C.E., have a unit of their own, which your instructor might or might not choose to emphasize. This so-called early music is also presented in historical sequence.

Throughout all this historical coverage, we have endeavored to choose the most moving, transformative, and enduring—to use those three words once more—individual works for you to study and listen to. Your listening will, we hope, be entertaining; but it will also be something deeper than entertainment. These musical works provide knowledge—or if not exactly knowledge, insight into the human experience as it extends over time. Music historians devote themselves not only to the appreciation of music from the past but also to an appreciation of the ways in which it captures experiences of past lives. It conveys these things in ways that are distinctly musical—different from the ways of a poem, a novel, a painting, or a statue.

Listening

The different ways music captures experiences bring us back once more to listening. Listening to recordings is the crucial assignment necessary for all those who would make productive use of this book. It is not the only way to experience music, of course. We hope that you will never forget about the possibility of *performing* music, at whatever level you can manage: from singing in the shower or strumming a guitar in your room to playing in your college symphony, forming a garage band, or singing in your college musical. We hope also that you will take advantage of opportunities around you to hear live music. Recordings are not the same as live music. No matter how faithful a reproduction of sound they are, they lack the physical pleasure of performing and the immediacy and empathy struck up among performers or among performers and audience in live-music situations.

Since, however, the main experience of music on which this book relies is listening to recordings, it is worth a few words to describe how we think this should be undertaken. Often you just *hear* music rather than listening to it—hear it out of the corner of your ear, so to speak. The center of your attention is somewhere else: on the car ahead of you cutting in from the next lane, on the organic chemistry you're studying while the music plays in the background, on the text message coming in from your friend, and so on. It's necessary to turn this hearing into true listening, to make a listening commitment to music, comparable in its way to the dedication of the composers and performers who create it. Background listening isn't enough, for real listening requires recognizing specific events in the music as it goes by in time, holding them in your memory, and relating them to one another in your mind. Classical music requires full attention to yield its full rewards.

J. K.
G. T.

How to Use This Book

To foster your appreciation of music, *Listen* contains a number of features to help focus your listening and further your understanding.

To help you listen closely to the music

Listening Charts for instrumental music are an integral feature of this text. In essence, the Listening Charts are tables of the main musical events of the pieces they represent, with brief explanatory notes where needed. Repeated listening is useful. We suggest that you first listen to the music by itself, then read the discussion of the piece of music in the text, and then listen again while following along with the Listening Chart. Read again, listen again. Interactive versions of these charts can be found in LaunchPad for *Listen* (see page xxxvii).

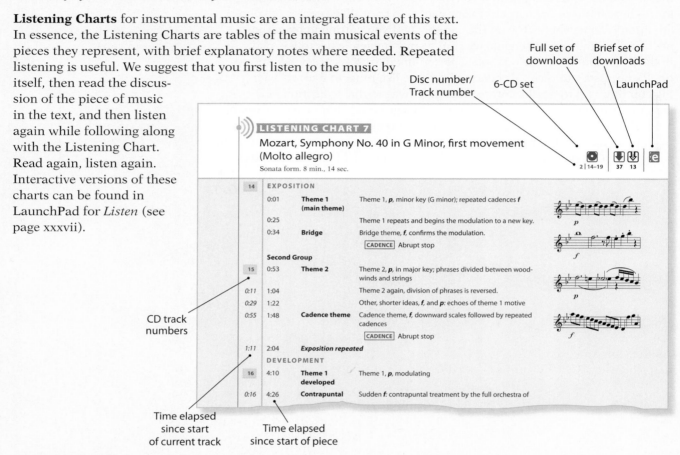

Listening Exercises in Unit I function in the same way to help you practice listening for fundamental elements of music such as rhythm, melody, and form. Music for these exercises can be found on the Unit I CD at the back of the book as well as in LaunchPad for *Listen*.

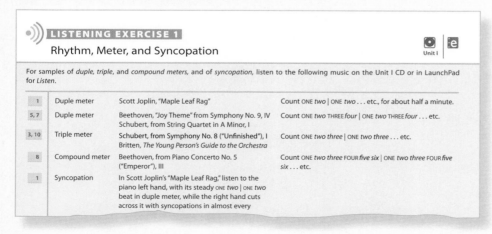

Listen guides are specially tailored for vocal music. They are similar to Listening Charts, but instead of explanatory notes, these charts contain the words of the piece in the original language and in an English translation.

Recordings are available for purchase in several different formats; visit **macmillanhighered.com/catalog/listen** for more information. For a complete list of the music discussed in *Listen*, see the Guide to Recordings on the inside front cover.

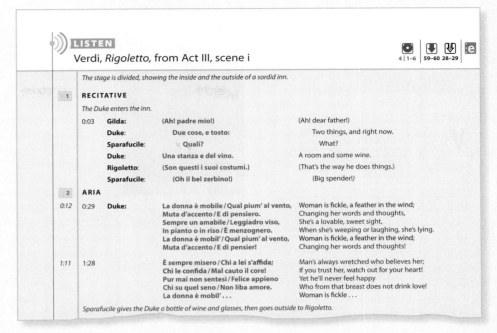

))) **LISTEN**

Verdi, *Rigoletto*, from Act III, scene i

4 | 1–6 | 59–60 28–29

The stage is divided, showing the inside and the outside of a sordid inn.

1 | **RECITATIVE**

The Duke enters the inn.

0:03	**Gilda:**	(Ah! padre mio!)	(Ah! dear father!)
	Duke:	Due cose, e tosto:	Two things, and right now.
	Sparafucile:	Quali?	What?
	Duke:	Una stanza e del vino.	A room and some wine.
	Rigoletto:	(Son questi i suoi costumi.)	(That's the way he does things.)
	Sparafucile:	(Oh il bel zerbino!)	(Big spender!)

2 | **ARIA**

0:12	0:29	**Duke:**	La donna è mobile / Qual pium' al vento,	Woman is fickle, a feather in the wind;
			Muta d'accento / E di pensiero.	Changing her words and thoughts,
			Sempre un amabile / Leggiadro viso,	She's a lovable, sweet sight,
			In pianto o in riso / È menzognero.	When she's weeping or laughing, she's lying.
			La donna è mobil' / Qual pium' al vento,	Woman is fickle, a feather in the wind;
			Muta d'accento / E di pensier!	Changing her words and thoughts!
1:11	1:28		È sempre misero / Chi a lei s'affida,	Man's always wretched who believes her;
			Chi le confida / Mal cauto il core!	If you trust her, watch out for your heart!
			Pur mai non sentesi / Felice appieno	Yet he'll never feel happy
			Chi su quel seno / Non liba amore.	Who from that breast does not drink love!
			La donna è mobil' . . .	Woman is fickle . . .

Sparafucile gives the Duke a bottle of wine and glasses, then goes outside to Rigoletto.

To help you understand the historical and cultural context

Prelude chapters introduce you to the historical and cultural background of four important eras of music — the Baroque and Classical eras, the nineteenth century, and the twentieth century to the present. Each prelude chapter also describes the stylistic features of the music you will study.

The Twentieth Century and Beyond

UNIT V

This unit covers music from around 1900 on and brings our survey up to the present. Looking back to the year 1900, we can recognize today's society in an early form. Large cities, industrialization, inoculation against disease, mass food processing, the first automobiles, telephones, movies, and phonographs—all were in place by the early years of the twentieth century. Hence the society treated in this unit will strike us as fairly familiar, compared to the societies of earlier centuries.

But the classical music produced in this period may strike us as anything but familiar. Around 1900, classical music experienced some of the most dramatic and abrupt changes in its entire history. Along with the changes came a wider variety of styles than ever before. At times it seemed almost as if each composer felt the need to create an entirely individual musical language. This tendency toward radical innovation, once it set in, was felt in repeated waves throughout the twentieth century. This vibrant, innovative, and unsettling creativity comes under the label "modernism."

Another development of great importance occurred around 1900: the widening split between classical and popular music. A rift that had started in the nineteenth century became a prime factor of musical life, giving rise to new traditions of American popular music. With the evolution of ragtime and early jazz, a vital rhythmic strain derived from African American sources was brought into the general American consciousness. This led to a long series of developments: swing, bebop, rhythm and blues, rock, rap, and more.

In this unit we sample the variety of musical modernism and glimpse the movement's outgrowths around the turn of the new millennium. The final chapter deals with America's characteristic popular music.

By the early twentieth century, industrialization had come to touch every aspect of life, from entertainment to warfare. In *The Twittering Machine*, from 1922, by Swiss-German artist Paul Klee (1879–1940), singing birds are attached to a crank apparatus. Is the image a message about the mechanization of music, or does its living song challenge the machine? *Digital Image © The Museum of Modern Art/Licensed by SCALA/Art Resource, NY.*

Chronologies at the beginning of each unit list the works you will study in the order in which they were composed and are accompanied by an overview of the relevant era.

Biography boxes throughout the book offer some personal background on each of the major composers you will study, as well as lists of additional works you might want to seek out for further listening.

Biography

Gustav Mahler (1860–1911)

Mahler's early life was not happy. Born in Bohemia to an abusive father, he lost five of his brothers and sisters to diphtheria, and others ended their lives in suicide or mental illness. The family lived near a military barracks, and the many marches incorporated into Mahler's music—often distorted marches—have been traced to his childhood recollections of parade music.

After studying for a time at the Vienna Conservatory, Mahler began a rising career as a conductor. His uncompromising standards and his authoritarian attitude toward the musicians led to frequent disputes with the orchestra directors. What is more, Mahler was Jewish, and Vienna at that time was rife with anti-Semitism. Nonetheless, he was acknowledged as one of the great conductors of his day and also as a very effective musical administrator. After positions at Prague, Budapest, Hamburg, and elsewhere, he came to head such organizations as the Vienna Opera and the New York Philharmonic.

It was only in the summers that Mahler had time to compose, so it is not surprising that he produced fewer pieces (though they are very long pieces) than any other important composer. Ten symphonies, the last of them unfinished, and six song cycles for voice and orchestra are almost all he wrote. The song cycle *The Song of* is often called Mahler's greatest masterpiece.

Mahler's wife was a famous Viennese beauty, Alma Schindler. By a tragic coincidence, shortly after he wrote his grim orchestral song cycle *Songs on the Death of Children*, his and Alma's youngest daughter died of scarlet fever.

Beyond this tragedy, Mahler's life was clouded by psychological turmoil, and he once consulted his famous Viennese contemporary Sigmund Freud. His disputes with the New York Philharmonic directors, which discouraged him profoundly, may have contributed to his premature death.

Chief Works: Ten lengthy symphonies, several with chorus, of which the best known are the First, Fourth, Fifth, and Ninth ■ Orchestral song cycles: *The Song of the Earth, Songs of a Wayfarer, The Youth's Magic Horn* (for piano or orchestra), *Songs on the Death of Children*

Encore: After Symphony No. 1, listen to the Adagietto from Symphony No. 5; *Songs of a Wayfarer*.

HOW DID EARLY MUSIC SOUND?

Because sound recording is only about a hundred years old, the hard truth is that we do not really know how the music of Beethoven sounded in 1800, or the music of Bach in 1700. We have the scores, and it may be that tradition, writings, anecdotes, and surviving instruments allow us to extrapolate from score to sound with some confidence. But what about early music—music from 1500, 1300, 1100?

Obsolete instruments have come down to us in an imperfect condition, and we can try to reconstruct them; but figuring out how they were actually played is much more speculative. As for singing, who can guess what a cathedral choir, to take just one example, sounded like in the Middle Ages? Since then, language itself has changed so much that it is hard enough to read a fourteenth-century poet such as Geoffrey Chaucer, let alone imagine how the words that he wrote were pronounced—or sung.

Another set of problems involves the way early music was written down. Its composers never indicated the tempo and rarely specified the instrumental or vocal forces that they anticipated for their music. With vocal pieces, they did not say whether one singer or a whole choir was to sing. It has taken generations of patient research and experiment to "reconstruct" the probable sounds of early music.

The Countess of Dia holding forth; she was one of a small number of women troubadours. *Bibliothèque Nationale de France.*

Additional boxes introduce you to interesting topics related to the music you're studying, such as events in music history, aspects of performance, or social and cultural trends.

Global Perspectives

Sacred Chant

The vast number of societies that exist or that have existed in this world all generated their own music—or, as we say, their own different "musics." Often they are very different indeed; the first time South African Zulus heard Christian hymn singing they were amazed as much as the missionaries were when they first heard Zulu music.

Yet for all their diversity, the musics of the world do show some parallels, as we are going to see in the Global Perspectives sections of this book. There are parallels of musical function in society, of musical technique, and sometimes of both together.

Often these parallels come about as the result of influences of one society on another—but influences are never accepted without modification and the blending of a foreign music with native music. At other times parallels appear in musics that have nothing whatsoever to do with one another. Considering all these parallels, we have to believe that certain basic functions for music and certain basic technical principles are virtually universal in humankind.

One of these near-universal features—and one of the most fundamental—is the role of music in the service of religion. Singing serves across the world as

of the Middle Ages (see pages 44–49) is only one of many traditions of monophonic religious chant, albeit one of the more elaborate.

Islam: Reciting the Qur'an

Another highly elaborate tradition of chant is found in Islam, practiced today by about a fifth of the world's population, and the dominant religion in some fifty nations. Across all of Islam, the revelations of the prophet Muhammad gathered in the Qur'an (or Koran) are chanted or sung in Arabic. Muhammad himself is said to have enjoyed this melodic recitation.

Usually Qur'anic recitation is rigorously distinguished from all types of secular music making. It is thought of as "reading" the sacred text aloud, not singing it; nonreligious activities such as singing or playing instruments might be referred to as music *(musiqi)*, but reading the Qur'an is not.

Given these distinctions, it is not surprising that

Global Perspectives sections provide brief glimpses of music from non-Western cultures. These sections point out some of the shared features as well as differences among a broad range of musical traditions.

To help you study and review

Goals for Review at the end of each chapter point out key concepts that you should review and understand before moving on to the next chapter.

Resources in LaunchPad for *Listen* are signaled by icons and cross-references throughout the book to **macmillanhigh-ered.com/listen8e**. LaunchPad includes an interactive e-book with streaming music, interactive versions of the Listening Charts, quizzes to help you study chapter concepts and practice your listening skills, and more. If your instructor recommends that you purchase LaunchPad, see the inside back cover for more information about how to get access.

from that need to resolve. Dissonance was to be free from the rule that says it must always be followed by the appropriate consonance.

Tonality, as we know, is the feeling of centrality, focus, or homing toward a particular pitch that we get from simple tunes and much other music. As melody grew more complex and harmony grew more dissonant, tonality grew more indistinct. Finally, some music reached a point at which no tonal center could be detected at all. This is **atonal** music.

Melody, harmony, tonality: All are closely related. Beleaguered conservatives around 1900 referred to them jokingly as the "holy trinity" of music. The "emancipation" of melody, harmony, and tonality all went together. This joint emancipation counts as the central style characteristic of the first phase of twentieth-century avant-garde music.

GOALS FOR REVIEW

▶ to understand artistic modernism c. 1900 as a response to innovation and its uncertainties

▶ to explore similar tendencies in modernist literature, pictorial art, and music

▶ to come to know some general stylistic features of early modernist music

macmillanhighered.com/listen8e
Reading Quiz for Chapter 20

Any recurring pattern of strong and weak beats, such as the ONE *two and* ONE *two three* we have referred to above, is called a **meter.** Meter is a strong/weak pattern repeated again and again.

Each occurrence of this repeated pattern, consisting of a principal strong beat and one or more weaker beats, is called a **measure**, or **bar.** In Western music there are only two basic kinds of meter: duple meter and triple meter.

• In **duple meter** the beats are grouped in twos (ONE *two* | ONE *two*) or in fours (ONE *two THREE four* | ONE *two THREE four*). Duple meter is instantly familiar from marches—such as "Yankee Doodle"—which tend always to use duple meter in deference to the human anatomy (LEFT *right,* LEFT *right,* LEFT *right*):

Glossary terms are highlighted throughout the text to help you identify and study key terms defined in the Glossary at the back of the book.

LISTEN

Fundamentals

UNIT I

The basic activity that leads to the love of music and to its understanding is listening to particular pieces of music again and again. The pages of this book are filled mostly with discussions of musical compositions—symphonies, operas, concertos, songs, and the like—that people have found more and more rewarding as they have listened to them repeatedly. These discussions are meant to introduce you to the contents of these works and their aesthetic qualities: what goes on in the music, and how it affects us.

For these discussions we need a familiarity with musical concepts and musical vocabulary, since analyzing things, pinpointing things, and even simply using the right names for things all make us more actively aware of them. This introductory unit provides this familiarity, covering the basic elements of music and their standard terminology.

Chapter 1 presents the most basic aspect of music, its organization in time, or rhythm, and introduces important features of this organization: meter and tempo. Chapter 2 takes up other basic features of musical sound—pitch, dynamics, and tone color—and also the instruments of the modern orchestra. Then Chapters 3 and 4 delve into some additional complexities of pitch—scales, melody, harmony, and more—and explore how musicians use these to organize pieces of music. Chapter 5 carries the discussion one stage further, to include musical form and style.

(Upper left) *Alvis Upitis/Getty Images.*
(Right) *Colorblind/Exactostock/Superstock.*
(Lower left) *Jim Wilson/The New York Times/Redux.*

Rhythm, Meter, and Tempo

CHAPTER 1

Music is the art of sound in time. Its unfolding in time is the most basic place to start understanding it. This aspect of music is summed up by the term **rhythm**.

1 | Rhythm

The fundamental role of rhythm in the experience of music is taken for granted in our culture—and in most other cultures as well. Rhythm is the main driving force in music both popular and classical, music of all ages and all cultures.

In a more specific sense, "*a* rhythm" refers to the actual arrangement of durations—long and short notes—in a particular melody or some other musical passage. Of course, the term *rhythm* is also used in other contexts, about quarterbacks, poems, and even paintings. But no sport and no other art handles rhythm with as much precision and refinement as music.

Beat and Accent

Beats provide the basic unit of measurement for time in music; if ordinary clock time is measured in seconds, musical time is measured in beats. When listening to a marching band or a rock band, to take two clear examples, we

> "Rhythm might be described as, to the world of sound, what light is to the world of sight. It shapes and gives new meaning."
>
> *Edith Sitwell, poet and critic, 1965*

The repeating patterns in architecture often give an impression similar to repeating beats in music; in this instance, there seems to be no distinction of strong and weak beats. *Chris Hellier/Getty Images.*

sense a regular recurrence of short pulses. These serve as a steady, vigorous background for other, more complicated rhythms that we discern at the same time. Sometimes we can't help beating time to the music, dancing to it, waving a hand or tapping a foot. The simple pulse being signaled by waving, tapping, or dancing is the music's beat.

There is, however, an all-important difference between a clock ticking and a drum beating time. Mechanically produced ticks all sound exactly the same, but it is virtually impossible for people to beat time without making some beats more emphatic than others. This is called giving certain beats an **accent**. And accents are really what enable us to beat time, since the simplest way to do this is to alternate accented ("strong") and unaccented ("weak") beats in patterns such as ONE *two* | ONE *two* | ONE *two* . . . or ONE *two three* | ONE *two three* | ONE *two three*. . . . To beat time, then, is not only to measure time according to a regular pulse but also to organize it, at least into these simple two- and three-beat patterns.

2 | Meter

Any recurring pattern of strong and weak beats, such as the ONE *two* and ONE *two three* we have referred to above, is called a **meter**. Meter is a strong/weak pattern repeated again and again.

Each occurrence of this repeated pattern, consisting of a principal strong beat and one or more weaker beats, is called a **measure**, or **bar**. In Western music there are only two basic kinds of meter: duple meter and triple meter.

• In **duple meter** the beats are grouped in twos (ONE *two* | ONE *two*) or in fours (ONE *two* THREE *four* | ONE *two* THREE *four*). Duple meter is instantly familiar from marches—such as "Yankee Doodle"—which tend always to use duple meter in deference to the human anatomy (LEFT *right,* LEFT *right,* LEFT *right*):

Yan-kee	doo-dle	came to	town . . .
ONE	*two*	ONE	*two*

• In **triple meter** the beats are grouped in threes (ONE *two three* | ONE *two three*). Our oldest national songs, "The Star-Spangled Banner" and "My Country, 'Tis of Thee," are in triple meter:

Oh,	say	can	you	see . . .	My	coun-	try,	'tis	of thee . . .
ONE	*two*	*three*	ONE		ONE	*two*	*three*	ONE	*two*	*three*

Two other national songs, "America the Beautiful" and "God Bless America," are in duple meter.

• Often the main beats of duple and triple meter are subdivided into quicker pulses. This usually happens by dividing the main beat into either twos or threes. When the main beats are divided in twos, the meter is called a **simple meter**. Dividing the main beats in threes creates **compound meters** with two or three main beats and six or nine quicker ones:

ONE	two	ONE	two	three
ONE *two three*	FOUR *five six*	ONE *two three*	FOUR *five six*	SEVEN *eight nine*

The round "Row, Row, Row Your Boat" is in compound duple meter. While the first voice is moving at a fast six-beat clip at the words "Merrily, merrily, merrily, merrily," the second voice comes in pounding out the basic duple meter, "ROW, *row,* ROW":

Row,	row,	row your	boat	gently	down the	stream,		Merrily,	merrily,	merrily,	merrily,
1 2 3	4 5 6	1 2 3	4 5 6	1 2 3	4 5 6	1 2 3	4 5 6	1 2 3	4 5 6	1 2 3	4 5 6
ONE	*two*	ONE	*two*	ONE	*two*	ONE	*two*	ONE	*two*	ONE	*two*

			second voice:	Row,	row,	row . . .
				ONE	*two*	ONE *two*

- Meters with five beats, seven beats, and so on have never been used widely in Western music, though they are found frequently enough in some other musical cultures. It was an unusual choice for nineteenth-century composer Pyotr Ilyich Tchaikovsky to have featured quintuple meter, five beats to a bar, in his popular Sixth Symphony.

Rhythm and Meter

Rhythm in the most general sense refers to the entire time aspect of music and, more specifically, *a* rhythm refers to the particular arrangements of long and short notes in a musical passage. In most Western music, duple or triple *meter* serves as the regular background against which we perceive music's actual rhythms.

We can see that the musical rhythms need not always coincide with the regular beats of the meter. And, as the rhythm first coincides with the meter, then cuts across it independently, then even contradicts it, all kinds of variety, tension, and excitement can result.

Musical notation has developed a conventional system of signs (see Appendix B) to indicate relative durations, or long and short notes; combining various signs is the way of indicating rhythms. Following are examples of well-known tunes in duple and triple meters. Notice from the shading (even better, sing the tunes to yourself and *hear*) how the rhythm sometimes corresponds with the beats of the meter and sometimes departs from them. The shading indicates passages of rhythm-meter correspondence:

The above examples should not be taken to imply that meter is always emphasized behind music's rhythms. Often the meter is not explicitly beaten out in the music's rhythms. It does not need to be, for the listener can almost always sense it under the surface. Naturally, meter is strongly stressed in music designed to stimulate regular body movements, such as marches, dances, and much popular music.

At the other extreme, there is *nonmetrical* music. In such music, the rhythms suggest no underlying pattern of strong and weak beats at all. For example, the meandering, nonmetrical rhythms of Gregorian chant contribute to the cool, otherworldly, and spiritual quality that devotees of this music cherish.

Syncopation

One way of obtaining interesting, striking effects in music is to move the accents in a foreground *rhythm* away from their normal position on the beats of the background *meter*. This may seem counterintuitive, but it works. In **syncopation**, as it is called, accents can be displaced so they go *one* TWO | *one* TWO (*weak* STRONG | *weak* STRONG) instead of the normal ONE *two* | ONE *two* (STRONG *weak* | STRONG *weak*). Or syncopation can occur when an accent is placed *in between* beats ONE and *two*, as in this Christmas ballad:

Ru-*dolf*__ the red - nosed rein - deer _____

ONE   *two* | ONE   *two* | ONE   *two* | ONE   *two*

The consistent use of syncopation is the hallmark of African American–derived popular music, from ragtime to rap. See Chapter 24, and listen to the lively, uneven, *syncopated* rhythms of Scott Joplin's "Maple Leaf Rag" in Listening Exercise 1.

3 | Tempo

Our discussion so far has referred to the *relative* **duration** of sounds—all beats are equal; some notes are longer than others, and so on—but nothing has been said yet about their *absolute* duration, in fractions of a second. The term for the speed of music is **tempo**; in metrical music, the tempo is the rate at which the basic, regular beats of the meter follow one another.

 **LISTENING EXERCISE 1**
Rhythm, Meter, and Syncopation

Unit I

For samples of *duple, triple,* and *compound meters,* and of *syncopation,* listen to the following music on the Unit I CD or in LaunchPad for *Listen.*

1	Duple meter	Scott Joplin, "Maple Leaf Rag"	Count ONE *two*	ONE *two* . . . etc., for about half a minute.
5, 7	Duple meter	Beethoven, "Joy Theme" from Symphony No. 9, IV Schubert, from String Quartet in A Minor, I	Count ONE *two THREE four*	ONE *two THREE four* . . . etc.
3, 10	Triple meter	Schubert, from Symphony No. 8 ("Unfinished"), I Britten, *The Young Person's Guide to the Orchestra*	Count ONE *two three*	ONE *two three* . . . etc.
8	Compound meter	Beethoven, from Piano Concerto No. 5 ("Emperor"), III	Count ONE *two three FOUR five six*	ONE *two three FOUR five six* . . . etc.
1	Syncopation	In Scott Joplin's "Maple Leaf Rag," listen to the piano left hand, with its steady ONE *two*	ONE *two* beat in duple meter, while the right hand cuts across it with syncopations in almost every measure.	

Tempo can be expressed exactly and measured by the **metronome**, a mechanical or electrical device that ticks out beats at any desired tempo. When composers give directions for tempo, however, they usually prefer approximate terms. Rather than freezing the music's speed by means of a metronome, they prefer to leave some latitude for different performers. Because all European music looked to Italy when this terminology first came into use, the conventional terms for tempo are Italian:

COMMON TEMPO INDICATIONS		LESS COMMON TEMPO INDICATIONS	
adagio:	slow	*largo, lento, grave:*	slow, very slow
andante:	on the slow side, but not too slow	*larghetto:*	somewhat faster than *largo*
moderato:	moderate	*andantino:*	somewhat faster than *andante*
allegretto:	on the fast side, but not too fast	*vivace, vivo:*	lively
allegro:	fast	*molto allegro:*	faster than *allegro*
presto:	very fast	*prestissimo:*	very fast indeed

It's interesting that in their original meaning many of these Italian words refer not to speed itself but rather to a mood, action, or quality that can be associated with tempo only in a general way. Thus, *vivace* is close to our "vivacious," *allegro* means "cheerful," and *andante*, derived from the Italian word for "go," might be translated as "walking along steadily."

An early metronome owned by Beethoven; its inventor was a friend of his. A clockwork mechanism made the bar swing side to side, ticking at rates controlled by a movable weight. *Musée de la Musique — Cité de la Musique, Paris, France/Giraudon, The Bridgeman Art Library.*

 **LISTENING EXERCISE 2**
Rhythm, Meter, and Tempo

Unit I | 2

A more advanced exercise: Our excerpt, from the middle of *Rhapsody on a Theme by Paganini*, for piano and orchestra, by Sergei Rachmaninov, consists of four continuous segments in different meters and tempos, here labeled A, B, C, and D.

0:00	**A**	The piano starts in **duple meter** (ONE *two* | ONE *two*). The loud orchestral interruptions are **syncopated**. (After the interruptions the meter is somewhat obscured, but it gets clearer.)
0:33		Clear duple meter by this time; then the music comes to a stop.
0:49	**B**	No meter. The piano seems to be engaged in a meditative improvisation, as if it is dreaming up the music to come.
1:45		Orchestral instruments suggest a slow **duple meter**? Not for long.
2:24	**C**	Slow **triple meter** (ONE *two three* | ONE *two three*)
3:47		**Ritardando** (getting slower)
3:56	**D**	Fast **triple meter**, assertive (note one or two syncopated notes)
4:26		Faster **triple meter**

The most important terms to remember are those listed under "common tempo indications" on page 8. Composers often use tempo indications alone as headings for major sections, called movements, in long works. Musicians refer to the "Andante" of Beethoven's Fifth Symphony, meaning a certain movement of the symphony (the second), which Beethoven specified should be played at an *andante* tempo.

GOALS FOR REVIEW

▶ to distinguish rhythm from meter

▶ to distinguish rhythm and meter from tempo

▶ to listen for duple, triple, and compound meter

 macmillanhighered.com/listen8e
Music for Listening Exercises 1 and 2
Listening Quiz for Chapter 1
Reading Quiz for Chapter 1

Pitch, Dynamics, and Tone Color

CHAPTER 2

If you have taken a course in physics, you know that sound is produced by vibrations that occur when objects are struck, plucked, stroked, or agitated in some other way. These vibrations are transmitted through the air and picked up by our ears.

For the production of sound in general, almost anything will do—the single rusted hinge on a creaky door as well as the great air masses of a thunderstorm. For the production of musical sounds, the usual objects are taut strings and membranes and columns of air enclosed in pipes of various kinds. These produce relatively simple vibrations, which translate into clearly focused or, as we say, "musical" sounds. Often the membranes are alive: They are called vocal cords.

Sound-producing vibrations are very fast; the range of sound that humans can hear extends from around 20 to 20,000 cycles per second. The vibrations are also very small. To be heard, they often need to be *amplified*, either electronically or with the aid of something physical that echoes or *resonates* along with the vibrating body. In a guitar or violin, the resonator is the hollow box that the strings are stretched across.

Musical sounds can be high or low, loud or soft, and can take on different qualities depending on the materials used to produce them. The musical terms for these aspects of sound are pitch, dynamics, and tone color.

Natural objects can serve as resonators for musical instruments. Gourds are a favorite on two continents, used in Latin American maracas and the kalimba, an African "finger piano." *Saed Hindash/Star Ledger/CORBIS.*

1 | Pitch

The scientific term for the rate of sound vibration is **frequency**. On the level of perception, our ears respond differently to sounds of high and low frequencies, and to very fine gradations in between. Indeed, people speak about "high" and "low" sounds quite unselfconsciously, as though they know that the latter actually have a low frequency—relatively few cycles—and the former a high frequency.

The musical term for this quality of sound, which is recognized so instinctively, is **pitch**. Low pitches (low frequencies) result from *long* vibrating elements, high pitches from *short* ones—a trombone sounds lower than a flute.

Noises, with their complex, unfocused vibrations, do not have pitch. Your college chorus divides up high and low pitches among four different groups of voices: sopranos (high females), altos (low females), tenors (high males), and basses (low males).

The totality of musical sounds serves as a kind of quarry from which musicians of every age and every society carve the exact building blocks they want for their music. We hear this totality in the sliding scale of a siren, starting low and going higher and higher. But musicians never (or virtually never) use the full range of pitches. Instead they select a limited number of fixed pitches from the sound continuum. These pitches are calibrated scientifically (European-style orchestras these days tune to a pitch with a frequency of 440 cycles), given names (that pitch is labeled A), and collected in *scales*. Scales are discussed in Chapter 3.

2 | Dynamics

In scientific terminology, *amplitude* is the level of strength of sound vibrations—more precisely, the amount of energy they contain and convey. As big guitar amplifiers attest, very small string vibrations can be amplified until the energy in the air transmitting them rattles the eardrums.

In musical terminology, the level of sound is called its **dynamics**. Musicians use subtle dynamic gradations from very soft to very loud, but they have never worked out a calibrated scale of dynamics, as they have for pitch. The terms used are only approximate. Like the indications for tempo, the terms used for dynamics are in Italian.

 **LISTENING EXERCISE 3**

Pitch and Dynamics

Unit I | 3

High and low **pitch** and loud and soft **dynamics** are heard so instinctively that they hardly need illustration. Listen, however, to the vivid way they are deployed in one of the most famous of classical compositions, the "Unfinished" Symphony by Franz Schubert. Symphonies usually consist of four separate big segments, called movements; musicologists are still baffled as to why Schubert wrote two superb movements for this work and started but never finished the rest.

		PITCH	DYNAMIC
0:00	Quiet and mysterious	Low range	**pp**
0:15	Rustling sounds	Middle range	
0:22	Wind instruments	High	
0:35	Single sharp accent		**sf** (*sforzando*, "forcing")
0:47	Gets louder	Higher instruments added	Long **crescendo**, leading to **f**, then **ff**, more accents
1:07	Sudden collapse		**piano** followed by **diminuendo**
1:15	New tune	First low, then high	(Marked **pp** by Schubert, but usually played **p** or **mp**)
1:52	Cuts off sharply; big sound		**ff**, more accents

(Similar pitch and dynamic effects for the rest of the excerpt)

3:07	Sinking passage	Individual pitches, lower and lower	
3:45	Ominous	Lowest pitch of all	**pp**

The main categories are simply loud and soft, **forte** (pronounced fór-teh) and **piano**, which may be qualified by expanding to "very loud" or "very soft" and by adding the Italian word for "medium," **mezzo** (mét-so):

pianissimo	*piano*	*mezzo piano*	*mezzo forte*	*forte*	*fortissimo*
pp	**p**	**mp**	**mf**	**f**	**ff**
very soft	soft	medium soft	medium loud	loud	very loud

Changes in dynamics can be sudden (*subito*), or they can be gradual—a soft passage swells into a loud one (*crescendo*, "growing"), or a powerful blare fades into quietness (*decrescendo* or *diminuendo*, "diminishing").

3 | Tone Color

At whatever pitch, and whether loud or soft, musical sounds differ in their general *quality*, depending on the instruments or voices that produce them. **Tone color** and **timbre** (tám-br) are the terms for this quality.

Tone color is produced in a more complex way (and a more astonishing way) than pitch and dynamics. Piano strings and other sound-producing bodies vibrate not only along their total length but also at the same time in half-lengths, quarters, eighths, and so on.

STRING VIBRATIONS

Full-Length:

Half-Length:

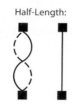

Quarter-Length and Three-Quarter-Length Simultaneously:

The diagrams above attempt to illustrate this. Musicians call these fractional vibrations **overtones**. They are much lower in amplitude—that is, softer—than the main vibrations; for this reason, we hear overtones not as distinct pitches, but somehow as part of the string's basic or fundamental pitch. The amount and exact mixture of overtones are what give a sound its characteristic tone color. A flute has few overtones. A trumpet has many.

Musicians make no attempt to tally or describe tone colors; about the best one can do is apply imprecise adjectives such as *bright, warm, ringing, hollow,* or *brassy*. Yet tone color is surely the most easily recognized of all musical elements. Even people who cannot identify instruments by name can distinguish between the smooth, rich sound of violins playing together, the bright sound of trumpets, and the woody croaking of a bassoon.

The most distinctive tone color of all, however, belongs to the first, most beautiful, and most universal of all the sources of music—the human voice.

The singing voice, the most beautiful and universal of all sources of music: Renée Fleming, star of the Metropolitan Opera in New York, excels in an unusually wide variety of roles and is often heard singing popular standards. *Nigel Norrington/ArenaPal/The Image Works.*

MUSICAL INSTRUMENTS

Different voices and different instruments produce different tone colors, or timbres. Enormous numbers of devices have been invented for making music over the course of history and across the entire world, and the range of tone colors they can produce is almost endless.

This section will discuss and illustrate the instruments of Western music that make up the orchestra, and a few others. Later, in our Global Perspectives sections, we will meet some instruments from other musical traditions.

Musical instruments can be categorized into four groups: *stringed instruments* or *strings, woodwinds, brass,* and *percussion.* Musical sound, as we know, is caused by rapid vibrations. Each of the four groups of instruments produces sound vibrations in its own distinct way.

Stringed Instruments

Stringed instruments produce their sound by means of taut strings attached to a *sound box,* a hollow box containing a body of air that resonates (that is, vibrates along with the strings) to amplify the string sound.

The strings themselves can be played with a bow, as with the violin and other orchestral strings; the bow is strung tightly with horsehair, which is coated with a substance called rosin so that the bow grips the strings to make them vibrate. With guitars and harps, the strings are plucked or strummed by the fingers or a small pick. Strings can be plucked on bowed instruments, too, for special effects. This is called **pizzicato** (pit-tzih-cáh-toe).

The Violin and Its Family   The **violin** is often called the most beautiful instrument used in Western music. It is also one of the most versatile instruments; its large range covers alto and soprano registers and many much higher pitches. As a solo instrument, it can play forcefully or delicately, and it excels in both brilliant and songlike music. Violinists also play chords by bowing two or more of the four strings at once, or nearly so.

As with a guitar, the player *stops* the (four) violin strings with a finger—that is, presses the strings against the neck of the violin—to shorten the string length and get different pitches (see the illustrations below). Unlike a guitar, a violin has no frets, so the player has to learn the exact places to press.

The violin is an excellent ensemble instrument, and it blends especially well with other violins. An orchestra violin section, made up of ten or more instruments playing together, can produce a strong yet sensitive and flexible tone. Hence the orchestra has traditionally relied on strings as a solid foundation for its composite sound.

Like most instruments, violins come in *families,* that is, in several sizes with different pitch ranges. Two other members of the violin family are basic to the orchestra. The **viola** is the tenor-range instrument, larger than a violin by several inches. It has a throaty quality in its lowest range, yet it fits especially smoothly into accompaniment textures. The viola's highest register is powerful and intense.

Cello, violin, viola, and electric keyboard on London's Millennium Bridge. *Mike Kemp/In Pictures/Corbis.*

Violin and bow. *Tom Chance/ Westend61/CORBIS.*

Chinese American cellist Yo-Yo Ma is perhaps this country's preeminent instrumentalist, and certainly the most versatile and most honored and admired. He has assumed the role of a national resource, playing at state occasions such as President Obama's 2009 inauguration. In 1998 he founded the Silk Road Project, a program of intercultural musical exchange along the Silk Road, the ancient trading route between China and the Mediterranean. His complete recordings to date fill over a hundred CDs! *Jim Wright/Star Ledger/CORBIS.*

The **cello**, short for *violoncello*, is the bass of the violin family. Cellists play seated, with the instrument propped on the floor between their knees. Unlike the viola, the cello has a rich, gorgeous sound in its low register. It is a favorite solo instrument as well as an indispensable member of the orchestra.

Double Bass   Also called **string bass** or just **bass**, this deep instrument is used to back up the violin family in the orchestra. (However, in various details of construction the bass differs from members of the violin family; the bass actually belongs to another, older stringed instrument family, the *viol* family.)

Played with a bow, the double bass provides a splendid deep support for orchestral sound. It is often (in jazz, nearly always) plucked to give an especially vibrant kind of accent and to emphasize the meter.

Harp   **Harps** are plucked stringed instruments with one string for each pitch available. The modern orchestral harp is a large instrument with forty-seven strings covering a wide range of pitches. In most orchestral music, the swishing, watery quality of the harp is treated as a striking occasional effect rather than as a regular timbre.

Woodwind Instruments

As the name suggests, woodwind instruments were once made of wood. Some still are, while others today are made of metal and even plastic. Sound in these instruments is created by setting up vibrations in the column of air in a tube. A series of precisely spaced holes are bored in the tube, which players open or close with their fingers or with a lever device (a *key*). In effect this creates columns of different lengths, producing different pitches.

Of the main woodwind instruments, *flutes, clarinets,* and *oboes* have approximately the same range. All three are used in the orchestra because each has a quite distinct tone color, and composers can obtain a variety of effects from them. It is not hard to learn to recognize and appreciate the different sounds of these woodwinds.

The Flute and Its Family   The **flute** is simply a long cylinder, held horizontally; the player sets the air vibrating by blowing across a side hole. The flute is the most agile

Double bass. © *Jack Vartoogian/FrontRowPhotos.*

Flute, recorder, and clarinet. *John Henley/ Corbis.*

of the woodwind instruments and also the gentlest. It nonetheless stands out clearly in the orchestra when played in its high register.

The **piccolo**, the smallest, highest member of the flute family, adds special sparkle to band and orchestral music. The **alto flute** and **bass flute**—larger and deeper flutes—are less frequently employed.

The **recorder**, a different variety of flute, is blown not at the side of the tube but through a special mouthpiece at the end. Used in older orchestral music, the recorder was superseded by the horizontal, or *transverse,* flute because the latter was stronger and more agile. In the late twentieth century recorders made a comeback for modern performances of old music using reconstructed period instruments. The instrument is also popular (in various family sizes) among musical amateurs today. The recorder is easy to learn and fun to play.

Clarinet The **clarinet** is a slightly conical tube made, usually, of ebony (a dark wood). The air column is not made to vibrate directly by blowing into the tube, as with the flute. The player gets sound by blowing on a *reed*—a small piece of cane fixed at one end—in much the same way as one can blow on a blade of grass held taut between the fingers. The vibrating reed vibrates the air within the clarinet tube itself.

Compared to the flute, the clarinet sounds richer and more flexible, more like the human voice. The clarinet is capable of warm, mellow tones and strident, shrill ones; it has an especially intriguing quality in its low register.

The small **E-flat clarinet** and the large **bass clarinet** are family members with a place in the modern orchestra. The tube of the bass clarinet is so long that it has to be bent back, like a thin black saxophone.

Oboe The **oboe** also uses a reed, like the clarinet, but it is a double reed—two reeds lashed together so that the air must be forced between them. (You can see the effort involved in the picture below.) This kind of reed gives the oboe its clearly focused, crisply clean, and sometimes plaintive sound.

The **English horn** is a larger, lower oboe, descending into the viola range. It is often called by the French equivalent, *cor anglais;* in either language, the name is all

Oboe (left) and bassoon. *Rahav Segev/ZUMA Press/Corbis.*

wrong, since the instrument is not a horn but an oboe, and it has nothing to do with England.

Bassoon   The **bassoon** is a low (cello-range) instrument with a double reed and other characteristics similar to the oboe's. It looks somewhat bizarre: The long tube is bent double, and the reed has to be linked to the instrument by a long, narrow pipe made of metal. Of all the double-reed woodwinds, the bassoon is the most varied in expression, ranging from the mournful to the comical.

The **contrabassoon**, also called the **double bassoon**, is a very large member of the bassoon family, in the double bass range.

Saxophone   The **saxophone**, invented by the Belgian instrument maker Adolphe Sax, was first used around 1840 in military bands. The instrument is sometimes included in the modern orchestra, but it really came into its own in jazz. Saxophones are close to clarinets in the way they produce sound. Both use single reeds. Since the saxophone tube is wider and made of brass, its tone is even mellower than that of the clarinet, yet at the same time more forceful. The long saxophone tube has a characteristic bent shape and a flaring *bell*, as its opening is called.

Most common are the **alto saxophone** and the **tenor saxophone**. But the big family also includes *bass, baritone,* and *soprano* members.

Brass Instruments

The brass instruments are the loudest of all the wind instruments because of the rather remarkable way their sound is produced. The player's lips vibrate against a small cup-shaped mouthpiece of metal. The lip vibration itself vibrates the air within the brass tube. All brass instruments have long tubes, and these are almost always coiled in one way or another. This is easy to do with the soft metal they are made from.

Trumpet   The **trumpet**, highest of the main brass instruments, has a bright, strong, piercing tone that provides the ultimate excitement in band and orchestral music alike. Pitch is controlled by three pistons, or *valves*, that connect auxiliary tubes with the main tube or disconnect them, so as to lengthen or shorten the vibrating air column.

French Horn   The **French horn** has a lower, mellower, thicker tone than the trumpet. It is capable of mysterious, romantic sounds when played softly; played loudly, it can sound like a trombone. Chords played by several French horns in harmony have an especially rich, sumptuous tone.

Trombone   The **tenor trombone** and the **bass trombone** are also pitched lower than the trumpet. The pitch is controlled by a sliding mechanism (thus the term *slide trombone*) rather than a valve or piston, as in the trumpet and French horn.

Less bright and martial in tone than the trumpet, the trombone can produce a surprising variety of sounds, ranging from an almost vocal quality in its high register to a hard, powerful blare in the low register.

Tuba   The **bass tuba** is typically used as a foundation for the trombone group in an orchestra. It is less flexible than other brass instruments. And like most other deep bass instruments, it is not favored for solo work.

Other Brass Instruments   All the brass instruments described so far are staples of both the orchestra and the band. Many other brass instruments (and even whole families of instruments) have been invented for use in marching bands and have then sometimes found their way into the orchestra.

Two French horns, trumpet, trombone, and tuba. *Jonathan Blair/CORBIS.*

Among these are the *cornet* and the *flügelhorn*, both of which resemble the trumpet; the *euphonium, baritone horn,* and *saxhorn,* which are somewhere between the French horn and the tuba; and the *sousaphone,* a handsome bass tuba named after the great American bandmaster and march composer John Philip Sousa.

Finally there is the *bugle.* This simple trumpetlike instrument is very limited in the pitches it can play because it has no piston or valve mechanism. Buglers play "Taps" and military fanfares, and not much else.

Percussion Instruments

Instruments in this category produce sound by being struck (or sometimes rattled, as with the South American maraca). Some percussion instruments, such as drums and gongs, have no fixed pitch, just a striking tone color. Others, such as the vibraphone, have whole sets of wooden or metal elements tuned to regular scales.

Timpani The **timpani** (or *kettledrums*) are large hemispherical drums that can be tuned precisely to certain low pitches. Used in groups of two or more, timpani have the effect of "cementing" loud sounds when the whole orchestra plays, so they are the most widely used percussion instruments in the orchestra.

Timpani are tuned by tightening the drumhead by means of screws set around the rim. During a concert, one can often see the timpani player, when there are rests in the music, leaning over the drums, tapping them quietly to hear whether the tuning is just right.

Pitched Percussion Instruments Pitched percussion instruments are *scale instruments,* capable of playing melodies and consisting of whole sets of metal or wooden bars or plates struck with sticks or hammers. While they add unforgettable special sound effects to many compositions, they are not usually heard consistently throughout a piece, as the timpani are.

These instruments differ in their materials:

The **glockenspiel** has small steel bars. It is a high instrument with a bright, penetrating sound.

The **xylophone** has hardwood plates or slats. It plays as high as the glockenspiel but also lower, and it has a drier, sharper tone.

The **marimba,** an instrument of African and South American origins, is a xylophone with tubular resonators under each wooden slat, making the tone much mellower.

The **vibraphone** has metal plates, like a glockenspiel with a large range, and is furnished with a controllable electric resonating device. This gives the "vibes" an echoing, funky quality unlike that of any other instrument.

Also like the glockenspiel, the **celesta** has steel bars, but its sound is more delicate and silvery. This instrument,

unlike the others in this section, is not played directly by a percussionist wielding hammers or sticks. The hammers are activated from a keyboard; a celesta looks like a miniature piano.

Tubular bells, or **chimes,** are hanging tubes that are struck with a big mallet. They sound like church bells.

Unpitched Percussion Instruments In the category of percussion instruments without a fixed pitch, the following are the most frequently found in the orchestra.

Cymbals are concave metal plates, from a few inches to several feet in diameter. In orchestral music, pairs of large cymbals are clapped together to support climactic moments in the music with a grand crashing sound.

The **triangle**—a simple metal triangle—gives out a bright tinkle when struck.

The **tam-tam** is a large unpitched gong with a low, mysterious quality.

The **snare drum, tenor drum,** and **bass drum** are among the unpitched drums used in the orchestra.

Timpani (kettledrums), with a vibraphone behind them. *David Redfern/Getty Images.*

The Orchestra

The orchestra has changed over the centuries, just as orchestral music has. Bach's orchestra in the early 1700s was about a fifth the size of the orchestra required today. (See pages 108, 157, and 227 for the makeup of the orchestra in various historical periods.)

So today's symphony orchestra has to be a fluid group. Eighty musicians or more will be on the regular roster, but some of them sit out some of the pieces on many programs. And freelancers have to be engaged for special compositions in which composers have imaginatively expanded the orchestra for their own expressive purposes. A typical large orchestra today includes the following sections, also called *choirs*.

Strings: about thirty to thirty-six violins, twelve violas, ten to twelve cellos, and eight double basses.

Woodwinds: two flutes and a piccolo, two clarinets and a bass clarinet, two oboes and an English horn, two bassoons and a contrabassoon.

Brass: at least two trumpets, four French horns, two trombones, and one tuba.

Percussion: one to four players, who between them manage the timpani and all the other percussion instruments, moving from one to the other. Unlike the violins, for example, the percussion instruments seldom have to be played continuously throughout a piece.

There are several seating plans for orchestras; which is chosen depends on at least two factors. The conductor judges which arrangement makes the best sound in the particular hall. And some conductors feel they can control the orchestra better with one arrangement, some with another. One such seating plan is shown on page 19.

Snare drums and cymbals. *WaringAbbott/Getty Images.*

 **LISTENING EXERCISE 4**

The Orchestra in Action

Unit I | 10–15

Take a break from reading now and listen to *The Young Person's Guide to the Orchestra,* a work devised by Benjamin Britten in 1946 to introduce the many tone colors of orchestral instruments. A full chart of this work is given on page 41. For now, the chart below will lead you one by one through the various sections and instruments of the orchestra.

10	0:00	**Full orchestra**
	0:42	**WOODWIND choir**
	1:11	BRASS choir
	1:42	**STRING choir**
	2:07	**PERCUSSION**
	2:26	**Full orchestra**
11	2:50	**Flutes and piccolo**
0:39	3:29	**Oboes**
1:41	4:32	**Clarinets**
2:24	5:14	**Bassoon**
12	6:11	**Violins**
0:45	6:56	**Violas**
1:34	7:45	**Cellos**
2:32	8:43	**Double bass**
3:29	9:40	**Harp**
13	10:31	French horns
0:40	11:11	Trumpets
1:16	11:47	Trombones, tuba
14	12:48	**PERCUSSION**
15	14:43	**Full orchestra**

Keyboard Instruments

Though most orchestras today include a pianist, the piano is a relatively new addition to the symphony orchestra. In earlier times, the orchestra regularly included another keyboard instrument, the harpsichord.

The great advantage of keyboard instruments, of course, is that they can play more than one note at a time. A pianist, for example, can play a whole piece without requiring any other musicians at all. Consequently the solo music that has been written for piano, harpsichord, and organ is much more extensive and important than (accompanied) solo music for other instruments.

Odile Noel/Lebrecht/The Image Works.

ORCHESTRAL SEATING PLAN

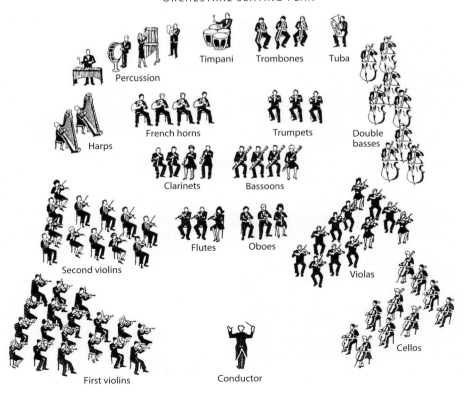

An organ with five(!) keyboards. The player pulls out the white knobs (stops) to change the sets of pipes that sound. *Lawrence Migdale/Science Source.*

Piano   The tuned strings of a **piano** are struck by felt-covered hammers, activated from a keyboard. Much technological ingenuity has been devoted to the activating mechanism, or *action*.

The hammer must strike the string and then fall back at once, while a damping device made of felt touches the string to stop the sound instantly. All this must be done so fast that the pianist can play repeated notes as fast as the hand can move. Also, many shades of loudness and softness must lie ready under the player's fingers. This dynamic flexibility is what gave the piano its name: *piano* is short for *pianoforte*, meaning "soft-loud."

The list of virtuoso pianists who were also major composers extends from Mozart through Frédéric Chopin to Sergei Rachmaninov. In the nineteenth century, the piano became *the* solo instrument. At the same time, nearly every middle-class European and American household had a piano. Piano lessons served and still serve for millions of young people as an introduction to the world of music.

Harpsichord   The **harpsichord** is an ancient keyboard instrument that was revived in the 1900s for the playing of Baroque music, in particular.

Like the piano, the harpsichord has a set of tuned strings activated from a keyboard, but the action is much simpler. There is no damping, and instead of hammers striking the strings, the key lifts up a quill that plucks the string. This means, first, that the tone is brittle and ping-y. Second, it means that the player cannot vary dynamics; when a string is plucked in this way, it always sounds the same.

Harpsichord makers compensated for this limitation in dynamics by adding one or two extra full sets of strings, controlled by an extra keyboard. One keyboard could be soft, the other loud. A mechanism allowed the keyboards to be coupled together for the loudest sound of all.

In spite of its brittle tone and its lack of flexibility in dynamics, the harpsichord can be a wonderfully expressive instrument. Good harpsichord playing requires, first and foremost, great rhythmic subtlety.

Another keyboard instrument of early times, the **clavichord,** has the simplest action of all. Its tone is much too quiet for concert use.

Organ   Called "the king of instruments," the **pipe organ** is certainly the largest of them (see page 147). This instrument has to provide enough sound to fill the large spaces of churches and cathedrals on a suitably grand scale. The organ has a great many sets of tuned pipes through which a complex wind system blows air, again activated from a keyboard. The pipes have different tone colors, and most organs have more than one keyboard to control different sets of pipes. A pedal board—a big keyboard on the floor, played with the feet—controls the lowest-sounding pipes.

Each set of tuned pipes is called a *stop;* a moderate-sized organ has forty to fifty stops, but much bigger organs exist. One organ in Atlantic City, New Jersey, has 1,477 stops, for a total of 33,112 pipes. A large organ is capable of an almost orchestral variety of sound.

The organ is not a member of the orchestra, but because the grandest occasions call for orchestra, chorus, vocal soloists, and organ combined (e.g., Handel's *Messiah* at Christmastime; see page 142), a major symphony hall has to have its organ—usually an imposing sight.

Electronic Keyboard Instruments Today *keyboard* or *organ* generally means an electronic instrument. Synthesizers simulate the sound of organs, pianos, and harpsichords—and many other sounds as well.

Modern concert music, from the 1960s on, has occasionally used electronic keyboards. On the whole, however, synthesizers have been used more to compose concert music than to play it. And of course electronic keyboards play major roles in today's popular music.

Plucked Stringed Instruments

Plucked stringed instruments figure much less in art music of the West than in Asian countries such as India and Japan, as we shall see. One exception is the orchestral harp; see page 14. The acoustic **guitar** and the **mandolin** are used very widely in Western popular music, but only occasionally in orchestras.

However, a now-obsolete plucked instrument, the **lute**, was of major importance in earlier times. One of the most beautiful-looking of instruments, the lute sounds rather like a gentle guitar. Large members of the lute family were the **theorbo** and the **archlute** (see page 117).

Like keyboard instruments, plucked stringed instruments have been revolutionized by electronic technology. **Electric guitars** dominate rock music, though they have only occasionally found their way into concert music.

Artists loved to paint the lute—a beautiful instrument and a triumph of woodworking craft. Here Francesco Trevisani includes also a violin, a recorder, and a harpsichord. *Francesco Trevisani (1656–1746),* Personification of Music: A Young Woman Playing a Lute. *Private Collection/Photo © Christie's Images/The Bridgeman Art Library.*

GOALS FOR REVIEW

▶ to distinguish pitch from rhythm and meter

▶ to listen for different dynamic levels

▶ to differentiate the timbres or tone colors of some of the main instruments of classical music

 macmillanhighered.com/listen8e
Instruments of the Orchestra
Music for Listening Exercises 3 and 4
Listening Quiz for Chapter 2
Reading Quiz for Chapter 2

Scales and Melody

CHAPTER 3

In Chapter 2 we learned that music generally does not use the total continuous range of musical sounds. Instead, it draws on only a limited number of fixed pitches. These pitches can be assembled in a collection called a **scale**. In effect, a scale is the pool of pitches available for making music.

1 | Scales

There are many different scales used in the musical cultures of the world. From them, musicians everywhere build an infinite array of melodies and other musical structures. If you sing to yourself the melody of one of your favorite songs, you will have employed the pitches of a scale. But how do scales—in particular the scales basic to Western art music—work?

The Octave

Any two pitches will have a certain distance, or difference in highness and lowness, between them. Musicians call this distance an **interval**. Of the many different intervals used in music, one called the **octave** has a special character that makes it particularly important.

If successive pitches are sounded one after another—say, running from low to high up the white keys on a piano—there comes a point at which a pitch seems in some sense to "duplicate" an earlier pitch, but at a higher level. This new pitch does not sound identical to the old one, but somehow the two sounds are very similar. They blend extremely well; they almost seem to melt into each other. This is the octave.

What causes the phenomenon of octaves? Recall from Chapter 2 that when strings vibrate to produce sound, they vibrate not only along their full length but also in halves and other fractions, creating overtones (page 12). A vibrating string that is exactly half as long as another will *reinforce* the longer string's strongest overtone. This reinforcement causes the duplication effect of octaves, and pitches that are an octave apart have frequencies related in a 2:1 ratio.

As strings go, so go vocal cords: When men and women sing along together, they automatically sing in octaves, duplicating each other's singing an octave or two apart. If you ask them, they will say they are singing "the same song"—not many will think of adding "at different octave levels."

As a result of the phenomenon of octaves, the full continuous range of pitches that we can hear seems to fall into a series of "duplicating" segments. We divide these octave segments into smaller intervals, thereby creating scales.

The Diatonic Scale

The scale originally used in Western music is a set of seven pitches within the octave, called the **diatonic scale**. Dating from ancient Greek times, the diatonic scale is still in use today. When the first of the seven pitches is repeated at a higher duplicating pitch, the total is eight—hence the name *octave,* meaning "eight span."

Anyone who knows the series *do re mi fa sol la ti do* is at home with the diatonic scale. You can count out the octave for yourself starting with the first *do* as *one* and ending with the second *do* as *eight*. The set of white keys on a keyboard plays this scale. Shown in the following diagram is a keyboard and diatonic scale notes running through two octaves. The scale notes (pitches) are marked with their conventional letter names. Because there are seven pitches, only the letters up to G are used before returning to A.

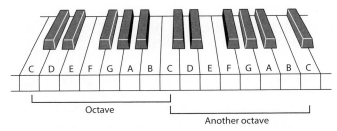

The Chromatic Scale

The diatonic scale was the original, basic scale of Western music. At a later period, five more pitches were added between certain of the seven pitches of the diatonic scale, making a total of twelve. This is the **chromatic scale**, represented by the complete set of white and black keys on a keyboard.

The chromatic scale did not make the diatonic scale obsolete. For centuries Western composers used the chromatic scale freely while favoring the diatonic scale embedded in it. Keyboards reflect this practice, with chromatic notes set back and thinner, and colored differently than diatonic ones.

These five extra pitches caused a problem for musical notation. The pitches of the diatonic scale are indicated on the lines and spaces of the staff (see the diagram on page 24); there are no positions in between, so no place for the new five pitches. To solve this problem, symbols such as those shown in the margin were introduced. B♭ stands for B **flat**, the pitch inserted between A and B; C♯ stands for C **sharp**, the pitch between C and D, and so on.

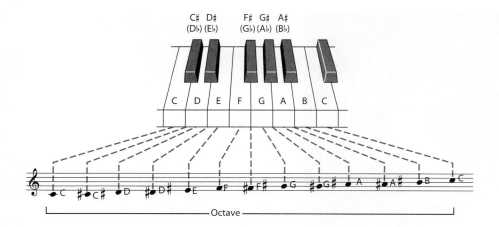

Octave

Half Steps and Whole Steps

You learned before that the difference, or distance, between any two pitches is called the interval between them. There are many different intervals between the notes of the chromatic scale, depending on which two notes you choose, including the octave that encompasses them all.

For our purposes, only two other interval types need be considered:

- The smallest interval is the **half step**, or semitone, which is the distance between any two successive notes of the chromatic scale. On a keyboard, a half step is the interval between the closest adjacent notes, white or black. The distance from E to F is a half step; so is the distance from C to C sharp (C♯), D to E flat (E♭), and so on.

As the smallest interval in regular use, the half step is also the smallest that most people can "hear" easily and identify. Many tunes, such as "The Battle Hymn of the Republic," end with two half steps, one half step going down and then the same one going up again ("His truth is *march-ing on*").

- The **whole step**, or whole tone, is equivalent to two half steps: C to D, D to E, E to F♯, and so on. "Three Blind Mice" starts with two whole steps, going down.

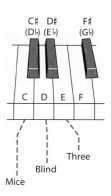

The chromatic scale consists exclusively of half steps. The diatonic scale, instead, includes both half steps and whole steps. As you can see in the keyboard picture on page 25, between B and C and between E and F of the diatonic scale, the interval is a half step—there is no black key separating the white keys. Between the other pairs of adjacent notes, however, the interval is twice as big—a whole step.

In this way the diatonic and chromatic scales differ in the intervals between their adjacent pitches. In the diagram on page 25, the two scales are shown in music notation in order to highlight the differences in the intervals they contain. The mixing of half steps and whole steps is a defining feature of the diatonic scale.

2 | Melody

A **melody** is an organized series of pitches. Melodies can be built from any scale. Think for a moment of pitch and time as the two coordinates of a musical graph (see the diagram shown in the margin). A series of single pitches played in a certain rhythm will appear as dots, high or low, on the pitch/time grid. If we connect them by a line, we get a picture of the melody's overall shape or contour. And in fact, musicians commonly speak of "melodic line," or simply line, in this connection.

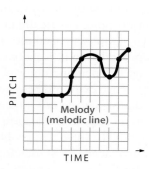

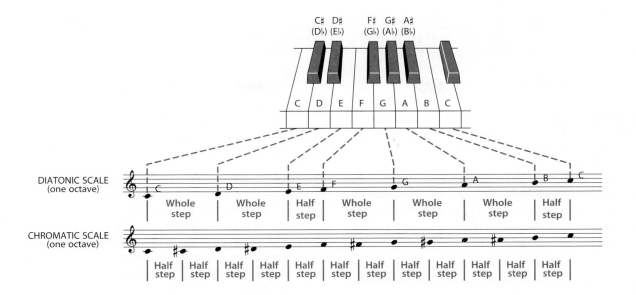

DIATONIC SCALE (one octave)

| C | | D | | E | F | | G | | A | | B | C |
| Whole step | | Whole step | | Half step | | Whole step | | Whole step | | Whole step | | Half step |

CHROMATIC SCALE (one octave)

| Half step | Half step | Half step | Half step | Half step | Half step | Half step | Half step | Half step | Half step | Half step | Half step |

Melodies come in an unlimited array of shapes, and they convey a huge variety of emotional characters. A melody involving a leap from low notes to high can seem to soar; a low note can feel like a setback; a long series of repeated notes on the same pitch can seem to wait ominously. The listener develops a real interest in how the line of a satisfactory melody is going to come out.

Of all music's structures, melody is the one that moves people the most, that seems to evoke human sentiment most directly. Familiar melodies register simple qualities of feeling instantly and strongly. These qualities vary widely: strong and assertive—like a bugle call—in "The Battle Hymn of the Republic," mournful in "Summertime" or "Yesterday," serene in "Amazing Grace," extroverted and cheerful in "Happy Birthday."

"Always remember that in listening to a piece of music you must hang on to the melodic line. It may disappear momentarily. . . . But reappear it surely will."

Composer Aaron Copland, 1939 (see page 349)

Tunes

A simple, easily singable, catchy melody such as a folk song, a Christmas carol, or many popular songs is a **tune**. A tune is a special kind of melody. *Melody* is a term that includes tunes, but also much else.

"The Star-Spangled Banner," which everyone knows, illustrates the general characteristics of tunes. See the box on page 26.

Motives and Themes

Tunes are relatively short; longer pieces, such as symphonies, may have tunes embedded in them, but they also contain other musical material. Two terms are frequently encountered in connection with melody in longer pieces of music: **motive** and **theme**.

A *motive* is a distinctive fragment of melody, distinctive enough so that it will be easily recognized when it returns again and again within a long composition. Motives are shorter than tunes, shorter even than phrases of tunes; they can be as short as two notes. Probably the most famous motive in all music is the four-note DA-DA-DA-**DAAA** motive in Beethoven's Fifth Symphony. It is heard literally hundreds of times in the symphony, sometimes up front and sometimes as a restless element in the background.

DA DA DA **DAAA**

The best way to grasp the characteristics of tunes is by singing one you know, either out loud or in your head.

Division into Phrases Tunes fall naturally into smaller sections, called **phrases**. This is, in fact, true of all melodies, but with tunes the division into phrases is particularly clear and sharp.

In tunes with words (that is, songs), phrases tend to coincide with poetic lines. Most lines in a song lyric end with a rhyming word and a punctuation mark such as a comma. These features clarify the musical phrase divisions:

> And the rockets' red **glare**,
> The bombs bursting in **air**

Singing a song requires breathing—and the natural tendency is to breathe at the end of phrases. You may not need to breathe after phrase 1 of our national anthem, but you'd better not wait any longer than phrase 2:

Oh _ say can you see   By the dawn's ear-ly light

Balance between Phrases In many tunes, all the phrases are two, four, or eight bars long. Blues tunes, for example, usually consist of three four-measure phrases, hence the term *twelve-bar blues*.

Most phrases of "The Star-Spangled Banner" are two measures long (see phrase 1 and phrase 2 above). But one phrase broadens out to four measures, with a fine effect: "Oh say, does that star-spangled banner yet wave." You don't want to breathe in the middle of this long phrase.

Other phrase lengths—three measures, five, and so on—can certainly occur in a tune and make for welcome contrast. For a good tune, the main requirement is that we sense a balance between the phrases, in terms of phrase lengths and in other terms, too, so that taken together the phrases add up to a well-proportioned whole.

Parallelism and Contrast Balance between phrases can be strengthened by means of *parallelism*. For example, phrases can have the same notes but different words ("Oh, say can you see," "Whose broad stripes and bright stars"). Others have the same rhythm but different pitches ("Oh, say can you see," "By the dawn's early light").

Sometimes phrases have the same general melodic shape, but one phrase is slightly higher or lower than the other ("And the rockets' red glare," "The bombs bursting in air"). Such duplication of a phrase at two or more different pitch levels, called **sequence**, occurs frequently in music, and is a hallmark of certain musical styles.

Composers also take care to make some phrases *contrast* with their neighbors—one phrase short, another long, or one phrase low, another high (perhaps even *too* high, at "O'er the land of the *free*"). A tune with some parallel and some contrasting phrases will seem to have a satisfying coherence and yet will avoid monotony.

Climax and Cadence A good tune has *form:* a clear, purposeful beginning, a feeling of action in the middle, and a firm sense of winding down at the end.

Many tunes have a distinct high point, or **climax**, which their earlier portions seem to be heading toward. Feelings rise as voices soar; a melodic high point is always an emotional high point. The climax of our national anthem emphasizes what was felt to be the really crucial word in it—"free." Patriot Francis Scott Key put that word in that place. (Key wrote the words of "The Star-Spangled Banner"—the words only, adapted to an older melody.)

Then the later part of the tune relaxes from this climax, until it reaches a solid stopping place at the end. Emotionally, this is a point of relaxation and satisfaction. In a less definite way, the music also stops at earlier points in the tune—or, if it does not fully stop, at least seems to pause. The term for these interim stopping or pausing places is **cadence**.

Composers can write cadences with all possible shades of solidity and finality. "And the home of the brave" is a very final-sounding cadence; "That our flag was still there" has an interim feeling. The art of making cadences is one of the most subtle and basic processes in musical composition.

Early sheet music for "The Star-Spangled Banner," "A famous Song for the Union." *Corbis.*

The second term, *theme,* is the most general term for the basic subject matter of longer pieces of music. *Theme* is another name for "topic": The themes or topics of an essay you might write are the main points you announce, repeat, develop, and hammer home. A composer treats musical themes in much the same way. The theme of Beethoven's Fifth Symphony consists of the brief DA-DA-DA-**DAAA** motive repeated over and over at different pitches—that is, played in *sequence* (see the key term on page 26). The famous theme of the last movement of Beethoven's Ninth Symphony is a full tune, which we will hear several times in the music recordings (see page 30).

LISTENING EXERCISE 5
Melody and Tune

Unit I | 4

Division into phrases*, *parallelism* and *contrast* between phrases, *sequence*, *climax*,** and ***cadence: These are some characteristics of tunes that we have observed in "The Star-Spangled Banner." They are not just inert characteristics — they are what make the tune work, and they are present in tunes of all kinds. Our example is a song by George and Ira Gershwin from the Depression era, which was also the jazz era: "Who Cares?" from the musical comedy *Of Thee I Sing* (1931).

In "The Star-Spangled Banner" the *climax* matches the text perfectly at "free." Here "jubilee" makes a good match for the climax, and a melodic *sequence* fits the words "I care for you / you care for me" neatly. "Who cares?" comes at 0:57 on our recording by the great jazz singer Ella Fitzgerald, after an introduction (called the *verse*) typical of such songs — a sort of subsidiary tune, with words that will not be repeated.

0:12	**Verse**: Let it rain and thunder . . . (eight more lines)	Includes a long ***sequence***
0:48		Tempo changes
0:57	**Tune**: Who cares if the sky cares to fall in the sea?	First phrase of the tune
	Who cares what banks fail in Yonkers?	***Contrasting*** phrase
	Long as you've got a kiss that conquers.	***Parallel*** phrase — starts like the preceding, ends higher
	Why should I care? Life is one long jubilee,	Threefold ***sequence*** ("Should I care / life is one / jubilee")
		Climax on "jubilee"
	So long as I care for you and you care for me.	Free ***sequence*** ("I care for you"/"you care for me") — ***cadence***
1:55	**Tune** played by the jazz band, today's "big band"	

George Gershwin and Ira Gershwin, "Who Cares? (So Long As You Care For Me)" from *Of Thee I Sing*. Music and lyrics by George Gershwin and Ira Gershwin. Copyright © 1931 (Renewed) WB Music Corp. All Rights Reserved. Used by permission of Alfred Music.

GOALS FOR REVIEW

▶ to understand the importance of octave, half step, and whole step in making scales

▶ to distinguish diatonic and chromatic scales

▶ to build a vocabulary for melody or tune: phrase, cadence, motive, theme

macmillanhighered.com/listen8e
Music for Listening Exercise 5
Listening Quiz for Chapter 3
Reading Quiz for Chapter 3

Harmony, Texture, Tonality, and Mode

A single melody is enough to qualify as music—sometimes, indeed, as great music. When people sing in the shower and when parents sing to their babies they are producing melody, and that is all, to everyone's full satisfaction. The same was true of the early Christian church, whose music, Gregorian chant, consisted of more than two thousand different melodies—and melodies alone.

Today, however, after a long and complicated historical development, it seems very natural to us to hear melodies together with other sounds. We are accustomed to hearing a folk singer singing and playing a guitar at the same time—*accompanying* herself on the guitar, as we say. In church, the congregation sings the hymns while the organist supplies the *accompaniment*.

Two concepts of basic importance in thinking about the way pitches sound together with each other are *harmony* and *texture*.

1 | Harmony

The most general word musicians use to refer to the sounding at the same time of different pitches is **harmony**. The folk singer's melody is said to be **harmonized**. She uses a number of standard groupings of simultaneous pitches that work well in combination. These groupings are called **chords**. The changing chords provide a shifting sound background for the melody. Any melody can be harmonized in different ways using different chords, and the overall effect of the music depends to a great extent on the nature of these chords, or the harmony in general.

In most of the music we hear, harmony is almost as important an element as melody. And, like melody, harmony is a powerful stimulus to our emotional responses to music.

Consonance and Dissonance

A pair of terms used in discussions of harmony are **consonance** and **dissonance**, meaning (roughly speaking) chords that sound at rest and those that sound tense, respectively. *Discord* is another term for dissonance. These qualities depend on the particular combinations of pitches that are sounding simultaneously to make up these chords. Octaves are the most consonant of intervals. Half steps are the most dissonant, as you can hear by striking any two adjacent keys on a piano at the same time.

In everyday language, *discord* implies something unpleasant; discordant human relationships are to be avoided. But music does not avoid dissonance, for

Melody and harmony: Abigail Washburn with her banjo. © *Jack Vartoogian/FrontRowPhotos.*

"Medicine, to produce health, must know disease; music, to produce harmony, must know discord."

Plutarch, c. 46–120 c.e.

a little discord supplies the subtle tensions that are essential to make music flow along. A dissonant chord leaves a feeling of expectation; it seems to demand a consonant chord following it to complete the gesture and to make the music come to a point of stability. This is called *resolution;* the dissonance is said to be *resolved.* Without dissonance, music would be bland, like food without salt or spices.

2 | Texture

Texture is the term used to refer to the way the various sounds and melodic lines occurring together in music interact or blend with one another. The word is adopted from textiles, where it refers to the weave of the various threads—loose or tight, even or mixed. A cloth such as tweed or denim, for instance, leaves the different threads clearly visible. In fine silk the weave is so tight and smooth that the threads are almost impossible to detect.

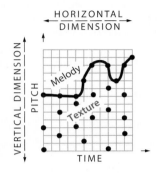

Thinking again of the pitch/time graph on page 24, we can see that it is possible to plot more than one pitch for every time slot. Melody exists in the horizontal dimension, from left to right; texture in the vertical dimension, from top to bottom. (For the moment, we leave the lower dots below the melody unconnected.)

Monophony

Monophony (mo-náh-fuh-nee) is the term for the simplest texture, a single unaccompanied melody: Gregorian chant; singing in the shower; "Row, Row, Row Your Boat" before the second person comes in. Simple as this texture is, some very beautiful and sophisticated **monophonic** music has been composed, just as artists have done wonderful things with line drawings.

Homophony and Polyphony

When there is only one melody of real interest and it is combined with other, less prominent sounds, the texture is called **homophonic**. A harmonized melody is an example of homophonic texture; for instance, one person singing the tune of "Yesterday" while playing chords on a guitar. We might indicate a chord on the pitch/time graph by a vertical box enclosing the dots (see margin). Each box represents a chord; the sum of these boxes represents the harmony. **Homophony** can be thought of as a tight, smooth texture—like silk, among textiles.

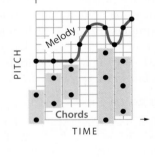

When two or more melodies are played or sung simultaneously, the texture is described as **polyphonic**. In **polyphony** (po-líf-uh-nee), the melodies are felt to be independent and of approximately equal interest. The whole is more than the sum of the parts, however; the way the melodies play off one another makes for the possibility of greater richness and interest than if they were played singly. In the textile analogy, polyphony would be compared to a rough fabric in which the strands are all perceptible, such as a multicolored woolen blanket.

It's also important to recognize that polyphonic music automatically has harmony. For at every moment in time, on every beat, the multiple horizontal melodies create vertical chords; those chords make harmony. A word often used for polyphonic texture is **contrapuntal**, which comes from the word **counterpoint**, the technique of writing two or more melodies that fit together.

Imitation

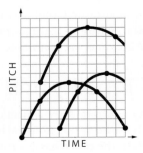

Polyphonic texture, like so many other musical elements, cannot be categorized with any precision. One useful and important distinction, however, is between *imitative polyphony* and *non-imitative polyphony.*

A famous passage from Beethoven furnishes a clear example of **monophonic, polyphonic,** and **homophonic textures** — the initial presentation of the so-called Joy Theme in Symphony No. 9, the "Choral" Symphony. The theme, a tune known around the world, takes its name from the words set to it, an enthusiastic ode to the joy that comes from human freedom, companionship, and reverence for the deity. The words are sung by soloists and a chorus.

But before anyone sings, the theme is played several times by the orchestra, in a way that suggests that joy is emerging out of nothingness into its full realization. Beginning with utterly simple *monophony,* and growing successively higher and louder, it is enriched by *polyphony* and then reaches its grand climax in *homophony.*

5	0:00	Joy Theme	Low register	**Monophony:** a single melodic line; cellos and double basses playing together, with no accompaniment
	0:49	Theme	An octave higher	**Polyphony, non-imitative:** the theme with two lines of **counterpoint,** in low strings (cello) and a mellow wind instrument (bassoon)
	1:36	Theme	Two octaves higher	
	2:21	Theme	Three octaves higher	**Homophony:** full orchestra with trumpets prominent

Our example of **imitative polyphony** comes from the *Symphony of Psalms,* another symphony with chorus, a major work by the twentieth-century composer Igor Stravinsky.

6	0:00	A slow, winding melody, unaccompanied, played by an oboe
	0:25	The same melody enters in another instrument, a flute, as the oboe continues with new material; this produces two-part **imitative counterpoint.**
	0:58	Third entry, second flute plays in a lower register — three-part counterpoint
	1:20	Fourth entry, second oboe — four-part counterpoint

Imitative polyphony results when the various lines sounding together use the same or fairly similar melodies, with one coming in shortly after another. The simplest example of imitative polyphony is a round, such as "Row, Row, Row Your Boat" or "Frère Jacques"; the richest kind is a fugue (see Chapter 10). In the following music example, you can see that each voice enters with the same notes but in staggered fashion; the second and third voices *imitate* the first:

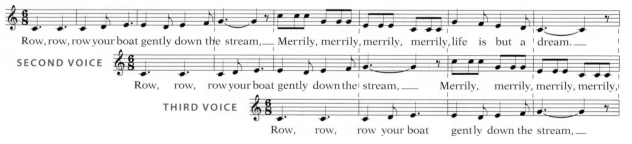

FIRST VOICE

Row, row, row your boat gently down the stream,— Merrily, merrily, merrily, merrily, life is but a dream.—

SECOND VOICE

Row, row, row your boat gently down the stream,— Merrily, merrily, merrily, merrily,

THIRD VOICE

Row, row, row your boat gently down the stream,—

Non-imitative polyphony occurs when the melodies are different from one another. An example that many will know is the typical texture of a New Orleans jazz band, with the trumpet playing the main tune, flanked top and bottom by the clarinet and the trombone playing exhilarating melodies of their own.

3 | Tonality and Mode

Tonality and mode are aspects of melody as well as harmony, and as such they might have been taken up earlier. We have deferred them till last because, even more than the other basic structures of music, they require careful explanation.

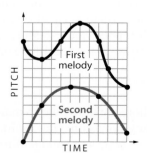

Tonality

We start with a basic fact about melodies and tunes: Melodies nearly always give a sense of focusing around a single "home" pitch that feels more important than all the other pitches of the scale. Usually this is **do** in the *do re mi fa sol la ti do* scale (C D E F G A B C). This pitch feels fundamental, and the melody seems to come to rest most naturally on it. The other notes in the melody all sound close or distant, dissonant or consonant, in reference to the fundamental note, and some of them may actually seem to lean or lead toward it.

This homing instinct that we sense in melodies is called **tonality**. The music in question is described as **tonal**. The home pitch (*do*) is called the *tonic pitch,* or simply the **tonic**.

The easy way to identify the tonic is to sing the whole melody through, because the last note is almost invariably *it.* Thus "The Star-Spangled Banner" ends on its tonic, *do:* "and the home of the *brave.*" An entire piece of music, as well as just a short melody, can give this feeling of focusing on a home pitch and wanting to end there.

Major and Minor Modes

Turn back to page 23 and the diagram for the diatonic scale, the basic scale of Western music. This diagram, of course, shows only a portion of a longer scale extending all the way up the octaves, from the lowest limits of hearing to the highest. Our portion, covering two octaves, starts on C because most melodies are oriented around C (*do*), as we've just explained.

The following diagram shows another portion of the diatonic scale, starting on A (*la*), because another class of melodies in Western music is oriented around A, not C:

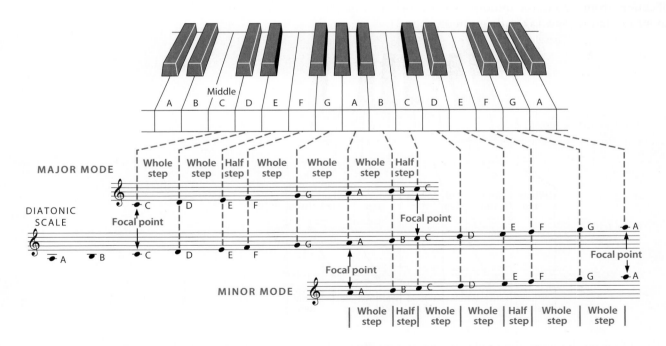

Look carefully at the diagram: Moving up through the octave from C to C, you encounter a different sequence of whole and half steps than you do moving from A to A. This difference gives melodies oriented around A a quality different from those oriented around C. The term for these different ways of centering or organizing the diatonic scale is **modality**; the different home pitches are said to determine the different **modes** of music. Music with the *do* (C) center is in the **major mode**. Music with the *la* (A) orientation is in the **minor mode**.

Keys

Mode and key are concepts that are often confused. Let us see if we can clarify them.

We have just seen how the two modes, the major with its tonic or home pitch on C and the minor on A, are derived from the *diatonic* scale. However, if you use all twelve notes of the *chromatic* scale, you can construct both the major and the minor modes starting from any note at all. Whichever note you choose as tonic, starting from there you can pick out the correct sequence of half steps and whole steps. This is because the chromatic scale includes *all* possible half steps and whole steps.

Thanks to the chromatic scale, then, major and minor modes can be constructed starting on any pitch. These different positions for the modes are called **keys**. If the major mode is positioned on C, the music is said to be in the key of C major, or just "in C"; positioned on D, the key is D major. Likewise we have the keys of C minor, D minor, and—as there are twelve pitches in the chromatic scale—a grand total of twenty-four different keys (twelve major and twelve minor).

Listening for the Major and Minor Modes

On paper, it is easiest to show the difference between major and minor if we compare major and minor keys that share the same tonic. So yet another diagram, below, compares C major with C minor. C minor is derived by duplicating, from C to C, the minor-mode arrangement of whole and half steps from A to A that we saw in the diagram on page 31.

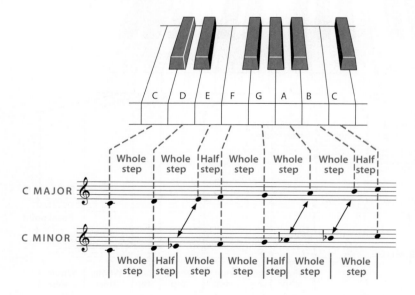

The difference between the modes is easy to see. Three of the scale degrees are lower in the minor (hence the term *minor*, of course); they are the pitches connected by arrows in the diagram. The arrangement of intervals is not the same when you sing up or down the scales, and this in turn makes a great difference in the feel of melodies built from these scales.

Hearing the difference between music in the major and minor modes comes easily to some listeners, less easily to others. As a result of the three lower scale degrees, music in the minor mode tends to sound more subdued, more clouded than music in the major. It is often said that major sounds cheerful and minor sounds sad, and this is true enough in a general way; but there are many exceptions, and in any case people can have different ideas about what constitutes sadness and cheerfulness in music.

Learning to distinguish the major and minor modes requires comparative listening. Listen especially for the third scale degree up from the tonic. "Joshua Fit the Battle of Jericho" and "We Three Kings" are both in the minor mode. Singing them through, we can practice recognizing the characteristic minor-mode sound involving the third scale degree at the final cadence.

Is it right to represent the major and minor modes by comedy and tragedy masks? Yes, but only in a general sense — there are many nuances between these extremes. ©68/GK Hart/Vikki Hart/ Ocean/Corbis.

Joshua Fit the Battle of Jericho

walls came tum-blin' down.

We Three Kings

fol-low-ing yon-der star.

Compare this with the third note up from the tonic at the end of major-mode songs such as "My Country, 'Tis of Thee," "Row, Row, Row Your Boat," "The Star-Spangled Banner," and many others. It sounds brighter, more positive.

My Country, 'Tis of Thee

let — free - dom ring!

Row, Row, Row Your Boat

life is but a dream.

The Star-Spangled Banner

home of the brave.

Listening for Keys and Modulation

The major and minor modes can be said to differ from one another intrinsically, for in each mode the pitches form their own special set of intervals and interval relationships. As we have seen, C major and C minor, while sharing the same central or tonic pitch, have their own individual arrangements of half- and whole-step intervals.

Different keys, however, merely entail the same set of intervals moved to a new position within the pitch continuum. This is a significant difference, but not an intrinsic one. In baseball, first base is different from second base, but only because the same sort of bag has been put in a significant new place.

As for actually *hearing* keys—that is, recognizing the different keys—for some listeners this presents an even greater problem than hearing modality, though to others it comes more easily. The important thing is not to be able to identify keys in themselves, but rather to be able to hear when keys change. Changing the key of music changes its mood or the way it feels; generations of composers have used this resource for some of their most powerful effects. Such changes of key—that is, changes of the tonic or home pitch—are called **modulations**. You will have many opportunities to hear the effects modulations can create; here you should try Listening Exercise 7, the most challenging one yet, listening for changes in mode and key.

Modality is probably most obvious when you hear a minor-mode melody (or phrase of melody) and then hear it with the mode changed to major. A short passage from the String Quartet in A Minor by Franz Schubert is a lovely illustration of this change.

| 7 | 0:00 | **pp** | A melancholy melody in the **minor mode**. Listen to the first violin above the rustling accompaniment in the lower stringed instruments. |
| | 0:47 | | The beginning of the melody returns, changed to the **major mode**. |

Listen to more of the Schubert quartet for a change in **key**:

	1:04	**ff**	Agitated; back in the minor mode. Lower instruments alternate with the solo violin.
	1:39	**p**	A quiet cadence, still in the same key, but followed by **modulation**
	1:56	**p**	Reaching a **new key**, for a new theme. This theme is in the major mode, calm and sunny.

For a series of **modulations** to several different keys, listen to the passage from Beethoven's Piano Concerto No. 5, the "Emperor" Concerto. Here the key changes stand out clearly because the modulations are carried out so abruptly — a Beethoven specialty.

8	0:00	Lively music for the piano, **f**, followed by a **f** response from the orchestra
	0:28	Modulation (French horns)
		New key: Similar music for piano, but **pp**, followed by the same orchestral response, **f**
	1:03	Similar modulation (French horns). The music seems to be searching for a place to settle.
		Another new key: piano, **p**, and orchestra, **f**, as before
	1:36	The piano bursts in, **f**, in the same key but in the **minor mode**. It begins modulating to further new keys in a more complicated way than before.

GOALS FOR REVIEW

► to define harmony and build a vocabulary for it: consonance, dissonance, and chord

► to listen for different textures: monophony, homophony, polyphony (counterpoint)

► to understand the concept of tonality, with its central pitch or tonic

► to distinguish major and minor modes

► to understand the difference between mode and key, and to listen for both

macmillanhighered.com/listen8e
Music for Listening Exercises 6 and 7
Listening Quiz for Chapter 4
Reading Quiz for Chapter 4

Musical Form and Musical Style

CHAPTER 5

Form is a general word with a long list of dictionary definitions. As applied to the arts, **form** is an important concept that refers to the shape, arrangement, relationship, or organization of the various elements. In poetry, for example, the elements of form are words, phrases, meters, rhymes, and stanzas; in painting, they are lines, colors, shapes, and space.

1 | Form in Music

In music, the elements of form and organization are those we have already discussed: rhythm, dynamics, tone color, melody, harmony, and texture. A musical work, whether a simple song or a whole symphony, is formed or organized by means of repetitions of some of these elements, and by contrasts among them. The repetitions may be strict or free (that is, exact or with some variation). The contrasts may be of many different kinds—the possibilities are virtually limitless—conveying many different kinds of feeling.

Over the centuries and all over the world, musicians have learned to create long and impressive pieces in this way: symphonies, operas, works for the Javanese gamelan or Japanese gagaku orchestras, and more. Each piece is a specific sound experience in a definite time span, with a beginning, middle, and end, and often with subtle routes between. Everyone knows that music can make a nice effect for a minute or two. But how does music extend itself—and hold the listener's interest—for ten minutes, or half an hour, or three whole hours at a time?

This is one of the main functions of musical form. Form is the relationship that connects those beginnings, middles, and ends.

> "The content of music is tonally moving forms."
>
> *Music critic Eduard Hanslick, 1854*

Form and Feeling

Form in art also has a good deal to do with its emotional quality; it is much more than a merely structural or intellectual matter. Think of the little (or big) emotional click we get at the end of a limerick or any poem with a "punch line," where the accumulated meanings of the words are summed up with the final rhyme. On a small scale, this is an effect to which form contributes. Similarly, when a melody heard before comes back at the end of a symphony, with new orchestration and new harmonies, the special feeling this gives us emerges from

Form in Painting

A Madonna by Raphael Sanzio (1483–1520), built out of two skillfully nested triangles. To balance the boys at the left, the Virgin faces slightly to the right, her extended foot "echoing" their bare flesh. On a larger scale, the activity at the left is matched by a steeper landscape. *Mondadori Portfolio/Electa/ Sergio Anelli/The Bridgeman Art Library.*

a flood of memory; we remember the melody in its earlier version. That effect, too, is created by form.

How easy is it, actually, to perceive form in music and to experience the feelings associated with form? Easy enough with a short tune, such as "The Star-Spangled Banner"—that's what the analysis on page 26 was all about. The various phrases of this tune, with their repetitions, parallel features, contrasts, and climax, provide a microcosm of musical form in longer pieces. A large-scale composition such as a symphony is something like a greatly expanded tune, and its form is experienced in basically the same way.

To be sure, a symphony requires more from the listener—more time and more attention—than a tune does. Aware of the potential problem here, composers scale their musical effects accordingly. The larger the piece, the more strongly the composer is likely to help the memory along by emphasizing the repetitions and contrasts that determine the musical form.

Form and Forms

Like the word *rhythm* (see page 4), the word *form* has a general meaning and also a more specific one. "Form" in general refers to the organization of elements in a musical work, but "*a form*" refers to one of many standardized formal patterns that composers have used over the centuries. The ones treated later in this book are listed in the margin.

The fixed elements in such forms provide a welcome source of orientation for listeners, but they are always general enough to allow composers endless possibilities on the detailed level. The quality and feeling of works in the same standardized or conventional form can therefore vary greatly.

Form in Poetry

Fleas:
Adam
Had 'em.

The poet creates rhyme and meter to add a little lift, and a smile, to the prose observation "Adam had fleas" (or "Ever since Adam and Eve, we've all suffered").

Musical forms, as standardized patterns, are conventionally expressed by letter diagrams, such as **A B A** or **a b a** (small letters tend to be used for shorter sections of music). They will be used again and again in this book. More complicated forms can be indicated through "nesting" capital and lowercase letters:

A	**B**	**A**
a b a	**c d c**	**a b a**

As we have said, two basic factors create musical form: *repetition* and *contrast*. In **A B A** form, one of the simplest, the element of repetition is **A** and the element of contrast is **B**. Some sort of tune or theme or other musical section is presented at the beginning (**A**), then comes another section (**B**) that contrasts with the first, and then the first one again (**A**). If **A** returns with significant modification, this can be indicated by a prime mark: **A'**.

It seems clear enough. Yet the letters tell us only so much. With any particular work, what about the specific music they stand for? Is **B** in a different mode or a different key? Does it present material that contrasts in rhythm, texture, or tone color—or does it work its contrast by ringing changes on the original material, on **A**? The returns to **A** material in **A B A'** form, too, can convey very different feelings. One return can sound exciting, another unexpected, while yet another provides a sense of relief.

So diagramming forms—getting the letters right—is just a first step in music appreciation. We need also to understand the way composers refine, modify, and personalize conventional forms for their own expressive purposes.

Musical Genres

One often hears symphonies, sonatas, and operas referred to as "forms" of music. Actually this is loose terminology, best avoided in the interests of clarity, because symphonies and other works can be composed in completely different standardized forms. Thus, the last movement of Joseph Haydn's Symphony No. 95 is in rondo form, whereas the last movement of Hector Berlioz's *Fantastic Symphony* follows no standard form whatsoever.

Form in Architecture

Many have noted the analogy between musical form and architectural form; "I call architecture frozen music," said the famous German poet Goethe (see page 234). The musical form frozen in this building might have three statements of the same music, each more emphatic than the last, followed by a strong cadence.
© *Platinum GPics/Alamy.*

"The Star-Spangled Banner" (not included in our recordings) has one of the simplest forms, **a a b**. "Oh, say can you see . . . the twilight's last gleaming" is **a**, "Whose broad stripes . . . gallantly streaming" is the second **a**, and the rest of the anthem is **b**. Section **b** makes a definite contrast with **a** by means of its new melody and higher range, as we've seen on page 26.

When sections of music are not identical but are considered essentially parallel, they are labeled **a**, **a′**, **a″**, and so on. The first theme of Schubert's String Quartet in A Minor is in **a a′ a″ form**.

7			
0:00	**a**	Melancholy
0:21	**a′**	Begins like **a**, but the melody lasts longer and goes higher and lower than in **a**
0:47	**a″**	The beginning now turns luminously to the major mode.

Smaller form elements (**a**, **b**, **a′**) can be nested in larger ones, marked with capital letters: **A**, **B**, **A′**. A more extended example comes from an all-time classical favorite, the Christmas ballet *The Nutcracker* by Pyotr Ilyich Tchaikovsky. Tchaikovsky used the "Dance of the Sugar-Plum Fairy" mainly to show off the celesta, a rare instrument (see page 17). The **A B A′** form of the dance breaks down into **a a′ b b a a′**.

9			
0:00			Introduction: The 2/4 meter is previewed by low stringed instruments.
0:08	**A**	**a**	Solo for celesta, with comments by a bass clarinet
0:23		**a′**	Begins like **a**, but the ending is different—on a new pitch and harmony
0:37	**B**	**b**	Contrast with **a**
0:44		**b**	
0:51			Transition: The music has a preparatory quality.
1:07	**A′**	**a**	Celesta an octave higher, with a quiet new click in the violins; the high celesta is a very striking sound.
1:22		**a′**	

The new orchestration is what gives this **A B A′** form its prime mark—not changes in melody or harmony, as is usually the case. More strictly, the form could be marked ***introduction*** **A** (**a a′**) **B** (**b b**) ***transition*** **A′** (**a″ a‴**), but this level of detail is seldom needed.

The best term for these general categories or kinds of music is **genre** (jáhn-ruh), borrowed from French. A genre can be defined by its text (a madrigal has Italian verses of a specific kind), or by its function (a Mass is written for a Roman Catholic service), or by the performing forces (a quartet is for four singers or instrumentalists). The main genres of Western music taken up in *Listen* are listed in the margin on page 39.

2 | Musical Style

Style, like *form*, is another of those broad, general words—general but very necessary. The style of a tennis player is the particular way he or she reaches up for the serve, follows through on the forehand, rushes the net, hits the ball deep or short, and so on. A lifestyle means the whole combination of things one does and doesn't do: the food one eats, the way one dresses and talks, one's habits of thought and feeling.

The style of a work of art, similarly, is the combination of qualities that make it distinctive. One composer's style may favor jagged rhythms, simple harmonies, and tunes to the exclusion of other types of melody. Another may prefer certain kinds of tone color or texture; still another may concentrate on a particular form. The type of emotional expression a composer cultivates is also an important determinant of musical style.

One can speak of the lifestyle of a generation as well as the lifestyle of a particular person. Similarly, a distinction can be made between the musical style of a particular composer and the style of a historical period. For example, to a large extent George Frideric Handel's manner of writing falls within the parameters of the Baroque style of his day. But some features of Handel's style are unique, and perhaps it is those features in particular that embody his musical genius.

Musical Style and Lifestyle

In any historical period or place, the musical style bears some relation to the lifestyle in general; this seems self-evident, even if the correlations are hard to pinpoint. Perhaps the point is clearest with popular music, where distinct (and distinctly different) worlds are evoked by rock, rap, and country music, to say nothing of earlier styles such as 1950s rhythm and blues or 1930s swing.

Older styles of music, too, relate to total cultural situations, and we will suggest some of these cultural connections to music of the various historical periods. In the Prelude chapters for each time period in this book, we sketch certain aspects of the culture, history, and lifestyle of the time. We then briefly outline the musical style and, wherever possible, suggest correlations. Then, in the chapters that follow, the musical style is examined in more detail through individual composers and individual pieces of music.

These individual pieces are our principal concern—not history, or culture, or concepts of musical style in the abstract. Learning the basic concepts of music (as we have tried to do in this unit) is useful only insofar as it focuses and sharpens the process of listening to actual music. This book is called *Listen,* and it rests on the belief that the love of music depends first and foremost on careful listening to particular pieces. But such listening never happens in a vacuum; for all of us it takes place in a vivid, experienced context of some kind. The general information presented here on history, culture, styles, and genres is intended to remake, in some small way, our own listening contexts. In this way it can play a role in our listening experiences.

As we come to the end of Unit I, after a lot of prose and a number of hasty musical excerpts, let's listen to a whole composition at some length: *The Young Person's Guide to the Orchestra*—the young of all ages—by Benjamin Britten, who was the leading English composer of the twentieth century.

Benjamin Britten (1913–1976), *The Young Person's Guide to the Orchestra* (1946)

Unit I | 10–15

Benjamin Britten wrote a lot of music for children, and he undertook *The Young Person's Guide to the Orchestra* as an educational responsibility, in order to teach listeners the timbres of orchestral instruments. We have already listened to the piece with this aim in mind (see page 18). But Britten also set out to create a coherent and interesting musical composition. Listening to it again, we can review several of the concepts introduced in Unit I.

The work uses one basic *theme*—a short, rather bouncy *tune* by an earlier English composer, Henry Purcell (see page 88). Britten first displays the tune in a grand setting for full orchestra, *harmonized* with his own rich *chords*. Then he has each of the four *orchestral choirs* play it: woodwinds, brass, strings . . . but he knew he had to cheat when he got to the percussion. (The main percussion instruments

theme, page 25

tune, page 25

orchestral choirs, page 18

are pitch-impaired and can't play tunes.) It was clever, then, to prepare for the not-very-thematic percussion statement at 2:07 by freeing up the theme a little in the preceding brass and stringed statements, and afterward to remind us of the original tune, played verbatim by the full orchestra again. (Britten makes up for his cheat by a particularly brilliant percussion episode later.)

So far everything has been in the *minor mode* and in *triple meter*. But next comes a series of *variations* on the theme, versions of the theme varied in melody, rhythm, texture, mode, tempo—anything and everything. We study the variation form on page 169. The first section of the piece has given us a theme in the minor mode and its repetitions, but the first variations already switch to the major mode. Variation 3, in a swinging *triple meter*, is followed at once by a variation in *duple meter*. Many variations—Variations 1, 3, and 4, to begin with—involve a great deal of repetition of a single *motive*. There are variations in fast *tempo* that last for hardly more than half a minute, and others in slow tempo that take nearly three times as long. Along the way, in keeping with Britten's teaching aims in the work, each variation features a particular instrument (or family of instruments) from the orchestra.

In variation form, variety is the order of the day. This central variation section of the *Young Person's Guide* offers, in addition to the catalogue of instrumental sounds, an equally dazzling catalogue of the endlessly varied moods that can be represented in music.

At the end, Britten writes an extremely vigorous *fugue*, based on yet another version of the Purcell tune. We study fugue on page 126. For now, notice that this section of the *Young Person's Guide* provides an excellent example of *imitative polyphony*.

And our virtuoso composer has still one more trick up his sleeve: He brings the tune back triumphantly just before the end, unvaried, while the fugue is still going on. Both can be heard simultaneously. This is non-imitative polyphony. The return of the tune wraps up the whole long piece very happily as a unique variety of **A B A′** *form*.

major and minor modes, page 32

duple and triple meter, page 5

motive, page 25

tempo, page 7

polyphony, page 29

form, page 35

Britten, *The Young Person's Guide to the Orchestra*
17 min., 13 sec.

10	0:00	**THEME**	Full orchestra	Note the prominent *sequence* in the middle of the Purcell tune. You will hear snatches of this in some of the variations.
	0:23	**Transition**		*Diminuendo* (getting softer). Further transitions occurring between thematic statements and variations will not be indicated on this chart.
	0:42	Theme	WOODWIND choir	
	1:11	Theme	BRASS choir	Ending is changed.
	1:42	Theme	STRING choir	**Theme is changed further.**
	2:07		PERCUSSION	"Theme" only in principle; only some rhythms remain.
	2:26	THEME	Full orchestra	Same as the first time
11	2:50	**Variation 1**	**Flutes and piccolo**	**(harp accompaniment)**
0:14	3:04			**Piccolo and flute play in harmony.**
0:39	3:29	**Variation 2**	**Oboes**	**Beginning of the tune transformed into a slow, romantic melody in oboe 1; oboe 2 joins in two-part *polyphony*.**
1:42	4:32	**Variation 3**	**Clarinet family**	**Two clarinets trade agile figures, swinging from high to low pitches.**
2:24	5:14	**Variation 4**	**Bassoon**	**Typical qualities of the bassoon: *staccato* (comic effect) and *legato* (melodious)**
12	6:11	**Variation 5**	**Violins**	**With chordal accompaniment — particularly clear *homophonic* texture**
0:45	6:56	**Variation 6**	**Violas**	**Slower**
1:34	7:45	**Variation 7**	**Cellos**	**Another slow, romantic melody: falls into a a′ form (clarinet in the background)**
2:32	8:43	**Variation 8**	**Double bass**	**Solo — humorous**
3:29	9:40	**Variation 9**	**Harp**	**In the background is a string *tremolo*, caused by bowing a single note extremely rapidly, so that it sounds like a single trembling note.**
13	10:31	Variation 10	French horns	
0:40	11:11	Variation 11	Trumpets	With snare drum, suggesting a fast military march
1:16	11:47	Variation 12	Trombones, tuba	Typical qualities of the trombone: humorously pompous, and mysterious chords
14	12:48	Variation 13	PERCUSSION	Timpani and bass drum (heard throughout the variation), cymbals (0:18), tambourine (0:28), triangle (0:32), snare drum (0:40), Chinese block (0:44), xylophone (0:50), castanets (1:01), gong (1:07), whip (1:14), xylophone and triangle (1:41)
				Percussion instruments are described on page 17.
15	14:43	**FUGUE**	Full orchestra	*Imitative polyphony* starts with flutes, then oboe, clarinet (same order as above!).
1:47	16:30	**THEME**	Full orchestra	Climax: slower than before. The tune combined with the fugue: *non-imitative polyphony*.

GOALS FOR REVIEW

▶ to think about form in music and relate it to form in poetry, art, and architecture

▶ to listen for simple musical forms

▶ to diagram musical forms with letters

▶ to differentiate three key terms: *form*, *genre*, and *style*

 macmillanhighered.com/listen8e
Music for Listening Exercise 8
Interactive Listening Chart 1
Listening Quiz for Chapter 5
Reading Quiz for Chapter 5

Early Music: An Overview

UNIT II

Western art music extends from the great repertory of Gregorian chant, first assembled around the year 600 C.E., to compositions circulating electronically on the Internet today. The scope and variety of all this music is almost bewildering; there's too much of it by far to cover in a single semester or quarter course—too much, that is, if one is going to do more than skim the music, picking up a few stray facts and figures about it without really *listening* carefully.

But listening carefully is the crucial thing; so we needed to make choices, limiting the range of music covered in *Listen*. The most attentive coverage begins in the eighteenth century, with Unit III and the music of Bach and Handel, who are the earliest composers with a long-standing place in the standard repertory of concert music. By *standard repertory* we mean a large body of music from which concert artists and conductors usually draw their programs.

As a concise introduction to all this, Unit II presents an overview of the rich traditions of Western art music before the eighteenth century. This so-called early music, from the Middle Ages, the Renaissance, and the early Baroque period, was forgotten for centuries and revived mainly in the second half of the twentieth century. The revival itself shows that musical life keeps changing, and these days many concert series and even opera companies include early music on their schedules. Through these performances and through recordings, what was once forgotten has found its way back into today's classical music mainstream.

The Virgin Mary was venerated very widely in the Middle Ages and the Renaissance. Music written for her ranges from hymns by St. Ambrose in the fourth century C.E., to Notre Dame organum in the twelfth century, to twelve Marian Masses by Palestrina in the sixteenth century—and far beyond. Music is played for her in many pictures. In this charming Madonna by the German painter Stefan Lochner, Mary appears lost in deep meditation of the Christian mystery, apparently oblivious to the Christ Child, the Holy Ghost (the dove), and even God above her. *Artothek.*

Chronology

The Middle Ages

CHAPTER 6

"The Middle Ages" is a catchall term for nearly a thousand years of European history, extending from the collapse of the Roman Empire in the fifth century C.E. to the advent of new learning, technology, and political organization in the age of Columbus. Even though life and culture changed slowly in those days, this is obviously too broad a span of time to mean much as a single historical period.

Nowhere is this clearer than in music. Music changed radically from the beginning to the end of the Middle Ages, more than in any other historical period. Two of the central features of later Western music, *tune* and *polyphony*, originated around the middle of this long period.

1 | Music and the Church

The early history of Western music was determined by the Christian church to an extent that is not easy for us to grasp today. The church cultivated, supported, and directed music as it did art, architecture, poetry, and learning. Composers were priests, clerics, or monks, and most musicians got their training as church choirboys. Exception must be made for popular musicians—called minstrels and **jongleurs** (jawn-glérs)—but we know little about their lives or their music. The only people who wrote music down were monks and other clerics, who could not have cared less about preserving popular music.

The music fostered by the church was the singing or chanting of sacred words in services, and we might pause for a moment to ask why singing was so important for Christian worship. Singing is a way of uttering words; words denote concepts, and singing words gives concepts in prayer or doctrine a special status, a step above merely speaking them. Music provides words with special emphasis, force, mystery, even magic. Throughout human history, this heightening by music has served the basic aim of religion: to bring humans into beneficial contact with unseen spirits, with deities, or with a single God.

Music and Church Services: Liturgy

The basic difference between music in church in the Middle Ages and now is that now the music is usually a matter of free choice by the minister—think of gospel music—whereas then it was fixed by a higher authority. This was true even in humble parish churches—that is, local churches for ordinary people—and all the more so for the higher ranks of Christendom: monks and nuns in monasteries, and priests and clerics attached to the great cathedrals.

The higher authority was called the **liturgy**. A whole set of services was arranged according to the calendar, specifying how to worship in summer or winter, on Sunday or a weekday, at night or in the morning, and how to celebrate All Saints' Day or Christmas, mark the beginning of Lent, or pray to the Virgin Mary or a patron saint.

All the largest world religions—Islam, Hinduism, and Buddhism as well as Christianity and Judaism—have complex systems of worship, or liturgies, and they all involve singing or chanting. Zen, for example, has a particular liturgy within Buddhism. Liturgies also include prescriptions for dress, incense, candles, movements, and so on. In Christianity, the central dates of the liturgy concern the life of Christ (his birth at Christmas, his crucifixion and resurrection at Easter) and the main saints, especially the Virgin Mary (her birthday, the day she ascended to heaven).

Monks and nuns in the Middle Ages spent an amazing amount of their time in prayer. Besides the Mass, a lengthy ceremony that might happen more than once a day, there were no fewer than eight other prayer services through the day and night. Large portions of all these services were sung. Each prayer was assigned its own music, in traditions built up over the years through small additions and adjustments to a traditional prototype.

Listening to this singing was not so much listening as worshipping, while allowing music to expand the devotional experience. Hearing liturgical chant today, one feels less like a listener in the modern sense than like a privileged eavesdropper, someone who has been allowed to attend a select occasion that is partly musical, but mainly spiritual. The experience is an intimate and tranquil one—cool and, to some listeners, especially satisfying.

Plainchant

The official music of the Catholic Church in the Middle Ages and far beyond was a great repertory of melodies designated for the liturgy. This is the system of **plainchant** (or plainsong), widely known as **Gregorian chant**.

"God is gone up with a shout, the LORD with the sound of a trumpet. Sing praises to God, sing praises; sing praises unto our King, sing praises."

Psalm 47:5–6

Monks singing plainchant, depicted within an illuminated initial letter *C* in a late medieval manuscript. The whimsical little stringed-instrument player is outside the *C*, for instrumental music was taboo in church. *Lambeth Palace Library, London, UK/The Bridgeman Art Library.*

It is called "plain" because it is unaccompanied, monophonic (one-line) music for voices; it takes the form of a melody and nothing more. And it is called "Gregorian" after the famous pope and church father Gregory I (c. 540–604). He is reputed to have assembled and standardized, with divine aid, all the basic chants required for the church services of his time — though in fact much Gregorian chant dates from centuries after him.

Characteristics of Plainchant

Plainchant comes in many genres, or types, differing widely in melodic style depending on their religious function. Some plainchants consist of simple recitation on a monotone, with only slight deviations from that single pitch; in monasteries, the entire set of 150 psalms had to be sung in this fashion every week. (That in itself is a lot of sung prayer.) Other chants are intricate songs with hundreds of notes ranging well over an octave. And still others count as the first real tunes that are known in Western music.

In whatever style or genre, plainchants share two characteristic features. First, they are typically *nonmetrical;* they have no clearly established meter, and therefore the rhythm is free. A distinctive beat is lacking in this music.

Second, plainchant is not constructed in the major/minor system, but according to one of the **medieval modes**. (*Medieval* means "from the Middle Ages.") As discussed in Unit I, the original scale of Western music was the diatonic scale, equivalent to the "white-note" scale on the piano. We still use this scale today, centered on the pitches C or A as the home pitch, or tonic (see page 31). Oriented around C, the music is said to be in the major mode, oriented around A, in the minor mode.

Musicians of the Middle Ages organized the scale differently — not around C or A, but around D, E, F, or G. The result was music in other modes, different from the modern major or minor. These modes were given Greek names, since medieval scholars traced them back to the modes of ancient Greek music, as discussed by Plato and others. The medieval modes are these:

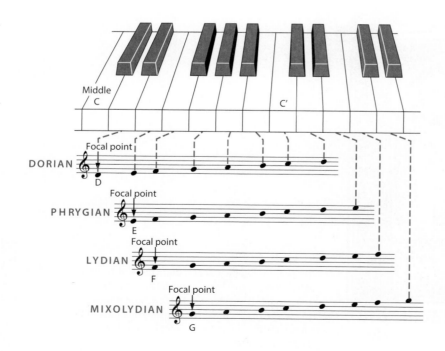

The essential difference between the modern major and minor modes comes in the different arrangement of half steps and whole steps in their scales. The medieval modes provide four additional arrangements. (Compare the preceding diagram with the one on page 31.) So medieval tunes sound different from modern tunes; and since there are more possible arrangements, medieval plainchant is actually richer and more subtle than music in the major/minor system. The artistic effect of plainchant—music without harmony or definite rhythm—is concentrated in melody built on this rich modal system.

Gregorian Recitation and Gregorian Melody

As we have said, the huge repertory of Gregorian chant ranges from simple recitation on a single pitch, with scarcely any variation, to long melodies that can make one dizzy with their endless, ecstatic twists and turns. Recitation was used for texts considered fairly routine in the services, such as lengthy readings from the Old Testament. In Gregorian recitation, the pitch on which the text is sung, called the **reciting tone**, is repeated again and again except for small, formulaic variations at beginnings and ends of phrases. These punctuate the text and make it easier to understand—and sing, since they give the singers time for a breath.

Elaborate melody, instead, was saved for more significant occasions, such as prayers at Mass and processions. One of the simplest genres showing such melody is the **antiphon**. Antiphons are usually workaday little pieces, but some exceptional ones can be very moving.

Anonymous (c. ninth century), Plainchant antiphon, "In paradisum"

In the liturgy for the dead, this antiphon is sung in procession on the way from the final blessing of the corpse in church to the graveyard where burial takes place. "In paradisum" is in the Mixolydian (G) mode. The special nature of this mode, which makes it different from the modern major mode, is heard twice in this melody, at cadences on the words "Chorus Ang*el*orum" (line 4) and "quondam pau*pere*" (line 5).

The way to experience "In paradisum" is to set this track on repeat and imagine yourself a medieval monk or nun who has lost a brother or sister. Candles have all been extinguished in the church after the Requiem Mass (so called because you have prayed for the soul's eternal rest—in Latin, *requiem aeternam*). As the coffin is lifted up, the priest begins "In paradisum," and then the entire religious community joins in. You sing this brief antiphon again and again, for as long as it takes the somber procession to reach the graveyard.

The melodic high point comes in line 5, where the text refers to Lazarus, the poor beggar in the Bible who went to heaven while a rich man went to hell—a point of identification for the mourners, all of whom had taken the vow of poverty, like the deceased. This haunting melodic figure was etched in the memory of the Middle Ages through an endless succession of last rites.

The beginning of "In paradisum" reveals a distant derivation from recitation: In the opening phrases notes of the same pitch—the relic of a reciting tone—are sung for most of the syllables of the text. Afterward the music grows more and more melodic, with many single syllables accommodating groups of two or three notes (or even five, at "ae-*ter*-nam"). These groups of notes on one syllable are called melismas, and on page 53 we will see much longer melismas in a chant genre that is less simple than the antiphon.

 **LISTEN**

Plainchant antiphon, "In paradisum"

| 0:00 | **In paradisum deducant te Angeli: in tuo adventu suscipiant te Martyres, et perducant te in civitatem sanctam Jerusalem.** | May the Angels lead you to paradise, and the Martyrs, when you arrive, escort you to the holy city of Jerusalem. |
| 0:36 | **Chorus Angelorum te suscipiat, et cum Lazaro quondam paupere aeternam habeas requiem.** | May the Angel choir sustain you, and with Lazarus, who was once poor, may you be granted eternal rest. |

Hildegard of Bingen (1098–1179), Plainchant sequence, "Columba aspexit"

To the Catholic Church she is St. Hildegard, venerated by a special liturgy on September 17. To musicians she is the first great woman composer. Five hundred years after Gregory I, the first compiler of Gregorian chants, Hildegard composed plainchant melodies in her own highly individual style, to go with poems that she wrote for special services at the convent of Bingen, in western Germany, under her charge as abbess. She also wrote a famous book describing her religious visions, books on natural science and medicine, even biographies.

"Columba aspexit" was composed in honor of a now-forgotten saint, St. Maximinus. It belongs to a late medieval plainchant genre called the sequence, a much more elaborate kind of melody than the antiphon, consisting of a series of short tunes sung twice, with some variation: **A A′ B B′ C C′ . . . N.** A soloist sings **A,** the choir **A′,** and so on. Modal cadences—Mixolydian, once again—at the beginning of the melody ("fe*ne*strae," "*ei*us") give it a deceptively humble quality that contrasts with its ecstatic soaring later. Like "In paradisum," "Columba aspexit" grows more and more *melismatic*—that is, it shows more melismas—as it goes along.

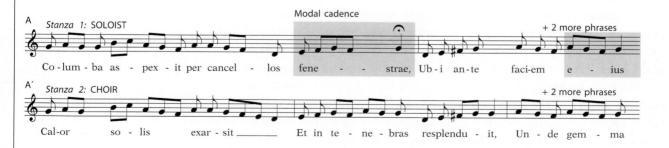

Our recording includes an instrumental *drone*—a single two-note chord running continuously. Drones are known from music around the world as well as from European folk music, and there is evidence that drones were sometimes used to accompany plainchant. The drone, the mystical words of Hildegard's poem, and the free, surging melody work together to produce a feeling of serene yet intense spirituality.

 LISTEN

Hildegard of Bingen, "Columba aspexit"

0:02	**A**	Columba aspexit Per cancellos fenestrae Ubi ante faciem eius Sudando sudavit balsamum De lucido Maximino.	The dove entered Through the lattices of the window, Where, before its face, Balm emanated From incandescent Maximinus.
0:28	**A'**	Calor solis exarsit Et in tenebras resplenduit; Unde gemma surrexit In edificatione templi Purissimi cordis benevoli.	The heat of the sun burned And dazzled into the gloom, Whence a jewel sprang forth In the building of the temple Of the most pure loving heart.
0:56	**B**	Iste turis . . .	He is the high tower of Lebanon . . .
1:29	**B'**	Ipse velox . . .	The swift hart sped to the fountain . . .
2:03	**C**	O pigmentarii . . .	O you makers of incense . . .
3:15	**D**	O Maximine . . .	O Maximinus . . .
			(two more stanzas)

A miniature illustration of Hildegard of Bingen, in one of her manuscripts, shows the miracle by which fire came down from heaven to engulf and inspire her. Her secretary, a monk named Volmar, looks on in wonder. *Erich Lessing/Art Resource, NY.*

2 | Music at Court

Over the long span of the Middle Ages, kings and barons gradually gained political power at the expense of the church. They also came to assume leadership in artistic matters. In the later Middle Ages, the princely courts joined the monasteries and cathedrals as major supporters of music.

Troubadour and Trouvère Songs

Large groups of court songs have been preserved from the twelfth and thirteenth centuries, the Age of Chivalry. The noble poet-composers of these songs—who, we are told, also performed the songs themselves—were called **troubadours** in the south of France, **trouvères** in the north, and **Minnesingers** in Germany (*Minne* means ideal or chivalric love). Among them were knights and princes, even kings—such as the most famous of all chivalric heroes, Richard I of England, "the Lion-Hearted." Troubadour society (but not trouvère society) also allowed for women composers and performers, such as Countess Beatriz of Dia (see page 51) and Maria di Ventadorn.

Perhaps some of these noble songwriters penned the words only, leaving the music to be composed by *jongleurs,* the popular musicians of the time. The music is relatively simple—just a tune, in most cases, with no indication of any accompaniment. We hear of jongleurs playing instruments while the trouvères sang; they probably improvised some kind of accompaniment, or played a drone, such as we heard in Hildegard's "Columba aspexit."

My love and I keep state
In bower,
In flower,
Till the watchman on the tower
Cry:
 "Up! Thou rascal, Rise,
 I see the white Light
 And the night Flies."

Troubadour alba

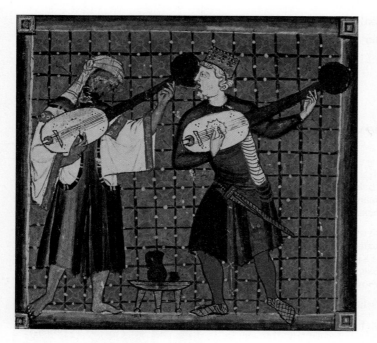

The meeting of cultures in medieval music: At a time when half of Spain was in Arab (Moorish) hands, a Moor and a Spaniard are shown playing large vihuelas together. Plucked stringed instruments like the vihuela, ancestors of the modern guitar, were an important novelty brought to medieval Europe from Arab countries. *Album/Art Resource, NY.*

There are some moving and beautiful troubadour poems—crusaders' songs, laments for dead princes, and especially songs in praise of the poets' ladies or complaints of their ladies' coldness. One interesting poetic type was the **alba**, the "dawn song" of a knight's loyal companion who has kept watch all night and now warns him to leave his lady's bed before the castle awakes.

Bernart de Ventadorn (c. 1135–1194), Troubadour song, "La dousa votz"

Bernart was one of the finest troubadour poets and probably the most important musically; other troubadour and trouvère songs imitated his. Originally of humble background, he came to serve the powerful Queen Eleanor of Aquitaine, wife of Henry II of England.

Like hymns and folk songs, troubadour songs set all their stanzas to the same melody, resulting in what is called *strophic* form (**A A A . . .**); often each stanza is in **a a′ b** form. "La dousa votz" is in the G (Mixolydian) mode:

La dousa votz ai au-zi - da Del rosin - ho-let sau - va-tge Et es m'insel cor salhi - da Si que tot lo co-si - rer

The performance on the recording stresses secular (that is, nonreligious) aspects of Bernart's song, including an imaginative reconstruction of a possible instrumental accompaniment. It sounds far removed indeed from the serene spirituality of Hildegard.

The language the troubadours spoke and wrote was Provençal, now almost extinct. It combines elements from Old French and Old Spanish.

0:07	*St. 1:* **La dousa votz ai auzida**	I have heard the sweet voice
	Del rosinholet sauvatge	Of the woodland nightingale
	Et es m'insel cor salhida	And my heart springs up
	Si que tot lo cosirer	So that all the cares
	E'ls mals traihz qu'amors me dona,	And the grievous betrayals love has given me
	M'adousa e m'asazona.	Are softened and sweetened;
	Et auria'm be mester	And I would thus be rewarded,
	L'autrui joi al meu damnatge.	In my ordeal, by the joys of others.
0:48	*St. 2:* **Ben es totz om d'avol vida**	In truth, every man leads a base life
	C'ab joi non a son estatge . . .	Who does not dwell in the land of joy . . .
1:28	*St. 3:* **Una fausa deschauzida**	One who is false, deceitful,
	Trairitz de mal linhage	Of low breeding, a traitress
	M'a trait, et es traida . . .	Has betrayed me, and betrayed herself . . .

The Estampie

A few—a very few—instrumental dances also survive from the same court circles that produced the chivalric trouvère repertory. Called **estampies** (ess-tom-pées), they are unassuming one-line pieces in which the same or similar musical phrases are repeated many times in varied forms. (This suggests that estampies may have been written-down jongleur improvisations.) Estampies are marked by lively and insistent rhythms in triple meter. Modern performers often add

HOW DID EARLY MUSIC SOUND?

Because sound recording is only about a hundred years old, the hard truth is that we do not really know how the music of Beethoven sounded in 1800, or the music of Bach in 1700. We have the scores, and it may be that tradition, writings, anecdotes, and surviving instruments allow us to extrapolate from score to sound with some confidence. But what about early music—music from 1500, 1300, 1100?

Obsolete instruments have come down to us in an imperfect condition, and we can try to reconstruct them; but figuring out how they were actually played is much more speculative. As for singing, who can guess what a cathedral choir, to take just one example, sounded like in the Middle Ages? Since then, language itself has changed so much that it is hard enough to read a fourteenth-century poet such as Geoffrey Chaucer, let alone imagine how the words that he wrote were pronounced—or sung.

Another set of problems involves the way early music was written down. Its composers never indicated the tempo and rarely specified the instrumental or vocal forces that they anticipated for their music. With vocal pieces, they did not say whether one singer or a whole choir was to sing. It has taken generations of patient research and experiment to "reconstruct" the probable sounds of early music.

The Countess of Dia holding forth; she was one of a small number of women troubadours. *Bibliothèque Nationale de France.*

a touch of spice with the help of percussion instruments. This is a modest beginning to the long and important history of European dance music, which we will pick up again in Chapter 7.

3 | The Evolution of Polyphony

Polyphony—the simultaneous combination of two or more melodies—must have arisen in medieval Europe because people took pleasure in the sensuous quality of music, in the rich sounds of intertwining melodic lines with their resulting harmony. However it got started, the development of polyphonic music in the late Middle Ages represents a decisive turn in the history of Western music.

We know about the earliest European polyphony only from its uses within the church (for, once again, most of what we know about very early music comes from the writing of monks and other clerics). And within the church, the sensuous aspect of polyphony had to be carefully controlled. Polyphony was justified as a way of embellishing Gregorian chants—that is, as yet another way of enhancing the all-important liturgy.

Organum

The earliest type of polyphony is called **organum** (plural: *organa*). First described in music theory treatises around 900 C.E., actual organum has survived in musical notation from around 1000. Early organum consists of a traditional plainchant melody to which a composer/singer/improviser has added another melody, sung at the same time with the same words.

The history of organum provides a fascinating record of growing artistic ambition and technical invention. A number of clear stages can be identified between about 1000 and 1200 C.E.:

• Originally, the added melody (itself called "the counterpoint") was sung closely parallel to the chant melody—that is, note against note with the same interval, or distance, between them. This is little more than singing along in thirds (or in octaves). The rhythm of this early, so-called *parallel organum* was the free rhythm of Gregorian chant.

• Soon the added melody (the counterpoint) was treated more independently— it would sometimes go up when the chant went down, and vice versa.

• Next, singers began to decorate the melody, using melismas—several notes at the same time as a single chant note. As more and more notes were crowded in, making richer and richer added melodies, the single chant notes were slowed down to surprising lengths, sounding finally like long drones.

• Someone then had the idea of adding two counterpoints to the chant. This certainly provided a more lush sound but required much greater skill, since the second counterpoint had to fit the first counterpoint as well as the chant.

• Perhaps to lessen the difficulty of having two counterpoints, definite rhythms, controlled by meter, replaced the chantlike free rhythms of the counterpoints— and ultimately of the underlying chant itself.

Organum of these last, highly developed kinds flourished at the Cathedral of Notre Dame in Paris, which was built slowly over the period 1163–1345. The names of two composers of the so-called Notre Dame school are recorded: Master Léonin and his follower Pérotin (called "the Great"). Pérotin astonished thirteenth-century Paris by creating impressive organa for as many as four simultaneous melodies.

Notre Dame Cathedral in Paris. Flying buttresses—the great medieval engineering feat that made such tall buildings possible—support the main structure (the nave). With its lofty front towers and its spire, Notre Dame seems to reach up to heaven itself. *JRoss/RobertHarding.*

Pérotin (c. 1200), Organum, "Alleluia. Diffusa est gratia"

Many organa were composed for services devoted to the Virgin Mary, the patron saint of Notre Dame Cathedral (*Notre Dame* means "Our Lady"). Our example is added to a lengthy chant for the Mass, "Alleluia. Diffusa est gratia." The music was probably written by Pérotin, though we cannot be certain.

At first the chant is sung—in the usual monophonic way:

Phrase 1   Phrase 2   Phrase 3   Phrase 4

Al-le - - - - - lu - - - - - ia. (a)_____

The whole chant is much longer, but this opening "Alleluia" section is the most important part—it comes back twice before the chant is over—and the most beautiful. The exclamation *alleluia* often calls for especially long melismas (see page 48), passages of pure, joyful vocalism. The melisma on the syllable *-lu* seems to rouse the melody, which then springs up still higher in phrase 2; then this melodic climax is balanced by a quiet, sinking "answer" in phrases 3 and 4. This alleluia is a beautiful example of the characteristics of tunes discussed in Unit I (see page 26).

Then the organum starts. The voices begin with a strange, static harmony, which comes to life when the upper voices start to intertwine in quick, triple-time rhythms of the kind shown in the margin. They are singing long melismas on the syllables *Dif- fu- sa,* and so on.

Underneath, the lowest voice is singing the rest of the chant—but no longer in the characteristic free rhythm of Gregorian chanting. Sometimes the chant plods along in a stiff, regular rhythm (as at 1:21). Sometimes it is slowed down enormously (at 0:37, 1:07, and 1:33); at these points the chant is unrecognizable—it has been reduced to a series of lengthy drones. The plainchant has become a sort of musical scaffolding for the added counterpoints, a constructive element supporting the ecstatic upper-voice melodies, which are the main focus of interest in this music.

Our recording omits part of this lengthy organum (the section indicated by italics). It ends with a huge melisma on *de-* and a sort of shudder on the final syllable *-us*. Then plain chanting is resumed, as the original "Alleluia" music returns twice, first with new words, *in aeternum,* and then with its original *alleluia*—a peaceful close.

 **LISTEN**

Pérotin, "Alleluia. Diffusa est gratia"

Italics indicate the section omitted from the recording.

0:00	**Chant**	ALLELUIA, ALLELUIA ——	Hallelujah.
0:37	**Organum**	**Diffusa est gratia in labiis tuis;** *propterea benedixit te* **deus**	Grace has been poured out upon your lips; therefore, God has blessed you
2:36	**Chant**	**in aeternum.**	eternally.
3:06		ALLELUIA, ALLELUIA ——	

4 | Later Medieval Polyphony

After 1200 C.E. the most significant development in polyphonic music was its gradual distancing from church services. In one important new genre, composers took a fragment of a Gregorian chant and repeated it several times over in the bottom voice. On top of it they layered two more voices, each with its own words: love poems, commentaries on political developments of the day, even the cries of Parisian street vendors. This was a radical and strange development; how many kinds of music do you know today that present simultaneously two different sets of lyrics?

In such music, despite the fragment of chant on which it was built, there was little sign left of the church. The genre was named after its proliferation of words in the upper voices: **motet**, from the French *mot* ("word").

Anonymous (late thirteenth century), Round, "Sumer Is Icumen In"

A very different approach to polyphony marks the astonishingly original "Sumer Is Icumen In," the one piece of music from this whole period that is still sung regularly by student choirs and others. This piece is a canon or round, like "Row, Row, Row Your Boat" and "Frère Jacques," but the melody is much longer. It survives in one manuscript, with no author's name. Its words, a bucolic celebration of the arrival of summer, form one of the earliest lyric poems in English—Middle English, that is, a much earlier stage of today's English. Here is a free translation of it:

Summer is a-coming in,
Loudly sing cuckoo!
Groweth seed, bloometh the meadow,
And springs the wood anew;
Sing cuckoo!
Ewe bleateth after lamb,

Cow after calf makes moo;
Bullock stamps and deer champs,
Merry sing cuckoo!
Cuckoo, cuckoo,
Well singest thou, cuckoo,
Be never still, cuckoo!

Four voices carry the tune; two more voices below them repeat "sing cuckoo" over and over again. Our recording starts with them and goes on to add the main melody sung by one voice, then, in staggered fashion, by two, then by four. Written sometime after 1250 in the major mode, not one of the medieval ones, the song packs an infectious swing that sounds like five (or eight) centuries later.

Ars Nova

We are moving through history very rapidly. After 1300 the technical development of polyphony reached new heights of sophistication. Composers and music theorists of the time began to speak of an **ars nova**, a "new art" or "new technique." The motet continued to develop as an important genre, incorporating ars nova ingredients; but the organum of the Notre Dame composers, now many years old, was regarded as "ancient art," **ars antiqua**.

Some historians have compared the fourteenth century with the twentieth, for it was a time of the breakup of traditions—an age of anxiety, corruption, and worse. Bubonic plague, the "Black Death," carried away an estimated 75 million people, at a time when the church had broken apart and two rival popes claimed the allegiance of European Christendom.

Polyphonic music grew increasingly intricate and even convoluted, as did the painting, architecture, and poetry of the time. Motets reflected such intricacy in a structural technique they employed called **isorhythm**. Here rhythmic patterns many notes long were repeated over and over—*isorhythm* means equal rhythm—but with different pitches each time. This went along with other schematic and numerical procedures, meant for the mind rather than the ear. Mathematics was also making great strides in this period.

The leading composers, Philippe de Vitry (1291–1361) and Guillaume de Machaut (c. 1300–1377), were both churchmen—Vitry ended his life as a bishop—but they were political churchmen serving the courts of France and Luxembourg. Machaut was also the greatest French poet of his time, admired (and imitated) by his younger English contemporary Geoffrey Chaucer.

Of instrument of strings in accord
Heard I so play a ravishing sweetness
That God, that Maker is of all, and Lord,
Ne heard never better, as I guess.

Geoffrey Chaucer, 1375

Guillaume de Machaut (c. 1300–1377), Chanson, "Dame, de qui toute ma joie vient"

1 | 6   6

Machaut left us numerous examples of secular polyphony, that is, polyphony independent from the church. He composed many motets using isorhythmic techniques. And, though he was still close enough to the trouvères to write beautiful monophonic songs, he also adapted their old tradition of chivalric love songs to complex, *ars nova* polyphony. These songs, or **chansons** (shahn-sohn), had no trace in them of Gregorian chant.

"Dame, de qui toute ma joie vient," a chanson with four voices, is an excellent example of non-imitative polyphony, *the* characteristic texture of Machaut's music. The top line was clearly intended to be sung, but the other three might have been meant for either vocal or instrumental performance; if he had a preference, Machaut didn't tell us. On our recording, all four parts are sung. The words are parceled out slowly, with long melismas on many syllables, a feature that looks back to the style of organum.

Because of this melismatic style, the song is much longer than Bernart's "La dousa votz." Each stanza takes about two minutes in our performance, and only the first is included here. Still, the form of "Dame, de qui toute ma joie vient" is identical to that of Bernart's song. Each stanza falls into an **a a′ b** arrangement; this was one of several standardized song forms Machaut adapted from the trouvères. Given the length of Machaut's song, a letter now stands for a whole section rather than a melodic phrase or two. Each section comes to a clear stop on a strong cadence. The three sections are signaled in the Listen box that follows.

The most general impression of this song is of a lively and flowing set of intertwining melodies. The words—hard to follow because of the abundant melismas—seem to be little more than an excuse for the complex polyphony. Certainly the music does not show any obvious attempt to reflect the meaning or emotion of the poem. We will see in Chapter 7 that, by the time of the Renaissance, this rather neutral relation of music and words would change.

Scenes of medieval music making. These and the miniature on page 50 are from *Songs of the Virgin Mary,* written (or perhaps compiled) by King Alphonso X of Spain, "the Wise" (1252–1284), renowned for his support of learning and the arts. *Images: Album/Art Resource, NY.*

LISTEN

1 | 6   6

Machaut, "Dame, de qui toute ma joie vient"

0:00	**a**	Dame, de qui toute ma joie vient Je ne vous puis trop amer et chierir	Lady, source of all my joy, I can never love or cherish you too much,
0:35	**a′**	N'assés loer, si com il apartient Servir, doubter, honourer n'obeïr.	Or praise you as much as you deserve, Or serve, respect, honor, and obey you.
1:19	**b**	Car le gracious espoi, Douce dame, que j'ay de vous vëoir, Me fait cent fois plus de bien et de joie Qu'en cent mille ans desservir ne porroie.	For the gracious hope, Sweet lady, I have of seeing you, Gives me a hundred times more joy and boon Than I could deserve in a hundred thousand years.

GOALS FOR REVIEW

▶ to understand basic features of medieval church services: liturgy, plainchant

▶ to listen for different styles of Gregorian plainchant: recitation and melody

▶ to sample the variety of plainchant genres: antiphon and sequence

▶ to distinguish church music from court music

▶ to witness the emergence of polyphonic church music in the late Middle Ages: organum

▶ to sample genres of medieval polyphony outside of church: a round and a chanson by Guillaume de Machaut

 macmillanhighered.com/listen8e
Listening Quizzes for Chapter 6 and Global Perspectives: Sacred Chant
Reading Quizzes for Chapter 6 and Global Perspectives: Sacred Chant

Sacred Chant

The vast number of societies that exist or that have existed in this world all generated their own music—or, as we say, their own different "musics." Often they are very different indeed; the first time South African Zulus heard Christian hymn singing they were amazed as much as the missionaries were when they first heard Zulu music.

Yet for all their diversity, the musics of the world do show some parallels, as we are going to see in the Global Perspectives sections of this book. There are parallels of musical function in society, of musical technique, and sometimes of both together.

Often these parallels come about as the result of influences of one society on another—but influences are never accepted without modification and the blending of a foreign music with native music. At other times parallels appear in musics that have nothing whatsoever to do with one another. Considering all these parallels, we have to believe that certain basic functions for music and certain basic technical principles are virtually universal in humankind.

One of these near-universal features—and one of the most fundamental—is the role of music in the service of religion. Singing serves across the world as an essential means of marking off the rituals of worship, signaling their special status and their difference from other, secular pursuits. The repertory of Gregorian chant developed in the Christian church of the Middle Ages (see pages 44–49) is only one of many traditions of monophonic religious chant, albeit one of the more elaborate.

Islam: Reciting the Qur'an

Another highly elaborate tradition of chant is found in Islam, practiced today by about a fifth of the world's population, and the dominant religion in some fifty nations. Across all of Islam, the revelations of the prophet Muhammad gathered in the Qur'an (or Koran) are chanted or sung in Arabic. Muhammad himself is said to have enjoyed this melodic recitation.

Usually **Qur'anic recitation** is rigorously distinguished from all types of secular music making. It is thought of as "reading" the sacred text aloud, not singing it; nonreligious activities such as singing or playing instruments might be referred to as music *(musiqi)*, but reading the Qur'an is not.

Given these distinctions, it is not surprising that Qur'anic recitation, like Gregorian chant, is monophonic and nonmetric, and does not involve instruments. It aims, above all else, to convey the Qur'anic text in a clearly comprehensible manner. Unlike plainchant, it has been passed along in oral tradition down to the present day; it has resisted the musical notation that came to be a part of the Gregorian tradition already in the Middle Ages. To this day, great Islamic chanters sing the whole 114-chapter Qur'an from memory.

"Ya Sin"

1 | 28   101   49

Our excerpt is the beginning of a long recitation of one of the most highly revered chapters from the Qur'an. It is titled "Ya Sin" and is recited in times of adversity, illness, and death. A skilled reciter, Hafíz Kadir Konya, reads the verses in a style midway between heightened speech and rhapsodic melody. His phrases correspond to lines of the sacred text, and he pauses after every one. He begins:

> In the name of Allah, the Beneficent, the Merciful.
>
> Ya Sin.
>
> By the wise Qur'an,
>
> Lo! thou art of those sent

The azan: A muezzin high in a minaret calls the faithful to prayer in Cairo, Egypt. *Christine Osborne/CORBIS.*

On a straight path,

A revelation of the Mighty, the Merciful,

That thou mayst warn a folk whose fathers were not
warned, so they are heedless.

Already hath the word proved true of most of them, for
they believe not.

In his first phrases, Konya begins at a low tonic and gradually expands his range to explore pitches around it. By 0:39, he reaches a pitch central to his melody, higher than the tonic. The succeeding phrases circle around this pitch, reciting words on it and decorating it with ornamental melodic formulas of varying intricacy. In this regard, it is a bit like Gregorian recitation, only more elaborate in its melodies.

The Azan

Like Gregorian chant, Islamic chanting has developed a wide variety of approaches and styles. The best-known type of Islamic chant employs a style related to recitation, though it does not take its words from the Qur'an: the singing of the *adhan,* or **azan**. This is a call to worship issued five times daily by a special singer called a *mu'adhdhin,* or *muezzin*. That an entire society comes to a stop five times a day for prayer reveals the tremendous force of Islamic religion.

The muezzin traditionally delivers his azan from the minaret, a tower attached to the mosque, and later inside the mosque to begin the prayers. In Islamic cities today, the azan is often broadcast over loudspeakers to enable it to sound over modern urban noises.

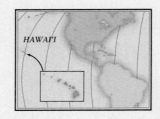

1 | 29   102

Hawai'ian Chant

We should not be too surprised to find certain broad similarities between Qur'anic and Gregorian chant. Both Christianity and Islam emerged from the same region, the Middle East, and Muhammad drew on elements of Christian doctrine in forming his new religion. He counted Jesus Christ as one of the Islamic prophets.

It is more surprising to find some of the same features in religious chant from halfway around the globe, in Polynesia—in Hawai'ian prayer songs, or **mele pule** (mél-eh póol-eh). By reciting these prayers, Hawai'ians sought to bring to life images of their gods fashioned of wood, stone, or feathers, animating them with divine powers.

Our brief example combines fragments of two chants (the division comes at 0:24). The first is a song to the fire goddess Pele, the second an invocation to a godlike chief. Like Gregorian and Qur'anic recitation, and like all traditional Hawai'ian song, these mele are monophonic. They are also almost monotonal, with only one prominent pitch other than the central reciting tone.

The chants take their rhythms from the words and show little trace of meter. Their simple melody is ornamented subtly with various shifts of vocal delivery. The most prominent of these is a clear, pulsating,

Hawai'ian singers in traditional garb.
They strike large, double gourds on the
ground to accompany their song.
Courtesy of the National Park Service.

almost sobbing *vibrato*, or wavering pitch, that the singer, Kau'i Zuttermeister, introduces on long syllables. This technique, called *i'i*, is a stylistic feature prized in many types of traditional Hawai'ian song. It is felt to endow melodies with special, deep emotion.

A Navajo Song

One more example of chant comes to us from Native American traditions. In these, too, singing is closely allied with the sacred. Song plays a role in healing, hunting, social rituals, and—embracing all these activities—in human relations with gods, spirits, and ancestors. Most Native North American song is monophonic, like the Hawai'ian, Arabic, and Western chants we have heard. Unlike them, it is usually accompanied by drums or rattles of one sort or another.

Our example comes from the Navajo nation of the Four Corners area of the American Southwest. It is called *"K'adnikini'ya',"* which means "I'm leaving," and it dates from the late nineteenth century.

Just as individual Gregorian chants have their assigned places in Catholic services, so this chant has its own special role. It is sung near the end of the Enemy Way ceremony, a central event of Navajo spiritual life. In this solemn ceremony, warriors who have come in contact with the ghosts of their enemies are purified and fortified. Such purification is still performed today, sometimes for the benefit of U.S. war veterans.

"K'adnikini'ya'" falls into a group of Navajo sacred songs known as *ho'zho'ni'* songs, and you will hear the related word *ho'zhon'go* ("beautiful," "holy") sung alongside *k'adnikini'ya'* to end each of the seven central phrases of the song. Every phrase of the song begins with the syllables *hé-yuh-eh, yáng-a-ang-a*. These are *vocables*, syllables having no precise meaning. Vocables are sometimes called "nonsense syllables" and likened to the "tra-la-las" and "hey-diddle-diddles" of European nursery rhymes. But they are hardly nonsensical. They can carry secret, venerable, and even mystical significance.

The melody of "K'adnikini'ya'," like the other chants we have examined, is organized around a prominent reciting tone (the pitch of *hé-yuh-eh*); each phrase turns upward at its end (on *k'adnikini'ya'*). The song's meter,

At a powwow in British Columbia. *Gunter Marx Photography/ CORBIS.*

given the regular drum strokes, is more pronounced than in any of our other examples. The formal plan consists of a refrain at the beginning and end, with a group of parallel phrases in between.

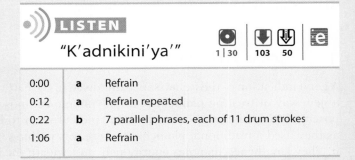

LISTEN

"K'adnikini'ya'"   1 | 30   103   50

0:00	**a**	Refrain
0:12	**a**	Refrain repeated
0:22	**b**	7 parallel phrases, each of 11 drum strokes
1:06	**a**	Refrain

The Renaissance

CHAPTER 7

Renaissance ("rebirth") is the name given to a complex current of thought that worked deep changes in Europe from the fourteenth to the sixteenth century. It began in Italy. By rediscovering and imitating their ancient Greco-Roman forebears, Italians hoped they could bring about the rebirth of their glorious past. It was an unrealistic idea, which came to nothing in political terms. Instead of becoming a new Roman empire, Italy at the end of the Renaissance consisted of the same pack of warring city-states that had been at each other's throats all through the Middle Ages.

However, the revival of Greek and Roman culture provided a powerful model for new values, first in Italy and then the rest of Europe. In the words of a famous nineteenth-century historian, the Renaissance involved "the discovery of the world and of man." This was the age of Columbus and Magellan, Leonardo da Vinci, Copernicus, Galileo, and Shakespeare. Medieval society was stable, conservative, authoritarian, and oriented toward God. The Renaissance laid the groundwork for the dynamic Western world we know today, a world in which human beings and nature, rather than God, have become the measure in philosophy, science, and art.

Renaissance artists strove to make their work more relevant to people's needs and desires. They began to reinterpret the world around them—the architect's world of space and stone, the painter's world of images, the musician's world of sound—in new ways to meet these ambitions.

> "Music is a thing which delighteth all ages and beseemeth all states; a thing as seasonable in grief as in joy. The reason hereof is an admirable facility which music hath to express . . . the turns and varieties of all passions."
>
> *Anglican bishop and theologian Richard Hooker, 1593*

Compare two Madonnas shown in this book: One (page 43) is a late medieval masterpiece from northern Europe, the other from the new world of Renaissance Italy (page 36; painted only fifty years later). Uncrowned, uncluttered, the mother here smiles, the children play—God and His angels do not encircle this Madonna by Raphael as they do Lochner's on page 43. *Mondadori Portfolio/Electa/Sergio Anelli/The Bridgeman Art Library.*

1 | New Attitudes

A good indication of the Renaissance mind-set, in the early fifteenth century, was a new way of treating plainchant in polyphonic compositions. Medieval composers writing organum or isorhythmic motets seem to have felt that so long as they used a traditional plainchant, there was nothing wrong with distorting it. They lengthened its notes enormously underneath the added counterpoints. They recast the meterless chant into fixed, arbitrary rhythms.

Renaissance composers no longer felt obliged always to use plainchants; but when they did, they tended to treat them as melodies to listen to, not as scaffolding for polyphonic structures. They embellished chants with extra notes, set them in graceful rhythms, and smoothed out passages that struck them as awkward or old-fashioned. This procedure is known as **paraphrase**.

The church singers in these famous panels by Florentine sculptor Luca della Robbia (1400–1482) are handsome boys who seem to be taking the same sensuous pleasure in their singing as Luca did in sculpting them. *Both images: Scala/Art Resource.*

Renaissance composers using paraphrase emphasized the sonorous, sensuous aspect of the chant rather than its function as structure and control—its authoritarian function, one might say. (**Sonority** means either tone color or, more loosely, rich tone color.) A new sensitivity to sonority and melody was one of the first signs of Renaissance attitudes toward music.

Having transformed plainchants into modern melodies with a more attractive profile, composers put them not at the bottom of the polyphony but on top, in the soprano, where they could be heard most clearly.

Early Homophony

The fifteenth century also saw the beginning of composed *homophony*—that is, music in a harmonic, chordal texture (see page 29). In the simpler plainchant paraphrases of the time, the melody is often highlighted by an accompaniment that does not really sound polyphonic. Though there are still several polyphonic voices, most of the time their independence vanishes because they move along together and form simple chords.

The effect is of a melody on top supported by a harmonization below. Once again the emphasis is on sensuous effect rather than on the more intellectual process of polyphony.

Guillaume Dufay (c. 1400–1474), Harmonized hymn, "Ave maris stella"

1|7   7

Guillaume Dufay (or Du Fay) was born and bred in the north of France near modern Belgium, a region that supplied the whole of Europe with musicians for many generations. For over twenty-five years he worked in Italy, where he came to know artists and thinkers of the Renaissance and (no less important) the princely patrons who supported them. His later years were spent in a glow of celebrity at the important French cathedral of Cambrai.

Dufay's "Ave maris stella" is a homophonic setting of a Gregorian **hymn**, one of the most tuneful of plainchant genres. A short tune is sung through many stanzas, followed by an Amen—much like a modern hymn, in fact. One of the loveliest of Gregorian hymns, "Ave maris stella" was also one of the best known, because it was addressed to the Virgin Mary and sung on all of the many special feasts in her honor, and on most Saturdays, too. Note how line 1 contains the words AVE MARI(*s stell*)A—"hail, Mary."

"Ave maris stella" is in the D (Dorian) mode. You may be able to hear that the third note in the tune (the sixth note of the scale) is higher than would be normal in the modern minor mode. The hymn itself has six or seven stanzas; Dufay set only the even-numbered ones to his own music, leaving the others to be sung Gregorian-style in alternation. This makes it fairly easy to hear how he embellished the plainchant.

His music for stanzas 2, 4, and 6 is the same each time—almost entirely homophonic and quite suave. The top voice sings a paraphrased, somewhat longer version of the hymn tune, as shown below, where the dashed lines mark the notes taken directly from the chant, shown screened in blue. The embellishment consists of a few extra notes and extensions, with the free rhythm of Gregorian chant channeled into a graceful triple meter.

Gregorian hymn, "Ave maris stella"

A - ve_ ma-ris_ stel-la,_

De - i Ma - ter _ al - ma,

At-que sem-per Vir-go,_

Fe - lix coe-li por - ta.

Beginning of stanza 2 of Gregorian hymn, "Ave maris stella," with Dufay's paraphrased melody beneath it

Su - mens ____ il - lud A - ve ____ Ga-bri-e - lis o - re ____ etc.

 LISTEN

Dufay, "Ave maris stella"

 1|7   7

	STANZA 1: Plainchant	
0:00	Ave maris stella,	Hail, star of the ocean,
	Dei Mater alma,	Kind Mother of God,
	Atque semper Virgo,	And also still a virgin,
	Felix coeli porta.	Our blessed port to heaven.
	STANZA 2: Dufay's paraphrase	
0:22	Sumens illud Ave	May that blessed "Ave"
	Gabrielis ore,	From Angel Gabriel's mouth
	Funda nos in pace,	Grant us peace,
	Mutans Hevae nomen.	Reversing the name "Eva."
	STANZA 3: Plainchant	
1:13	Solve vincla reis . . .	
	STANZA 4: Paraphrase	
1:35	Monstra te esse matrem . . .	
	STANZA 5: Plainchant	
2:26	Virgo singularis . . .	
	STANZA 6: Paraphrase	
2:48	Sit laus Deo Patri,	Praise be to God the Father,
	Summo Christo decus,	To Christ on high,
	Spiritui Sancto,	To the Holy Spirit:
	Tribus honor unus,	Three honored as one.
	Amen.	Amen.

Dufay and another fifteenth-century composer, Gilles Binchois (c. 1400–1460), with a harp. Portable small organs (called *portatives*) were in use at the time. *Bibliothèque Nationale de France, Paris/Giraudon — The Bridgeman Art Library.*

"Ave maris stella" counts as a rather simple composition for Dufay, whose fame was and is based on longer, more elaborate pieces; he wrote some of the first polyphonic Masses, for example—the important genre we take up next. Still, plainsong harmonizations make up an appreciable proportion of his output, and they show the new Renaissance attitudes with particular clarity.

The Mass

The new treatment of traditional plainchant, as in the technique of paraphrase, shows Renaissance composers taking a relaxed attitude toward medieval authority. The same can be said of their reaction to medieval intricacy, as represented by intellectual musical devices such as isorhythm. Fourteenth-century composers like Machaut (page 55) had used isorhythm even when writing love songs. Composers now cultivated a much simpler style for their polyphonic songs, or chansons: simpler, gentler, and more supple. The modest style of these new chansons was sometimes used for sacred texts, including portions of the Mass.

The rejection of isorhythm did not mean, however, that composers abandoned the technical development of their craft, which had taken such impressive strides from the early days of organum. Rather, such efforts now were focused on large-scale musical construction. For the first time, compositions were written to last—and to make sense—over twenty or thirty minutes.

The problem of large-scale construction that fascinated fifteenth-century composers was how to write music that would hold together throughout the **Mass**, the largest and most important prayer service of the Christian liturgy. The Mass contains numerous items that were sung in plainchant, and as we have seen, for centuries—from the time of organum to the time of harmonized hymns—composers had been embellishing plainchants with polyphony to be sung in services. The next step was to set the words that had been chanted to new music, instead of embellishing the existing chant music. Composers settled on these five items of the Mass for their new music:

Kyrie	A simple prayer:	"Lord have mercy, Christ have mercy"
Gloria	A long hymn, beginning:	"Glory to God in the highest"
Credo	A recital of the Christian's list of beliefs, beginning:	"I believe in one God, the Father almighty"
Sanctus	Another, shorter hymn:	"Holy, holy, holy, Lord God of hosts"
Agnus Dei	Another simple prayer:	"Lamb of God . . . have mercy on us"

In this way the polyphonic Mass was standardized into a five-section form, and it has retained this form down to the present day, in settings by Palestrina, Bach, Mozart, Liszt, Stravinsky, and many others.

One of the earliest ways to unify these disparate elements was simply to use the same music to open each movement. Another way was to base each movement on the same Gregorian chant—one belonging not to the Mass, but perhaps to the liturgy of some special day on which the Mass was celebrated. This would make the Mass especially appropriate for Christmas or Easter or (as we will see shortly) Corpus Christi, a celebration held every year in springtime.

So large a structure presented composers with a challenge, and they took this up in a spirit of inventiveness and ambition characteristic of the Renaissance. What the symphony was to nineteenth-century composers and their audiences, the Mass was to their fifteenth-century counterparts: a brilliant, monumental test of artistic prowess.

2 | The High Renaissance Style

Around 1500 a new style emerged for Masses, motets, and chansons that would hold sway for much of the sixteenth century. The chief characteristic of this High Renaissance musical style was a careful blend of two kinds of musical texture, *imitative counterpoint* and *homophony* (see pages 29–30).

Imitation

Most polyphony at the beginning of the fifteenth century was non-imitative; most polyphony at the end of the century was imitative. This remarkable change is due partly to the fact that imitative polyphony, or imitation, reflects the ideals of moderation and balance that also characterize the visual arts of the High Renaissance. In the Madonna by Raphael shown on page 36, the calm, dignified repose expressed by the figures and faces is as striking as the beautiful balance among all the pictorial elements.

By its very nature, imitative texture depends on a carefully controlled balance among multiple voice parts. A first voice begins with a motive (see page 25) designed to fit the words being set. Soon other voices enter, one by one, singing the same motive and words, but at different pitch levels; meanwhile the earlier voices continue with new melodies that complement the later voices. Each voice has a genuinely melodic quality, none is mere accompaniment or filler, and none predominates for very long.

We can get an impression of the equilibrium of imitative polyphony from its look on the page, even without reading the music exactly. The following excerpt is from the score of Josquin Desprez's *Pange lingua* Mass:

A Kyrie from a dazzling Renaissance book of Mass music. Such handcrafted treasures were rarely used in music making, though many plainer manuscripts saw much use. The man who commissioned this one is shown praying with an angel in the top left. *Austrian National Library, Vienna.*

Homophony

Almost all polyphony involves some chords, as a product of its simultaneously sounding melodies. But in the music of Machaut, for example, the chords are more of a by-product. Late medieval composers concentrated on the horizontal aspects of texture at the expense of vertical ones (see page 29), delighting in the separateness of their different voice parts. The chords that resulted from the interplay of these parts were a secondary consideration.

A major achievement of the High Renaissance style was to create a rich chordal quality out of polyphonic lines

Another Kyrie, this one printed around 1500—the earliest beginnings of music-printing technology. The circulation of music (as of books, maps, images, and data in general) skyrocketed with the great Renaissance invention of the printing press.

that still maintain a quiet sense of independence. Composers also used simple homophony—passages of *block chord* writing. They learned to use homophony both as a contrast to imitative texture and as an expressive resource in its own right.

Other Characteristics

The ideal tone color at this time, especially for sacred music, becomes **a cappella** performance—that is, performance by voices alone. Tempo and dynamics change little in the course of a piece. The rhythm is fluid, without any sharp accents, and shifts unobtrusively all the time. The melodies never go very high or very low in any one voice; the ups and downs are carefully balanced. This music rarely settles into the easy swing of a dance rhythm or into the clear patterns of an actual tune.

Music in the High Renaissance style can sometimes strike modern listeners as vague, but if we listen more closely—and always listen to the words as well as the music—its flexibility, sensitivity, and rich expressive potential begin to come clear. Does it remind us of a wonderfully musical and subtle speaking voice? The sixteenth century would have been pleased to think so.

Josquin Desprez (c. 1450–1521), *Pange lingua* Mass (c. 1510)

1 | 8–9   8–9   2

The first master of the High Renaissance style was Josquin Desprez. Like Dufay, he was born in the north of France, and like Dufay and many other of his countrymen, in early life he traveled to Italy. The list of Josquin's patrons reads like a Renaissance who's who: Pope Alexander VI, the notorious Sforza family of Milan, the Estes of Ferrara, Louis XII, king of France.

An amazingly imaginative composer, Josquin brought the fifteenth-century Mass to a brilliant climax and pioneered whole new expressive genres, such as the sixteenth-century chanson and motet. He was famous both for his technical prowess and for his expressive innovations—for the prayerful serenity of his motet "Ave Maria" as well as the grief-stricken accents of "Planxit autem David," a setting of King David's lament for his dead son Absalom.

Josquin wrote eighteen different settings of the Mass—all large pieces in the standard five-section form. The *Pange lingua* Mass, one of his masterpieces, derives its melodic material largely from a hymn called "Pange lingua" (Proclaim the Mystery). This is a Gregorian hymn of the same kind as "Ave maris stella," which we have heard in Dufay's harmonized setting. "Pange lingua" (and hence Josquin's Mass) is designed for Corpus Christi, a feast celebrating the Holy Eucharist, or Communion.

This is a four-part Mass (that is, a Mass for a choir with four separate melodic lines). In Josquin's day, boys sang the high parts and men the lower ones; Josquin probably started his musical career as a choirboy. Today women usually substitute for boys in music of this period.

We shall examine the first two sections of Josquin's *Pange lingua* Mass.

Kyrie   The men in the choir sing line 1 of the hymn "Pange lingua," in simple monophony, before the first section of the *Pange lingua* Mass. This first section, the Kyrie, is an elemental prayer consisting of three subsections:

Kyrie I:	Kyrie eleison.	Lord have mercy.
Christe:	Christe eleison.	Christ have mercy.
Kyrie II:	Kyrie eleison.	Lord have mercy.

For Kyrie I, Josquin wrote a **point of imitation**—a brief passage of imitative polyphony usually using a single melodic motive. Here the motive is a paraphrase (see page 60) of line 1 of the hymn:

Gregorian hymn, "Pange lingua"

TENORS   Ky - ri - e   e - le - i - son

This motive enters many times in the various voice parts, sometimes with delays in between: tenor, bass, *wait*, soprano, alto, *wait*, bass, tenor, soprano. Josquin did not invent this motive—it was derived from the plainchant hymn, as shown above—but his paraphrase is very beautiful, especially at the end.

The Christe section has two points of imitation, also derived from the hymn, for the words *Christe* and *eleison;* the motives of these points are rhythmically similar. Kyrie II has a new point of imitation for the words *Kyrie eleison,* followed by free material not paraphrased from the hymn—a descending sequence and, prior to the drawn-out final cadence, a powerful oscillating passage.

Gregorian hymn, "Pange lingua"

Pan-ge lin-gua _ glo-ri-o-si

Cor - po-ris mys-te-ri-um, _

San-gui-nis-que pre-ti-o-si,

Quem in mun-di pre-ti-um _

Fruc-tus ven-tris ge-ne-ro-si

Rex ef-fu-dit _ gen - ti-um.

 LISTEN

Josquin, *Pange lingua* Mass, Kyrie

0:09	**Kyrie eleison.**	Lord have mercy.
0:53	**Christe eleison.**	Christ have mercy.
2:10	**Kyrie eleison.**	Lord have mercy.

Gloria   The four remaining sections of the Mass—the Gloria, Credo, Sanctus, and Agnus Dei—introduce countless new points of imitation, which are interspersed with occasional passages of homophony.

In the second subsection of the Gloria, beginning with the words *Qui tollis,* polyphony and homophony are contrasted in a highly expressive way. At the beginning, we can almost envisage one or two persons timidly invoking Him "who takes away the sins of the world" (polyphony), and then the whole congregation—or, symbolically, the whole of Christendom—urgently responding together with a plea for mercy and relief: "have mercy" (homophony). This music gives a dramatic sense of communal worship.

The "Qui tollis" subsection as a whole includes eight points of imitation and four homophonic or nearly homophonic phrases. (The imitation on "Tu solus Dominus" is illustrated on page 64.) Even in the imitative phrases, the vocal lines fit together smoothly into chords, and while the sequence of these chords seems hard to predict, at least for modern ears, it does not seem arbitrary. The remarkable mood of Josquin's music—at once sober, quietly energetic, and reverential—owes much to its Phrygian (E) mode. Like the hymn "Pange lingua," the *Pange lingua* Mass is in this mode.

LISTEN

Josquin, *Pange lingua* Mass, from the Gloria

Capital letters indicate phrases sung in homophony.

0:00	**Qui tollis peccata mundi,**
	  MISERERE NOBIS.
		You who take away the sins of the world,
		  have mercy upon us.

0:34	**Qui tollis peccata mundi,**
	  SUSCIPE DEPRECATIONEM **nostram.**
	Qui sedes ad dexteram Patris,
	  miserere nobis.
		You who take away the sins of the world,
		  hear our prayer.
		You who sit at the right hand of the Father,
		  have mercy upon us.

1:18	**Quoniam tu solus sanctus,**
	  tu solus Dominus,
	  tu solus altissimus,
	  Jesu Christe,
	cum sancto spiritu,
	  in gloria Dei Patris.
	  AMEN.
		For you alone are holy,
		  you alone are the Lord,
		  you alone are the most high,
		  Jesus Christ,
		With the Holy Spirit,
		  in the glory of God the Father.
		  Amen.

3 | Music as Expression

In parts of Josquin's *Pange lingua* Mass, as we have just seen, the music does not merely enhance the liturgy in a general way, but seems to address specific phrases of the Mass text and the sentiments behind them. Music can be said to "illustrate" certain words and to "express" certain feelings. The exploration of music's power to express human feelings was a precious contribution by musicians to the Renaissance "discovery of the world and of man."

Josquin Desprez, Chanson, "Mille regrets"

Josquin's polyphonic chanson, or song, "Mille regrets," a lover's lament at leaving his or her beloved, illustrates his attention to the words he set to music. Though the poem is little more than a string of clichés, its sorrowful tone seems to have moved the composer and is perfectly captured in his music: in its somber harmonies, its drooping melodies, its slow-moving rhythms. Particularly effective are two homophonic moments in this song. The first singles out the phrase *J'ai si grand deuil* ("I feel such great sorrow"); the second, after a short point of imitation on *Qu'on me verra*, ends the song with repeated affirmations of *brief mes jours déffiner* ("my days are numbered").

It is revealing to compare "Mille regrets" with Guillaume de Machaut's chanson "Dame, de qui toute ma joie vient," an earlier polyphonic love song (see page 55). There we have the sense of an exuberant interplay of melodies rather than an expression of the poetry's sentiments. In Josquin's chanson, in keeping with Renaissance expressive ideals, we experience instead a straightforward musical rendering of the grief of the words.

Josquin, "Mille regrets"

Mille regrets de vous abandonner	A thousand regrets at leaving you
Et d'élonger votre face amoureuse.	and departing from your loving look.
J'ai si grand deuil et peine douloureuse	I feel such great sorrow and grievous pain
Qu'on me verra brief mes jours déffiner.	that all will see my days are numbered.

Renaissance composers derived inspiration for their exploration of music's expressive powers from reports of the music of ancient Greece, just as artists, architects, and writers of the time were also looking to ancient Greece and Rome for inspiration. Philosophers such as Plato had testified that music was capable of arousing emotions in a very powerful way. In the Bible, when Saul is troubled by an evil spirit, David cures him by playing on his harp; there are similar stories in Greek myth and Greek history.

How modern music could recapture its ancient powers was much discussed by music theorists after the time of Josquin. They realized that both music and words could express emotions, and they sought to match up the means by which they did so. Composers shared this expressive aim of matching words and music; in fact, devotion to the ideal of musical expression, by way of a text, was one of the main guiding ideas for musicians of the later Renaissance. This led to two important new developments in the music of the time:

• First, composers wanted the words of their compositions to be clearly heard. They strove for accurate **declamation**—that is, they made sure that words were sung to rhythms and melodies that approximated normal speech.

This may seem elementary and obvious, but it is simply not true of most medieval polyphony (or of many plainchants). The Renaissance was the first era when words were set to music naturally, clearly, and vividly.

- Second, composers began matching their music to the *meaning* of the words that were being set. The phrase **word painting** is used for this musical illustration of the text. Words such as *fly* and *glitter* were set to rapid notes, *up* and *heaven* to high ones, and so on:

Fly,   Love, a - loft   to heav'n to seek out   for - tune . . .

Sigh was typically set by a motive including a rest, as though the singers have been interrupted by sighing. *Grief, cruel, torment, harsh,* and exclamations such as *alas* — words found all the time in the language of Renaissance love poetry — prompted composers to write dissonant or distorted harmony. First used extensively in the sixteenth century, word painting has remained an important expressive resource of vocal music. For examples from the Baroque period, when it was especially important, see pages 86, 88, 143, and 147.

The move toward personal expression in Renaissance music was matched in the pictorial arts, and individualized portrait-painting came into its own. Here is Eleonora Gonzaga, Duchess of Urbino, painted by the Venetian master Titian (c. 1488–1576). *Erich Lessing/Art Resource, NY.*

4 | Late Renaissance Music

The High Renaissance style established by the generation of Josquin Desprez proved remarkably stable. Yet it was also flexible enough that composers were able to do new things with it all the way to the end of the sixteenth century. While its use was clearest in the church music of the time, important

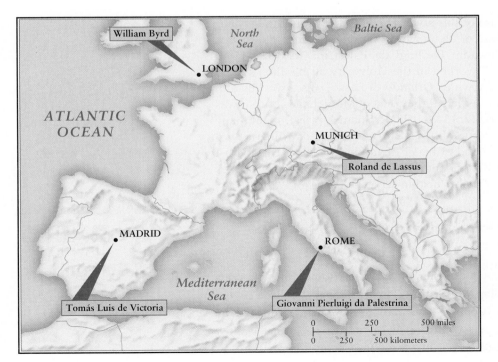

The dispersion of the High Renaissance style across Europe

Music at court: instrumentalists of the Bavarian Court Chapel in 1565, under Roland de Lassus. Each man and boy is carefully and solemnly depicted. With this imposing picture (and another, of an equally large group of court singers), the duke showed off the size and distinction of his retinue — a reflection, of course, of his own glory. *De Agostini Picture Library/The Bridgeman Art Library.*

new secular genres also made use of this style. The broad appeal of the style is shown by the geographical spread of its four most famous masters, Palestrina, Lassus, Victoria, and Byrd. Giovanni Pierluigi da Palestrina (c. 1525–1594) was born just outside Rome and worked in the Holy City all his life. Roland de Lassus (c. 1532–1594), also known as Orlando di Lasso, was a worldly and much-traveled Netherlander who settled at the court of Munich. His output was enormous. Tomás Luis de Victoria (c. 1548–1611), a Spanish priest, spent many years in Rome working for the Jesuits but ended up in Madrid. William Byrd (1540–1623) was organist of England's Chapel Royal under Queen Elizabeth I but also a member of the English dissident Catholic minority. He wrote Masses for illegal and highly dangerous services held in secret in barns and attics.

Giovanni Pierluigi da Palestrina (c. 1525–1594), *Pope Marcellus* Mass (1557)

1 | 11   11

Palestrina was a singer in, or choirmaster of, many of Rome's most famous churches and chapels, including the Sistine (Papal) Chapel. He lived in the repressive atmosphere of the Counter-Reformation movement, launched by the pope in 1545 to combat a growing revolt in northern Europe against Catholicism as then practiced. (That revolt was the Protestant Reformation.) In his youth Palestrina wrote secular compositions, some of which were widely popular, but later he recanted and apologized for them. He composed over a hundred Masses; some of the earliest of them were published with a highly symbolic illustration of the kneeling composer presenting his music to the pope.

Because singing is so powerful a force in religion, as we noted on page 44, societies have felt a need to control it carefully. Christianity has witnessed periodic reforms to prune church services of musical features that came to be seen as extravagant. The Counter-Reformation staged just such a reform. Palestrina's most famous composition, the *Pope Marcellus* Mass, was supposed to have convinced the pope and his council that composers of complicated polyphonic church music could still set the sacred words clearly enough that the congregation could hear them. Partly because of this legend, and partly because of the serenity and careful control of his musical style, Palestrina became the most revered Renaissance composer for later centuries. His works are still treasured by Catholic choir directors today.

Gloria A section from the Gloria of the *Pope Marcellus* Mass, the "Qui tollis," shows how the High Renaissance a cappella style changed after the time of Josquin. Compared with Josquin's setting of these same words in his *Pange lingua* Mass (see page 65), Palestrina's setting employs much more homophony. Apart from some fuzziness on a few individual words, only the last and longest line of Palestrina's composition uses polyphony; this contrast makes for a fine climax.

Beyond this, we notice at once that vocal sonority is of major importance in Palestrina's setting. He uses a larger and richer choir than Josquin—six vocal parts, rather than four—and keeps alternating between one and another subgroup, or semichoir, drawn from the total choir. Thus the first phrase, in high voices, is answered by the second, in low voices, and so on. The whole choir does not sing all together until the word *suscipe.*

What matters most to Palestrina are the rich, shifting tone colors and harmonies, which he uses to produce a generalized spiritual aura, sometimes ethereal, sometimes ecstatic. And with the aims of the Counter-Reformation in mind, he is certainly careful to declaim the words very clearly.

The frontispiece of Palestrina's *First Book of Masses* (1554) announces to all the world that this music has the pope's blessing. The book in Palestrina's hands is open to the papal Mass *Ecce Sacerdos magnus* (Behold the great priest). *Bettmann/CORBIS.*

1 | 11   11

Palestrina, *Pope Marcellus* Mass, from the Gloria

Capital letters indicate phrases sung in homophony.

0:00	QUI TOLLIS PECCATA MUNDI, MISERERE NOBIS. QUI TOLLIS PECCATA MUNDI, **Suscipe** DEPRECATIONEM NOSTRAM.	You who take away the sins of the world, have mercy upon us. You who take away the sins of the world, hear our prayer.
1:23	QUI SEDES AD DEXTERAM PATRIS, MISERERE NOBIS.	You who sit at the right hand of the Father, have mercy upon us.
2:00	QUONIAM TU SOLUS SANCTUS, TU SOLUS DOMINUS, TU SOLUS ALTISSIMUS, JESU CHRISTE,	For you alone are holy, you alone are the Lord, you alone are the most high, Jesus Christ,
2:36	CUM SANCTO SPIRITU, IN GLORIA DEI PATRIS. **Amen.**	With the Holy Spirit, in the glory of God the Father. Amen.

The Motet

The term *motet*, we saw in Chapter 6, was invented in the late Middle Ages. It has lived on and been applied to very different kinds of music over the centuries since. Thus motets by Palestrina or Byrd have little in common with motets by Machaut or even Dufay. The sixteenth-century **motet** is a relatively short composition with Latin words, made up of short sections in the homophony and imitative polyphony that were the staples of the High Renaissance style. The words are nearly always religious, taken from a variety of sources—sometimes directly from the Bible. As compared with the Mass of the same time, the motet is basically similar in *musical style*, but different in *scope* and, of course, in text.

It was the variety of possible words in the motet, as contrasted to the invariable words of the Mass, that recommended it to sixteenth-century composers. By providing them with new words to express, motets allowed church composers to convey religious messages in their music with more verve and power than ever before.

The Italian Madrigal

It was in secular music, however, that the Renaissance ideal of music as expression made the greatest impact. This took place principally in an important new Italian genre, after around 1530, called the **madrigal**.

The madrigal is a short composition set to a one-stanza poem—typically a love poem, with a rapid turnover of ideas and images. Ideally it is sung by one singer per part, in an intimate setting. The music consists of a sometimes equally rapid turnover of sections in imitative polyphony or homophony. Essentially, then, the plan is the same as that in High Renaissance sacred works such as Masses and motets.

But with secular words came a decisive change of emphasis. The points of imitation were shorter, and the imitation itself less strict; there was generally much more homophony; and the words assumed more and more importance. Both declamation and word painting were developed with great subtlety. For three generations a line of Italian madrigal composers, or *madrigalists*, pioneered an amazing variety of techniques to make words more vivid and to illustrate and illuminate them by musical means. Many thousands of their madrigals were published at the time and have come down to us.

The English Madrigal

A genre like the madrigal, tied so closely to its words—Italian words—would seem difficult to transplant. Even so, Italian madrigals became all the rage in Elizabethan England and led to the composition of madrigals in English. This popularity may well have reflected the taste and interests of Queen Elizabeth I herself. The Virgin Queen not only maintained a splendid musical establishment, like all other ambitious monarchs and princes of the time, but also became an accomplished musician in her own right.

"If therefore you will compose madrigals, you must possess yourself of an amorous humor, so that you must be wavering like the wind, sometimes wanton, sometimes drooping, sometimes grave and staid, otherwhile effeminate; and show the very uttermost of your variety, and the more variety you show the better shall you please."

From a music textbook by madrigal composer Thomas Morley, 1597

Queen Elizabeth I playing the lute. This miniature portrait is reproduced close to its original size. *Berkeley Castle, Gloucestershire, UK/The Bridgeman Art Library.*

In 1601, twenty-three English composers contributed madrigals to a patriotic anthology in Elizabeth's honor, called *The Triumphs of Oriana*. All the poems end with the same refrain: "Then sang the shepherds and nymphs of Diana: Long live fair Oriana!" Oriana was a pseudonym for Elizabeth, and the nymphs and shepherds of Diana—the goddess of virginity—were her subjects. The *Triumphs* was obviously a court-inspired project, and as such it reminds us vividly of one of the main functions of court music in all ages: flattery.

Thomas Weelkes (c. 1575–1623), Madrigal, "As Vesta Was from Latmos Hill Descending" (1601)

Thomas Weelkes never rose beyond the position of provincial cathedral organist-choirmaster; in fact, he had trouble keeping even that post in later life, when the cathedral records assert that he became "noted and found for a common drunckard and notorious swearer and blasphemer." Although he is not a major figure—not in a league with the other composers treated in this unit—he is one of the best composers of madrigals in English.

Weelkes's contribution to *The Triumphs of Oriana* is a fine example of a madrigal of the lighter kind. (Weelkes also wrote serious and melancholy madrigals.) After listening to the music of Josquin and Palestrina, our first impression of "Vesta" is one of sheer exuberant brightness. Simple rhythms, clear harmonies, crisp melodic motives—all look forward to music of the Baroque era and beyond. This music has a modern feel about it.

The next thing likely to impress us is the elegance and liveliness with which the words are declaimed. Weelkes nearly always has his words sung in rhythms that would seem quite natural if the words were spoken, as shown in the margin (where—stands for a long syllable, ˘ for a short one). The declamation is never less than accurate, and it is sometimes expressive: The rhythms make the words seem imposing in the second phrase, dainty in the third.

Leav-ing their God-dess all a-lone

Then sang the shep-herds and nymphs of Di-a-na

To whom Di-a-na's dar-lings

As for the word painting, that can be shown in a tabular form:

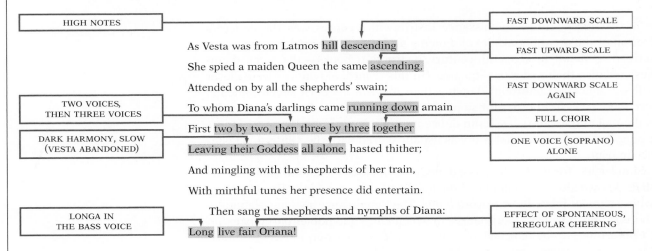

(The "maiden Queen" is Elizabeth, and "Diana's darlings" are the Vestal Virgins, priestesses of Vesta, the Roman goddess of hearth and home. The archaic word *amain* means "at full speed.")

This brilliant six-part madrigal uses two sopranos, alto, two tenors, and bass. Weelkes makes particularly good use of this group in his extended imitative setting of the poem's last line. Here we can easily imagine six loyal voices (or many more) endlessly cheering their queen in a spontaneous, irregular way, one after another. Shakespeare and his contemporaries, Weelkes among them, were very fond of puns. Weelkes has the word *long* sung by the bass voice on a note four times the duration of a whole note—a note whose Latin name was *longa*. So this madrigal has its esoteric, in-joke side for musicians as well as its public, political side for Elizabeth's subjects.

5 | Instrumental Music: Early Developments

The best sixteenth-century composers concentrated almost entirely on vocal genres, on music with words. Except for the English master William Byrd, none of them devoted much attention to music for instruments alone. This is in keeping with the Renaissance preoccupation with expression in music, achieved through the association of music with words.

Nevertheless, instruments and music for instruments developed significantly during this period. The first violins and harpsichords date from the sixteenth century; many other instruments such as the lute (see page 21) were perfected during this time. Originally from the Near East, the lute was as popular then as the guitar is today. Instrumental music was to become one of the great glories of the Baroque era, and the basis for this was laid in the Renaissance.

Around 1500, hardly any music was written specifically for instruments. Instrumentalists would either play along with singers in vocal music or else play motets, chansons, and other vocal genres by themselves, without words. The principal vocal genre after 1550, however—the madrigal—would not have made much sense performed without its words. By this time new genres were emerging specifically for instrumental performance.

Renaissance Dances

The most widespread of Renaissance instrumental genres was the dance, a reflection of the great popularity of dancing at the time. Many dance types are described in detail in sixteenth-century instruction books—the steps themselves, and also their order or sequence. (In this regard, old dances were closer to square dances or ballroom dancing than to some modern social dancing, where there is no fixed order for steps or movements.) One of the most popular was the **pavan** (pa-váhn), a solemn dance in duple meter, with the participants stepping and stopping formally. It was usually paired with the **galliard**, a faster dance in triple meter.

Simpler, less formal Renaissance dance types include the Italian *saltarello;* the Irish *jig*, known also in Scotland and the north of England; and the French *bransle*, whose name is related to our word *brawl*. The Renaissance also saw elaborately choreographed ballets, court dances in which kings and nobles participated.

Conforming to the dance steps, dance music was written in easy-to-follow phrases, almost always four to eight bars long. Ending with especially clear cadences, the phrases were each played twice in succession to produce forms such as **a a b b** or **a a b b c c**.

Instrumental music at work: a dance at the French royal court, c. 1580. The leaping couple tells us the dance is a lively one. *Musée des Beaux-Arts, Rennes, France/Giraudon/The Bridgeman Art Library.*

Anonymous (sixteenth century), Galliard, "Daphne"

The title of this melodious Elizabethan dance suggests that originally it may have been a song. But if so, at some point the song was pressed into galliard form, **a a b b c c:**

Played in our recording by an early violin ensemble, "Daphne" is mainly homophonic. The meter is kept very clear, and the distinct quality of the phrases ending **a, b,** and **c** makes it easy for the dancers to remember the place in the dance step sequence. The first violin improvises ornaments at the second playing—an instrumental practice as old as the estampie (see page 51) and as new as jazz (page 386).

Anonymous (sixteenth century), "Kemp's Jig"

Will Kemp was an Elizabethan actor, comedian, and song-and-dance man, immortalized for having created comic roles in Shakespeare, such as Dogberry, the addle-headed constable in *Much Ado about Nothing*. Kemp specialized in a type of popular dance number, called a jig, that was regularly presented in Elizabethan theaters after the main play. He accompanied himself with pipe (a type of simple flute, blown like a recorder) and tabor (a snare drum).

"Kemp's Jig" is a lively—perhaps *perky* is the right word—and very simple dance tune in **a a b** form. Both **a** and **b** end with the same cadence. The tune is played several times on our recording, first by a recorder and then by a viol, an early stringed instrument in the cello range; ornaments are piled on, first to the repeated phrase **a** and then to all the repetitions. A lute accompanies.

Will Kemp of "Kemp's Jig"; his musician accompanies with traditional tools of the trade, a pipe and tabor (flute and drum). © *The British Library Board. Harley 3885 f19.*

GOALS FOR REVIEW

▶   to understand the technique of paraphrasing an earlier melody

▶   to listen for melodic paraphrase and homophonic texture in a Renaissance hymn

▶   to understand the imitative polyphony at the heart of the high Renaissance style

▶   to gain an overview of the Mass, the most important element of Christian liturgy

▶   to listen to polyphonic settings of individual prayers or sections of the Mass by Josquin Desprez and Giovanni Pierluigi da Palestrina

▶   to understand the new Renaissance emphasis on musical expression, and to hear it at work in a madrigal by Thomas Weelkes

▶   to witness the growing importance of instrumental music, especially dances

Global Perspectives

Music and Early European Colonialism

In introducing the Renaissance, on page 60, we echoed the words of a historian who saw in it "the discovery of the world and of man." But we have not yet said much about the *world* part of this formulation.

The period from 1480 to 1620 marks the first great phase of European expansion into other parts of the world. The most famous European voyages of exploration, by Bartolomeu Dias, Vasco da Gama, Columbus, and Magellan, were followed by countless others. Trade routes to Africa and the New World were quickly established—so quickly that from 1492 on, only one year passed without European journeys to the Americas.

The voyages of exploration were more than sheer adventurism or innocent trading ventures. They were also expeditions of military conquest and territorial expansion. They marked the beginning of aggressive European colonization of large portions of the rest of the globe that would last almost five hundred years, well into the 1900s, and would profoundly shape the modern world.

Cultural Conquest and Music

The European attempt to conquer was cultural as well as military. In the immediate wake of European soldiers and conquistadors came missionaries aiming to convert the native peoples to Christian beliefs—whether by persuasion or harsher measures. Wherever they went,

A European depiction from the 1590s of the song and dance of the Tupi Indians of Brazil. *Private Collection / The Stapleton Collection / Bridgeman Images.*

soldiers, missionaries, and merchants reported back to a fascinated Europe on the novelties they found.

These reports—some precise and evidently accurate, others very fanciful—often made room for descriptions of music. They inform us of musical traditions that today are at least much changed and, in many cases, simply extinct. From the 1590s comes a description of African music in the Congo. (For discussion of West African drumming, see page 397.) English mariners report on Native North American song and dance (see page 59), and Dutch explorers tell about the elaborate gong orchestras, or *gamelans*, still played today in Indonesia (see page 199). The Jesuit Father Matteo Ricci, the first European allowed to reside in the imperial capital of Beijing, was scandalized by Chinese opera, "a curse," in his view, "more prone to vice" than any other activity (for more on Chinese opera, see page 297).

Music of the Aztecs and Incas

The Aztec and Inca empires were the greatest civilizations Europeans came upon in the New World. They amazed their conquerors with their cultural achievements and complexity, their riches, and their astonishing capitals: Tenochtitlán, in the middle of a Mexican lake that has long since disappeared under Mexico City, and Cuzco, built so high up in the Andes that the Spaniards established Lima, a low-lying city on the coast, for themselves.

Since they had elaborate religious institutions of their own, the Mexicans and Andeans presented the European missionaries with their first great challenges for religious conversion in the New World. The missionaries systematically studied Aztec and Inca culture to determine how best to achieve their goal, and they taught the natives all the elements of a Christian life as they saw it. Prominent among their studies was native music; central to their teachings was European music.

Inevitably, the two musics were thrust into confrontation. A Mexican church council of the sixteenth century ruled that native musicians "shall sing polyphonic music only when their singing conforms to standards we consider acceptable . . . and they shall not be permitted to sing songs that remind people of their old idolatrous customs." A church council at

A church procession in seventeenth-century Cuzco, with the Virgin Mary atop a wagon carrying musicians (not painted to scale). The aristocrat at the far left wears traditional Inca garb.

Lima tried to abolish altogether singing and dancing at native harvest festivals. Meanwhile, the missionaries *encouraged* native song and dance in *Christian* festivals, hoping that they would hasten the Andeans' acceptance of the new, foreign religion.

These efforts could not succeed completely. We know that native singers preserved their traditional songs, often singing them secretly, away from the eyes and ears of the authorities. At the same time they easily learned and adopted the European music the missionaries pressed on them. By the mid-seventeenth century Native Americans were composing European-style church music in more than one newly built cathedral.

Inca Processional Music

The song "Hanaq pachap kusikuynin" is a fascinating case of the musical merging of two cultures. Published in 1631 by a Franciscan friar named Bocanegra, it is the first piece of elaborate music to be published anywhere in the New World. The words of the song are in the native Andean language Quechua (*ket*-chwa). Was it the work of Bocanegra himself, or one of the new Indian composers? We cannot be sure.

The song is a hymn to the Virgin Mary. Bocanegra says that it was sung during religious processions honoring her, like the one pictured above. Imagine the scene in 1630 in front of the still unfinished cathedral of Cuzco, built on the sturdy foundations of an Inca palace: Native singers march in procession across the plaza, wearing the traditional garb still permitted for Christian festivals, singing Quechua words set to European-style music, and accompanying themselves on Andean flutes and drums.

As they enter the church, they regroup as a choir for services including Gregorian chant, now with Latin words—perhaps "Ave maris stella," the widely used hymn to the Virgin that we have already studied. Next comes newly composed polyphonic music. Such are the cultural mixes that arise in colonial situations.

Our performance of "Hanaq pachap kusikuynin" is tamer than this—no instruments are used. The music is simple but moving. It sets the phrases of the Quechua text one by one, in the straightforward homophonic texture we have heard in Dufay's harmonization of "Ave maris stella" and Palestrina's *Pope Marcellus* Mass (see pages 61 and 70).

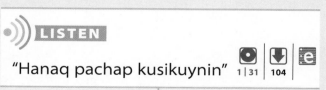

LISTEN

"Hanaq pachap kusikuynin" 1 | 31 104

Hanaq pachap kusikuynin **Waranqakta much'asqayki**	Bliss of heaven, A thousand times I adore you.
Yupay ruru puquq mallki **Runakunap suyakuynin** **Kallpannaqpa q'imikuynin** **Waqyasqayta**	Tree of myriad fruits, Hope of peoples, Pillar of the weak: Hear my cry.
	(one more stanza)

The Early Baroque Period

In the years around 1600, music underwent rapid changes at the sophisticated courts and churches of northern Italy. Composers began to write motets, madrigals, and other pieces more directly for effect—with less artifice of imitative polyphony and also with the use of exciting new performing forces. A new style, the style of the early Baroque period, took hold all over Italy and, soon, in most of the rest of Europe.

1 | From Renaissance to Baroque

The madrigal, we saw in Chapter 7, was the most "advanced" form in late Renaissance music. Toward the end of the sixteenth century, the search for expression led madrigal composers to increasingly extreme—even weird—kinds of word painting. Previously taboo dissonances and rhythmic contrasts were explored to illustrate emotional texts in a more and more exaggerated fashion. The fluid High Renaissance style broke down.

At the same time, a reaction set in *against* the madrigal. In Florence, an influential group of intellectuals mounted an attack on the madrigalists' favorite technique, word painting. It was artificial and childish, they said, and the many voices of a madrigal ensemble could not focus feeling or express it strongly.

True emotionality could be projected only by a single human agent, an individual, a singer who would learn from great actors how to move an audience to laughter, anger, or tears. A new style of solo singing was developed, *recitative,* that aimed to join together features of music and speech. This led inevitably to the stage and, as we shall see, to opera. Invented in Florence around 1600, opera became one of the greatest and most characteristic products of the Baroque imagination.

"Why cause words to be sung by four or five voices so that they cannot be distinguished, when the ancient Greeks aroused the strongest passions by means of a single voice supported by a lyre? Renounce counterpoint . . . and return to simplicity!"

A Florentine critic, 1581

Music in Venice

Meanwhile, there were important developments in Venice, the city of canals. The "Most Serene Republic," as Venice called itself, cultivated especially brilliant styles in all the arts—matched, it seems, to the city's dazzling physical beauty.

Wealthy and cosmopolitan, Venice produced architects whose flamboyant, varied buildings were built of multicolored materials, and painters—the Bellinis,

Venice, the most colorful of European cities, and one of the most musical. Several major painters made a specialty of Venetian scenes, which were very popular; this one, of an aquatic fete across from the central square, the Piazza San Marco, is by Canaletto (1697–1768). The Bucintoro Returning to the Molo *(oil on canvas), ©The Bowes Museum, Barnard Castle County Museum, UK/The Bridgeman Art Library.*

Titian, Tintoretto—who specialized in warm, rich hues. Perhaps, then, it is more than a play on words to describe Venetian music as "colorful."

From the time of Palestrina's *Pope Marcellus* Mass (see page 70), composers of the sixteenth century had often divided their choirs into low and high groups of three or four voice parts each. These semichoirs would alternate and answer or echo each other. Expanding this technique, Venetian composers would now alternate two, three, or more whole choirs. Homophony crowded out counterpoint as full choirs answered one another in stereo, seeming to compete throughout entire motets and Masses, then joining together for climactic sections of glorious massed sound.

The sonic resources were enriched even further when Venetian composers started designating the choirs for instruments on some parts as well as the usual voices on others. Even whole choirs could be made up of instruments and pitted against the choirs of voices. As the sonorous combinations of Venetian music grew more and more colorful, magnificence and extravagance became the new ideals, well suited to the pomp and ceremony for which Venice was famous. And as Venice became the tourist center of Europe, its distinctive music proved to be one of its big attractions.

Extravagance and Control

Wherever they looked, knowledgeable travelers to Italy around 1600 would have seen music bursting out of its traditional forms, styles, and genres. Freedom was the order of the day. But they might have been puzzled to notice an opposite tendency as well: In some ways musical form was becoming more rigorously controlled and systematic. As composers sought to make music more untrammeled in one respect, it seems they found they had to organize it more strictly in another. Listeners could not be allowed to lose track of what was happening.

The clarity and control composers exercised over Baroque form, in other words, was an appropriate response to Baroque extravagance and emotionality of expression.

Giovanni Gabrieli, Motet, "O magnum mysterium" (c. 1610)

1 | 15   15

The most important composers in Venice were two Gabrielis, Andrea (c. 1510–1586) and his nephew Giovanni. As organists of St. Mark's Basilica, the cathedral of Venice, both of them exploited the special acoustics of that extraordinary building, which still impress tourists today. By placing choirs of singers and instrumentalists in some of St. Mark's many different choir lofts, they obtained brilliant echo effects that even modern audio equipment cannot duplicate.

Giovanni's "O magnum mysterium," part of a larger motet, was written for the Christmas season. The words marvel that lowly animals—the ox and the ass—were the first to see the newborn Jesus. This naïve, touching text made "O magnum mysterium" a favorite for motet settings at the time; there are lovely versions by Victoria and Byrd (page 70).

Gabrieli's music marvels along with the text. In the manner of a madrigal, the exclamation *O* is repeated like a gasp of astonishment. Then lush chord progressions positively make the head spin, as the words *O magnum mysterium* are repeated to the same music, but pitched higher (that is to say, in sequence—see page 48).

Gabrieli uses two choirs, each with three voice parts and four instrumental parts, plus organ, though at first all we hear is a sumptuous blend of brass instruments and voices in a mainly homophonic texture. A more polyphonic texture emerges for the first time at the word *sacramentum*. Solo voices, first tenors, then boy sopranos, imitate one another during the line *iacentem in presepio*. Their motive is finally taken up by the brass.

Gabrieli unleashes his musical resources in a big way at the choral "Alleluia" section. The music moves in quick triple meter, matching the jubilation of repeated *alleluias*, and the choirs echo back and forth across the sound space:

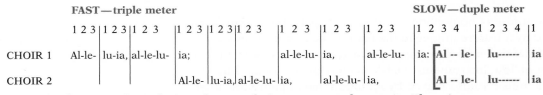

To make a grand conclusion, the two choirs come together again. There is another wash of voice-and-brass sonority as the tempo slows and the meter

"Sometimes there sung 16 or 20 men together, having their master or moderator to keep them in order, and when they sung the instrumental musicians played also. Sometimes 16 played together: 10 sagbuts, 4 cornets, and 2 violdegamboes of an extraordinary greatness, sometimes 2, a cornet and a treble viol. "

Venetian music in 1611, as reported by an English tourist

sagbut: an early trombone
cornet: a woodwind instrument played with a trumpet mouthpiece
viola da gamba: a cello-like instrument

changes to duple for a climactic *alleluia*. And for still more emphasis, Gabrieli repeats the entire "Alleluia" section, both the fast triple-time alternations and the massive slow ending. This kind of clear sectional repetition shows one way Baroque composers worked to impose clarity and control on flamboyant chords and the solo rhapsodies.

 **LISTEN**

Gabrieli, "O magnum mysterium"

1 | 15   15

0:00	**O magnum mysterium,**	O, what a great mystery,
0:29	**et admirabile sacramentum**	and what a wonderful sacrament—
0:51	**ut animalia viderunt Dominum natum**	that animals should see the Lord new born
1:16	**iacentem in presepio:**	lying in the manger.
1:51	**Alleluia, alleluia.**	Hallelujah, hallelujah.

2 | Style Features of Early Baroque Music

Music from the period of approximately 1600 to 1750 is usually referred to as *baroque,* a term that captures its excess and extravagance. (It was originally a jeweler's term for large pearls of irregular shape.) A number of broad stylistic features unify the music of this long period.

Rhythm and Meter

Rhythms become more definite, regular, and insistent in Baroque music; a single rhythm or similar rhythms can be heard throughout a piece or a major segment of a piece. Compare the subtle, floating rhythms of Renaissance music, changing section by section as the motives for the imitative polyphony change. (Renaissance dance music is an exception, and in the area of dance music there is a direct line from the Renaissance to the Baroque.)

Related to this new regularity of rhythm is a new emphasis on meter. One technical feature tells the story: Bar lines begin to be used for the first time in music history. This means that music's meter is systematically in evidence, rather than being downplayed as it was in the Renaissance. (Full disclosure: For ease of reading, we have added bar lines to our examples in Chapters 6 and 7, but there are no bar lines in the original music.) The strong beats are often also emphasized by certain instruments, playing in a clear, decisive way. Strong rhythms and clear meter are conspicuous in Gabrieli's motet "O magnum mysterium."

Texture: Basso Continuo

Some early Baroque music is homophonic and some is polyphonic, but both textures are enriched by a feature unique to the period, the **basso continuo**.

In Baroque music the bass line is performed by bass voices (as in Renaissance music) or low instruments such as cellos or bassoons. But the bass part in Baroque music is also played by an organ, harpsichord, or other chord instrument. This instrument not only reinforces the bass line but also adds chords continuously to go with it. The basso continuo, as it was called, meaning "continuous bass," has the double effect of clarifying the harmony and making the texture bind or jell. Baroque music players today usually call it simply the **continuo**.

One can see how the continuo responds to the growing reliance of Baroque music on harmony (already clear from Gabrieli's motet). Originally, the continuo was simply the bass line of the polyphony reinforced by chords; but later the continuo with its chords was mapped out first, and the polyphony above adjusted to it. Baroque polyphony, in other words, has systematic harmonic underpinnings.

This fact is dramatized by a musical form that is characteristically Baroque, the **ground bass**. This is music constructed from the bottom up. In ground-bass form, the bass instruments play a single short melody many times, generating the same set of repeated harmonies above it (played by the continuo chord instruments). Over this ground bass, upper instruments or voices play (or improvise) different melodies or virtuoso passages, all adjusted to the harmonies determined by the bass.

Baroque ground-bass compositions discussed in this book are "Dido's Lament" from the opera *Dido and Aeneas* by Henry Purcell (page 88), and Vivaldi's Violin Concerto in G, Op. 4, No. 12 (page 117).

Another name for the ground bass comes from Italian musicians of the Baroque: **basso ostinato**, meaning "persistent" or "obstinate" bass. By extension, the term **ostinato** is also used to refer to any short musical gesture repeated over and over again, in the bass or anywhere else, especially one used as a building block for a piece of music. Ostinatos are found in most of the world's musical traditions (see page 94).

A ground bass
(the Pachelbel Canon)

Andante

= repeated
many times

Functional Harmony

Inevitably, in view of these new techniques, the art of harmony evolved rapidly at this time. Whereas Renaissance music had still used the medieval modes, although with important modifications, Baroque musicians developed the modern major/minor system, which we discussed on pages 31–33. Chords became standardized, and the sense of tonality—the feeling of centrality around a tonic or home pitch—grew much stronger.

Composers also developed a new way of handling the chords so that their interrelation was felt to be more logical or coherent. Each chord now assumed a special role, or function, in relation to the tonic chord (the chord on the home pitch). Thus when one chord follows another in Baroque music, it does so in a newly predictable and purposeful way. **Functional harmony**, in this sense, could also be used as a way of organizing large-scale pieces of music, as we will see later.

In a Baroque composition, as compared with one from the Renaissance, the chords seem to be going where we expect them to—and we feel they are determining the sense or the direction of the piece as a whole. Harmonies no longer seem to wander, detour, hesitate, or evaporate. With the introduction of the important resource of functional harmony, Baroque music brings us firmly to the familiar, to the threshold of modern music.

3 | Opera

Opera—drama presented in music, with the characters singing instead of speaking—is often called the most characteristic art form of the Baroque period. Baroque opera combined many different arts: not only music, drama, and poetry but also dancing, highly elaborate scene design, and spectacular special effects. Ingenious machines were contrived to portray gods descending to earth, shipwrecks, volcanos, and all kinds of natural and supernatural phenomena. Scene designers often received top billing, ahead of the composers.

Opera began in Florence; the early operas were court entertainments put on to celebrate royal weddings and the like. But an important step was taken in 1637 with the opening of the first public opera theater. Opera soon became the leading form of entertainment in the whole of Italy. By the end of the century, seven opera houses in Venice fulfilled much the same function as movie theaters in a comparable modern city (around 145,000 people).

Opera was a perfect answer to the general desire in the early Baroque era to portray individual emotion. Opera provided a stage on which the single individual could step forward to express his or her feelings in the most direct and powerful fashion. Indeed, composers felt a need to relieve the constant emotional pressure exerted on their characters by the ever-changing dramatic action. They had to contrive moments of relaxation, moments when the characters could stop and reflect. This led to a standard dualism that has been with opera ever since: *recitative* and *aria*.

Recitative and Aria

Recitative (reh-sih-ta-téev), from the Italian word for "recitation," is the technique of declaiming words musically in a heightened, theatrical manner. It is descended from the careful declamation practiced by late Renaissance composers (see page 68).

The singing voice closely follows the free rhythm of highly emotional speech; it mirrors and exaggerates the natural ups and downs that occur as an actor raises his or her voice at a question, lowers it in an aside, or cries out inw distress. The accompaniment is usually kept to a minimum—most often one or two continuo instruments—ensuring that all the words can be heard clearly.

Recitative is used for plot action, dialogue, and other situations in the drama where it is particularly important for the words to be brought out. On the other hand, where spoken drama would call for soliloquies or meditations, opera uses arias.

An **aria** is an extended piece for solo singer that has much more musical elaboration and coherence than a passage of recitative. The vocal part is more melodic, the rhythm is more consistent, the meter clearer, and typically the accompaniment includes the entire orchestra. Here the singer-actor mulls over his or her feelings at some leisure, instead of reacting moment by moment, as in recitative. Emotion is controlled and frozen into a tableau

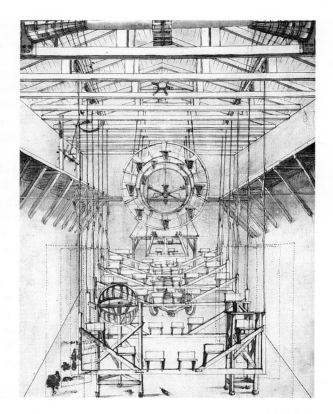

Stage designers of Baroque opera specialized in rapidly moving scenery for their most dazzling effects. Shown here are the machinery for one such set and a drawing of how the effects looked to the audience. *Bibliothèque Nationale de France.*

or picture. Paradoxically, when the music gets more elaborate, the emotion stands still.

Recitative required great singing actors, and arias required artists who could convert the notes of a score into these tableaus of furious, sensuous, or tragic emotion. Opera houses in the seventeenth century became showcases of vocal virtuosity—as they still are today. Ever since the Baroque era, dramatic expression and vocal display have vied with one another as the driving forces of opera.

Claudio Monteverdi (1567–1643)

One figure stood out above all others in music around 1600, just as Josquin Desprez had around 1500. Claudio Monteverdi, an enormously imaginative and innovative composer, also has the distinction of being the first great composer whose music was attacked for being too radical. Radical it was. Monteverdi has aptly been called "the last great madrigalist and the first great opera composer"; indeed, while his earliest madrigals are close in style to those of Thomas Weelkes, some of his later ones are more like small, self-contained opera scenes.

Monteverdi's career was long and fortunate. He was a quick starter, publishing a little book of sacred songs while only fifteen, and he was still composing operas into his seventies. He first worked at the music-loving court of Mantua, in northern Italy. There he wrote his first opera, *Orfeo* (Orpheus, 1607), famous in music history as the first masterpiece of opera. He was then appointed choirmaster of St. Mark's Cathedral in Venice, the most prestigious musical position in Europe, where the Gabrielis had held forth. (Even before moving to Venice he had composed a collection of motets that rivaled anything the Gabrielis produced, in its rich amalgam of solo voices, multiple choirs, and instruments.) At the end of his long career, in the 1640s, Monteverdi helped inaugurate public opera, Venice's greatest contribution to the history of music.

After *Orfeo*, none of Monteverdi's operas were printed, and some have been completely lost—a grievous loss indeed. All we have left of his *Arianna* is the heroine's big lament, one of the greatest hits of the day, which Monteverdi published in several different arrangements. Fortunately, two late masterpieces have survived: *The Return of Ulysses* and *The Coronation of Poppea*.

Monteverdi as a young man. *Conservatory of St. Peter, Naples, Italy/Giraudon — The Bridgeman Art Library.*

SINGING ITALIAN

The Coronation of Poppea is the first of many Italian texts printed in this book. To follow the recordings, it will help to know a few simple rules about Italian pronunciation and singing conventions.

- The consonants *c* and *g* are soft (pronounced, respectively, "ch" and "j") when followed by *e* or *i* (cello, Genoa, cappuccino, DiMaggio). They are hard when followed by other letters, including *h* (Galileo, spaghetti con Chianti).

- In poems, when an Italian word *ending* with a vowel is followed by another word *beginning* with a vowel, the two vowels are elided, run together as one.

- In Italian (and German) *z* is pronounced *dz* or *tz* (pizza, Mozart).

Lines from our selection from *The Coronation of Poppea* are sung as indicated below:

3 Pur teco io stò	= Pur téc'yo stó
19 tu a me verrai	= tw'a méh verráh-ee
27 Il core accarezzando	= Il cór' accar-etzándo
30 E mi circondi intanto	= E mi chircond' intánto
35 Per me guerreggia Amor	= Per méh gwerréj' Amór

Claudio Monteverdi, *The Coronation of Poppea* (1642)

Even today, the story of *The Coronation of Poppea* can shock by its startling and cynical dramatic realism. Poppea, mistress of the notorious Roman emperor Nero, schemes to get his wife, Ottavia, deposed and his eminent adviser, Seneca, put to death. She succeeds in both. In a counterplot, Ottavia blackmails Ottone, Poppea's rejected lover, into an attempt on Poppea's life. Ottone tries but fails. The counterplotters are all exiled. As an added cynical touch, Poppea's ruthless maneuvering to be crowned empress of Rome is shown to be aided by the God of Love and the Goddess of Fortune.

After a prologue sung by the mythological characters, Act I begins with Ottone arriving at Poppea's house at daybreak, and retreating in dismay after he sees Nero's guards outside it. In an ironic alba (see page 50), the guards curse military life and gossip about Poppea's scheming. This is a vivid prelude to the first of the opera's several steamy love scenes.

Recitative   Enter Nero and Poppea, who tries to wheedle Nero into staying with her. Delaying his departure as long as possible, she makes him promise to return. Accompanied by a lute as continuo instrument—a voluptuous sound, in this context—she repeats the question *"Tornerai?"* ("Won't you return?") in increasingly seductive accents until Nero stops evading the issue and agrees: *"Tornerò"* ("I will return"). The vocal line does not form itself into real melodies, but goes up or down or speeds or slows, following the words in speechlike fragments. This is characteristic of the recitative style.

Monteverdi in old age, pictured on the title page for a book of poems honoring him, published in Venice ("In VENETIA") just after his death. The title page shows a fine collection of old instruments, including four lutes, shown in front and back views. *Bettmann/CORBIS.*

Nero's most extended evasion is a short aria-like fragment, called an **arioso**. Then the recitative resumes. On the final *addio*s—some of them melting, others breathless—the singers say good-bye, improvising delicate vocal ornaments.

Aria   As soon as Nero leaves, Poppea shows her true colors in a jubilant aria, a sort of victory dance. Accompanied by a small orchestra, it contains three short sections. The first is an orchestral tune (strings and recorder) to which Poppea sings her first two lines of text:

Allegro
POPPEA (with strings, recorder)

Speran - za _____ tu mi va - i   il core ac - ca - rez - zando __

Note that a moment of uncertainty ("a mantle that is . . . illusory") is marked by a momentary lapse into recitative. Her mood becomes harder and more determined in the aria's second section. Finally, in section 3, she sings lighthearted, fast military fanfares—this is word painting in the madrigal tradition—as she exults that the gods are fighting on her behalf.

Mercurial, manipulative, fearless, dangerously sensual: Poppea has been characterized unforgettably by Monteverdi's music in this scene.

 **LISTEN**

Monteverdi, *The Coronation of Poppea*, from Act I

1 | 16–17   16–17

Italics indicate repeated words and lines. For a word about singing Italian, see page 85.

		RECITATIVE		
16	0:00	**Poppea:**	Tornerai?	Won't you return?
		Nero:	Se ben io vò,	Though I am leaving you,
			Pur teco io stò, *pur teco stò* . . .	I am in truth still here . . .
		Poppea:	Tornerai?	Won't you return?
		Nero:	Il cor dalle tue stelle	My heart can never, never be torn away
			Mai mai non si disvelle . . .	from your fair eyes . . .
		Poppea:	Tornerai?	Won't you return?
		ARIOSO		
	0:20	**Nero:**	Io non posso da te, *non posso*	I cannot live apart from you
			da te, da te viver disgiunto	
			Se non si smembra l'unità del punto . . .	Unless unity itself can be divided . . .
		RECITATIVE		
	0:52	**Poppea:**	Tornerai?	Won't you return?
		Nero:	Tornerò.	I will return.
		Poppea:	Quando?	When?
		Nero:	Ben tosto.	Soon.
		Poppea:	Ben tosto, me'l prometti?	Very soon — you promise?
		Nero:	Te'l giuro.	I swear it!
		Poppea:	*E me l'osserverai?*	And will you keep your promise?
		Nero:	*E s'a te non verrò,*	If I do not come, you'll come to me!
			tu a me verrai!	
	1:19	**Poppea:**	Addio . . .	Farewell . . .
		Nero:	Addio . . .	
		Poppea:	Nerone, Nerone, addio . . .	
		Nero:	Poppea, Poppea, addio . . .	
		Poppea:	Addio, Nerone, addio!	Farewell, Nero, farewell!
		Nero:	Addio, Poppea, ben mio.	Farewell, Poppea, my love.
17	2:18	**ARIA**	(Section 1)	
0:11	2:29	**Poppea:**	Speranza, tu mi vai	O hope, you
			Il core accarezzando;	Caress my heart;
			Speranza, tu mi vai	O hope, you entice my mind;
			il genio lusingando;	
			E mi circondi intanto	As you cloak me
			Di regio si, ma immaginario manto.	In a mantle that is royal, yes, but illusory.
			(Section 2)	
0:51	3:09		No no, non temo, no, *no no,*	No, no! I fear no adversity:
			non temo, no di noia alcuna:	
			(Section 3)	
1:08	3:26		Per me guerreggia, *guerreggia,*	I have fighting for me,
			Per me guerreggia Amor,	I have fighting for me Love and Fortune.
			guerreggia Amor e la Fortuna, *e la Fortuna.*	

Many men's roles in early opera were written for castrati, male soprano singers (see page 137). On our recording, Nero is sung by a female mezzo-soprano, Guillemette Laurens.

Henry Purcell (1659–1695)

Italy was the undisputed leader in music throughout the seventeenth century. However, music in Baroque styles also flourished in France, Germany (or what is now Germany), and other countries, always under Italian influence. The greatest English composer of the Baroque era, Henry Purcell, was the organist at Westminster Abbey and a member of the Chapel Royal, like several other members of his family. In his short lifetime he wrote sacred, instrumental, and theater music, as well as twenty-nine "Welcome Songs" for his royal masters. Purcell combined a respect for native traditions, represented by the music of William Byrd, Thomas Weelkes, and others, with a lively interest in the more adventurous French and Italian music of his own time. He wrote the first English examples of a new Italian instrumental genre, the sonata.

Our Songs and our Musick
Let's still dedicate
To *Purcell,* to *Purcell,*
The Son of *Apollo,*
'Til another, another,
Another as Great
In the Heav'nly Science
Of Musick shall follow.

Poet Thomas d'Urfey, seventeenth century (Apollo was the Greek god of music.)

Henry Purcell, *Dido and Aeneas* (1689)

1 | 18–19   18–19   3

Though Purcell composed a good deal of music for the London theater, his one true opera, *Dido and Aeneas,* was performed at a girls' school (though there may have been an earlier performance at court). The whole thing lasts little more than an hour and contains no virtuoso singing roles at all. *Dido and Aeneas* is an exceptional work, then, and a miniature. But it is also a work of rare beauty and dramatic power—and rarer still, it is a great opera in English, perhaps the only great opera in English prior to the twentieth century.

Background Purcell's source was the *Aeneid,* the noblest of all Latin epic poems, written by Virgil to celebrate the glory of Rome and the Roman Empire. It tells the story of the city's foundation by the Trojan prince Aeneas, who escapes from Troy when the Greeks capture it with their wooden horse. After many adventures and travels, Aeneas finally reaches Italy, guided by the firm hand of Jove, king of the gods.

In one of the *Aeneid*'s most famous episodes, Aeneas and the widowed Queen Dido of Carthage fall deeply in love. But Jove tells the prince to stop dallying and get on with his important journey. Regretfully he leaves, and Dido kills herself—an agonizing suicide, as Virgil describes it.

In Acts I and II of the opera, Dido expresses apprehension about her feelings for Aeneas, even though her courtiers keep encouraging the match in chorus after chorus. Next we see the plotting of some witches—a highly un-Virgilian touch, but ever since Shakespeare's *Macbeth,* witches had been popular with English theatergoers, perhaps especially with school-age ones. For malicious reasons of their own, these witches make Aeneas believe that Jove is ordering his departure.

In Act III, Aeneas tries feebly to excuse himself. Dido spurns him in a furious recitative. As he leaves, deserting her, she prepares for her suicide.

Recitative Dido addresses this regal, somber recitative to her confidante, Belinda. Notice the imperious tone as she tells Belinda to take her hand, and the ominous word painting on *darkness.* Purcell designed the melody of this recitative as a long, gradual descent, as if Dido's life force is already ebbing away.

Aria The opera's final aria, usually known as "Dido's Lament," is built over a slow ground bass or ostinato (see page 83), a descending bass line with

Henry Purcell. *National Portrait Gallery, London, UK/The Bridgeman Art Library.*

An incident sparking the affair of Dido and Aeneas, depicted in Act II of Purcell's opera, is a hunting party disrupted by a violent storm. Here Thomas Jones (1742–1803) captures the oblivious passion of the lovers. *AKG-Images/The Image Works.*

chromatic semitones (half steps) repeated a dozen times. The bass line sounds mournful even without accompaniment, as in measures 1–4. Violins in the string orchestra imitate this line while Dido is singing, and especially after she has stopped. As often happens in arias, the words are repeated a number of times; Dido has little to say but much to feel, and the music needs time to convey the emotional message. We experience an extended emotional tableau. Whereas recitative makes little sense unless the listener understands the exact words, with arias a general impression of them may be enough. Indeed, even that is unnecessary when the song is as poignant as Purcell's is here.

The most heartbreaking place comes (twice) on the exclamation "ah," where the bass note D, harmonized with a major-mode chord during the first six appearances of the ground bass, now supports a new minor chord:

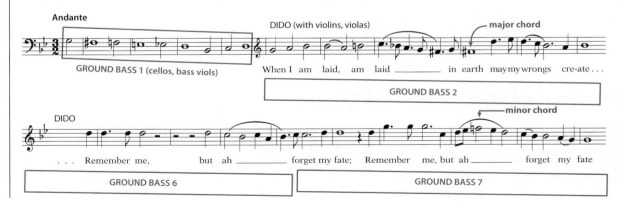

Chorus The last notes of this great aria run into a wonderful final chorus. We are to imagine a slow dance, as groups of sorrowful cupids (first graders, perhaps) file past the bier. Now Dido's personal grief and agony are transmuted into a sense of communal mourning. In the context of the whole opera, this chorus seems even more meaningful, because the courtiers who sing it have matured so much since the time when they thoughtlessly and cheerfully urged Dido to give in to her love.

The general style of the music is that of the madrigal—imitative polyphony and homophony, with some word painting. (The first three lines are mostly imitative, the last one homophonic.) But Purcell's style clearly shows the inroads of functional harmony and of the definite, unified rhythms that had been developing in the seventeenth century. There is no mistaking this touching chorus for an actual Renaissance madrigal.

Like "Dido's Lament," "With drooping wings" is another emotional tableau, and this time the emotion spills over to the opera audience. As the courtiers grieve for Dido, we join them in responding to her tragedy.

 **LISTEN**

Purcell, *Dido and Aeneas*, Act III, final scene   1 | 18–19 | 18–19 | 3

Italics indicate repeated words and lines. Colored type indicates words treated with word painting.

			RECITATIVE
18	0:00	**Dido:**	Thy hand, Belinda! **Darkness** shades me;
			On thy bosom let me rest.
			More I would—but death invades me:
			Death is now a welcome guest.
			ARIA
	0:58	**Dido:**	When I *am laid* in earth
			May my wrongs create
			No trouble in thy breast;
			(repeated)
	2:17		*Remember me, but ah, forget my fate;*
			Remember me, but ah, forget my fate. (stabs herself)
			CHORUS
19	4:01	**Courtiers:**	*With **drooping** wings, ye cupids come*
			And scatter roses on her tomb.
			***Soft, soft** and gentle as her heart.*
1:30	5:31		Keep *here* your watch;
			Keep here your watch, and never part.

4 | The Rise of Instrumental Music

The development of instrumental music—music without words, music that does not depend on words—counts as one of the most far-reaching contributions of composers in the early Baroque period. Broadly speaking, we can trace their instrumental music to three main sources.

- *Dance,* the first of these sources (and one we have already discussed), reaches all the way back to the Middle Ages (see page 74). In the Baroque period dance received a special impetus from opera, the genre that most fascinated people at the time. Opera was firmly linked to ballet, with frequent and sometimes elaborate dance episodes. We have seen a modest example of this in the final chorus of *Dido and Aeneas.* Musicians, especially in France, the center of ballet at the time, would put together sets of dances selected from operas or ballets. These dance **suites,** as they were called—groups of dances—could then be played by an orchestra and enjoyed apart from an actual stage performance.

  Composers also wrote many dances and suites for harpsichord. These are *stylized* dances, pieces written in the style or the form of dance music but intended for listening rather than dancing, for mental rather than physical pleasure.

- *Virtuosity* was the second source from which composers of instrumental music drew. As long as instruments have existed there have surely been virtuoso players ready to show them off—and audiences ready to applaud the show. But the art of early virtuosos was improvised and scarcely ever written down; only in the sixteenth and seventeenth centuries was some of their art incorporated systematically into written-out compositions. Even then, not all the virtuosity on which the compositions depended for their effect was notated. Much was left to be improvised, and so modern performers often have to learn how to play a good deal more than what appears in the old scores.

- *Vocal music* was the third source for instrumental music. More specifically, the principal technique of vocal music, imitative polyphony (imitation), was transferred to the instrumental medium. In fact, this had happened already toward the end of the Renaissance, when several instrumental genres were modeled on vocal music in this way. Each genre consists of a series of points of imitation (see pages 64 and 66) built on different motives, like a motet or a madrigal.

  From these genres emerged the characteristic polyphonic genre of the Baroque era, the **fugue** (fewg). A typical fugue uses only one theme throughout—like a single extended point of imitation—and often treats that theme with great contrapuntal ingenuity and learning. The art of improvising and writing fugues was practiced especially by keyboard players: organists and harpsichordists. We will discuss fugue more fully in Chapter 10.

  Vocal music influenced instrumental music in another way as well. It gave instrumentalists a fund of materials they could use as the basis for sets of **variations**—that is, sectional pieces in which each section repeats certain musical elements while others change around them.

Girolamo Frescobaldi (1583–1643)

The three main sources of instrumental music are all evident in the keyboard works of Girolamo Frescobaldi. Frescobaldi was the foremost organ virtuoso of the early seventeenth century, famed through much of Europe for his expressive and even extravagant improvising and composition. Organist of St. Peter's in Rome, he was an influential teacher, and his influence reached far beyond his own pupils. A century later Johann Sebastian Bach—keyboard virtuoso in his own right and composer of an immense body of organ and harpsichord works—carefully studied Frescobaldi's music.

Girolamo Frescobaldi. *Scala/Art Resource, NY.*

We will hear Frescobaldi's music on a modern organ specially modeled on an instrument of his own time. The player employs different *registrations*, that is, different combinations of the organ's many sets of pipes (see page 20).

Frescobaldi composed organ works in several distinct genres:

- **Toccatas**, free-formed pieces meant to capture the spirit of Frescobaldi's own improvisation. (*Toccata* means "touched" in Italian, as in the touching of keys.)

- **Canzonas**, more rigorously organized works emphasizing imitative texture—the ancestors of later fugues.

- Stylized dances, formed of two phrases each, one or both of them repeated to yield the pattern **a a b** or **a a b b** (for similar Renaissance patterns, see page 74); these dances are sometimes grouped together in small suites.

- Sets of variations on melodic or harmonic patterns borrowed from contemporary vocal music.

Girolamo Frescobaldi, Canzona, Balletto, and Corrente (1627–1637)

1 | 20–22   20–22

From Frescobaldi's organ works we sample two genres: an imitative canzona, ancestor of the later fugues, and a pair of dances.

20 ***Canzona*** This piece opens with a point of imitation (see page 66) using a theme that begins with long leaps followed by running sixteenth notes:

After four entries of this theme the music comes to a cadence. Then a new theme enters at the top of the texture, this one marked by three repeated notes at its start (see the example in the margin). Frescobaldi immediately combines the second theme in counterpoint with the first, pitting the two against each other until he brings the music to a solid cadence.

21 22 ***Balletto and Corrente*** Each of these dance movements consists of two phrases, both of which are repeated: **a a b b**. Careful listening reveals that the two dances are related, especially by their bass lines:

While sharing a bass line, however, the dances also contrast strongly in their meters—the first duple, the second triple. Such metrical contrast from one dance to the next was a basic principle of suites from the late Renaissance on. (Compare the pavan and galliard—see page 74.)

The instrumental music of the early seventeenth century was the precursor to an explosion of new instrumental styles and genres in the late Baroque era. We go on to discuss this in Unit III, after an introductory Prelude chapter dealing with the history and culture of the time.

GOALS FOR REVIEW

▶ to hear an example of the Baroque mixing of expressive extravagance with formal control

▶ to understand the new techniques of *basso continuo* and *basso ostinato* (or ground bass)

▶ to listen for the dichotomy of recitative and aria in an early opera by Claudio Monteverdi

▶ to appreciate the expressive power of an ostinato lament by Henry Purcell

▶ to witness the continued growth of instrumental music

 macmillanhighered.com/listen8e
Listening Quizzes for Chapter 8 and Global Perspectives: African Ostinato Forms
Reading Quizzes for Chapter 8 and Global Perspectives: African Ostinato Forms

African Ostinato Forms

Though we borrow the term *ostinato* from Italian Baroque music, the technique is much older than the seventeenth century and is dispersed around the globe. The organizational principle at stake is, indeed, basic: Set up a brief repeating musical unit and use it as the foundation for other, more varied melodies and harmonies.

Musical forms built according to this principle come in a wide variety of shapes and patterns. We have already appreciated one variety in "Dido's Lament" by Purcell: a free-flowing melody over an unchanging bass line.

Nowhere in the world is ostinato form more prominent, or practiced with a richer array of techniques, genres, and instruments, than in Africa. Up and down the continent, ostinato forms multiply in fascinating variety: from North and West African nations, with ancient traditions of troubadour-like singers accompanying themselves on a single instrument, all the way to South Africa, with its electrified, rock and roll–derived Township Jive. (Rock itself is a great repository of ostinato forms.)

The two examples of African ostinato forms heard here come from Gambia, a small nation lying along the West African coast, and from the Mbuti pygmies of the rain forests of Congo in central Africa.

A Minstrel's Song

1 | 32   105

In the Gambian excerpt, a singer-reciter named Foday Musa Suso accompanies himself on a plucked stringed instrument called a *kora*. This is a complicated affair, a cross between a lute and a harp, with two sets of strings, twenty-one in all. The player, as our picture shows, holds it facing himself, plucking the strings with the thumbs and index fingers of both hands. Traditions of a singer accompanying himself on an instrument like the kora or harp or lyre are very ancient around the Mediterranean Sea, whether in Europe, the Middle East, or Africa—think of the biblical David with his harp or of Homer singing the *Iliad* and *Odyssey* to the lyre.

In West Africa, singers to the kora often belong to guilds, with musical expertise passed down in families from generation to generation. Foday Musa Suso comes from such a family and guild. For centuries these singers have fulfilled a wide variety of social roles, singing the praises of patrons and rulers, narrating in song historical or legendary events, contributing to weddings and other celebrations, and—especially in recent times—simply providing informal entertainment. Their styles have also fed into recent developments in African pop music. In fact, Foday Musa Suso himself emigrated from Gambia to Chicago in the 1970s, where he made a name for himself playing music that fuses jazz, pop, and traditional African styles.

Our recording is an early one, from before Foday's move, and offers a brief example of the kind of praise song a West African minstrel might sing for a wealthy patron. But our main point in introducing it is to sample an African ostinato form. After a short introductory flourish on the kora, Foday lays down an ostinato pattern, plucked mainly on the low-pitched strings with his thumbs. He overlays this here and there with quick, cascading melodies, played on the

Foday Musa Suso, with kora, crossing over to jazz performance. *Peter Gannushkin/DOWNTOWNMUSIC.net.*

higher strings with the index fingers. Enriching the texture further is his singing, a freely repeated melodic phrase that starts high and drifts languidly down (first heard at 0:22). In between these phrases, Foday seems to be absorbed in his kora playing, singing quietly along with the fast melodies he plucks above the ever-present ostinato (listen especially from 1:01). To bring the performance to a close, he reserves a special effect: two strings, dissonant with each other, plucked in syncopated rhythms high above the ostinato (starting at 2:11).

Pygmy Polyphony

Since it was first recorded in the 1950s, singing in Mbuti pygmy communities has become famous for its delicate and complex polyphony. Pygmy polyphony is created in improvised group singing, sometimes in rituals central to the society, sometimes to accompany work, sometimes for simple pleasure and relaxation.

Pygmy polyphony involves a technique common to many kinds of African music: *interlocking ostinatos*. In a pygmy chorus, various voices form an intricate, repetitive texture by singing over and over again their own short melodic motives—often only one or two notes—in quick alternation. The overall effect is of a multistranded, hypnotically recycling ostinato. This choral ostinato can be savored on its own or else, as in our example, used as the foundation for freer melodies of lead singers.

A Hunting Song for Chorus

1 | 33   106

Two exclamations for the whole chorus announce the beginning of a song describing the bravery and daring of an elephant hunt. At first, we hear no clear ostinato. Instead, two lead singers alternate prominent melodic phrases while, underneath them, the chorus softly sings—almost murmuring—an indistinct, ostinato-like melody.

Then something marvelous happens. At about 0:44 the individual melodic motives of a polyphonic ostinato begin to crystallize in the chorus. We hear the polyphony taking shape. (How many distinct components of the ostinato can you make out?) By 1:30 the choral ostinato is fully formed and clearly articulated; it continues through to the end of the song (not heard here) underneath the soloists.

The singing is underlaid throughout by the simplest of instrumental accompaniments: two sticks struck together to mark the beat. The Mbuti rarely employ more elaborate instruments in their choral singing, though in other contexts they regularly play on drums, flutes, musical bows, and other instruments.

This song was recorded in the mid-1950s by Colin Turnbull, a British anthropologist who was among the first to study the pygmies. He described their society poetically and lovingly in a book still read today, *The Forest People,* but he didn't give the names of the singers of this song.

Mbuti villagers, singing and dancing to tall drums. *Giacomo Pirozzi/Panos Pictures.*

The Eighteenth Century

UNIT III

The century of Bach and Handel and Mozart and Haydn spans two very different styles, those of the late Baroque era and of Viennese Classicism. In the following pages we will define these styles and identify their differences.

You may ask why in spite of these differences we treat the eighteenth century as a unit. The reason is that the eighteenth century as a whole contrasts in one basic criterion from the nineteenth century, covered in Unit IV. This criterion is not musical style, at least not directly, but rather the quality of musical expression. There is a certain objectivity in the feelings that eighteenth-century music seems to express or depict. It keeps some distance from the listener, even when it is powerful and moving. Music of the nineteenth century comes on as more demonstrative, more personal, more obviously intense; it is not accidental that this music is called "Romantic."

This broad distinction in expressive quality sprang in part from the differing social and economic conditions under which composers worked. In our "Prelude" chapters, Chapters 9 and 12, we look at the cultural background and the social setting of eighteenth-century music and suggest how these factors influenced musical style and expression. The other chapters in this unit look into specific works by leading late Baroque and Classical composers.

The eighteenth century begins with the music of Bach, Handel, and Vivaldi and ends with that of Haydn and Mozart. The change involves many things, but it is in part one from music of intricate complexity to music of accessible, tuneful simplicity. In *The Music Lesson*, from late in the century, the French painter Jean-Honoré Fragonard captures a young amateur being trained in this new music. *Louvre, Paris, France/ Giraudon/The Bridgeman Art Library.*

Chronology

The Late Baroque Period

CHAPTER 9

Music from the period of around 1600 to 1750 is usually referred to as "Baroque," a term borrowed from art history. Art historians themselves borrowed the term from seventeenth-century jewelers, who applied it to large pearls of irregular shape. At one time, then, Baroque art was considered imperfect, bizarre, or at least erratic. With changing taste over the centuries, however, what was originally a negative implication has turned positive.

And over the last seventy-five years or so, with the help of recordings, Baroque music has grown more and more popular. Instruments of the period have been revived to play it, among them the harpsichord, the recorder, and a special high-pitched trumpet without valves. (Some of these instruments were discussed on pages 13–21.) Most of the Baroque music heard today dates from the eighteenth century—from about 1700 to 1750, a subperiod sometimes classified as "late Baroque." Johann Sebastian Bach and George Frideric Handel were the greatest composers of this period, and among their most important contemporaries were Alessandro Scarlatti and Antonio Vivaldi in Italy, François Couperin and Jean-Philippe Rameau in France, Domenico Scarlatti (the son of Alessandro) in Spain, and Georg Philipp Telemann in Germany.

1 | Absolutism and the Age of Science

Baroque is a period term used by art historians and musicologists. Historians are more likely to speak of the period from 1600 to 1750 as the Age of Absolutism. This was the time of belief in the divine right of kings, the idea that the right of kings to rule was absolute—total, unlimited—because they were chosen by God. Louis XIV of France became the most powerful monarch in all of European history, and also one of the most ruthless. Absolutism is still with us, in the form of (usually godless) dictatorships.

Students of the history of ideas, on the other hand, speak of this as the Age of Science. In this era, the telescope and the microscope revealed their first secrets; Newton and Leibniz invented calculus; Newton developed his laws of mechanics and the theory of gravity. These discoveries affected both technology and philosophy—not only the formal philosophy of the great empiricist thinkers Descartes, Locke, and Hume, but also philosophy in a more informal sense. People began to think about ordinary matters in a new way, influenced by the newly acquired habits of scientific experimentation and proof. The mental climate stimulated by science significantly affected the music and the art we call Baroque.

Louis XIV's palace of Versailles, with a procession of carriages arriving in the great courtyard. Note the formal gardens and canal. *Pierre Patel,* Carriages Arriving at Versailles, *1688. Photo: Bridgeman-Giraudon/Art Resource, NY.*

Absolutism and science were two of the most vital currents that defined life in the seventeenth and early eighteenth centuries. The result was an interesting dualism that can be traced throughout Baroque art: pomp and extravagance on the one hand, system and calculation on the other. The same dualism can be traced in Baroque music.

Art and Absolutism

As far back as ancient times, rulers in Europe sponsored the arts. Before the Baroque era, the artistic glories of the Renaissance were supported by powerful merchant-princes, such as the Medici family in Florence, who were determined to add luster to the city-states they ruled. But sponsorship of the arts rose to new heights in the seventeenth century, and one state loomed larger than any other in the scope and grandeur of its projects: France under Louis XIV (1638–1715), "the Sun King."

All of French life orbited around the royal court, like planets, comets, and asteroids in the solar system. Pomp and ceremony were carried to extreme lengths: The king's *levée*—his getting-up-in-the-morning rite—involved dozens of functionaries and routines lasting two hours. Artists of all kinds were supported lavishly, so long as their work symbolized the majesty of the state (and the state, in Louis's famous remark, "is me"—*"L'état, c'est moi"*).

The influence of this monarch and his image extended far beyond France, for other European princes and dukes envied his absolute rule and did everything they could to match it. Especially in Germany—which was not a united country, like France, but a patchwork of several hundred political units—rulers competed with one another in supporting artists who built, painted, and sang to their glory. Artistic life in Europe was kept alive for many generations by this sort of patronage. The brilliance and grandeur of much Baroque art derives from its political function.

Art was to impress, even to stupefy. Thus Louis XIV built the most enormous palace in history, Versailles, with over three hundred rooms, including the eighty-yard-long Hall of Mirrors, and formal gardens extending for miles around. Many nobles and high-ranking churchmen built little imitation-Versailles palaces, among them the archbishop of Würzburg in Germany, whose magnificent residence was built in Bach's lifetime. The rooms were decorated by the Venetian artist Giovanni Battista Tiepolo, a master of Baroque ceiling painting.

Look at the ceiling shown on page 101, and try to imagine its true dimensions. You may well be dazzled by the figures in excited motion, caught up in great gusts of wind that whirl them out of the architectural space. Ceiling painting provides a vivid example of the extravagant side of Baroque dualism.

Art in the service of royalty: a *very* idealized portrait of Louis XIV by the greatest sculptor of the day, Gianlorenzo Bernini (1598–1680). *Scala/Art Resource, NY.*

Design for an opera stage set by G. G. Bibiena. Such fantastic architecture did not exist in the real world, even at the palace of a king (see page 99). *G. G. Bibiena, stage set for Metastasio's* Didone Abbandonata. *Photo: Blauel/Gnamm/Artothek.*

The Music of Absolutism

Just as painting and architecture could glorify rulers through color and designs in space, music could glorify through sound. The nobility maintained horn players for their hunts, trumpeters for their battles, and orchestras for balls and entertainments. Smaller groups of musicians would play *Tafelmusik* ("table music"), background music during lengthy banquets. A special "festive" or "celebratory" orchestra featuring military instruments—trumpets and drums—was used to pay homage to kings and princes; by extension, it also glorified God, the "King of Kings," as he is called in Handel's Hallelujah Chorus. The words sung by the chorus in this famous work praise God, but the accompanying orchestra with its trumpets also pays splendid homage to King George II of England (see pages 143–44).

But the main musical vehicle of Baroque absolutism was opera. Opera today is a very expensive entertainment in which a drama is presented with music and stage spectacle. So it was in the Baroque era. The stage set shown

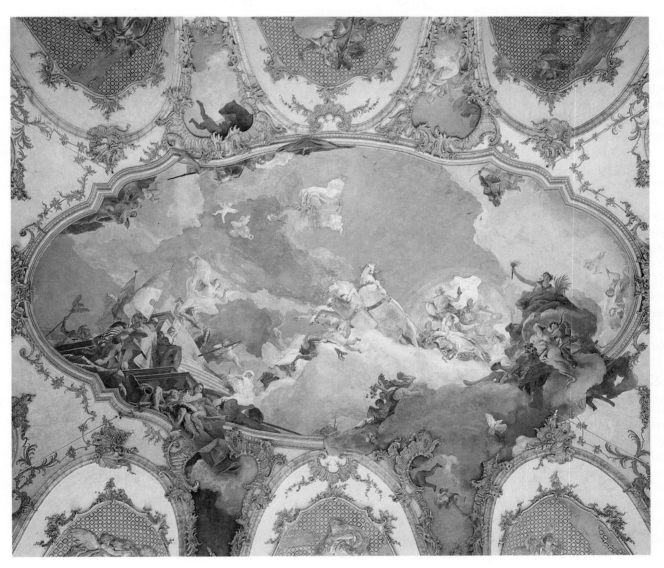

Baroque grandeur: a ceiling painting by Giovanni Battista Tiepolo (1696–1770). The oval measures 30 feet by 60 feet. *Giovanni Battista Tiepolo, painted ceiling, Residenz, Würzburg. Photo: Scala/ Art Resource, NY.*

on page 100 was created by a member of the Bibiena family, the foremost set designers of the time. It conveys the majestic heights and distances of an ideal Baroque palace by means of perspective, though the stage was actually quite shallow. The figures gesture grandly, but they are dwarfed by pasteboard architecture that seems to whirl as dizzily as does the painted architecture on Tiepolo's ceiling (see page 101).

One aspect of Baroque opera is unlike opera today: The stories were indirect tributes to the glory and supposed virtue of those who paid for them. For example, one favorite Baroque opera story tells of the Roman emperor Titus, who survives a complicated plot on his life and then magnanimously forgives the plotters. Strange as it may seem today, this story was set to music by dozens of court composers. It told courtiers that if they opposed their king, he might well excuse them out of the godlike goodness of his heart (for he claimed to rule by divine right). But it also reminded them that he was an absolute ruler—a modern Roman tyrant—who could do exactly the reverse if he pleased. Operas flattered princes while at the same time stressing their power and wealth.

Art and Theatricality

Opera was invented in Italy around the year 1600. Indeed, opera counts as Italy's great contribution to the seventeenth century's golden age of the theater. This century saw Shakespeare and his followers in England, Corneille and Racine in France, and Lope de Vega and Calderón in Spain.

The theater is first and foremost a place where strong emotion is on display, and it was this more than anything else that fueled the Baroque fascination with it. The emotionality that we generally sense in Baroque art has a theatrical quality; this is true even of much Baroque painting. Compare Raphael's calm Renaissance Madonna on page 36 with the early Baroque Madonna by Guercino (right). Jesus seems to be falling out of the picture as he twists away from his mother, and she twists the other way; the background is not a serene landscape but a turbulent cloudscape, and the stagey lighting contrasts bright patches of flesh with dark shadows.

Science and the Arts

All this may seem some distance away from the observatories of Galileo and Kepler and the laboratories where William Harvey discovered the circulation of the blood and Antoni van Leeuwenhoek first viewed microorganisms through a microscope. And indeed, the scientific spirit of the time had its most obvious effect on artists who were outside the realm of absolutism. The Dutch were citizens of free cities, not subjects of despotic kings. In Jan Vermeer's painting of his own city, Delft, the incredibly precise depiction of detail reflects the new interest in scientific observation. The painter's analysis of light is worthy of Huygens and Newton, fathers of the science of optics. There is something scientific, too, in the serene objectivity of this scene.

Madonna and Child with a Swallow, by G. F. Barbieri (1591–1666), known as Il Guercino (meaning "the squinter"; Guercino was cross-eyed). *Guercino (Giovanni Francesco Barbieri) (1591–1666), Madonna della Rondinella (oil on canvas)/Palazzo Pitti, Florence, Italy/The Bridgeman Art Library.*

View of Delft, by Jan Vermeer (1632–1675). *Scala/Art Resource, NY.*

Human control over nature is also symbolized by Baroque formal gardens. Today, landscape architecture is not usually regarded as one of the major arts, but it was very important in the age of the Baroque palace. Baroque gardens regulate nature strictly according to geometrical plans, as you can see in the painting of Versailles on page 99. Bushes are clipped, lawns tailored, and streams channeled, all under the watchful eye of big statues of Venus, Apollo, Hercules, and the rest, lined up in rows. Such gardens spell out the new vision of nature brought to heel by human reason and calculation.

Science and Music

Various aspects of Baroque music reflect the new scientific attitudes that developed in the seventeenth century. Scales were tuned, or *tempered*, more exactly than ever before, so that for the first time all the twenty-four major and minor keys were available to composers. Their interest in exploring this resource is

The Age of Absolutism and the Age of Science converge in this painting of Louis XIV founding the Academy of Sciences. *Bridgeman-Giraudon/Art Resource, NY.*

evident from collections such as Bach's *The Well-Tempered Clavier*, containing preludes and fugues in every key. Harmony was systematized so that chords followed one another in a way that seemed to have a new, logical direction guiding it.

Regularity became the ideal in rhythm, and in musical form—the distribution of sections of music in time—we find a tendency toward clearly ordered, even schematic plans. Whether consciously or not, composers seem to have viewed musical time in a quasi-scientific way. They divided it up and filled it systematically, almost in the spirit of the landscape architects who devised Baroque formal gardens.

In the important matter of musical expression, too, science was a powerful influence. Starting with the French philosopher-mathematician René Descartes, thinkers sought to apply the new rational methods to the analysis and classification of human emotions. It had always been felt that music had a special power to express and arouse emotions. Now it seemed that there was a basis for systematizing—and hence maximizing—this power.

Thus scientifically inclined music theorists made checklists of musical devices and techniques corresponding to each of the emotions. Grief, for example, could be projected by a specific kind of melodic motive and a specific kind of rhythm—even by a specific key. By working steadily with these devices and saturating their pieces with them, composers assumed they could achieve the maximum musical expressivity.

The emotions of Hope and Fear, as represented in a Baroque scientific treatise. Like composers of the time, the artist felt that feelings could be isolated and depicted in the abstract.

2 | Musical Life in the Early Eighteenth Century

The eighteenth century was a great age for the crafts—the age of Stradivarius in violin making, Chippendale in furniture, and America's own Paul Revere in silver, to name just a few. Composing music was also regarded as a craft. The Romantic idea of the composer—the lonely genius working over each masterpiece as a long labor of love expressing an individual personality—was still far in the future. Baroque composers were more likely to think of themselves as servants with masters to satisfy. They were artisans with jobs, rather than artists with a calling. They produced music on demand to fill a particular requirement.

This is why many Baroque pieces do not seem especially individualized in their expression. They are not so much unique masterpieces as satisfactory examples of their style and genre, of which there are many other equally satisfactory examples.

There were three main institutions where composers could make a living by practicing their craft. In order of increasing glamour, these were the church, the court, and the opera house.

• *The church*. In the cathedrals, monasteries, and town churches of the Baroque era, it was taken for granted that the organists or choirmasters would compose their own music, then play and conduct it. Organists had to improvise or write out music to accompany certain parts of the church services. They played long pieces to see the congregation out when the service was over.

At large institutions, important occasions called for elaborate music scored for chorus, soloists, and instruments: a Catholic Mass for the installation of an archbishop, for example, or a Lutheran church cantata for the anniversary of the Reformation. Church musicians were also responsible for training the boys who sang in their choirs, often in special choir schools.

• *The court*. Under the patronage of kings or members of the nobility, a musician was employed on the same terms as a court painter, a master of the hunt, or a head chef. Musicians had to work entirely at the whim of their masters; still, they could count on a fairly secure existence, a steady demand for their services, and a pension.

Naturally, conditions varied from court to court, depending on the ruler's taste. For some, music was a good deal less interesting than hunting or banqueting. Others could not have enough of it. Frederick the Great of Prussia was an enthusiastic flutist, so at his court concertos and sonatas for flute were composed at an especially healthy rate. He wrote many himself.

Court musicians kept in better touch with musical developments than church musicians, since they were required to travel with their employers. They made extended trips to major cities, where diplomacy was eased along by music composed for the occasion.

• *The opera house*. Although many opera houses were attached to courts, others were maintained by entrepreneurs in major cities. (The public opera house existed before the public concert hall; in the Baroque era, public concerts were not a regular feature of musical life.) Composers traditionally conducted their own operas, sitting at the harpsichord. Audiences were alert to the most exciting new singers, and it was part of the composer's job to keep the singers well supplied with music that showed off their talents. Opera revivals always required recomposition—often by a new composer—in order to satisfy new singers. It was an exciting, unpredictable life, promising great rewards as well as daunting reverses.

A Baroque opera performance (Turin, 1740). The stage set represents a larger-than-life palace hall; the characters are striking various extravagant attitudes. Note the orchestra, a boy selling oranges, and a security guard. *Oliviero,* Performance at Teatro Reggio, *Turin.* Photo: Scala/Art Resource, NY.

The life stories of the two greatest composers of the late Baroque period show a good deal about the interaction between musicians, the patrons who supported them, and the institutions that required music. Johann Sebastian Bach labored as a church organist, a court musician, and then a major composer-administrator for the Lutheran Church. George Frideric Handel, who also had a court position, became an independent opera composer and opera promoter. Their biographies are given on pages 127 and 141.

3 | Style Features of Late Baroque Music

If any one characteristic can be singled out as central to the music of the late Baroque period, it would be its thorough, methodical quality. Much of a Baroque composition (or at least a segment of that composition) consists of inspired repetition and variation. It is as though the composers had intended to draw their material out to the maximum extent and wring it dry, as it were.

Indeed, the shorter pieces we will be examining in Chapters 10 and 11—pieces like the prelude and fugue from Bach's *The Well-Tempered Clavier* and the aria from Handel's opera *Julius Caesar*—contain little if any notable contrast in rhythm, dynamics, melody, texture, or tone color (see pages 129 and 138). Baroque composers preferred thoroughness and homogeneity.

With longer pieces, Baroque composers tended to break them up into blocks of music that contrast with one another in obvious ways, but are still homogeneous in themselves. This is the case with Bach's *Brandenburg* Concerto No. 5, for example, where the orchestral and solo sections contrast clearly enough. Within each orchestral or solo section, however, things are usually quite regular (see page 123).

Rhythm

Baroque music is brimming with energy, and this energy is channeled into a highly regular, determined sort of motion. Like today's popular music, Baroque music gets its rhythmic vitality by playing off distinctive rhythms against a very steady beat. The meter nearly always stands out, emphasized by certain instruments in the ensemble. Most characteristic of these "marking-time" instruments is the busy, crisp harpsichord.

Attentive listening will also reveal another aspect of regularity in the steady *harmonic rhythm*—that is, a Baroque piece tends to change chords at every measure or at some other set interval. (Do not expect to hear this happening all the time, but it happens often enough so that we can speak of a tendency.)

Dynamics

Another steady feature of Baroque music is dynamics. Composers infrequently used loud and soft indications (*f* and *p*) in their scores, and once a dynamic was chosen or set, it remained at about the same level for the whole section—sometimes even for the whole composition.

Neither in the Baroque period nor in any other, however, have performers played or sung music at an absolutely even level of dynamics. Instrumentalists made expressive changes in dynamics to bring out rhythmic accents, and singers certainly sang high notes louder than low ones. But composers did not go much beyond natural variations of these kinds.

Gradual buildups from soft to loud, and the like, were rarely used. Abrupt dynamic contrasts were preferred—again, between fairly large sections of a longer piece, or whole movements. A clear *forte/piano* contrast is built into the concerto genre, with its alternating blocks of music for the full orchestra and for one or more quieter solo instruments. When, exceptionally, a Baroque composer changed dynamics in the middle of a section or a phrase of music, he could count on the great surprise—even the amazement—of his listeners. A famous sudden *forte* in Handel's Hallelujah Chorus has been known to electrify the audience, to bring them to their feet (see page 144).

We spoke earlier of a characteristic dualism between extravagance and order in Baroque culture (see page 99). The methodical, regular quality of Baroque musical style that we are tracing here reflects the orderly, quasi-scientific side of this dualism. But Baroque music can also be highly dramatic, bizarre, or stupendous—a reflection of the other side of the dualism. Indeed, the magnificent momentary effects that occur occasionally in Handel and Bach are all the stronger because of the regular music around them.

Tone Color

Tone color in Baroque music presents something of a contradiction. On the one hand, the early part of the period evinced a new interest in sonority, and the end of it echoed with some very sophisticated sounds: Handel's imaginative orchestration in his operas, Bach's sensitive writing for the flute, and the refined harpsichord textures developed by several generations of composers in France. There are distinctive and attractive Baroque sounds that we do not hear in other periods: the harpsichord, the bright Baroque organ, the virtuoso recorder, and what we will call the festive Baroque orchestra, featuring high trumpets and drums.

On the other hand, a significant amount of music was written to allow for multiple or alternative performing forces. Thus it was a regular practice to designate music for harpsichord *or* organ, for violin *or* oboe *or* flute. Bach wrote a sonata for two flutes and rewrote it as a sonata for viola da gamba (a cello-like instrument) and harpsichord. Handel took solo arias and duets and rewrote them as choruses for his oratorio *Messiah*. In the last analysis, then, it seems the original tone color was often not critical in Baroque music.

The Baroque Orchestra

The core of the Baroque orchestra was a group of instruments of the violin family. The famous orchestra maintained by Louis XIV of France was called "The Twenty-Four Violins of the King"—meaning twenty-four instruments of the violin family: six violins, twelve violas, and six cellos. A great deal of Baroque music was written for such an orchestra or a similar one that today would be called a "string orchestra": violins, violas, cellos, and one or two basses.

To this was added a keyboard instrument as continuo (see page 110)—usually a harpsichord in secular music and an organ in church music.

Woodwinds and brass instruments were sometimes added to the string orchestra, too, but there was no fixed complement, as was to be the case later. For special occasions of a festive nature—music celebrating a military victory, for example, or Christmas music ordered for the town cathedral—composers augmented the basic Baroque orchestra with trumpets or French horns, timpani, bassoons, and oboes and/or flutes. This festive orchestra has a particularly grand, open, and brilliant sound.

Melody

Baroque melody tends toward complexity. Composers liked to push melodies to the very limits of ornateness and luxuriance. Baroque melodies may extend over two whole octaves; they twist and turn in an intricate way as they reach high

THE BAROQUE ORCHESTRA as in Vivaldi's Concerto in G (page 117)	
STRINGS	**KEYBOARD**
Violins (divided into two groups, called violins 1 and violins 2) Violas Cellos Bass (playing the same music as the cellos an octave lower)	Harpsichord or organ

THE FESTIVE BAROQUE ORCHESTRA as in Handel's Minuet from the *Royal Fireworks Music* (page 133)				
STRINGS	**WOODWINDS**	**BRASS**	**PERCUSSION**	**KEYBOARD**
Violins 1 Violins 2 Violas Cellos Bass	2 Oboes 1 Bassoon	3 Trumpets	2 Timpani (kettledrums)	Harpsichord or organ

and low. It can be maintained that in the European classical tradition, the art of melody reached a high point in the late Baroque era, a point that has never been equaled since.

These long melodies, with their wealth of decorations added to the main direction of the line, are not easy to sing. Shown below is the first-movement theme of Bach's *Brandenburg* Concerto No. 5. Almost anyone can learn to sing the first two bars, but if you can sing the rest you have a very good ear:

One easily recognized feature of Baroque melodies is their frequent use of sequence (see page 26). A (slightly free) sequence is shaded near the end of the melody above. Near the beginning (also shaded) the melody catches hold of a simple gesture—just two different pitches—and repeats it again and again at many pitch levels. Sequences provide Baroque music with one of its most effective means of forward motion.

Ornamentation

Not all melodies of the time are as complicated as the one shown above, however, and some, such as the simpler Baroque dances, are exceptions to the rule. On the other hand, the most highly prized skill of the elite musicians of the era, opera singers, was improvising melodic extras in the arias they sang night after night in the theater. This practice is called **ornamentation.**

Before the present era of sound amplification, when volume does much of the work, audiences thrilled to brilliant, fast, very high (or very low) music played and especially improvised by singers and instrumentalists. This is still very much the case with jazz—and when was the last event you went to or watched on TV where "The Star-Spangled Banner" was sung absolutely straight, without ornamentation?

In the Baroque era, enough improvisations were written down, as guides for lesser musicians, to give us some idea of the art of the greatest virtuosos—such as the singers Bordoni and Cuzzoni (see page 146) and the violinist-composer Vivaldi (see page 119). They would spontaneously add all kinds of ornaments (jazz

Soul legend Aretha Franklin singing "My Country, 'Tis of Thee" at President Obama's first inauguration — with added ornamentation. *AP Photo/Ron Edmonds.*

players would call them "riffs" or "licks") to whatever scores composers placed before them. Artists today have re-created Baroque ornamentation, or something like it; for a splendid example, listen to Handel's aria "La giustizia" on page 138.

Texture

The standard texture of Baroque music is polyphonic (or contrapuntal). Even many Baroque pieces that consist of just melody and bass count as contrapuntal because of the independent melodic quality of the bass. And large-scale pieces spin a web of contrapuntal lines filling every nook and cranny of musical space-time. While cellos, basses, bassoons, and organ pedals play the lowest line, the other stringed instruments stake out their places in the middle, with oboes and flutes above them and the trumpets piercing their way up into the very highest reaches of the sound universe. The density achieved in this way is doubly impressive because the sounds feel alive—alive because they are all in motion, because they are all parts of moving contrapuntal lines.

Again, some exceptions should be noted to the standard polyphonic texture of Baroque music. Such are the homophonic orchestra sections (the *ritornellos*) in the concerto, Bach's Prelude in C Major from *The Well-Tempered Clavier* (see page 129), and his highly expressive harmonizations of old German hymns, as in his Cantata No. 4 (see page 147). But it is no accident that these textures appear *within pieces that feature polyphony elsewhere*. The ritornello in Bach's *Brandenburg* Concerto No. 5 alternates with polyphony played by the solo flute, violin, and harpsichord (see page 123). The harmonized hymn in his Cantata No. 4 comes at the very end, where it has the effect of calming or settling the complex polyphony of all the preceding music. And the Prelude is paired with a fugue, the high point of imitative polyphonic art in the Baroque era.

The Continuo

Yet all this polyphony is supported by a solid scaffold of harmony. The central importance of harmony in Baroque music appears in the universal practice of the *basso continuo,* or just **continuo**.

The continuo is a bass part (the lowest part in polyphonic music) that is always linked to a series of chords. These chords are played by a harpsichord, organ, or lute as support or accompaniment for the important melodies in the other instruments. Indeed, we might say "mere accompaniment," for composers did not bother to write the chords out in detail, but only notated them in an abstract way by a numerical shorthand below the bass part. (Another name for continuo, **figured bass**, derives from this numerical shorthand.)

This left continuo players with a good deal to do, even though their role was considered subsidiary. By reading the basso continuo part, the harpsichordist or organist would play along with the cellos or bassoons—this with the left hand, which doubles the bass line. But the right-hand chords could be played in many ways: high or low, widely or closely spaced, smoothly connected or not. A certain amount of quick, on-the-spot improvisation was (and still is) required to "realize" a continuo—that is, to derive actual chords from abstract numbers.

Continuo part, as written: cello and harpsichord, left hand

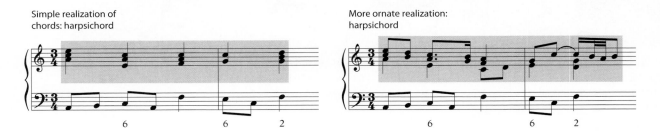

Simple realization of chords: harpsichord

More ornate realization: harpsichord

Continuo chords provide the basic harmonic framework against which the contrapuntal lines of Baroque music trace their airy patterns. This Baroque texture may be described as *polarized*—a polarity of voices between a strong bass and a clear, high (soprano) range, the domain of the melody. Less clearly defined is a middle space containing the improvised chords. In Baroque works on the largest scale, this space is also filled in by polyphonic lines drawn from the median range of the orchestra and chorus, such as violas, tenors, and altos. In more modest works a characteristic texture is a hollow one: one or two high instruments (violins, flutes) or voices, a bass instrument, and subsidiary chord improvisation in the middle.

Baroque music is usually easily identified by the presence of the continuo—by the continuous but discreet sound of the harpsichord or organ playing continuo chords in the background. Indeed, the Baroque era in music was once called the basso continuo era, not a bad name for it.

Musical Form

Musical forms are clearer and more regular in the Baroque period than in most other historical periods. Two factors that appear to have contributed to this, one of them social, the other intellectual, were mentioned earlier.

The social factor is the patronage system, whereby the court and the church demanded a large amount of music and expected it to be produced in a hurry, almost as soon as it was ordered. Therefore composers needed to rely on formulas that could be applied quickly and efficiently. What is amazing about the church cantatas that Bach wrote every week (at one point in his career) is how imaginatively he varied the standard forms for the various components of a cantata. But it was very helpful—in fact, it was absolutely necessary—for him to have those standard forms in place as a point of departure.

In this typical ensemble for Baroque chamber music, two violins play melodies in the upper register, the cello plays the bass line, and the harpsichord and lute fill in chords in between. Cello, harpsichord, and lute together make up the basso continuo. *Clive Barda/ArenaPal/Topham/ The Image Works.*

The other factor is the scientific spirit of the age, which affected composers only indirectly, but affected them nonetheless. One can detect the composer's ambition to map the whole range of a piece of music and to fill it in systematically in an orderly, logical, quasi-scientific way. This ambition seems to have been based on the conviction that musical time could be encompassed and controlled at will, an attitude similar to that of scientists, philosophers, and craftsmen of the age.

The music of Bach, in particular, shows this tendency on various levels. Look, for example, at the symmetrical arrangement of the seven sections of his Cantata No. 4, diagrammed on page 148. The last fugue in his *Art of Fugue*, a composite work containing twenty items, is a more famous example. An ordinary fugue, as we shall see, is a polyphonic composition that deals exclusively with a single theme. This fugue deals with *four* themes, one after another, in four sections; then in the last section all four themes combine in four-part counterpoint. Theme No. 4 spells "Bach" in a musical code! Even Bach's shortest compositions can have schematic features, as we will see on page 129.

4 | The Emotional World of Baroque Music

All music, it seems safe to say, is deeply involved with emotion. But in the music of different cultures, and also in the music of different historical eras within a single culture, the nature of that involvement can be very different. The emotional effect of Baroque music strikes the modern listener as very powerful and yet, in a curious way, also impersonal. Baroque composers believed firmly that music could and should mirror a wide range of human feelings, or *affects*, such as had been analyzed and classified by the scientifically oriented psychology of the day. But these composers did not believe that it was their task to mirror feelings of their own. Rather, they tried to isolate and analyze emotions in general—at a distance—and then depict them consistently.

The exhaustiveness of their musical technique made for a similar exhaustiveness of emotional effect. A single movement or aria was usually restricted to depicting one specific emotion, feeling, or mood. As the rhythms and themes are repeated, the music intensifies a single strong feeling. Sadness in Baroque music is presented as the deepest gloom, calmness as profound quiet, brightness as pomp and splendor, happiness as loud rejoicing. These are extreme sentiments; the people who can be imagined to experience them would have to be almost larger than life.

All this fits into place with the Baroque fascination with the theater. The Baroque theater concentrated on grand gestures and high passion, on ideal emotions expressed by ideal human beings. Kings and queens were shown performing noble actions or vile ones, experiencing intense feelings of passion or fury, delivering thunderous speeches, and taking part in lavish stage displays. How these personages looked and postured can be seen in the picture on page 106.

Theatrical emotion has the virtues of intensity, clarity, and focus; it must, if it is to get past the footlights and reach its audience. Actors analyze the emotion they are asked to depict, shape it and probably exaggerate it, and then project it by means of their acting technique. It is not their personal emotion, though for the moment they *make* it their own. We may come to feel that Baroque composers worked in a similar way, not only in their operas—actual stage works set to music—but also in their oratorios and church cantatas, and even in their instrumental concertos and sonatas.

GOALS FOR REVIEW

► to gain an overview of European culture in the early eighteenth century

► to differentiate the musical worlds of church, court, and theater

► to understand the general stylistic features of late Baroque music, especially in rhythm, melody, texture, and form

► to explore late Baroque attitudes toward the expressive powers of music

 macmillanhighered.com/listen8e
Reading Quiz for Chapter 9

Baroque
Instrumental Music

CHAPTER 10

In the early music of Europe, music with words was the norm; strictly instrumental music was less common and less important. In the Middle Ages, words for the church services were sung by monks and nuns as Gregorian chant, and later some of these same words were set to new polyphonic music for cathedral choirs and royal chapels. Troubadours set their love poems as solo songs. Later, in the Renaissance, polyphonic church music proliferated and love poetry was set to music as madrigals, intricate part-music for a small group of solo singers. Vocal music remained very important in the Baroque era, when opera was invented.

But part of the importance of the Baroque era was that for the first time, listeners and musicians began to take instrumental music much more seriously. A momentous change was set in motion, one that came about gradually. It is revealing of the trend that the foremost composer at the very beginning of the Baroque period, Claudio Monteverdi (see pages 85–87), composed no strictly instrumental music, so far as we know. At the end of the period, instead, Bach, Handel, and Vivaldi alone left us many hundreds of instrumental compositions.

The reasons for the rise of instrumental music are not entirely clear. It can hardly be a coincidence, however, that it took place at the same time as improvements in the technology of instrument making. The name of Antonio Stradivarius (1644–1737) is known to many because of auctions where prices soar into the millions for one of his violins, unmatched after three hundred years. (They rarely come on the market. "Strad" cellos are even rarer.) Instruments by other master builders of the era, less well known, can still sound glorious: the organs of Gottfried Silbermann, the harpsichords of François Étienne Blanchet, the viols of Barak Norman.

In any case, the rise of instrumental music meant that there had to be a basic understanding between composers and audiences about instrumental forms and genres. To pose the most basic question: When the music starts, what should the listener expect, and how long should the composer keep going? With vocal music, the answer was (roughly speaking): until the words end. For instrumental music, there was no such answer. Conventional forms and genres, understood by both composers and listeners, had to supply it.

In this chapter we look at the most important instrumental forms and genres established in the Baroque era. Baroque vocal music will be treated in Chapter 11.

Violins are varnished and sun-dried in Cremona, a little town in northern Italy famous for its violin makers since the 1600s. Violinist-composers such as Vivaldi (see page 119) wrote for instruments by Antonio Stradivarius and other master craftsmen. *David Lees/Corbis.*

1 | Concerto and Concerto Grosso

The **concerto** and the **concerto grosso** (plural: *concerti grossi*) are the most important orchestral genres of the Baroque era. The basic idea underlying these genres is contrast between an orchestra and a soloist (in the concerto) or a small group of soloists (in the concerto grosso). Indeed, the word *concerto* comes from the Latin word *concertare,* to contend—an origin that accurately indicates a sort of contest between solo and orchestra. This contest pits the brilliance of the soloist or soloists against the relative power and stability of the orchestra. Contrast comes to these genres naturally.

Concertos and concerti grossi exemplify a large-scale approach to instrumental composition that was new in the Baroque era. Composers wanted large-scale forms because audiences, then as now, were more impressed by extended compositions than by short ones. They wanted them also because they could afford the opportunity to portray several different emotions or affects.

Movements

One way to extend a composition was, and is, to lay it out in several movements (or, to put it another way, join together several movements as a single composite work). A **movement** is a self-contained section of music that is part of a larger work; movements can be compared to chapters in a book. Movements in a multimovement work will always show some variety in tempo, meter, key, musical form, and mood.

The typical late Baroque concerto has three movements. The *first* movement is a bright, extroverted piece in a fast tempo. After this, the *second* movement strikes an obvious contrast: It is quieter, slower, and more emotional. The *third* movement is fast again—if anything, faster than the first.

In the first concerto we study, Vivaldi's Violin Concerto in G, the three movements exploit two conventional forms of the Baroque era. The first and last movements are in ritornello form, the second movement in ground-bass form. To understand these forms and their contrast, we examine the first two movements.

Ritornello Form

Many concerto movements are in *ritornello form*, from **ritornello**, the name for the orchestral music that typically starts the movement off. Contrast is basic to the concerto, and ritornello form focuses on contrast between two musical ideas, or groups of ideas—one belonging to the orchestra and the other to the soloist. The orchestral material (the ritornello) tends to be solid and forceful, the solo material faster and more brilliant.

Ritorno, the Italian word for "return," tells us that the function of the ritornello in ritornello form is to return many times as a stable element of the form. Usually it returns only in part, and usually it is played in different keys as the movement proceeds. As for the musical ideas for the solo, sometimes these are virtuoso passages, sometimes themes, sometimes larger sections including themes and other material. To end the movement, the orchestral ritornello returns in the tonic key and, often, at full length.

Ritornello form can be diagrammed as follows, where RIT stands for the entire ritornello; [RIT] for any part of the ritornello; and Solo 1, 2, 3, etc., for the solo sections:

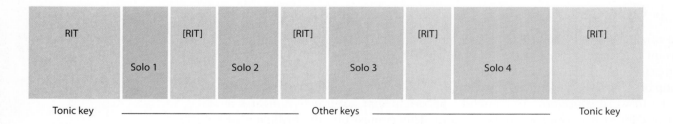

| RIT | Solo 1 | [RIT] | Solo 2 | [RIT] | Solo 3 | [RIT] | Solo 4 | [RIT] |

Tonic key ——————————— Other keys ——————————— Tonic key

We need not worry too much about the exact number of ritornello fragments, the keys, and other details shown in such form diagrams; these change from concerto to concerto. More important is the general impression that the form gives: the sense of a sturdy, reliable support in the orchestra for rapid and sometimes fantastic flights by the solo or solo group. Alongside the almost improvisational freedom of the solo instruments, the ritornello is always there, ready to bring them back down to earth and remind us of the original point of departure.

Antonio Vivaldi, Violin Concerto in G, *La stravaganza*, Op. 4, No. 12 (1712–1713)

1 | 23   23   4

The undisputed champion of the concerto was the Venetian composer Antonio Vivaldi. Vivaldi wrote hundreds of concertos. He published relatively few of them, in sets of six or twelve; each set was given an opus, or work, number (*opus* is Latin for "work"). To some opuses he gave titles that evoke the extravagant side of the Baroque dualism (see page 99), such as "Harmonic Whims" (*L'estro armonico*, Opus 3) and "Extravagance" (*La stravaganza*, Opus 4). This Concerto in G is the last and one of the best of his Opus 4.

It is a concerto for solo violin. In the age of Antonio Stradivarius, violin maker supreme, a great deal of music was composed at least partly to show off this favorite instrument. The violin's brilliance was especially prized, as was its ability to play expressively.

The violin soloist is pitted against the basic Baroque orchestra of strings and continuo (see page 108); on our recording the continuo chords are played by a large lute (an *archlute*). The orchestra is quite small.

Archlute. *Gianni Dagli Orti/Corbis.*

First Movement (Spiritoso e non presto) "Spirited, not too fast," writes Vivaldi at the start of this triple-meter movement. The first and second violins of the orchestra echo each other brightly. Read the following material about the first movement, and listen, following along with the Listening Chart—see page xxxiv if anything about the chart (or the icons) is not clear. Read again, listen again.

The opening ritornello—with its typical loud, extroverted sound, marked *f*—consists of three short parts. The first begins with a couple of loud chords to catch the audience's attention and set the tempo (**a**); then comes a central section with a distinct sequence (**b**), and then a cadential section where the dynamic changes to *p* for a moment (**c**):

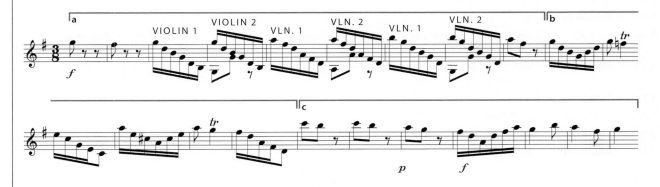

Once the ritornello ends with a very solid cadence (another typical feature of Baroque ritornellos), the solo violin enters, first with music moving at about the same speed as the ritornello, but soon speeding up. Virtuosity for the

Baroque violinist meant jumping from the high strings to the low, executing fast scales, in fact any and all kinds of fast playing.

Ritornello 2 is an exact repetition of **c** from the first ritornello. The second solo has several subsections, which makes it much longer than any of the others; in one section the continuo drops out entirely. Ritornello 3 begins with derivatives of **a** and **c** but then wanders off freely and ends in a minor key. This provides a springboard for some expressive playing in the next solo. Ritornello 4 is freer still; it takes just enough from the original ritornello (especially part **b**) so that it seems to fit in with it and, indeed, to grow out of it spontaneously.

Vivaldi seems to have wanted his first four ritornellos to feel freer and freer, before he finally pulls the piece back in line. After the last solo (following Ritornello 4) cuts in very energetically, he ends the movement with a literal statement of **b** and **c**. (Absent is **a**, perhaps because its attention-getting function is no longer needed.) Compare the particular form of this movement with the generalized formal scheme shown in the diagram on page 116.

RIT **a b c**		[RIT 2] **c**		[RIT 3] **(a c)**		[RIT 4] free		[RIT 5] **b c**
	Solo 1		Solo 2		Solo 3		Solo 4	

LISTENING CHART 2

Vivaldi, Violin Concerto in G, *La stravaganza*, first movement

Ritornello form. 2 min., 46 sec.

1 | 23   23   4

0:00	**Ritornello**	**a**	
0:11		**b**	
0:18		**c**	
0:26	**Solo 1**	Contrasting solo violin music	
0:41	**Ritornello 2**	**c**	
0:49	**Solo 2**	Virtuoso solo violin music; several different sections Continuo drops out for a short time.	
1:17	**Ritornello 3**	Part of this is derived from **a** and **c**; the rest is free. CADENCE in a minor key	
1:33	**Solo 3**	More expressive	
1:52	**Ritornello 4**	Even freer than Ritornello 3	
2:10	**Solo 4**	Very fast	
2:24	**Ritornello 5**	**b c**	

Baroque Variation Form: The Ground Bass

Variation forms are among the simplest and most characteristic of Baroque forms. Although they are not as common as other forms, they project the Baroque desire for systematic, thorough structures in a very direct way. This

The son of a Venetian violinist, Antonio Vivaldi was destined to follow in his father's footsteps. He entered the priesthood—where his bright red hair earned him the nickname "the Red Priest"—and in 1703 became a music teacher at the Seminario Musicale dell'Ospedale della Pietà, a Venetian orphanage for girls. The Ospedale was one of several such institutions in Venice that were famous for the attention they paid to the musical training of their students. A large proportion of Vivaldi's works were composed for the school, whose concerts were a great tourist attraction.

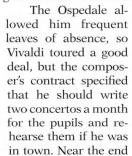

The Ospedale allowed him frequent leaves of absence, so Vivaldi toured a good deal, but the composer's contract specified that he should write two concertos a month for the pupils and rehearse them if he was in town. Near the end of his life, Vivaldi left Venice permanently to settle in Vienna.

Internationally renowned as a virtuoso violinist, Vivaldi is remembered today chiefly for his brilliant concertos. He wrote more than four hundred of these, including concertos for harp, mandolin, bassoon, and various instrumental combinations; we know of more than 250 solo violin concertos, including our Concerto in G from *La stravaganza* and *Spring* from *The Four Seasons*. Critics of the day complained that Vivaldi's music was thin and flashy and that the composer was always playing for cheap effects. But the young Bach, before writing his *Brandenburg* Concertos, carefully copied out pieces by Vivaldi as a way of learning how to write concertos himself.

Chief Works: Solo concertos for many different instruments, including the very famous *Four Seasons* ▪ Concerti grossi for various instruments ▪ twenty-one extant operas; oratorios; cantatas

Encore: After the Violin Concerto in G and *Spring*, listen to all of *The Four Seasons;* Concerto for Two Violins in A Minor, Op. 3, No. 8.

Image credit: Bettmann/CORBIS.

---

is because **variation form** entails the successive, uninterrupted repetition of one clearly defined melodic unit, with changes that rouse the listener's interest without ever losing touch with the original unit, or theme.

That theme may be a complete melody in the soprano range or a shorter melodic phrase in the bass. Given the emphasis in the Baroque era on the basso continuo (see page 82), it is not surprising that Baroque variations tend to occur above repeating bass patterns. A name for such patterns is **basso ostinato**, meaning "persistent" or "obstinate" bass. Sometimes the bass itself is slightly varied—though never in such a way as to hide its identity. Dynamics, tone color, and some harmonies are often changed in variations. Tempo, key, and mode are changed less often.

There are a number of names for compositions in variation form, which grew up independently all over Europe, first as improvisations—opportunities for impromptu display on various instruments—and then as written-out compositions. Besides the French *chaconne* and the Italian *passacaglia* (pah-sa-cáhl-ya), there was the English term *ground* (the repeating bass figure being called the **ground bass**). One seventeenth-century Italian composer, Girolamo Frescobaldi, left a passacaglia for organ with exactly a hundred variations. More compact examples of variation form sometimes appear as one movement in a larger Baroque genre, such as a concerto.*

---

* We examine an earlier example of variation (ground bass) form on page 88: "Dido's Lament" from *Dido and Aeneas* by Henry Purcell.

The term *ostinato* has come to be used more broadly than just for repeating Baroque bass lines. It can refer to any short musical unit repeated many times, in the bass or anywhere else, especially one used as a building block for a piece of music. Ostinatos are by no means unique to European music; in some form they are found in almost all musical traditions (see, for example, pages 94 and 201).

Antonio Vivaldi, Violin Concerto in G, *La stravaganza,* Op. 4, No. 12 (1712–1713)

1 | 24   24   5

Second Movement (Largo)   As is typical, Vivaldi's Violin Concerto in G has three contrasting movements—the first and third vigorous and brilliant, the second gentle and slow. This slow movement is in basso ostinato (ground bass) variation form.

Our first impression of this music is probably of its texture and timbre—the gentle throbbing, the ingenious weaving in and out of the orchestral violins and the solo violin, and the delicate, subsidiary continuo sounds. There is, however, not much melody to listen to in the violin's music. There is less, in fact, as the movement goes along and the texture changes.

Sooner or later we notice that the only real melody is in the bass, where a solemn, quiet theme (the ground bass) is heard repeatedly in the cellos and bass viol. The theme sinks down and down, ending with a strong cadence:

Theme, Variations 1–4, 7

Variations 5–6

etc.

We develop a sort of double listening for music like this, listening simultaneously to the unchanging theme and to the changing material presented above that theme. (This is a little like taking in a distant view while noticing someone in the foreground.) After the theme's initial statement, four more statements with violin variations follow, during which the solo violin plays faster and faster material above the unvaried ground bass. In its quiet way, this movement is showing off the violinist's ability to play music that is fast and sleek.

After Variation 4, however, there is a marked stop. Variation 5 makes a grand contrast of the kind relished by Baroque composers and audiences. The continuo stops, and since the texture is now thin and ethereal, the ground bass (played by the orchestra violins) can be heard more clearly—and what we hear is that the theme itself has been varied. It is now in the minor mode.

The mood becomes muted and melancholy; the violin is now showing off not its speed, but its expressive capabilities. The mood deepens in Variation 6. Rather abruptly, after this, the original theme returns in the full orchestra and continuo, played just as it was at the beginning, to end the movement.

The construction of this movement as a set of variations over a ground bass exemplifies the thorough, methodical quality of so much Baroque music. The effect of the contrast that Vivaldi has added with Variations 5 and 6 is not diminished by the steadily repeating, even obsessive bass. On the contrary, double listening can make the contrast seem richer and more interesting.

Vivaldi, Violin Concerto in G, *La stravaganza*, second movement

Variation (ground-bass) form. 2 min., 59 sec.

0:00	**Theme**	**Orchestra and Solo**: descending bass	
0:22	**Var. 1**	**Solo**:	Flowing material
0:41	**Var. 2**		Faster flowing material
1:03	**Var. 3**		Even faster music, though now in spurts
1:23	**Var. 4**		Faster yet: rapid figuration
		CADENCE	Brief stop at the cadence ending Variation 4
1:44	**Var. 5**		Thin texture (organ and lute drop out), with expressive violin material over a varied bass: in the minor mode
2:04	**Var. 6**		Like Variation 5, but the violin is a little faster and more expressive.
2:26	**Theme**	**Orchestra and Solo**: as at the beginning (i.e., back to the major mode, and the continuo returns)	

Vivaldi's Greatest Hits

In our day, a set of four concertos by Vivaldi is a runaway leader among favorite works from the Baroque era; it has been recorded over a hundred times! The set is called *The Four Seasons*, and it is special not just because of its virtuosic music for string orchestra and violin soloist but also because of what this music *depicts*. Each concerto is associated with a poem describing a season—its weather especially, but also activities, sights, and sounds: shepherd and sheep hiding from the blazing sun of summer, hunters coming out at dawn in the fall, the poet slipping on the ice of winter. Vivaldi captured all these things in the music of his concertos; so as to leave us no doubt, he even indicated in his published music which lines of poetry correspond to which passages of music.

This depiction makes *The Four Seasons* an early example of **program music**, instrumental music that tries to convey a story, actions, or events. Program music became especially popular in the nineteenth century, and we will come back to it for a closer look in Chapter 16.

Antonio Diziani (1737–1797) specialized in painting landscapes and scenes of Venice. Here he captures a springtime country outing that recalls Vivaldi—but without the thunderstorm. *De Agostini Picture Library/A. Dagli Orti/The Bridgeman Art Library.*

Antonio Vivaldi, Violin Concerto in E, *Spring,* Op. 8, No. 1 (before 1725)

The most famous movement of all is the first movement from *Spring (La Primavera)*. The poetry associated with this movement describes (in order) the singing birds and murmuring streams, a sudden thunderstorm silencing the birds, and their return after it clears; the relevant lines are translated in Listening Chart 4. With returns of the ritornello in between, Vivaldi depicts each of these moments, as the chart shows.

The ritornellos could hardly be simpler—or catchier. The opening ritornello consists of two phrases, bright and fanfare-like, heralding spring. Each phrase is stated, then immediately repeated more quietly: **a (loud)** a (soft) **b (loud)** b (soft). All of the ritornellos after the first are made up of one or two statements of the **b** phrase—all but one: The next-to-last ritornello introduces new melodies, related to the ritornello, for the full orchestra. The ritornello that comes after the thunderstorm sounds darker than the rest, almost ominous; it is in the minor mode, while the others are in the major.

The solo sections, because of the depiction involved, are slightly more complicated than we might expect. The first and third of them, portraying the birds singing, require three violins, not just the single soloist. In these moments the movement sounds more like a concerto grosso (a concerto with more than one soloist) than like a solo concerto. The sections depicting the murmuring breezes and streams and the thunderstorm are not really solo sections at all, but for the full orchestra. Nevertheless, the soloist gets to show off during the thunderstorm, with streaking (musical) bolts of lightning.

))) LISTENING CHART 4

Vivaldi, Violin Concerto in E, *Spring,* first movement (Allegro)

Ritornello form. 3 min., 10 sec.

0:00	**Ritornello 1**	a (loud)	
0:06		a (soft)	
0:13		b (loud)	
0:20		b (soft)	
0:28	**Solo 1**	Three violins: birds	
0:59	**Ritornello 2**	b	
1:07	**Breezes**	Full orchestra	
1:28	**Ritornello 3**	b	
1:34	**Solo 2**	Thunderstorm (orchestral thunder, solo lightning bolts)	
1:57	**Ritornello 4**	b, now in the minor mode	
2:06	**Solo 3**	Three violins: Birds resume songs.	
2:25	**Ritornello 5**	New melodies, related to a and b	
2:37	**Solo 4**		
2:50	**Ritornello 6**	b (loud) b (soft)	

Springtime has arrived, and the birds greet her return with festive song, and the streams, caressed by the breezes, flow with soft murmurs. Then lightning and thunder, announcing the spring, cast their dark mantle over the heavens. When these grow quiet, the birds take up again their enchanting songs.

Johann Sebastian Bach, *Brandenburg* Concerto No. 5, for Flute, Violin, Harpsichord, and Orchestra (before 1721)

2 | 1–5   26   7

A concerto grosso is a concerto for a group of several solo instruments (rather than just a single one) and orchestra. In 1721 Johann Sebastian Bach sent a beautiful manuscript containing six of these works to the margrave of Brandenburg, a minor nobleman with a paper title—the duchy of Brandenburg had recently been merged into the kingdom of Prussia, Europe's fastest-growing state. We do not know why this music was sent (if Bach was job-hunting, he was unsuccessful) or if it was ever performed in Brandenburg.

To impress the margrave, presumably, Bach sent pieces with six different combinations of instruments, combinations that in some cases were never used before or after. Taken as a group, the *Brandenburg* Concertos present an unsurpassed anthology of dazzling tone colors and imaginative treatments of the concerto contrast between soloists and orchestra.

Brandenburg Concerto No. 5 features as its solo group a flute, violin, and harpsichord. The orchestra is the basic Baroque string orchestra (see page 108). The harpsichordist of the solo group doubles as the player of the orchestra's continuo chords, and the solo violin leads the orchestra during the ritornellos.

First Movement (Allegro)   In ritornello form, the first movement of *Brandenburg* Concerto No. 5 opens with a loud, bright, solid-sounding orchestral ritornello. We have seen this music before, as an example of a typical Baroque melody—intricate, wide-ranging, and saturated with sequences (see page 109). The brackets show the three segments of the ritornello, **a**, **b**, and **c**, that recur in the movement:

Once the ritornello ends with a solid cadence, the three solo instruments enter with rapid imitative polyphony. They dominate the rest of the movement. They introduce new motives and new patterns of figuration, take over some motives from the ritornello, and toss all these musical ideas back and forth between them. Every so often, the orchestra breaks in again, always with clear fragments of the ritornello, in various keys. All this makes an effect very, very different from Vivaldi's Violin Concerto in G and *Spring* concerto, not only because of the sheer length of the movement but also because of the richness of the counterpoint and the harmony.

During a particularly striking solo section in the minor mode (the first section printed in blue in Listening Chart 5), the soloists abandon their motivic style and play music with even richer harmonies and intriguing, special

"I Shall

1. set the boys a shining example of an honest, retiring manner of life, serve the School industriously, and instruct the boys conscientiously

2. Bring the music in both the principal Churches of this town [Leipzig] into a good state, to the best of my ability

3. Show to the Honorable and Most Wise Town Council all proper respect and obedience."

Bach's contract at Leipzig, 1723—the first three of fourteen stipulations

textures. After this, you may be able to hear that all the remaining solos are closely related to solos heard before the minor-mode section—all, that is, except the very last. Here (the second blue-printed section in the Listening Chart) the harpsichord gradually outpaces the violin and the flute, until finally it seizes the stage and plays a lengthy virtuoso passage, while the other instruments wait silently.

An improvised or improvisatory solo passage of this kind within a larger piece is called a **cadenza**. Cadenzas are a feature of concertos in all eras; the biggest cadenza always comes near the end of the first movement, as in *Brandenburg* Concerto No. 5.

In this cadenza, the harpsichord breaks out of the regular eighth-note rhythms that have dominated this long movement. Its swirling, unexpectedly powerful patterns prepare gradually but inexorably for the final entrance of the orchestra. This is an instance of Bach's masterful ability to ratchet up harmonic tension and expectancy.

Finally the whole ritornello is played, exactly as at the beginning; after nine minutes of rich and complex music, we hear it again as a complete and solid entity, not in fragments.

FLUTE

VIOLIN

etc.

An elaborately painted eighteenth-century harpsichord, with two keyboards.
AKG-Images/The Image Works.

Bach, *Brandenburg* Concerto No. 5, first movement

Ritornello form. 9 min., 44 sec.

2 | 1–5   26   7

1	0:00	**Ritornello (a, b, and c)**	Complete ritornello is played by the orchestra, **forte**: bright and emphatic.
	0:20	**Solo**	Harpsichord, flute, and violin in a contrapuntal texture. Includes faster rhythms; the soloists play new themes and also play some of the motives from the ritornello.
	0:44	**Ritornello (a only)**	Orchestra, ***f***
	0:49	**Solo**	Similar material to that of the first solo
	1:09	**Ritornello (b)**	Orchestra, ***f***
	1:15	**Solo**	Similar solo material
	1:36	**Ritornello (b)**	Orchestra, ***f***; minor mode
	1:41	**Solo**	Similar solo material at first, then fast harpsichord runs are introduced.
2	2:23	**Ritornello (b)**	Orchestra, ***f***
0:06	2:29	**Solo**	This solo leads directly into the central solo.
0:31	2:54	**Central solo**	**Quiet flute and violin dialogue (accompanied by the orchestra, *p*) is largely in the minor mode. The music is less motivic, and the harmonies change less rapidly than before.**
0:55	3:19		**Detached notes in cello, flute, and violin; sequence**
1:34	3:52		**Long high notes prepare for the return of the ritornello.**
3	4:06	**Ritornello (a)**	Orchestra, ***f***
0:04	4:10	**Solo**	
0:48	4:54	**Ritornello (a and b)**	Orchestra, ***f***; this ritornello section feels especially solid because it is longer than the others and in the tonic key.
1:00	5:05	**Solo**	
1:27	5:34	**Ritornello (b)**	Orchestra, ***f***
1:33	5:40	Solo	**Fast harpsichord run leads into the cadenza.**
4	6:18	**Harpsichord cadenza**	*Section 1:* a lengthy passage developing motives from the solo sections
1:46	8:05		*Section 2:* very fast and brilliant
2:11	8:30		*Section 3:* long preparation for the anticipated return of the ritornello
5	9:14	**Ritornello (a, b, and c)**	Orchestra, ***f***, plays the complete ritornello.

Second Movement (*Affettuoso*)   After the forceful first movement, a change is needed: something quieter, slower, and more emotional (*affettuoso* means just that, emotional). As often in concertos, this slow movement is in the minor mode, contrasting with the first and last, which are in the major.

Baroque composers had a simple way of reducing volume: They could omit many or even all of the orchestra instruments. So here Bach employs only the three solo instruments—flute, violin, and harpsichord—plus the orchestra cello playing the continuo bass.

Third Movement (Allegro)   The full orchestra returns in the last movement, which, however, begins with a lengthy passage for the three soloists in imitative, or fugal style (see the next section of this chapter). The lively compound meter with its triple component—*one* two three *four* five six—provides a welcome contrast to the duple meter of the two earlier movements.

2 | Fugue

Fugue is one of the most impressive and characteristic achievements of Baroque music, indeed of Baroque culture altogether. In broad, general terms, fugue can be thought of as systematized imitative polyphony (see pages 29–30). Composers of the Middle Ages first glimpsed imitative polyphony, and Renaissance composers developed it; Baroque composers, living in an age of science, systematized it. The thorough, methodical quality that we pointed to in Baroque music is nowhere more evident than in fugue.

This painting is thought to depict a viola da gamba player of Bach's time named C. F. Abel and his musician sons. It is a symbolic picture: The kindly, soberly dressed father is holding his continuo instrument (the viol) as a support for the upper lines of the boys, who wear the frothy costumes of a later era. One of them would become a major composer.

Biography

Johann Sebastian Bach (1685–1750)

During the Baroque era, crafts were handed down in family clans, and in music the Bach clan was one of the biggest, providing the region of Thuringia, in central Germany, with musicians for many generations. Most of the Bachs were lowly town musicians or Lutheran church organists; only a few of them gained court positions. Johann Sebastian, who was himself taught by several of his relatives, trained four sons who became leading composers of the next generation.

Before he was twenty, Bach took his first position as a church organist in a little town called Arnstadt, then moved to a bigger town called Mühlhausen. Then he worked his way up to a court position with the Duke of Weimar. As a church organist, Bach had to compose organ music and sacred choral pieces, and at Weimar he was still required to write church music for the ducal chapel as well as sonatas and concertos for performance in the palace. The way his Weimar position terminated tells us something about the working conditions of court musicians. When Bach tried to leave Weimar for another court, Cöthen, the duke balked and threw him in jail for several weeks before letting him go. At Cöthen the prince happened to be a keen amateur musician who was not in favor of elaborate church music, so Bach concentrated on instrumental music.

In 1723 Bach was appointed cantor of St. Thomas's Church in Leipzig, a center of Lutheran church music in Germany. He had to not only compose and perform but also organize music for all four churches in town. Teaching in the choir school was another of his responsibilities. Almost every week in his first years at Leipzig, Bach composed, had copied, rehearsed, and performed a new cantata—a religious work for soloists, choir, and orchestra containing several movements and lasting from fifteen to thirty minutes.

Bach chafed under bureaucratic restrictions and political decisions by town and church authorities. The truth is, he was never appreciated in Leipzig. Furthermore, at the end of his life he was regarded as old-fashioned by modern musicians, and one critic pained Bach by saying so in print. Indeed, after Bach's death his music was neglected by the musical public at large, though it was admired by composers such as Mozart and Beethoven.

Bach had twenty children—seven with his first wife (a cousin) and thirteen with his second (a singer), for whom he prepared a little home-music anthology, *The Note-Book of Anna Magdalena Bach.* The children were taught music as a matter of course, and also taught how to copy music; the performance parts of many of the weekly cantatas that Bach composed are written in their hands. From his musical response to the sacred words of these cantatas and from other works, it is clear that Bach thought deeply about religious matters. Works such as his Passions and his Mass in B Minor emanate a spirituality that many listeners find unmatched by any other composer.

Bach seldom traveled, except to consult on organ construction contracts (for which the fee was often a cord of wood or a barrel of wine). Blind in his last years, he continued to compose by dictation. He had already begun to assemble his compositions in orderly sets: organ chorale preludes, organ fugues, preludes and fugues for harpsichord. He also clearly set out to produce works that would summarize his final thoughts about Baroque forms and genres; such works are the Mass in B Minor, the thirty-three *Goldberg* Variations for harpsichord, and *The Art of Fugue,* an exemplary collection of fugues all on the same subject, left unfinished at his death. Bach was writing for himself, for his small devoted circle of students, perhaps for posterity. It is a concept that would have greatly surprised the craftsmen musicians who were his forebears.

Chief Works: More than 200 sacred and secular cantatas; two Passions, with words from the gospels of St. Matthew and St. John; Mass in B Minor ▪ *The Well-Tempered Clavier,* consisting of forty-eight preludes and fugues in all major and minor keys for harpsichord or clavichord ▪ Three sets of suites (six each) for harpsichord—the French and English Suites and the Partitas; solo cello suites; violin sonatas; *Goldberg* Variations ▪ Organ fugues and chorale preludes ▪ *Brandenburg* Concertos, other concertos, orchestral suites, sonatas ▪ Late composite works: *A Musical Offering* and *The Art of Fugue* ▪ Chorale (hymn) harmonizations

Encore: After *Brandenburg* Concerto No. 5, listen to the Concerto for Two Violins; Mass in B Minor (Gloria section).

Image credit: Bettmann/CORBIS.

A **fugue** is a polyphonic composition for a fixed number of instrumental lines or voices—usually three or four—built on a single principal theme. This theme, called the fugue **subject**, appears again and again in each of the instrumental or vocal lines.

The term *fugue* itself comes from the Latin word *fuga,* which means "running away"; imagine the fugue subject being chased from one line to another. Listening to a fugue, we follow that chase. The subject stays the same, but it takes on endless new shadings as it turns corners and surrounds itself with different melodic and rhythmic ideas.

Fugal Exposition

A fugue begins with an **exposition** in which all the voices present the subject in an orderly, standardized way. (The contrapuntal lines in fugues are referred to as *voices,* even when the fugue is written for instruments. We will refer to the four lines in our Bach fugue for keyboard as the *soprano, alto, tenor,* and *bass.*)

First, the subject is announced in the most prominent fashion possible: It enters in a single voice without any accompaniment, while the other voices wait. Any voice can begin, and any order of entry for the other voices is possible; in the first diagram below, we follow the order of the example on our recording (alto, then higher up for the soprano, then below the alto for the tenor, and finally, lowest of all, the bass). After leading off, voice 1 continues with new material of its own while the subject enters in voice 2. Next, the subject arrives in voice 3—with 1 and 2 continuing in counterpoint with it (and with each other), using more new material, and so on. This section of a fugue, the exposition, is over when all the voices have stated the subject.

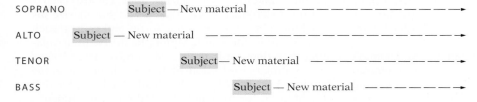

After the exposition, the subject enters at intervals; usually it is spaced out by passages of other music. It may come at the top of the texture (in the soprano), the bottom (bass), or half hidden away in the middle; see the diagram on page 129. Some of these later **subject entries** come in different keys. Although the modulations to these other keys may not be very obvious, without them the music would be dull and stodgy.

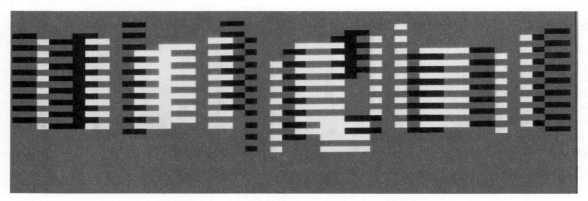

Fugue by Josef Albers (1888–1976). One can almost see the exposition and the subsequent subject entries. *Gianni Dagli Orti/The Art Archive at Art Resource, NY.*

The passages of music separating the later subject entries are called **episodes**. They provide a contrast to the subject entries. This is true even though their motives are often derived from the subject; in such cases, the episodes present not the subject in full but fragments of it, and so they stand apart from subject entries. After the exposition, the form of a fugue falls into an alternating pattern: Episodes of various lengths come between subject entries in various voices and in various keys. Here is a diagram of a typical short fugue:

Exposition	Episode	Entry	Episode	Entry	Longer Episode	Entry
Subject Subject Subject Subject		Subject		Subject Subject		Subject
TONIC KEY		ANOTHER KEY		ANOTHER KEY		TONIC KEY

Fugal Devices

Many specialized techniques can enter into the imitative polyphony of fugues, and the art of composing them has been so often analyzed and taught in the wake of Bach that a whole terminology has grown up. In addition to *exposition*, *subject*, and *episode*, there is the **countersubject**, a kind of second subject that fits together in counterpoint with the first, shadowing it in all its appearances after the beginning.

Composers may lengthen or shorten all the notes in the subject, making it twice as slow or twice as fast. They might turn the melody of the subject upside down, *inverting* its every interval (so that where the original subject went up a step, the **inversion** will go down, and so forth). Very often they shorten the space between subject entries from what was heard in the exposition, so that the entries follow one another faster and are stacked almost on top of each other. This technique is called **stretto** (the Italian word for "narrow"). All these possibilities and more are basic to the ingenious contrapuntal art of the fugue.

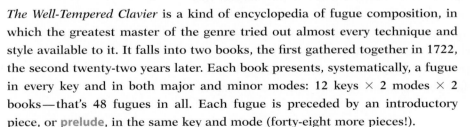

Johann Sebastian Bach, Prelude and Fugue in C Major, from *The Well-Tempered Clavier*, Book 1 (1722)

1 | 26–27   27–28 8–9

The Well-Tempered Clavier is a kind of encyclopedia of fugue composition, in which the greatest master of the genre tried out almost every technique and style available to it. It falls into two books, the first gathered together in 1722, the second twenty-two years later. Each book presents, systematically, a fugue in every key and in both major and minor modes: 12 keys × 2 modes × 2 books—that's 48 fugues in all. Each fugue is preceded by an introductory piece, or **prelude**, in the same key and mode (forty-eight more pieces!).

Some of the fugues give the impression of stern regimentation, some are airy and serene; some echo counterpoint from a century before, others sound like up-to-date dances; some even seem to aim for comic effect. Bach was unsurpassed in the expressive variety he could milk from fugal techniques.

Clavier (or *Klavier*) is today the German word for piano. In Bach's time it referred to a variety of keyboard instruments, including the harpsichord and the very earliest pianos (but not including the church organ). The term *well-tempered* refers to a particular way of tuning the keyboard, among the several employed in the eighteenth century. *The Well-Tempered Clavier* was probably played in Bach's time on various instruments, but most often on harpsichord. Our prelude and fugue are played on piano by a modern master of Bach interpretation, Glenn Gould (see page 131).

Prelude Like the fugues, the preludes in *The Well-Tempered Clavier* display a wide variety of moods, from gentle and lyrical to aggressive and showy, and they explore many musical textures (though usually not the imitative polyphony that features in the fugues to follow). Each prelude tends to occupy itself in an almost obsessive manner with a single musical gesture, repeating it over and over across shifting harmonies. The preludes are, in their different way, systematic like the fugues that follow.

The most famous of them—and also one of the easiest for the novice pianist to work through—is the first, in C major. Its basic gesture is an upward-moving **arpeggio**—that is, a chord "broken" so that its pitches are played in quick succession rather than simultaneously. The wonder of this simple prelude is the rich array of chords Bach devised for it. We feel at its end as if we have taken a harmonic journey, ranging away from our starting point, exploring some rather rocky pathways (that is, dissonant harmonies), and finally—satisfyingly—arriving back home.

Fugue Perhaps because this fugue takes pride of place in *The Well-Tempered Clavier*, Bach crafts it with extraordinary economy and single-mindedness. There are no episodes here, and there is no countersubject to speak of. There are only incessant entries of the subject—twenty-four in all. (Was Bach, who loved number games, referring to the number of fugues in the whole of Book 1?) Many of them overlap in stretto fashion.

The subject is introduced in a spacious exposition—soprano, tenor, and bass follow the alto at even time intervals. The subject moves stepwise up the scale in even rhythms at first, only to reverse course with a quick twist downward. Listen carefully for this twist; it will help you pick out the many subject entries to come. (The whole subject is shown in Listening Chart 6.)

After the exposition, however, all bets are off, fugally speaking. Instead of the more usual episodes alternating with orderly entries of the subject, this fugue is all about stretto. The first stretto comes as soon as the exposition is complete, with two voices overlapping, and from then on entries begin to pile up.

But an overall order underlies all these strettos. The fugue comes, exactly at its midpoint, to a strong cadence on a key different from our starting key, and in the minor mode. This articulates but does not stop the action, as the stretto

> "The bearer, *Monsieur* J. C. Dorn, student of music, has requested the undersigned to give him a testimonial as to his knowledge in *musicis*. . . . As his years increase it may well be expected that with his good native talent he will develop into a quite able musician."
>
> *Joh. Seb. Bach (a tough grader)*

The Prelude in C Major from *The Well-Tempered Clavier*, Book 1—in Bach's own musical handwriting, beautiful and intricate.

Glenn Gould (1932–1982)

The Canadian pianist Glenn Gould is remembered for making Bach, and especially his keyboard works, widely popular from the 1950s on. At that time the preferred medium was the harpsichord, which had been revived so that Bach could be played on his own instrument; audiences were specialized, to say the least, and pianists didn't play much Bach. Significantly, Gould's first great success was a best-selling three-LP recording of one of Bach's encyclopedic works, the *Goldberg* Variations. In a stroke he created a uniquely modern Bach sound by imitating the harpsichord on the piano, joining the crisp, even attack of the older instrument with the potent dynamic range of the newer one.

Thus his playing of Bach's Prelude No. 1 in C sounds less like chords made by a swishing harp than a hollow series of pings; yet the dynamics fall and rise, rise and fall so purposefully that this simple piece produces an almost majestic effect. Notice how carefully *p* and *f* moments are coordinated with the harmonies spelled out by the chords. In the fugue, Gould is in his element—every entry is loud and clear!

Like many performers, old and new, classical and popular, Gould derived some of his fame from his eccentricities. At concerts he had to have the piano bench very low and the temperature in the hall very high. On our recording you will hear weird little noises behind the music; even the top recording engineers couldn't filter out Gould's constant humming or yelping when he played.

Gould was also a popular broadcaster, promoting his pet ideas. For example, he thought that concerts were

Michael Ochs Archive/Getty Images.

outmoded and the future of music lay with recordings. He was wrong, but it worked for him; for nearly twenty years at the end of his life, he concentrated on building up an extraordinary archive of recordings but played no concerts at all.

)))) LISTENING CHART 6

Bach, Fugue 1 in C Major, from *The Well-Tempered Clavier*

1 min., 55 sec.

0:00	**Exposition**	*Fugue subject in:*
0:00		**A** (alto)
0:06		**S** (soprano)
0:12		**T** (tenor)
0:18		**B** (bass)
0:24	First **stretto, S** and **T**	
0:32	Subject entry: **A**	
0:38	More **stretto** entries: **B, A, T**	
0:51	CADENCE minor mode	
0:52	Quickest voice entries yet in **stretto: A, T, B, S**	
1:01	More **stretto: S, A, T, B,** etc.	
1:33	CADENCE major mode, home key; but three more entries follow quickly in **stretto: T, A, S**	

entries of the subject begin again immediately, back in the home key. Indeed, as if to counterbalance the clarity of the cadence, the entries here come faster than anywhere else in the fugue—eight of them in quick succession. At one moment four entries all overlap, the last beginning before the first has finished.

After this frenzy of entries, even a big cadence back in the home key takes a moment to sink in, as three more entries of the subject quickly follow it. The energy of all this finally comes to rest in the soprano voice, which at the very end floats beautifully up to the highest pitch we have heard.

3 | Baroque Dances

We have sampled Italian and German music of the Baroque era, and turn now to the French tradition. All Europe associated France with dance music. Paris was a center for ballet, which has always been a particularly strong feature of French opera—and French opera of the Baroque era was particularly grand and spectacular. An admirer writes of the great opera composer Jean-Philippe Rameau: "As a composer of dances, he bewilders comparison."

The Dance Suite

Many different dance types existed in the Baroque era. What distinguished them were features originally associated with the dance steps—a certain meter, a distinctive tempo, and some rhythmic attributes. The **minuet**, for example, is a simple dance in triple time at a moderate tempo. The slower **sarabande** is a little more intricate; also in triple time, it has an accent on the second beat of the measure, as well as the normal accent on the first.

The custom all over Europe was to group a collection of miscellaneous dances together in a genre called the **suite**. Which dances occurred in a suite was not subject to any general rule, nor was there any specified order. But all the dances in a suite kept to the same key, and the last of them was always fast—frequently a **gigue**, a dance in compound meter that may have been derived from the Irish jig. Otherwise there was no standard overall structure to a suite.

Composers also wrote a great many dances and dance suites for the lute or the harpsichord. These are *stylized* dances, pieces written in the style and form of dance music but intended for listening rather than dancing, for mental rather than physical pleasure. Compared with dances written for the actual dance floor, stylized ones naturally allowed for more musical elaboration and refinement, while still retaining some of the typical features of the various dance-type.

Baroque Dance Form

A Baroque dance has two sections, **a** and **b**. Each ends with a strong cadence coming to a complete stop, after which the section is immediately repeated. Both sections tend to include the same motives, cadences, and other such musical details, and this makes for a sense of symmetry between them, even though **b** is nearly always longer than **a**. Hence Baroque dance form is diagrammed **a a b b**, abbreviated as |: **a** :||: **b** :| where the signs |: and :| indicate that everything between them is to be repeated. This form is also called **binary form**.

With shorter dances, composers tended to group them in pairs of the same type, with the first coming back after the second, resulting in a large-scale **A B A** form. (Don't confuse **A** with **a**, or **B** with **b**. Admittedly, the standard terminology is awkward.) The second, or **B**, dance in such a pair was called the **trio**, a relic

Concerts began late in the Baroque era. They were sometimes given in parks (such as the Vauxhall Gardens of London, shown here), where music accompanied gossip, flirtation, and food. *English School/London Metropolitan Archives, City of London/The Bridgeman Art Library.*

of orchestral dances from early French opera, when **B** had often been scored for only three instruments. This made for a simple, agreeable contrast with the full orchestration of the **A** dance.

Later the idea of contrast between **A** and **B** was always kept, with **B** quieter than **A**, or perhaps changed in mode. Thus a Baroque minuet and trio, to choose this type as an example, consists of one minuet followed by a second, contrasting minuet, and then the first one returns. This time, however, the repeats in the binary form are usually omitted:

	MINUET	TRIO	MINUET
	A	**B**	**A**
	a a b b	**c c d d**	**a b**
abbreviated as:	|: **a** :||: **b** :|	|: **c** :||: **d** :|	**a b**

The term *trio,* to indicate a contrasting, subsidiary section, lasted until well after the Baroque period. Band players know it from the marches of John Philip Sousa and others.

George Frideric Handel (1685–1759), Minuet from the *Royal Fireworks Music* (1749)

2|6   29

We will discuss Handel as a composer of opera and oratorio in Chapter 11, on Baroque vocal music. One of his best-loved instrumental works is a dance suite for a huge band to celebrate the end of one of England's many wars in the eighteenth century, the War of the Austrian Succession. The minuet from this suite was not

\|: **a** :\|\|: **b** :\|
8   8

meant to be danced, then, but music like this certainly encourages body movement. On our recording, the minuet is played twice, the second time with full military honors.

The rehearsal of the Fireworks Music at London's Vauxhall Gardens (see page 133) was attended by 12,000 people, causing a historic traffic jam. At the celebration itself, which was led off by a hundred brass cannons, things got much worse: The stage set caught fire, the crowd stampeded, two people died, and the man in charge of the fireworks had a mad fit. Music should stay indoors.

Johann Sebastian Bach, Gigue from Cello Suite No. 2 in D Minor (c. 1720)

2 | 7   30   10

Bach wrote three important sets of suites for harpsichord, with six suites each. His set of six suites for cello solo have become very popular; if you search on Amazon.com for "Bach" today (we can't vouch for tomorrow), the cello suites top any of his other music. This is the most stylized of dance music, far from the dance floor or ballet stage.

|: **a** :||: **b** :|
16   22

One can play chords on a stringed instrument by bowing any two adjacent strings, and Bach does this very effectively in both **a** and **b** sections of his D-minor gigue. The range of this music provides much of its exhilaration; the cello races up and down more than three whole octaves. Bach's genius lies in making these athletic lines sound like wide-ranging melodies and broken chords supporting them, all at the same time.

GOALS FOR REVIEW

▶   to witness the explosion of instrumental music in the late Baroque period

▶   to distinguish concerto grosso from solo concerto

▶   to listen for the basic formal design of Baroque concerto movements: ritornello form

▶   to understand the principles of fugue, develop a vocabulary for them, and listen to them in action

▶   to follow the development of late Baroque dance music

▶   to survey the lives and works of Antonio Vivaldi and Johann Sebastian Bach

macmillanhighered.com/listen8e
Interactive Listening Charts 2–6
Listening Quiz for Chapter 10
Reading Quiz for Chapter 10

Baroque Vocal Music

CHAPTER 11

Vocal music—music for solo voices, choruses, or both—formed a major part of the output of most Baroque composers. We have seen that composers were supported by three main institutions: the church, the opera house, and the court. Each of these demanded vocal music. Indeed, of the three, only the court was a major venue for instrumental music—and every court had its chapel, for which the court composers were also required to provide vocal music. Courts often had their own opera theaters, too.

Theories of musical expression in the Baroque era were touched on in Chapter 9 (page 112). It was believed at the time that emotions could be isolated, categorized, and listed in a fairly simple way, and that music could enhance or even arouse each emotion by means of certain musical devices applied consistently throughout a piece. Theorists developed checklists of musical devices corresponding to each of the "affects," as they called emotions conceived in this way.

It was particularly in vocal music—where the words that are sung define or suggest a specific emotion—that this musical vocabulary of the emotions was developed and exploited. If a text refers to "rejoicing," for example, a Baroque composer would match this with fast, lively runs; a mention of "victory" would probably require trumpets and drums in the accompanying instruments to evoke battle music—or at least fanfare motives in the violins. "Sorrow" would call forth sighing melodic gestures and intense, dissonant harmonies, and so on.

1 | Opera

The principal genre of secular vocal music of the Baroque era was opera. Introduced around the year 1600, opera soon flourished mightily all over Europe, and became the most glamorous and probably the most adventurous and influential artistic genre of the Baroque era.

Any general description of the emotional world of Baroque art must feature its theatrical quality (see page 113). The Baroque was fascinated by the theater, and especially by opera—the ultimate multimedia experience of its day, combining poetry, drama, music, vocal virtuosity, scenic splendor, dance, and more. Spectacle was of the essence in Baroque opera—spectacular singing, to be sure, but also spectacular stage architecture, featuring amazing transformation scenes and the like. Systems of pulleys and counterweights

In contrast to the painting on page 106, this is a much more informal picture of a Baroque opera performance—evidently during a recitative, to judge from the interaction of the characters on stage and the inattention of the audience. (The painting is perhaps by Antonio Longhi, 1702–1785.) *School of Pietro Longhi, Opera Seria. Photo: Scala/Art Resource, NY.*

could rapidly change the set from a palace to a magic garden, with gods and goddesses descending from the heavens in a fiery chariot. Opera offered a wealth of satisfactions, then—most obviously, no doubt, for the vocal connoisseurs of the day, the fans of great singers. They are said to have gossiped, gambled, and flirted in the boxes while waiting for the special moments when their favorites sang.

But opera's ability to project emotion was the real basis of its appeal. First and foremost, opera offered a stage on which individual singers could step forward to express feelings in the most direct and powerful fashion. Since the singers were portraying characters in a drama, they were repeatedly thrown into situations that made it seem natural for them to experience (and express) intense emotions.

Such emotions were made all the more intense by music. Emotion could be intensified by great vocal virtuosity, too. The most obvious kind of vocal virtuosity is *coloratura* singing—fast brilliant runs, scales, high notes, vocal cadenzas, and so on, stressing technique for its own sake. But the legendary singers of old moved their audiences not only by singing faster than anyone else but also by singing more beautifully, more delicately, and more emotionally.

Italian Opera Seria

The principal type of Italian Baroque opera was **opera seria**, or serious opera. The plots—mostly derived from ancient history, with all kinds of alterations and additions—were designed to stir up powerful emotions, such as passion, rage, grief, and triumph. Such plots gave the singers many opportunities to excel in one kind of expression or another. Opera seria consisted mainly of solo singing by sopranos and mezzo-sopranos, including castrati (see the box below). Brilliant high voices were prized above all. Tenors and basses played subordinate roles, and there were few duets or choruses.

The words of an opera are called the *libretto* ("little book"), and their author is the *librettist*. Librettists had to build up the drama as a whole from a series of brief texts, alternating with one another, for *recitatives* and *arias*.

Recitative

Recitative (reh-sih-ta-téev), from the Italian word for "recite," is a technique of declaiming words musically in a heightened, theatrical manner. There is always an instrumental accompaniment. The singing voice closely follows the free rhythm of emotional speech; it mirrors and indeed exaggerates the natural ups and downs that occur as an actor raises his or her voice at a question, lowers it in "asides," or cries out angrily. The composer makes no effort to organize these speechlike utterances into real melodies; the point is speechlike song.

THE CASTRATO

Intimately tied up with Italian opera seria was the castrato singer (plural: *castrati*). The starring male roles in opera were hardly ever sung by tenors or basses but rather by men who had submitted to castration at puberty in order to preserve their voices in the soprano or alto range. At its best, the castrato voice was a prized virtuoso instrument, more powerful and brilliant than a woman's soprano.

This practice seems an outrage to us today, as it did to everybody outside Italy at the time (and to many in Italy itself). Nevertheless, in Italy and across most of Europe—France was a notable exception—castrati were gladly accepted because of their spectacular singing and given top billing, along with women prima donnas. But the presence of frankly unnatural men in the main opera roles, which were of course usually romantic roles, made it hard to believe in the ideal of opera as serious drama in music. Contributing to the sideshow quality, it was common in opera seria plots for male characters to disguise themselves as women (and vice versa). Then the male soprano voice was used for female impersonation.

The most famous castrati were international stage figures. Some were pampered stars and objects of ridicule at the same time, such as Caffarelli, who was once jailed for indecent gestures during a performance. Others led more dignified careers. Carlo Broschi, whose stage name was

Farinelli, the most famous of all, was also a composer and later in life an influential figure at the royal court of Spain.

Most castrati, however, labored far from the limelight, singing in Italian churches. The last known castrato, Alessandro Moreschi, a member of the Sistine Choir in Rome who was born as late as 1858, made recordings in 1902–03; you can listen to some of them on YouTube.

You can also rent the 1994 film *Farinelli*, for which a virtual castrato voice was invented by digital wizardry.

Farinelli. *Royal College of Music, London, UK/The Bridgeman Art Library.*

Recitative was used for plot action, dialogue, and other places in the drama where it is particularly important for the words to be brought out. Text phrases and individual words are not ordinarily repeated any more than they would be in speech.

Most of the time, recitative accompaniment was kept to a minimum—basso continuo (typically cello and harpsichord) alone—so that the singer could interpret the dialogue or the action as spontaneously as possible. Italians at the time called recitative with continuo accompaniment **secco recitative**, from the Italian meaning "dry" (think of the sound of the harpsichord).

In every opera seria, however, one or two of the most excited, emotion-filled recitatives were provided with orchestral accompaniment of one kind or another. This type is called **accompanied recitative**.

Aria

An **aria** is a set piece for solo singer that has much more musical elaboration and coherence than recitative. The vocal part is more melodic, and ordinarily the accompaniment includes the orchestra, not just the continuo, as in secco recitative. Here the singer-actor is mulling over his or her emotions at some leisure, "getting his feelings out," instead of reacting moment by moment, as in recitative. Consequently in arias the repetition of poetic phrases or words is common and, in principle, appropriate.

The standard form for the Baroque Italian opera aria is **da capo** form, **A B A** (less usual is free da capo form, **A B A′**). Both the words and music of **A** are repeated after **B**; *da capo* ("from the head") is a direction on scores meaning repeat from the beginning. The composer wrote the music for **A** and **B** only, leaving the performers to do the rest. Indeed, the singer would do more than just repeat **A**. He or she would also ornament the music with improvised runs, cadenzas, and so on, so as to create an exciting enhanced effect the second time around.

For connoisseurs of the day, a great deal depended on the **A** repeats, since it was there that the star singers really dazzled their audiences. Many modern singers have relearned the lost improvisational art of the Baroque era, and we can recapture some of the original excitement on recordings.

George Frideric Handel, *Julius Caesar* (1724)

2 | 8   31

As a young man, Handel wrote a few German operas for the Hamburg opera company (most of the music is lost) and a few Italian operas for theaters in Florence and Venice. In his maturity he wrote as many as forty Italian operas for London, where he helped start a fad for imported Italian opera. Probably the most famous of them is *Julius Caesar (Giulio Cesare in Egitto)*, one of a trio of Handel masterpieces written in the years 1724–25, the others being *Rodelinda* and *Tamerlano*.

Background Like most opera seria of the late Baroque era, *Julius Caesar* draws on Roman history. Cleopatra, the famous queen of Egypt, applied her formidable charms to Julius Caesar and then, after Caesar's assassination, also to his successor Mark Antony. Shakespeare deals with the second of these famous affairs in his play *Antony and Cleopatra;* Handel tackles the first.

Handel's librettist added a great deal of nonhistorical plot material. History tells that Pompey—who comes into the story because he waged war on Caesar and lost and fled to Egypt—was murdered by one of his soldiers, but in the opera the murderer is Cleopatra's brother Ptolemy. Pompey's widow, Cornelia, is thrown into Ptolemy's harem and has to resist his advances (among others'). Her son Sextus rattles around the opera swearing vengeance on Ptolemy and finally kills him. The historical Cleopatra poisoned Ptolemy, but her character in the opera is whitewashed, and she gets to sing some of the most ravishing, seductive music while disguised as her own maid. All this gives a taste of the typical complications in an opera seria plot.

Although the role of Sextus, for mezzo-soprano, was presumably meant for a castrato, at the first performance it was sung by a woman singer who was one of Handel's regulars.

Aria, "La giustizia"   Sextus promises revenge on Ptolemy, not for the first time, in the aria "La giustizia" (Justice). This aria is preceded—or, rather, set up—by a recitative (as usual). Since it makes more sense to study recitative when the words are in English, we leave that discussion until we get to Handel's *Messiah*.

The aria starts with a ritornello played by the string orchestra, like the opening section of a concerto movement (see page 116). It establishes the mood right away:

The "affect" Handel means to convey by this strenuous, vigorous music is anger, and Sextus starts up with the same music. We will hear this ritornello three more times, once in a shortened form, prior to the second **A** section.

Apart from this shortened ritornello, "La giustizia" is in strict **A B A** (da capo) form. In the **A** section Handel goes through the words three times, with the orchestra interjecting to allow the singer to catch her breath. (These short spacers are not marked in the Listen box.) Notice how the music tends to explode angrily on certain key words, principally by the use of *coloratura* (fast scales and turns), as on "ven-*det*-ta" (vengeance) and "tradi-*tor*" (traitor). Even more vivid are the sudden high notes on "pu-*ni*-re" (punish) and a suspense-making long note on "tradi-*tor*."

There is a flamboyant effect typical of the Baroque near the end of **A**, where Sextus dramatically comes to a stop. After a breathless pause, he moves on to make a very forceful final cadence. Revenge is nigh!

The aria's **B** section introduces new words and some new keys for contrast; both features are typical in da capo arias. Otherwise it is brief and seems rather subdued—the strings drop out, leaving only the continuo as accompaniment. What the audience is waiting for is the repeat of **A**, where we can forget about Sextus and get to admire a display of vocal virtuosity. Lorraine Hunt Lieberson, the singer on our recording, adds brilliant improvised flourishes to the high notes on "pu-*ni*-re" and the long note on "tradi-*tor*." When she gets to the fermata in **A** she fills it in with a cadenza (see page 124), and her (ornamented) final cadence sweeps us away. Anyone who can carry off a feat like this, the aria seems to say, will be more than a match for Ptolemy.

Vocal cadenzas at the time were short, because they were supposed to be sung in a single breath—thus showing off virtuoso breath control as well as vocal technique and inventiveness.

 **LISTEN**

Handel, *Julius Caesar*, Aria "La giustizia"

2|8   31

For a note on Italian pronunciation, see page 85: "La joostidzia (ah) jah sool arco."

0:00	A	RITORNELLO		
0:16		*St. 1*: first time	La giustizia ha già sull' arco Pronto strale alla vendetta Per punire un traditor	Justice now has in its bow The arrow primed for vengeance To castigate a traitor!
0:50		*St. 1*: second time	*La giustizia . . . etc.*	
1:10		*St. 1*: third time	*La giustizia . . . etc.*	
1:31		RITORNELLO		
1:47	B	*St. 2*:	Quanto è tarda la saetta Tanto più crudele aspetta La sua pena un empio cor.	The later the arrow is shot, The crueler is the pain suffered By a dastardly heart!
2:15	A	RITORNELLO (abbreviated)		
2:22			*La giustizia . . . etc.*	Justice . . . etc.

2 | Oratorio

Sacred, or religious, vocal music of the Baroque era exhibits much diversity in style and form. Most of it was written directly for church services, and so its style and form depend first of all on whether those services were of the Roman Catholic, Lutheran, or Anglican rite. Every service has places where music is appropriate, or even specified by the liturgy. In principle, each place gives rise to a different musical genre.

There are, however, two general factors that are important for all Baroque sacred-music genres—oratorio and passion, cantata, Mass, and motet. One of these factors is traditional in origin; the other is specific to the Baroque era.

• The traditional factor is the participation of the choir. A simple point, perhaps; choral music has had a functional place in the religious music of virtually all rites and ages. For when one person utters a religious text, he or she speaks as an individual, but when a choir does so, it speaks as a united community. A church choir can be said to speak for the whole church, even for the whole of Christianity.

• The other important fact about Baroque sacred vocal music is its strong tendency to borrow from secular vocal music—which is to say, from opera. In an era fascinated by the theater, the church grew more and more theatrical. Arias inspired by Italian opera seria appear even in Baroque settings of the Catholic Mass. Solo singers could display their vocal prowess at the same time as they were presenting parts of the divine service.

"On Tuesday the 2nd day of May will be performed, the Sacred Story of Esther, an Oratorio in English. Formerly composed by Mr. Handel, and now revised by him, with several Additions. . . . *N.B.* There will be no Action on the Stage."

London newspaper announcement, 1731

The most operatic of all religious genres was oratorio, which existed in Catholic and Protestant countries alike. An **oratorio** is basically an opera on a religious subject, such as an Old Testament story or the life of a saint. It has a narrative plot in several acts, real characters, and implied action—even though oratorios were not staged, but presented in concert form, that is, without scenery, costumes, or acting. Oratorio takes over such operatic features as recitatives and arias. On the other hand, it also makes much use of the chorus—a major difference from Italian opera of the time, where the chorus played little role.

Unlike most other religious genres, an oratorio was not actually part of a church service. Indeed, in opera-crazed Italy, the oratorio was prized as an

Biography

George Frideric Handel (1685–1759)

Georg Friedrich Händel—he anglicized his name to George Frideric Handel after settling in England—was one of the few composers of early days who did not come from a family of musicians. His father was a barber-surgeon and a valet at a court near Leipzig. He disapproved of music, and the boy is said to have studied music secretly at night, by candlelight. In deference to his father's wishes, Handel studied law for a year at Halle, one of Germany's major universities, before finally joining the orchestra at Hamburg, Germany's leading center of opera.

From then on, it was an exciting, glamorous life. Still in his teens, Handel fought a duel with another Hamburg musician about which of them was to get top billing. In 1706 he journeyed to the homeland of opera and scored big successes in Venice, Florence, and Rome. Though he became a court musician for the elector of Hanover, in northern Germany, he kept requesting (and extending) leaves to pursue his career in London, a city that was then beginning to rival Paris as the world capital.

Here Handel continued to produce Italian operas, again with great success. He also wrote a flattering birthday ode for Queen Anne and some big pieces to celebrate a major peace treaty; for this he was awarded an annuity. In 1717, after the elector of Hanover had become George I of England, Handel got back into his good graces by composing music to be played in a royal celebration on barges on the River Thames. This famous *Water Music* consists of two suites for the Baroque festive orchestra.

As an opera composer, Handel had learned to gauge the taste of the public and also to flatter singers, writing music for them that showed off their voices to the best advantage. He now became an opera impresario—today we would call him a promoter—recruiting singers and negotiating their contracts, planning whole seasons of opera, and all the while composing the main attractions himself: an opera every year, on average, in the 1720s and 1730s.

He also had to deal with backers—English aristocrats and wealthy merchants who supported his opera companies and persuaded their friends to take out subscriptions for boxes.

Handel made and lost several fortunes, but he always landed on his feet, even when Italian opera went out of style in Britain, for he never lost a feel for his audience. After opera had failed, he popularized oratorios—retellings of Bible stories (mostly from the Old Testament) in a half-operatic, half-choral form. Opera audiences had always been ready to identify opera's virtuous Roman emperors with local princes. Now they were delighted to identify oratorio's virtuous People of Israel with the British nation.

Handel was a big, vigorous man, hot-tempered but quick to forgive, humorous and resourceful. When a particularly temperamental prima donna had a tantrum, he calmed her down by threatening to throw her out the window. At the end of his life he became blind—the same surgeon operated (unsuccessfully) on both him and Bach—but he continued to play the organ brilliantly and composed by dictating to a secretary.

Chief Works: Forty Italian operas, including *Giulio Cesare* (Julius Caesar) ■ Near-operatic works in English: *Semele* and *Acis and Galatea* ■ Oratorios, including *Messiah*, *Israel in Egypt*, *Samson*, and *Saul* ■ Concerti grossi and organ concertos ■ *Water Music*, written for an aquatic fete on the river Thames, and *Royal Fireworks Music*, celebrating the end of the War of the Austrian Succession, in 1747 ■ Sonatas for various instruments

Encore: After *Messiah*, listen to *Acis and Galatea*; Concerto Grosso in B-flat, Op. 6, No. 7.

Image credit: Bettmann/CORBIS.

entertainment substituting for opera during Lent, a somber season of abstinence from opera as well as other worldly diversions.

In England also, the oratorio substituted for opera, though in a different sense. Thanks largely to Handel, Italian opera became very popular in London for a quarter of a century, but finally audiences tired of it. At that point, Handel, already in his mid-fifties, began composing oratorios, and these turned out to be even more popular, the pinnacle of his long career.

George Frideric Handel, *Messiah* (1742)

Handel's oratorio *Messiah*, his most famous work, is also one of the most famous in the whole of Western music. It is the only composition of its time that has been performed continuously—and frequently—since its first appearance. Today it is sung at Christmas and Easter in hundreds of churches around the world, as well as at symphony concerts and "*Messiah* sings," where people get together just to sing along with the Hallelujah Chorus and the other well-known choral numbers, and listen to the well-loved arias.

Unlike most oratorios, *Messiah* does not have actual characters depicting a biblical story in recitative and arias, although its text is taken from the Bible. In a more typical Handel oratorio, such as *Samson*, for example, Samson sings an aria about his blindness and argues with Delilah in recitative, while choruses represent the People of Israel and the Philistines. Instead, *Messiah* works with a group of anonymous narrators, relating episodes from the life of Jesus in recitative. The narration is interrupted by anonymous commentators who react to each of the episodes by singing recitatives and arias.

All this is rather like an opera in concert form; but in addition, the chorus has a large and varied role to play. On one occasion, it sings the words of a group of angels who actually speak in the Bible. Sometimes it comments on the story, like the soloists. And often the choristers raise their voices to praise the Lord in Handel's uniquely magnificent manner.

The first two numbers in *Messiah* we examine cover the favorite Christmas story in which an angel announces Christ's birth to the shepherds in the fields. Included are a recitative in four brief sections and a chorus.

Recitative *Part 1 (secco)* Sung by a boy soprano narrator accompanied by continuo (cello and organ), this recitative has the natural, proselike flow typical of all recitatives. Words that would be naturally stressed in ordinary speech are brought out by longer durations, higher pitches, and pauses: "*shep*herds," "*field*," "*flock*," and "*night*." As is typical in recitative, but unlike aria, no words are repeated.

Part 2 (accompanied) Accompanied recitative is used for special effects in operas and oratorios—here the miraculous appearance of the angel. The slowly pulsing high-string background furnishes the angel with a sort of musical halo. It is also a signal for more vigorous declamation: The words *lo*, *Lord*, and *glory* are brought out with increasing emphasis. The end of this brief accompanied recitative is heavily punctuated by a standard cadence formula, played by the continuo. This formula is an easily recognized feature of recitatives.

Part 3 (secco) Notice that the angel speaks in a more urgent style than the narrator. And in ***Part 4 (accompanied),*** the excited, faster pulsations in the high strings depict the beating wings, perhaps, of the great crowd of angels. When Handel gets to what they will be saying, he brings the music to a triumphant high point, once again over the standard recitative cadence.

Chorus, "Glory to God" "Glory to God! Glory to God in the *highest!*" sing the angels—the *high* voices of the choir, in a bright marchlike rhythm. They are accompanied by the orchestra, with the trumpets prominent. The *low* voices alone add "and peace on *earth,*" much more slowly. Fast string runs following "Glory to God" and slower reiterated chords following "and peace on earth" recall the fast and slow string passages in the two preceding accompanied recitatives.

good will to-ward men

After these phrases are sung and played again, leading to another key, the full chorus sings the phrase "good will toward men" in a fugal style. The important words are *good will,* and their two-note motive is happily sung (in imitation) again and again by all the voices of the angel choir. To conclude, the "good will" motive is singled out in an enthusiastic ascending sequence.

good will. . .

The whole chorus is quite concise, even dramatic; the angels do not stay long. At the very end, the orchestra gets quieter and quieter—a rare effect in Baroque music, here indicating the disappearance of the shepherds' vision.

 **LISTEN**

Handel, *Messiah,* Recitative "There were shepherds" and Chorus "Glory to God"

2 | 9   32   11

Bold italic type indicates accented words or syllables. *Italics indicate phrases of text that are repeated.*

	RECITATIVE PART 1 (secco)	
0:01	There were **shep**herds abiding in the **field**, keeping **watch** over their **flock** by **night**.	
	PART 2 (accompanied)	
0:22	And **lo!** the angel of the **Lord** came upon them, and the **glory** of the Lord shone round about them; and they were sore afraid.	**Standard cadence**
	PART 3 (secco)	
0:42	And the angel said unto **them**: **Fear** not, for be**hold**, I bring you good **ti**dings of great **joy**, which shall **be to all peo**ple.	**Standard cadence**
	For unto you is born this **day** in the city of **Da**vid a **Sa**viour, which is **Christ** the **Lord**.	**Standard cadence**
	PART 4 (accompanied)	
1:39	And **sud**denly there was with the **an**gel a **mul**titude of the heavenly **host**, praising **God**, **and saying**:	**Standard cadence**
	CHORUS	
1:51	Glory to God, *glory to God,* in the highest, and peace on earth,	
2:30	good will toward men *good will*	
2:48	*Glory to God*	

Hallelujah Chorus This famous chorus brings Act II of *Messiah* to a resounding close. Like "Glory to God," "Hallelujah" makes marvelous use of monophony ("King of Kings"), homophony (the opening "Hallelujah"), and polyphony

("And he shall reign for ever and ever"); it is almost a textbook demonstration of musical textures. Compare "and peace on earth," "Glory to God," and "good will toward men" in the earlier chorus.

Hallelujah, Hallelujah, Hallelujah, Hallelujah, Halle - lujah.

and he shall reign for ever and ev-er

In a passage beloved by chorus singers, Handel sets "The Kingdom of this world is become" on a low descending scale, *piano*, swelling suddenly into a similar scale in a higher register, *forte*, for "the kingdom of our Lord and *of his Christ*"—a perfect representation of one thing becoming another thing, similar but newly radiant. Later the sopranos (cheered on by the trumpets) solemnly utter the words "King of Kings" on higher and higher long notes as the other voices keep repeating their answer, "for ever, Hallelujah!"

George II of England, attending the first London performance of *Messiah*, was so moved by this chorus that he stood up in his box—prompting everyone else to stand—honoring the King of Kings, no doubt, but also reminding everyone of his own majesty, which was being acclaimed by the typical Baroque festive orchestra. Audiences still stand during the Hallelujah Chorus.

Elite opera and oratorio were not the only music in Handel's London. This famous scene by William Hogarth (1697–1764) shows a violinist, sometimes identified as a player in Handel's orchestra, enraged by lowbrow music and noise beneath his window. *William Hogarth (1698–1764)*, The Enraged Musician *1741 (engraving)/© Yale Center for British Art, New Haven, USA/ Transfer from the School of Music/The Bridgeman Art Library.*

Italics indicate phrases of text that are repeated.

0:06	Hallelujah, *Hallelujah!*
0:23	For the Lord God omnipotent reigneth. *Hallelujah!* *For the Lord God omnipotent reigneth.*
1:09	The Kingdom of this world is become the kingdom of our Lord and *of his Christ.*
1:26	And He shall reign for ever and ever, *and he shall reign for ever and ever.*
1:48	KING OF KINGS *for ever and ever, Hallelujah!* AND LORD OF LORDS *for ever and ever, Hallelujah!*

3 | The Church Cantata

Second in importance to oratorio among Baroque sacred-music genres is the church cantata. *Cantata* is a general name for a piece of moderate length for voices and instruments. Many Baroque cantatas, especially Italian ones, are not sacred music, but in Germany church cantatas were written to be performed during Lutheran church services. Lutheran churches had (and still have to-day) fixed readings and hymns specified for every Sunday of the year as well as for special occasions such as Easter and Christmas. The words of cantatas addressed the religious content of the day in question. Sung before the sermon, the cantata was in effect a second, musical sermon.

As cantor, or music director, of Leipzig's biggest church (the Thomaskirche), Bach was required to produce cantatas for the entire year—a stupendous task that kept him very busy indeed for years after he was appointed. Over two hundred cantatas by Bach have survived, each of them with several movements. Most are sacred works, but they include some secular cantatas written for court or civic celebrations and for functions at the University of Leipzig.

The Lutheran Chorale

The content and structure of Bach's cantatas varied from one work to the next. But in general they tend to fall into a short series of operatic arias and recitatives with one or more choral movements, like an excerpt from an oratorio. (Most secular cantatas, likewise, resemble a scene or two from an opera.) A special feature of nearly all Lutheran cantatas is their use of traditional congregational hymns. Lutheran hymns are called chorales (co-ráhls), from the German word for hymn (*Choral*).

Martin Luther, the father of the Protestant Reformation, placed special emphasis on hymn singing by the congregation when he decided on the format of Lutheran services. Two hundred years later, in Bach's time, a large body of chorales served as the foundation for Lutheran worship, both in church services and also at informal pious devotions in the home. Everybody knew the words and melodies of these chorales. You learned them as a small child and sang them in church all your life. Consequently when composers introduced chorale tunes into cantatas (and other sacred-music genres), they were drawing on a rich source of association.

Before the twentieth century, opportunities for women were limited. Though some women worked as teachers, nurses, and laborers, society viewed women's primary role as that of wife and mother. Occasionally accidents of royal succession placed a woman in a position of great power, and the eighteenth century saw two amazingly long-lasting cases: Catherine the Great, empress of Russia, who ruled from 1762 to 1796, and Maria Theresa, de facto empress of the Austrian Empire from 1740 to 1780. But what we now think of as careers were simply not open to women, with few exceptions.

Bordoni. *Mary Evans Picture Library.*

Music provided one of those exceptions. It did so by way of the theater, because an opera singer, like an actress or a ballet dancer, could attain fame and fortune and the opportunity to develop her talents in the same way as men in those same fields. Indeed, opera depended on female singers; without them the genre could never have developed or survived.

The names—although not, alas, the voices—of opera's legendary prima donnas have come down to us, along with those of opera's great composers: from **Anna Renzi**

Cuzzoni. *Mary Evans Picture Library.*

(c. 1620–c. 1660), who sang in Monteverdi's *Poppea* (see page 86), to the notorious rival sopranos **Faustina Bordoni** (1700–1781) and **Francesca Cuzzoni** (1698–1770) in the age of Handel, and beyond. Cuzzoni sang in the star-studded premiere of Handel's *Julius Caesar* (see page 138).

Women of the theater paid a price for their career opportunities, of course. They were displaying themselves—their legs or their voices—for the enjoyment of, mainly, men, who paid for the privilege. There was always a question about the respectability and marriageability of opera singers.

While female opera singers were a fixture in the musical workplace of the Baroque, female instrumentalists were much rarer. Women composers were simply flukes. Remember that composers, such as Bach and Handel (and Farinelli—see page 137), were also always performers; a notable harpsichordist-composer of the Baroque era was **Elizabeth-Claude Jacquet** (1667–1729), a Mozart-style prodigy who was sponsored by Louis XIV himself. Famous as a harpsichordist, she composed music of all kinds, including an opera that was put on at the forerunner of the Paris Opéra—then as now the grandest venue for opera in Europe.

There was no respectability problem with Jacquet; by the time she was seventeen she was married to an organist, one Marin de la Guerre, whose name is usually hyphenated with hers.

Just how were tunes introduced? There were many ways. The last movement of a Bach cantata is usually a single hymn stanza sung straight through, in much the same simple way as the congregation would sing it, but with the orchestra playing and a homophonic harmonization of the melody added.

Longer cantata movements present the individual lines or phrases of the chorale one by one, with gaps in between them. Newly composed music by Bach runs on continuously, both during the chorale phrases (that is, in counterpoint with them) and during the gaps. In such a gapped chorale, the chorale melody is delivered in spurts. It can be sung, or it can be played by one prominent instrument—an oboe, say, or a trumpet—while the continuous music goes along in the other instruments and/or voices.

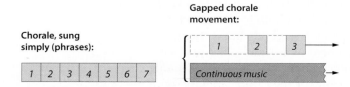

Chorale, sung simply (phrases):

| 1 | 2 | 3 | 4 | 5 | 6 | 7 |

Gapped chorale movement:

| 1 | 2 | 3 |

Continuous music

Johann Sebastian Bach (1685–1750), Cantata No. 4, "Christ lag in Todesbanden" (1707)

In his positions as an organist and cantor, Bach made multiple settings of many hymns. We will study just one of his settings of the Easter chorale "Christ lag in Todesbanden" (Christ Lay in Death's Dark Prison).

This rugged old tune, given below in its entirety, had been fitted with even more rugged words by Martin Luther himself, in 1524. The seven stanzas of the chorale, each ending with "Hallelujah!," tell in vivid language of mankind's struggle with Death and the victory achieved through Christ's sacrifice. The fact that this hymn is in the minor mode throws a tough, sober shadow over all the rejoicing; the mood is unforgettable.

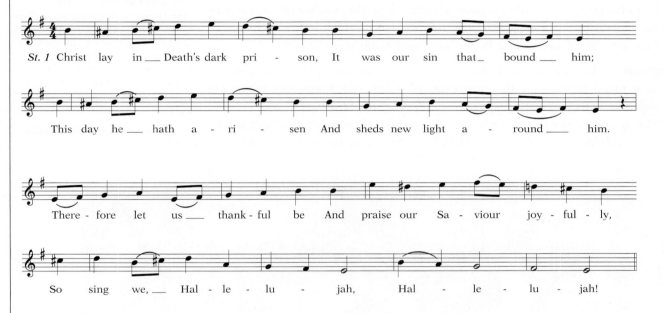

The cantata based on "Christ lag in Todesbanden," one of Bach's earliest, employs simple forces: voices and a string orchestra, with continuo. The words of the seven movements are Martin Luther's words of the seven stanzas of the famous Easter chorale.

Bach set these seven stanzas with a sharp eye (or ear) for symmetry. Not all of the voices sing in all of the stanzas. The following diagram tallies the voices that sing in each one, with the shading indicating which voices sing the chorale melody itself.

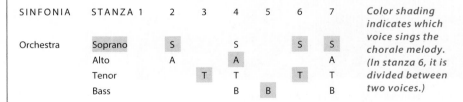

After a short orchestral prelude—Bach calls it "sinfonia," or symphony—all the stanzas except the last are set as gapped chorales of some sort.

Stanza 3   The tenor sings the gapped chorale tune; follow him along with the music on page 147. Accompanied by the continuo (played on the organ), a violin plays an urgent melody at both ends of the piece and in the gaps between the lines. At the word *nichts* ("nothing") the music comes to a wrenching stop and a slowdown, a quite astonishing effect. Then the violin starts up again as though nothing had happened. The sudden absence of music tells us what is left of Death's power: *nichts*, zilch!

Stanza 4   Here it is the alto (doubled by organ) that sings the gapped chorale tune, more slowly than the tenor of stanza 3. The continuous music is assigned to the other voices singing faster imitative polyphony to the same words. Their music always uses fragments of the chorale melody; in this way Bach works the old chorale even into his own, newly composed music. Perhaps all this busy imitative polyphony makes a good illustration of the warfare described with such gusto in this stanza. Perhaps, too, the jaunty rhythm at *Ein Spott* can indeed be heard as mocking Death, who has lost his sting.

Stanza 7   No longer gapped, this is a straightforward presentation of the hymn as it might be sung by the congregation. Bach's rich harmonies below the soprano melody are sung by the lower voices, doubled by the instruments. The cantata comes to a restful conclusion at last, as the text turns from battles to the confidence of faith. Even "Hallelujah!" can now be uttered simply.

"When Bach seated himself at the organ, he used to choose some theme and treat it in all the various forms of organ composition. First, he used this theme for a prelude and fugue, with the full organ. Then he showed his art of using the stops for a trio, quartet, etc., on the same theme. Afterwards followed a chorale, the melody of which was playfully surrounded by the same theme in three or four contrapuntal parts."

Bach the improviser, from the earliest biography, 1802

Church organs of Bach's time were not only the largest and loudest musical instruments in existence; they often numbered among the most beautiful. The ornament on this organ, from a pilgrimage church in southern Germany, seems to complete the tracery on the grillwork in front of it and the designs on the columns to either side. *Egon Bümsch/imagebrok/imagebroker.net/SuperStock.*

11	*Stanza 3:* **Jesus Christus, Gottes Sohn,**	Jesus Christ, the Son of God,
	An unser Statt ist kommen,	Has come on our behalf,
	Und hat die Sünde weggetan,	And has done away with our sins,
	Damit den Tod genommen	Thereby robbing Death
	All' sein Recht und sein' Gewalt;	Of all his power and might;
	Da bleibet *nichts* — denn Tod's Gestalt;	There remains nothing but Death's image;
	Den Stach'l hat er verloren.	He has lost his sting.
	Hallelujah!	Hallelujah!
12	*Stanza 4:* **Es war ein wunderlicher Krieg,**	It was a marvelous war
	Da Tod und Leben rungen;	Where Death and Life battled.
	Das Leben da behielt das Sieg,	Life gained the victory;
	Es hat den Tod verschlungen.	It swallowed up Death.
	Die Schrift hat verkündiget das	Scripture has proclaimed
	Wie ein Tod den andern frass;	How one Death gobbled up the other;
	Ein Spott aus dem Tod ist worden.	Death became a mockery.
	Hallelujah!	Hallelujah!
13	*Stanza 7:* **Wir essen und leben wohl**	We eat and live fitly
	Im rechten Osterfladen.	On the true unleavened bread of Passover;
	Der alter Sauerteig nicht soll	The old yeast shall not
	Sein bei dem Wort der Gnaden.	Contaminate the word of grace.
	Christus will die Koste sein	Christ alone will be the food
	Und speisen die Seel' allein,	To feed the soul:
	Der Glaub' will keins andern leben.	Faith will live on nothing else.
	Hallelujah!	Hallelujah!

GOALS FOR REVIEW

▶   to follow late Baroque vocal music into theater and church

▶   to understand the dichotomy of recitative and aria in late Baroque opera

▶   to listen for the standardized form of late Baroque opera arias: da capo form

▶   to distinguish opera from oratorio and get to know Handel's *Messiah*

▶   to hear the difference between accompanied and *secco* recitative

▶   to understand and listen to the structure of a church cantata by Bach

▶   to survey the life and works of George Frideric Handel

macmillanhighered.com/listen8e
Listening Quiz for Chapter 11
Reading Quiz for Chapter 11

Music and the Enlightenment

CHAPTER

12

In the second part of the eighteenth century, a new musical style emerged in Europe. Called the Classical style, it had important pioneers in Italy and northern Germany; one of them was Carl Philipp Emanuel Bach, the eldest son of Johann Sebastian, working in Berlin. But the Classical style was developed particularly by composers active in Vienna, capital of Austria. Here conditions seem to have been ideal for music. Geographically, Austria stands at the crossroads of four other musical nations—Germany, Bohemia (now in the Czech Republic), Hungary, and Italy—and Vienna was also central in political terms. As the capital of the mighty Hapsburg empire, Vienna was plunged into every European conflict of the time and exposed to every new cultural and intellectual current.

Vienna flourished under the Hapsburg empress Maria Theresa and emperor Joseph II. Maria Theresa was one of Europe's most powerful monarchs over a period of forty years, and Joseph was one of the most enlightened. During his short but golden reign from 1780 to 1790, Joseph emancipated the peasantry, furthered education, and reduced the power of the clergy; he supported music and literature with his patronage and encouraged a free press. In a city of only 150,000 people, it is said there were 300 newspapers and journals during Joseph's reign, representing every shade of opinion.

In this liberal atmosphere, Franz Joseph Haydn of nearby Eisenstadt became recognized as Europe's leading composer; his symphonies were commissioned from far-off Paris and London. The young Wolfgang Amadeus Mozart was drawn to the capital in 1781 from Salzburg, a hundred miles to the west, to spend his brilliant last decade there. And in 1792 a young musician from the other end of Germany, who had composed a long cantata mourning Emperor Joseph's death, decided to come to this great musical center to launch his career. His name was Ludwig van Beethoven.

1 | The Enlightenment and Music

To describe Joseph II as an "enlightened" ruler is both to commend him and also to locate him in European intellectual history. Like a number of other rulers of the time, Joseph II was strongly influenced by an important intellectual movement of the eighteenth century known as the Enlightenment. This movement also helped to define the music that flourished under his reign.

Centered in France, the Enlightenment had strong roots in British philosophy and strong offshoots in Germany and Austria. Its original source was the faith in reason that led to the great scientific discoveries of the Baroque period, from Galileo to Newton and Leibniz. Now, however, the emphasis moved away from the purely intellectual and scientific toward the social sphere. People were less intent on controlling natural forces by science than on turning these forces to human benefit. People also began to apply the same intelligence that solved scientific problems to problems of public morality, education, and politics.

Social injustice came under especially strong fire in the eighteenth century; so did established religion. For the first time in European history, religion ceased to be an overriding force in many people's minds. There were currents of agnosticism and even outright atheism—to the outrage of the English poet and mystic William Blake:

> Mock on, mock on, Voltaire, Rousseau:
> Mock on, mock on, 'tis all in vain!
> You throw the sand against the wind,
> And the wind blows it back again.

The two French philosophers named by Blake are always mentioned in connection with the Enlightenment: François Marie Arouet, who wrote under the pen name Voltaire (1694–1778), tireless satirist and campaigner for justice and reason, and the younger, more radical, more disturbing Jean-Jacques Rousseau (1712–1778). Rousseau is one of the few major figures of European philosophy who had a direct effect on the history of music, as we shall see.

Voltaire, by Jean-Antoine Houdon (1740–1828), master sculptor of the neo-Roman busts that were much favored at the time. (All the other portrait busts in this chapter are also by Houdon.) *Bibliothèque de la Comedie Française, Paris, France — Peter Willi/Bridgeman Images.*

The phrase *Viennese Classical style* brings to mind Haydn, Mozart, and Beethoven; each of them came to the capital city from other, smaller centers.

In the Classical era, lighter entertainments took over the stage, in place of the heavy drama characteristic of the Baroque. Compare this picture (a London ballet of 1791) with the opera seria shown on page 106. Even the attitudes and attentions of this audience seem more varied and playful than those of the Baroque audience. (The box to the far right is particularly instructive!) *London Metropolitan Archives, City of London/The Bridgeman Art Library.*

"The Pursuit of Happiness"

"Life, liberty, and the pursuit of happiness": The last of these three famous rights, too, was very much of its time. One can imagine the medieval barons who forced King John to accept the Magna Carta insisting on life and liberty, of a sort, but it would never have occurred to them to demand happiness as a self-evident right for all. Voltaire and Rousseau fought passionately for social justice so that people might live good lives according to their own convictions.

The eighteenth century was an age of good living, then, an age that valued intelligence, wit, and sensitivity. The age cultivated elegant conversation, the social arts, and hedonism. One of its inventions was the salon—half party, half seminar: a regular gathering in a fashionable lady's home where notables would discuss books, music, art, and ideas. Another innovation of the time was the coffeehouse. Another was the public concert.

In political terms, the Enlightenment has special resonance for America, for it was also the occasion for our first great contribution to Western civilization. In colonial days, the austere Puritan spirit was hardly in step with the growing secularization of European society, but the Declaration of Independence and the Federalist Papers proved to be the finest flowers of Enlightenment idealism. The notion that a new state could be founded on rational principles, set down on a piece of paper, and agreed to by men of goodwill and intelligence—this could only

Thomas Jefferson. *The Bridgeman Art Library.*

have emerged under the influence of the political and philosophical writings of the eighteenth century.

Art and Entertainment

Entertainment, for most people, contributes to the good life—though certainly Thomas Jefferson was thinking of more than entertainment when he wrote of "the pursuit of happiness." However, the pursuit of entertainment was not something that the eighteenth century looked down upon at all. Art was expected to *please* rather than to instruct, impress, or even express, as had been the case in the Baroque era. The result of this attitude is evident in the style of all the arts in the eighteenth century.

For a time at midcentury a light and often frothy style known as *Rococo* was fashionable in painting, decoration, furniture, and so on. Our illustration—a ceramic plaque—catches the spirit of this entertainment art with special charm. Wreathed in leaves that fit in with the border, two well-dressed court gentlemen cavort in an ideal countryside; one plays the flute while the other dances. The silly subject, the feathery designs on the frame, even the pretty rim itself, are all characteristic of the light art of the Rococo.

A French Rococo ceramic plaque. *Bridgeman — Giraudon/Art Resource, NY.*

Music of the mid-eighteenth century, just before the formation of the Viennese Classical style, was also very light—charming at best, but often frivolous. A genre that was typical of the time was the **divertimento**, a piece designed to divert, amuse, and entertain. Elegant figurines of musicians and ornamented music boxes, playing little tunes, were extremely popular.

The Viennese Classical music of Haydn and Mozart that we will study is far from this light style, yet these composers never put pen to paper without every expectation that their audiences were going to be "pleased." Every historical era, of course, has had its entertainment music. But only in the Classical era was great music of the highest quality put forth quite frankly and plainly as entertainment.

Jean-Jacques Rousseau and Opera

Jean-Jacques Rousseau was a dazzlingly many-sided figure—acclaimed novelist, autobiographer, philosopher, fiery publicist, and self-taught composer, who made his living for many years as a music copyist. He was Europe's first "alienated intellectual," forever blasting the social institutions of his day as stifling to the individual. "Natural man," he proclaimed, was born good but corrupted by civilization. This conviction, incidentally, led Rousseau to idealize the so-called primitive peoples in the Americas, peoples whom Europeans had colonized and enslaved for over two hundred years. If Rousseau had lived longer, we can be sure he would have joined those who denounced the double standard of the Founders in demanding liberty for whites but not for blacks.

Rousseau viewed music as more "natural," and therefore more basic and archaic, than speech. So he launched a great attack on the aristocratic music of the late Baroque era. This meant attacking opera, the most important, extended, and glamorous musical genre of the time. For Rousseau, the complicated plots

Benjamin Franklin, who sat for Houdon during a stay in Paris, brought the sculptor back home to portray Washington, Jefferson, Lafayette, and Robert Fulton, the steamboat inventor. *Musée des Beaux-Arts, Orléans, France/Roger-Viollet, Paris/The Bridgeman Art Library.*

of Baroque operas were as impossibly artificial as their complicated music. He demanded a kind of opera that would portray real people in actual life—simple people, close to nature, singing natural music.

In fact, short comic operas filling this prescription were already being developed in Italy, and Rousseau pounced on one that was playing in Paris. In G. B. Pergolesi's *La serva padrona* (*The Maid as Mistress,* 1733), the music is lively and catchy, with no elaborate coloratura singing, rich harmonies, or exaggerated emotional outpourings. The plot is little more than one big joke. Rousseau not only praised this little piece to the skies but also wrote an opera of his own that was just as slight—and almost as popular.

Thanks to Pergolesi and Rousseau—and to Mozart—comic opera became the most progressive operatic form of the later part of the century. It dealt not with Roman emperors and their idealized noble sentiments, but with contemporary middle- and lower-class figures expressing everyday feelings in a relatively vivid and natural way. *Opera buffa,* as Italian comic opera was called, is discussed on pages 189–90.

The Novel

This new kind of opera can be compared to the most important new literary genre that grew up at the same time. This was the novel, which—together with the symphony—counts as the Enlightenment's greatest artistic legacy to more recent times.

Precursors of the novel go back to ancient Rome, but the genre did not really capture the European imagination until around 1750. Among the best-known early novels are Henry Fielding's *Tom Jones,* the tale of a rather ordinary young man and his adventures in town and country, and Samuel Richardson's *Pamela,* a domestic drama that manages to be sexually explicit, sentimental, and moralistic all at the same time. Rousseau wrote several very popular novels; Voltaire wrote *Candide.* At the end of the century, Jane Austen began her subtle explorations of the social forces at work on the hearts of her very sensitive (and sensible) characters in novels such as *Pride and Prejudice, Emma, Persuasion,* and others. These novels are still alive and well in Hollywood and on PBS.

Sharp, realistic observation of contemporary life and sensitive depiction of feeling—these are the ideals shared by late eighteenth-century opera and the novel. Within a few years of their publication, both *Tom Jones* and *Pamela* were turned into major operas, one French, the other Italian.

In Mozart, opera buffa found a master equal to Jane Austen in the sensitive response to feeling and action. In his opera *Don Giovanni,* for example, the three women involved with the hero—the coquettish country girl, Zerlina; the steely aristocrat, Donna Anna; and the sentimental Donna Elvira—are depicted and distinguished from one another in music with the greatest psychological insight and sympathy. One can come to feel that the same qualities are reflected in Mozart's symphonies and concertos.

2 | The Rise of Concerts

A far-reaching development in the sociology and economics of music was the rise of public concerts. Occasional concerts had been given before, in taverns, private homes, palaces, and theaters, but it was only in the middle of the eighteenth century that they became a significant force in musical life. Concert series, financed by subscription, were put on by the forerunners of today's promoters. Concerts for the benefit of charity were set up on a regular basis as major society events.

In 1748 Europe's first hall designed especially for concerts was built in a college town, Oxford. Still in use, the Holywell Music Room holds about 150 people.

Jean-Jacques Rousseau. *Musée Lambinet, Versailles, France/Lauros/Giraudon/The Bridgeman Art Library.*

Rousseau himself composed a very successful opera of the uncomplicated kind he recommended. Pictured is a scene from Rousseau's *Le Devin du Village* (The Village Soothsayer), 1752. *Bibliothèque des Arts Décoratifs, Paris, France/Archives Charmet/The Bridgeman Art Library.*

Music of all kinds was presented at these new public concerts. One major series—the Parisian *Concert spirituel*, founded in 1725—started out with sacred vocal music. But orchestral music was the staple, and the importance of concerts lay mainly in the impetus they gave to the composition of symphonies and concertos. For there were, after all, other public forums for church music (churches) and opera (opera houses). Now purely orchestral music, too, moved into the public domain, and its importance and prestige grew rapidly.

However, the livelihood of musicians still depended principally on court patronage, the opera house, and the church (see page 105). Concerts were certainly a factor in the careers of both of the masters of Classical style already mentioned: Haydn wrote his last symphonies, called the *London* symphonies, for concerts on two celebrity tours to that city, and Mozart wrote most of his piano concertos—among his greatest works—for concerts he himself put on in Vienna. But public concerts were a resource that Haydn did not draw upon much until the end of his long life, and they were not a reliable enough resource, alas, to sustain Mozart.

Michael Angelo Rooker (1743–1801) spent much of his career painting scene backdrops for the Haymarket Theater in London. Here he portrays an episode from Henry Fielding's novel *Tom Jones*, a wildly popular comedy of (sometimes scandalous) manners. *Eileen Tweedy/ The Art Archive at Art Resource, NY.*

3 | Style Features of Classical Music

In discussing the musical style of the late Baroque period, we started with a single guiding concept. There is a thorough, even rigorous, quality in the ways early eighteenth-century composers treated almost all aspects of music, and this quality seems to underpin the expressive gestures of grandeur and overstatement that are characteristic of the Baroque.

Classical music cannot be discussed quite as easily as this. We have to keep two concepts in mind to understand it, concepts that were constantly on the lips of men and women of the time. One was "natural," and the other was "pleasing variety." In the late eighteenth century, it was taken for granted that these two artistic ideals went hand in hand and provided mutual support.

Today we can see that sometimes they pulled in opposite directions. For although "variety" was called on to ward off boredom, it was also an invitation to complexity, and complexity would seem to run counter to "natural" simplicity and clarity. In any case, in Classical music one or the other—and sometimes both—of these qualities can be traced in all the elements of musical technique: in rhythm, dynamics, tone color, melody, texture, and form. A new expressive quality developed in this music as a result of its new technique.

Rhythm

Perhaps the most striking change in music between the Baroque and Classical periods came in rhythm. In this area the artistic ideal of "pleasing variety" reigned supreme. The unvarying rhythms of Baroque music came to be regarded as obvious and boring.

Classical music is highly flexible in rhythm. Throughout a single movement, the tempo and meter remain constant, but the rhythms of the various themes tend to differ in both obvious and subtle ways. In the first movement of Mozart's Symphony in G Minor, for example, the first theme moves almost entirely in eighth notes

For the Benefit of Mr. F L A G G.
This Evening,
A public CONCERT of
Vocal and Instrumental MUSIC,
Will be performed at Concert Hall in Queen-street.
The Vocal part to be performed by Four Voices, and to conclude with the BRITISH GRENADIERS.——N. B. *TICKETS* to be had at the Printers, or at the London Bookstore, at *HALF a DOLLAR* each.——To begin precisely at half after seven.
*** The last Concert this Season.

The rise of concerts: With only around 15,000 inhabitants, pre-Revolutionary Boston already had a concert hall and a concert promoter (bandmaster Josiah Flagg). This advertisement is from the *Boston Chronicle* of 1769.

and quarters, whereas the second theme is marked by longer notes and shorter ones—dotted half notes and sixteenths.

Audiences wanted variety in music; composers responded by refining the rhythmic differences between themes and other musical sections, so that the differences sound like more than differences—they sound like real contrasts. The music may gradually increase or decrease its rhythmic energy, stop suddenly, press forward by fits and starts, or glide by smoothly. All this gives the sense that Classical music is moving in a less predictable, more interesting, and often more exciting way than Baroque music does.

First theme

Second theme

Dynamics

Variety and flexibility were also introduced into dynamics. Passages were now conceived more specifically than before as loud, soft, very loud, and so on, and marked *f*, *p*, *ff*, etc,. by composers accordingly. Composers made variety in dynamics clearly perceptible and, we must suppose, "pleasing."

Furthermore, instead of using the steady dynamics of the previous period, composers now worked extensively with gradations of volume. The words for growing louder (*crescendo*) and growing softer (*diminuendo*) first came into general use in the Classical period. Orchestras of the mid-eighteenth century were the first to practice long crescendos, which, we are told, caused audiences to rise up from their seats in excitement.

A clear sign of the times was the rise in popularity of the piano, at the expense of the ever-present harpsichord of the Baroque era. The older instrument could manage only one sound level (or at best a few sound levels, thanks to more than one set of strings). The new pianoforte could produce a continuous range of dynamics from soft to loud; the name means "soft-loud" in Italian. It attracted composers because they wanted their keyboard instruments to have the same flexibility in dynamics that they were teaching to their orchestras.

Tone Color: The Classical Orchestra

Classical composers also devoted increasing attention to tone color. The clearest sign of this was the emergence of the Classical orchestra. The orchestra standardized in this period formed the basis of the symphony orchestra of later times.

The heart of the Classical orchestra was still (as in the Baroque orchestra) a group of stringed instruments: violins, divided into two groups, first violins and second violins; violas; and cellos, with a few basses playing the same music as the cellos an octave lower. As we saw on pages 108–09, there was a basic Baroque orchestra consisting of just these instruments plus the continuo, and various other possibilities, including the festive Baroque orchestra:

THE BAROQUE ORCHESTRA

STRINGS	KEYBOARD
Violins (divided into two groups, called violins 1 and violins 2)	Harpsichord or organ
Violas	
Cellos	
Bass (playing the same music as the cellos an octave lower)	

THE FESTIVE BAROQUE ORCHESTRA

STRINGS	WOODWINDS	BRASS	PERCUSSION	KEYBOARD
Violins 1	2 Oboes	3 Trumpets	2 Timpani (kettledrums)	Harpsichord or organ
Violins 2	1 Bassoon			
Violas				
Cellos				
Bass				

In the Classical orchestra, however, the woodwind and brass instruments were given clearly defined, regular roles. With the strings as a framework, woodwind instruments were added: in the high range, pairs of flutes, oboes, and (a bit later) clarinets; in the low, bassoons. These instruments provided "pleasing variety" by playing certain melodies and other passages; each of the woodwinds contributed its own intriguing tone color or timbre. They also strengthened the strings in loud sections.

THE CLASSICAL ORCHESTRA

STRINGS	WOODWINDS	BRASS	PERCUSSION
Violins 1	2 Flutes	2 French horns	2 Timpani (kettledrums)
Violins 2	2 Oboes	2 Trumpets*	
Violas	2 Clarinets*		
Cellos	2 Bassoons		
Basses	*Optional	*Optional	

Brass instruments were added in the middle range. The function of French horns and trumpets was mainly to provide solid support for the main harmonies, especially at points such as cadences, when the harmonies needed to be made particularly clear. But sometimes they played lively (short) solos. The only regular percussion instruments used were two timpani, which generally played along with the brass.

The great advance in the orchestra from the Baroque to the Classical era was in flexibility—flexibility in tone color and also in rhythm and dynamics. The orchestra now became the most varied and versatile musical resource that composers could employ, as well as the grandest.

Domestic music making in the eighteenth century: a group portrait by Johann Zoffany (1733–1810), one of many fashionable painters in Britain (and British India). It was not uncommon for members of the gentry—including, here, an earl—to order pictures showing off their musical accomplishments. *Yale Center for British Art, Paul Mellon Collection, USA/The Bridgeman Art Library.*

Melody: Tunes

The Enlightenment ideal of "pleasing variety" was a secondary issue when it came to Classical melody. Rather the demand was for plainness, for relief from the complex, richly ornamented lines of the Baroque period. When people at the time demanded "natural" melodies, what they meant were tunes: uncomplicated, singable melodies with clear phrases (and not too many of them), melodies with easily grasped parallelisms and balances.

In their move toward melodic simplicity, composers of the Classical period moved much closer to popular music, even folk music, than their Baroque predecessors had done. There is a definite popular lilt in Haydn's music that people have traced to the Croatian folk melodies he heard as a child. Short tunes—or, more often, attractive little phrases that sound as though they might easily grow into tunes—are heard again and again in Classical symphonies and quartets. Tunes are not the only melodic material to be heard in these works, as we will see in a moment. Nevertheless, by comparison with a Baroque concerto, a Classical symphony leaves listeners with a good deal more to hum or whistle as they leave the concert.

Indeed, entire tunes were often worked into larger compositions. For example, variation form (theme and variations) grew popular both for separate pieces improvised by virtuosos and for movements in multimovement genres. Haydn wrote variations on a tune of his devising that would later become the German national anthem, and Mozart wrote variations on "Twinkle, Twinkle, Little Star," in its original French version, "Ah vous dirai-je, maman" (Oh mama, I must tell you). Occasionally, popular songs were even introduced into symphonies. There is a contemporary opera tune in Mozart's "Jupiter" Symphony, the last he composed, and one of his greatest.

Texture: Homophony

The predominant texture of Classical music is homophonic. In Classical compositions, melodies are regularly heard with a straightforward harmonic accompaniment in chords, without counterpoint and without even a melodic-sounding bass line. Again, this was thought (with some reason) to be a more "natural," clearer way of presenting a melody than polyphony.

All this made, and still makes, for easy listening. The opening of Mozart's famous Symphony No. 40 in G Minor proclaims the new sonorous world of the late eighteenth century:

A single quiet chord regrouped and repeated by the violas, the plainest sort of bass support below, and above them all a plaintive melody in the violins—this simple, sharply polarized texture becomes typical of the new style.

Homophony or melody with harmony was not, however, merely a negative reaction to what people of the time saw as the heavy, pedantic complexities of Baroque counterpoint. It was also a positive move in the direction of sensitivity.

When composers found that they were not always occupied in fitting contrapuntal parts to their melodies, they also discovered that they could handle other elements of music with more "pleasing variety." In particular, a new sensitivity developed to harmony for its own sake.

One aspect of this development was a desire to specify harmonies more precisely than in the Baroque era. The first thing to go was the continuo, which had spread its unspecified (because improvised) chord patterns over nearly all Baroque music. Classical composers, newly alert to the sonorous quality of a particular chord, wanted it spaced and distributed among various instruments just so. They refused to allow a continuo player to obscure the chord with unpredictable extra notes and rhythms.

It may seem paradoxical, then, but the thrust toward simplicity in texture and melody led through the back door to increased subtlety in other areas, especially in rhythm and in harmony.

Classical Counterpoint

The rise of homophony in the Classical period represents a major turnaround in musical technique, for though Baroque composers wrote some homophonic pieces, as we have seen, the predominant texture of their music was polyphonic.

Yet it is not the way of history to abandon important resources of the past completely. Classical composers rejected Baroque music, but they cautiously retained the basic principle of counterpoint. They were able to do this by refining it into a more delicate, unobtrusive kind of counterpoint than that of the Baroque era. And there was a sharper awareness now of counterpoint's expressive possibilities. In a texture that was mostly "natural" and homophonic, counterpoint attracted special attention; this texture could be used to create the impression of tension, of one line rubbing against another. The more intense, artificial texture of polyphony stood out against natural homophonic texture.

Hence, as we will see in the next chapter, the section in Classical sonata form called the development section, whose basic function is to build up tension, typically involves contrapuntal textures. Sonata form was the most important musical form of the time, and so counterpoint was often heard.

4 | Form in Classical Music

How can a piece of music be extended through a considerable span of time when listeners expect everything to be natural, simple, and easily understood? This was the problem of musical form that composers of the Viennese Classical era faced. They arrived at a solution of considerable elegance and power, involving several elements.

Repetitions and Cadences

First, themes in Classical music tend to be *repeated* immediately after their first appearance, so that listeners can easily get to know them. (In earlier music, this happened only in dance music, as a general rule.) Later in the piece, those same themes are repeated again.

Second, themes are *led into* in a very distinctive manner. The music features prominent transitional passages that do not have much melodic profile, only a sense of urgency about arriving someplace—the place where the real theme will be presented (and probably presented twice).

Third, after themes have been played, they are typically *closed off* just as distinctly. Often there are quite long passages consisting of cadences repeated two, three, or more times, as though to assure the listener that one musical idea is over and another is coming up. Composers would devise little cadential phrases, often with minimal melodic interest, that could be repeated and thus allow for such multiple cadences.

Multiple cadences are a characteristic and easily recognizable feature of Classical music, particularly, of course, at the very ends of movements. We will hear examples of this in Haydn, Mozart, and—with special force—in Beethoven.

Classical Forms

A third feature designed to cope with the problem of musical form in Classical music is perhaps the most far-reaching. Composers and their audiences came to rely on a limited number of *forms,* or standard formal patterns, the most important of which are *sonata form, minuet form, rondo form,* and *theme and variations form.*

These provided a commonly understood frame of reference for composing music and appreciating it. Broadly speaking, after listening for just a short time to some new piece, an eighteenth-century music lover could always tell what sort of themes and keys it would include, when they would return, and about how long the piece would last. This frame of reference is not so obvious today, so the four Classical forms just mentioned will be taken up in some detail in Chapter 13.

The repetitions, self-conscious transitions, and emphatic cadences that are so characteristic of the Classical style all help clarify the forms. And the forms themselves were a special necessity at a time when composers were filling their compositions with contrasts of all kinds. It is a mark of the aesthetic success of Classical music that the contrasts don't sound too drastic, because the forms control and, in effect, tame them. The seemingly inexhaustible emotional range of Classical music is directly proportional to the extent of those contrasts, on the one hand, and, on the other, to the elegance of their control by musical form.

Houdon's most informal portrait bust: his wife. *Photo: Gerard Blot. Musée du Louvre, Paris, France © RMN-Grand Palais/Art Resource, NY.*

GOALS FOR REVIEW

▶ to understand the impact of the Enlightenment on music in the late eighteenth century

▶ to witness the rise of public concerts and of the modern orchestra

▶ to contrast stylistic features of late Baroque music and Classical music

▶ to think about general features of form in Classical music

---

macmillanhighered.com/listen8e
Reading Quiz for Chapter 12

The Symphony

The genres of music that arose in the Classical period, replacing those of the Baroque era, continued to hold their own in the nineteenth century, and all the way through the first half of the twentieth. Indeed, they are still in use today, at least in the sense that their names are still encountered. Not surprisingly, the style, the number of movements, and the forms employed today bear little relation to norms from two hundred and more years ago. But it is still true that if you compose a large, impressive concert piece for orchestra, the best way to convey that fact to conductors, musicians, and audiences is to name it a **symphony**.

One reason for the prominence of the symphony in the Classical era is its close association with a crucial development in the sociology of music, discussed in Chapter 12: the growth of public concerts. As concerts became more and more frequent, people felt a need for some genre that would make an effective, substantial focus for these occasions. Symphonies answered the need—and in turn required more variety and flexibility of sound than anything orchestras of the early eighteenth century could provide. The symphony spurred a major technical development within music, the evolution of the Classical orchestra (see page 156).

The symphony, then, is rightly viewed as the crowning achievement of Viennese Classical music—but when any musician acknowledges this, he or she wants to add a plea in the same breath: Please don't forget the other genres that grew up alongside the symphony, for in these genres you will find music just as beautiful, music that has become for us just as precious. In Chapter 14 we study the sonata, the Classical concerto, the string quartet, and—in the field of opera—Italian *opera buffa* (comic opera).

1 | The Movements of the Symphony

As with Baroque genres, works in the Classical period consist of several movements, which contrast in tempo and are composed in different musical forms. Compare the following brief description of the four movements of a typical symphony with the description given on page 115 for the Baroque concerto:

- The *first* movement of a symphony is a substantial piece in fast or moderate tempo, written in the most important new form, of the time, sonata form, which we will study in the next section. Sometimes this fast music is preceded by a short but solemn *introduction* in a slower tempo.

- The *second* movement strikes an obvious contrast with the first by its slow tempo and its quiet mood. It can assume a variety of forms.

- The *third* movement contrasts in another way, by its persistent dance rhythms: It is always a minuet and trio. A minuet is a moderately paced dance in triple meter, inherited from the Baroque period. See page 132.

- The *fourth*, closing movement is fast again—if anything, faster than the first. It may be in sonata form, like the first movement, though rondo is also a common choice.

If we compare the symphony table with a parallel table for the Baroque concerto, both below, we see many differences, but also certain similarities. The forms used for the movements are entirely different, and there is the extra minuet. However, in the broadest terms, the sequence from *fast/complex* to *slow/quiet* to *fast/brilliant* is the same.

MOVEMENTS OF THE SYMPHONY

	OPENING MOVEMENT	SLOW MOVEMENT	MINUET (WITH TRIO)	CLOSING MOVEMENT
Tempo	Fast/Moderate	Slow/very slow	Moderate	Fast/very fast
Form	Sonata form (sometimes preceded by a slow introduction)	Sonata form, variations, rondo form, or other	Minuet form	Sonata form or rondo form

MOVEMENTS OF THE BAROQUE CONCERTO

	OPENING MOVEMENT	SLOW MOVEMENT	CLOSING MOVEMENT
Tempo	Fast/Moderate	Slow/very slow	Fast/very fast
Form	Ritornello form	No standard form	Ritornello form

A word of caution: This symphony table represents the norm, but there are always exceptions. Some famous ones are Mozart's *Prague* Symphony, lacking a minuet, and Haydn's *Farewell* Symphony, with an extra slow movement—five movements in all. (There were exceptions also to the Baroque scheme: Bach's *Brandenburg* Concerto No. 1 has two dance movements added to the usual three for the concerto.)

2 | Sonata Form

A new form developed at this time, called **sonata form**, is closely associated with the symphony—even though it turns up in much other music in other genres. The opening movement of every symphony is in sonata form, and this movement counts as the intellectual and emotional core of the whole work. Many Classical works have two or even three movements in this same form.

The reason for this wide use, perhaps, was that more than any other form, sonata form exploited what was the overriding interest of Classical composers. Their interest was in contrasts of every kind—especially contrast of musical themes and contrast of key, or tonality. Composers found that sonata form enabled a special flexibility of expression. They could use it for forceful, brilliant, pathetic, even tragic opening movements, gentle or dreamy slow movements, and lively, often humorous closing movements.

Viewed on the highest level, sonata form is simple enough—a very large-scale example of **A B A′** form, usually with repetitions: |: **A** :||: **B A′** :| or |: **A** :|| **B A′**. What is less simple, and what makes sonata form different from other **A B A** forms, is the nature and the function of the musical material in each letter section. This is implied by the special names given to them: **A** is called the *exposition*, **B** the *development*, and **A′** the *recapitulation*. What do these terms signify?

Exposition (A)

The **exposition** of a sonata-form movement is a large, diverse section of music in which the basic material of the movement is presented (or "exposed"). (It is not related to the opening section of a fugue, though they share the same name; see page 128.) The material of a sonata-form exposition consists of the following elements:

• To begin, a main theme is presented in the first key, the home or tonic key (see page 31; this key is the key of the piece as a whole—in Mozart's Symphony in G Minor, the tonic is G minor). This **first theme** may be a tune, a group of small phrases that sound as though they might grow into a tune, or just a motive or two (see page 25) with a memorable rhythmic character.

• After the first theme is firmly established, often with the help of a repetition, there is a change in key, or *modulation*. The subsection of the exposition that accomplishes this change is called the **bridge**, or the *transition*.

The modulation in the bridge is an essential feature (even *the* essential feature) that gives sonata form its sense of dynamic forward movement. With a little experience, it is not hard to hear the contrast of key and sense the dynamism, for the idea is not to make the crucial modulation sound too smooth.

Freemasonry in the eighteenth century was a high-minded society of intellectuals and aristocrats, promulgating ideas that were often radical. "Enlightened" emperor Joseph II tolerated them, barely. Mozart joined the group and wrote music for their secret meetings; this extraordinary painting shows him seated at the far right. *Wien Museum Karlsplatz, Vienna, Austria/The Bridgeman Art Library.*

There has to be some tension in the way the new themes, now to be introduced, "sit" in the new key.

- Next comes a group of themes or other musical ideas in the new key, called the **second group**. At least some of these new themes contrast with the first theme in melody, rhythm, dynamics, and so on, as well as in key. Usually one new theme stands out by its melodious quality; this is called the **second theme**.

- The last theme in the second group, the **cadence theme**, or *closing theme,* is constructed to make a solid ending prior to a full stop and the big repeat. The very end of the exposition is marked by a loud series of repeated cadences, as though the composer wanted listeners to know exactly where they are in the form. This exposition (**A**) section is usually repeated.

Development (B)

All this musical variety is built into the exposition. The following section, the **development**, heightens the tensions set up by the contrasting themes and keys of the exposition. The themes are "developed" by being broken up, recombined, reorchestrated, extended, and in general shown in unexpected and often exciting new contexts. Most development sections use counterpoint to create a sense of breakup and turmoil.

This section moves around restlessly from key to key. Its modulations can often be easily heard. The music sounds unstable and less clearly oriented than in the exposition.

After considerable tension has been built up, the last modulation of the development section returns to the first key. The passage that accomplishes this, called the **retransition**, has the function of relieving the tension and creating a sense of expectancy for the recapitulation to come. Classical composers were amazingly inventive in finding ways to make this crucial juncture of the form seem fresh, logical, and inevitable.

Recapitulation (A′)

With a real sense of relief or resolution, we now hear the first theme again, followed by all the other themes and other elements of the exposition. There may be minor changes, but in principle everything comes back in its original order. Hence the name for this section—the **recapitulation**, meaning a step-by-step review.

But there is an important difference: The music now remains in the same key, the tonic key. (In practical terms, this means that the whole second group is relocated in the tonic. To allow for this, the bridge has to be rewritten—often in an imaginative way.) Stability of key in the recapitulation is especially welcome after the instability and restlessness of the development section. Basically, as we have said, sonata form depends on a strong feeling of balance between exposition and recapitulation (**A B A′**). But it is a weighted balance, because **A′** has achieved a new solidity.

The entire **B A′** sequence (development and recapitulation) may be repeated. Whether this happens or not, another section in the tonic is often added at the very end, a postmortem or wrap-up for the main action. This optional section is called the **coda** (in fact, coda is a general term applied to a concluding section in any musical form).

In the following schematic diagram for sonata form, changes of key are shown on a continuous band. Notice the tonal stability of the recapitulation, where the steady horizontal band contrasts with the modulation of the exposition and the fluctuations of the development.

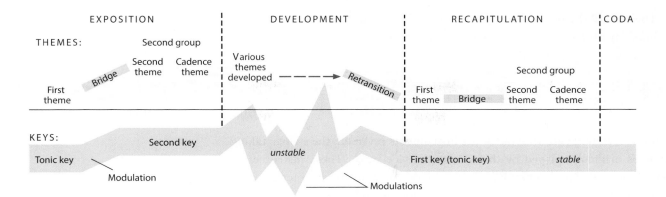

It may not be accidental that the terms used in discussing sonata form resemble those used in discussions of drama. We speak of the "exposition" of a play, where the initial situation is set forth, and of the "development" of the plot. Indeed, sonata form has a dramatic quality compared with the more architectural quality of Baroque music such as a fugue or a ritornello form (compare the chart on page 116 to the one above). In a Classical symphony, the themes seem almost like characters in a play or a novel to whom things are happening. They seem to change, take part in various actions, and react to other themes and musical processes.

Wolfgang Amadeus Mozart, Symphony No. 40 in G Minor, K. 550* (1788)

2 | 14–19   37   13

Mozart's Symphony in G Minor is one of the most famous and admired of all his works. The opening movement, with its sharp contrasts and clear demarcations, makes an arresting introduction to sonata form.

Not many Classical compositions convey as dark and uneasy a mood as does this symphony. (Not many Classical symphonies are in the minor mode.) It suggests some kind of muted struggle against inescapable constraints. Mozart's themes alone would not have created this effect; expressive as they are in themselves, they only attain their full effect in their setting. Mozart needed sonata form to manage these expressive themes—in a sense, to give them something to struggle against.

We have already cited the first movement's opening texture—melody with a strictly homophonic accompaniment—as characteristic of the Viennese Classical style (see page 158). So also are the delicate dynamic changes toward the end of the theme and the loud repeated cadences that terminate it. The unique nervous energy of this theme, a blend of refinement and subdued agitation, stamps the first movement unforgettably.

VIOLINS

Exposition The first theme is played twice. The second playing already begins the modulation to the exposition's second key, and a forceful bridge passage completes this process, after which the music comes to an abrupt stop. Such stops will come again and again in this movement.

---

*Mozart's works are identified by *K numbers,* after the chronological catalog of his works compiled by Ludwig von Köchel. The first edition (1862) listed 626 works composed by Mozart in his short lifetime; later editions add many more that have come to light since then.

The second theme, in the major mode, is divided up, measure by measure or phrase by phrase, between the strings and the woodwinds:

Then it is repeated with the role of the instruments reversed, the strings taking the notes originally played by the winds, and vice versa. These instrumental alterations contribute something absolutely essential to the character of the theme, and show Mozart's fine ear for tone color, or timbre.

The second appearance of the second theme does not come to a cadence, but runs into a series of new ideas that make up the rest of the second group. All of them are brief and leave little impression on the rest of the movement, so it is best not to consider these ideas actual themes. One of these ideas repeats the motive of the first theme.

A short cadence theme, *forte*, and a very insistent series of repeated cadences bring the exposition to a complete stop. (We still hear the rhythm of theme 1.) After one dramatic chord, wrenching us back from major to the original minor key, the whole exposition is repeated.

Development Two more dramatic chords—different chords—and then the development section starts quietly. The first theme is accompanied as before. It modulates (changes key) at once, and seems to be losing itself in grief, until the rest of the orchestra bursts in with a furious contrapuntal treatment of that tender, nervous melody.

The music seems to exhaust itself. It comes to another stop. But in the following *piano* passage, the modulations continue, with orchestral echoes based on smaller and smaller portions of the first theme, as shown on page 165. Breaking up a theme in this way is called *fragmentation*.

Passion breaks out anew in another *forte* passage; but the modulations have finally ceased. The fragmentation reaches its final stage. At last the harmony seems to be waiting or preparing for something, rather than shifting all the time. This passage is the *retransition*.

Recapitulation After its fragmentation in the development section, the first theme somehow conveys new pathos when it returns in its original form, and in the original tonic key. The bassoon has a beautiful new descending line.

And pathos deepens when the second theme and all the other ideas in the second group—originally heard in a major-mode key—are now recapitulated in the tonic key, which is a minor key. The result is a great many small alterations of the exposition material—small, but they change the mood decisively. The recapitulation is more stable than the exposition—for one thing, both the first and the second groups are now in the same mode (minor), as well as in the same key. The bridge theme, much expanded, also hammers away at the minor mode, recalling the contrapuntal outburst of the development section. It is a passage of great power.

Coda In a very short coda, Mozart refers one last time to the first theme. It sounds utterly disheartened, and then battered by the usual repeated cadences.

Original

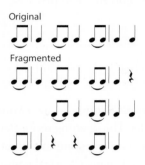

Fragmented

Mozart, Symphony No. 40 in G Minor, first movement (Molto allegro)

Sonata form. 8 min., 14 sec.

2 | 14–19   37   13

14		**EXPOSITION**		
	0:01	**Theme 1 (main theme)**	Theme 1, *p*, minor key (G minor); repeated cadences *f*	
	0:25		Theme 1 repeats and begins the modulation to a new key.	
	0:34	**Bridge**	Bridge theme, *f*, confirms the modulation.	
			CADENCE Abrupt stop	
		Second Group		
15	0:53	**Theme 2**	Theme 2, *p*, in major key; phrases divided between woodwinds and strings	
0:11	1:04		Theme 2 again, division of phrases is reversed.	
0:29	1:22		Other, shorter ideas, *f*, and *p*: echoes of theme 1 motive	
0:55	1:48	**Cadence theme**	Cadence theme, *f*, downward scales followed by repeated cadences	
			CADENCE Abrupt stop	
1:11	2:04	***Exposition repeated***		
16		**DEVELOPMENT**		
	4:10	**Theme 1 developed**	Theme 1, *p*, modulating	
0:16	4:26	**Contrapuntal passage**	Sudden *f*: contrapuntal treatment by the full orchestra of theme 1	
0:44	4:54	**Fragmentation**	Sudden *p*: beginning of theme 1 echoes between strings and woodwinds; theme fragmented from ♪♪ ♩ ♪♪ ♪♩ ♩♩ to ♪♪ ♩ ♪♪ ♩ ♩ ♩ and finally to ♪♪ ♩ ♩.	
1:01	5:11		Retransition *f* (full orchestra), *p* (woodwinds), which leads into the recapitulation	
17		**RECAPITULATION**		
	5:26	**Theme 1**	Theme 1, *p*, G minor, as before	
0:24	5:50		Theme 1, modulating differently than before	
0:33	5:59	**Bridge**	Bridge, *f*, longer than before	
			CADENCE Abrupt stop	
		Second Group		
18	6:41	**Theme 2**	Theme 2, *p*, this time in the minor mode (G minor)	
			All the other second-group themes are in the tonic key (minor mode); otherwise much the same as before.	
1:00	7:42	**Cadence theme**	Scale part of the cadence theme, *f*	
19		**CODA**		
	7:54		New imitative passage, *p*, strings; based on theme 1 motive	
0:10	8:04		Repeated cadences, *f*	
			Stop, this time confirmed by three solid chords	

Wolfgang Amadeus Mozart (1756–1791)

Mozart was born in Salzburg, a picturesque town in central Austria, which today is famous for its music festivals. His father, Leopold, was a court musician and composer who also wrote an important book on violin playing. Mozart showed extraordinary talent at a very early age. He and his older sister, Nannerl, were trotted all over Europe as child prodigies; between the ages of six and seventeen, Wolfgang never spent more than ten successive months at home. His first symphony was played at a London concert when he was only eight years old.

But mostly Wolfgang was displayed at courts and salons, and in a somewhat depressing way this whole period of his career symbolizes the frivolous love of entertainment that reigned at midcentury. The future queen Marie Antoinette of France was one of those for whose amusement the six-year-old prodigy would name the keys of compositions played to him, and sight-read music at the piano with a cloth over his hands.

It was much harder for Mozart to make his way as a young adult musician. As usual in those days, he followed in his father's footsteps as a musician at the court of Salzburg, which was ruled by an archbishop. (Incidentally, one of their colleagues was Joseph Haydn's brother Michael.) But the archbishop was a disagreeable autocrat with no patience for independent-minded underlings. Mozart hated working for him. In 1781, he extricated himself from his court position, not without an ugly scene, and set himself up as a freelance musician in Vienna.

It seems clear that another reason for Mozart's move was to get away from his father, who had masterminded the boy's career and now seemed to grow more and more possessive as the young man sought his independence. Leopold disapproved of Wolfgang's marriage around this time to Constanze Weber, a singer. (Mozart had been in love with her older sister, Aloysia—a more famous singer—but she rejected him.)

Mozart wrote his greatest operas in Vienna, but only the last of them, *The Magic Flute,* had the success it deserved. Everyone sensed that he was a genius, but his music seemed too difficult—and he was a somewhat difficult personality. He relied for his living on teaching and on the relatively new institution of concerts. Every year he set up a concert at which he introduced one of his piano concertos. In addition, the program might contain arias, a solo improvisation, and an overture by somebody else.

But as happens with popular musicians today, Mozart seems (for some unknown reason) to have suddenly dropped out of fashion. After 1787, his life was a struggle, though he did receive a minor court appointment and the promise of a church position, and finally scored a really solid hit with *The Magic Flute.* When it seemed that financially he was finally getting out of the woods, he died suddenly at the age of thirty-five.

He died under somewhat macabre circumstances. He was composing a Requiem Mass, that is, a Mass for the Dead, commissioned by a patron who insisted on remaining anonymous. Mozart became ill and began to think he was writing for his own demise. When he died, the Requiem still unfinished, a rumor started that he had been poisoned by the rival composer Antonio Salieri.

Unlike Haydn, the other great master of the Viennese Classical style, Mozart allowed a note of disquiet, even passion, to emerge in some of his compositions (such as the Symphony in G Minor). The Romantics correctly perceived this as a forecast of their own work. Once we recognize this, it is hard not to sense something enigmatic beneath the intelligence, wit, and sheer beauty of all Mozart's music.

Chief Works: The comic operas *The Marriage of Figaro, Don Giovanni, Così fan tutte* (That's What They All Do), and *The Magic Flute* ▪ *Idomeneo,* an opera seria ▪ Church music: many Masses, and a Requiem (Mass for the Dead) left unfinished at his death ▪ 41 symphonies, including the *Prague,* the G minor, and the *Jupiter* ▪ String quartets and quintets ▪ Concertos for various instruments, including nearly thirty much-loved piano concertos ▪ Piano sonatas; violin sonatas ▪ Lighter pieces (such as divertimentos, etc.), including the famous *Eine kleine Nachtmusik*

Encore: After Symphony No. 40, listen to the Clarinet Quintet and *The Marriage of Figaro* (Act I).

Image credit: Ali Meyer/CORBIS.

Mozart's musical handwriting. *University of California at Berkeley Music Library.*

3 | Classical Variation Form

Variation form, as we saw on pages 118–19, entails the repetition of a clearly defined melodic unit, the *theme*, with various changes at each repetition. In the Baroque era, the theme was usually a bass pattern (sometimes called a ground bass). The same basic principle is at work in Classical variation form, but now the theme is a tune in the upper register.

We can understand why the Baroque era, which developed the idea of the basso continuo supporting harmonies from below, would have cultivated variations on a bass pattern, whereas the Classical era, with its emphasis on simple melody, preferred variations on short tunes in the upper register.

The point of variations is to create many contrasting moods with the same theme, which is transformed but always somehow discernible under the transformations. In principle, nothing distracts from this process, at least until the end, where composers usually add a coda. There are no contrasting themes, transitions, cadence sections, or development sections, as there are in sonata form movements (and in many rondos).

A Classical **theme and variations** movement begins with a theme that is typically in |: **a** :||: **b** :| or |: **a** :||: **ba** :| form. This miniform nests within the larger variation form:

Theme	Variation 1	Variation 2 . . .	Coda
|: a :||: b :|	|: a^1 :||: b^1 :|	|: a^2 :||: b^2 :|	(free)

Variations were part of the stock-in-trade of virtuosos of the Classical era. At a musical soiree, someone might suggest a popular opera tune, and the pianist would improvise variations on the spot, for as long as his or her imagination held out. Twelve was a common number for these variations when they were published; virtuosos piled them up for maximum effect. In symphonies and concertos, theme and variations movements are less extended, since they have to fit into a time scale with all the other movements.

Symphonies of Haydn

Even before Mozart's maturity, his older colleague Joseph Haydn was already a master of the Classical symphony. He composed over a hundred of them, averaging more than one a year over the last two decades of his active career, from 1780 to 1800. His most famous symphonies are the last twelve, written for concerts in London, where Haydn enjoyed enormous acclaim on two tours after his retirement from the court of the Esterházy princes. For our examples of second, third, and fourth movements from Classical symphonies, we select from Haydn's so-called *London* symphonies.

Variations in the visual arts: Claude Monet (1840–1926) painted dozens of pictures of Rouen Cathedral at different times of the day and in different lights. Variations in music could also be said to show their theme in "different lights." *Musée d'Orsay, Paris, France/Lauros/Giraudon/ The Bridgeman Art Library.*

Franz Joseph Haydn, Symphony No. 94 in G ("The Surprise," 1791)

The second movement of a symphony is the slow movement, a restful episode to contrast with the vigorous first movement. There is no standardized form for slow movements, either in symphonies or in other genres, such as sonatas or concertos. Mozart, in his late symphonies, preferred sonata form or some derivative of it. Haydn favored his own version of variation form, and indeed tuneful and witty variations movements in symphonies were a specialty of his. One of his most beloved variations movements is the Andante from his Symphony No. 94, nicknamed "The Surprise" Symphony.

For the theme of this movement Haydn devised a tune as charming as it is simple:

It is presented at the beginning almost in the |: **a** :||: **b** :| form we might expect, except that Haydn alters each repetition slightly. The repeat of the **b** phrase adds flutes, oboes, and horns not present the first time through, while the second **a** phrase is played more quietly than the first until its final chord—a crashing *fortissimo* stroke that gave the symphony its nickname.

Now the variations start—four in all, plus a brief coda—and in each of them the original theme can be clearly heard, while much else is varied. The normal expectation would be the basic scheme shown in the margin, as discussed on page 169. Haydn wrote dozens of variations movements in this "standard" form—though not, interestingly, in symphonies. He seems to have felt it would be boring for a concert audience and that he needed to do something freer. Instead of repeating **a** and **b** phrases in the variations exactly, he might write variations within variations, as indicated by prime marks in the following diagram:

Theme	**a**	**a**	**b**	**b**
"Normal" variation	a_1	a_1	b_1	b_1
Variation within variation	a_1	a_1'	b_1	b_1'

Variation 1 in this movement is of the "normal" kind, leading us gently toward the greater changes to come. The lower strings present the theme and its harmonic support, while the first violins, aided for a moment by the flutes, add a graceful new melody above them.

Variation 2 sets a different tone entirely, as it shifts to the minor mode and presents the first phrase of the theme *ff*. This phrase, a_2, then modulates off to end in a new key—and back in the major mode. (Classical composers tended not to linger for long in the minor mode in their variations movements.) Phrase a_2 is literally repeated, leading us to think we are about to embark on the b_2 phrases of a normal variation. Haydn has other plans, however; instead of

Basic Variation

THEME	|: **a** :| |: **b** :|
Variation 1	|: a_1 :| |: b_1 :|
Variation 2	|: a_2 :| |: b_2 :|
Variation 3	|: a_3 :| |: b_3 :|

|: **b₂** :|, we get loud, tumultuous music, with the opening motive from the theme developed in the lower strings. This works its way to a sense of harmonic expectancy and a pause, leaving only the first violins. It is as if Haydn momentarily shifted to sonata form and wrote a miniature development section, complete with retransition.

The violins lead us smoothly to Variation 3, a variation within a variation. For **a₃** the theme, back in the major mode, is presented in quicker rhythms by a solo oboe. The next phrase, **a₃′**, offers a duet of flute and oboe high above the theme in the strings. This arrangement continues through **b₃** and **b₃′**, with quiet French horns added in **b₃′**.

LISTENING CHART 8

Haydn, Symphony No. 94 in G ("The Surprise"), second movement (Andante)

Variation form. 6 min., 47 sec.

2 | 20–25   38   14

20	THEME			
	0:00	**a**		
	0:19	**a′**	Ends with **ff** chord, full orchestra	
	0:38	**b**		
	0:57	**b′**	Adds woodwinds	
21	VARIATION 1			
0:00	1:15	**a₁**	Violins (later with flute) add a new melody above the theme.	
0:17	1:33	**a₁**		
0:35	1:51	**b₁**		
0:52	2:08	**b₁**		
22	VARIATION 2			
0:00	2:25	**a₂**	Begins in minor mode, **ff**, then modulates	
0:17	2:43	**a₂**		
0:35	3:00	**b₂**	Free, development-like section plus retransition	
23	VARIATION 3			
0:00	3:39	**a₃**	Oboe solo, playing theme in quick rhythms	
0:16	3:55	**a₃′**	Oboe and flute duet, theme in strings	
0:34	4:13	**b₃**	Oboe and flute duet continues.	
0:52	4:31	**b₃′**	Horns added	
24	VARIATION 4			
0:00	4:49	**a₄**	Full orchestra, including trumpets and drums; **ff**	
0:17	5:06	**a₄′**	Strings plus bassoons	
0:35	5:24	**b₄**		
0:53	5:42	**b₄′**	Full orchestra, **ff**	
25	CODA			
0:00	5:57			
0:19	6:17		*Diminuendo* to **pp**; new, mysterious harmonies for theme	

Variation 4 begins triumphantly with the complete orchestra, including trumpets and drums; the winds present the theme while the violins play a quick countermelody, all *ff*. But this is another variation within a variation, and Haydn quiets the jubilant mood abruptly in a_4' and b_4, played mainly by the strings, before restoring it in b_4'.

The return of the triumphant mood seems to signal the end of the movement, and indeed it leads straight into a brief coda. For this Haydn reserves one more surprise—a bigger one, even, than the crashing chord at the beginning that gave the symphony its nickname. The last, incomplete statement of the theme grows softer and softer, over mysterious and dissonant harmonies that seem to recall the minor-mode variation in the middle of the movement. The theme of this movement is simple, to be sure—but not without its secrets, it turns out.

4 | Minuet Form (Classical Dance Form)

Stylized dances—music in the style and form of dances, but intended for listening rather than dancing—reached a state of high development in the Baroque era. In Chapter 10 we saw how various dance types were assembled into suites. Unlike the Baroque era, which developed a single genre made up of different dances, the Classical era focused on a single stylized dance and introduced it into many different genres.

The sole dance type from the Baroque suite to survive in the multimovement genres of the Classical period was the **minuet**. One reason for its endurance was simply the dance itself: Originally popularized at the court of Louis XIV in the seventeenth century, it continued as one of the major fashionable social dances in the eighteenth. However much the minuet movement of a symphony differed from a simple dance tune, it was always a reminder of the aristocratic courts that had originally established orchestras.

Another reason was more technical. As a moderately paced piece in triple meter, the minuet makes an excellent contrast to the quick duple meter that was by far the most common meter in the opening and closing movements of Classical symphonies, quartets, and the like.

Works with four movements—symphonies and string quartets—always included a minuet, usually as a light contrast after the slow movement. Mozart even managed to fit a minuet into some of his piano concertos, though traditionally the concerto, as a three-movement genre, did not leave room for one.

Baroque and Classical Dance Form

A Baroque minuet consists of two sections; each comes to a complete stop and is immediately repeated (|: **a** :||: **b** :|). See page 132. Minuets tend to come in pairs, alternating in an **A B A** pattern. The second dance, **B**, is called the **trio**, because in early days it was often played by only three instruments.

As a whole, a Baroque minuet movement can be diagrammed as follows. (Remember that |: :| means repeat, and that in the second **A** the parts are usually not repeated.)

MINUET	TRIO	MINUET
A	B	A
|: **a** :||: **b** :|	|: **c** :||: **d** :|	**a b**

Biography
Franz Joseph Haydn (1732–1809)

Unlike so many other composers, Haydn did not come from a family of professional musicians. But his father, an Austrian village wheelwright, was a keen amateur musician. As a boy Joseph had a beautiful voice, and at the age of eight he was sent to Vienna to be a choirboy in St. Stephen's Cathedral. After his voice broke, he spent several difficult years as a free-lance musician in Vienna before obtaining the position of Kapellmeister with Prince Paul Anton Esterházy, one of the most lavish patrons of music at the time.

After this, Haydn's career reflects the changing social situation in the later eighteenth century, when the old system of court patronage coexisted with an early form of the modern concert system. Indeed, there is no finer tribute to the system of court patronage than Haydn's thirty-year career with the Esterházys. The post of Kapellmeister involved managing and writing music not only for the prince's chapel (the *Kapell*) but also for his private opera house, his marionette theater, and for palace chamber music and orchestral performances. Haydn had a good head for administration. Hiring his own musicians, he was able over many years to experiment with the symphony and other genres and develop his style under ideal conditions.

Haydn's output is staggering. He composed 104 symphonies; 83 string quartets; numerous divertimentos, trios, and sonatas; and over 20 operas. He also had to write a great deal of music for baryton—a bizarre archaic instrument fancied by the next Esterházy prince, Nikolaus, which was something like a cello with extra strings that could be plucked, like guitar strings.

The Esterházys had a splendid estate some miles outside of Vienna, but Haydn's duties there did not prevent him from spending a good deal of time in the capital. In the 1770s his string quartets made a particularly strong impression in the metropolis. In the 1780s he befriended Mozart, and the two actually played together in an amateur string quartet.

Meanwhile the spread of Haydn's international fame accelerated with the growth of public concerts. At first his symphonies were picked up by French concert organizers (who paid Haydn nothing). Then in the 1780s his six *Paris* symphonies were commissioned for concerts in that city, and in the 1790s twelve *London* symphonies were written for two highly successful tours to Britain.

Toward the end of his life Haydn turned to choral music: six impressive Latin Masses for soloists, chorus, and orchestra, and two German oratorios inspired by Handel, *The Creation* and *The Seasons*, admired by his contemporaries as the apex of an exemplary career in music.

Haydn's most famous composition is a simple Austrian patriotic song:

It appears with variations in his *Emperor* Quartet, Op. 76 No. 3 (1797). The tune was adopted for the German national anthem, "Deutschland über Alles," and for the hymn "Glorious Things of Thee Are Spoken."

One of the most attractive personalities in the gallery of the great composers, Haydn was shrewd but generous-minded, humorous, always honorable, and though fully aware of his own worth, quite ready to praise his young, difficult colleague Mozart. "Friends often flatter me that I have some genius," he once said—without contradicting them—"but he stood far above me."

Haydn's music combines good-humored simplicity of melody with a very sophisticated delight in the manipulations of musical form and technique. No composer has ever enjoyed a (musical) joke more. In his reasonableness, his wit, and his conviction that his art should serve humanity (a conviction he both expressed and acted upon), Haydn is a true musical representative of the Enlightenment.

Chief Works: 104 symphonies; the last twelve, composed for London in 1791–95, include the "Surprise," "Clock," and "Drum Roll" symphonies ■ A cello concerto and a delightful trumpet concerto ■ Over 80 string quartets; piano trios and piano sonatas ■ Choral music in his late years: six Masses and the oratorios *The Creation* and *The Seasons*

Encore: After movements from Symphonies No. 94, No. 99, and No. 101, listen to the whole of Symphony No. 102; Trumpet Concerto.

Top image credit: Royal Collection Trust/ © HM Queen Elizabeth II, 2014/Bridgeman Images.

Baryton. *Image copyright: Metropolitan Museum of Art. Image source: Art Resource.*

An eighteenth-century minuet, with music and notation for the dance steps. *Lebrecht/The Image Works.*

Classical composers extended the internal form of minuets (and trios) by developing internal **a b a** structures according to one of the following schemes:

MINUET	TRIO	MINUET		MINUET	TRIO	MINUET
A	B	A	or	A	B	A
|: **a** :||: **b a** :|	|: **c** :||: **d c** :|	**a b a**	(more often)	|: **a** :||: **b a′** :|	|: **c** :||: **d c′** :|	**a b a′**

Prime marks (**a′** and **c′**) indicate changes or extensions to the original **a** and **c** sections. Classical dance form is sometimes called **ternary form**, acknowledging its **a b a′** order.

Franz Joseph Haydn, Symphony No. 99 in E-flat (1793)

2 | 26–28   39   15

Minuet movements in Haydn's symphonies often seem to take us on a small mental journey from the ballroom to the countryside, with the genteel demeanor of the minuet countered by the more rustic mood of the trio. In the minuet and trio of Symphony No. 99, Haydn appears to poke fun at this division by reversing it. It is the minuet that seems a bit bumptious and clumsy, the trio that exudes suave charm.

Minuet The **a** section of this |: **a** :|: **b a′** :|, or *ternary*, form begins with question-and-answer phrases: The high strings play a downward–moving melody immediately countered—loudly, almost rudely—by the full orchestra. This happens twice—2 bars + 2 bars, 2 bars + 2 bars—then the music proceeds more smoothly to end on repeated cadences (repeated, however, just a bit too insistently). The **b a′** section begins with an upward-moving melody, turning on its head the melody beginning **a**. The return to **a′** comes about abruptly, wrenching us back from a minor-mode key Haydn has led us to. It leads to an unexpected pause for the whole orchestra, and then the minuet closes with cadences more insistent than before. We have seen (page 159) that repeated cadences are a general feature of the Classical style; here they are used to give the minuet a feel rather far from gentility.

Trio After these repeated cadences, two oboes are left hanging on a single note. One of them takes up, along with the violins and accompanied by the other strings, an alluring, legato tune; there is no trace here of insistence or rude response. The music, also, slides from the oboes' note into an unexpected key, adding to its sense of distance from the mood of the minuet. The trio, like the minuet, is in ternary form (that is, |: **c** :|: **d c′** :|), though it is a shorter one than in the minuet, without repeated cadences.

Minuet When the trio ends, Haydn has carried us so far from the key—and the feeling—of the minuet that he needs a brief passage of transition to help bring us back. This is an unconventional addition to minuet and trio form, but Haydn was a composer never unwilling to bend the rules, as we saw also in the miniature development section that breaks out in the variations movement from "The Surprise" Symphony. Then the minuet is played again unchanged, except for the omission of repeats: | **a** | **b a′** |.

Pencil drawing of Haydn, which he once singled out as the best likeness he had ever seen: not the choice of a vain man. Compare page 174. *Bettmann/Corbis.*

))) **LISTENING CHART 9**

Haydn, Symphony No. 99 in E-flat, third movement (Allegretto)

Minuet form. 5 min., 13 sec.

2 | 26–28   39   15

26		MINUET (A)		
	0:00	**a**	Descending melody, staccato	
	0:19		Repeated cadences	
	0:28	**a**	*Repetition*	
	0:55	**b**	Ascending melody	
	1:12	**a′**		
	1:25		Pause for full orchestra on expectant harmony	
	1:34		Repeated cadences	
	1:42	**b a′**	*Repetition*	
27		TRIO (B)		
0:00	2:29		Two oboes, alone	
0:02	2:32	**c**	Tune, legato	
0:13	2:43	**c**	*Repetition*	
0:24	2:53	**d**		
0:33	3:03	**c′**		
0:46	3:16	**d c′**	*Repetition*	
1:09	3:39		Transition back to minuet	
28		MINUET (A)		
	3:59		*Repetition of a b a′*	

Allegretto

p   *f*

VIOLINS AND CLARINETS

p cantabile

VIOLINS AND OBOE

5 | Rondo Form

The **rondo** is a form with popular leanings, dating back to the Baroque era. In the symphonies and other multimovement genres of the Classical era, it was used mainly for fast, closing movements.

The formal principle of the rondo is a simple one. A rondo begins with a full-fledged tune (**A**) and comes back to it after episodes (**B**, **C**, etc.) serving as spacers between its appearances. Longer rondo tunes may return in shortened form. For example, if **A** is in the favorite |: **a** :|: **b a′** :| pattern of the time, the recurrence of **A** throughout the rondo may present **a b a′**, **b a′**, or even **a** alone. There is always enough of the tune for the listener to recognize it.

In simple rondos, the episodes feature additional tunes contrasting with **A**; this results in formal designs such as those shown in the margin. In symphonies, the episodes may present transitions to new themes, cadence formulas, and even sonata form–style development sections using motives from **A**. (The most complex rondos of this kind are sometimes called *sonata rondos*; they were a favorite of Haydn in the symphonies from late in his career.) Various schemes are possible, and often a coda is added. Whatever the specific structure, the regular return of the main theme **A** is the critical feature of rondo form.

Rondo Schemes

A B A C A coda
A B A C A B A
A B A C A D A
—and others

A famous performance of Haydn's oratorio *The Creation* from 1808. The elderly Haydn is seated in the foreground, and Beethoven stands before him with a cane. The picture shows how much smaller orchestra and chorus were in the early nineteenth century; today's typical performing forces for such a work would double the number onstage here. *De Agostini Picture Library/A. Dagli Orti/The Bridgeman Art Library.*

A modern view of Esterháza palace, near Vienna, where Haydn spent much of his career. *Lebrecht/The Image Works.*

Franz Joseph Haydn, Symphony No. 101 in D ("The Clock," 1793–1794)

2 | 29–33   40   16

If rondo form is typically used in fast finales, here it is *very* fast and closes one of the most effervescent and joyous of all Haydn's symphonies. Like Symphony No. 94, No. 101 also has earned a nickname—"The Clock," for a steady, tick tock motive in the second movement.

In largest outline the fourth movement shows many typical features of rondo form. Its main theme (**A**) takes on the |: **a** :|: **b a** :| form; here is the complete **a** melody:

Also typically, when **A** first comes back, it is presented in abbreviated fashion, without repeats. (The melody also is varied when it returns: **a** becomes **a′** and then **a″**.) The movement as a whole presents **A** three times, with two episodes in between: **A B A C A**.

For their part, the episodes are not simple tunes but complex music reminiscent of sonata-form developments—loud, busy, and contrasting strongly with the sprightly **A** theme. This is common in symphonic rondos and especially in Haydn's. The second episode starts off with furious, stormy music in the minor mode, briefly threatening the lightheartedness of the movement. Each episode has a quiet moment in its midst with a new melody, which begins in a way reminiscent of the **a** melody but then veers off with *syncopated* rhythms:

The second episode ends on a broad, expectant pause, and the last return of **A** begins with something unexpected: a fugue, taking as its *subject* another varied version of the **a** melody:

This is a very free fugue. There is scarcely room in the middle of this rondo for the kind of systematic imitative counterpoint we might expect from Bach. Nevertheless, it persists, complete with a quick-moving melody that accompanies it (in fugue terminology, a *countersubject*), until it rises up to a culminating statement of the subject in the full orchestra. After the fugue, a final, short statement of **a** leads to the kind of emphatic, repeated closing cadences common at the end of Classical works—but especially needed here to ground the freewheeling musical energies Haydn has generated.

LISTENING CHART 10

Haydn, Symphony No. 101 in D ("The Clock"), fourth movement (Finale. Vivace)

Rondo. 4 min., 29 sec.

2 | 29–33   40   16

29	0:00	**A (Tune)**	**a**
	0:07		**a**
	0:14		**b**
	0:24		**a**
	0:31		**b a**
30	0:48	**B (Episode 1)**	**f**, quick running scales in the strings; trumpet fanfares
0:29	1:17		New theme, **p**, derived from **a**, with syncopations
0:41	1:29		More loud running scales
0:58	1:46		Quiet close leads to return of:
31	1:54	**A**	**a' b a"**
32	2:24	**C (Episode 2)**	**f**, minor mode, stormy
0:15	2:39		New theme from **B** again, major mode, now **f**
0:29	2:53		Stormy music resumes, minor mode
0:43	3:07		Expectant pause signals return to:
33	3:10	**A**	Fugue!
0:52	4:02		Final, quiet return of **a**
1:01	4:11		Running scales lead to final cadences.

GOALS FOR REVIEW

► to understand the standard movement types of the Classical symphony

► to understand the forms associated with these movement types

► to develop a vocabulary for the various elements of sonata form

► to listen carefully to all the elements of a sonata form movement

► to understand and listen to theme and variation form

► to understand and listen to minuet form

► to understand and listen to rondo form

► to get to know the lives and works of Wolfgang Amadeus Mozart and Franz Joseph Haydn

 macmillanhighered.com/listen8e
Interactive Listening Charts 7–10
Listening Quiz for Chapter 13
Reading Quiz for Chapter 13

Other Classical Genres

In Chapter 13 we examined the symphony as exemplified by Mozart's Symphony No. 40 in G Minor and three movements from Haydn's *London* symphonies. We go on in this chapter to examine the other main genres of music in the Viennese Classical era: the sonata, the Classical concerto, the string quartet, and opera buffa, the name for Italian comic opera of the time.

It would be somewhat redundant to spend the same amount of detail on each of these genres as on the symphony, for many features of the symphony are duplicated in these other genres. Indeed, for Classical instrumental music, the symphony can be used as a sort of prototype. Bear in mind the symphony outline from Chapter 13; we reprint it here.

In the following pages we discuss the sonata, concerto, and string quartet, emphasizing the specific features that differentiate each genre from the symphony. We finish by turning from instrumental music to opera buffa.

MOVEMENTS OF THE SYMPHONY

	OPENING MOVEMENT	SLOW MOVEMENT	MINUET (WITH TRIO)	CLOSING MOVEMENT
Tempo	Fast/moderate	Slow/very slow	Moderate	Fast/very fast
Form	Sonata form (sometimes preceded by a slow introduction)	Sonata form, variations, rondo form, or other	Minuet form	Sonata form or rondo form

1 | The Sonata

The word **sonata** has multiple meanings. We already know it from the term *sonata form*, the scheme employed in the first movements of symphonies, but the word goes back to before the Classical period and simply meant a piece for a small number of instruments or a single one. (In Italian, *sonata* means "sounded," that is, played.) In the Classical period the term usually referred to compositions for one or two instruments only.

Sonatas were not designed for concerts, which in any case were still rare at this time, but for private performances, often by amateurs. The symphony is a public genre, the sonata a domestic one—and increasingly the domestic clientele was made up of women (see the next page). Although professional

From the late eighteenth century on, musical accomplishment was regarded as a highly desirable social asset for women: for a French baroness (painted by Elisabeth Vigée-LeBrun, a fashionable court painter, 1755–1842) or an American First Lady — Louisa C. (Mrs. John Quincy) Adams — at a later period. Left: *Musée des Augustins, Toulouse, France/Giraudon/The Bridgeman Art Library*. Right: *Smithsonian American Art Museum, Washington, DC/Art Resource, NY*.

female instrumentalists were still rare, more and more women played music in the home. Given their amateur audience, some (not all!) sonatas are easy to play and may be limited in expressive range.

Piano sonatas were composed for solo piano, the favorite new instrument of the time, and *violin sonatas* were composed for violin and piano. (The early piano was called the *fortepiano;* see page 187.) In Classical sonatas with violin, the piano is not a mere accompaniment but an equal partner; it holds its own in such combinations in a way that the earlier harpsichord usually did not.

Compare the three-movement plan for the sonata, shown below, with the four-movement symphony prototype on the previous page; they are similar except for the omission of the minuet movement in the sonata. But sonatas are much less uniform than symphonies, concertos, or quartets. Of Mozart's sonatas, for example, only about two-thirds follow the plan, leaving many exceptions. None of them has more than three movements, however, and the movements are always shorter than those of a symphony. Some sonatas have only two movements — including two ever-popular ones by the youthful Beethoven.

In Chapter 15 we will return to the piano sonata, examining a movement by Beethoven.

MOVEMENTS OF THE SONATA

	OPENING MOVEMENT	SLOW MOVEMENT	CLOSING MOVEMENT
Tempo	Fast/moderate	Slow/very slow	Fast/very fast
Form	Sonata form	Sonata form, variations, rondo form, or other	Often rondo form

2 | The Classical Concerto

On page 115 we discussed the Baroque concerto and concerto grosso at the time of Bach and Vivaldi in terms of the basic concerto idea—the contest between soloist and orchestra. This basic idea was refined and sharpened by the Viennese Classical composers.

Instrumental virtuosity, in the person of the soloist, remained a central feature of the Classical concerto. At the same time, the orchestra was growing and becoming a richer expressive force. With its well-coordinated string, woodwind, and brass groups, the Classical orchestra afforded more variety than the Baroque concerto orchestra could ever do.

So the balance between the two contesting forces—solo instrument and orchestra—presented a real problem, a problem that Mozart worked out in a series of seventeen superb piano concertos written during his years in Vienna, mostly for his own concert use. (Counting earlier works, he composed twenty-seven piano concertos in all.) Mozart pitted the soloist's greater agility, brilliance, and expressive capability against the orchestra's increased power and variety of tone color. The contestants are perfectly matched; neither one emerges as the definite winner.

Compare the movement plan for the Classical concerto below with the symphony prototype on page 181. Concertos have long opening movements and no minuet movements.

MOVEMENTS OF THE CLASSICAL CONCERTO

	OPENING MOVEMENT	SLOW MOVEMENT	CLOSING MOVEMENT
Tempo	Fast/moderate	Slow/very slow	Fast/very fast
Form	Double-exposition sonata form; cadenza near the end	Sonata form, variations, rondo form, or other	Rondo form (occasionally variation form)

Double-Exposition Form

For the first movements of concertos, Mozart developed a special form to capitalize on the contest that is basic to the genre. Though the diagram for **double-exposition form** may look rather cluttered, it is in fact simply an extended variant of sonata form. Compare the sonata-form diagram on page 165:

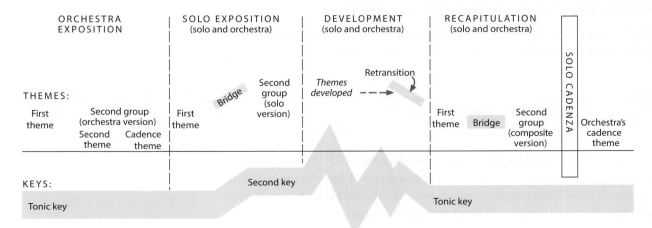

In sonata form, the exposition presenting all the basic material is repeated. In the concerto, instead, each of the competing forces presents the musical themes in its own somewhat different version. The two times through the exposition of a symphony, in other words, are here apportioned between the orchestra (first time) and the soloist (second time). But the two statements of the concerto exposition differ not merely in the instruments that play them. Unlike the exposition in a symphony, in a concerto the **orchestra exposition** does not modulate. The change of key (which counts for so much in sonata-form composition) is saved until the **solo exposition**. The listener senses that the orchestra can't modulate and the soloist can—evidence of the soloist's superior range and mobility. This is demonstrated spectacularly by the soloist playing scales, arpeggios, and other brilliant material, making the solo exposition longer than the orchestral one.

The recapitulation in double-exposition form amounts to a composite of the orchestral and solo versions of the exposition. Typically the orchestra's cadence theme, which has been crowded out of the solo exposition to make room for virtuoso activity, returns at the end to make a very satisfactory final cadence.* Shortly before the end, there is a big, formal pause for the soloist's cadenza (see page 124). The soloist would improvise at this point—to show his or her skill and flair by working out new thematic developments on the spot, and also by carrying off brilliant feats of virtuosity.

---

* Double-exposition form, like sonata form, may also have a coda—a feature exploited by Beethoven more than Mozart and Haydn.

> "These piano concertos are a happy medium between too easy and too difficult; they are very brilliant, pleasing to the ear, and natural, without being simple-minded. There are passages here and there which only connoisseurs will be able to appreciate, but less learned listeners will like them too, without knowing why."
>
> *Letter from Mozart to his father, 1782*

Wolfgang Amadeus Mozart (1756–1791), Piano Concerto No. 23 in A, K. 488 (1786)

2 | 34–38   41

This favorite Mozart concerto proceeds from one of his most gentle and songful first movements to a second movement that is almost tragic, followed by an exuberant, sunny finale. The first movement might almost have been intended as a demonstration piece for double-exposition form, except for one unique feature: a new theme introduced halfway through.

No fewer than four themes in this movement could be described as gentle and songful—though always alert. For a work of this character, Mozart uses a reduced orchestra, keeping the mellow clarinets but omitting the sharper-sounding oboes as well as trumpets and timpani.

Orchestra Exposition   Theme 1, played *piano* by the strings and repeated by the woodwinds, is answered by a vigorous *forte* response in the full orchestra.

This response idea returns many times, balancing the quiet themes, and often leading to something new—here, theme 2, another quiet melody, full of feeling. An agitated passage interrupts, suddenly emotional, touching on two different minor keys, but only briefly. This whole section remains in the major tonic key, without any actual modulation. The cadence theme that ends the section maintains the gentle mood.

Solo Exposition   The solo exposition expands on and illuminates the orchestra exposition, with the piano taking over some of it, while also adding fast-moving scales or other figuration of its own. The main difference comes at the bridge; the modulation, needed to give the music a lift, is engineered by the piano. The orchestral second theme sounds especially intimate and lovely when played on the piano—as Mozart planned. And at the end, instead of the gentle cadence theme, the piano has a moment of brilliant passage work, culminating in a drawn-out, triumphant cadence with a long trill.

Showy cadences of this kind are a regular feature of Classical concertos; the orchestra always answers with loud music of its own, like a cheer. Here it is the orchestra's response passage again. But this time it stops in midcourse, as though the orchestra has suddenly remembered something intimate and a little serious. A new theme (yet another quiet, gentle melody, this time with a thoughtful character) appears out of nowhere:

New theme, exposition

Development
CLARINET

PIANO

After the orchestra plays the new theme, the solo repeats it in an elaborated version, and we slip into the development section.

Development   The basic idea behind concertos, the contest between orchestra and soloist, is brought out wonderfully here. Mozart sets up a rapid-fire dialogue between the two contestants; fragments of the new theme in the woodwinds seem to discuss or argue with the piano, as the music modulates to minor-mode keys and the material is developed.

The new theme turns unexpectedly anxious in the retransition (see the music in the margin, to the right). Finally, with a brief cadenza, the piano pulls out of the dialogue and steers the way to the recapitulation.

STRINGS

Recapitulation   At the start of the movement, the songful first theme was claimed in turn by the orchestra and the solo in their respective expositions. In the recapitulation, a composite of the two expositions, they share it.

Otherwise, the recapitulation resembles the solo exposition, though the bridge is altered so that the whole remains in the tonic key. There is a beautiful extension at the end, and when the response passage comes again, it leads to a heavy stop, with a fermata—the standard way for the orchestra to bow out, after preparing for the soloist's grand re-entrance for the main cadenza. Compared to the cadenza in Bach's *Brandenburg* Concerto—see page 123—this one is much more varied. Written out by Mozart himself, it includes both modest moments and brilliant ones.

The solo's showy cadence at the end of the cadenza is cheered along once again by the orchestra's response passage, which we have heard so many times before. This time it leads to something we have *not* heard many times—only

Cadence theme

once, nine minutes back: the quiet cadence theme of the orchestra exposition. Do you remember it? It makes a perfect ending for the whole movement, with an extra twist: a little flare-up to *forte* that subsides almost at once.

LISTENING CHART 11

Mozart, Piano Concerto No. 23 in A, K. 488, first movement (Allegro)

Double-exposition form. 11 min., 42 sec.

2 | 34–38   41

On this chart, the column arrangement distinguishes the main orchestra and solo sections.

34	**ORCHESTRA EXPOSITION**			
	0:00	Theme 1, *p*	Orchestra	Strings; woodwinds for the second playing
	0:34	*f* response		
	0:58	Theme 2, *p*		
	1:29	"Deflection" passage		Two minor-mode keys are suggested.
	2:01	Cadence theme, *p*		
35	**SOLO EXPOSITION**			
	2:11	Theme 1		SOLO: Melody is increasingly ornamented.
0:29	2:40	*f* response	Orchestra, with SOLO cutting in	
0:38	2:49	Bridge — modulates		
1:00	3:11	Theme 2		
1:31	3:42	"Deflection" passage		
1:59	4:10	Solo virtuoso passage		
36	4:26	*f* response, leads to		
0:13	4:39	**New theme**	Orchestra	
0:25	4:51			SOLO *ornaments* the new theme.
	DEVELOPMENT			
0:39	5:05		Orchestra and SOLO: *dialogue* around the new theme; modulations	
1:23	5:49	Retransition		
1:45	6:11	Short CADENZA		in free time; ends with a fermata
37	**RECAPITULATION**			
	6:30	Theme 1, *p*	Orchestra, with SOLO cutting in for the second playing	
0:30	7:00	*f* response	Orchestra, with SOLO cutting in again	
0:38	7:08	Bridge		
1:00	7:30	Theme 2		
1:30	8:00	"Deflection" passage		
38	8:35	**New theme** (longer virtuoso passage)		(the first time the SOLO plays it without ornaments)
0:43	9:18	*f* response, leads to		
0:57	9:32	**New theme**		
1:13	9:48	Main CADENZA		SOLO free, improvised passage
2:30	11:05	*f* response	Orchestra	
2:44	11:19	Cadence theme, *p*		
2:52	11:27	Brief ending *f* ⟶ *p*		

Cadence theme

Mozart's fortepiano, the forerunner of today's piano. In the smaller fortepiano, the strings were strung less tightly because the frame was wood, not iron; hence the volume was lower. The fortepiano makes up for this by its responsive touch and delicacy of tone. © *Internationale Stiftung Mozarteum.*

3 | The String Quartet

Developed in the Classical era, the **string quartet** is a genre for four instruments: two violins, a viola, and a cello. The plan for a string quartet, with its four movements, is close to that of the symphony; compare page 181. Indeed, next to the symphony the quartet counts as the most important genre of Classical music.

MOVEMENTS OF THE STRING QUARTET

	OPENING MOVEMENT	SLOW MOVEMENT	MINUET (WITH TRIO)	CLOSING MOVEMENT
Tempo	Fast/moderate	Slow/very slow	Moderate	Fast/very fast
Form	Sonata form	Sonata form, variations, rondo form, or other	Minuet form	Sonata form or rondo form

The quartet may have as many movements as the symphony, but of course it doesn't have as many instruments, and it cannot match the symphony's range of volume and tone color. This can disappoint listeners today. For the eighteenth century, however, volume was no issue, because quartets were never intended for concert listening. They were intended primarily for the performers, with small, informal audiences—or none at all. History tells of a quartet session with Haydn and Mozart playing along with two other well-known musicians of the time, the only audience being Mozart's family and their two servants.

As for range of tone color, the quartet compensates for lack of variety by its own special qualities: nuance, delicacy, and subtlety. Without any conductor, the quartet players are partners responding to one another as only old, close friends can. As developed by Haydn, the four instruments of the quartet grow more and more similar in their actual musical material, and more and more interdependent. There is a fine interplay as they each react to musical gestures by the others, sometimes supporting them, sometimes countering.

This interplay has been aptly compared to the art of cultivated conversation—witty, sensitive, always ready with a perfectly turned phrase—that was especially prized in eighteenth-century salons (see page 152).

There are dozens of wonderful string quartets by Haydn and ten equally wonderful ones by Mozart. Beethoven's sixteen string quartets, composed from the beginning to the end of his career, today stand at the heart of the repertory. To get an idea of the varieties of intimate expression these four instruments could achieve, go back to Listening Exercise 7 (page 34) and listen to the beginning of a string quartet movement by Franz Schubert.

Chamber Music

The string quartet was the main but not the only genre developed at this time for small forces in relatively intimate circumstances. **Chamber music** is a term for music designed to be played in a room (a chamber)—in a palace drawing room or in a small hall. Chamber music can be taken as encompassing compositions for from two to nine players. Other types are the piano trio (violin, cello, piano: a favorite of Haydn) and string quintets (string quartet plus another low instrument; Mozart wrote four superb quintets with two violas, and one of Schubert's great masterpieces is a quintet with two cellos).

Broadly speaking, what has been said above about the intimate character of the quartet applies to all chamber music, though it's probably clear enough that a string octet, with eight players, must be less subtle and more orchestral than a string trio, with three players.

String quartets, then (above) and now (page 189). Nineteenth-century quartets were often led by celebrated violin soloists; shown here is a group led by a virtuosa of the time, Wilma Norman-Néruda (1838–1911). From left to right: two violins, viola (slightly larger), and cello. © *Bettmann/CORBIS*.

4 | Opera Buffa

In the late eighteenth century, comic opera grew to equal in importance the serious opera that was a hallmark of the Baroque era (see page 137). Roman emperors and their courtly confidants gave way to contemporary peasant girls and soldiers; castrati were edged aside by basses specializing in comical rants and exasperations, the so-called *buffo* basses (*buffone* is Italian for "buffoon"). Happy endings were the result of tricks and schemes rather than the decrees of magnanimous princes.

Comic opera stars had to be funny; they had to act, not just sing. The new flexibility of the Classical style was perfectly suited to the unexpected and swift effects that are the essence of comedy. As much as its humor, it was this "natural," lifelike quality of comedy that appealed to audiences of the Enlightenment. Enlightened monarch Joseph II of Austria actively promoted comic opera.

Italian comic opera was the most important, though there were also parallel developments in Germany, France, and England. Serious Italian opera was called *opera seria;* comic Italian opera was called **opera buffa**. Just as Italian opera seria was very popular in London in Handel's time, so was Italian opera buffa in Vienna at the time of Haydn and Mozart. Thus Haydn, whose court duties with the Esterházys included running their opera house, wrote twelve comic operas—all in Italian. Mozart in his mature years wrote six—three in German and three in Italian.

The Ensemble

Baroque opera seria, as we have seen (page 137), employs two elements in alternation: recitatives for the dialogue and the action, and numbers that are fully musical—almost always arias—for static meditation and "tableaus" of emotional expression. Classical opera buffa works with the same elements, except that the fully musical numbers include *ensembles* as well as solo arias.

An **ensemble** is a number sung by two or more people. And given the Classical composers' skill in incorporating contrast into their music, they were

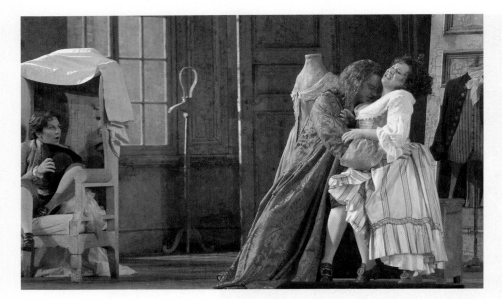

able to make their ensembles depict the different sentiments of the participating characters simultaneously. This meant that sentiments could be presented much more swiftly and vividly: swiftly, because we don't have to wait for the characters to sing whole arias to find out what they are feeling, and vividly, because the sentiments stand out in sharp relief one against the other.

The music also depicts these sentiments in flux. For in the course of an ensemble, the action proceeds and the situation changes. And changing sentiments are usually projected by means of new musical sections with different tempos, keys, and themes. A Classical opera ensemble, then, is a sectional number for several characters in which the later sections represent new plot action and the characters' new reactions to it.

Think back to the da capo aria of Baroque opera seria (see page 138). There the return of the opening music—**A** in the **A B A** form—told us that the dramatic situation was just where it had been when the aria started. But at the end of a Classical ensemble, the drama has moved ahead by one notch or more. The music, too, has moved on to something different. The Baroque aria was essentially a static number, the Classical ensemble a dynamic one. The ensemble transformed opera into a much more dramatic genre than had been possible within the Baroque aesthetic.

Wolfgang Amadeus Mozart, *Don Giovanni* (1787)

2 | 39–41   42–44

Mozart wrote *Don Giovanni* in 1787 for Prague, the second-largest city of the Austrian Empire, where his music was enjoying a temporary spurt in popularity. While technically it counts as an opera buffa, *Don Giovanni* is neither a wholly comic drama nor wholly tragic. A somewhat enigmatic mixture of both—what might be called today a dark comedy—it seems to convey Mozart's feeling that events have both comical and serious dimensions, and that life's experiences cannot be pigeonholed.

Background Don Giovanni is the Italian name for Don Juan, the legendary Spanish libertine. The tale of his endless escapades and conquests is meant to stir up incredulous laughter, usually with a bawdy undertone. Certainly a subject of this kind belongs to opera buffa.

"On Monday the 29th the Italian opera company gave the eagerly awaited opera by Maestro Mozart, *Don Giovanni,* or *The Stone Guest.* Connoisseurs and musicians say that Prague had never heard the like. Herr Mozart conducted in person; when he entered the orchestra he was received by three-fold cheers, as also happened when he left. The opera is extremely difficult to perform."

Prague newspaper, 1787

But in his compulsive, completely selfish pursuit of women, Don Giovanni ignores the rules of society, morality, and God. Hence the serious undertone of the story. He commits crimes and mortal sins—and not only against the women he seduces. He kills the father of one of his victims, the Commandant, who surprises Giovanni struggling with his daughter.

This action finally brings Don Giovanni down. Once, when he is hiding from his pursuers in a graveyard—and joking blasphemously—he is reproached by the marble statue that has been erected over the Commandant's tomb. (Yes, the statue speaks.) He arrogantly invites the statue home for dinner. The statue comes, and when Giovanni refuses to mend his ways drags him off to *its* home, which is hell. The somber music associated with the statue was planted ahead of time by Mozart in the orchestral overture to *Don Giovanni,* before the curtain rises.

Thanks to Mozart's music, our righteous satisfaction at Don Giovanni's end is mixed with a good deal of sympathy for his verve and high spirits, his bravery, and his determination to live by his own rules, not those of society, even if this dooms him. The other characters in the opera, too, awaken ambivalent feelings. They amuse us and move us at the same time.

Act I, scene iii A chorus of peasants is celebrating the marriage of Masetto and Zerlina. Don Giovanni enters with his manservant Leporello and immediately spots Zerlina. He promises Masetto various favors, and then tells him to leave—and tells Leporello to take him away by force if need be.

Aria, "Ho capito" This opera buffa aria, sung by Masetto, shows how vividly (and rapidly!) Mozart could define character in music. Singing almost entirely in very short phrases, Masetto almost insolently tells Don Giovanni that he will leave only because he has to; great lords can always bully peasants. Then he rails at Zerlina in furious, fast asides. She has always been his ruin! He sings a very sarcastic little tune, mocking Don Giovanni's promise that he is going to make her into a fine lady:

ORCHESTRA   MASETTO

Fac-cia il nostro ca-va-lie - re Ca - va - lie - ra ancora te, ca-va-liera ancora te!
No doubt this fine lord will make you his fine lady, too!

Toward the end of the aria he forgets Don Giovanni and the opening music he used to address him, and thinks only of Zerlina, repeating his furious words to her and their sarcastic tune. He gets more and more worked up as he sings repeated cadences, so characteristic of the Classical style. A variation of the tune, played by the orchestra, ends this tiny aria in an angry rush.

The total effect is of a simple man (judging from the music he sings) who nonetheless feels deeply and is ready to express his anger. There is also a clear undercurrent of class conflict: Masetto the peasant versus Don Giovanni the aristocrat. Mozart was no political radical, but he himself had rebelled against court authority; and the previous opera he had written, *The Marriage of Figaro*, was based on a notorious French play that had been banned because of its anti-aristocratic sentiments. Two years after *Don Giovanni* was composed, the French Revolution broke out in Paris.

Recitative   Next comes an amusing secco recitative, sung with just continuo accompaniment, as in Baroque opera (see page 137). The dialogue moves forward quickly, as the words are sung in speechlike, conversational rhythms. Giovanni invites Zerlina up to his villa, promising to marry her and make her into a fine lady, just as Masetto had ironically predicted.

Don Giovanni and Zerlina, in an early engraving; see page 194 for a modern production. *Bettmann/Corbis.*

Duet, "Là ci darem la mano"   Operas depend on memorable tunes, as well as on musical drama. The best opera composers write melodies that are not only beautiful in themselves but also further the drama at the same time. Such a one is the most famous tune in *Don Giovanni*, in the following **duet** (an ensemble for two singers) between Don Giovanni and Zerlina.

Section 1 (Andante)   The words of this section fall into three stanzas, which the music accommodates in an **A A′ B A″ coda** form. Don Giovanni sings the first stanza to a simple, unforgettable tune (**A**) that combines seductiveness with a delicate sense of banter:

Andante

Là ci darem la   mano,   Là mi di-rai di si;   Ve - di, non è lon - ta - no; Par-tiam, ben mio, da   qui.
There you'll give me your hand, there you'll tell me yes;   You see, it isn't far—Let's go there, my dear!

Mozart, *Don Giovanni*, from Act I, scene iii

Italics indicate phrases of the text that are repeated.

39

ARIA: "Ho capito"

0:03	**Masetto:** (to Don Giovanni)	Ho capito, *signor, si!* Chino il capo, e me ne vò Ghiacche piace a voi così Altre repliche *non fò.* . . . Cavalier voi siete già, Dubitar non posso affè, Me lo dice la bontà, Che volete *aver per me.*	I understand you, *yes, sir!* I touch my cap and off I go; Since that's what you want I have nothing else to say. After all, you're a lord, And I couldn't suspect you, oh no! You've told me of the favors You mean to do for me!
0:31	(aside, to Zerlina)	(Briconaccia! malandrina! *Fosti ognor la mia ruina!)*	(You wretch! you witch! You have always been my ruin!)
	(to Leporello)	Vengo, vengo!	Yes, I'm coming —
	(to Zerlina)	(Resta, resta! È una cosa molto onesta;	(Stay, why don't you? A very innocent affair!
0:46		Faccia il nostro cavaliere *cavaliera ancora te.)*	No doubt this fine lord Will make you his fine lady, too!)

(last seven lines repeated)

RECITATIVE
(with continuo only)

40

1:37	**Giovanni:**	Alfin siam liberati, Zerlinetta gentil, da quel scioccone. Che ne dite, mio ben, so far pulito?	At last, we're free, My darling Zerlinetta, of that clown. Tell me, my dear, don't I manage things well?
	Zerlina:	Signore, è mio marito!	Sir, he's my fiancé!
	Giovanni:	Chi? colui? vi par che un onest' uomo Un nobil Cavalier, qual io mi vanto, Possa soffrir che qual visetto d'oro, Quel viso inzuccherato, Da un bifolcaccio vil sia strapazzato?	Who? him? you think an honorable man, A noble knight, which I consider myself, Could suffer your pretty, glowing face, Your sweet face, To be stolen away by a country bumpkin?
	Zerlina:	Ma signore, io gli diedi Parola di sposarlo.	But sir, I gave him My word that we would be married.
	Giovanni:	Tal parola Non vale un zero! voi non siete fata Per esser paesana. Un'altra sorte Vi procuran quegli occhi bricconcelli, Quei labretti sì belli, Quelle dituccie candide e odorose, Parmi toccar giuncata, e fiutar rose.	That word Is worth nothing! You were not made To be a peasant girl. A different fate Is called for by those roguish eyes, Those beautiful little lips, These slender white, perfumed fingers, So soft to the touch, scented with roses.
	Zerlina:	Ah, non vorrei —	Ah, I don't want to —
	Giovanni:	Che non voreste?	What don't you want?
	Zerlina:	Alfine Ingannata restar! Io so che raro Colle donne voi altri cavalieri Siete onesti e sinceri.	To end up Deceived! I know it's not often That with women you great gentlemen Are honest and sincere.
	Giovanni:	È un' impostura Della gente plebea! La nobiltà Ha dipinta negli occhi l'onestà. Orsù non perdiam tempo; in quest'istante Io vi voglio sposar.	A slander Of the lower classes! The nobility Is honest to the tips of its toes. Let's lose no time; this very instant I wish to marry you.

		Zerlina:		Voi?	You?
		Giovanni:		Certo io.	Certainly, me;
				Quel casinetto è mio, soli saremo;	There's my little place; we'll be alone —
				E là, gioella mio, ci sposeremo.	And there, my precious, we'll be married.

DUET: "Là ci darem la mano"

SECTION 1   Andante, 2/4 meter

41	3:24	Giovanni:	**A**	Là ci darem la mano	There [in the villa] you'll give me your hand,
				Là mi dirai di si!	There you'll tell me yes!
				Vedi, non è lontano;	You see, it isn't far —
				Partiam, ben mio, da qui!	Let's go there, my dear!
		Zerlina:	**A′**	Vorrei, e non vorrei;	I want to, yet I don't want to;
				Mi trema un poco il cor.	My heart is trembling a little;
				Felice, è ver, sarei,	It's true, I would be happy,
				Ma può burlarmi ancor.	But he could be joking with me.
0:45	4:09	Giovanni:	**B**	Vieni, mio bel diletto!	Come, my darling!
		Zerlina:		Mi fa pietà Masetto . . .	I'm sorry for Masetto . . .
		Giovanni:		Io cangierò tua sorte!	I shall change your lot!
		Zerlina:		Presto non son più forte . . .	All of a sudden I'm weakening . . .

(repetition of phrases [both verbal and musical] from stanzas 1–3)

1:10	4:34	Giovanni:	**A″**	Vieni, vieni! Là ci darem la mano	
		Zerlina:		Vorrei, e non vorrei . . .	
		Giovanni:		Là mi dirai di si!	
		Zerlina:		Mi trema un poco il cor.	
		Giovanni:		Partiam, ben mio, da qui!	
		Zerlina:		Ma può burlarmi ancor.	
1:41	5:04	Giovanni:	**coda**	Vieni, mio bel diletto!	
		Zerlina:		Mi fa pietà Masetto . . .	
		Giovanni:		Io cangierò tua sorte!	
		Zerlina:		Presto *non son più forte* . . .	
		Giovanni; *then* Zerlina:		*Andiam!*	

SECTION 2   Allegro, 6/8 meter

2:09	5:33	**Both:**		Andiam, andiam, mio bene,	Let us go, my dear,
				A ristorar le pene	And relieve the pangs
				D'un innocente amor.	Of an innocent love.

Don Giovanni leads Zerlina on. *Jack Vartoogian/Getty Archive Photos.*

(words and music repeated)

When Zerlina sings the same tune to the second stanza (**A′**), we know she is playing along, even though she hesitates (notice her tiny rhythmic changes and her reluctance to finish the tune as quickly as Giovanni—she stretches it out for two more measures).

In stanza 3 (**B**), Don Giovanni presses more and more ardently, while Zerlina keeps drawing back. Her reiterated "non son più forte" ("I'm weakening") makes her sound very sorry for herself, but also coy. But when the main tune comes back (**A″**), repeating words from earlier, Giovanni and Zerlina share it phrase by phrase. Their words are closer together than before, and the stage director will place them physically closer together, too.

Section 2 (Allegro) Zerlina falls into Don Giovanni's arms, echoing his "andiam" ("let us go"). The "innocent love" they now mean to celebrate is depicted by a little rustic melody (Zerlina is a peasant girl, remember) in a faster tempo. But a not-so-innocent sensuous note is added by the orchestra after the singers' first phrase in this section.

How neatly and charmingly an operatic ensemble can project dramatic action; this whole duet leads us step by step through Don Giovanni's seduction line, and shows us Zerlina wavering before it. By portraying people through characteristic action or behavior—Don Giovanni winning another woman, Zerlina playing her own coy game—Mozart exposes their personalities as convincingly as any novelist or playwright.

"17 MAY 1788. To the Opera. *Don Giovanni.* Mozart's music is agreeable and very varied."

Diary of a Viennese opera buff, Count Zinzendorf

GOALS FOR REVIEW

▶ to recognize some Classical genres other than the symphony

▶ to listen to double-exposition form, the variant of sonata form heard in Classical concertos

▶ to gain a familiarity with Mozart's *opera buffa* (comic opera), and to contrast it with late Baroque *opera seria*, especially in the new importance of the ensemble

macmillanhighered.com/listen8e
Interactive Listening Chart 11
Listening Quizzes for Chapter 14 and Global Perspectives: Musical Form
Reading Quizzes for Chapter 14 and Global Perspectives: Musical Form

Musical Form: Two Case Studies from Asia

As we have seen, musical forms in the Classical style become quite elaborate. It is certainly no accident that these intricate designs emerged across the eighteenth century, just when independent instrumental music was gaining unprecedented prestige in the European tradition. Instrumental music often seems to require such complexities. It is as if the removal of other determinants of form—a poem set to music, a specific religious ritual, or a pattern of dance steps—calls for a different, more abstract musical organization.

Taking the broadest view of these complex forms, however, we can see that they work changes through a simple process. Composers state a tune and then repeat it throughout a movement, joining with it contrasting elements either complex (sonata form, first-movement concerto form) or simple (minuet and trio, most rondos and slow movements). Such a basic concept of repetition and change may be realized in many ways, according to the imagination and inclination of the composer, and result in an unlimited array of individual styles.

Other traditions of instrumental music around the world also start from this concept and elaborate it, building intricate forms. In this segment we offer a historical snapshot of two Asian instrumental traditions, from Japan and Indonesia, and we examine music from each.

Japan

The symphony orchestra as we know it emerged in the seventeenth century as a reflection of the power and splendor of European courts (see page 99). In Japan, a court orchestra had been established a thousand years earlier. This was the period in Japanese history, from the sixth century C.E. to the eighth, when the first centralized control of the islands emerged. The new Japanese central government, many of its institutions, and even its newly constructed capital city of Nara were modeled on the greatest empire in Asia, China. In the process, many elements of Chinese culture were imported to Japan—most importantly Buddhism, which had in turn come to China from India centuries before.

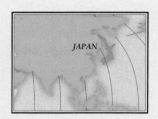

The new Japanese court also imported various musical styles from continental Asia. These were altered and developed into an independent Japanese tradition, which came to play an important role in the court's ceremony and ritual. Altogether, these styles are known as **gagaku** (gáh-gáh-koo), from Chinese characters meaning "elegant music," though their sources are more than just Chinese.

The gagaku repertory is divided into two parts. One, known as *togaku* (tóh-gáh-koo), consists of music

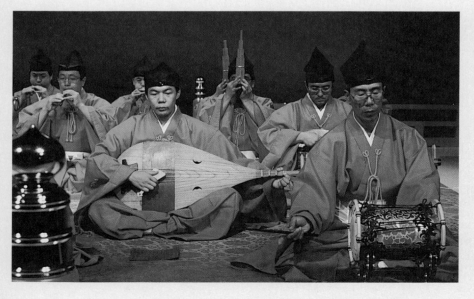

The togaku orchestra:
from left: hichiriki, biwa, sho, and kakko.
© *Jack Vartoogian/FrontRowPhotos.*

derived from Chinese styles (with ingredients from India and Southeast Asia as well). The other, *komagaku* (ko-máh-gáh-koo), is made up of works of Korean and Manchurian origin. Further distinctions are made when gagaku accompanies dance, which is often the case, just as with European Baroque orchestral music.

The Japanese Togaku Orchestra The togaku orchestra is so distinctive, and so different from any European orchestra, that we should spend a moment getting to know the various instruments. While European orchestras are dominated by strings, all gagaku orchestras feature wind instruments. The instruments all have specific functions:

• The sliding, wailing double-reed *hichiriki* (hée-chee-ree-kée) carries the main melody. Several are heard on our recording, playing together.

• The side-blown flute called *ryuteki* (ree-óo-tay-kée) is the first instrument heard. It plays the melody along with the hichirikis, though in a slightly different version. This is called a *heterophonic* texture; heterophony is an important feature in many non-Western musics.

• The *sho*, a mouth reed-organ with seventeen pipes, plays chordal clusters of tones derived from the main melody. This unusual instrument contributes a haunting background of harmonic haze to the texture.

• The *kakko*, a two-headed barrel drum played with sticks, is used for single strokes or short rolls. It is the first drum heard.

Sho. © *Jack Vartoogian/FrontRowPhotos.*

• A deep, larger barrel drum, *tsuridaiko* (tzóo-ree-díe-koh; its first beat is heard at 0:13), marks off long phrases of the melody with two successive strokes, the first soft and the second louder.

The togaku orchestra: tsuridaiko suspended on the large stand, back right, and, in the foreground, ryuteki, gakuso, and a small suspended gong not heard on our recording, called shoko. © *Jack Vartoogian/FrontRowPhotos.*

- A *biwa,* or four-stringed lute (bée-wah, first plucked at 1:11), strums across several strings quickly, punctuating the melody.

- A *gakuso,* a zither with thirteen strings (gáh-kóo-so, first heard at 1:31), plays short motives, mainly of three notes related, again, to the melody. Both the biwa and the gakuso take a more active role as this performance proceeds, finally even playing some of the main melody.

Etenraku *Etenraku* is the most famous piece for the togaku orchestra. Its name means "music of divinity," and it emanates a deep, powerful calm associated with Buddhist contemplation. This is probably the oldest music on our recordings; in some form it reaches back almost to the origins of gagaku itself.

The musical form of this piece exhibits three characteristics of gagaku music. *First,* the piece as a whole is constructed from a single melody, according to a predetermined plan and without improvisation. In *Etenraku* the melody consists of three phrases, labeled **a**, **b**, and **c** in the musical example and Listen box on this page. Each phrase is 32 beats long. (The beats move by slowly at first, so slowly that the phrases can be hard to discern until you get used to the melody.)

Second, the instruments of the orchestra are introduced gradually and in a predetermined order as they fulfill their various functions. The melody is played through by some of the instruments and punctuated by others, as described above.

Third, the beat quickens, the meter is more clearly marked, and the general musical activity increases as the performance proceeds. At first, while the flute alone carries the melody, the beats are very slow and flexible—the music seems almost to have no meter at all. (Each pair of beats on the tsuridaiko, however, coming 16 very slow beats after the last, provides a certain sense of regularity and meter.) When the double-reed hichirikis enter, they play the melody along with the flute to a more prominent beat. Then, at the **c** phrases of the melody, the tsuridaiko doubles its pace, beating twice every 8 beats instead of every 16.

Meanwhile the tempo gradually quickens: At the outset the beats come every 2–3 seconds (*very* slow!), while at the close they move by at about one per second.

LISTEN

Etenraku

3 | 34   107

0:00	**a**	Ryuteki, kakko, tsuridaiko only
0:51		Sho and hichirikis enter.
1:11	**a**	Biwa enters.
1:31		Gakuso enters, completing the orchestra.
2:18	**b**	
3:15	**b**	
4:04	**c**	Paired beats of tsuridaiko every 8 beats
4:46	**c**	Gakuso and biwa gradually play more and more fragments of the main melody, joining in the heterophony of hichirikis and ryuteki.
5:25	**a**	
6:02	**a**	
6:37	**b**	
7:11	**b**	After the phrase is completed (at 7:55), biwa and gakuso end the piece with a brief coda.

Even at this relatively quick tempo, the music never loses its sense of restraint. Virtuosic playing is strictly avoided. *Etenraku*'s aura of quiet, inward-looking Buddhist contemplation characterizes the gagaku repertory as a whole.

Indonesia

The Southeast Asian Republic of Indonesia consists of some six thousand islands in all, half of them inhabited. The central island is Java. Across Indonesia, ensembles playing traditional musics thrive—alongside, these days, many kinds of pop, rock, and world beat ensembles, especially in large urban centers such as Jakarta. A traditional musical ensemble in Indonesia is called a **gamelan**.

The Indonesian Orchestra: Gamelan Gamelans assume a wide, even bewildering variety of shapes and sizes, as we might expect of musical traditions that extend back many centuries and that have served an array of religious, political, and social functions. Gamelans may involve three or four musicians, or they may involve dozens. They sometimes include singers. They frequently accompany drama or dance: sacred temple dances, danced dramas, or the famous Indonesian shadow-puppet plays enacting stories from Hindu epics. The music gamelans play may have been passed down over hundreds of years, or it may be recently composed.

At the heart of gamelan music stands a great variety of gongs and **metallophones** (instruments like a xylophone, with metal keys). Indeed the word *gong* itself comes to us from Java, where it names (and also evokes the sound of) the largest gamelan instrument.

Balinese Gamelans Nowhere in Indonesia are gamelans more prevalent than on Bali, a good-sized island to the east of Java. In 1980 it was estimated that there was a gamelan for every 350 inhabitants of the island—a staggering number, in a population of around 2 million!

Gamelans seem to have come to Bali in the sixteenth century, brought from Java by aristocratic refugees when their Hindu kingdom fell to Islamic invaders from the Asian mainland. Balinese gamelans, at least the elaborate ones with many instruments, were associated especially with temples and princely courts. When Bali came under colonial control of the Netherlands in 1906, the courts declined, but their traditions of gamelan music did not simply disappear. Instead they were taken over more and more by village gamelan clubs, and these are the main venue in which Balinese gamelan music continues today.

Gamelan Pelegongan *Gamelan pelegongan,* heard on our recording, is a type of Balinese orchestra used primarily to accompany elaborate dance-dramas. It takes its name from this dance, called *legong.* The primary instruments in gamelan pelegongan are:

- Two hand-beaten drums. (The drummers direct the ensemble.)

- Several gongs of varying sizes.

- A large group of metallophones, some low-pitched, some high. Most of these have five metal keys each, with a range of a single octave, while some have thirteen keys and a wider range. The sounds, construction, and names of these metallophones vary, but all of them can be called by the umbrella term *gangsa,* "bronze."

- One or two bamboo flutes. What Western ears might hear as "out of tune-ness" in their playing is a quality cultivated and prized by Balinese musicians.

Form in Gamelan Music A traditional piece for gamelan is usually organized around the repetition of a long, symmetrical melody. This melody is made up of smaller, equal phrases, generally 8 or 16 beats long, so that the whole melody will last a multiple of these numbers, especially 64 or 128 beats. A central group of instruments in the gamelan presents this melody. At the same time it may be played by other instruments in a simpler version, mainly in even note values, creating a heterophonic presentation.

An ornate gamelan pelegongan from the Balinese village of Kapal, photographed in the 1930s. Large and small gangsas are arrayed on both sides of the large suspended gong; other players sit behind this front row. *Courtesy of the Colin McPhee Collection, UCLA Ethnomusicology Archive.*

A legong dancer and part of the gamelan pelegongan: A drum, a small floor gong, and a thirteen-key gangsa are prominent. © *Jack Vartoogian/FrontRowPhotos.*

At the end of each statement of the melody, the largest, deepest gong in the orchestra sounds. The unit between one gong stroke and the next, known as a *gongan*, is considered the basic structural unit for the piece. The gongan is divided into smaller units by other instruments in the gamelan: first into two units by a higher-sounding gong, then into four by other gongs, then into eight, and so forth. A 64-beat melody, for example, breaks down audibly into units of 32 beats, 16 beats, 8 beats, 4 beats, and so on.

This process of division continues right through the rhythmic level of the main melody, so that certain instruments elaborate upon its pitches twice as fast, four times as fast, perhaps even eight times as fast.

The whole texture, then, is an elaborately *stratified* polyphony, with rhythmic layers ranging from the gongan itself all the way down to subdivisions of individual beats. Each instrument or each instrumental group plays a single role, occupying one of these rhythmic strata. In the midst of it all is the melody of the piece

A gamelan at a Balinese funeral. The large array of gongs in the foreground is not found in gamelan pelegongan. *Roman Soumar/Corbis.*

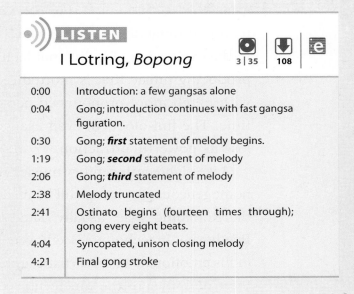

at hand, presented in one version or simultaneously in distinct versions.

Bopong The piece on our recording, *Bopong*, is not a full dance piece but instead a sort of brief overture, played before the dancing begins. It was composed by I Lotring, a famous Balinese master musician born about 1900 and involved in many stylistic innovations of the 1920s and 1930s.

The main melody is played through three times; this is the heart of the piece. Before it we hear introductory material, partly based on the main melody. After it comes a lengthy, separate section with an ostinato (see page 119), and then a new concluding melody played by the whole gamelan.

The beats of the melody move slightly faster than one beat per second. The melody is 64 beats long and composed of four phrases of 16 beats each. The large gong sounds at the end of the 64-beat cycle.

The core melody, the most prominent melody you hear, is played by some of the gangsas and by two flutes, one high-pitched and one lower and less easy to hear. At the same time other gangsas play a simpler, unadorned version of this melody in slow notes. They are omitted from the beginning of the melody; listen for them starting at 0:42.

Around this melody is woven faster figuration, dividing each beat you count into four, played by brittle-sounding gangsas. They fall silent at the start of each statement of the melody. Then they enter, softly at first, finally asserting themselves with a clamorous outburst (the first instance occurs at 0:58). Such outbursts are a famous hallmark of the newer, postcourt styles of Balinese gamelan music.

The third statement of the melody speeds up toward the end but does not quite finish. An entirely new melodic phrase breaks in to start a different section of the piece. Beginning at 2:41, some of the gangsas play a single, eight-beat ostinato, repeated many times; other gangsas and the flutes play along with a slightly elaborated version. Meanwhile the brittle-sounding gangsas contribute spectacular figuration, moving eight times as fast as the main beat. The large gong, sounding at the end of every ostinato—hence every 8 beats now, instead of every 64—adds to the feeling of rhythmic climax.

Finally, all this energy is channeled into a single closing melody with striking syncopations (see page 7), played in unison by most of the gamelan.

LISTEN

I Lotring, *Bopong*   3 | 35   108

0:00	Introduction: a few gangsas alone
0:04	Gong; introduction continues with fast gangsa figuration.
0:30	Gong; ***first*** statement of melody begins.
1:19	Gong; ***second*** statement of melody
2:06	Gong; ***third*** statement of melody
2:38	Melody truncated
2:41	Ostinato begins (fourteen times through); gong every eight beats.
4:04	Syncopated, unison closing melody
4:21	Final gong stroke

The Nineteenth Century

UNIT IV

Starting with the towering figure of Beethoven in the first quarter of the nineteenth century, famous names crowd the history of music: Schubert, Schumann, Chopin, Wagner, Verdi, Brahms, Tchaikovsky, Mahler, and others. These composers created a repertory of music that stands at the heart, still today, of symphony concerts, piano recitals, and seasons at the opera house. You might be surprised to realize how many nineteenth-century tunes you recognize in a general sort of way. They tend to turn up as background music to movies and television; some of them are metamorphosed into pop tunes and advertising jingles; and many of them are available as ringtones.

Nineteenth-century music was a great success story. Only at this juncture in European history was music taken entirely seriously as an art on the highest level. Music, more than any other art, was thought to mirror inner emotional life; we tend still today to adopt this view. Composers were accorded a new, exalted role in the expression of individual feeling. They responded magnificently to this role, producing music that is more direct and unrestrained in emotional quality, and with much more pronounced personal attributes, than the music of any earlier time. The full-blooded, even exaggerated, emotion of this music seems never to lose its powerful attraction.

Like eighteenth-century music, music of the nineteenth century is not stylistically homogeneous, yet it can still be regarded as a larger historical unit. We shall take up the Romantic style, usually dated from the 1820s, after discussing the music of Beethoven. In technique Beethoven was clearly a child of the eighteenth century; but in his emotionalism, his artistic ambition, and his insistence on individuality, he was the true father of the nineteenth century. Understanding Beethoven is the key to understanding Romantic music.

In the nineteenth century, many came to feel that music could carry them toward mysterious and awesome expressive realms—*sublime* realms, in the favorite word of the day. The sublime was discovered also in the natural world. In this painting by the German Caspar David Friedrich, it is rendered as a sea of fog, viewed by a lone hiker perched on a mountain crag. *DEA Picture Library/De Agostini/Getty Images.*

Chronology

Beethoven

CHAPTER 15

If any single composer deserves a special chapter in the history of music, that composer is Ludwig van Beethoven (1770–1827). Probably no other figure in the arts meets with such a strong universal response. People may pity van Gogh, respect Michelangelo and Shakespeare, and admire Leonardo da Vinci, but Beethoven instantly summons up a powerful, positive image: that of the tough, ugly, angry genius staring down adversity and delivering one deeply expressive masterpiece after another. Beethoven's music has enjoyed broad-based, uninterrupted popularity from his own day to the present. Today its place is equally secure with casual listeners and with the most learned musicians.

There is a sense, furthermore, in which music may be said to have come of age with Beethoven. For despite the great music that came before him—by Bach, Mozart, and many other composers we know—the art of music was never taken so seriously until Beethoven's symphonies and sonatas struck listeners of his time as a revelation. They were almost equally impressed by the facts of his life, in particular his deafness, the affliction that caused him to retire from a career as a performing musician and become solely a composer.

A new concept of artistic genius was evolving at the time, and Beethoven crystallized this concept powerfully for his own age. No longer a mere craftsman, the artist suffers and creates; endowed not just with greater talent but with a greater soul than ordinary mortals, the artist creates for humanity. Music is no longer merely a product of bodily parts like the ear or the fingers. It flows from the highest reaches of the artist's spirit.

"There is much to be done on earth, do it soon!

I cannot carry on the everyday life I am living; art demands this sacrifice too. Rest, diversion, amusement—only so that I can function more powerfully in my art."

From Beethoven's journal, 1814

1 | Between Classicism and Romanticism

Beethoven is special in another sense, in the unique position he occupies between the eighteenth-century Viennese Classical style and nineteenth-century Romanticism. Beethoven's roots were firmly Classical. He was a student of Haydn when the latter was at the height of his fame. Beethoven remained committed to the principles of the Classical style until the end of his life.

Committed to the *principles* of Classicism—but not to every one of its features, and certainly not to the mood behind it. There is almost always a sense of urgency and striving in Beethoven's music that makes it instantly distinguishable from Haydn's or Mozart's. It can be very violent; it can be solemn, severe, or exceptionally gentle. These qualities emerged in response to Romantic stirrings that are the subject of our next chapter.

The French Revolution

Romanticism, as we shall see, was originally a literary movement. Though well under way by the beginning of the nineteenth century, it was not yet influential in Vienna; and, in any case, Beethoven did not have a very literary sensibility. At the root of Romanticism, however, lay one great political upheaval that made an enormous impact on the composer's generation. This was the French Revolution. Beethoven was one of many artists who felt compelled to proclaim their sympathy with the ideal of freedom symbolized by that cataclysmic event.

When the Parisian crowd stormed the Bastille in 1789, Beethoven was a highly impressionable eighteen-year-old, already grounded in liberal and humanistic ideals. In 1803 his admiration for Napoleon Bonaparte as hero of the revolution led him to an extravagant and unprecedented gesture—writing a descriptive symphony called *Bonaparte*. Retitled the *Eroica* (Heroic) Symphony, it was the decisive breakthrough work of Beethoven's maturity, the first work to show his full individual freedom as an artist.

Before Beethoven could send the symphony off to Paris, liberal Europe received an ominous jolt: Napoleon crowned himself emperor of France. Beethoven scratched out the dedication on his score in a fury, and his feelings for Napoleon and France were never the same again. But idealism dies hard. To many at the time, the French Revolution still stood for an ideal of perfectibility— not so much of human society (as Beethoven himself acknowledged by deleting Napoleon's name) as of human aspiration. That ideal, too, is what Beethoven realized by his own triumph over his deafness. The point was not lost on those of his contemporaries who were swept away by his music.

And that is what listeners have responded to ever since. Listening to the *Eroica* Symphony, we sense that it has less to do with Napoleon than with the composer's own self-image. The quality of heroic striving and inner triumph is what emerges so magnificently in Beethoven's most famous compositions.

Storming the Bastille, an eighteenth-century engraving of the most famous event of the French Revolution. *Leemage/Corbis.*

The revolution betrayed, as painted by Jacques-Louis David: After crowning himself emperor, Napoleon crowns his wife, Josephine, empress of France in 1804. Today this huge (20 by 30 feet) and pompous painting repels some viewers almost as much as the actual event it depicts enraged Beethoven. *Bridgeman-Giraudon/Art Resource, NY.*

2 | Beethoven and the Symphony

As we have said, what sets Beethoven instantly apart from Haydn or Mozart is his mood of excitement and urgency. This he achieved by maximizing virtually all musical elements. Higher and lower registers, sharper syncopations, stronger accents, harsher dissonances yielding to more profound resolutions — all of these are found in Beethoven's music. He made new demands on instruments, expanded the orchestra, and stretched Classical forms to their limits.

Given all this, it is not surprising that this composer should be especially associated with the symphony, the most public of Classical genres, with the greatest range of expression, variety, and sheer volume. In fact, Beethoven wrote fewer symphonies (nine) than piano sonatas (thirty-two) or string quartets (sixteen) — and no musician would rank these works any lower than the symphonies. But at the height of his career, from around 1800 to 1810, even many of his piano sonatas and string quartets sound like symphonies. The torrents of sound Beethoven summoned up in these works demanded whole new techniques of piano and string playing.

Biography
Ludwig van Beethoven (1770–1827)

Probably the first musician to make a career solely from composing, Beethoven was regarded as a genius even in his lifetime. Like Mozart, he followed his father as a court musician; the Beethovens served the archbishop-elector of Bonn in western Germany. But Ludwig's father—unlike Wolfgang's—was a failure and an alcoholic who beat the boy to make him practice. A trip to Vienna to make contacts (he hoped to study with Mozart) was cut short by the death of his mother. Still in his teens, Beethoven had to take charge of his family because of his father's drinking.

Nonetheless, Bonn was an "enlightened" court, ruled by the brother of Emperor Joseph II of Austria. The talented young musician could mix with aristocrats and audit classes at the liberal University. The idealism that is so evident in Beethoven's later works—such as his Ninth Symphony, ending with a choral hymn to universal brotherhood—can be traced to this early environment.

Compared to Mozart, Beethoven was a slow developer, but by the age of twenty-two he had made enough of an impression to receive a sort of fellowship to return to Vienna, this time to study with Haydn. He was soon acclaimed as a powerful virtuoso pianist, playing his own compositions and improvising brilliantly at the palaces of the music-loving aristocracy of that city. He remained in Vienna until his death.

After the age of thirty, he became progressively deaf—a devastating fate for a musician, which kept him from making a living in the traditional manner, by performing. The crisis that this caused in Beethoven's life is reflected by a strange, moving document (called the "Heiligenstadt Testament," after the town where it was written, in 1802) that is half a proclamation of artistic ideals, half suicide note. But Beethoven overcame his depression and in 1803 wrote the first of his truly powerful and individual symphonies, the Third (*Eroica*).

Beethoven all but demanded support from the nobility in Vienna, who were awed by his extraordinarily forceful and original music as well as by his uncompromising character. An alarmingly brusque and strong-willed person, he suffered deeply and seemed to live for his art alone. His domestic life was chaotic; one anecdote has him pouring water over himself to cool off in summer and being asked by his landlord to leave. (He moved an average of once a year.) By the end of his life he was well known in Vienna as an eccentric, teased by street boys.

Like many leftists—for the French Revolution invented the Left as we know it—Beethoven grew more conservative in later years. After life in Vienna was disrupted by French occupations, he went into a slump and kept himself going by writing music for counterrevolutionary celebrations. Ironically, he was never so famous or so well-off. He came out of the slump to write some of his greatest music, but it was mostly beyond the comprehension of his contemporaries.

Beethoven had an immense need to receive and to give affection, yet he never married, despite various love affairs. After he died, passionate letters to a woman identified only as his "Immortal Beloved" were found; we now know she was the wife of a Frankfurt merchant. In his later years Beethoven adopted his own orphan nephew, but this was a catastrophe. His attitude was so overprotective and his love so smothering that the boy could not stand it and attempted suicide.

Beethoven had always lived with ill health, and the shock of this new family crisis hastened his death. Twenty thousand attended his funeral; his eulogy was written by Vienna's leading poet.

Taste in many matters has changed many times since Beethoven's lifetime, but his music has always reigned supreme with audiences and critics. The originality and expressive power of his work seem never to fade.

Chief Works: Nine symphonies, the most famous being the Third (*Eroica*), Fifth, Sixth (*Pastoral*), Seventh, and Ninth (*Choral*) ■ The opera *Fidelio* (originally called *Leonore*), for which he wrote four different overtures; overtures to the plays *Egmont*, by Goethe, and *Coriolan* ■ Violin Concerto and five piano concertos, including the "Emperor" (No. 5) ■ Sixteen string quartets ■ Thirty-two piano sonatas, including the *Pathétique, Waldstein, Appassionata,* and the late-period *Hammerklavier* Sonata ■ Mass in D (*Missa solemnis*)

Encore: After Symphony No. 5 and the Piano Sonata in E, Op. 109, listen to the "Moonlight" Sonata; Sonata in A-flat, Op. 110; Symphonies No. 6 and 9.

Image credit: AKG-Images/The Image Works.

We can approach Beethoven's "symphonic ideal" through his Fifth Symphony, written in 1808. Three main features of this work have impressed generations of listeners: its rhythmic drive, its motivic consistency or unity, and the sense it gives of a definite psychological progression. The first feature can be grasped at once, the second by the end of the opening movement, and the third only after we have experienced all four of the symphony's movements.

- *Rhythmic drive.* Immediately apparent is the drive and blunt power of the rhythmic style. Beethoven hammers the meter, piles accent upon accent, and calculates long time spans with special power: a far cry from the elegance and wit of the Classical style.

- *Motivic consistency.* During the first movement of the Fifth Symphony, a single motive is heard constantly, in many different forms. They are not random forms; the motive becomes more and more vivid and significant as the work proceeds. People have marveled at the "organic" quality of such music, which seems to them to grow like a plant's leaves out of a simple seed.

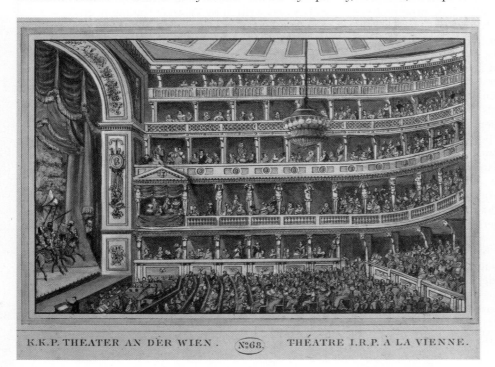

DA DA DA DAAA

- *Psychological progression.* Over the course of the Fifth Symphony's four movements, Beethoven seems to trace a coherent and dramatic psychological progression in several stages. "There Fate knocks at the door!" he is supposed to have said about the first movement—but after two eventful middle stages, Fate is nullified in the last movement, trampled under by a military march.

In Beethoven's hands, the multimovement symphony seems to trace an inspirational life process, one so basic and universal that it leaves few listeners unmoved. This was, perhaps, the greatest of all his forward-looking innovations.

The Scherzo

Another of Beethoven's technical innovations should also be mentioned. On the whole, Beethoven continued to use Classical forms for his symphonies and other multimovement works. As early as his Second Symphony, however, he replaced

K.K.P. THEATER AN DER WIEN.   N°68.   THÉATRE I.R.P. À LA VIENNE.

The Theater an der Wien, a famous opera theater and concert house that opened in Vienna in 1801. Many of Beethoven's best-loved works were first performed here, including, in 1808, his Fifth Symphony. *Erich Lessing/Art Resource, NY.*

the traditional minuet with another kind of movement, which he called the **scherzo** (scáir-tzo). This is a fast, rushing movement in triple meter—inherited from the minuet—and in the basic minuet-and-trio form, **A B A**. Beethoven's scherzos sometimes go so fast that they need more repetitions to make their point; **A B A** can be extended to **A B A B A**.

The word *scherzo* means "joke" in Italian. Beethoven's brand of humor is very different from, say, Haydn's: It is broad, brusque, jocular, even violent. Originally associated with the court of Louis XIV, the minuet still stood for eighteenth-century formality and elegance; one can see why Beethoven rejected it. The scherzo became an ideal vehicle for Beethoven's characteristic rhythmic drive. See page 214.

Ludwig van Beethoven, Symphony No. 5 in C Minor, Op. 67 (1808)

3 | 1–15   45–48   17–20

Beethoven composed his Fifth Symphony together with his Sixth (*Pastoral*) for one of the rare concerts in which he was able to showcase his own works. This concert, in December 1808, was a huge success, even though it ran on for five hours and the heating in the hall failed.

First Movement (Allegro con brio)   Motivic consistency, as we have said, is a special feature of Beethoven's work. The first movement of the Fifth Symphony is famously saturated by a single rhythmic motive, ♪♪♪ ♩. This motive forms the first theme in the exposition and it initiates the bridge. It is even heard as a subdued background to the lyrical, contrasting second theme; and it emerges again at full force in the cadence material:

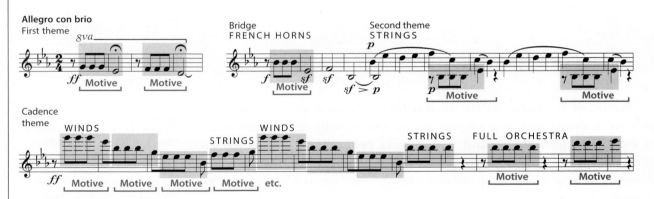

The motive then expands further in the development section and continues growing in the long coda.

How is this different from Classical motivic technique? In such works as Mozart's Symphony No. 40, a single motive is likewise developed with consistency and a sense of growth. But Beethoven's use of the same device gives the Fifth Symphony its particular gripping urgency. The difference is not in the basic technique but in the way it is being used—in the expressive intensity it is made to serve. It is a Classical device used for non-Classical ends. Let us see how this works.

Exposition The movement begins with an arresting presentation of the first theme, in the key of C minor (shown on page 209). The meter is disrupted by two fermatas (a fermata ⌒ indicates an indefinite hold of the note it comes over). These give the music an improvisational, primal quality, like a great shout. Even after the theme surges on and seems to be picking up momentum, it is halted by a new fermata, making three fermatas in all.

The horn-call bridge (see page 209) performs the usual function of a bridge in an unusually dramatic way. That function is to cement the new key—a major key—firmly and usher in the second theme effectively.

The second theme introduces a new gentle mood, despite the main motive rumbling away below it. But this mood soon fades—Beethoven seems to brush it aside impatiently. The main motive returns in a stormy cadence passage, which comes to a satisfying, complete stop. The exposition is repeated.

Development The development section starts with a new eruption, as the first theme makes a (very clear) modulation, a modulation that returns to the minor mode. There is yet another fermata. It sounds like the crack of doom.

For a time the first theme (or, rather, its continuation) is developed, leading to a climax when the ♩♩♩ rhythm multiplies itself furiously, as shown to the right. Next comes the bridge theme, modulating through one key after another. Suddenly the *two middle pitches* of the bridge theme are isolated and echoed between high wind instruments and lower strings. This process is called fragmentation (for an example from Mozart, see page 166). The two-note figure fragments further, and the echoing process shrinks down to just one note:

Beethoven is famous for the tension he builds up in retransitions, the sections in sonata form that prepare for the recapitulations (see page 164). In the Fifth Symphony, the hush at this point becomes almost unbearable. Finally the whole orchestra seems to grab and shake the listener by the lapels, shouting the main motive again and again until the first theme settles out in the original tonic key.

Recapitulation The exposition version of the main theme was interrupted by three fermatas. Now, in the recapitulation, the third fermata is filled by a slow, expressive passage for solo oboe, a sort of cadenza in free rhythm. This extraordinary moment provides a brief rest from the continuing rhythmic drive. Otherwise the recapitulation stays very close to the exposition—a clear testimony to Beethoven's Classical allegiance.

Coda On the other hand, the action-packed coda that follows is an equally clear testimony to Beethoven's freedom from Classical formulas.

Learning to Appreciate Beethoven, Part 1

"Went to a German charitable concert [the American premiere of Beethoven's Fifth Symphony]. . . . The music was good, very well selected and excellently well performed, as far as I could judge. The crack piece, though, was the last, Beethoven's Sinfonia in C minor. It was generally unintelligible to me, except the Andante."

Diary of a New York music lover, 1841

In the exposition, we recall, the stormy cadence passage was defused by a satisfying Classical cadence and a complete stop. At the end of the recapitulation, the parallel passage seems to reject any such easy solution. Instead a new contrapuntal idea appears, with French horns below and strings above:

In the melody for French horns we hear the four main-theme *pitches* (G E♭ F D; see page 209). But they are played in the *rhythm* of the bridge: ♪♪♪ | ♩ ♩ | ♩. Then the two middle notes of this melody are emphasized by a long downward sequence.

The sequence evolves into a sort of grim minor-mode march—a moment of respite from the endless thematic evolutions of the main motive. A final, defiant appearance of the original theme leads this time to continuations that are unexpectedly poignant. But the very end of the movement consists of affirmative cadences, built once again out of the main motive.

The Remaining Movements The defiant-sounding final cadence of the first movement feels like a standoff at the end of a heroic struggle. Beethoven now builds on this feeling to give the impression of a dramatic psychological progression, another characteristic feature of his symphonic writing.

The later movements of the Fifth Symphony feel like responses to—and, ultimately, a resolution of—all the tension Beethoven had summoned up in the first movement. We are never allowed to forget the first movement and its mood, not until the very end of the symphony, mainly because a form of the first movement's rhythmic *motive*, ♪♪♪♩, is heard in each of the later movements. This motive always stirs uneasy recollections. Furthermore, the later movements all refer to the *key* of the first movement. Whenever this key returns in its original minor mode (C minor), it inevitably recalls the struggle that Beethoven is said to have associated with "Fate knocking at the door." When it returns in the major mode (C major), it signifies (or foretells) the ultimate resolution of all that tension—the triumph over Fate.

Don't worry about recognizing C major or distinguishing it from any other major-mode key. Almost any time you hear a very loud, triumphant theme in the later movements, it is in the key of C major. As important as the melody of those themes and their orchestration (often with brass) is the fact that they come in the major mode, thus negating the first movement's struggle.

A special abbreviated Listening Chart for the entire symphony is provided on page 213. All the C-major sections are indicated in color.

Second Movement (Andante con moto) The first hint of Beethoven's master plan comes early in the slow movement, after the cellos have begun with a graceful theme, which is rounded off by repeated cadences. A second graceful theme begins, but is soon derailed by a grinding modulation—to C

Learning to Appreciate Beethoven, Part 2

"I expected to enjoy that Symphony [Beethoven's Fifth], but I did not suppose it possible that it could be the transcendent affair it is. I've heard it twice before, and how I could have passed by unnoticed so many magnificent points—appreciate the spirit of the composition so feebly and unworthily—I can't imagine."

Diary of the same New Yorker, 1844

LISTENING CHART 12

Beethoven, Symphony No. 5 in C Minor, first movement

Sonata form. 7 min., 18 sec.

3 | 1–9   45   17

EXPOSITION

1	0:00	**Theme 1**	Main theme with *two fermatas*, followed by the *first continuation* (based on ♩♩♩ ♩); *another fermata (the third)*
	0:20		Main motive (♩♩♩ ♩), *ff*, is followed by a *second continuation:* timpani, crescendo.
2	0:46	**Bridge theme**	French horn, *f*

Second Group

0:02	0:49	**Theme 2**	Major mode, *p*, strings and woodwinds (♩♩♩ ♩ in background)
3	1:17	**Cadence theme**	Based on ♩♩♩ ♩ motive
0:05	1:22		CADENCE
0:10	1:26	***Exposition repeated***	

DEVELOPMENT

4	2:52		First modulation, using ♩♩♩ ♩ motive; French horns, *ff*; minor mode
0:05	2:58		Development of *first continuation* of theme 1
0:29	3:21		Climactic passage of powerful reiterations: ♩♩♩	♩♩♩♩	♩♩♩♩	♩
0:36	3:28		Development of bridge theme
5	3:39		Fragmentation of bridge theme to two notes, alternating between strings and winds
0:10	3:49		Fragmentation of bridge theme to one note, alternating between strings and winds, *p*
0:29	4:07	**Retransition**	Based on ♩♩♩ ♩, *ff*, runs directly into the recapitulation

RECAPITULATION

6	4:13	**Theme 1**	Harmonized; *two fermatas*. *First continuation* of theme; woodwind background.
0:18	4:31		***Slow oboe cadenza in place of the third fermata***
0:33	4:46		*Second continuation* of theme 1
0:53	5:06	**Bridge Theme**	Bassoons, *f*

Second Group

7	5:09	**Theme 2**	Strings and winds, *p* (♩♩♩ ♩ in timpani); major mode
0:33	5:42	**Cadence theme**	This time it does not stop.

CODA

8	5:49		Another climax of reiterations (as in the development)
0:15	6:04		Returns to the minor mode; new expanded version of bridge theme, in counterpoint with new scale figure
0:30	6:19		New marchlike theme, brass; winds and strings build up.
9	6:51		Theme 1: climactic presentation in brass. ***Last fermatas.***
0:08	6:59		*First continuation* of theme 1, with a pathetic coloration; oboe and bassoon figures
0:13	7:04		Strong conclusion on ♩♩♩ ♩

major, where the second theme starts again. Blared out by the trumpets, *ff*, it's no longer graceful—it would sound like a brutal fanfare if it didn't fade almost immediately into a mysterious passage where the ♪♪♪♩ rhythm of the first movement sounds quietly. Beethoven is not ready to resolve the C-minor turmoil of the first movement just yet. Variations of the first theme follow (one is in the minor mode), but there is something aimless about them. What stays in the memory from this movement are two shattering brass fanfares in C major.

Third Movement (Allegro)   This movement, in **3/4** time, is one of Beethoven's great scherzos (though the composer did not label it as such, probably because its form is so free). There are two features of the smooth, quiet opening theme (**a**) that immediately recall the mood of the first movement—but in a more muted, apprehensive form. One is the key, C minor. The other is the interruption of the meter by fermatas.

First movement (**a**):

Third movement (**b**):

Then a very forceful second theme (**b**), played by the French horns, recalls in its turn the first movement's rhythmic motive. The two themes alternate and modulate restlessly, until the second makes a final-sounding cadence.

When now a bustling and somewhat humorous fugal section starts in the major mode—in C major—we may recognize a vestige of the old minuet-and-trio form, **A B A** (though the **A** section, which you have heard, with its two sharply contrasted themes **a** and **b**, has nothing in common with a minuet beyond its triple meter). **B**, the major-mode "trio," is in the traditional |: **c** :||: **d c'** :| form, but with an all-important modification. The second **d c'**, instead of being repeated exactly, is reorchestrated, becoming quieter and quieter.

After this, the opening minor-mode music returns, as we would expect in a conventional minuet and trio movement. But it has now been transformed in tone color into something quiet and almost stealthy. Hushed *pizzicato* (plucked) strings for **a** and a brittle-sounding oboe for **b** replace the smooth and forceful sounds heard before. Everything now breathes an unexpected mood of mystery.

Fourth Movement (Allegro)   The point of this reorchestration appears when the section does not reach a cadence but runs into a truly uncanny transition, with timpani tapping out the rhythm of **b**—the original DA–DA–DA–DAAA motive, again—over a strange harmony. The music grows louder and clearer until a veritable military march erupts—in the key, needless to say, of C major.

Minor mode cedes to major, *pp* to *ff*, mystery to clarity; the arrival of this symphony's last movement, after the continuous transition from the scherzo, has the literal effect of triumph over some sort of adversity. This last movement brings in three trombones for the first time in the symphony. (They must have really awakened the freezing listeners at that original 1808 concert.)

The march makes a splendid first theme of a sonata-form movement, in which the later themes are marchlike, too. The second theme includes a speeded-up version of the DA-DA-DA–DAAA rhythm, with a slower, upward-stepping bass that will drive the development section. The bridge and the cadence theme are wonderfully gutsy.

Beethoven, Symphony No. 5 in C Minor, complete work

31 min., 31 sec.

3 | 10–15 | 46–48 18–20

	FIRST MOVEMENT (Allegro con brio, 2/4; sonata form)			C minor, **ff**
	See Listening Chart 12.			
10	**SECOND MOVEMENT (Andante, 3/8; variations)**			A♭, major, **p**
	0:00	**Theme 1**	Ends with repeated cadences	
	1:03	**Theme 2**	Played by clarinets and bassoons	
	1:26		Trumpets enter.	**(goes to C MAJOR, ff)**
	2:12	**Theme 1**	Variation 1, played by strings	
	3:06	**Theme 2**	Clarinets and bassoons	
	3:29		Trumpets enter.	**(goes to C MAJOR, ff)**
	4:16	**Theme 1**	Variations 2–4 (without repeated cadences), ending **f**; then a long, quiet transition: woodwinds	
	6:13	**Theme 2**	Trumpets	**C MAJOR, ff**
11	6:58	**Theme 1**	Variations 5 (minor; woodwinds) and 6 (full orchestra); cadences	
1:30	8:29	**Coda**		A♭, major
	THIRD MOVEMENT (Allegro, 3/4; A B A′)			C minor, **pp**
12	**Scherzo (A)**			
	0:00	**a b**		
	0:41	**a′b′**		
	1:21	**a″b″**	Ends with a loud cadence built from **b**	
13	**Trio (B)**			**C MAJOR, ff**
	1:52	**|: c :|**	**Fugal**	
0:33	2:25	**d c′**		
1:03	2:56	**d c′**	*Reorchestrated, p; runs into scherzo* (goes back to C minor, **pp**)	
	Scherzo (A′)			
1:38	3:30		Scherzo repeated, shorter and *reorchestrated*, **pp**	
2:54	4:46	**Transition**	Timpani; leads directly into the fourth movement	
	FOURTH MOVEMENT (Allegro, 2/2; sonata form)		**(goes to C MAJOR, ff)**	
14	**Exposition**			**C MAJOR, ff**
	0:00	**Theme 1**	**March theme**	
	0:34	**Bridge theme**	**Low horns and bassoons**	
	1:00	**Theme 2**		
	1:27	**Cadence theme**		
	Development			
	1:57		Development begins; modulation.	
	2:02		Theme 2 and its bass developed	
15	3:31	**Retransition**	Recall of the scherzo (**A′, 3/4** meter)	(recall of C minor, **pp**)
	Recapitulation			**C MAJOR, ff**
0:32	4:03	**Theme 1**		
1:07	4:38	**Bridge theme**		
1:36	5:07	**Theme 2**		
2:02	5:33	**Cadence theme**		
	Coda			
2:30	6:01		**Coda; three sections, accelerating; uses parts of the bridge, cadence theme, and theme 1**	**C MAJOR, ff**

(music notation examples at right:)

ff

p

f TRUMPETS

a CELLOS **p**

b FRENCH HORNS **f**

c DOUBLE BASSES **f** fugue subject

with TROMBONES **ff**

ff

bass:

Then, at the end of the development, Beethoven offers another example of his inspired manipulation of musical form. The second theme (**b**) *of the previous movement*, the scherzo, comes back quietly once again, a complete surprise in these surroundings (there is even a change from the **4/4** meter of the march back to **3/4**). This theme now sounds neither forceful nor mysterious, as it did in the scherzo, but rather like a dim memory. Perhaps it has come back to remind us that the battle has been won.

All that remains is a great C-major jubilee, in the recapitulation and then later in a huge accelerating coda. "There Fate knocks at the door"—but fate and terror alike yield to Beethoven's optimistic major-mode vision.

3 | Beethoven's "Third Period"

Beethoven's music is traditionally divided into three style periods. The first period (until 1800, in round numbers) covers music building on the style of Haydn and Mozart. The middle period contains characteristically "heroic" works like the *Eroica* and Fifth symphonies.

In the third period (from around 1818 to 1827) Beethoven's music loses much of its earlier tone of heroism. It becomes more introspective and tends to come framed in more intimate genres than the symphony, such as the piano sonata, the string quartet, and the piano miniature (a new genre that looks to the future; see page 229). The strength of his earlier music seems to be tempered by a new gentleness and spirituality. (However, Beethoven's mightiest symphony, the Ninth, also dates from this period.)

Beethoven's late music also becomes more abstract—a difficult quality to specify. In part the abstractness involves his free exploration of cerebral formal designs, such as long fugues looking back on Bach, or variation forms that range farther from their themes than any before them. In part it is a matter of the themes themselves, which are reduced to fragments or to elemental musical materials: scales, quick-moving arpeggios or "broken" chords, and the like. And in part the abstractness comes from an almost miraculous control of contrast and musical flow that Beethoven now managed. This is especially evident in movements still showing the outlines of sonata form. Here themes and sections of the form are often condensed, and transitional moments are boiled down to carefully judged juxtapositions. While disruption was always a feature of Beethoven's music—think of the fermatas in the first movement of the Fifth Symphony, and the C-major trumpets in the second—now the breaks in the musical fabric can be bewildering, even unnerving.

This picture of Beethoven at work, painted about 1890, captures the conception of him that grew strong after his death: the solitary genius wrestling with his celestial art, oblivious to the worldly disarray around him. The picture, however, conveys an irony: One thing Beethoven could *not* do late in his career, given his deafness, was try out each musical idea at the piano. *The Granger Collection, NYC. All rights reserved.*

Ludwig van Beethoven, Piano Sonata in E, Op. 109 (1820)

2 | 42–45   49

Gentleness and spirituality certainly characterize this extraordinary transformation of sonata form. Two expressive themes contrast in every possible way, even in tempo and meter. The first barely murmurs its way into our consciousness, with its playful repeated ♪♩. rhythm:

The second theme breathes considerable passion and draws on some brilliant piano effects:

Both themes sound inconclusive, even fragmentary, and the second follows on the heels of the first with almost shocking abruptness. (*Is* it a second theme? A bridge theme?)

After a cadence theme that dwindles to little more than a scale, a brief development-like passage shows theme 1, with its characteristic rhythm, growing into a new melody that rises up in pitch and volume. At its high point, a sense of harmonic expectancy reminds us of the retransitions of conventional

LISTENING CHART 14

Beethoven, Piano Sonata in E, Op. 109, first movement (Vivace)

42–45   49

Free sonata form. 4 min., 4 sec.

42	EXPOSITION		
	0:00	Theme 1	
	0:13	Theme 2	
	0:58	Cadence theme	
43	**DEVELOPMENT**		
0:00	1:11	Theme 1 developed	New melody appears.
0:35	1:46	Retransition	Harmonic expectancy
44	**RECAPITULATION**		
0:00	1:54	Theme 1	Now *f*
0:13	2:07	Theme 2	New dynamics, harmonies
0:57	2:51	Cadence theme	Varied from exposition version
45	**CODA**		
	3:12	Theme 1	Melody varied, but quiet as at first

sonata forms, and indeed it ushers in the first theme, but now *f*, its tranquillity disturbed. In this recapitulation, the second theme introduces new juxtapositions of dynamics (*p* → *ff*) and of unexpected harmonies.

The closing theme leads to an especially benign coda. It focuses on the rhythm of the first theme, restoring the theme's original tenderness in a version of it that reintroduces the melody from the development, quietly now, and closes with repeated cadences.

GOALS FOR REVIEW

▶ to locate Ludwig van Beethoven between the Classical and Romantic styles

▶ to understand the unique historical impact of Beethoven's symphonic style

▶ to listen to Beethoven's transformation of Classical forms and techniques in his Symphony No. 5

▶ to sample the innovative turn in Beethoven's late style

macmillanhighered.com/listen8e
Interactive Listening Charts 12–14
Listening Quiz for Chapter 15
Reading Quiz for Chapter 15

Music after Beethoven: Romanticism

CHAPTER

16

Many terms we use for historical periods in the arts came into use only after the fact. *Baroque,* as a designation for a style period in music, was adopted from the field of art history by musicologists in the twentieth century. The term *Romantic,* instead, was used by the Romantics themselves. It first took hold in literature, and by the time the earliest Romantic composers began their careers in the 1820s, their literary contemporaries were already excitedly talking about "Romantic" music.

This tells us two important things about music after the time of Beethoven. One is that, largely thanks to Beethoven, people had become highly aware of music as a major art. Music was treated with a new respect in cultivated circles; it was taken seriously in a way it never had been before.

The other is that it seemed quite natural for observers of the time to link up developments in music with parallel developments in literature. From Homer and Virgil to Shakespeare and Milton, literature had always been considered the most important and most convincing of the arts. The prestige and power of literature were now freely extended to music.

This fact is illustrated in a painting much admired at midcentury, showing a group of literary lions and lionesses listening reverently to Franz Liszt at the piano (see page 219). Their expressions tell us how profoundly the music moves them; their aesthetic experience is very different, clearly, from the casual enjoyment of eighteenth-century listeners pictured on page 133. The painting shows also how important Beethoven was in bringing about this change. Liszt gazes soulfully at Beethoven's larger-than-life bust. Does it rest on the books stacked on the piano, or loom outside the window, gigantic, against the turbulent sky?

1 | Romanticism

Romantic literature and literary theory flourished particularly in and around the first two decades of the nineteenth century. In England, this was a great age of poetry: Wordsworth, Coleridge, Shelley, Keats, and Byron. There was also a brilliant outpouring of German Romantic literature during the same period, though the names of its writers are less familiar in the English-speaking world: Tieck, Novalis, Kleist, Hölderlin, and E. T. A. Hoffmann.

For us, the word *romantic* refers to love; this usage dates from the nineteenth century and derives from the literary movement. But the glorification of love was only one of the many themes of Romantic literature, themes that were also central to the music of the nineteenth century.

The power of Romantic music: Liszt as the inspiration for novelists Alexandre Dumas, Victor Hugo, George Sand, and Daniel Stern (on the floor). Daniel Stern was the pseudonym of the Countess d'Agoult (see page 247). In the back, opera composer Gioacchino Rossini embraces violin virtuoso Niccolò Paganini. *Bettmann/CORBIS*.

The Cult of Individual Feeling

Striving for a better, higher, ideal state of being was at the heart of the Romantic movement. Everyday life seemed dull and meaningless; it could be transcended only through the free exercise of individual will and passion. The rule of feeling, unconstrained by convention, religion, or social taboo (or anyone else's feelings, often enough)—this became the highest good. Emotional expression became the highest artistic goal. "Bohemians," as they were disparagingly called at the time, proclaimed romantic love, led irregular lives, and wore odd clothes. We have the Romantics to thank for this familiar image of the artist, still around today.

These attitudes may be laid at the door of Jean-Jacques Rousseau—the same Enlightenment philosopher who had spoken up in the mid-eighteenth century for "natural" human feelings, as opposed to the artificial constraints imposed by society (see page 153). Hailed as the philosophical father of the French Revolution, Rousseau provided the Romantics with the ideal of individual, as well as political, freedom and fulfillment. We have also seen Rousseau as a proponent of a "natural" music, and indeed his own music was still being played at French revolutionary rallies and pageants.

But there was more than philosophy behind the new attitudes. The Industrial Revolution had already begun its inexorable course, and increasingly as the nineteenth century went on, people felt their helplessness in the face of the factories, slag heaps, and inhuman working conditions of developing capitalism. The smokestacks of what William Blake called "these dark, Satanic mills" now loomed over the European landscape. There was an understandable element of escapism in Romantic striving.

Romanticism and Revolt

In the wake of the Industrial Revolution came actual revolution—the central fact in the politics of the age. It began with our own American Revolution. Then the French Revolution of 1789 rocked all of Europe. It was followed by a whole set of aftershocks up to 1848, a year of major upheavals in France, Germany, Austria, and Italy.

The Romantics were inevitably cast in the role of rebels against the established order. Many musicians (like many poets and painters) associated themselves with libertarian politics, starting with Beethoven, who wrote a symphony named *Bonaparte* (which he renamed the *Eroica;* see page 205). In a later generation, Liszt briefly espoused a strange half-communistic, half-religious movement that took hold in French intellectual circles. Giuseppe Verdi's name became an acronym for the Italian liberation movement (see page 261). Richard Wagner was thrown out of Germany in 1849 for inflammatory speeches he made from the revolutionary barricades in the town of Dresden.

Along with political revolution went social revolution. The barriers of hereditary nobility were breached, and the lower and middle classes gained more social mobility. Thus Liszt, who was the son of an estate foreman, could conduct glamorous liaisons—one stormy, the other stable—with a French countess and a Russian princess. The importance of this was not lost on Liszt's contemporaries; the countess is another of the celebrities included in the picture of Liszt at the piano (though the artist tactfully hid her face).

Artistic Barriers

The Romantics' search for higher experience and more intense expression provoked a reaction against the restraints of artistic form and genre. Artists resisted all rules and regulations. They distrusted abstract notions of "beauty" and rules of "decorum" that they felt might hamper their spontaneity.

Eighteenth-century drama, for example, was hemmed in by such rules until the Romantics overturned them. Against the rules they cited the works of Shakespeare, where locations change scene by scene, tragedy mixes with farce, rich poetry collides with bawdy prose, and noble characters share the stage with clowns. The lifelike turbulence and loose form of these plays made Shakespeare enormously popular in the nineteenth century. Dozens of composers wrote music associated with them, including Mendelssohn, Berlioz, Tchaikovsky, Wagner, and Verdi.

In music itself, composers worked to break down barriers of harmony and form. All the Romantic composers experimented with chords, or chord progressions, that had previously been forbidden. From the time of Schubert on,

La Marseillaise, the great rallying song of the French Revolution. *The Granger Collection, NYC. All rights reserved.*

Nightmare, by Henry Fuseli (1741–1825), an eighteenth-century pre-Romantic painter, poet, and revolutionary who emigrated from Switzerland to England for political reasons. *Detroit Institute of Arts, USA/Founders Society purchase with Mr. and Mrs. Bert L. Smokler/and Mr. and Mrs. Lawrence A. Fleischman funds/The Bridgeman Art Library.*

their music was enriched by imaginative new harmonies. Sonata form, the hallmark of Classicism, was already treated freely by Beethoven, especially in his late style, as we saw in his Piano Sonata in E, Op. 109 (see page 216). The Romantic composer Robert Schumann went further, treating the form so freely in his piano sonatas that he finally labeled the last (and greatest) of them "Fantasy." It was a proclamation of his spontaneity on the one hand, and insurance against accusations of rule-breaking on the other.

Music and the Supernatural

The supernatural—often linked to the bizarre or macabre—loomed large in the Romantic firmament, as we might expect of a movement so intent on transcending the ordinary. In *Nightmare,* a weird picture by the early Romantic painter Henry Fuseli, dream is made concrete, visible, and public in the figure of a horrible ogre (see above). The magician Faust pledging his soul to the Devil for a single moment of transcendent happiness became the subject of the greatest poem of the time, Goethe's *Faust.* Franz Schubert wrote "The Erlking," about a demon who claims a terrified child, in 1815 (see page 234); Mary Shelley wrote *Frankenstein* in 1818. The titles of some of the most famous operas of the time—*Robert the Devil, The Vampire, The Magic Bullet*—speak for themselves.

In music, the new freedoms aided this aspect of Romanticism. Composers cultivated strange harmonies and sinister orchestral sounds that can still be heard for special effect on video and movie soundtracks today. A famous scene of devilish conjuration in a deep forest, the Wolf's Glen scene in Carl Maria von

Weber's opera *Der Freischütz* (The Magic Bullet, 1821), was an early monument to Romanticism in music (see page 256). Spooky music was devised by Verdi for the witches in his Shakespeare opera *Macbeth*, and by Wagner for the ghost ship and its crew in *The Flying Dutchman*. And in his *Fantastic* Symphony, as we shall see (page 249), Hector Berlioz wrote a movement called "Dream of a Witches' Sabbath" that bears comparison with Fuseli's *Nightmare*.

Music and the Other Arts

Shakespearean, individualist in outlook, emotive, contemptuous of handed-down conventions—these are the general traits of Romantic art. In this climate new efforts were made to blend the arts together: Poetry became more "musical," paintings and musical works were given "poetic" titles, and poetry, drama, music, and stagecraft all merged in Wagner's unique and enormously influential "total artwork," or *Gesamtkunstwerk* (see page 266). Within individual arts, blurred effects were cultivated—half-obscure verbal meanings, ambiguous shapes and color blends, and musical sounds that are imprecise but rich and evocative.

No one went further in this respect than the English landscape painter J. M. W. Turner. In one of his most famous pictures, *The "Fighting Téméraire,"* the grandeur of nature and the horrors of industrialization merge in dizzy, almost

The "Fighting Téméraire" Tugged to Her Last Berth to Be Broken Up, 1838 by J. M. W. Turner (1775–1851).
© National Gallery, London/Art Resource, NY.

In *The Bard* by John Martin, man is dwarfed by nature—nature depicted as both menacing and thrilling. *Yale Center for British Art, Paul Mellon Collection, USA/Paul Mellon Collection/The Bridgeman Art Library.*

abstract swirls of color. If Rousseau had admired nature for its simplicity, now Turner aimed at its "sublime" quality: the majesty and mystery of nature, its boundlessness, even its menace. The great Romantic artists stared unblinkingly at the infinite and tried to set it down in their art.

And it was exactly the boundless quality of music that gave it its special prestige and status. Music, people felt, could express inner experience more deeply than the other arts because the musician's imagination is not tied down to the meaning of words (like the poet's) or to the representation of things (like the painter's). This led philosophers of the time to incorporate music at the heart of their views. Here, too, Rousseau had pointed the way; he was followed by Arthur Schopenhauer (who influenced Wagner) and Friedrich Nietzsche (whom Wagner influenced) in Germany.

"All art aspires to the condition of music," wrote a famous Victorian critic, Walter Pater. All Romantic art tried to capture music's depth and freedom of emotional expression and its continuous, "infinite" quality.

"Music is a strange thing. I would almost say it is a miracle. For it stands halfway between thought and phenomenon, between spirit and matter."

Poet Heinrich Heine

2 | Concert Life in the Nineteenth Century

So much for ideals. What about the marketplace?

Public concerts, first introduced in the Baroque era during the age of aristocratic patronage of the arts, grew more important in the days of Haydn, Mozart, and Beethoven. As the nineteenth century progressed, the concert hall together with the opera house came to dominate the presentation of music. Every town of any size had its symphony association, organized by merchants, government officials, lawyers, and other members of the middle class. Halls built to accommodate symphony concerts were expressions of civic pride, as they still are today. In 1891 the New York Symphony, that city's second orchestra (the New York Philharmonic was founded in 1842), proudly presented a five-concert music festival led by Tchaikovsky in brand-new Carnegie Hall.

By the end of the century even intimate, domestic musical genres, designed for the drawing room or the studio, were presented on the concert stage. Concerts of *Lieder* (German songs) and string quartet concerts became established, though they were never as important as orchestral concerts. In an age before technologies for sound recording, concerts made more music available to more and more people.

Improved transportation, meanwhile, brought musicians on tour to remote areas, such as the American West. Italian Romantic opera in particular spread far and wide — to New York and Philadelphia, to San Francisco (where Italian immigrant dockworkers were drafted to sing the choruses), to Buenos Aires, and even up the Amazon River.

The Artist and the Public

The institutionalization of concert life also had its negative aspect, in that audiences gradually became more conservative in their musical tastes. The old aristocratic system had actually been more neutral in this respect. While many aristocratic patrons cared less about music than display, and some exercised the most whimsical of tastes, others actually encouraged composers to pursue new paths, or at least left them alone to do so. On the other hand, the concert public tended to conservatism. The mainly middle-class buyers of concert tickets naturally wanted value, as with anything else they bought. What counted as value was something already established as a masterpiece, something that they already knew and liked.

Composers with an interest in innovation — and that includes every composer discussed in this unit — often felt that their work was being neglected by the concert world. A paradoxical situation developed. The composers' dependence on the public was tinged with resentment, and the public's admiration for composers — never before higher — was tinged with distrust, even hostility.

In this climate the composer Robert Schumann started an important magazine to campaign for Romantic music in the face of public indifference to serious art and preference for what he regarded as flashy trivia. Editor Schumann invented a "League of David" to slay the "Goliath" of the concert audience. (In the Bible, Goliath was the champion of the Philistines; it was around this time that the adjective *philistine* came to mean "uncultured.") Later, the music of Liszt and Wagner was attacked by hostile critics as formless, dissonant, and overemotional. Later still, the symphonies of Gustav Mahler were repeatedly rejected by audiences in Vienna, in spite of Mahler's important position as head of the Opera there.

The gap between innovative music and a conservative concert public, which opened up in the nineteenth century, widened in the twentieth, as we shall see. Here as elsewhere, the nineteenth century set the tone for modern musical life.

"Alas, if one could only reduce the public to an assembly of fifty sensible and intelligent persons, how blissful it would be to be an artist!"

Hector Berlioz

Groundbreaking ceremony for Carnegie Hall in New York. The bearded man visible behind one of the vertical ropes is the famous railroad and steel baron Andrew Carnegie, the donor. Program: *Hulton Archive/Getty Images*. Photo: *Courtesy of Carnegie Hall Archives*.

3 | Style Features of Romantic Music

Since the main artistic value in the Romantic era was the integrity of personal feeling, every genuine artist was expected to have a personal style. Many artists carried this very far, cultivating styles that were highly personal and even eccentric. Furthermore, Romanticism's constant striving after ever-new kinds of expression put a premium on innovation; this could be seen as an exciting breaking down of artistic barriers on the one hand, and as a heroic personal breakthrough on the other. Consequently it is harder to define the Romantic style in general than to spot innovations, novelties, and individual peculiarities.

Nevertheless, nineteenth-century composers were united by some common interests: technical considerations concerning melody, harmony, rhythmic freedom, tone color, and, perhaps especially, musical form. But it is important to remember that one such common interest was to sound different from everybody else.

Romantic Melody

The most instantly recognizable feature of Romantic music is its melodic style. Melody in the Romantic era was more emotional, effusive, and demonstrative than before. Often the melodic lines ranged more widely than the orderly, restrained tunes of the Classical era; often, too, they built up to more sustained climaxes. Melodies became more irregular in rhythm and phrase structure, so as to make them sound more spontaneous.

A fine example is the so-called Love theme of Tchaikovsky's Overture-Fantasy, *Romeo and Juliet* (see page 279). It begins with a great outburst—a climax, at the very start, shaded blue in the music below—and then sinks down an octave and more, in melodic curves whose yearning quality grows more and more sensuous. Especially striking is the second part of the melody, where a rhythmic figure surges up in sequence, seven times in all, in preparation for a free return of the opening climax, now *ff* (also shaded blue):

When one thinks of Romantic melody, what comes first to mind is this kind of grand, exaggerated emotionality. Some Romantic melodies are more intimate, however—and they are no less emotional for sparing the tears and handkerchief. Each in an individual way, Romantic composers learned to make their melodies dreamy, sensitive, passionate, ecstatic, or whatever shade of feeling they wished to express.

Romantic Harmony

Harmony was one of the areas in which Romantic music made the greatest technical advances. On the one hand, composers learned to use harmony to underpin melody in such a way as to bring out its emotionality. Romantic melody is, in fact, inseparable from harmony. In the *Romeo and Juliet* Love theme, for example, a rich new chord goes hand in hand with the warm upward scoop of the melodic line in measure 5.

On the other hand, harmony was savored for its own sake, and composers experimented freely with new chord forms and new juxtapositions of chords. These, it was found, could contribute potently to those mysterious, sinister, rapturous, ethereal, or sultry moods that Romantic composers sought to evoke.

Chromaticism is a term for a style that liberally employs all twelve notes of the chromatic scale (see page 23). Romantic composers pursued chromaticism to a greater extent than Baroque and Classical ones, in order to expand the expressive range of both their melodies and their harmony. If you look closely at the *Romeo and Juliet* theme, you will find nearly all twelve notes of the chromatic scale included—something that seldom happens in earlier music. Chromaticism was carried furthest in the nineteenth century by Richard Wagner, and further yet by the early twentieth-century modernists.

The increased chromaticism of nineteenth-century music spawned this bizarre experimental harp, which is really two harps, crisscrossed, to accommodate all the notes of the chromatic scale. *Image copyright © The Metropolitan Museum of Art. Image source: Art Resource, NY.*

Rhythmic Freedom: Rubato

The general Romantic tendency to blur all sharp edges found its musical counterpart in the rhythmic practice of *tempo rubato,* or just **rubato**. Rubato means that in musical performance the rhythm is handled flexibly; the meter itself may waver, or else the beat is maintained strictly in the accompaniment while the melody is played or sung slightly out of phase with it. (Literally, *tempo rubato* means "robbed time"—that is, some time has been stolen from the beat.)

Rubato was practiced in the service of greater individual expressivity. Though seldom indicated in a score—indeed, no one has ever found an accurate way to indicate rubato in musical notation—its practice is documented by old recordings, made around 1900 by musicians who were close to the Romantic composers (or even by the composers themselves). Improvisation, in the sense of adding ornaments or other notes to a score, was all but abolished by the end of the nineteenth century. Let no mere performer tamper with notes which had been set down by a composer of transcendent genius! But performers of the time improvised *rhythmically,* in that they applied rubato freely to nearly every score they played.

Considered a sign of bad taste in Baroque or Classical music, at least when applied extensively, rubato is an essential expressive resource in the playing, singing, and conducting of Romantic music. A musician's sensitivity and "feeling" depends to a great extent on his or her artistic use of rubato.

The Expansion of Tone Color

While tone color had been treated with considerable subtlety by the Viennese Classical composers, the Romantics seized on this aspect of music with particular enthusiasm. For the first time in Western music, the sheer sensuous quality of sound assumed major artistic importance on a level with rhythm, melody, and musical form.

So it is no accident that all instruments went through major technical developments during the nineteenth century—the piano not least. As orchestral instruments reached their present-day forms, the orchestra was expanded, soon reaching its present standard makeup. The chart below for a typical Romantic orchestra, when compared with the Classical orchestra chart on page 157, shows how the ranks of the brass, woodwind, and percussion sections were filled out:

A TYPICAL ROMANTIC ORCHESTRA

STRINGS	WOODWINDS	BRASS	PERCUSSION
First violins (12–16 players)	2 Flutes	4 French horns	3 Timpani
Second violins (12–16)	1 Piccolo	2 Trumpets	Bass drum
Violas (8–12)	2 Oboes	3 Trombones	Snare drum
Cellos (8–12)	1 English horn	1 Bass tuba	Cymbals
Basses (6–10)	2 Clarinets		Triangle
	1 High E♭ clarinet		Tubular bells
	1 Bass clarinet		
Note: Each string section is sometimes divided into two or more subsections, to obtain richer effects.	2 Bassoons		
	1 Contrabassoon		
2 Harps			Piano

What such charts cannot show, however, are the ingenious new *combinations* of instruments that were now investigated. Composers learned to mix instrumental colors with something of the same freedom with which painters mix actual colors on a palette. Berlioz wrote a treatise on "orchestration," or the use and combination of the instruments of the orchestra, which is still read today. In his and other composers' practice, the clear, sharply defined sonorities of the Classical era were replaced by multicolored shades of blended orchestral sound.

Romantic composers and audiences alike were fascinated by the symphony orchestra, and for the first time conductors came to the fore—conductors wielding batons. (Berlioz also wrote a treatise on conducting.) In earlier times, orchestras had simply followed the first violinist or the continuo player, but now they needed experts to control and balance out those special blended effects.

The orchestra also became increasingly important in nineteenth-century opera. Major opera composers, such as Weber, Meyerbeer, and Wagner, specialized in orchestral effects that sometimes even threatened to put the voices in the shade. If today, when one thinks of classical music, the symphony orchestra comes to mind almost automatically, that is a holdover from the Romantic nineteenth century.

4 | Program Music

Program music is a term for instrumental music written in association with a poem, a story, or some other literary source—or even just a highly suggestive word or two. While program music was certainly not new in the Romantic era, it gained new importance and prestige, for program music answered the general Romantic demand for transcending inter-art boundaries. Instrumental music could be made even more expressive, many felt, by linking it to poetry and ideas.

The term *program music* is sometimes restricted to music that tells or at least traces a story, the story being the "program." In 1829, at the premiere of his *Fantastic* Symphony, the composer Hector Berlioz actually handed out a pamphlet containing his own made-up program, and the music of the symphony behaves like a narrator a good deal of the time. From the weird shrieks and groans at the start of the symphony's last movement, through the riotous welcome of the heroine, to the final frenzied round dance, we are treated to musical events that follow the events of the story step by step (see page 252).

Another type of program music adopts a different strategy. Instead of telling a story, it attempts to capture the general flavor of a mood associated with some extramusical state, concept, or personality. The single word *nocturne*, as the title for a whole genre of compositions by Frédéric Chopin, is enough to set up expectations of nighttime romance—and the music does the rest (see page 245). In short piano pieces, Schumann drew portraits of his friends (and even of himself; see page 244).

Program music sparked a great debate in the nineteenth century, a debate that still goes on. Does the music *really* illustrate or represent the program? Suppose the music is played without listeners being given the program—could they tell it from the music? Shouldn't the music make complete sense on its own terms, even if we grant that the program provides an added dimension to it?

But the point is that the Romantics did not *want* to be without the program. They did not necessarily *want* the music to "make sense on its own terms." And it seems they were prepared to live with this apparent inconsistency: On the one hand, they revered purely instrumental music as the highest form of art; on the other hand, they embraced program music, music that is less "pure" because it mixes in nonmusical elements.

More and more complex orchestras required conductors, and conductors required batons. Before sticks came into use, the German opera composer Carl Maria von Weber (see page 258) seems to have used a tight scroll of paper (a score?). *Bettmann/CORBIS.*

5 | Form in Romantic Music

Individual spontaneity was an important goal of the Romantic movement. And if there was any area in which the composer wanted to seem particularly free and spontaneous, it was the area of musical form. The music should bubble out moment by moment, irrepressible and untrammeled, like churning emotion itself. But composers faced a problem: how to control that spontaneity? They had to provide their music with enough sense of coherence that listeners could follow it.

In their approach to musical form, nineteenth-century composers broke with Classical norms. They wanted each work of art to express its individuality in its form as well as its style (melody, harmony, timbre, etc.). They distrusted conventional, standardized forms just as they flouted society's other conventions. Even when they followed forms such as sonata form, rondo, and so on, they tended to follow them so loosely that it gets to be a matter of opinion whether they are doing so at all. Themes tend to blend into one another, and there is much less of the neat, clear cadencing of Classical music.

Some Romantic compositions deliberately break down the boundary between music and nonmusical silence. Robert Schumann's song "Im wunderschönen Monat Mai" (see page 238) begins hesitantly, as though it is already in the middle of a transition; we feel we have just begun hearing music that started long ago. Instead of ending with a decisive cadence, the song comes to a questioning dissonance, then—silence. The vague, atmospheric quality at the start and the suggestion of infinity at the end are typically Romantic.

Yet the music had to avoid real formlessness if it was to hold the attention of an audience. Once again, for Romantic composers the problem was how to create the impression of spontaneous form while at the same time giving the listener some means of following the music. They developed a number of interesting and characteristic solutions.

Miniature Compositions

While many Romantic compositions last for about as long as works from the eighteenth century, special classes of music arose with quite different dimensions.

First, composers cultivated what we will call **miniatures**, pieces lasting only a few minutes—or even less. Mostly songs and short piano pieces, these were designed to convey a particularly pointed emotion, momentary and undeveloped. In this way the composer could commune with the listener intensely but intimately, as though giving him or her a single short, meaningful glance. The meaning might well be hinted at by a programmatic title.

Though short pieces were also written in earlier times, of course—think of minuet movements in classical symphonies—usually they were components of larger units, where their effect was balanced by other, longer movements. Romantic miniatures, though they were often published in sets, as we will see, nevertheless were composed so as to stand out as individuals in their own right, apart from their sets. Miniatures for piano were sometimes given general titles, such as Schubert's Impromptus (Improvisations) and Brahms's Capriccios (Caprices). Sometimes they masqueraded as dances, like Chopin's Mazurkas (a Polish dance). Often they were given more suggestive, programmatic titles: *Years of Pilgrimage* by Franz Liszt; *Spring Song* by Felix Mendelssohn; *To a Wild Rose* by Edward MacDowell, America's leading late Romantic composer. Schumann was something of a specialist in such titles: *The Poet Speaks, Confession, The Bird as Prophet,* and—*Why?*

The man has put down his violin to sit with the woman at the piano; we can imagine the four-hand music they are playing, perhaps, but we cannot see their faces. This picture catches both the intimacy and privacy of the Romantic miniature and also its characteristic location, the middle-class living room. *Blauel/Gnamm/Artothek.*

In miniatures the problem of musical form was not so much solved as avoided. They are over before the listener begins to wonder where the music is going, what the next effect will be.

Grandiose Compositions

Another Romantic tendency was diametrically opposed to the miniatures. Many composers wrote what may be called grandiose compositions—larger and larger symphonies, cantatas, and so on, with more and more movements, increased performing forces, and a longer (sometimes much longer) total time span. For example, Hector Berlioz's symphony *Romeo and Juliet* of 1839 lasts for nearly an hour and a half. (A typical Haydn symphony lasts twenty minutes.) Starting with an augmented symphony orchestra, Berlioz added soloists and a chorus in certain of the movements and a narrator between them, and then threw in an off-stage chorus for still other movements. In the field of opera, Richard Wagner's *The Nibelung's Ring* takes the prize. It goes on for four evenings, with a huge orchestra including specially invented instruments, a cast of thirty, and fifteen separate stage sets (see page 268).

The total effect of these grandiose compositions involved not only music but also poetry, philosophical or religious ideas, story lines, and (in operas) dramatic action. Listeners were impressed, even stupefied, by a combination of opulent sounds, great thoughts, powerful emotions, and sheer length.

The grandiose compositions of the nineteenth century occasioned many cartoons—amusing enough, but not in the last analysis friendly to the advanced music of the time. Here it is Berlioz who is lampooned. *The Pierpont Morgan Library/Art Resource, NY.*

These works met what we have called the problem of musical form in their own way. The bigger the work, the bigger the problem, but to help solve it composers could draw on extramusical factors—on the words of a vocal work, or the program of an instrumental one. Music could add emotional conviction to ideas or stories; in return these extramusical factors could supply a rhyme and reason for the sequence of musical events—that is, for the musical form.

The Principle of Thematic Unity

An important general principle developed by Romantic composers was that of thematic unity. There was an increasing tendency to maintain some of the same thematic material throughout whole works, even (or especially) when these works were in many movements.

In nineteenth-century symphonies and other such works, several different levels of thematic unity can be distinguished:

• Most obviously, themes from one movement may come back literally and quite clearly in other movements. We have already heard this happen in Beethoven's Fifth Symphony, when the scherzo theme returns in the last movement.

• In other compositions, new *versions* of a single theme are used at important new points in the music, either later in the same movement or in later movements.

While these new versions are really nothing more than variations of the original theme, this procedure differs fundamentally from Classical theme and variations form (see page 169). In Classical variation form, the theme is an entire tune, and the variations follow one another directly. In the new Romantic procedure, the theme is (generally) much more fragmentary than a tune, and the new versions of the theme appear at irregular intervals in the midst of other, unrelated music.

The term **thematic transformation** is used for this variation-like procedure in Romantic music, whereby short themes are freely varied at relatively wide and unpredictable intervals of time. A precedent for it can be traced to works such as Beethoven's Fifth Symphony, where the 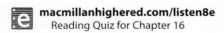 motive of the first movement is evoked freely in each of the later ones.

• In still other nineteenth-century pieces, we hear themes with even looser relationships among them. Clearly different, they nonetheless exhibit mysterious inner similarities—similarities that seem to help unify the music, though they are too shadowy to count as transformations in the Romantic definition, let alone as variations in the Classical style. Wagner's operas are famous for such themes.

Of all the levels of thematic unity employed by nineteenth-century composers, this last is the most typical of all. Vague similarity rather than clear likeness, suggestion rather than outright statement, atmosphere rather than discourse, feeling rather than form: All these go to the heart of Romanticism. We cannot appreciate Romantic music fully if we approach it in too literal a frame of mind. In much of this music, the special spontaneous form of the individual piece, as distinct from standard forms such as sonata and rondo form, is tied to the principle of thematic unity. Listening to Romantic music requires ears that are not only attentive but also imaginative, exploratory, and more than a little fanciful.

GOALS FOR REVIEW

▶ to gain an overview of the culture and arts of the Romantic movement

▶ to understand the new place of the composer in nineteenth-century concert life

▶ to see, in general, new features of style and new genres in the Romantic period

▶ to understand new ways of connecting instrumental music to nonmusical things: program music

▶ to think about the contrast of miniature and grandiose works by Romantic composers

macmillanhighered.com/listen8e
Reading Quiz for Chapter 16

The Early Romantics

Perhaps the most brilliant generation of composers in the entire history of music was that of the early Romantics. Franz Schubert was born in Vienna in 1797; then the ten-year period between 1803 and 1813 saw the births of Robert Schumann, Frédéric Chopin, Felix Mendelssohn, Franz Liszt, Hector Berlioz, Richard Wagner, and Giuseppe Verdi. It was a brilliant generation, but not a long-lived one. Only the last four of these composers survived to continue their major work into the second half of the century.

Two general points are worth making about this early Romantic galaxy. First, Beethoven's music had a profound effect on them, though this was naturally felt more strongly by German composers than by non-Germans. Schubert, who lived in Vienna under Beethoven's shadow, was influenced by the older master much more directly than Chopin, a Pole who lived in Paris.

The second important point is that these composers were deeply influenced by literary Romanticism, which had flourished since before they were born. Schubert wrote many songs to texts by Romantic poets such as Goethe, Novalis, and Friedrich Schlegel, and Schumann's enthusiasm for the German Romantic novelist Jean Paul Richter was reflected in his music as well as in his own prose writings. We have mentioned that Shakespeare was particularly admired by the Romantics; nearly all the composers mentioned here wrote music associated with Shakespeare's plays.

1 | The Lied

The ordinary German word for song is *Lied* (plural, *Lieder*—pronounced "leader"). The word also has a special application: the **lied** is a particular type of German song that evolved in the late eighteenth century and flourished in the nineteenth. As such, the lied is one of the most important "miniature" genres of the Romantic era.

Though one cannot generalize about the melodies of these songs—some consist of little more than a tune, others are melodically much more complex—they share some other characteristic features.

• *Accompaniment.* A lied is nearly always accompanied by piano alone, and the accompaniment contributes significantly to the artistic effect. Indeed, the pianist becomes more of a discreet partner to the singer than a mere accompanist.

• *Poetry.* The text of a lied is usually a Romantic poem of some merit (at least in the composer's estimation). Hence, although we need to understand the words of almost any vocal music, with the lied we should also try to appreciate how the poem's words and meanings fit together as poetry. The art of the lied depends on the sensitivity of the composer's response to the poetic imagery and feeling.

• *Mood.* A third characteristic, harder to explain, is the intimacy of expression that is captured by these pieces. The singer and the pianist seem to be sharing an emotional insight with just you, rather than with an entire audience; words and music are uttered softly, inwardly. Composers intended lieder for the intimacy of a living room, not a formal concert hall, and that is where they are best heard.

Franz Schubert, "Erlkönig" (The Erlking) (1815)

3 | 16   50   21

The earliest and (for most musicians) greatest master of the lied is Franz Schubert. He wrote close to seven hundred songs in his short lifetime. In his eighteenth year, 1815, he averaged better than a song every two days! Many of these are quite short tunes with simple piano accompaniments, but Schubert's tunes are like nobody else's; he was a wonderfully spontaneous melodist. Later in life his melodies became richer but no less beautiful, and taken together with their poems, the songs often show remarkable psychological penetration.

One of those songs from 1815 was an instant hit: "Erlkönig" (The Erlking), published as the composer's opus 1, and still today Schubert's best-known lied. In those early years, Schubert wrote a considerable number of long, narrative songs, though this one stands out from the others in its dramatic intensity.

The poem is by Johann Wolfgang von Goethe, the greatest literary figure of the day—by turns a Romantic and a Classical poet, novelist, playwright, naturalist, and philosopher, and a favorite source of texts for many generations of lied composers. Cast in the old storytelling ballad form, which enjoyed a vogue in the Romantic era, and dealing with death and the supernatural, the poem is famous in its own right.

Title page of the first edition of "The Erlking." Note the stunted tree; the literal meaning of "Erlkönig" is king of the alders, or birches—in effect, a forest troll.

Schubert playing at an evening with the Schubertians (see page 237). To the left is Johann Vogel, an older singer, one of his main supporters. Their friend Moritz von Schwind started this picture but didn't quite finish it. *Wien Museum Karlsplatz, Vienna, Austria/The Bridgeman Art Library.*

Though Goethe's poem consists of eight parallel stanzas, they are not set to the same music. Schubert provided the later stanzas with different or modified music; such a song is said to be **through-composed**. (A song that repeats the same music over and over for all its stanzas is called **strophic**; see page 50.) The poem certainly invites this kind of musical setting, as its mood changes dramatically as it goes along. A father rides furiously through the night with a child who is presumably running a high fever, for he claims to see and hear a murderous demon. The Erlking first beckons the child, then cajoles him, then threatens and assaults him. The father—uncomprehending, even impatient—tries to quiet the boy, but by the time they reach home the boy is—dead!

The opening piano introduction sets the mood of dark, tense excitement. The right hand hammers away at harsh repeated notes in triplets, representing the horse's hooves, while the left hand has an agitated motive:

Schubert invented different music for the poem's three characters (and also the narrator). Each "voice" characterizes the speaker in contrast to the others. The father is low, stiff, and gruff, the boy high and frantic. Marked **ppp**, and inaudible to the father, the ominously quiet and sweet little tunes crooned by the Erlking, offering his "schöne Spiele"—lovely games—add a chilling note.

Two things help hold this long song together. First, the piano's triplet rhythm continues ceaselessly, until the very last line, where recitative style lets us know that the ride is over. (The triplets are muffled during the Erlking's speeches—because the child is hearing him in a feverish daze?) Second, there are some telling musical repetitions: the agitated riding motive (stanzas 1–2 and 8), and a desperately strained phrase sung higher and higher by the boy as he appeals to his father (stanzas 4, 6, and 7).

 **LISTEN**

Schubert, "Erlkönig"

3 | 16   50   21

0:23	**Wer reitet so spät, durch Nacht und Wind?** **Es ist der Vater mit seinem Kind;** **Er hat den Knaben wohl in dem Arm,** **Er fasst ihn sicher, er hält ihn warm.**	Who rides so late through the night and wind? It is the father with his child. He holds the youngster tight in his arm, Grasps him securely, keeps him warm.
0:56	**"Mein Sohn, was birgst du so bang dein Gesicht?"** **"Siehst, Vater, du den Erlkönig nicht?** **Den Erlenkönig mit Kron' und Schweif?"** **"Mein Sohn, est ist ein Nebelstreif."**	"My son, what makes you afraid to look?" "Don't you see, Father, the Erlking there? The King of the forest with his crown and train?" "Son, it's only a streak of mist."
1:29	**"Du liebes Kind, komm, geh mit mir!** **Gar schöne Spiele spiel' ich mit dir;** **Manch' bunte Blumen sind an dem Strand;** **Meine Mutter hat manch' gülden Gewand."**	*"Darling child, come away with me!* *I will play some lovely games with you;* *Many bright flowers grow by the shore;* *My mother has many golden robes."*
1:52	**"Mein Vater, mein Vater, und hörest du nicht** **Was Erlenkönig mir leise verspricht?"** **"Sei ruhig, bleibe ruhig, mein Kind:** **In dürren Blättern säuselt der Wind."**	"Father, Father, do you not hear What the Erlking is softly promising me?" "Calm yourself, be calm, my son: The dry leaves are rustling in the wind."
2:14	**"Willst, feiner Knabe, du mit mir gehn?** **Meine Töchter sollen dich warten schön;** **Meine Töchter führen den nächtlichen Reihn** **Und wiegen und tanzen und singen dich ein."**	*"Well, you fine boy, won't you come with me?* *My daughters are ready to wait on you.* *My daughters lead the nightly round,* *They will rock you, dance for you, sing you to sleep!"*
2:32	**"Mein Vater, mein Vater, und siehst du nicht dort** **Erlkönigs Töchter am düstern Ort?"** **"Mein Sohn, mein Sohn, ich seh es genau:** **Es scheinen die alten Weiden so grau."**	"Father, Father, do you not see The Erlking's daughters there in the dark?" "My son, my son, I see only too well: It is the gray gleam in the old willow trees."
3:01	**"Ich liebe dich, mich reizt deine schöne Gestalt,** **Und bist du nicht willig, so brauch' ich Gewalt."** **"Mein Vater, mein Vater, jetzt fasst er mich an!** **Erlkönig hat mir ein Leids getan!"**	*"I love you, your beauty allures me,* *And if you're not willing, then I shall use force."* "Father, Father, he is seizing me now! The Erlking has hurt me!"
3:26	**Dem Vater grauset's, er reitet geschwind,** **Er hält in Armen das ächzende Kind,** **Erreicht den Hof mit Müh und Not;** **In seinen Armen das Kind war tot.**	Fear grips the father, he rides like the wind, He holds in his arms the moaning child; He reaches the house hard put, worn out; In his arms the child was—dead!

Biography
Franz Schubert (1797–1828)

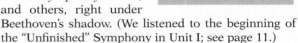

Schubert was the son of a lower-middle-class Viennese schoolmaster. There was always music in the home, and the boy received a solid musical education in the training school for Viennese court singers. His talent amazed his teachers and also a number of his schoolmates, who remained devoted to him throughout his career. Schubert began by following in his father's footsteps as a schoolteacher, without much enthusiasm, but soon gave up teaching to devote all his time to music.

Schubert was an endearing but shy and unspectacular individual who led an unspectacular life. However, it was the sort of life that would have been impossible before the Romantic era. Schubert never married — it is believed he was gay — and never held a regular job. He was sustained by odd fees for teaching and publications and by contributions from a circle of friends who called themselves the Schubertians — young musicians, artists, writers, and music lovers. One of the Schubertians, Moritz von Schwind, who became an important painter, has left us many charming pictures of the group at parties, on trips to the country, and so on (see page 235).

It was an atmosphere especially conducive to an intimate musical genre such as the lied. Schubert wrote nearly seven hundred lieder and many choral songs. For a time he roomed with a poet, Johann Mayrhofer, who provided him with gloomy texts for about fifty of them.

But it's unfortunate that Schubert's wonderful songs have tended to overshadow his symphonies, sonatas, and chamber music. Starting out with Classical genres, Schubert in his very short lifetime transformed them under the influence of Romanticism. He never introduced himself to Beethoven, even though they lived in the same city; perhaps he instinctively felt he needed to keep his distance from the overpowering older master. It speaks much for Schubert that he was able to write such original and powerful works as the "Unfinished" Symphony, the so-called *Great* Symphony in C, and others, right under Beethoven's shadow. (We listened to the beginning of the "Unfinished" Symphony in Unit I; see page 11.)

A few of Schubert's instrumental works include melodies taken from his own songs: the popular *Trout* Quintet, the String Quartet in D Minor (*Death and the Maiden*), and the *Wanderer* Fantasy for piano.

Schubert died in a typhoid fever epidemic when he was only thirty-one. He never heard a performance of his late symphonies, and much of his music came to light only after his death.

Our portrait shows Schubert around the time he wrote *The Erlking*.

Chief Works: Lieder, including the song cycles *Die schöne Müllerin*, *Winterreise*, and *Schwanengesang*, "The Erlking," "Gretchen at the Spinning Wheel," "Hedgerose," "Death and the Maiden," "The Trout," and hundreds of others ▪ "Character" pieces for piano; waltzes ▪ Symphonies, including the "Unfinished"—Schubert completed only two movements and sketches for a scherzo—and the *Great* Symphony in C ▪ Piano sonatas; *Wanderer* Fantasy for piano ▪ Four mature string quartets; a string quintet; the genial *Trout* Quintet for piano and strings (including double bass)

Encore: After "The Erlking," listen to the "Unfinished" Symphony and songs from *Winterreise*.

Image credit: Kunsthistorisches Museum, Vienna, Austria/The Bridgeman Art Library.

The Song Cycle

A song cycle is a group of songs associated by a common poetic theme or an actual story. For the words of the songs, composers either found whole coherent groups of poems to set, or else made their own selections from a larger collection of a poet's work. Schubert, who wrote two great song cycles relatively late in his career, was able to use ready-made groups of poems published by a minor Romantic poet named Wilhelm Müller: *Die schöne Müllerin* (The Fair Maid of the Mill) and *Winterreise* (Winter Journey).

The advantage of the song cycle was that it extended the rather fragile expression of the lied into a larger, more comprehensive, and hence more impressive unit. It was, in a sense, an effort to get beyond "miniaturism," even while composing miniatures. The unity of such larger units, however, is always loose. The individual songs can often be sung separately, as well as in sequence with the rest of the cycle.

Robert Schumann, *Dichterliebe* (A Poet's Love) (1840)

3 | 17–18   51–52   22

"Schubert died. Cried all night," wrote the eighteen-year-old Robert Schumann in his diary in 1828. Yet living in Zwickau, Germany, far from Schubert's Vienna, Schumann did not know many of the older composer's best-known works, his lieder. He loved Schubert's piano music, and indeed, for the first ten years of his own career as a composer, Schumann wrote only piano music.

> "To cast light into the depths of the human heart — the artist's mission!"
>
> *Robert Schumann*

Then in 1840, the year of his marriage, he suddenly started pouring out lieder. Given this history, it is not surprising that in Schumann's songs the piano is given a more complex role than in Schubert's. This is particularly true of his most famous song cycle, *Dichterliebe*, the first and last songs of which (nos. 1 and 16) we will examine here. *Dichterliebe* has no real story; its series of love poems traces a psychological progression from cautious optimism to disillusionment and despair. They are the work of another great German poet, Heinrich Heine, a man who reacted with bitter irony against Romanticism, while acknowledging his own hopeless commitment to its ideals.

"Im wunderschönen Monat Mai" (In the wonderfully lovely month of May)   The song begins with a piano introduction, halting and ruminative—which seems at first to be a curious response to the "wonderfully lovely" month of May. The piano part winds its way in and out of the vocal line, ebbing and flowing rhythmically and sometimes dwelling on quiet but piercing dissonant harmonies.

What Schumann noticed was the hint of unrequited longing in Heine's very last line, and he ended the song with the piano part hanging in midair, without a true cadence, as though in a state of reaching or yearning: a truly Romantic effect. Technically, the last sound is a dissonance that requires resolution into a consonance (see page 28) but does not get it (until the next song).

In this song, both stanzas of the poem are set to identical music. As mentioned earlier, such a song is called *strophic;* strophic setting is of course familiar from folk songs, hymns, popular songs, and many other kinds of music. For Schumann, this kind of setting had the advantage of underlining the similarity in the text of the song's two stanzas, both in meaning and in actual words. Certainly his music deepens the tentative, sensitive, hope-against-hope quality of Heine's understated confession of love.

The qualities of intimacy and spontaneity that are so important to Romantic miniatures can be inhibited by studio recording. Our recording of Schumann's song was made at a concert (you will hear applause as the artists enter).

"Die alten, bösen Lieder" (The hateful songs of times past)   After many heart-wrenching episodes, the final song in the *Dichterliebe* cycle begins strongly. The insistent rhythm in the piano part sounds a little hectic and forced, like the black humor of Heine's poem. Although basically this is a through-composed

LISTEN

Schumann, "Im wunderschönen Monat Mai"

0:28	**Im wunderschönen Monat Mai,**	In the wonderfully lovely month of May,
	Als alle Knospen sprangen,	When all the buds were bursting,
	Da ist in meinem Herzen	Then it was that in my heart
	Die Liebe aufgegangen.	Love broke through.
1:05	**Im wunderschönen Monat Mai,**	In the wonderfully lovely month of May,
	Als alle Vögel sangen,	When all the birds were singing,
	Da hab' ich ihr gestanden	Then it was I confessed to her
	Mein Sehnen und Verlangen.	My longing and desire.

LISTEN

Schumann, "Die alten, bösen Lieder"

0:05	**Die alten, bösen Lieder,**	The hateful songs of times past,
	Die Träume bös' und arg,	The hateful, brutal dreams,
	Die lasst uns jetzt begraben:	Let's now have them buried;
	Holt einen grossen Sarg.	Fetch up a great coffin.
0:23	**Hinein leg' ich gar Manches,**	I've a lot to put in it —
	Doch sag' ich noch nicht, was.	Just what, I won't yet say;
	Der Sarg muss sein noch grösser	The coffin must be even bigger
	Wie's Heidelberger Fass.	Than the Great Cask of Heidelberg.
0:41	**Und holt eine Todtenbahre**	And fetch a bier,
	Und Bretter fest und dick,	Boards that are strong and thick;
	Auch muss sie sein noch länger	They too must be longer
	Als wie zu Mainz die Brück'.	Than the river bridge at Mainz.
0:59	**Und holt mir auch zwölf Riesen,**	And fetch me, too, twelve giants
	Die mussen noch stärker sein	Who must be stronger
	Als wie der starke Christoph	Than St. Christopher, the great statue
	Im Dom zu Köln am Rhein.	At the Cathedral of Cologne on the Rhine.
1:18	**Die sollen den Sarg forttragen**	It's they that must haul the coffin
	Und senken in's Meer hinab,	And sink it in the sea,
	Denn solchem grossen Sarge	For a great coffin like that
	Gebührt ein grosses Grab.	Deserves a great grave.
1:49	**Wisst ihr, warum der Sarg wohl**	Do you know why the coffin really
	So gross und schwer mag sein?	Has to be so huge and heavy?
	Ich senkt' auch meine Liebe	Because I sank all my love in it,
	Und meinen Schmerz hinein.	And all of my great grief.

song, the opposite of strophic form, there are some musical parallels between many of the stanzas, and the music of stanza 1 comes back in stanza 5.

But there is a sudden reversal of mood in stanza 6, as the poet offers to tell us what this morbid list of funeral arrangements is all about. In the music, first the accompaniment disintegrates and then the rhythm. All the poet's self-dramatization vanishes when he speaks of his grief in recitative-like rhythms; the end of the song would be a whimper if Schumann at the piano were not quietly and firmly in control.

Instead, in a lovely meditative piano solo, music takes over from words. Not only does the composer interpret the poet's words with great art, both in the hectic early stanzas and the self-pitying final one, but he adds something entirely his own in this final solo. The sixteen vignettes by Heine and Schumann in *Dichterliebe* add up to a memorable anthology of the endless pains and pleasures of love celebrated by the Romantics.

A rather amazing nineteenth-century score of a Schumann lied. The poem is given in ornate calligraphy and illustrated in the richest, most opulent Romantic style. The picture might well be for Clara Schumann's "The Moon Has Risen Softly" (actually, it is for Robert's similar song "Moonlit Night"). Then, at the bottom, the music begins. *AKG/Science Source.*

Biography
Robert Schumann (1810–1856)

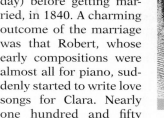

Robert Schumann's father, a bookseller and writer, encouraged the boy's musical talent and started him studying the piano at the age of six. When his father died, his mother wanted him to go into law; he attended the University of Leipzig, but finally persuaded her to let him pursue the career of a piano virtuoso. He had to give this up, however, after an injury sustained when he tried to strengthen his fingers with a mechanical device.

Besides his musical talent, Schumann had a great flair for literature, no doubt inherited from his father. When he was only twenty-three, Schumann founded a magazine to campaign for a higher level of music, *Die Neue Zeitschrift für Musik* (The New Music Journal—it is still being published). For several years he wrote regular music criticism, often couched in a fanciful romantic prose style. For example, he signed some of his reviews with the names "Florestan" or "Eusebius," representing the opposite (but both thoroughly romantic) sides of his character—the impetuous side and the tender, dreamy side. He encouraged fledgling composers such as Chopin and (later) Brahms.

Schumann's piano works—among his most important music—are mostly "character pieces," often with imaginative titles, and occasionally signed "Eu." or "Fl." at the end. They are arranged in loosely organized sets, with titles such as *Butterflies, Scenes from Childhood,* and *Carnaval.*

Schumann fell in love with Clara Wieck, the daughter of his piano teacher; at the age of fifteen she was already a famous pianist. Thanks to her father's fanatical opposition—he did not think Robert was a very savory character—they had to wait until she was twenty-one (minus one day) before getting married, in 1840. A charming outcome of the marriage was that Robert, whose early compositions were almost all for piano, suddenly started to write love songs for Clara. Nearly one hundred and fifty songs were composed in this so-called song year.

A little later, he also turned to the composition of larger works: concertos, symphonies, chamber music, choral music, and one opera. Thereafter he worked as a teacher and conductor, but his withdrawn personality made him less than successful. Schumann suffered from mood swings and had experienced breakdowns in his youth, and now he began to show tragic signs of insanity. In 1854, tormented by voices, hallucinations, and loss of memory, he tried to drown himself in the river Rhine and was committed to an asylum. He died two years later.

Chief Works: Sets of miniatures for piano, among them *Scenes from Childhood, Album for the Young, Papillons* (Butterflies), and *Carnaval* ■ Songs (lieder) and song cycles: *Woman's Life and Love, Dichterliebe* ■ Piano Fantasy (a free sonata); Piano Concerto and the first important concerto for cello; four symphonies ■ Chamber music: a quintet and a quartet for piano and strings ■ An opera, *Genoveva;* incidental music to Byron's *Manfred* and Goethe's *Faust;* choral works

Encore: After *Dichterliebe* and *Carnaval,* listen to the Piano Concerto in A Minor.

Image credit: Bettmann/CORBIS.

Clara Schumann, "Der Mond kommt still gegangen" (The moon has risen softly) (1843)

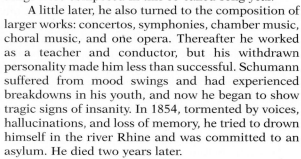

3 | 19   53   23

This lied is another perfect Romantic miniature, in spite of the cliché-filled poem, with its moonlight, its dreams of love, and its downhearted lover. Both melody and piano accompaniment are very plain, but the slightly unusual chords chosen by Schumann create a unique pensive mood. The form, too, is simple: modified strophic form, **A A A′**. Some modification, however slight, had to occur in stanza 3, where the poem's speaker, catching sight of the lit-up windows in the house, registers his excitement by crowding his poetic lines with extra words and extra syllables—which require extra notes.

There is an obvious, banal way of setting such crowded lines: See page 243, in the Listen box. But instead Schumann very skillfully pulls the words out of

Clara Wieck (Clara Schumann) (1819–1896)

Clara Wieck was the eldest child (she had two younger brothers) of a highly ambitious music teacher named Friedrich Wieck (pronounced *Veek*). Wieck had his own piano method, and he determined to make Clara a leading pianist. By the age of fifteen she was widely known as a prodigy. Like most virtuosos of the time, she also composed music to play at her own concerts: variations on popular opera arias, waltzes, a piano concerto.

Robert and Clara Schumann figure in what must be music's greatest love story. Still, there seems to have been just a little friction between them because she was so much better a pianist; she, on her part, felt diffident about composing under his shadow, though he did encourage her to some extent, and they published one song cycle jointly, containing music by both of them. Clara often wrote songs to give Robert on his birthdays. The last of these is dated 1853, the year before he was committed to an insane asylum.

Even before that, Robert's depression and instability made life difficult for Clara. She continued her career as best she could, but more and more she had to take care of the family. During the 1848 revolution in Leipzig, for example, it was up to her to get the five Schumann children out of town (three more were born later).

Things were difficult in another way when Robert died. At the age of thirty-seven, after losing the husband whom she loved and revered, Clara found herself more than half in love with his twenty-two-year-old protégé Johannes Brahms (see page 288). It is not known which of them withdrew from the relationship. They remained close friends; Brahms was a lifelong bachelor, and she did not remarry.

Today we tend to regret that Clara decided to give up composing, for she left enough good pieces to make us wish there were more. But she knew it would have been an uphill battle, given the common nineteenth-century view that important music couldn't be written by a woman. With children to support, she can hardly be blamed for concentrating instead on activities that had already earned her admiration and respect—and a good living: concertizing and teaching.

Clara Schumann went on to further establish herself as one of Europe's leading pianists and a much-sought-after pedagogue. She concertized and toured widely. Brahms (who always asked her to critique his new compositions) was just one in the eminent circle of her friends and associates. Outliving Robert by forty years, Clara became a major force in late nineteenth-century music.

Chief Works: Miniatures for piano, with names such as *Romances* and *Soirées musicales* (Musical Evenings); songs ▪ A piano concerto and a trio for piano, violin, and cello ▪ *Piano Variations on a Theme by Robert Schumann* (Brahms wrote a set of variations on the same theme)

Encore: After "Der Mond," listen to *Romances* for piano and the piano concerto.

Image credit: De Agostini Picture Library/A. Dagli Orti/Bridgeman Art Library.

---

phase with the musical phrases, achieving beautiful rhythmic matches for some of the extra words: slower for *drunten* (down), livelier for *funkeln* (light—literally, sparkle), and very slow for *still* (silently):

St. 1:   ¹The moon has ri - sen soft - ly ²With gleaming rays of gold, ³Be - neath its shin - ing splendor ⁴The wea - ry earth's at rest.
St. 2:   ¹And on the drifting breez - es ²From man - y faith - ful minds ³Endearing thoughts by the thousand ⁴Waft down on those who sleep.

St. 3:   ¹Und drun - ten im Ta - le,   da funkeln ²Die Fenster von Lieb - chens Haus;   ³Ich a - ber blikke im Dunkeln ⁴Still . . .
         ¹And down in the val-ley,   a light can ²Be seen in my loved_ one's house;   ³But I   keep staring, in darkness, ⁴Silently

Clara Schumann, "Der Mond kommt still gegangen"

0:03	*St. 1:* ¹**Der Mond kommt still gegangen** ²**Mit seinem goldn'en Schein,** ³**Da Schläft in holdem Prangen** ⁴**Die müde Erde ein.**	The moon has risen softly With gleaming rays of gold, Beneath its shining splendor The weary earth's at rest.
0:34	*St. 2:* ¹**Und auf den Lüften schwanken** ²**Aus manchem treuen Sinn** ³**Viel tausend Liebesgedanken** ⁴**Über die Schläfer hin.**	And on the drifting breezes From many faithful minds Endearing thoughts by the thousand Waft down on those who sleep.
1:05	*St. 3:* ¹**Und drunten im Tale, da funkeln** ²**Die Fenster von Liebchens Haus;** ³**Ich aber blicke im Dunkeln** ⁴**Still in die Welt hinaus.**	And down in the valley, a light can Be seen in my loved one's house; But I keep staring, in darkness, Silently out to the world.

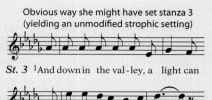

Obvious way she might have set stanza 3 (yielding an unmodified strophic setting)

St. 3 ¹And down in the val-ley, a light can

²Be seen in my loved one's house;—

And three things help make the climactic word *Liebchens* (loved one) radiant: the new long high note, the new harmony, and the expansive phrase (five bars in place of four). Schumann's piano postlude adds a wistful minor-mode aftertaste. As with many great lieder, the music here far transcends the words.

2 | The Character Piece for Piano

Besides the lied, the other chief type of Romantic miniature composition was the short piano piece. Such pieces were written in great profusion in the nineteenth century, and they appeared under many names. Frédéric Chopin preferred simple genre titles such as Nocturne, Waltz, Scherzo, or **Étude** (study). Robert Schumann preferred descriptive titles. Piano miniatures were composed at all levels of difficulty, ranging from virtuoso showpieces, which hardly anyone but their composers could manage, to unassuming pieces playable (and enjoyed) by beginning students.

A good general name for these short Romantic piano pieces (one sometimes used by the Romantics themselves) is **character pieces**, for the essential point about them is that each portrays some definite mood or character. In principle, at least, this is as true of the brilliant virtuoso works as of the simple ones. Each conveys an intense, distinct emotion—an emotion often hinted at by an imaginative title supplied by the composer.

This explains why the Romantic character piece can be thought of as analogous to the Romantic song, or lied, though without its poem. Indeed, six books of such piano pieces by Felix Mendelssohn are entitled *Songs without Words*. Some of them have descriptive subtitles that stress still further their similarity to lieder: "Spinning Song," "Spring Song," "Venetian Boat Song."

Franz Schubert, Moment Musical No. 2 in A-flat (1827?)

Creative publishers gave Franz Schubert's piano miniatures their titles: "Momens musicals" (spelled wrong!) and "Impromptus" (improvisations— Johannes Brahms would later call some of *his* miniatures "caprices").

In Moment Musical No. 2, the main idea, **A**, is a gentle rocking figure, with a nostalgic mood characteristic of Schubert. The mood deepens when **A'** is provided with a relatively long coda, which seems reluctant ever to let go. In between comes **B**, a sad melody in the minor mode; the piano texture changes from cloudy chords in **A** to plain melody with a steady moving accompaniment in **B**. As usual in piano miniatures, the form is simple, at least on the surface: **A B A′ B′ A″**.

But in fact this is an excellent example of how much these schematic form diagrams can hide. After **A B A′** with its coda, after four minutes, we think that the piece must be over—except, perhaps, for a hint when the piano moves to an unusually high register at the coda's final cadence. **B** returns again, or rather explodes—*fortissimo,* in the high register, no longer sad but terribly anguished, a cry of pain. In the wake of this climax, there is a momentary switch from the minor mode to the major, a Schubert fingerprint we also noted in Listening Exercise 7 (page 34). Does this change heal the pain? By the end of **A″** the high register no longer hints at anything. It simply hovers at the border of hearing, a true Romantic effect, a Romantic evocation of the ineffable.

 **LISTEN**

Moment Musical No. 2

		A	
20	0:00	**a, *p***	
	0:29	**a′**	
		B	
21	1:06	**b**: minor, ***p***	
		A′	
22	2:18	**a″** (longer)	
0:47	3:05	coda	
		B′	
23	3:42	**b′**: minor, ***ff***	
			Turns to the major
		A″	
1:11	4:53	**a‴, *p***	
1:49	5:31	coda	

Robert Schumann, *Carnaval* (1833–1835)

3 | 24–25   55–56   24–25

Schumann's style of piano writing has a warmth and privacy that set it apart from the music of any of the other pianist-composers of his day. A favorite marking on his scores is the German word *innig,* meaning "inward," "intimate," or "heartfelt." Schumann typically assembled his piano pieces into collections with some general title and, often, some interesting musical means of connection among them. Just as the Romantic character piece for the piano is analogous to the Romantic lied, so these collections by Schumann are analogous to song cycles.

Such a collection is *Carnaval,* a set of twenty short character pieces that really *are* characters—musical portraits of masked guests at a Mardi Gras ball. After the band strikes up an introduction, the sad clown Pierrot arrives, followed by the pantomime figures Harlequin and Columbine, Schumann himself, two of his girlfriends masquerading under the names Estrella and Chiarina, and even the composers Paganini and Chopin. This diverse gallery provided Schumann with an outlet for his whimsy and humor, as well as all his Romantic melancholy and passion.

"Eusebius"   Eusebius was Schumann's pen name for his tender, dreamy self, and this little piece presents him at his most introspective. In the passage below, the yearning effect of the high notes (shaded) is compounded by the vague, languorous rhythm:

"Eusebius: In sculpture, the actor's art becomes fixed. The actor transforms the sculptor's forms into living art. The painter turns a poem into a painting. The musician sets a picture to music. Florestan: The aesthetic principle is the same in every art; only the material differs."

Robert Schumann, 1833

The right-hand groups of five and three blur with the left-hand quarter notes, especially when played with Romantic rubato. The somewhat unusual form is **aa ba b′a′ ba**, in which **b′a′** stands out, although it differs from **ba** only in its much thicker chords, heightening the emotional warmth, and its use of the pedal.

"Florestan"   After "Eusebius" ends very tentatively, Schumann's impetuous other self makes his entrance. "Florestan" is built out of a single explosive motive; the piece moves in fits and starts. At first the motive contrasts with a calmer one, but then it gets faster and faster, almost madly, ending completely up in the air. This non-cadence is resolved only in the next number.

Frédéric Chopin, Nocturne in F-sharp, Op. 15, No. 2 (1831)

Chopin's twenty-one **nocturnes**, meaning "night pieces," written throughout his career, are as different as twenty-one different nights. But each features a particularly striking tune—a languid serenade, for example, or a dark, secret lament. Something else—a musical contrast—is usually heard or overheard in the night, too, such as a distant procession, a passionate encounter, or even a fragment of a dance or a folk song.

The opening tune in Chopin's Nocturne in F-sharp has an elegance unique to the composer, an elegance that stems partly from the wonderfully graceful rhythm, partly from the Romantic turns of harmony, and partly from the pianistic decorations of the melodic line. We have seen decorated melodies before, but

LISTEN

Nocturne in F-sharp

0:00	**a**
0:27	**a′** ornamented
0:58	**b**
1:28	**c**
2:13	**a″**
2:55	**coda**

Was this striking painting, by a minor late nineteenth-century artist, done with Chopin's nocturnes in mind? Called *Notturno*, its cool elegance, twilight sensuality, and vaguely apprehensive quality might suggest so. *Blauel/Gnamm/Artothek.*

Biography
Frédéric Chopin (1810–1849)

Chopin was born near Warsaw, where his father, a Frenchman who had emigrated to Poland and married a Polish lady, ran a private school for young gentlemen. In this atmosphere Fryderyk—later he adopted the French form Frédéric—acquired his lifelong taste for life in high society. Provided with the best teachers available, he became an extraordinary pianist. There are many reports of the exquisite delicacy of his playing, and his miraculous ability, as it seemed at the time, to draw romantic sounds out of the piano.

Furthermore, his set of variations on Mozart's "Là ci darem la mano" (see page 192), written when he was seventeen, was already an impressive enough composition to earn a rave review from Robert Schumann.

Chopin settled in Paris, where he found ready acceptance from society people and from other artists and intellectuals, such as the novelist Honoré de Balzac and the painter Eugène Delacroix, who produced the famous portrait of the composer shown here. Chopin made his way as a fashionable piano teacher and by selling his music to publishers. The facts that he was Polish and that Poland was being overrun by Russia at that time seem to have made him even more glamorous to the French. Among Chopin's piano miniatures are over fifty Mazurkas and sixteen Polonaises, which are stylized Polish dances.

Chopin was a frail and fastidious personality. Though he sometimes played in public, he truly disliked the hurly-burly of concert life and preferred to perform for select audiences in great houses.

More than any other of the great composers, he restricted his work to music for *his* instrument, the piano. Even his works that combined orchestra with piano—two concertos and a few other works—were all from his pre-Paris days.

The major event of his personal life was his ten-year romance with Aurore Dudevant, an early feminist and a famous novelist under the pen name George Sand. (They were introduced by Liszt, who wrote an admiring book about Chopin after his death.) The relationship was a rocky one; Sand sketched some unkind scenes from their life together in one of her novels. After the affair ended in 1847, Chopin's health declined with his spirits. He toured England and Scotland unhappily in 1848 and died the next year, aged thirty-nine, of tuberculosis, a major killer in the nineteenth century.

Chief Works: Character pieces for piano: Preludes (including the "Raindrop" prelude), Nocturnes, Études, Ballades, Waltzes (including the "Minute" waltz), and Polish Mazurkas and Polonaises ■ Three piano sonatas, including one with a famous funeral march as the slow movement ■ Two piano concertos ■ A cello sonata; a few Polish songs

Encore: Listen to the Nocturne in D-flat Major, the Fantasy-Impromptu, and the Ballade in G Minor.

Image credit: Louvre, Paris, France/Giraudon/The Bridgeman Art Library.

Chopin's have an almost liquid quality, caused partly by chromaticism—by the free use of all the notes of the chromatic scale, as in this fragment:

Romantic form contributes to the Romantic effect. Chopin avoids sharp demarcations and literal returns; the music seems to grow spontaneously, in an almost improvisational way. The main tune, **A (a a′ b)**, does not really end, but gives way to plaintive sounds emerging out of nowhere, which surge up to a moment of real passion. Then the return of the tune (**a″**) is fragmentary—though in a way more intense—and the whole is capped by an unexpected and delicious little coda. Free rhythm in the performance (rubato) mirrors the freedom of form.

Biography
Franz Liszt
(1811–1886)

There are some important composers whose music we unfortunately have to pass over in this book because of space limits. In this box and the one on page 248, we give the biographies of three of them, together with some account of their roles in the history of Romantic music.

Franz Liszt learned music from his father on the Hungarian estate of the princes Esterházy, whom Haydn had once served. At age eleven, the boy gave his first piano concert in Vienna, where he met Beethoven. He later settled in Paris, home of another great émigré pianist-composer, Chopin.

Liszt's dashing looks and personality and his liaisons with married noblewomen—Countess d'Agoult and, later, Princess Sayn-Wittgenstein—dazzled Europe as much as his incredible pianistic technique. No one had heard such virtuosity. He drew crowds like a modern rock star and cultivated a lifestyle to match.

After his relationship with d'Agoult came to a stormy end in 1839, Liszt spent a few years giving sensational concerts all over Europe. Tiring of concert life, he then took a position as conductor and director of the theater at Weimar, in Germany, where there was still a court that supported the arts in the old eighteenth-century manner. There he wrote his most radical and influential music.

Like many other Romantic composers, Liszt was a writer of note, as well as a musician. He was a strong advocate of the music of Richard Wagner; the two men learned much from each other. Both friend

Liszt's phenomenal virtuosity as a pianist inspired many a cartoonist. The sword here refers to his many decorations; he has a halo because he had turned to religion and become an unordained priest. "The Abbé Liszt" was known to break, if not pianos, piano strings, and this helped ruin one Viennese piano maker (Graf). *Mary Evans Picture Library*.

and foe linked Wagner's "music dramas" with Liszt's symphonic poems as "Music of the Future." In his personality, however, Liszt was as magnanimous as Wagner was self-centered and devious.

Liszt really had two major careers. The first, at Paris, his career as a fantastic piano virtuoso, underpins a musical ideal that is still alive and well in music conservatories today. It left a mass of fiercely difficult piano music, including the *Transcendental Études* (the name says it all!) and the popular *Hungarian Rhapsodies*—important early products of nationalism in music (see page 282).

Liszt's second career, at Weimar, focused on orchestral music: program symphonies and symphonic poems. We take up these genres on pages 249 and 279.

3 | Early Romantic Program Music

The lied and the character piece for piano—the two main forms of early Romantic miniature compositions—were intimately tied up with nonmusical, usually poetic, ideas. Furthermore, in a work such as Schumann's *Carnaval*, the various piano portraits are juxtaposed in such a way as to hint at their interaction—hint, that is, at a shadowy story line. Poems, stories, and nonmusical ideas in general were also associated with large-scale instrumental pieces.

As we have seen, *program music* is a term used for instrumental compositions associated with poems, stories, and the like. Program music for orchestra grew up naturally in opera overtures, for even in the eighteenth century it was seen that an overture might gain special interest if it referred to moods or ideas in the opera to come by citing (or, rather, forecasting) some of its themes.

This happens in Mozart's *Don Giovanni,* in which the next-to-last scene has Don Giovanni carried off to hell by the statue of the murdered Commandant (see page 190). The otherworldly music associated with the statue is first heard in the opera's overture, even before the curtain has gone up. Lively, effervescent music follows; but the serious undertone of Mozart's opera is already loud and clear at the start of the work's overture.

The Concert Overture: Felix Mendelssohn

A further step, conceptually, was the **concert overture**, never intended to be followed by a stage play or an opera—never intended, indeed, for the theater. Robert Schumann wrote an overture to *Hermann und Dorothea,* by Goethe, which is not a play but an epic poem. Hector Berlioz wrote overtures to literary works of various kinds: plays (Shakespeare's *King Lear*), long poems (*The Corsair* by Byron, a special hero for the Romantics), and novels (*Waverley* by Sir Walter Scott).

Public composer and private composer: Felix Mendelssohn and his sister Fanny. *Both images: Bettmann/CORBIS.*

Biography
Felix Mendelssohn (1809–1847)

Felix Mendelssohn may be the only great composer who has ever come from an upper-class family, a family of converted Jews who were in banking. Their home was a meeting place for artists and intellectuals over generations. Felix and his sister Fanny were brought up with music and every other advantage that came with a life of privilege. (Felix also became a fine amateur painter.)

By the time he was fifteen Felix was conducting the family orchestra in his own music. He went on to a stellar career, not only as an enormously successful composer but also as a pianist, organist, conductor, educator—he founded the Leipzig Conservatory of Music—and even musicologist. His performance of Bach's *St. Matthew Passion* was a landmark in the revival of "early music."

This action was typical, for from the start Mendelssohn showed a great respect for, even deference toward, the classics. His music never goes as far as, say, Schumann or Chopin in acceding to Romantic tendencies, but always keeps a firm foundation of Classical technique.

One of Mendelssohn's most significant fields of activity was the concert overture, an early genre of Romantic program music, discussed above. In his lifetime he was admired even more for his oratorios *St. Paul* and *Elijah,* and for popular sets of piano miniatures he called *Songs without Words.* His Violin Concerto and "Italian" Symphony are special favorites.

Fanny Mendelssohn (1805–1847)

Fanny Mendelssohn, Felix's older sister, was also a highly prolific composer. The siblings were always very close; music was one of their bonds, for Fanny showed as much talent as her brother. Married to a painter named Wilhelm Hensel, she devoted herself to weekly concerts at the Mendelssohn home in Berlin, for which she composed music of all kinds, including even oratorios.

However, Fanny's music did not pass beyond the threshold of the Mendelssohn mansion. Only a small percentage of it found its way into print, at the end of her short life. Fanny is often seen as a victim of patriarchal society and of the general refusal in the past to take women composers seriously. Like Mozart's sister Nannerl, she watched as her younger brother built a great career, while she was expected—indeed, conditioned—to put motherhood and family first, music second. But we should remember that unlike other successful women composers of the nineteenth century—from Louise Farrenc (1804–1875) to Clara Schumann (1819–1896) to Cécile Chaminade (1857–1944) and Ethel Smythe (1858–1944)—Fanny Mendelssohn belonged to the upper class. Few members of this class, male or female, had ever pursued public careers in the arts. They didn't need the rat race. Workaholic Felix was an exception.

Fanny's sudden death at age forty-one devastated Felix and hastened his own death only six months later.

Probably the best-known and best-loved concert overtures are by Felix Mendelssohn. He wrote his concert overture to Shakespeare's *A Midsummer Night's Dream* when he was seventeen; the play was a special favorite with both Felix and his sister Fanny. He had no theatrical occasion in mind, though years later the overture was indeed used in productions of the Shakespeare play. At that time Mendelssohn also added other music, and a suite derived from this piece has become a popular concert number.

A work in sonata form, following Classical models quite clearly, the overture to *A Midsummer Night's Dream* nonetheless includes representational features. Music illustrates the delicate, fluttering fairies in the service of King Oberon and Queen Titania, the sleep induced by Puck's magic flower, and the braying of Bottom the Weaver when he is turned into a donkey.

Another fine example by Mendelssohn is the *Hebrides* Overture, an evocative, moody depiction of lonely Scottish islands rich in romantic associations. Surging string music suggests the swell and the spray of waves; woodwind fanfares suggest seabird calls, perhaps, or romanticized foghorns. This is evidently program music, but what makes it an overture? Nothing more than the fact that it follows the standard scheme for overtures at the time—namely, a single movement in sonata form.

The Program Symphony: Hector Berlioz

PROGRAM OF THE SYMPHONY: A young musician of unhealthy sensibility and passionate imagination poisons himself with opium in a fit of lovesick despair. Too weak to kill him, the dose of the drug plunges him into a heavy sleep attended by the strangest visions, during which his sensations, emotions, and memories are transformed in his diseased mind into musical thoughts and images. Even the woman he loves becomes a melody to him, an *idée fixe* [an obsession], so to speak, that he finds and hears everywhere.

"Love or music—which power can uplift man to the sublimest heights? It is a large question; yet it seems to me one should answer it in this way: Love cannot give an idea of music; music can give an idea of love. But why separate them? They are the two wings of the soul."

From the Memoirs of Hector Berlioz, *1869*

So begins a long pamphlet that the French Romantic composer Hector Berlioz distributed at performances of his first symphony—a symphony which he could justifiably call *Fantastic,* and which to this day remains his most famous work. It certainly represents a more radical approach to program music than that of the concert overture. Berlioz, too, had written several concert overtures, but he now felt the need for a broader canvas. In his **program symphonies**—entire symphonies with programs spelled out movement by movement—Berlioz set the tone for the grandiose compositions that were to become as characteristic of Romanticism as its musical miniatures.

Hector Berlioz, *Fantastic* Symphony: Episodes in the Life of an Artist (1830)

3 | 27–33   58   27

Clearly Berlioz had a gift for public relations, for the program of his *Fantastic* Symphony was not a familiar play or novel, but an autobiographical fantasy of the most lurid sort. Here was music that encouraged listeners to think it had been written under the influence of opium, the drug of choice among the Romantics, which shocked society at large. What is more, half of Paris knew that Berlioz was madly in love (from afar) with an Irish actress, Harriet Smithson, who had taken the city by storm with her Shakespearean roles.

Audiences have never been quite sure how seriously to take it all, but they continue to be bowled over by the sheer audacity of the whole conception and the rambunctious way it is realized. Then there are the young Berlioz's effects of tone color. He demanded an orchestra of unprecedented size (see page 231!), which he used in the most original and imaginative ways. Also highly original was the notion of having a single theme recur in all the movements as a representation of the musician's beloved—his **idée fixe** or obsession, the Shakespearean Smithson. Here is the *idée fixe* theme as it first appears:

This typically Romantic melody takes its yearning quality from its slow struggle to move higher and higher in pitch; from measure 5 on, each phrase peaks a bit above the preceding phrase until the melody reaches its climax at measure 15. Near the end, measure 19 provides a positive shudder of emotion. Notice how many dynamic, rubato, and other marks Berlioz has supplied, trying to ensure just the right expressive quality from moment to moment.

To illustrate the drastic mood swings described in his program, Berlioz subjects the *idée fixe* to thematic transformation (see page 232) for all its other appearances in the opium dream. The last movement, for example, has a grotesque parody of the theme. Its new jerky rhythm and squeaky orchestration (using the small E-flat clarinet) thoroughly undermine the original Romantic mood:

Berlioz's expressive terms translate as follows:

Canto espressivo = expressive song
dolce = sweetly
poco = somewhat
poco a poco = bit by bit
animato = animated
ritenuto = slowed down (ritardando)
a tempo = back to the original tempo

First Movement: Reveries, Passions (Largo—Allegro agitato e appassionato assai) We first hear a short, quiet run-in—a typically Romantic touch suggesting that the music has grown up imperceptibly out of silence. Then the "soul-sickness" mentioned in the program is depicted by a halting, passionate melody. A faster section begins with the *idée fixe,* and the music picks up energy (the "volcanic love" of the program).

This fast section follows sonata form, but only very loosely. The *idée fixe* is the main theme, and a second theme is simply a derivative of the first. Some of the finest strokes in this movement run counter to Classical principles—for example, the arresting up-and-down chromatic scale that arrives in the development section without any logical connection to anything else. The recapitulation, too, is extended in a very un-Classical fashion; it actually includes a whole new melody for the oboe.

Near the end, beginning a very long coda, the *idée fixe* returns loudly at a faster tempo—the first of its many transformations. At the very end, slower music depicts the program's "religious consolations."

From Berlioz's Program: Movement 1

First he recalls the soul-sickness, the aimless passions, the baseless depressions and elations that he felt before first seeing his loved one; then the volcanic love that she instantly inspired in him; his jealous furies; his return to tenderness; his religious consolations.

Second theme

Biography

Hector Berlioz (1803–1869)

No other great composer has survived so unpromising a beginning to reach so unhappy an end as Hector Berlioz. Berlioz grew up in a country village in France and received a spotty musical education; he played the guitar and the flute, and as a hypersensitive child learned as much from reading books and scores as from his teachers. His father, a doctor, sent him to medical school in Paris. But, as Berlioz told it, he was so horrified when he got to the dissecting room, where rats were nibbling at the scraps, that he leaped out of the window and went to the Paris Conservatory of Music instead.

The anecdote is typical of his emotional and utterly Romantic personality. Berlioz thought the unthinkable in music; his grandiose program symphonies had simply no precedent and were not matched in ambition until the time of Gustav Mahler, about 1900. His imagination for orchestral tone color was extraordinary.

Like all other Romantic composers, he was inspired by literary models, including especially Shakespeare—his *Lélio* is a meditation on *Hamlet,* and his opera *Béatrice et Bénédict* is taken from *Much Ado about Nothing*—and Virgil. *The Trojans* (1858), his huge two-part opera derived from Virgil's *Aeneid,* was seldom performed until modern times, but it is now regarded as his masterpiece.

Berlioz had two wretched marriages, the first to the Irish Shakespearean actress Harriet Smithson, who is immortalized as the *idée fixe* in the *Fantastic Symphony.* In spite of suffering from constant ridicule from the musical establishment on the one hand, and terrible health on the other, Berlioz managed through sheer force of his impetuous personality to get most of his enormous compositions performed and to gain a good measure of recognition in musically conservative Paris.

Throughout his life, he was obliged to support himself with musical journalism, at which he was a master; his *Memoirs* is one of the most delightful books ever written about music. One of the first great conductors, Berlioz toured extensively to promote his own music, especially in Germany, where he was welcomed in progressive circles.

His last years were spent in physical pain and depression. During this time he dragged himself to Russia for conducting gigs—he said his pain stopped when he was on the podium. After 1862 he listened to little music and composed none. Berlioz died in Paris in 1869.

Chief Works: Program symphonies: *Fantastic* Symphony, *Harold in Italy, Romeo and Juliet* ■ Concert overtures: *The Corsair, The Roman Carnival* ■ Operas: *Benvenuto Cellini, The Trojans* (after Virgil's *Aeneid*) ■ Oratorios: *The Damnation of Faust, The Childhood of Christ* ■ A great Requiem Mass for orchestra, chorus, and four brass bands

Encore: After the whole *Fantastic* Symphony, listen to the program symphony *Harold in Italy* and the overture *The Corsair.* Read the *Memoirs.*

Image credit: Hulton-Deutsch Collection/CORBIS.

Second Movement: A Ball (Allegro non troppo)   A symphony needs the simplicity and easy swing of a dance movement, and this ballroom episode of the opium dream conveniently provides one. The dance in question is not a minuet or a scherzo, but a waltz, the most popular ballroom dance of the nineteenth century. The *idée fixe,* transformed into a lilting triple meter, first appears in the position of the trio (**B** in the **A B A** form) and then returns hauntingly in a coda.

Third Movement: Scene in the Country (Adagio) Invoking nature to reflect human emotions was a favorite Romantic procedure. The "pastoral duet" is played by an English horn and an offstage oboe (boy and girl, perhaps?). At the end, the English horn returns to the accompaniment of distant thunder sounds, played on four differently tuned timpani. Significantly, the oboe can no longer be heard.

In this movement the *idée fixe* returns in a new, strangely agitated transformation. It is interrupted by angry sounds swelling to a climax, reflecting the anxieties chronicled in the program.

Movement 2

He encounters his beloved at a ball, in the midst of a noisy, brilliant party.

Movement 3

He hears two shepherds piping in dialogue. The pastoral duet, the location, the light rustling of trees stirred gently by the wind, some newly conceived grounds for hope—all this gives him a feeling of unaccustomed calm. But *she* appears again . . . what if she is deceiving him?

Fourth Movement: March to the Scaffold (Allegretto non troppo)   This movement has two main themes: a long downward scale ("gloomy and wild") and an exciting military march ("brilliant and grand"), orchestrated more like a football band than a symphony orchestra. Later the scale theme appears divided up in its orchestration between plucked and bowed strings, woodwinds, brass, and percussion—a memorable instance of Berlioz's novel imagination for tone color. The scale theme also appears in a truly shattering inverted form (that is, moving up instead of down).

Berlioz had written this march or something like it several years earlier. As he revised it to go into the *Fantastic* Symphony, he added a coda that uses the *idée fixe* and therefore only makes sense in terms of the symphony's program. The final fall of the ax is illustrated musically by the sound of a guillotine chop and a military snare-drum roll, right after bars 1–2 of the *idée fixe*. "Berlioz tells it like it is," conductor Leonard Bernstein once remarked. "You take a trip and you end up screaming at your own funeral."

Fifth Movement: Dream of a Witches' Sabbath (Larghetto—Allegro)   Adding a fifth movement to the traditional four of the Classical symphony was a typical Berlioz innovation (although it can be traced back to the Beethoven he so admired). Now the element of parody is added to the astonishing orchestral effects pioneered earlier in the symphony. First we hear the unearthly sounds of the nighttime locale of the witches' orgy. Their swishing broomsticks are heard, and distant, echoing horn calls summon them. Mutes are used in the brass instruments—perhaps the first time mutes were ever used in a poetic way.

As Berlioz remarks, the "noble and timid" *idée fixe* sounds thoroughly vulgar in its last transformation, played in a fast jig rhythm by the shrill E-flat clarinet. (Compare the music examples on page 250.) The treatment of the *idée fixe* here is strictly "programmatic": When the theme first arrives, only two phrases are played before the orchestra breaks in, with a "roar of joy" welcoming Harriet Smithson to the orgy to mock her lover's death.

Movement 4

He dreams he has killed his beloved, that he is condemned to death and led to execution. A march accompanies the procession, now gloomy and wild, now brilliant and grand. Finally the *idée fixe* appears for a moment, to be cut off by the fall of the ax.

Movement 5

He finds himself at a Witches' Sabbath. . . . Unearthly sounds, groans, shrieks of laughter, distant cries echoed by other cries. The beloved's melody is heard, but it has lost its character of nobility and timidity. It is *she* who comes to the Sabbath! At her arrival, a roar of joy. She joins in the devilish orgies. A funeral knell; burlesque of the *Dies irae*.

Witches' Sabbath (detail), by Francisco de Goya (1746–1828), one of a number of dark, unsettling images Goya painted on the walls of his house in his last years. Satan, in the form of a goat, presides over the orgy. *Scala/Art Resource, NY.*

As the merriment is brought to an end by the tolling of funeral bells, Berlioz prepares his most sensational stroke of all—a burlesque of one of the most solemn and famous of Gregorian chants, the *Dies irae* (Day of Wrath). This chant is the centerpiece of Masses for the Dead, or Requiem Masses; in Catholic France, any audience would have recognized the *Dies irae* instantly. Three segments of it are used; each is stated first in low brasses, then faster in higher brasses, then, faster still and in the vulgar spirit of the transformed *idée fixe,* in woodwinds and plucked strings. It makes for a blasphemous, shocking picture of the witches' black Mass.

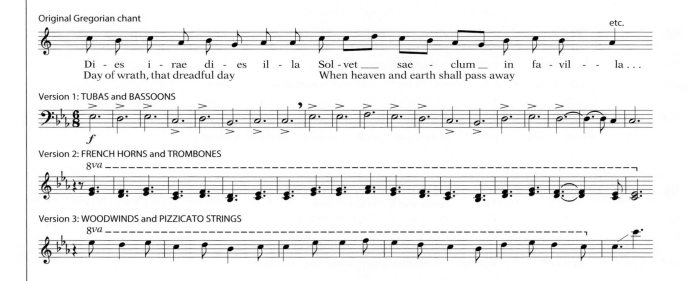

Original Gregorian chant

Di - es i - rae di - es il - la Sol - vet ___ sae - clum ___ in fa - vil - - la . . .
Day of wrath, that dreadful day   When heaven and earth shall pass away

Version 1: TUBAS and BASSOONS

Version 2: FRENCH HORNS and TROMBONES

Version 3: WOODWINDS and PIZZICATO STRINGS

The final section of the movement is the "Witches' Round Dance." Berlioz wrote a free fugue—a traditional form in a nontraditional context; he uses counterpoint to give a feeling of tumult and orgiastic confusion. The subject is an excited one:

The climax of the fugue (and of the symphony) comes when the round dance theme is heard together with the *Dies irae,* played by the trumpets. Berlioz wanted to drive home the point that it is the witches, represented by the theme of their round dance, who are parodying the church melody. The *idée fixe* seems at last to be forgotten.

But in real life Berlioz did not forget; he married Smithson and both of them lived to regret it.

Berlioz, *Fantastic* Symphony, fifth movement

9 min., 59 sec.

3 | 27–33 | 58 | 27

INTRODUCTION

27	0:00		Mysterious orchestral effects
	0:27	*Fanfare*	Like a distant summons: trombones, then flutes plus piccolo echoed by muted French horns
	0:57		Free repetitions: mysterious sounds, fanfare

IDÉE FIXE

	1:39		Prefatory statement: two phrases (only) of the *idée fixe;* note the bass drum. Riotous orchestral response, **ff**.
28	1:59	*Idée fixe*	Entire tune presented in a grotesque transformation, in **6/8** meter, played by "squeaky" E-flat clarinets
0:30	2:29	*Crescendo*	Big climax — the first of many
0:51	2:50	**Upward motive**	A short, expectant motive (later this motive initiates the fugue subject of the "Round Dance")
0:54	2:53	*Transition*	Quiet descending passage
1:12	3:11	**Funeral bells**	Three sets of three bells (the third set is muted); the upward motive also appears.

DIES IRAE

29	3:38	**Segment 1**	**Segment 1 of plainchant *Dies irae* is played in three versions:** **(1)** **tubas and bassoons — slow**
0:21	3:58		**(2)** **horns and trombones — faster**
0:31	4:08		**(3)** **woodwinds and pizzicato strings — faster still** **(the rhythm here recalls that of the *idée fixe*)**
0:37	4:14	**Segment 2**	**Segment 2 of the plainchant, same three versions**
1:00	4:37	**Segment 3**	**Segment 3 (begins like segment 1), same three versions**
1:34	5:11	*Transition*	The upward motive is developed; crescendo.

WITCHES' ROUND DANCE (free fugue)

30	5:28	**Exposition**	Four entries of the fugue subject
0:26	5:55	*Episode 1*	
0:46	6:15	**Subject entries**	*Three more entries, in stretto*
31	6:30	*Episode 2*	A passage starting with a loud rhythmic motive, derived from the subject, comes four times.
0:21	6:52		The music dies down.
0:40	7:10		**Fragments of the *Dies irae***
0:55	7:26		Long transition; crescendo over a drum roll
1:35	8:06	**Subject entry**	The original subject returns.
32	8:12	**Subject plus** *Dies irae*	The two themes together in a polyphonic combination. This is a climax; **trumpets play the *Dies irae* for the first time.**
0:31	8:44	**Subject entry**	Final appearance of subject: over strings *col legno* (played with the wood, that is, the back of the bow). Some notes are lengthened.
33	9:19	*Dies irae*	**Segment 1 of the *Dies irae* hastily recollected; big drum strokes**
0:09	9:28	**Conclusion**	Final passage of cadences: very loud

GOALS FOR REVIEW

▶ to come to know new genres in the early nineteenth century: lied, character piece for piano, and program symphony

▶ to listen carefully to examples of each of these genres

▶ to differentiate and hear strophic and through-composed form in the lied

▶ to diagram musical form in miniature piano pieces

▶ to see program music at work in miniature piano pieces (*Carnaval*) and a grandiose symphony (*Fantastic* Symphony)

▶ to appreciate the individuality of early Romantic styles: Franz Schubert, Robert Schumann, Clara Schumann, Frédéric Chopin, Hector Berlioz

 macmillanhighered.com/listen8e
Interactive Listening Chart 15
Listening Quiz for Chapter 17
Reading Quiz for Chapter 17

Romantic Opera

The nineteenth century was a golden age of opera, which flourished all over Europe from Germany, France, and Italy to Bohemia and Russia. This was true in part because opera tied into two important Romantic themes. The first was the idea of breaking down barriers between the arts. Combining music with poetry and other forms of literature, and even with philosophy, made perfect sense to Romantic composers and their audiences. The age that produced the lied—a German song with an important poetic dimension—was also committed to the union of music and drama.

The second Romantic theme was the celebration of music as the most profound of all the arts. Opera composers and librettists began to ponder the

"Carve this into your head, in letters of brass: An opera must draw tears, cause horror, bring death, by means of song."

Opera composer Vincenzo Bellini, 1834

The Wolf's Glen scene from Weber's *Der Freischütz*, most famous of early German Romantic operas (see page 258). *The Art Archive at Art Resource, NY.*

meaning and message of their work; they came to view opera as a type of serious drama in music, not just a vehicle for song, spectacle, and entertainment, as had often been the case before. Richard Wagner is famous for embracing and publicizing this notion. He put it into action with his "music dramas," as he called his operas—works that fascinated the later nineteenth century. Nevertheless, Wagner was not alone. Even when he was still an unknown provincial conductor, the attitudes he would build on were developing all over Europe.

In this climate many operas took their subjects from highly regarded Romantic novels, such as *Ivanhoe, The Lady of the Lake*, and *The Bride of Lammermoor*, by Sir Walter Scott. Other operas started from Romantic poems and plays by Lord Byron, or the French writer Victor Hugo (author, in his later days, of *Les Misérables*). Moreover, since Romantic writers looked with new enthusiasm to Shakespeare's plays, opera composers also drew on them widely. Giuseppe Verdi, to whom we now turn, set versions of Shakespeare's tragedies *Macbeth* and *Othello*, as well as the comedy *The Merry Wives of Windsor*.

1 | Verdi and Italian Opera

Giuseppe Verdi was the greatest of Italian opera composers and the dominant figure in nineteenth-century opera houses. For while Wagner's music dramas and his theories of opera attracted much excited attention, Verdi's operas got many more performances. Then as now, people were inevitably drawn to compare and contrast these two masters.

The heart of the contrast lies in Verdi's unswerving commitment to the human voice. In this, he was a faithful follower of the **bel canto** principles of his Italian predecessors Rossini, Donizetti, and Bellini (see page 258). Verdi never allowed the voice to be overshadowed by the orchestra, and from early on in his career he showed a special talent for writing both beautiful, Romantic melodies and catchy tunes. Opera was a singing art to Verdi, and generations of opera lovers before, during, and after his lifetime have enthusiastically agreed with him.

But while audiences have always loved Verdi's melodies, what he himself cared most about was the dramatic quality of his operas. First and foremost, Verdi was interested in people, people placed in situations in which strong, exciting actions bring out equally strong emotions. He sought out dramatic subjects full of stirring action, and he had a genius for finding just the right vocal melody to capture a dramatic situation.

Recitative and Aria: The Role of the Orchestra

Verdi's commitment to the human voice does not mean that the orchestra was unimportant to him. Instead it plays a much richer role in his operas than in those of any earlier Italian composer of operas. This was all but inevitable in the orchestra-intoxicated nineteenth century.

The role of the orchestra was especially expanded in passages of recitative or near recitative—the relic or descendant of the recitatives of Baroque opera seria and Classical opera buffa. Italian opera still held roughly to the old division of declamation (recitative) for the action and dialogue portions of an opera, and melody (arias) for reflective, emotional expression. (Ensembles encompassed both.) But plot action and dialogue were now always accompanied by the full

Romantic opera made its serious start in the 1820s, after the end of the Viennese Classical period. It sprang from the major opera houses of Italy, especially those in Naples and Milan, and from Paris. In Vienna, both Beethoven and Schubert felt threatened by the popular rage for the operas of Gioacchino Rossini, a young Italian whose meteoric career left a mark on the whole of Europe.

Gioacchino Rossini (1792–1868)

Rossini is most famous today for crisp, elegant opera buffas in a style that is not all that far from Mozart—the immortal *Barber of Seville* among them. The overtures of these operas, which are popular as concert pieces, are even written in sonata form, the true trademark of Classicism in music.

But in his own day Rossini was admired equally for his serious operas, which established the style and form of Italian Romantic opera. This is sometimes called *bel canto* opera because of its glorification of beautiful singing (*bel canto* means just that—"beautiful song"). Rossini's operas provided models of Romantic emotional melodic expression, such as Desdemona's "Willow Song" from his Shakespeare opera, *Otello*. The same operas are also well stocked with coloratura arias, showcases for the legendary virtuoso singers of that era.

To everyone's astonishment, Rossini gave up opera in 1829 after the success of *William Tell*, his greatest work.

Gaetano Donizetti (1797–1848)

Donizetti, who dominated Italian *bel canto* opera after Rossini's sudden retirement, moved decisively in the direction of simple, sentimental arias and blood-and-thunder action music. Enormously prolific, he wrote more than sixty operas in his short lifetime.

The most famous are *Lucia di Lammermoor*, based on the historical novel by Scott mentioned on page 257, and *Don Pasquale*, a very late example of opera buffa. In the 1970s, the American soprano Beverly Sills starred in a Donizetti trilogy featuring famous queens of English history: *Anna Bolena* (Anne Boleyn, the ill-fated second wife of Henry VIII), *Maria Stuarda* (Mary Stuart—Mary, Queen of Scots), and *Roberto Devereux* (about Queen Elizabeth I and Robert Devereux, Earl of Essex).

Vincenzo Bellini (1801–1835)

Vincenzo Bellini strikes listeners today as the most refined of the three early *bel canto* composers. He wrote many fewer operas than the others, and his most beautiful arias have a unique Romantic sheen. The title role in *Norma*, his finest work, is the final testing ground for sopranos, for it demands highly expressive singing, coloratura fireworks, and great acting, all in unusual quantities.

Verdi often expressed his admiration for the supremely melodious Bellini. All the same, he learned more from the more robust and dramatic Donizetti.

Carl Maria von Weber (1786–1826)

Weber was the founder of German Romantic opera. His most important work, *Der Freischütz* (The Magic Bullet), has the quality of a German folktale or ballad put to music. Max, a somewhat driven young huntsman, sells his soul to the Devil for seven magic bullets, but is redeemed by the love of his innocent fiancée, Agatha.

Two spiritual arias sung by Agatha in this opera show Romantic melody at its best. There are German choruses in folk-song style. A famous scene of devilish conjuration (see page 256) features sensational orchestral writing with spooky harmonic effects.

Supernatural subject matter with a strongly moral overtone—quite unlike the historical subjects chosen by Donizetti, for example—and emphasis on the orchestra became characteristic of German Romantic opera. These features are still evident in the mature works of Richard Wagner, who started out in the 1830s as an opera composer in Weber's mold. Otherwise, Wagner's "music dramas" leave early Romantic opera far behind.

Legendary singers of the *bel canto* era: Pauline Viardot (1821–1910; she was also a composer), Maria Malibran (1808–1836), and Giulia Grisi (1811–1869), along with a playbill for one of their favorite showcases, the opera *Norma* by Vincenzo Bellini. Left to right: *Scala/White Images/Art Resource, NY; Alfredo Dagli Orti/The Art Archive at Art Resource, NY; Album/Art Resource, NY; Bettmann/CORBIS.*

orchestra. Nowhere in Verdi will you hear passages of the old recitative of Mozart, accompanied by harpsichord alone. The orchestra, also, is usually not restricted to the simple chords that were normal in earlier recitative styles; it plays more active, motivic, and excited music that points up the words and urges the singers on.

Recitative is no longer a satisfactory name for this action music in Verdi's operas, though no other name exists. Highly melodramatic, it is always on the point of merging into a full-fledged melodic style. What distinguishes this music from actual arias is that arias are formally complete and distinct. Unlike passages of Verdian recitative, Verdian arias can be (and often are) extracted and sung separately, as concert numbers.

In arias and duets, the orchestra's role is smaller; here, however, Verdi uses another Romantic resource, that of rich harmonies underpinning melodic high points and climaxes. Many—though by no means all—of Verdi's arias might be described as simple strophic songs in his own exuberant style of Romantic melody. Some of his most famous music consists of timeless tunes such as the choral hymn "Va pensiero" from *Nabucco*, the soprano aria "Addio, del passato" from *La traviata*, and the tenor aria "Celeste Aida" from *Aida*.

Giuseppe Verdi, *Rigoletto* (1851)

4 | 1–6   59–60   28–29

Rigoletto was a daring subject for Verdi to take on, typical of his dramatic choices in its strong situations and violent emotions. For the source of this opera Verdi looked to a play by the literary lion of French Romanticism, Victor Hugo. Hugo's *Le roi s'amuse* (The King Amuses Himself) scandalized Paris in 1832 with its depiction of a dissolute, womanizing king and a jester who tries to have him assassinated; it was closed by the police after one performance. When Verdi settled on it the censors, who checked every operatic project in Italy at the time, demanded many changes. (The king was demoted to a mere duke, this apparently making his immorality less offensive.) Scandalous or not, *Rigoletto* was an immediate success; today it ranks among the most frequently performed operas.

The scene is set during the sixteenth century at the court of Mantua in northern Italy, where Rigoletto is the hunchbacked court jester of the Duke. He is a split character, divided between cynicism and hatred for the courtiers and his shining love for his daughter, Gilda, whom he keeps hidden from sight. The dashing, immoral, and rapacious Duke has gotten wind of her, however, and wants to add her to his list of conquests. Verdi's Duke of Mantua is descended clearly enough from Mozart's Don Giovanni.

Through turns of plot we will not trace, the Duke manages to seduce Gilda. She falls in love with him, believing he is a student who returns her love. Rigoletto, meanwhile, can think only of revenge. He hires an assassin, Sparafucile—half comical, but still one of the most menacing characters of nineteenth-century opera—to lure the Duke to his broken-down inn on the edge of the Mantuan marshes. Sparafucile (his name means something like "shotgun" in Italian) does so with the aid of his sister, Maddalena.

All this, in the terms of nineteenth-century operatic tragedy, can only end very badly for poor Gilda and her father.

"I want subjects that are novel, big, beautiful, varied and bold—as bold as can be!"

Giuseppe Verdi, 1853

We pick up the action at the beginning of the final act, as Rigoletto brings Gilda to Sparafucile's hovel to see for herself the Duke's habits. The scene is split, with the Duke and Maddalena inside the house, Rigoletto and Gilda eavesdropping from outside through a crack in the wall, and Sparafucile moving in between. (We are meant to understand that father and daughter sing to each other, unheard by those inside.)

Rigoletto and Gilda outside, the Duke and Maddalena inside: two images of the quartet, one from Verdi's day, the other a modern production. Left: *Bettmann/CORBIS.* Below: © *Jack Vartoogian/ FrontRowPhotos.*

Biography

Giuseppe Verdi (1813–1901)

The son of a storekeeper in a tiny village in northern Italy, Verdi had a spotty education. He played church organ and conducted the band of the neighboring little town. A local merchant, Antonio Barezzi, who became a patron and almost a second father to the young man, sent him to Milan to study music.

In those days, the center of musical life in Italy was Milan's opera house, La Scala. (It is still active and world famous today.) After several discouraging years in that city, Verdi scored a huge success with his biblical opera *Nabucco* (Nebuchadnezzar) when he was twenty-nine years old. For the next ten years he composed operas at a furious rate for opera houses in Italy, Paris, and London. Three great hits from the early 1850s are still his most popular works: *Rigoletto*, which we take up here; *Il trovatore*, a grisly tale set in the age of chivalry; and *La traviata*, about a Parisian courtesan with a noble heart. After this Verdi took more time with his operas, and his later works became richer and more subtle.

Italy was not an independent nation during Verdi's youth. He was an ardent supporter of the Risorgimento, or Italian liberation movement, and many of his early operas had patriotic themes. The most beloved number in *Nabucco* was a nostalgic hymn of the Hebrew slaves in Babylon—a clear reference to the Italians under the heel of the Austrian Empire. In the year of revolution, 1848, Verdi wrote the rousing *Battle of Legnano*. VERDI actually became a patriotic acronym for the popular choice for king—*Vittorio Emmanuele,*

Re d'Italia. After independence was achieved, the composer was made an honorary deputy in the first Italian parliament.

A dour character and a tough businessman, Verdi drove hard bargains with opera impresarios, bullied his librettists, and insisted on supervising the production of his new operas. After the premiere of *Aida* in 1871 in Cairo, Egypt—Verdi was internationally famous—he retired to a fine country estate near his birthplace and spent his later years hunting and raising livestock. He was coaxed out of retirement in the 1880s by his canny publisher and by an eminent librettist, Arrigo Boito. In his seventies, Verdi wrote his two greatest operas with Boito on Shakespearean subjects: the tragedy *Otello* and the comedy *Falstaff*.

Verdi's first marriage, to the daughter of his early patron Barezzi, ended when his young wife and two babies died within two years. The composer bore the emotional scars of this tragedy all his life, and it may be that the many moving scenes between fathers and daughters in Verdi's operas, including *Rigoletto*, served to channel his feelings about fatherhood. He later married a remarkable woman, Giuseppina Strepponi, a singer who had assisted him in his early career and starred in his first success, *Nabucco*. She had been Verdi's partner for many years before their marriage.

By the time he died, at the age of eighty-eight, Verdi was a national institution, and he was mourned throughout Italy. Schools closed. Eulogies were delivered in a special session of the senate in Rome. Nearly 300,000 people saw the old man to his grave. His operas remain the most popular of all in the international repertory.

Chief Works: Twenty-four operas, including *Nabucco, Macbeth, Rigoletto, Il trovatore, La traviata, Don Carlos, The Force of Destiny, Aida* ■ Two great Shakespeare operas composed in his seventies, *Otello* and *Falstaff* ■ A Requiem Mass, and a few other choral works; a string quartet

Encore: After *Rigoletto*, listen to *La traviata* (Act I), *Aida* (Act IV), *Otello* (Act I).

Verdi photograph: Bettmann/CORBIS.

A popular graffito of the Italian revolution: "Viva VERDI" (meaning "Long live Victor Emmanuel, King of Italy"). *Bettmann/CORBIS.*

The stage is divided, showing the inside and the outside of a sordid inn.

1   RECITATIVE

The Duke enters the inn.

0:03	**Gilda:**	**(Ah! padre mio!)**	(Ah! dear father!)
	Duke:	**Due cose, e tosto:**	Two things, and right now.
	Sparafucile:	**Quali?**	What?
	Duke:	**Una stanza e del vino.**	A room and some wine.
	Rigoletto:	**(Son questi i suoi costumi.)**	(That's the way he does things.)
	Sparafucile:	**(Oh il bel zerbino!)**	(Big spender!)

2   ARIA

0:12	0:29	**Duke:**	**La donna è mobile / Qual pium' al vento,**	Woman is fickle, a feather in the wind;
			Muta d'accento / E di pensiero.	Changing her words and thoughts,
			Sempre un amabile / Leggiadro viso,	She's a lovable, sweet sight,
			In pianto o in riso / È menzognero.	When she's weeping or laughing, she's lying.
			La donna è mobil' / Qual pium' al vento,	Woman is fickle, a feather in the wind;
			Muta d'accento / E di pensier!	Changing her words and thoughts!
1:11	1:28		**È sempre misero / Chi a lei s'affida;**	Man's always wretched who believes her;
			Chi le confida / Mal cauto il core!	If you trust her, watch out for your heart!
			Pur mai non sentesi / Felice appieno	Yet he'll never feel happy
			Chi su quel seno / Non liba amore.	Who from that breast does not drink love!
			La donna è mobil' . . .	Woman is fickle . . .

Sparafucile gives the Duke a bottle of wine and glasses, then goes outside to Rigoletto.

3   RECITATIVE

2:45	**Sparafucile:**	**È là il vostr'uom; viver dee, o morire?**	There's your man; does he live or die?
	Rigoletto:	**Più tardi tornerò l'opra a compire.**	I'll be back later to finish him off.

Sparafucile walks off; enter Maddalena, with the Duke inside; Gilda and Rigoletto remain outside.

4   QUARTET *(from midway through the fast section)*

0:02	**Duke:**	**La bella mano candida!**	What lovely hands you have!
	Maddalena:	**Scherzate voi, signore.**	You're joking, sir.
	Duke:	**No, no,**	No, no . . .
	Maddalena:	**Son brutta.**	I'm plain!
	Duke:	**Abbracciami!**	Kiss me!
	Gilda *(outside)*:	**(Iniquo!)**	(Villain!)
	Maddalena:	**Ebbro!**	You must be drunk
	Duke:	**. . . d'amore ardente!**	. . . with burning love!

Recitative   A quick rustling gesture in the orchestra signals the Duke bursting in, disguised as a military officer, and demanding service at the inn. Gilda cries out in dismay as she recognizes her "student" lover.

Aria: "La donna è mobile"   Waiting for his drink, the Duke holds forth on the fickleness of women. (*He* should talk!) This brief aria is one of Verdi's most famous and enduring tunes—one of those nineteenth-century melodies everyone knows, even if they can't identify it. It captures perfectly the compelling

	Maddalena:	Signor l'indifferente, Vi piace canzonar?	You couldn't care less, sir, You like your little joke.
	Duke:	No, no, ti vo' sposar.	No, I mean to marry you!
	Maddalena:	Ne voglio la parola.	Give me your word?
	Duke:	Amabile figliuola!	Silly girl!
	Rigoletto:	(E non ti basta ancor?)	(Isn't that enough for you?)
	Gilda:	(Iniquo traditor!)	(You horrible traitor!)

5   **QUARTET** (slow section)

	0:35	**Duke:**	Bella figlia dell'amore Schiavo son de' vezzi tuoi; Con un detto sol tu puoi Le mie pene consolar. Vieni, e senti del mio core Il frequente palpitar.	You gorgeous child of love, I'm enslaved by your charms; With one word you can Stop my suffering. Come and feel My heart pounding!
1:00	1:35	**Maddalena:**	Ah! Ah! rido ben di core Chè tai baie constan poco, Quanto valga il vostro gioco Mel credete, sò apprezzar. Son avvezza, bel signore, Ad un simile scherzare.	Ha, ha, I'm laughing out loud. Talk doesn't mean a thing; Believe me, I know how much Your game counts for. My dear sir, I'm used To such joking.
1:03	1:38	**Gilda:**	(Ah! così parlar d'amore! A me pur l'infame ho udito! Infelice cor tradito, Per angioscie non scoppiar!)	(Oh, to talk about love like that! The villain has said the same to me! My unhappy, betrayed heart— Don't burst with anguish!)
1:12	1:47	**Rigoletto:**	Taci, il piangere non vale, Ch'ei mentiva sei sicura. Taci, e mia sarà la cura La vendetta d'affrettar. Sì, pronta fia, sarà fatale, Io saprollo fulminar.	(Quiet! It's no use weeping. You can see he was lying. Hush, and I'll take good care To get quick revenge. Yes, it'll be swift and fatal, I'll know how to strike him down!)

6   **RECITATIVE**

	4:21	**Rigoletto:**	M'odi: ritorna a casa, Oro prendi, un destiero, Una veste viril che t'apprestai, E per Verona parti. Sarovvi io pur doman.	Listen: go back home, Take the money, get the horse, And the men's clothes I got you, And ride to Verona. I'll join you there tomorrow.
		Gilda:	Or venite.	Come with me now!
		Rigoletto:	Impossibil.	I can't.
		Gilda:	Tremo!	I'm frightened!
		Rigoletto:	Va!	Go!

energy of the Duke, sweeping all before it. The effect stems especially from the insistent repetitions, in sequence, of the short motive that opens (and dominates) the aria.

The aria is in strophic form, with each of the two strophes introduced by the orchestra. At the end of each strophe the opening words return as a refrain and lead the melody up to the tenor's highest pitches. On our recording the tenor adds a brief flourish (a vocal **cadenza**) at the end of the second stanza, finishing on his highest pitch of all.

Recitative   Instead of pausing for applause, Verdi keeps the orchestra moving, repeating the melody of "La donna è mobile" more and more quietly in the woodwinds as Sparafucile comes out to confirm that this is the man Rigoletto wants killed. It is a small but deft touch, turning the jaunty melody of the aria a bit sinister and making it an accompaniment for a quick recitative exchange. Sparafucile exits, leaving Rigoletto and Gilda (outside still) and the Duke and Maddalena (inside) to sing an **ensemble**—in this case, a quartet.

Quartet: "Bella figlia dell'amore" (Allegro) This is another of Verdi's most famous inspirations. It begins with a fast section, in which the Duke presses his attentions on Maddalena while she jokingly resists. Meanwhile, outside, Gilda is horrified. These recitative-like exchanges are sung to a lively, continuous orchestral melody that propels the action forward—one way Verdi blurred the distinction between recitative and full-fledged melody.

Our recording skips the beginning of this section, picking it up midway through. The fast section comes to a stop on a loud, expectant chord, with all four singers joining together.

Andante As a slower movement begins, the Duke, never at a loss for a beautiful tune, takes the lead, pursuing Maddalena with all the suavity Verdi's melodic genius could muster. His melody is a perfect sixteen measures, four phrases of four measures each, rising to a climax in its third, contrasting phrase: **a a' b a'**.

As he finishes, the other voices start up, one by one. Each sings a distinct melody that captures the emotions at stake: Maddalena laughing at the Duke's efforts, Gilda sobbing, and Rigoletto stern, determined, bent on revenge. We heard this kind of dramatic characterization through melody in *Don Giovanni*, in the duet of Giovanni and Zerlina (see page 193).

The Duke joins in, the four voices shift through rich, Romantic harmonies (and modulations) to come to another expectant pause, and then the Duke begins his melody again. Now, however, the others sing with him, and Verdi has skillfully managed their melodies so that each preserves its independent emotional stance in the counterpoint that results. The Andante ends with a long passage for all four voices.

Recitative The lush quartet could not contrast more with what follows: a stark, brusque recitative in which Rigoletto tells his daughter to go to Verona, where he will follow. To sharpen the contrast, Verdi omits the orchestra entirely.

Alas, Gilda does not obey her father's instructions. She returns to the scene and is murdered, in place of the Duke, during a climactic thunderstorm. Rigoletto comes back to gloat over the dead Duke, but finds instead his daughter, dying; he is left maddened with grief as the curtain falls.

2 | Wagner and Music Drama

Richard Wagner was, after Beethoven, the most influential of all nineteenth-century composers. His strictly musical innovations, in harmony and orchestration, revolutionized instrumental music as well as opera. In terms of opera, Wagner is famous for his novel concept of the "total work of art" (*Gesamtkunstwerk*) and his development of a special operatic technique, that of the "guiding motive" (leitmotiv).

Unlike earlier innovative composers, it seems Wagner could not just compose. He had to develop elaborate theories announcing what art, music, and

Biography

Richard Wagner (1813–1883)

Wagner was born in Leipzig during the turmoil of the Napoleonic Wars; his father died soon afterward. His stepfather was a fascinating actor and writer, and the boy turned into a decided intellectual. Wagner's early interests, literature and music (his idols were Shakespeare and Beethoven), later expanded to include philosophy, mythology, and religion.

As a young man he worked as an opera conductor, and he spent an unhappy year in Paris trying to get one of his works produced at the very important opera house there. The virulent anti-French sentiments in his later writings stemmed from this experience. Back in Germany, he produced the first of his impressive operas, *The Flying Dutchman* and *Tannhäuser*, and wrote *Lohengrin*. Though these works basically adhere to the early Romantic opera style of Carl Maria von Weber, they already hint at the revolutionary ideal for opera that Wagner was pondering.

This he finally formulated after being exiled from Germany (and from a job) as a result of his part in the revolution of 1848–49. He wrote endless articles and books expounding his ideas—ideas that were better known than his later operas, for these were extremely difficult to stage. His book *Opera and Drama* set up the principles for his "music drama" *The Rhine Gold*, the first segment of the extraordinary four-evening opera *The Nibelung's Ring*. He also published a vicious essay attacking Felix Mendelssohn, who had just died, and other Jews in music. Fifty years after Wagner's death, his anti-Semitic writings (and his operas) were taken up by the Nazis.

Wagner's exile lasted thirteen years. His fortunes changed dramatically when he gained the support of the young, unstable, and finally mad King Ludwig II of Bavaria. Thanks to Ludwig, Wagner's mature music dramas were at last produced (*The Rhine Gold*, completed in 1854, was not produced until 1869). Wagner then promoted the building of a special opera house in Bayreuth, Germany, solely for his music dramas—an amazing concept! These grandiose, slow-moving works are based on myths and characterized by high-flown poetry of his own, a powerful orchestral style, and the use of *leitmotivs* (guiding or leading

motives). To this day the opera house in Bayreuth performs only Wagner, and tickets to the yearly Wagner Festival are almost impossible to get.

A hypnotic personality, Wagner was able to spirit money out of many pockets and command the loyalty and affection of many distinguished men and women. His first marriage, to a singer, ended in divorce. His great operatic hymn to love, *Tristan and Isolde*, was created partly in response to his love affair with the wife of one of his patrons. His second wife, Cosima, daughter of Franz Liszt, had been married to an important conductor, Hans von Bülow, who nonetheless remained one of Wagner's strongest supporters. Cosima's diaries tell us about Wagner's moods, dreams, thoughts, and musical decisions, all of which he shared with her. After the death of "the Master," Cosima ruled Bayreuth with an iron hand.

Half con man and half visionary, bad poet and very good musician, Wagner created a storm of controversy in his lifetime that has not died down to this day. He was a major figure in the intellectual life of his time, a thinker whose ideas were highly influential not only in music but also in other arts. In this sense, at least, Wagner was the most important of the Romantic composers.

Chief Works: Early operas: *The Flying Dutchman, Tannhäuser*, and *Lohengrin* ▪ Mature "music dramas": *Tristan and Isolde, The Mastersingers of Nuremberg* (a brilliant comedy), *Parsifal*, and *The Nibelung's Ring*, a four-opera cycle consisting of *The Rhine Gold, The Valkyrie, Siegfried*, and *Twilight of the Gods* ▪ *Siegfried Idyll*, for small orchestra (based on themes from *Siegfried;* a surprise birthday present for Cosima after the birth of their son, also named Siegfried)

Encore: After selections from *The Valkyrie*, listen to "Wotan's Farewell" from the same work (Act III); Prelude and Liebestod (love-death) from *Tristan and Isolde*.

Image credit: Richard Wagner Museum, Lucerne, Switzerland.

opera ought to be like. (Indeed, he also theorized about politics and philosophy, with very unhappy results.) Wagner's extreme self-consciousness as an artist was prophetic of attitudes toward art of a later period.

His theory of opera had its positive and negative sides. First, Wagner wanted to do away with all the conventions of earlier opera, especially the French and Italian varieties. Opera, he complained, had degenerated from its original

RICHARD WAGNER, /₌ GILL.

Wagner, Cosima, and their son Siegfried, who followed Cosima as director of the Wagner festivals at Bayreuth. *Contrasto/Archivio GBB/Redux.*

Wagner was God's gift to cartoonists. *Private Collection/ The Bridgeman Art Library.*

form as serious drama in music—Wagner was thinking of ancient Greek drama, which he knew had been sung or at least chanted—into a mere concert in costume. He particularly condemned arias, which were certainly at the heart of Italian opera, as hopelessly artificial. Why should the dramatic action keep stopping to allow for stretches of pretty but undramatic singing?

The Total Work of Art

The positive side of Wagner's program was the development of a new kind of opera in the 1850s, for which he reserved a special name: **music drama**. Music, in these works, shares the honors with poetry, drama, and philosophy—all furnished by Wagner himself—as well as the stage design and acting. Wagner coined the word **Gesamtkunstwerk**, meaning "total work of art," for this powerful concept. He always insisted on the distinction between music drama and ordinary "opera."

Since words and ideas are so important in the *Gesamtkunstwerk*, the music is very closely matched to the words. Yet it is also unrelievedly emotional and intense, as Romantic doctrine required. The dramas themselves deal with weighty philosophical issues, or so at least Wagner and his admirers believed, and they do so under the symbolic cover of medieval German myths and legends.

This use of myths was another Romantic feature, one that strikingly anticipated Freud, with his emphasis on myths (for example, the myth of Oedipus) as embodiments of the deepest unconscious truths. Wagner employed the old romance of Tristan and Iseult, the saga of the Nordic god Wotan, and the Arthurian tale of Sir Perceval to present his views on love, political power, and religion, respectively. Wagner's glorification of Germanic myths in particular made him the semiofficial voice of German nationalism, which in turn paved the way for Hitler.

One of the first great conductors and a superb orchestrator, Wagner raised the orchestra to new importance in opera, giving it a role modeled on

"*Drama* is the most comprehensive work of art; it can only be fully realized when *all the other arts* in their full realization are present in it."

Wagner pondering the Gesamtkunstwerk, *1850*

WAGNER'S *TRISTAN AND ISOLDE* (1859)

Wagner's first completed music drama was the great love story of Tristan and Isolde, taken from medieval legend. There was already a mystical undertone to the legend, which Wagner, writing the opera's libretto, refined under the sway of Romantic thinking.

The composer was only too pleased to find support in the writings of a contemporary philosopher, Arthur Schopenhauer, who had made his own formulation of the Romantic insight into the central importance of music in emotional life. All human experience, said Schopenhauer, consists either of emotions and drives—which he called "the Will"—or of ideas, morals, and reason, which he downgraded by the term "Appearance." He insisted that the Will always dominates Appearance, and that our only direct, unencumbered sense of it comes through music.

"Through *my* music!" we can almost hear Wagner exclaiming. And in a music drama, what would exemplify the Will better than the strongest human drive that is known, sexual love?

Tristan and Isolde is not just a great love story, then, but something more. It is a drama that presents love as the dominant force in life, one that transcends every aspect of worldly Appearance. Many love stories hint at such transcendence, perhaps, but Wagner's story makes it explicit, on the basis of an actual philosophy that the composer espoused.

The plot shows step by step the growing power of love, and the music—with its hypnotic orchestral web of leitmotivs and Romantic harmonies of unmatched richness—grows more and more powerful, too. In Act I, love overpowers Isolde's fierce pride, which had previously made her scorn Tristan as her blood enemy, and also Tristan's chivalry, which had demanded that he escort Isolde safely to her marriage to King Mark of Cornwall, his uncle and liege lord. In Act II, love overcomes the marriage, when the pair meet in the longest unconsummated love scene in all of opera. Their tryst is discovered, and Tristan is mortally wounded—but love overcomes the wound, too. In Act III he simply cannot or will not die until Isolde comes to him from over the seas. Isolde comes; Tristan dies in her arms; she sinks down in rapture and expires also. For both of them, death is not a defeat but an ecstatic expression of love.

At this point (if not earlier) the plot passes the bounds of reality—which was exactly what Wagner wanted to show. Tristan and Isolde, hardly characters anymore but stand-ins for the Will, move in a realm where conventional attitudes, the rules of society, and even life and death have lost their powers. Transcendence is a recurring theme of Romanticism; here passion becomes the ultimate experience, beyond reality. Music, which is itself beyond reality, explores the insecure borderland between love, sensuality, and death.

In Act II of Wagner's opera, Isolde signals Tristan that all is clear for their fatal meeting. *Alfredo Dagli Orti/The Art Archive at Art Resource, NY.*

Beethoven's symphonies with their motivic development. Leitmotivs (see below) were among the motives he used for this symphonic continuity. The orchestra was no longer used essentially as a support for the singers (which was still the situation, even in Verdi); it was now the orchestra that carried the opera along. Instead of the alternation of recitatives, arias, and ensembles in traditional opera, music drama consisted of one long orchestral web, cunningly woven in with the singing.

Leitmotivs

A **leitmotiv** (líte-moh-teef)—guiding, or leading, motive—is a musical motive associated with some person, thing, idea, or symbol in the drama. By presenting and developing leitmotivs, Wagner's orchestra guides the listener through the story.

Leitmotivs are easy to ridicule when they are used mechanically—when, for example, the orchestra obligingly sounds the Sword motive every time the hero reaches for his weapon. On the other hand, leitmotivs can suggest with considerable subtlety what the hero is thinking or feeling even when he is saying something else—or saying nothing. Wagner also became very skillful in **thematic transformation**, the characteristic variation-like technique of the Romantic composers (see page 232). By transforming the appropriate motives, he could show a person or an idea developing and changing under the impact of dramatic action.

And since, for the Romantics, music was the undisputed language of emotion, leitmotivs—being music—could state or suggest ideas in *emotional* terms, over and above the intellectual terms provided by mere words. This was Wagner's theory, a logical outcome of Romantic doctrine about music. Furthermore, the complex web of leitmotivs provided his long music dramas with the thematic unity that Romantic composers sought. On both counts, psychological and technical, leitmotivs were guaranteed to impress audiences of the nineteenth century.

The Nibelung's Ring (1848–1874)

Wagner's *Der Ring des Nibelungen* (The Nibelung's Ring) is a huge music drama in four parts, stretching over four separate nights of three to five hours each. This work, a quarter century in the making, counts as the supreme example of the Romantic tendency toward the grandiose (see page 230). *The Ring* (as it is commonly called) grew so large because of the sprawling material Wagner wanted to cover, large portions of the most famous of all Germanic or Norse legends. It involves gods and goddesses, giants and dwarfs, magical prophecies and transformations, a dragon, an invisibility cloak that lives on in Harry Potter novels—and, in the midst of it all, very human feelings and actions. *The Ring* counts as one of the towering artworks of all time, comparable to the Taj Mahal, the *Iliad* and the *Odyssey*, and Michelangelo's Sistine Chapel (comparisons the megalomaniac Wagner would have enjoyed).

The first night, *Das Rheingold* (The Rhine Gold), shows us events whose consequences will be played out over the following three nights: A precious lump of gold at the bottom of the Rhine River is stolen from its rightful owners, the mermaids of the Rhine, by the dwarf Alberich, and then is taken again from him by the gods. The stolen gold, forged into the ring of Wagner's title by the dwarfs whom Alberich commands, carries with it a curse. It makes all who possess it, even Wotan, the leader of the gods, renounce the love that could save

"The language of music consists only of *feelings* and *impressions*. It expresses to the utmost the emotions . . . independently of the language of words, which has become a purely rational system of communication."

Wagner in a public letter to his supporters, 1851

them from its corruption. *Love* is meant here in the broadest sense, to include human compassion in all its forms. Over the following three nights of *The Ring—Die Walküre* (The Valkyrie), *Siegfried,* and *Götterdämmerung* (Twilight of the Gods)—generations pass. We see the gods, humans, and dwarfs—and a giant transformed into a dragon—brought to grief by their lust for the gold. An innocent hero, Siegfried, is born who can defy the gods and their corrupt order, but even he dies through treachery arising from everyone else's pursuit of the ring.

Wagner employs all this elaborate mythology to tell a simple modern tale. His basic theme is the moral decline of the world, brought about by greed for money and hunger for power. In the guise of Norse gods, gnomes, and warriors, one group after another of nineteenth-century society is shown destroying itself in the pursuit of gold. Even the renunciation of love entailed in possessing the ring is an allegory, turning the old myth into an indictment of modern bourgeois biases toward work and discipline and away from emotion.

Richard Wagner, *The Valkyrie* (1851–1856)

4 | 7–12 | 61 | 30

The Valkyrie is the second of the four nights of *The Ring.* Much of the opera concerns a subplot in Wagner's tale. This story within a story brings together Siegmund and Sieglinde, two of Wotan's numerous children, a brother and sister separated in early childhood. Their irresistible attraction to each other results in an incestuous union (at the end of Act I), doubly illicit since Sieglinde is already married to Hunding. In Act II, Hunding fights a duel with Siegmund. Wotan, for reasons stemming from his fateful involvement with the ring, is powerless to intervene to help his son, and Siegmund is killed—another playing out of the gold's curse. Sieglinde escapes, however, to bear their child: the hero Siegfried, protagonist of the last two nights of *The Ring.*

The first scene of Act I shows us the meeting of Siegmund and Sieglinde. He stumbles into her dwelling, worn to exhaustion by a pack of enemies pursuing him in a raging thunderstorm. (The storm is depicted by the orchestral prelude that opens the work.) Siegmund collapses on the hearth to the sound of a leitmotiv we quickly come to associate with him, a descending scale that is a transformed version of the theme of the storm. This musical connection shows us that the storm is in Siegmund's soul as much as it is out in the elements.

Storm Motive

Siegmund Motive

Sieglinde enters from the back room and is startled to find a stranger unconscious on her floor. As she bends over him, concerned, the violins sound her leitmotiv—it rises up gently and falls back—while cellos underneath continue to play Siegmund's. Wagner's orchestral music has already joined the two characters.

What follows is one of the great portrayals of love at first sight in all of opera. Or nearly at first sight: Siegmund and Sieglinde's attentions are riveted to each other almost from the moment he regains consciousness, but the intensity of their emotional connection grows quickly during this scene.

Sieglinde Motive
A little livelier

CELLOS   VIOLINS

Siegmund Motive

General Features Along the way the audience witnesses the primary features of Wagner's revolutionary music drama.

• The orchestra, carrying the leitmotivs, plays a role far beyond merely accompanying the singers. It depicts for us the characters' thoughts and especially their feelings, even during long stretches when they are not singing.

The images evoked over the years by *The Valkyrie* and Wagner's other operas are wonderfully diverse. Shown here are Wagner's favorite tenor, Ludwig Schnorr von Carolsfeld, in a typical costume of the day; Sieglinde with a drinking horn for Siegmund by book illustrator Arthur Rackham, from 1910; and Brünnhilde, the Valkyrie of the title, complete with face tattoos, from a production of 2011. Top left: *Lebrecht/The Image Works*. Top right: *Private Collection/Photo © Chris Beetles Ltd, London/The Bridgeman Art Library*. Bottom: *David Beloff*.

It yields a sense of psychological depth and complexity in the characters—a sense conveyed, in typical Romantic fashion, more by music than by words.

• The leitmotivs hardly ever appear in exactly the same way twice but instead are transformed slightly for each new appearance. In this way their psychological portrayal shifts along with the drama. This probing, shifting depiction of the characters' feelings is one of the hallmarks of Wagnerian drama.

• The singers, meanwhile, do not as a rule sing the leitmotivs, and their melodies show none of the tunefulness or lyrical song forms of Verdi's *Rigoletto*. Instead they deliver a free-formed declamation of the words, something like recitative, that blossoms forth now and then to approach tunefulness but never gives way to full-fledged aria.

The First Drink   As Sieglinde leans over him, Siegmund awakes and cries out for a drink. She hurries outside to fill a drinking horn for him. While she does so the orchestra takes over, building to a miniature climax before falling back; in its music we still hear Siegmund's and Sieglinde's leitmotivs. Siegmund drinks, and his eyes fix on Sieglinde for the first time. A new melody grows in the orchestra, warmly scored for solo cello and other low strings, and richly harmonized. It is the leitmotiv of their blossoming love:

Now the characters exchange information, for their benefit and the audience's. Sieglinde tells him that she is Hunding's wife; he tells her how he came to her home, and of the relief from his misery she has brought him: "Now the sun smiles on me anew."

The Second Drink   At this, Sieglinde spontaneously hurries to her storeroom to fill a horn with mead (a fermented honey drink) for him. This action, parallel to her fetching water earlier, summons from the orchestra an intensified version of its earlier climax. (See the Listen box, first and second orchestral climaxes.)

The lovers share the mead, their eyes now fixed on each other, and the love motive sounding in the orchestra also wells up—until Siegmund rouses himself with a deep sigh accompanied in the orchestra by a loud dissonant chord. He is ill-fated; misfortune follows wherever he goes (Wagner sets the crucial, repeated word *Misswende* to additional dissonant chords); and he would not for the world bring such misery on her (Love motive)—he must leave. Sieglinde cannot let him go. She stops him in his tracks with an impulsive admission: She is as ill-fated as he!

Communion   At Sieglinde's last word a hesitant new, warm melody begins low in the orchestra; we immediately hear it as an affirmation of the deep empathy they already feel for each other. It is played first in sequence—a favorite of Wagner's techniques for developing his leitmotivs. Then, when Siegmund announces he

Sorrow/empathy Motive

The inside of a dwelling, built around a huge ash tree in its midst; to the right a hearth, and behind it an inner storeroom. Siegmund, exhausted, enters from outside as the storm subsides.

7	0:00	**Siegmund:**	**Wess' Herd dies auch sei,** **hier muss ich rasten.**	Whoever's hearth this may be, I must rest here.

Siegmund Motive

He sinks back and lies motionless. Sieglinde enters, thinking her husband has returned; she is surprised to find instead a stranger. Hesitantly she approaches him closer and closer.

		Sieglinde:	**Ein fremder Mann?** **Ihn muss ich fragen.** **Wer kam ins Haus** **und liegt dort am Herd?** **Müde liegt er von Weges Müh'n:** **schwanden die Sinne ihm?**	A stranger here? I must ask him: Who has come into this house and lies on the hearth? He's weary and travel-worn. Is he unconscious?
	1:23		**Wäre er siech?** **Noch schwillt ihm der Atem;** **das Auge nur schloss er.** **Mutig dünkt mich der Mann,** **sank er müd' auch hin.**	Could he be sick? No, he is still breathing; he's only sleeping. He seems to me valiant, even though he's exhausted.

Sieglinde Motive

		Siegmund:	*(suddenly raises his head)* **Ein Quell! Ein Quell!**	A drink! A drink!
		Sieglinde:	**Erquickung schaff' ich.**	I'll bring some water.
8	2:08	**FIRST ORCHESTRAL CLIMAX**		

She quickly takes a drinking horn and goes out. She returns with the horn filled and offers it to Siegmund.

			Labung biet' ich **dem lechzende Gaumen:** **Wasser, wie du gewollt!**	Moisten your dry lips with this drink I've brought: water, as you wished!

0:51	2:59	*Siegmund drinks and gives the horn back. As he nods his head in thanks, his eyes fix on her face with growing interest.*		

Love Motives

1:58	4:06	**Siegmund:**	**Kühlende Labung** **gab mir der Quell,** **des Müden Last** **machte er leicht;** **erfrischt ist der Mut** **das Aug' erfreut** **des Sehens selige Lust.** **Wer ist's, der so mir es labt?**	The water brings me cooling relief; it lightens my weary load; my heart is refreshed, my eyes relish a beautiful, glorious sight. Who is it who so revives me?
9	5:05	**Sieglinde:**	**Dies Haus und dies Weib** **sind Hundings Eigen;** **gastlich gönn' er dir Rast:** **harre, bis heim er kehrt!**	This house and this wife belong to Hunding; he'll welcome you as guest; wait here until he returns!
		Siegmund:	**Waffenlos bin ich:** **dem wunden Gast** **wird dein Gatte nicht wehren.**	I am weaponless; a wounded guest will not threaten your husband.
		Sieglinde:	**Die Wunden weise mir schnell!**	You're wounded? Where?
0:28	5:33	**Siegmund:**	**Gering sind sie,** **der Rede nicht wert;** **noch fügen des Leibes** **Glieder sich fest.** **Hätten halb so stark wie mein Arm** **Schild und Speer mir gehalten,** **nimmer floh ich dem Feind;** **doch zerschellten mir** **Speer und Schild.**	It's nothing, pay no heed; my body is still strongly knit. If my shield and spear had been half as strong as my body, I never would have fled my foe. But spear and shield were shattered;

0:46	5:51		Der Feinde Meute hetzte mich müd', Gewitterbrunst brach meinen Leib; doch schneller, als ich der Meute, schwand die Müdigkeit mir; sank auf die Lider mir Nacht, die Sonne lacht mir nun neu.	the horde of enemies chased me down, the thunderstorm broke body and spirit; but now—faster than I fled my weariness flees from me! Darkness sank on my eyes, but now the sun smiles on me anew!	Storm Motive

10 6:24 **SECOND ORCHESTRAL CLIMAX**

Sieglinde goes to the storeroom and fills a horn with mead; she returns and offers it to Siegmund.

	Sieglinde:	Des seimigen Metes süssen Trank mög'st du mir nicht verschmähn.	Surely you'll not refuse a sweet drink of honeyed mead.
	Siegmund:	Schmecktest du mir ihn zu?	Would you not taste it first?

11 7:21 **LOVE MOTIVES RETURN**

Sieglinde drinks from the horn and gives it back. Siegmund takes a long drink, watching her all the while with growing warmth. At 8:33 (1:12) he sighs deeply and his eyes sink to the ground.

	Siegmund:	Einen Unseligen labtest du: Unheil wende der Wunsch von dir! Gerastet hab' ich und süss geruht: weiter wend ich den Schritt.	You've helped an unhappy man; may I keep Ill-fate from you! I have rested—rested sweetly; now I must go on my way.
	Sieglinde:	Wer verfolgt dich, dass du schon fliehst?	Who follows you, making you flee?

2:01	9:22	**Siegmund:**	Misswende folgt mir, wohin ich fliehe; Misswende naht mir, wo ich mich zeige.	Ill-fate follows me, wherever I run; Ill-fate approaches, wherever I linger.
2:33	9:54		Dir, Frau, doch bleibe sie fern! Fort wende ich Fuss und Blick.	You, wife, keep your distance! I must turn my path from you.

He turns to leave. She calls after him impetuously.

12	10:10	**Sieglinde:**	So bleibe hier! Nicht bringst du Unheil dahin, wo Unheil im Hause wohnt!	No, remain here! Ill-fate is nothing new here, where Ill-fate makes its home!	Sorrow/empathy Motive

He turns back, looks searchingly at her; she lowers her eyes in sadness and shame.

	Siegmund:	Wehwalt hiess ich mich selbst: Hunding will ich erwarten.	I myself named me Wehwalt— Woebound; I'll wait for Hunding.

EMPATHY MOTIVE DEVELOPED

Hunding Motive

He rests against the hearth, his eyes fixed on her; she raises her eyes to his, and they regard each other with deep emotion. At 12:26 (2:16) Sieglinde starts as she hears Hunding outside.

---

will stay, the orchestra cannot restrain itself; it pours forth a lush, Romantic harmonization of the new melody, the soon-to-be lovers gazing at each other all the while. In the midst of this beautiful passage, other leitmotivs are heard: first Sieglinde's, later the Love motive, and finally Siegmund's drooping scale.

The passage comes to no cadence—another favorite trick of Wagner's—but is cut off by a new, ominous leitmotiv in the low brasses. Hunding has returned, and the second scene begins.

Wagner's drama often moves at a ponderous, slow pace, and it has sometimes been criticized for this. (And lampooned, too; there is a Bugs Bunny cartoon that takes on *The Ring*.) In the first scene of *The Valkyrie* we have the sense that searching looks and sighs are stretched out to exaggerated length. Other than

Sieglinde's fetching two drinks for Siegmund, there is little stage action. At the same time, however, especially because of his orchestra with its leitmotivs, Wagner manages to pack a lot into the minimal gestures of his characters. By the end of scene i, barely a quarter hour into the drama, we have been introduced to two protagonists and gained knowledge of their history and a subtle sense of their emotional lives. And, before our eyes and ears, their love has burgeoned.

3 | Late Romantic Opera

Opera continued to flourish after Wagner and Verdi. The orchestra retained the important role it had achieved, if in different ways, with both of these composers. The Romantic emphasis on strong emotions, alongside powerful music to convey and probe them, continued.

These emotional passages now tended to break down into ever freer and more fragmentary melodic forms, and the distinction between recitative and aria, blurred in Verdi, became even harder to maintain. Wagner's leitmotiv technique was employed in most operas, in one form or another; its dramatic and psychological powers were acknowledged by composers and audiences alike.

What composers and audiences turned away from, however, was Wagner's mythical, quasi-philosophical ideal for opera. "Music drama" in Wagner's sense gave way to new realistic tendencies. Modern-day subjects were chosen for operas, showing up-to-date middle- or lower-class characters, rather than kings and queens, gods and heroes. A few of Verdi's operas had already pointed in this direction, most notably *La traviata* (see page 261).

Late Romantic realistic operas typically emphasized the sordid and violent aspects of life, as far as the censorship of the day would allow—in this they carried further a tendency we can already glimpse in *Rigoletto*. A famous and masterful example is *Carmen* (1875), by the French composer Georges Bizet. Set in contemporary Spain, it tells the tale of a fiery, sexually irresistible Gypsy woman who works in a cigarette factory and a soldier who falls under her spell. Having abandoned his fiancée and deserted his regiment for her, he loses her to a devil-may-care matador; at the final climax, mad with jealousy, he stabs her to death. All this is very distant from the mythical setting, the minimal action, the lingering gazes, and the psychological probing of *The Valkyrie*.

Giacomo Puccini (1858–1924)

Giacomo Puccini was the main Italian opera composer after Verdi; indeed, he may be said to have brought to an end the great tradition of Italian Romantic opera, which had begun a century before. Several operas Puccini composed around 1900 are perennial favorites, thanks to his special gift for short, intense vocal melodies and his canny sense of the stage.

Most of Puccini's operas are touched by the new realistic tendencies in late Romantic opera, but they also tend to distance the audience from what would otherwise be quite harsh dramatic messages. The locales of his operas range from contemporary Japan to the American Wild West, and from Rome in 1800, under Napoleon, to Beijing in the distant

Bettmann/CORBIS.

past. In these remote, even exotic sites, Puccini found it easier to view realistic stories through a Romantic and sentimental lens.

Capitalizing on Romantic psychological depiction in opera, Puccini specialized in intimate portraits of helpless women in hopeless situations. Such is the actress Tosca, propositioned by the police chief of Rome as the price for her lover's life (*Tosca*); or the poor seamstress Mimi, dying of tuberculosis (*La Bohème*); or the geisha Cho-Cho-San (*Madame Butterfly*), whose plight we take up now.

Giacomo Puccini, *Madame Butterfly* (1904)

4 | 13   62   31

Puccini's *Madame Butterfly*, derived from a play by the American author David Belasco, has a disturbingly true-to-life story. In the wake of the opening of Japan to trade with the United States in the 1850s, a cynical young naval officer, Lieutenant Pinkerton, marries a naïve fifteen-year-old geisha, Cho-Cho-San, whom he calls "Madame Butterfly." He then sails away with no intention of honoring the Japanese ceremony. Cho-Cho-San persists against all evidence in hoping he will return; but when he eventually does, he brings his "real" American wife with him, and Cho-Cho-San, now mother of Pinkerton's child, kills herself.

During Act II, in response to her maid's doubts, Cho-Cho-San sings the opera's most famous number, "Un bel dì," spinning a fantasy about Pinkerton's return. From the hills (she imagines) they will first see a little wisp of smoke, as the gunboat appears on the horizon. She sings this vision to a memorable melody that has a floating, disembodied quality in keeping with the fantasy it portrays—partly because it begins high in the soprano's range and slowly descends, partly because of its delicate orchestration.

After this melody, the aria takes on a freer formal cast. Cho-Cho-San sings varied music that mixes full-fledged melody (at "Poi la nave bianca . . .") with something closer to a recitative-like declamation (at "Mi metto là sul ciglio . . .").

But when she comes in her fantasy to the moment of remeeting Pinkerton ("Per non morire . . ."), she sings her heart out to a reprise of the aria's opening melody, now louder and with

The poster for the world premiere of *Madama Butterfly*. *Private Collection/The Bridgeman Art Library.*

redoubled, brass orchestration. It is a stroke of almost unbearable pathos, for it dramatizes the helpless growth of her fantasy. Originally linked to the hope that Pinkerton's ship would return, now the main melody expresses her joy at his reunion with her—which is sheer delusion. Puccini underscores the pathos when, at Cho-Cho-San's last words, the orchestra takes up the intensified melody once more to end the aria.

)))) LISTEN

Puccini, *Madame Butterfly*, Aria "Un bel dì" from Act II

4 | 13   62   31

0:00	**Un bel dì, vedremo** **levarsi un fil di fumo** **sull'estremo confin del mare;** **e poi la nave appare.**	One beautiful day, we'll see a tiny thread of smoke rise up on the horizon, out at sea; then the ship appears.
0:38	**Poi la nave bianca entra nel porto;** **romba il suo saluto. Vedi? È venuto!** **Io non gli scendo incontro — io no;**	Now the white ship sails into port; cannons roar a welcome. See? He has come! I don't run to meet him — not I;
1:24	**mi metto là sul ciglio del colle,** **e aspetto, e aspetto gran tempo,** **e non mi pesa la lunga attesa.**	I go to the brow of the hill and wait, and wait a long time, but the long wait doesn't bother me.
1:49	**E uscito dalla folla cittadina** **un uomo, un picciol punto,** **s'avvia per la collina.**	Out of the crowd down in the city a man, a tiny speck, sets out up the hill.
2:18	**Chi sarà, chi sarà? E come sarà giunto,** **che dirà, che dirà?** **Chiamerà: "Butterfly" dalla lontana . . .** **Io senza dar risposta** **me ne starò nascosta** **un po' per celia, e un po'**	Who is it? Who is it? And as he comes, what will he say? what will he say? He'll call out: "Butterfly" from afar . . . Without answering I'll hide myself, partly to tease him, and partly
2:56	**per non morire al primo incontro!** **Ed egli alquanto in pena chiamerà,** **chiamerà: "Piccina mogliettina,** **Olezza di verbena"—** **i nomi che mi dava al suo venire.**	so as not to die when we first meet! And then he'll be worried and call: "Little child-wife! Verbena blossom!"— the names he gave me when he first came.
3:40	**Tutto questo averrà, te lo prometto!** **Tienti la tua paura;** **io con sicura fede l'aspetto!**	All this will happen, I promise you! Don't be afraid; I await him knowing he'll come!

GOALS FOR REVIEW

► to experience the development of recitative, aria, and ensemble in Giuseppe Verdi's Romantic opera *Rigoletto*

► to see the changing relationship of voice and orchestra in opera

► to contrast Richard Wagner's revolutionary music drama with Italian Romantic opera

► to understand Wagner's use of leitmotivs and follow their use in a scene from *The Valkyrie*

► to gain an overview of early and late Romantic opera, before and after Verdi and Wagner

 macmillanhighered.com/listen8e
Listening Quiz for Chapter 18
Reading Quiz for Chapter 18

The Late Romantics

19

The year 1848 in Europe was a year of failed revolutions in France, Italy, and various German states. Political freedom, which for the Romantics went hand in hand with freedom of personal expression in life and art, seemed further away than ever. While not all the early Romantics lived in free societies, at least by today's standards, freedom was an ideal they could take seriously as a hope for the future. We recall Beethoven's enthusiasm for Napoleon as a revolutionary hero, reflected in the *Eroica* Symphony of 1803, one of the landmarks of nineteenth-century music. In the 1820s, artists and intellectuals thrilled to the personal role of one of them—Lord Byron, a poet—in the struggle for Greek independence. Then they lamented his death near the field of battle.

But the failure of the revolutions of 1848 symbolized the failure of Romantic aspirations. In truth, those aspirations had had little to nourish them since the days of Napoleon. Romanticism lived on, but it lived on as nostalgia.

The year 1848 is also a convenient one to demarcate the history of nineteenth-century music. Some of the greatest early Romantic composers—Mendelssohn, Chopin, and Schumann—died between the years 1847 and 1856. By a remarkable coincidence of history, too, the 1848 revolution transformed the career of Richard Wagner. Exiled from Germany for revolutionary activity, he had no opera house to compose for. Instead he turned inward and—after a long period of philosophical and musical reflection—worked out his revolutionary musical ideas. Wagner's music dramas, written from the 1850s on, came to dominate the imagination of musicians in the second half of the century, much as Beethoven's symphonies had in the first half.

Romanticism and Realism

European literature and art from the 1850s on was marked not by continuing Romanticism, but by realism. The novel, the principal literary genre of the time, grew more realistic from Dickens to Trollope and George Eliot in Britain, and from Balzac to Flaubert and Zola in France. In French painting, there was an important realist school led by Gustave Courbet. Thomas Eakins was a realist painter in America; William Dean Howells was our leading realist novelist. Most important as a stimulus to realism in the visual arts was that powerful new invention, the camera.

There was a move toward realism in opera at the end of the nineteenth century, as we have seen (page 274). On the other hand, the myth-drenched

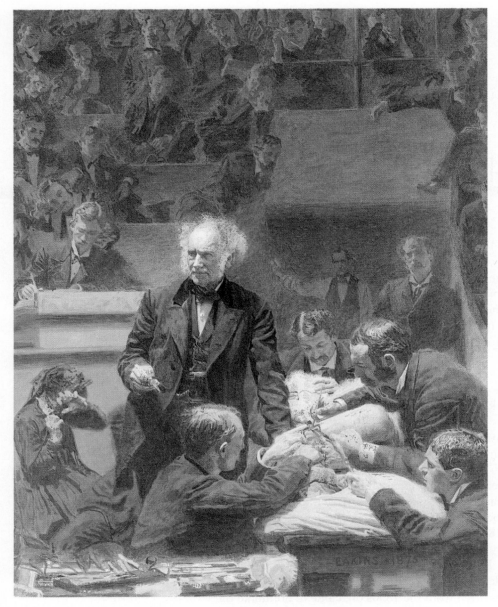

Realists in the arts of the nineteenth century tended toward glum or grim subject matter. The Philadelphia artist Thomas Eakins was so fascinated by surgery that he painted himself in among the students attending a class by a famous medical professor, Dr. S. D. Gross (*The Gross Clinic,* 1875). *The Philadelphia Museum of Art/Art Resource, NY.*

music dramas of Wagner were as unrealistic as could be. (Wagner thought he was getting at a deeper, psychological realism.) And what would "realism" in orchestral music be like? Given music's nature, it was perhaps inevitable that late nineteenth-century music came to function as an inspirational and emotional escape—an escape from political, economic, and social situations that were not romantic in the least.

Perhaps, too, music serves a similar function for many listeners of the twenty-first century. Significantly, concert life as we know it today, with its emphasis on great masterpieces of the past, was formed for the first time in the late nineteenth century.

1 | Late Romantic Program Music

Late Romantic program music took its impetus from an important series of works called *symphonic poems,* composed in the 1850s by Franz Liszt. A **symphonic poem** is a one-movement orchestral composition with a program, in a free musical form. By using the word *poem,* Liszt insisted on the music's programmatic nature.

It is not often that a great virtuoso pianist such as Liszt, who started out composing études and other miniatures of the kind cultivated by Chopin and Schumann, turns himself into a major composer of large-scale orchestral works. Liszt's formula was simply to write a one-movement piece for orchestra associated in one way or another with a famous poem, play, or narrative. In its single-movement format—unlike a Berlioz program symphony—the symphonic poem is descended from the concert overture as practiced by Mendelssohn (see page 248). But unlike the concert overture, it often is formally free, showing no sign of sonata form. Symphonic poems, also sometimes called *tone poems,* became very popular in the later nineteenth century.

Among Liszt's symphonic poems are *Hamlet, Orpheus, Prometheus,* and *Les Préludes,* the last loosely connected with a poem by the French Romantic poet Alphonse de Lamartine. But except for *Les Préludes,* these works are heard less often today than other symphonic poems written by composers influenced by Liszt's example. The most popular of later symphonic poems are those by Pyotr Ilyich Tchaikovsky and Richard Strauss (see page 335).

Pyotr Ilyich Tchaikovsky, Overture-Fantasy, *Romeo and Juliet* (1869, revised 1880)

4 | 14–25   63   32

Tchaikovsky wrote several symphonic poems, including one on a subject already used by Liszt and Berlioz, Shakespeare's *Hamlet.* Rather than *symphonic poem,* he preferred the descriptions *symphonic fantasia* or *overture-fantasy* for these works. They are substantial pieces in one movement, with free forms adopting some features from sonata form, rondo form, and so on.

In his *Romeo and Juliet,* Tchaikovsky followed the outlines of the original play only in a very general way, but one can easily identify his main themes with elements in Shakespeare's drama. The surging, romantic string melody clearly stands for the love of Romeo and Juliet. The angry, agitated theme suggests the vendetta between their families, the Capulets and the Montagues. More generally, it suggests the fate that dooms the two "star-cross'd lovers," as Shakespeare calls them. The hymnlike theme heard at the very beginning of the piece (later it sounds more marchlike) seems to denote the kindly Friar Laurence, who devises a plan to help the lovers that goes fatally wrong.

Slow Introduction   The slow introduction of *Romeo and Juliet* is already heavy with drama. As low clarinets and bassoons play the sober Hymn theme, the strings answer with an anguished-sounding passage forecasting an unhappy outcome. The wind instruments utter a series of solemn announcements, interspersed by strumming on the harp, as though someone (Friar Laurence?) was preparing to tell the tale. This sequence of events is repeated, with some variation, and then both the woodwind and string themes are briefly worked up to a climax over a dramatic drumroll.

> "The kernel of a new work usually appears suddenly, in the most unexpected fashion. . . . I could never put into words the joy that seizes me when the main idea has come and when it begins to assume definite shape. You forget everything, you become a madman."
>
> *Tchaikovsky letter to Madame von Meck about his composing, 1878*

Biography

Pyotr Ilyich Tchaikovsky (1840–1893)

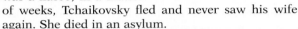

Tchaikovsky was born in the Russian countryside, the son of a mining inspector, but the family moved to St. Petersburg when he was eight. In nineteenth-century Russia, a serious musical education and career were not accorded the social approval they received in Germany, France, or Italy. Many of the famous Russian composers began in other careers and turned to music later in life, when driven by inner necessity.

Tchaikovsky was fortunate in this respect, for after working as a government clerk for only a few years, he was able to enter the new St. Petersburg Conservatory, founded by another Russian composer, Anton Rubinstein. At the age of twenty-six he was made a professor at the Moscow Conservatory. Once Tchaikovsky got started, after abandoning the civil service, he composed prolifically—six symphonies, eleven operas, symphonic poems, chamber music, songs, and some of the most famous of all ballet scores: *Swan Lake, Sleeping Beauty,* and *The Nutcracker.* Listen to a dance from *The Nutcracker* in Listening Exercise 8 (page 38).

Though his pieces may sometimes sound "Russian" to us, Tchaikovsky was not as devoted a nationalist as some other major Russian composers of the time (see page 284). Perhaps because of this, he had greater international renown than they. Of all the nineteenth-century Russian composers, Tchaikovsky had the most success in concert halls around the world. His famous Piano Concerto No. 1 was premiered in 1875 in Boston, and he toured America as a conductor in 1891.

Tchaikovsky was a depressive personality who more than once attempted suicide. He had been an extremely delicate and hypersensitive child, and as an adult he worried that his homosexuality would be discovered and exposed. In an attempt to raise himself above suspicion, he married a highly unstable young musician who was in love with him. The marriage was a fiasco; in a matter of weeks, Tchaikovsky fled and never saw his wife again. She died in an asylum.

For many years Tchaikovsky was subsidized by a wealthy, reclusive widow named Nadezhda von Meck. She not only commissioned compositions from him but actually granted him an annuity. By mutual agreement, they never met; nevertheless, they exchanged letters regularly over the thirteen years of their friendship. This strange arrangement was terminated, without explanation, by Madame von Meck.

By this time Tchaikovsky's position was assured, and his music widely admired. In a tragic mishap, he died after drinking unboiled water during a cholera epidemic.

Chief Works: Symphonies No. 4, 5, and 6 (*Pathétique*); a very popular Violin Concerto and Piano Concerto ▪ Operas: *The Queen of Spades* and *Eugene Onegin,* based on works by the Russian Romantic poet Alexander Pushkin ▪ Symphonic poems: *Romeo and Juliet, Hamlet, Overture 1812* (about Napoleon's retreat from Russia in that year) ▪ Ballet scores: *Swan Lake, Sleeping Beauty, The Nutcracker*

Encore: After *Romeo and Juliet,* listen to *The Nutcracker;* Symphony No. 4; Violin Concerto.

Image Credit: Bettmann/CORBIS.

Allegro The tempo changes to allegro, and we hear the Vendetta or Fate theme. It is made up of a number of short, vigorous rhythmic motives, which Tchaikovsky at once begins to develop. Then the Vendetta theme returns in a climax punctuated by cymbal crashes.

The highly romantic Love theme (illustrated on page 226) is first played only in part, by the English horn and violas—a mellow sound. It is halted by a curious but affecting passage built out of a little sighing figure:

LISTENING CHART 16

Tchaikovsky, Overture-Fantasy, *Romeo and Juliet*

20 min., 25 sec.

4 | 14–25   63   32

INTRODUCTION (Andante)				
14	0:00	**Hymn theme**	Low woodwinds, **pp**	
	0:35	**String motives**	Anguished quality; contrapuntal	
	1:28	**Strumming harp**	With "announcements" in the high woodwinds	
15	2:09	**Hymn theme**	High woodwinds with pizzicato strings. Followed by the string motives and harp; the "announcements" are now in the strings.	
2:00	4:08	**Buildup**	Ends with drumroll, **f**	
16	4:45	**Preparation**	Prepares for the main section; **p**, then *crescendo*	
MAIN SECTION (Allegro)				
17	5:26	**Vendetta theme**	Full orchestra, **f**	
0:25	5:51		Development of the Vendetta theme; contrapuntal	
0:54	6:20		Reaches a climax: cymbals	
1:07	6:33	**Vendetta theme**	Full orchestra, **ff**	
1:30	6:56		Relaxes, in a long slowdown	
2:18	7:44		Prefatory statement of Love theme (English horn): phrase **a**	
18	8:07		"Sighing" theme; muted strings, **pp**	
19	8:57	**Love theme**	Form is **a b a**, in the woodwinds, with the sighing motive played by the French horn.	
1:08	10:05		Harp. Cadences; the music dies down and nearly stops.	
DEVELOPMENT				
20	11:13	**Developmental combination**	Vendetta theme fragments are combined with the Hymn theme, which now sounds more like a march than a hymn.	
21	12:34		This works up to a climax, marked by a cymbal crash.	CYMBALS
0:25	13:00	**Hymn theme**	Played by trumpets; syncopated rhythm in the cymbals	
FREE RECAPITULATION (abbreviated)				
22	13:30	**Vendetta theme**	Full orchestra, **ff**	
0:26	13:56		Sighing theme	
1:08	14:38	**Love theme**	Form is **a b a**; ecstatically in the strings, with the sighing motive again in the French horn; the last **a** is **ff**.	
23	15:47		Fragments of the Love theme	
0:31	16:18	**(Love theme)**	Sounds like another ecstatic statement, but is interrupted	
0:41	16:28		Interruption by the Vendetta theme: conflict! Cymbals.	
0:51	16:39	**Developmental combination**	Vendetta theme fragments combined with the Hymn theme; buildup to **fff**	
1:33	17:21		Then dies down, rather unwillingly; ends on drumroll, **f**	
CODA (Moderato)				
24	17:55	**Love theme**	A broken version of the Love theme, with muffled funeral drums. The music seems to be ending.	
25	18:32	**New theme**	Woodwinds; ends with a transformation of the sighing motive	
0:59	19:31	**Love theme**	Section **a** in a slow cadential "transcendent" version. The strumming harp of the slow introduction has returned.	
1:31	20:03		Final cadences; a drumroll and solemn ending gestures	

After the Love theme dies down at some length, a lively development section begins (a feature suggesting sonata form). Confronted by various motives from the Vendetta theme, the Hymn theme takes on a marchlike character. We may get the impression of a battle between the forces of good and evil.

The Vendetta theme returns in its original form (suggesting a sonata-form recapitulation). The sighing motive and the lengthy Love theme also return, but the end of the latter is now broken up and interrupted—a clear reference to the tragic outcome of the drama. At one last appearance, the Vendetta theme is joined more explicitly than before with the Hymn theme.

Coda (slow)   A fragment of the Love theme appears in a broken version over funeral drum taps in the timpani. This must depict the pathos of Romeo's final speeches, where he refers to his love before taking poison. A new, slow theme in the woodwinds is really a transformation of the sighing motive heard earlier.

But the mood is not entirely gloomy; as the harp strumming is resumed, the storyteller seems to derive solace and inspiration from his tale. Parts of the Love theme return in a beautiful new cadential version, surging enthusiastically upward in a way that is very typical of Tchaikovsky. Doesn't this ecstatic surge suggest that even though Romeo and Juliet are dead, their love is timeless—that their love transcends death? The influence of Wagner's *Tristan and Isolde* (see page 267) was felt here as everywhere in the later nineteenth century.

2 | Nationalism

One legacy of Romanticism's passion for freedom played itself out all through the nineteenth century: the struggle for national independence. The Greeks struggled against the Turks, the Poles rose up against Russia, the Czechs revolted against Austria, and Norway broke free of Sweden.

As people all over Europe became more conscious of their national characters, they also came to prize their distinctive artistic heritages more and more. This gave rise to **nationalism** in music. The characteristic musical feature of this movement is simply the incorporation of national folk music into concert pieces, songs, and operas. Symphonic poems or operas also were based on programs or librettos that took up national themes—a hero of history such as Russia's Prince Igor; a national literary treasure such as the Finnish Lemminkaïnen legends; even a beloved river such as the Vltava (Moldau) in Bohemia. Such national themes were reinforced by the musical themes taken from folk song. The result was music that stirred strong emotions at home, and often made an effective ambassador abroad.

Although in the nineteenth century political nationalism was certainly a major factor all over Europe, composers in Germany, Italy, and France are usually not categorized with the musical nationalists, for musical nationalism also strove to make local music independent of Europe's traditional cultural leaders. Nationalist composers often deliberately broke the traditional rules of harmony, form, and so on. They did this both in a spirit of defiance and also in an effort to develop new, genuinely local musical styles.

> "A nation creates music—the composer only arranges it."
>
> *Mikhail Glinka (1804–1857), early Russian nationalist composer*

Exoticism

All this specifying of national styles had another effect: Audiences came to enjoy hearing folk music of *other* nations at concerts and the opera. French

Nationalism: For Finland, chafing under the rule of Russia, the epic poem *Kalevala* became a nationalist icon, drawn upon again and again by composer Jean Sibelius, as well as the Finnish painter Akseli Gallen-Kallela. In our picture, Kullervo, one of the saga's heroes, rides off to war; *Kullervo* by Sibelius is a grandiose symphonic poem. *Ateneum Art Museum, Finnish National Gallery, Helsinki, Finland/The Bridgeman Art Library.*

composers wrote Spanish music, Russians wrote Italian music, and Czechs wrote American music (George Bizet's opera *Carmen*, Tchaikovsky's orchestra piece *Capriccio Italien*, and Antonín Dvořák's famous *New World* Symphony, with its reference to spirituals). Such music cannot be called nationalistic, since its aim was not national self-definition, but it still had the effect of emphasizing the unique qualities of nations. It is usually simply called "exotic." Puccini's *Madame Butterfly* (see page 275) exemplifies this trend. Puccini even studied a few samples of Japanese music to find the right exotic sound for his opera.

The Russian *Kuchka*

A close group of five Russian nationalist composers were nicknamed (by one of their critic friends) the *kuchka*—sometimes translated as "the Mighty Five," but actually meaning a group or clique. They were an interesting and exceptionally talented group—even though they included only one trained musician, Mily Balakirev (1837–1910). Alexander Borodin (1833–1887) was a distinguished chemist, César Cui (1835–1918) an engineer, Nikolai Rimsky-Korsakov (1844–1908) a navy man, and Modest Musorgsky (1839–1881) an officer in the Russian Imperial Guard.

What held this group together was their determination to make Russian music "Russian," their deep interest in collecting folk songs, and their commitment to self-improvement as composers, relatively late in life.

Modest Musorgsky, *Pictures at an Exhibition* (1874)

4 | 26–29   64–67   33–34

The title of this interesting work refers to a memorial exhibit of pictures by a friend of Musorgsky's who had recently died, the Russian painter Viktor Hartmann. Like Musorgsky, Hartmann cared deeply about getting Russian themes into his work. *Pictures at an Exhibition* was originally written for piano solo, as a series of piano miniatures joined in a set, like Robert Schumann's *Carnaval* (see page 244). In 1922 the set was orchestrated by the French composer Maurice Ravel, and this is the form in which it is usually heard.

***Promenade** [1]* To provide some overall thread or unity to a set of ten different musical pieces, Musorgsky hit upon a plan that is as simple and effective as it is ingenious. The first number, "Promenade," does not refer to a picture, but depicts the composer strolling around the picture gallery. The same music returns several times in free variations, to show the promenader's changes of mood as he contemplates Hartmann's varied works.

The Promenade theme recalls a Russian folk song:

Ravel orchestrated this forceful theme first for brass instruments, later for wood-winds and strings. Quintuple meter (**5/4:** measures 1, 3, and 5) is a distinct rarity, and having this meter alternate with **6/4** (measures 2, 4, and 6) rarer still. The metrical oddity, in respect to usual classical procedures, gives the impression of folk music—and perhaps also of walking back and forth without any particular destination, as one does in a gallery.

Gnomus "Gnomus" is a drawing of a Russian folk-art nutcracker. The gnome's jaws crack the nut when his legs (the handles) are pulled together; the same grotesque figure, which could frighten a little child, comes to life and dances in Tchaikovsky's well-known Christmas ballet *The Nutcracker*. Musorgsky writes music that sounds suitably macabre, with a lurching rhythm to illustrate the gnome's clumsy walk on his handle-legs, and striking dissonant harmonies.

The lurching rhythms and dissonance of "Gnomus" and the **5/4** meter of "Promenade" are among the features of Musorgsky's music that break with the norms of mainstream European art music, in a self-consciously nationalistic spirit.

Promenade [2] Quieter now, the promenade music suggests that the spectator is musing as he moves along . . . and we can exercise our stroller's prerogative and skip past a number of Hartmann's pictures, which are not nationalistic in a Russian sense. Some refer to other peoples, and Musorgsky follows suit, writing music we would call exotic: "Bydlo," which is the name of a Polish cattle-cart, and "Il Vecchio Castello," Hartmann's Italian title for a conventional painting of a medieval castle, complete with a troubadour serenading his lady.

The Great Gate at Kiev, by Viktor Hartmann. *Private Collection, RIA Novosti, Bridgeman Images.*

The Great Gate at Kiev The last and longest number is also the climactic one. It illustrates—or, rather, spins a fantasy inspired by—a fabulous architectural design by Hartmann that was never executed.

Musorgsky summons up in the imagination a solemn procession with crashing cymbals, clanging bells, and chanting Russian priests. The Promenade theme is now at last incorporated into one of the musical pictures; the promenader himself has become a part of it and joins the parade. In addition, two real Russian melodies appear:

The ending is very grandiose, for grandiosity forms an integral part of the national self-image of Russia—and, unfortunately, of many other nations.

Modest Musorgsky (1839–1881)

Musorgsky (pronounced MOO-sorgsky) was the son of a well-to-do landowner. The social class into which he was born dictated that he become an officer in the Russian Imperial Guard. Musorgsky duly went to cadet school and joined a regiment after graduation, but he could not long ignore his deep-seated desire to become a composer.

In the meantime, the emancipation of the serfs and other political and economic changes in Russia caused the liquidation of his family estate. For a time Musorgsky tried to help run the family affairs, but in his twenties he was obliged to work at a clerical job. Meanwhile, he experimented with musical composition, struggling to master the technique of an art that he had come to late in life. It was around this time that he joined the circle of Russian nationalist composers that was dubbed the *kuchka* (the Group; see page 284).

Musorgsky never felt secure in his technique and relied on his skillful *kuchka* friend, Nikolai Rimsky-Korsakov, to criticize his work. But his intense nationalism formed his vision of what he wanted his work to be—truly Russian music. His masterpiece, the opera *Boris Godunov*, is based on the story of the sixteenth-century tsar as told by the great Russian poet Alexander Pushkin. It hardly had the success it deserved when it was finally revised and performed in St. Petersburg. Indeed, this and other works by Musorgsky only succeeded some time later, after their orchestration had been touched up (some say glamorized) by Rimsky-Korsakov.

Musorgsky led a rather grim life; his was a personality filled with self-doubt, and his instability was a constant concern to his friends. He became an alcoholic early in life. Musorgsky died of alcoholism and epilepsy in an army hospital at the age of forty-two.

Chief Works: Operas: *Boris Godunov* and *Khovanschina* ■ Orchestral program compositions: *Pictures at an Exhibition* (originally for piano) and *Night on Bald Mountain* ■ Songs, including the very impressive song cycles *The Nursery* and *Songs and Dances of Death*

Encore: After *Pictures*, listen to *Night on Bald Mountain* and *Boris Godunov*, Coronation Scene (scene ii).

Image credit: Bettmann/CORBIS.

3 | Responses to Romanticism

Tchaikovsky's *Romeo and Juliet* and many works of musical nationalism and exoticism reveal the continuing development of Romantic ideals well after the 1850s. But times were changing, and the new realism of literature and the arts embodied new ideals in keeping with a no-nonsense world increasingly devoted to industrialization and commerce. In the age of Victorian morality, a new work ethic gave short shrift to the heady emotion that the Romantics had insisted on conveying in their art. Romantic music came to seem out of step—or else it was prized exactly because it offered an escape, in the concert hall, to a never-never land with little connection to everyday events.

The work of the two greatest late nineteenth-century German composers can be viewed as two different responses to this situation. Johannes Brahms, though a devoted young friend of Robert Schumann, one of the most Romantic of composers, turned back to the Classicism of the Viennese masters. He saw this as a way of tempering the unbridled emotionalism of Romanticism, which he expressed only in a muted mood of restraint and resignation.

A younger composer, Gustav Mahler, reacted differently. Lament was his mode, rather than resignation; his music expresses an intense, bittersweet nostalgia for a Romanticism that seems to have lost its innocence, even its credibility. The lament for this loss is almost clamorous in Mahler's songs and symphonies.

OTHER NATIONALISTS

Nationalism enjoyed new life after 1900. Some of the most impressive nationalists were also among the earliest modernists, among them Béla Bartók in Hungary, Charles Ives in the United States, and—most important—Igor Stravinsky in Russia. We examine this new nationalism in Chapters 21 and 22, restricting ourselves here to a listing of the main late Romantic nationalists outside of Russia.

Bohemia   Bohemia, as the Czech Republic was then called, produced two eminent national composers: Bedřich Smetana (1824–1884), who wrote the symphonic poem *Vltava* (The Moldau) and the delightful folk opera *The Bartered Bride,* and Antonín Dvořák (1841–1904), composer of the popular *Slavonic Dances* as well as important symphonies and other large-scale works. Dvořák also spurred nationalist music in a distant land he visited—the United States of America.

Scandinavia   The Norwegian composer Edvard Grieg (1843–1907) wrote sets of piano miniatures with titles such as *Norwegian Mountain Tunes,* which were very popular at the time; also a well-known suite of music for *Peer Gynt,* the great drama by the Norwegian playwright Henrik Ibsen.

Jean Sibelius (1865–1957), a powerful late Romantic symphonist, produced a series of symphonic poems on the folklore of his native Finland: *The Swan of Tuonela, Kullervo, Finlandia,* and others.

Spain   Among Spanish nationalists were Enrique Granados (1867–1916), Joaquín Turina (1882–1949), and Manuel de Falla (1876–1946), best known for his *Nights in the Gardens of Spain* for piano and orchestra. Spain was also a favorite locale for exotic compositions with a Spanish flavor written by Frenchmen—among them Bizet's opera *Carmen* and orchestral pieces by Emmanuel Chabrier (*España*), Claude Debussy (*Ibéria*), and Maurice Ravel (*Boléro*).

Great Britain   The major English nationalist in music was Ralph Vaughan Williams (1872–1958). His *Fantasia on a Theme by Thomas Tallis* is a loving meditation on a tune written by an English composer from the time of Queen Elizabeth I, while his *Folk Song Suite,* incorporating traditional English melodies, remains a staple of the concert band repertory.

Less well known is Irish composer Sir Charles Villiers Stanford (1852–1924), who wrote *Irish Rhapsodies* for orchestra and the opera *Shamus O'Brien.*

The Renewal of Classicism: Brahms

Born in the dour industrial port city of Hamburg, Johannes Brahms gravitated to Vienna, the city of Haydn, Mozart, and Beethoven. The move seems symbolic. For Brahms rejected many of the innovations of the early Romantics and went back to Classical genres, forms, and, to some extent, even style.

Brahms devoted his major effort to traditional genres such as string quartets and other chamber music works, symphonies, and concertos. In these works, he found new life in the Classical forms—sonata, theme and variations, and rondo. The only typical Romantic genre he cultivated was the miniature—the lied and the character piece for piano; he never contemplated grandiose works such as philosophical program symphonies or mythological operas. Almost alone among the important composers of his time, he made no special effort to pioneer new harmonies or tone colors.

What impels a great composer—and Brahms *was* a great composer, not a timid traditionalist—to turn back the clock in this way? One can only speculate that he could not find it in himself to copy or continue the enthusiastic, open-ended striving of the early Romantics. In the late nineteenth century, this type of response no longer rang true, and Brahms recognized it.

On the other hand, the nobility and power of Beethoven inspired him with a lifelong model. Seen in this way, Brahms's effort was a heroic one: to temper the new richness and variety of Romantic emotion with the traditional strength and poise of Classicism.

Biography

Johannes Brahms (1833–1897)

The son of an orchestral musician in Hamburg, Brahms was given piano lessons at an early age. By the time he was seven, he was studying with one of Hamburg's finest music teachers. A little later he was playing the piano at dockside taverns and writing popular tunes.

A turning point in Brahms's life came at the age of twenty when he met Robert and Clara Schumann. These two eminent musicians befriended and encouraged the young man and took him into their household. Robert wrote an enthusiastic article praising his music. But soon afterward, Schumann was committed to an insane asylum—a time during which Brahms and Clara (who was fourteen years his senior) became very close. In later life Brahms always sent Clara his compositions to get her comments and suggestions.

With another musician friend, Joseph Joachim, who was to become one of the great violinists of his time, the young Brahms signed a foolish manifesto condemning the advanced music of Liszt and Wagner. Thereafter he passed an uneventful bachelor existence, steadily turning out music—chamber music, songs, and piano pieces, but no program music or operas. He was forty-three before his first symphony appeared, many years after its beginnings at his desk; it seemed that he was hesitating to invoke comparison with Beethoven, whose symphonies set a standard for the genre. In fact, this symphony's last movement contains a near quotation from Beethoven's Ninth Symphony that is more like a challenge. When people pointed out the similarity, Brahms snarled, "Any jackass can see that," implying that it was the differences between the two works that mattered, not their superficial similarities.

Brahms would eventually write four magnificent symphonies, all harking back to forms used by Beethoven and even Bach, but building a restrained Romantic yearning into their expressive effect.

For a time Brahms conducted a chorus, and he wrote much choral music, including *A German Requiem*, a setting of sober biblical texts in German. As a conductor, he indulged his traditionalism by reviving the music of Bach and even earlier composers, but he also enjoyed the popular music of his day. He wrote waltzes (Johann Strauss, "the Waltz King," was a valued friend), folk song arrangements, and the well-known *Hungarian Dances*.

Chief Works: Four symphonies, *Tragic* Overture, and the rather comical *Academic Festival* Overture ▪ Violin Concerto, Double Concerto for Violin and Cello, and two piano concertos ▪ Much chamber music—including quartets, quintets, and sextets; a trio for French horn, violin, and piano; a beautiful quintet for clarinet and strings ▪ Piano music and many songs ▪ Choral music, including *A German Requiem* and *Alto Rhapsody* ▪ Waltzes, *Hungarian Dances*

Encore: After the Violin Concerto, listen to the Clarinet Quintet; Symphony No. 3.

Image credit: Bettmann/CORBIS.

Brahms was a serious man; this is one of the few pictures of him smiling, with friends at a favorite Viennese tavern. *Snark/Art Resource, NY.*

Johannes Brahms, Violin Concerto in D, Op. 77 (1878)

Concertos are always written to show off great virtuosos—who are often the composers themselves, as with Mozart, Chopin, and Liszt. Brahms wrote his one violin concerto for a close friend, Joseph Joachim, a leading violinist of the time and also a composer. Even this late in his career—Brahms was then forty-five—he accepted advice about certain details of the composition from Joachim.

We can appreciate Brahms's traditionalism as far as the Classical forms are concerned by referring to the standard movement plan for the Classical concerto on page 183. Like Mozart, Brahms wrote his first movement in double-exposition sonata form; this must have seemed extremely stuffy to writers of Romantic concertos who had developed new and much freer forms. Also, Brahms's last movement is a rondo—much the most common Classical way to end a concerto. If it is a relatively simple movement, by Brahms's standards, that is because the last movements of Classical concertos were typically the lightest and least demanding on the listener.

Third Movement (Allegro giocoso, ma non troppo vivace)   *Giocoso* means "jolly"; the first theme in this rondo, **A,** has a lilt recalling the spirited Gypsy fiddling that was popular in nineteenth-century Vienna. Imitating Gypsy music in this work and others counts as a modest exotic feature in Brahms's music (see page 283).

The solo violin plays the theme (and much else in the movement) in *double stops,* that is, in chords produced by bowing two violin strings simultaneously. Hard to do well, this makes a brilliant effect when done by a virtuoso.

The theme falls into a traditional **a a b a**′ form; in Brahms's hands, however, this becomes something quite subtle. Since the second **a** is identical to the first, except in instrumentation, the last **a** (**a**′) might be dull unless it were varied in an interesting way. Brahms manages to extend it and tighten it up at the same time, by compressing the main rhythmic figure in quicker and quicker repetitions:

These seem for a moment to disrupt or contradict the prevailing meter, a characteristic fingerprint of Brahms's style. There are other examples in this movement.

The first rondo episode, **B**, a theme with a fine Romantic sweep about it, begins with an emphatic upward scale played by the solo violin, again employing double stops. This is answered by a *downward* scale in the orchestra in a lower range. When the orchestra has its turn to play **B**, the positions of the scales are reversed: The ascending scale is now in the low register, and the descending one in the high register.

Brahms, Violin Concerto in D, third movement
Rondo. 7 min., 43 sec.

4 | 30–35   68

30	0:00	**A (Tune)**	The entire tune is presented.
	0:00	**a**	Solo violin, with double stops
	0:11	**a**	Orchestra
	0:22	**b**	Solo violin
	0:35	**a'**	Orchestra
	0:46		The solo violin begins the cadences ending the tune, which lead into a transition.
	1:04		Fast scales prepare for **B**.
31	1:14	**B (Episode 1)**	Melody (emphatic upward scale) in the violin, with double stops; inverted scale below it, in the orchestra
0:20	1:34		Melody in the orchestra, with inverted scale above it
0:35	1:49		Cadential passage (orchestra), **f**
32	2:00	**A'**	
	2:00	**a**	Solo
0:11	2:11	**a"**	Orchestra
0:20	2:20		Transition (orchestra and solo), **p**
33	2:38	**C (Episode 2)**	Lyrical tune (solo and orchestra), **p**
0:33	3:11		Expressive climactic section, solo
0:44	3:22		Orchestra interrupts, **f**.
0:49	3:27		Scales prepare for **B**.
0:57	3:35	**B**	
34	4:22	**A"**	Starts with **b'** (solo)
0:20	4:43	**a'''**	In orchestra, extended; the real feeling of "return" comes only at this point.
0:46	5:08	**Short cadenza**	Solo, double stops again; orchestra soon enters.
1:02	5:25		Solo trills and scales; motive ♩♩♩
1:31	5:54		Passage of preparation: motive ♩♩♩ in low French horns
35	6:09	**Short cadenza**	
0:11	6:20	**Coda**	Mostly in **6/8** time. Starts with a marchlike transformation of phrase **a** (solo), over a drumbeat.
0:35	6:44		References to **B**
1:07	7:16		Final-sounding cadences
1:20	7:29		The music dies down and ends with three loud chords.

From Brahms's score of his Violin Concerto.

Violinist Joseph Joachim, for whom Brahms wrote his Violin Concerto, playing with another Brahms friend, Clara Schumann (see page 242). *Alfredo Dagli Orti/The Art Archive/Corbis.*

The second rondo episode, **C**, involves a shift of meter; this charming melody—which, however, soon evaporates—is in **3/4** time:

The coda presents a version of the **a** phrase of the main theme in yet another meter, **6/8**, in a swinging march tempo. Most of the transitions in this movement are rapid virtuoso scale passages by the soloist, who is also given two short cadenzas before the coda.

Romantic Nostalgia: Mahler

If, like Brahms, Gustav Mahler felt ambivalent about the Romantic tradition, he expressed this ambivalence very differently. He eagerly embraced all the excesses of Romanticism that Brahms had shrunk from, writing huge program symphonies (though he vacillated on the question of distributing the programs to his audiences) and symphonies with solo and choral singing. Mahler thought of the symphony as a mode of expression universal and encompassing—"like a world" in itself, as he once put it. This connects him clearly enough to the most visionary of earlier Romantics. Again and again his works set out to encode seemingly profound metaphysical or spiritual messages.

Yet Mahler felt unable to enter freely into this Romantic world. There is an uneasy quality to his music that sets it apart from other late Romantic music. For while *we* may feel that the emotion expressed in Tchaikovsky's music, for example, is exaggerated, we do not feel that Tchaikovsky himself thought so. Mahler's exaggeration seems deliberate and self-conscious.

Exaggeration spills over into another characteristic feature, distortion. Mahler tends to make more or less slight distortions of melody, motive, and harmony. Sometimes these distortions put a uniquely bittersweet touch on the musical material; sometimes they amount to all-out parody. The parody does not seem harsh, however, but affectionate, nostalgic, and ultimately melancholy. Distortion for Mahler was a way of acknowledging his inability—and the inability of his generation—to recapture the lost freshness of Romantic music.

To give an example: The slow movement of his Symphony No. 1 quotes the cheerful children's round "Frère Jacques," strangely distorted so as to sound like a funeral march. Mahler explained that this march was inspired by a well-known nursery picture of the time, *The Huntsman's Funeral Procession,* showing forest animals shedding insincere tears around the casket of a hunter (see page 294). But an innocent children's song was not distorted in this way in order to mock childhood or childish things. If anything, Mahler used it to lament his own lost innocence, and that of his time.

Biography

Gustav Mahler (1860–1911)

Mahler's early life was not happy. Born in Bohemia to an abusive father, he lost five of his brothers and sisters to diphtheria, and others ended their lives in suicide or mental illness. The family lived near a military barracks, and the many marches incorporated into Mahler's music—often distorted marches—have been traced to his childhood recollections of parade music.

After studying for a time at the Vienna Conservatory, Mahler began a rising career as a conductor. His uncompromising standards and his authoritarian attitude toward the musicians led to frequent disputes with the orchestra directors. What is more, Mahler was Jewish, and Vienna at that time was rife with anti-Semitism. Nonetheless, he was acknowledged as one of the great conductors of his day and also as a very effective musical administrator. After positions at Prague, Budapest, Hamburg, and elsewhere, he came to head such organizations as the Vienna Opera and the New York Philharmonic.

It was only in the summers that Mahler had time to compose, so it is not surprising that he produced fewer pieces (though they are very long pieces) than any other important composer. Ten symphonies, the last of them unfinished, and six song cycles for voice and orchestra are almost all he wrote. The song cycle *The Song of the Earth* of 1910, based on translated Chinese poems,

is often called Mahler's greatest masterpiece.

Mahler's wife was a famous Viennese beauty, Alma Schindler. By a tragic coincidence, shortly after he wrote his grim orchestral song cycle *Songs on the Death of Children,* his and Alma's youngest daughter died of scarlet fever.

Beyond this tragedy, Mahler's life was clouded by psychological turmoil, and he once consulted his famous Viennese contemporary Sigmund Freud. His disputes with the New York Philharmonic directors, which discouraged him profoundly, may have contributed to his premature death.

Chief Works: Ten lengthy symphonies, several with chorus, of which the best known are the First, Fourth, Fifth, and Ninth ■ Orchestral song cycles: *The Song of the Earth, Songs of a Wayfarer, The Youth's Magic Horn* (for piano or orchestra), *Songs on the Death of Children*

Encore: After Symphony No. 1, listen to the Adagietto from Symphony No. 5; *Songs of a Wayfarer.*

Photo Credit: Bettmann/CORBIS.

From the score Mahler was working on at his death—the unfinished Symphony No. 10.

Mahler's Symphony No. 8, called "Symphony of a Thousand," represents a peak in the nineteenth-century tradition of grandiose compositions (see page 230). One early performance (in Philadelphia) did indeed use 1,069 orchestral players, chorus singers, and soloists. © *Jack Vartoogian/FrontRowPhotos*.

Gustav Mahler, Symphony No. 1 (1888)

4 | 36–43 | 69 | 35

Mahler's first symphony went through as complicated a process of genesis as any major work of music. It started out as a symphonic poem in one movement, grew to a five-movement symphony, and was finally revised into four movements. As is also true of several of his other symphonies, Symphony No. 1 includes fragments from a number of earlier songs by Mahler. The program that Mahler once published for the whole symphony, but then withdrew, concerns the disillusion and distress of disappointed love, with the hero pulling himself together again in the finale.

An important general feature of Mahler's style is a special kind of counter-point closely tied up with his very individual style of orchestration. He picks instruments out of the orchestra to play momentary solos, which are heard in counterpoint with other lines played by other "solo" instruments. The changing combinations can create a fascinating kaleidoscopic effect, for the various bright strands are not made to blend, as in most Romantic orchestration, but rather to stand out in sharp contrast to one another.

Third Movement (Feierlich und gemessen, ohne zu schleppen—"With a solemn, measured gait; do not drag") This ironic funeral march is also a personal lament, for its trio is taken from an earlier song by Mahler about lost love. (Though the musical form of the movement is quite original, it is based on march and trio form, analogous to the Classical minuet and trio.)

Mahler conducting. *Bettmann/CORBIS*.

Section 1 Mahler had the extraordinary idea of making his parody funeral march out of the French round "Frère Jacques." He distorts the familiar tune by playing it in the minor mode at a slow tempo:

The mournful, monotonous drumbeat that accompanies the march is derived from the ending of the tune. (Note that Mahler slightly changed the ending of "Frère Jacques" as he transformed it into his march—he wanted only so much monotony.)

The slow march itself is played first by a single muted double bass playing in its high register—a bizarre, deliberately clumsy sonority. An additional figure that Mahler appends to his version of "Frère Jacques," played by the oboe, fits so naturally that we almost accept it as part of the traditional tune. The music dies out on the drumbeat figure (played by the harp), then on a single repeated note.

Section 2 This section is a study in frustration, as fragmentary dance-music phrases that sound distorted, parodistic, and even vulgar give way to equally fragmentary recollections of the funeral march. One dance starts up in band instruments, with a faster beat provided by *pizzicato* (plucked) strings; notice the exaggerated way in which its opening upbeat is slowed down. It is cut short by a new dance phrase—louder, more vulgar yet, scored with bass drum and cymbals. "With Parody," Mahler wrote on the score at this point:

The Huntsman's Funeral Procession, inspiration for the slow movement of Mahler's Symphony No. 1. *The New York Public Library/Art Resource, NY.*

LISTENING CHART 18

Mahler, Symphony No. 1, third movement, Funeral March

10 min., 20 sec.

4 | 36–43   69   35

SECTION 1

36	0:00	**Funeral March**	Drumbeat, then four main entries of the round "Frère Jacques" (minor mode), which is the march theme
	0:07		Entry 1: Double bass, muted
	0:28		Entry 2: Bassoon (a subsidiary entry follows: cellos)
	0:48		Entry 3: Tuba
	1:02		("Additional" fragment: oboe)
	1:15		Entry 4: Flute in low register
	1:35		("Additional" fragment). The march gradually dies away; the drumbeat finally stops.

SECTION 2

37	2:09	**Dance-Band Phrases**	**a**	Oboes, *p*, repeated (trumpets in counterpoint); pizzicato string beat
0:29	2:39		**b**	Faster, *mf*; high (E-flat) clarinets, bass drum, and cymbals
38	2:53		**a**	Strings, with varied repeat (trumpets in counterpoint)
0:31	3:24		**b'**	With new continuation
0:49	3:42	**Conclusion**		Descending cadential passage, a little slower, based on **a**
1:19	4:12	**Return to Funeral-March Motives**		The funeral-march drumbeat, which entered during the previous passage, continues in the background. The march dies away; the drumbeat almost stops.

SECTION 3

2:00	4:53	**Trio (Song)**	The rhythm gradually picks up: a gentle triplet accompaniment with a throbbing background.
39	5:09		A songlike melody starts in muted strings, then moves to the flute, two solo violins, clarinet, and oboe.
1:16	6:25		The trio dies away (violins).
40	6:43		Gong strokes
0:07	6:50		Flutes play two new phrases, as though waiting.

41	**SECTION 4**		
	7:02	**March**	Drumbeat, faster, in a new key: march ("Frère Jacques")
0:16	7:18		("Additional" fragment: E-flat clarinet, strings, flute)
42	7:36		March theme with new, parodistic counterpoint: trumpets
0:23	8:00		Dance-band phrase **b**: clarinets, cymbals, drums
43	8:17		March theme with new trumpet counterpoint; new sudden speedup: clarinets, *ff*
0:19	8:37	**Conclusion**	Descending cadential passage, based on **a**, with drumbeat as in section 2; slower
1:21	9:38		("Additional" fragment, in low range: bassoon)
1:35	9:53		The music dies down; gong strokes.

This phrase, too, is cut short, and a varied repetition of the material introduced so far does not proceed much further. Instead, a long, grieving cadential passage is heard over the funeral-march drumbeat. Other fragments of "Frère Jacques" are recalled. Mourning gives way to utter exhaustion.

Section 3   A note of consolation is sounded by this contrasting "trio," which begins with warm major-mode sounds and a triplet accompaniment on the harp. (The funeral-march beat is transformed into a faster but gentler throb.) The melody introduced is the one that belonged originally to a nostalgic song about lost love. Played first by muted strings, then the oboe and solo violins, the song melody soon turns bittersweet.

The rhythm is halted by quiet but dramatic gong strokes. Flutes play a few strangely momentous new phrases, also taken from the song.

Section 4   The final section combines elements from both sections 1 and 2. Soon after the "Frère Jacques" round commences, in a strange key, a new counterpoint joins it in the trumpets—another parodistic, almost whining sound:

One of the dance phrases from section 2 interrupts, picking up the tempo; and when "Frère Jacques" and the trumpet tune return, the tempo picks up even more for a wild moment of near chaos. But the mourning passage that ended section 2 returns, with its constant, somber drumbeat. The movement ends after another series of gong strokes.

GOALS FOR REVIEW

▶   to understand the cultural background of late Romantic art: realism, nationalism, and exoticism

▶   to follow the development of symphonic program music in works by Pyotr Ilyich Tchaikovsky and Modest Musorgsky

▶   to hear musical styles that offer responses to Romanticism: the renewal of Classicism in Johannes Brahms, the nostalgia and exaggeration of Gustav Mahler

   macmillanhighered.com/listen 8e
Interactive Listening Charts 16–18
Listening Quizzes for Chapter 19 and Global Perspectives: Musical Drama Worldwide
Reading Quizzes for Chapter 19 and Global Perspectives: Musical Drama Worldwide

Global Perspectives

Musical Drama Worldwide

We saw earlier (page 57) that most religious traditions make substantial use of singing of one sort or another. Likewise, most traditions of drama worldwide do not consist of plain speech and little else, but instead incorporate chanting, singing, instrumental music, and dance. In this way they resemble the European opera we have studied and other kinds of Western drama, from ancient Greek tragedy and comedy to today's megamusicals on Broadway.

Perhaps, in fact, this connection between music and drama is related at a very deep level to the connection between singing and religion. Just as the heightening of prayer in song seems to give readier access to invisible divinity, so music seems somehow compatible with the illusory, real-and-yet-unreal enactment of actions and events onstage.

Whatever the reason, from the ancient beginnings of drama down to the present day, music has been joined with acting more often than not.

Asia has developed particularly rich traditions of musical drama. These include the shadow plays of Indonesia, accompanied by gamelan music and relating stories from lengthy epic poems by means of the shadows of puppets cast on a screen (see page 199). In India, religious dance-dramas reach back hundreds of years. Today the main form of musical drama is on-screen: Movie musicals are the staple of the huge and lucrative Indian film industry.

In Japan, meanwhile, several types of musical drama have arisen over the centuries. One of the most important, **kabuki** (kah-bóo-kee) theater, arose in the seventeenth century and appealed to a new public made up of members of the urban merchant class that was emerging in Japan at this time. In a strikingly similar way, Baroque opera in Europe evolved from its aristocratic origins to become a cherished entertainment of new, upper-middle-class audiences (see page 00).

Chinese Opera

What we know as Beijing opera, the most famous variety of Chinese musical drama, is in China called **jingju** (chéeng-chu), meaning "theater of the capital." It is a rich amalgam of song, spoken dialogue, instrumental music, dance, elaborate costume, and martial arts.

Beijing opera is a relatively recent product of a long, complex history. Some of its stylistic features were introduced to the capital by provincial theater troupes at the end of the eighteenth century, while others developed

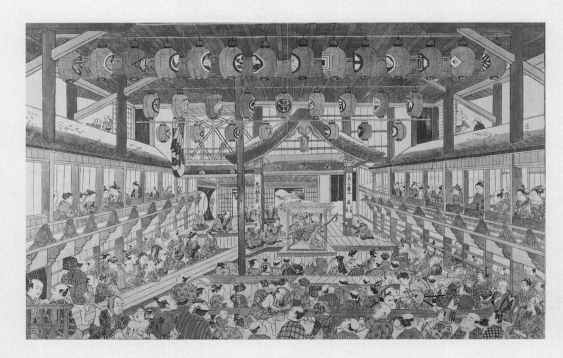

Inside a kabuki theater, c. 1745. *British Museum, London, UK/The Bridgeman Art Library.*

through much of the nineteenth century. Only by the late 1800s did Beijing opera assume the form we know today, and even that form has more recently undergone striking changes, especially during the Communist period of the last sixty-five years.

Voice Types in Beijing Opera In European opera, different voice types have been habitually associated with specific character types. In Romantic opera, tenors usually play young, vital, and amorous characters (for example, the Duke in Verdi's *Rigoletto*), and sopranos play their female counterparts (Gilda). Low male voices, baritone and bass, can variously have comic, evil, or fatherly associations (Rigoletto).

Such conventional connections of voice and character type are highly developed in Beijing opera, too—but the voice types are different. Young men of romantic, dreamy inclination sing in a high register and usually in falsetto. Older, bearded men, trusted and loyal advisers of one sort or another, sing in the high baritone range. Warriors sing with a forced, throaty voice; in addition they must be skilled acrobats in order to enact lively, athletic battle scenes.

Two other special male roles are the male comic, who speaks more than he sings, and the *jing*, or face-painted role, who may be a warrior, a dashing bandit, or even a god. His face is painted more elaborately than those of the other actors, with patterns whose colors symbolically reveal much about his character. The *jing* sings in a loud, hoarse manner that takes years to master.

The female roles in Beijing opera were, until the Communist era, almost always sung by male impersonators. They include a mature, virtuous woman, sung in a refined, delicate falsetto (when women sing these roles today, they imitate that male falsetto). A younger woman, lively and flirtatious, is sung in a suggestive, innuendo-laden falsetto. There is also an acrobatic female warrior.

The Orchestra The small orchestra of Beijing opera consists of a group of drums, gongs, and cymbals, a few wind instruments, and a group of bowed and plucked stringed instruments. These are all played by a handful of versatile musicians who switch from one instrument to another during the performance.

The percussion group is associated especially with martial music, accompanying battle scenes. But it also fulfills many other roles: It can introduce scenes, provide special sound effects, use conventional drum patterns to announce the entrances and social status of different characters, and play along with the frequent songs. The most important function of the stringed instruments is to introduce and accompany the songs.

Beijing Opera Songs In a way that is somewhat akin to the Western contrast of recitative and aria, Beijing opera shows a wide range of vocal styles, from full-fledged song through more declamatory song to stylized speech and even, for comic and minor characters, everyday speech. In general, the songs of Beijing opera are, like the arias of Italian opera, the musical heart of the drama,

Beijing opera: a female character and a *jing*. © *Jack Vartoogian/FrontRowPhotos.*

A Beijing opera orchestra: The player in front holds the banjo-like yueqin; behind him are an erhu player (partly visible), a player of reed pipes (called sheng), and, standing, percussion players. *Dean Conger/Corbis.*

marked off from the other singing around them by their lyrical style. The songs suggest the feelings and internal psychological states of their singers.

The Prince Who Changed into a Cat

4 | 44   109

Our recording presents the beginning of a scene from *The Prince Who Changed into a Cat*, one of the most famous of Beijing operas. The story concerns an Empress who is banished from Beijing through the machinations of one of the Emperor's other wives. (Her newborn son, the Prince of the title, is stolen from his cradle and replaced by a cat.) The present scene takes place many years later, when a wise and just Prime Minister meets the Empress and determines to restore her to her rightful position.

First the percussion plays, and then stringed instruments, along with a wooden clapper, introduce an aria sung by the Prime Minister (0:25). There are only three stringed instruments: a high-pitched, two-stringed fiddle played with a bow called a **jinghu** (chéeng-hoo), a similar but lower-pitched fiddle called an **erhu** (ár-hoo), and a plucked lute called a **yueqin** (yuéh-chin). All three play the same melody, the erhu doubling the jinghu an octave below, while the yueqin adds characteristic repeated notes created by the quick, banjo-like strumming of a string.

Finally, the singer enters (0:41). He sings the same melody as the stringed instruments, though he pauses frequently while they continue uninterrupted. This heterophonic texture is typical of Beijing opera arias. The Prime Minister is a bearded old-man role and sings in the appropriate high baritone range.

The Twentieth Century and Beyond

UNIT V

This unit covers music from around 1900 on and brings our survey up to the present. Looking back to the year 1900, we can recognize today's society in an early form. Large cities, industrialization, inoculation against disease, mass food processing, the first automobiles, telephones, movies, and phonographs—all were in place by the early years of the twentieth century. Hence the society treated in this unit will strike us as fairly familiar, compared to the societies of earlier centuries.

But the classical music produced in this period may strike us as anything but familiar. Around 1900, classical music experienced some of the most dramatic and abrupt changes in its entire history. Along with the changes came a wider variety of styles than ever before. At times it seemed almost as if each composer felt the need to create an entirely individual musical language. This tendency toward radical innovation, once it set in, was felt in repeated waves throughout the twentieth century. This vibrant, innovative, and unsettling creativity comes under the label "modernism."

Another development of great importance occurred around 1900: the widening split between classical and popular music. A rift that had started in the nineteenth century became a prime factor of musical life, giving rise to new traditions of American popular music. With the evolution of ragtime and early jazz, a vital rhythmic strain derived from African American sources was brought into the general American consciousness. This led to a long series of developments: swing, bebop, rhythm and blues, rock, rap, and more.

In this unit we sample the variety of musical modernism and glimpse the movement's outgrowths around the turn of the new millennium. The final chapter deals with America's characteristic popular music.

By the early twentieth century, industrialization had come to touch every aspect of life, from entertainment to warfare. In *The Twittering Machine,* from 1922, by Swiss-German artist Paul Klee (1879–1940), singing birds are attached to a crank apparatus. Is the image a message about the mechanization of music, or does its living song challenge the machine? *Digital Image © The Museum of Modern Art/Licensed by SCALA/Art Resource, NY.*

Chronology

Music and Modernism

CHAPTER

20

The period from about 1890 to 1940 saw profound changes in European and American societies and the art they created. These changes were outgrowths of trends whose beginnings we traced in Chapter 19—trends such as the collapse of Romantic political aspirations in 1848, accelerating industrialization, and increasingly pronounced nationalism. They came to a climax in the first half of the new century, with the cataclysms of World War I (1914–18) and World War II (1939–45).

The artists of this period responded in ways generally familiar also from the nineteenth century. Some pushed forward with ever bolder expression and technique (think of Wagner). Others searched for new vitality in modes of expression that by now seemed traditional (think of Brahms).

The first of these groups, the avant-garde modernists, riveted the attention of the artistic world in the period leading up to World War I because of the excitement (many thought scandal) generated by their experimentation and innovation. We take up these innovations in this Prelude and in Chapter 21. In Chapter 22 we consider responses between the world wars to the challenges and difficulties of this avant-garde.

1 | Varieties of Modernism

To start with, the terms *modernist* and *modernism* require a word of explanation. They mean something different from *modern* or *contemporary*, terms that refer to anything at all that happens to take place in the present; the *-ist* and *-ism* at the end of the word *modern* give them an extra twist. The terms refer to a special self-consciousness, on the part of the artists themselves, of their position at the forefront of new developments. The modernists of 1900 were artists and intellectuals who insisted on a particular vision of modernity: anti-traditionalism. They formed a specific movement marked by radical experimentation, which first peaked in the years 1890 through 1920—a period of breakthrough works by such figures as novelists Marcel Proust and James Joyce, poets Ezra Pound and T. S. Eliot, and painters Pablo Picasso and Henri Matisse.

The chief composers associated with the modernist movement in this early phase were Claude Debussy, Arnold Schoenberg, and Igor Stravinsky. They are often referred to as members of the musical "avant-garde." **Avant-garde**—meaning "vanguard"—was originally a military term, but it has long been embraced by radical artists and thinkers to denote the forefront of their activity. Later, about 1950, a second phase of avant-garde modernism set in, involving a new generation of composers.

Not all modernist composers were members of this avant-garde. The full variety of modernist music includes not only radical experimentation but also more modest kinds. It embraces late nationalist composers, striving to incorporate their nations' musical idioms in new ways. It also includes many composers who incorporated into their works the newly prominent gestures of popular music, as well as some who resisted the styles of the avant-garde, preferring to continue developing the spirit of late Romanticism. All these composers, alongside more radical innovators, showed the special self-consciousness of their place in music history that defines modernism.

Through the twentieth century, these many styles mixed, merged, and interacted with one another to form the colorful tapestry of modernist classical music. At certain times assertive avant-garde experiment seemed to gain the upper hand—for example, from 1900 to 1920 and from 1950 to 1970—while other times were periods of consolidation, for example in the 1920s and 1930s.

2 | Progress and Uncertainty

Industrialization is one of two overriding historical facts of the nineteenth century. The other one, the emergence of the modern nation-state, we spoke of earlier (pages 282–83). Ever since the first so-called age of science in the seventeenth century, technological discoveries had come faster and faster, and industry was transformed. The harnessing of steam power in the eighteenth century was matched by the capturing of electricity in the nineteenth. Europe and America were crisscrossed with railroads, built for the benefit of industry and commerce. By the early twentieth century, automobile and air travel were in their early stages of development, as were telephones, movies, and sound recordings.

What had been essentially rural societies, controlled by stable aristocracies, turned into modern nations, dominated by urban centers and run by self-made entrepreneurs. These changes occurred at breakneck speed, as people saw at the time. Yet no one could have forecast how the stresses caused by such social changes would lead on the one hand to the disturbing artistic-intellectual movement known as modernism, and on the other to the catastrophe of World War I.

For at the heart of nineteenth-century culture was a sense of confidence in progress. Progress in science and technology, it was thought, would be matched in due time by progress in human affairs. And although anyone could see evidence to the contrary—for example, in the appalling conditions of the new industrial poor, as exposed by the novels of Charles Dickens and the political writings of Karl Marx—this evidence was easily ignored by the rich and powerful who were profiting from technology's advances.

Another dark side of progress became evident in the development of weaponry. The deadly novelty of the American Civil War was the rifle, effective over five times the range of previous shoulder weapons. In World War I, tanks, submarines, and chemical weapons showed technology's terrible potential for destruction: an estimated forty million military and civilian dead from war, famine, and epidemic, and twenty million wounded. With World War I, nationalism reached its first, horrifying climax, as modern nation-states pitted themselves against one another. Nineteenth-century confidence in progress—a response to the successes of technology—was thrown into question by technology itself.

By this time, however, confidence was shaken also by nontechnological developments. Men and women were moved to question their most basic assumptions about life by startling advances in physics, biology, and psychology.

● The impact of Einstein's theory of relativity made its own contributions to the technology of weaponry later in the century, with the invention of nuclear weapons. At first, however, it was more philosophical than practical in nature. The idea that things depend on the standpoint of the observer and cannot be counted on according to the objective rules of Newtonian physics rocked people's sense of certainty.

● For many, this uncertainty deepened a crisis in religion that the Victorians had already experienced as a result of scientific theories of evolution. Here the key figure was Charles Darwin. Were human beings created by God in God's image, as the Bible teaches, or did they evolve by an impersonal process from lower animals? The disturbance that this idea caused in people's sense of stability is still reflected in today's disputes about creationism and "intelligent design."

Sigmund Freud was an avid collector of antiquities, a student of the history of civilization and art as well as of psychology. Here, in a portrait of 1914, he is surrounded by some of his treasures from ancient Egypt, China, Greece, and Rome. *Freud Museum, London, UK/Bridgeman Images.*

● Meanwhile the psychological theories of Sigmund Freud suggested that in spite of what people thought they were doing or feeling, they were in fact controlled by unconscious drives. The idea of men and women in the grip of irrational forces of their own (or their parents') making was, again, very disturbing. At the same time, the prospect of working out one's problems through psychotherapy gave the new century its paradigm for personality change.

3 | The Response of Modernism

If the traditional laws of physics, biblical authority, and psychological certainty could no longer be accepted, it seemed a small enough step to question the rules and assumptions surrounding the arts.

One such assumption was that visual art had to represent something from the external world. Once this idea was questioned, and then abandoned, the materials of painting and the other arts could be used for themselves—and a world of abstract painting opened up. (It is also called "nonrepresentational," because it doesn't faithfully *represent* objects in the world.) Avant-garde artists developed whole new languages for art—for example, the language of cubism, shown in the painting by Georges Braque, on page 305.

In literature, the basic assumption was that poets and novelists would use ordinary sentence structure, syntax, and grammar. Freedom from these assumptions opened up a whole new sphere of suggestion in tune with Freud's ideas about the mind's unconscious and irrational impulses. James Joyce's novel *Ulysses* of 1922 is one of the most famous instances of the so-called stream-of-consciousness method of writing. His last novel, *Finnegans Wake,* makes use of a language that is half English and half words he invented.

In music, the basic assumptions concerned the composing of melody and its close associates harmony and tonality. These assumptions too were thrown into doubt, and the logic of earlier musical styles was questioned or even rejected. Some avant-garde composers turned away from conventional presentation of rhythm and meter, while others wrote melodies that carried to new lengths the most complex of late Romantic melodic designs. Still others devised new harmonies more complicated and dissonant than those of earlier generations, or even harmonies derived from new scales, different from the major and minor.

There was a tendency about this time for artists of various kinds to join together in formal or informal groups, both for mutual encouragement and for the exchange of ideas. Thus Claude Debussy was friends with several avant-garde poets. Schoenberg, himself a painter as well as a musician, associated with a group of artists who set forth their ideas in *The Blue Rider,* a magazine named after a picture by the pioneer nonrepresentational painter Vasily Kandinsky (see page 308). Stravinsky and Maurice Ravel belonged to a group who called themselves the Apaches. With all this interchange, it is not surprising that one can sometimes detect similar tendencies in music and the other arts.

4 | Literature and Art before World War I

The new languages for art were unquestionably (and unapologetically) difficult. To this day, few people understand *Finnegans Wake.* Avant-garde music became detached from the concert- and opera-going public, and hence abstracted from a base in society.

At the same time, the modernists' concentration on artistic materials led to abstraction of another kind, the separation of technique from expression. This emphasis on technique was welcomed by some as a relief from the overheated emotionality of the late Romantic music of Tchaikovsky, Mahler, and the like. Especially in the 1920s, "objectivity" was an ideal espoused by many artists. Only too often, their works struck the public as cold, dry, and unengaging.

Characteristic of this phase of the avant-garde was the use of schematic, even mathematical devices in the arts. The Dutch painter Piet Mondrian made pictures out of straight lines at right angles to one another and juxtaposed planes of bright color. Among composers, Igor Stravinsky was known for his provocative statements extolling objectivity and attacking Romantic music—and certainly the brisk, mechanistic rhythms that characterize Stravinsky's style are diametrically opposed to rubato (see page 227), the rhythmic stretching that contributes so much to nineteenth-century music's emotionality.

Cubism was one of the earliest styles of abstract or near-abstract art, developed around 1910 by Pablo Picasso, Georges Braque, and others. It presented objects—in this painting by Braque, a violin and a musical score—as intersecting geometrical forms (not only cubes!), as if viewed simultaneously from several perspectives. Interestingly, Braque does not treat the artist's palette at the top in cubist fashion. *Solomon R. Guggenheim Museum, New York, USA/Mondadori Portfolio/Walter Mori/The Bridgeman Art Library.*

"Sheshell ebb music wayriver she flows"

James Joyce, Finnegans Wake

Several lesser composers, fascinated by machine rhythms, even tried to evoke machinery in their works: the American George Antheil (*Ballet mécanique*), the Russian A. V. Mosolov (*The Iron Foundry*), and the Swiss Arthur Honegger (*Pacific 231*—a locomotive). An Italian group called the Futurists—more famous for their well-publicized proclamations than for any actual music—called for "music of the machine age" and composed with industrial noises. They invented a mechanized "noise intoner" with dozens of categories ranging from explosions and crashes to crackles and howls.

Impressionists and Symbolists

Modernism got its start in the late nineteenth century and then peaked in the twentieth. The best-known modernist movement, **impressionism**, dates from the 1870s, when people were astonished by the flickering network of color patches used by impressionist painters to render simple scenes from everyday life (as in Edouard Manet's *In the Boat*, below). These painters claimed that they had to develop such a technique to catch the actual, perceived quality of light. They proudly called themselves "realists," in reaction to the idealized and overemotional art of Romanticism. Claude Monet's multiple views of Rouen Cathedral (see page 170) emphasize (even exaggerate!) how differences in daylight define the impressionist painter's reality.

Symbolism, a consciously *un*realistic movement, followed soon after impressionism. Symbolist poets revolted against the "realism" of words being used for reference—for the purpose of exact definition or denoting. They wanted words to perform their symbolizing or signifying function as freely as possible, without having to fit into phrases or sentences. The meaning of a cluster of words might be vague and ambiguous, even esoteric—but also rich, "musical," and endlessly suggestive.

Musical was a word the symbolists liked to apply to their language. They were fascinated by the music dramas of Richard Wagner, where again musical symbols—Wagner's leitmotivs—refer to elements in his dramas in a complex, multilayered fashion. All poets use musical devices such as rhythm and

Left: *In the Boat,* an impressionist painting by Edouard Manet (1832–1883). Right: Does nature imitate art? This snapshot of Debussy (second from the left) and some friends is startlingly similar in mood to the (earlier) painting by Manet. Painting: *Scala/Art Resource, NY.* Photograph: *De Agostini Picture Library/G. Dagli Orti/The Bridgeman Art Library.*

Horses and riders, painted by Vasily Kandinsky over a four-year period, show his path toward nonrepresentational painting. In the first picture, the figures are quite clear; in the last, they could be missed entirely. *All images © Artists Rights Society (ARS), New York/ADAGP, Paris.*
Top left: Couple on Horseback, *1907. Artothek.* Top right: Blue Mountain *(Der blaue Berg), 1908–09. Solomon R. Guggenheim Museum, New York. Solomon R. Guggenheim Founding Collection. By gift 41.505.* Bottom: Romantic Landscape, *1911. Artothek.*

rhyme, but the symbolists were prepared to go so far as to break down grammar, syntax, and conventional thought sequence to approach the elusive, vague reference of Wagner's music.

Claude Debussy is often called an impressionist in music because his fragmentary motives and little flashes of tone color seem to recall the impressionists' painting technique. Debussy can also—and more accurately—be called a symbolist, since suggestion, rather than outright statement, is at the heart of his aesthetic. Famous symbolist texts inspired two of Debussy's pathbreaking works: the orchestral *Prelude to "The Afternoon of a Faun"* (a poem by Stéphane Mallarmé) and the opera *Pelléas et Mélisande* (a play by Maurice Maeterlinck). In the opera Debussy's elusive musical symbols and Maeterlinck's elusive verbal ones combine to produce an unforgettable effect of mysterious suggestion.

Expressionists and Fauves

In Paris and Vienna—artistic centers that were also centers of avant-garde music—two émigré artists pursued separate but parallel paths toward completely abstract painting.

Our horse-and-rider pictures on page 307 by the Russian-born painter Vasily Kandinsky (1866–1944) show how the process was accomplished. Kandinsky belonged to a German movement in the arts called **expressionism**—not to be confused with impressionism—which sought to express the most extreme human feelings by divorcing art from everyday literalness. Anguish, even hysteria, could be conveyed by the harsh clashing of strong colors, irregular shapes, and jagged lines. What seems to be depicted is not something external but the artist's inner turbulence—most violently in the last Kandinsky picture, *Romantic Landscape,* which is almost entirely abstracted from the outer world.

Parallel to the expressionists was a short-lived group in Paris dubbed *Les fauves,* "the wild beasts." The fauves experimented with distorted images bordering on the grotesque; they also employed motifs from what they called "primitive" art as though in defiance of a decadent European culture. In Pablo Picasso's famous painting *Les Demoiselles d'Avignon* of 1907 (Avignon was a street in the red-light district of Barcelona), the quality of abstraction is evident in the angular bodies and the African-mask-like heads—a complete break with conventional European rules of human portrayal (see page 309). Picasso took a further step toward abstraction later when he turned to cubism.

There is violence in both Kandinsky's and Picasso's work of this period. Certainly that is how it struck a generation used to the nonthreatening art of the impressionists—painters of flickering summer landscapes, soft-edged nudes, and diaphanous action pictures of the ballet. Composers, too, courted violence in their music. The Hungarian composer Béla Bartók wrote a "barbarous" piano piece entitled *Allegro barbaro.* Stravinsky, in his ballet *The Rite of Spring,* depicted human sacrifice in the fertility ceremonies of primitive Slavic tribes.

5 | Modernist Music before World War I

The art of music never enjoyed (or suffered) a link to the tangible world that was comparable to representation in painting, or to the reference of words in literature. But it did have its own stable, generally accepted set of principles, its own traditional internal logic. This rested upon elements that we have discussed many times in this book: tune, motive, harmony, tonality, tone color, and rhythm.

The music of Bach, Beethoven, and Brahms was based on this logic, and so was the entire stream of Western European folk songs, popular songs, dances,

Those nymphs, I want to perpetuate them.
So clear
Their carnation flesh, that it flutters in the air,
Drowsy with tufted slumbers.
Was it a dream I loved?

Opening of the symbolist poet Stéphane Mallarmé's "The Afternoon of a Faun"

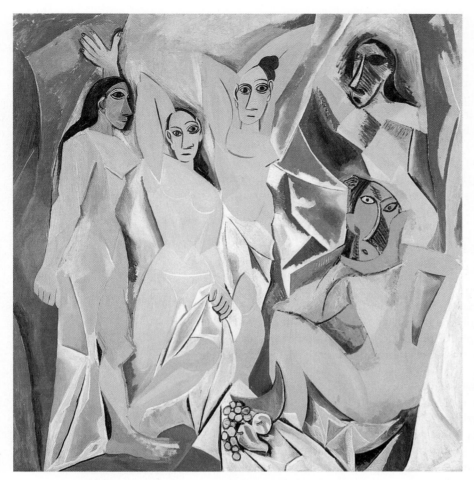

Picasso's famous shocker *Les Demoiselles d'Avignon* (1907). Picasso and other abstract painters designed sets for Diaghilev's Ballets Russes, sponsor of Stravinsky and other modernist composers. © *The Museum of Modern Art/licensed by SCALA/Art Resource, NY.* © *2014 Estate of Pablo Picasso/Artists Rights Society (ARS) New York.*

military marches, and the rest. Avant-garde modernist music moved away from this norm. Like abstract, nonrepresentational painting, this music worked out new principles based on the materials of the art itself.

With European music before World War I, we can lay special emphasis on developments in melody, harmony, and tonality, for on the whole, these features were the main preoccupations of avant-garde composers in that period. Developments in tone color and rhythm—or, more broadly, musical sonority and musical time—dominated a later stage of avant-garde music, after World War II.

Experiment and Transformation: Melody

Melody, harmony, and tonality all work closely together. In historical terms, harmony arose as a way of supporting and adorning melody, and tonality first arose as a means of clarifying both melody and harmony; later tonality functioned as a more general way of organizing music. Each of these functions was transformed in the early twentieth century.

The Viennese Classical composers brought tunes to the fore in their music, and the Romantics capitalized on tunes as the most emphatic means of conveying powerful emotion. Yet Wagner, despite the melodic quality of many of his leitmotivs, was criticized for the confusing quality of his singing lines, and

Mahler's audiences were puzzled and irritated by the bittersweet distortions that he applied to folklike tunes. In his later works, his long melodies surge, swoop, and yearn in a strange, almost painful manner.

By that time another Viennese composer, Arnold Schoenberg, was writing even more complex melodies that made little sense to contemporary listeners. The intense rhythms and the anguished intervals of Romanticism were exaggerated almost beyond recognition.

Outside of Vienna, the disintegration of tuneful melody was accomplished in other ways. In many (not all) of his works, Claude Debussy used only the most shadowy motives—a constant suggestion of melody without clear tunes. A little later Igor Stravinsky, writing in Paris, seized upon Russian folk songs but whittled them down into brief, utterly simple fragments—blank, "objective," and without emotion.

New Horizons, New Scales

Just as African masks influenced Picasso's *Demoiselles*, non-European musics began to make inroads into European classical music. At a world's fair that fascinated Paris in 1889—the fair for which the Eiffel Tower was built—Debussy heard his first non-Western music played by native musicians, under simulated native conditions. He tried to recapture the sounds of the Indonesian gamelan (see page 198) in several compositions, even taking a Balinese melody for the theme of a concerto movement.

Debussy sensed a resonance between his own music and the shimmering timbres of the gamelan, and also the scales used in Indonesian music. The traditional diatonic scale had served as the foundation of Western music for so long that it was almost regarded as a fact of nature. But now composers were beginning to reconsider the basic sound materials of music. Notable among these experimenters was Charles Ives, in America. New scales were employed for themes or even whole movements, first among them the **pentatonic scale**, a five-note scale playable on the black notes of the piano, imported from folk song and Asian music. Debussy featured a pentatonic theme in *Clouds*, which we take up in Chapter 21.

Two other new scales introduced at this time are (significantly enough) artificial constructions, derived not from non-European music but by systematically manipulating the total chromatic scale. The **whole-tone scale** divides the octave into six equal parts. All of its intervals are whole steps, and it yields a dreamy, ambiguous sound that Debussy in particular prized. The **octatonic scale**—a specialty with Stravinsky—fits eight pitches into the octave by alternating whole and half steps.

More important as a means of composition than the use of any of these scales was **serialism**, the "new language" for music invented in the 1920s by Arnold Schoenberg. As we will see in the next chapter, serialism in effect creates something like a special scale for every serial composition.

"The Emancipation of Dissonance"

As melody grew more complex, more fragmentary, or more vague, harmony grew more and more dissonant. The concepts of **consonance** and **dissonance**, as we noted on page 28, rest on the fact that certain combinations of pitches (consonant chords) sound stable and at rest, whereas others (dissonant chords) sound tense and need to resolve to consonant ones. In a famous phrase, Schoenberg spoke of "the emancipation of dissonance," meaning emancipation

Pentatonic scale

or

Debussy, *Clouds*

Whole-tone scale

Octatonic scale

from that need to resolve. Dissonance was to be free from the rule that says it must always be followed by the appropriate consonance.

Tonality, as we know, is the feeling of centrality, focus, or homing toward a particular pitch that we get from simple tunes and much other music. As melody grew more complex and harmony grew more dissonant, tonality grew more indistinct. Finally, some music reached a point at which no tonal center could be detected at all. This is **atonal** music.

Melody, harmony, tonality: All are closely related. Beleaguered conservatives around 1900 referred to them jokingly as the "holy trinity" of music. The "emancipation" of melody, harmony, and tonality all went together. This joint emancipation counts as the central style characteristic of the first phase of twentieth-century avant-garde music.

GOALS FOR REVIEW

▶ to understand artistic modernism c. 1900 as a response to innovation and its uncertainties

▶ to explore similar tendencies in modernist literature, pictorial art, and music

▶ to come to know some general stylistic features of early modernist music

macmillanhighered.com/listen8e
Reading Quiz for Chapter 20

Early Modernism

CHAPTER 21

The first major phase of avant-garde music took place in Paris and Vienna from around 1890 to 1914. Claude Debussy, Igor Stravinsky (a young Russian working in Paris), and Arnold Schoenberg were the leading figures in this brilliant era. And there were strong modernist rumblings in Russia, Hungary, Italy, and the United States.

It was a period of rapid development in all the arts, as we have seen, in which the basic tenets of nineteenth-century art were everywhere challenged. In music, nineteenth-century ideas of melody, harmony, tonality, rhythm, and tone color came under attack. Above all, it was the revolution in tonality—which went along with a radical reconsideration of melody and harmony—that caught the imagination of the early twentieth century.

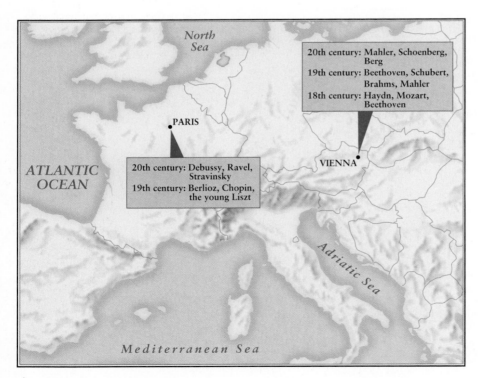

North
Sea

20th century: Mahler, Schoenberg, Berg
19th century: Beethoven, Schubert, Brahms, Mahler
18th century: Haydn, Mozart, Beethoven

•PARIS

ATLANTIC
OCEAN

20th century: Debussy, Ravel, Stravinsky
19th century: Berlioz, Chopin, the young Liszt

VIENNA•

Adriatic Sea

Mediterranean Sea

Paris and Vienna as musical centers.

1 | Debussy and Impressionism

Claude Debussy occupies the border area between late nineteenth-century and early twentieth-century styles. His investigation of sensuous new tone colors for orchestra and for piano, his development of new rich harmonies, and his search for new ways to express emotion in music all remind us of the Romantics. Yet while in some ways his work seems tied to Romanticism, in others it represents a direct reaction against it.

Debussy's tone colors avoid the heavy sonorities that were usual in late Romantic music, merging instead into subtle, mysterious shades of sound. His melodies and motives are usually fragmentary and tentative, his harmonies sound strangely vague, and the tonality of his music is often clouded. He often draws on the vague-sounding new scales mentioned in Chapter 20.

Debussy's orchestral sound differs sharply from that of his contemporary Gustav Mahler, another great innovator in orchestration. Mahler treated the orchestra more and more contrapuntally; each instrument tends to stand out from the others like a Romantic hero striving for his own say in the world. Debussy's orchestra is more often a single, delicately pulsing totality to which individual instruments contribute momentary gleams of color. In this it reminds us of an impressionist picture, in which small, separate areas of color, visible close-up, merge into unified color fields as the viewer stands back and takes in the painting as a whole (see page 306).

> "(... Sounds and perfumes sway in the evening air)"
>
> *Title of a Debussy "miniature" for piano; the parentheses and dots are his.*

Claude Debussy, *Clouds,* from Three Nocturnes (1899)

5 | 1–6   70   36

Debussy's Three Nocturnes, like most of his orchestral works, might be described as impressionist symphonic poems, though they have titles only, not narrative programs. They suggest various scenes without attempting to illustrate them explicitly.

The word *nocturne* evokes a nighttime scene, the great examples before Debussy being the piano nocturnes of Chopin (see page 245). But in fact Debussy's reference was to famous atmospheric paintings by an artist who was close to the impressionists, James McNeill Whistler (see page 314). The first of the nocturnes, *Clouds*, is a pure nature picture, the least nocturnal of the three. The second, *Festivals*, depicts mysterious nighttime fairs and parades. The third nocturne, *Sirens*, includes a women's chorus along with the orchestra, singing not words but vowels and adding an unforgettable timbre to the usual orchestra. The women's voices evoke the legendary sea maidens of the title, who tempt lonely sailors and pull them into the deep.

In *Clouds*, we first hear a quiet series of chords, played by clarinets and bassoons, that circles back on itself repeatedly. The chords seem to suggest great cumulus clouds, moving slowly and silently across the sky.

As a theme, however, these chords do not function conventionally. They make no strong declarations and lead nowhere definitive. This is also true of the next motive, introduced by the English horn—a haunting motive that occurs many times in *Clouds*, with hardly any change. (It is built on an octatonic scale; see page 310.) Yet even this muted gesture, with its vague rhythm and its fading conclusion, seems sufficient to exhaust the composition and bring it to a near halt, over a barely audible drumroll:

> "The title 'Nocturnes' should be taken here in a more general and especially in a more decorative sense.... *Clouds:* the unchanging aspect of the sky, the slow, melancholy motion of the clouds, fading away into agonized grey tones, gently tinged with white."
>
> *Claude Debussy*

After this near stop, the "cloud" music begins again, leading this time to a downward passage of remarkably gentle, murmuring chords in the strings. These chords all share the same rich, complex structure. Their pitches slip downward, moving parallel to one another without establishing a clear sense of tonality. This use of *parallel chords* is one of Debussy's most famous innovations.

Clouds might be said to fall into an **A B A′** form—but only in a very approximate way. Debussy shrinks from clear formal outlines; the musical form here is much more fluid than **A B A** structures observed in earlier music. Such fluidity is something to bear in mind when following *Clouds* and other avant-garde music with Listening Charts. By design, avant-garde composers break down the sharp and (to them) oversimple divisions of older musical styles. If they use form types such as rondo or sonata form at all, they do so in very free, imaginative ways.

In the **A** section of *Clouds*, the return of the cloud theme after a more active, restless passage suggests an internal **a b a′** pattern as well. The next idea, **B**, sounds at first like a meditative epilogue to **A**; it is built on a pentatonic scale (see page 310). But when the little pentatonic tune is repeated several times, it begins to feel like a substantial section of contrast. The return, **A′**, is really just a reference to some of **A**'s material, notably the English-horn figure. Then at the end the bassoons play a dim, disturbed fragment of the cloud theme; the flute hovers for a moment on the **B** tune; and the drumroll is extended—so as to suggest distant thunder, perhaps.

Nocturne in Black and Gold — The Falling Rocket. This impression of the night sky with fireworks, by American expatriate James McNeill Whistler (1834–1903), shocked London viewers when it was shown in 1878. The most powerful critic of the day likened it to "flinging a pot of paint in the public's face"; Whistler sued him. *Detroit Institute of Arts, USA/Gift of Dexter M. Ferry Jr./The Bridgeman Art Library.*

LISTENING CHART 19

Debussy, *Clouds,* from Three Nocturnes

7 min., 3 sec.

1	0:00	**A**	**a**	Cloud theme: clarinets and bassoons
	0:15			English-horn motive
	0:20			Quiet timpani roll — music almost stops.
	0:34			Cloud theme: high strings
2	0:47			Downward parallel chord passage
0:15	1:02			Further development: strings
0:34	1:21			English-horn motive, with a new echo in the French horn
1:02	1:49			Downward chord passage
3	2:10		**b**	Rising section, more restless: woodwinds added
0:30	2:41			Brief climax
0:37	2:48			English-horn motive (with new even-note rhythm accompaniment) is repeated several times, until it dies away.
4	3:38		**a′**	Cloud theme, with new solo viola counterpoint
0:16	3:54			Downward chord passage
5	4:12	**B**		A new tune enters tentatively, but then repeats itself; flute and harp.
0:27	4:40			Tune in strings and solo violin
0:44	4:56			Tune in flute and harp
		(A′)		*Not a real "return" of* **A**, *only of selected elements standing in for* **A**
6	5:19			English-horn motive, with its echo
0:31	5:51			Quiet timpani and low strings — prominent until the end
				Recollection of thematic fragments:
0:54	6:14			Cloud theme: bassoons, then cellos
1:13	6:32			**B** tune fragment
1:21	6:40			French-horn echo to the English-horn motive

ENGLISH HORN

FLUTE

2 | Stravinsky: The Primacy of Rhythm

Stravinsky's earliest work followed from that of his teacher, Russian nationalist composer Nikolai Rimsky-Korsakov. But in three famous ballet scores written for the Ballets Russes (Russian Ballet) in Paris, Stravinsky rapidly developed his own powerful, hard-edged avant-garde style, a style that can be compared to the contemporary fauve style in French painting (see page 308). These ballets reveal a fascinating progression toward a more and more abstract use of folk tunes. Compare the development of abstraction in art by Kandinsky and Picasso (pages 307 and 309).

The first ballet, *The Firebird* (1910), spins a romantic fairy tale about the magical Firebird, the ogre Kastchei, and Prince Ivan Tsarevitch, son of the tsar. Its rich, half-Asian setting is matched by beautifully colored folk music and orchestral sound worthy of Debussy. But in the next ballet, Stravinsky moved from the steppes to the urban marketplace, to Mardi Gras in St. Petersburg. *Petrushka* (1911), the story of a carnival barker and his

Claude Debussy (1862–1918)

Claude Debussy went through the strict curriculum of the famous Paris Conservatory of Music, which he entered at the age of ten. He did not do well in the piano exams, or at least not well enough, but won various awards in theory and composition. He was finally awarded the coveted Grand Prix (Top Prize)—a three-year fellowship to study in Rome.

Before this, Debussy took a job with Madame von Meck, the eccentric patron of Tchaikovsky, playing in a trio at her house in Moscow. Russian music (see page 284) was one of several vivid influences on the young composer; another was the Indonesian gamelan (see page 198), which he encountered at the world's fair in Paris in 1889. Visits to Bayreuth, the shrine of Wagner's music dramas, afforded another, even stronger influence. But Debussy soon turned against Wagner and German music in general.

Debussy settled into Parisian café life, becoming a familiar bearded figure in his broad-brimmed hat and flowing cape. A long-term relationship with a mistress came to a bad end, as did Debussy's first marriage when he eloped with a married woman, who later became his wife. They had a daughter—Debussy wrote the well-known *Children's Corner* Suite for her before she was old enough to play the piano.

In his early thirties Debussy seems to have rather suddenly crystallized his musical style, reflecting the influences of the French symbolist poets and impressionist painters. One remarkable work after another was given its premiere, greeted with a flurry of controversy, and then generally accepted by the critics and the public. His one opera, *Pelléas et Mélisande* (1902), was written directly to the words of a play by the prominent symbolist Maurice Maeterlinck. He planned a second opera, on Edgar Allan Poe's story "The Fall of the House of Usher," but never finished it.

Debussy is famous for his innovations in orchestration and in piano writing. His Preludes and Études for the piano are the most impressive "miniatures" since the time of the early Romantics; some would say the same for his songs. One of his later works, music for the ballet *Jeux* (Games), dissolves melody, theme, and rhythm so far that it was taken up as a model by the avant-garde after World War II.

For a short time Debussy wrote music criticism, in which he expressed in pungent prose the anti-German attitudes that were already manifest in his music. Debussy died of cancer in Paris during World War I, while the city was being bombarded by the Germans he hated.

Chief Works: For orchestra, *Prelude to "The Afternoon of a Faun"* (a famous poem by the French symbolist poet Mallarmé); Three Nocturnes; *La Mer* (The Sea); *Ibéria; Jeux* (Games) ▪ The opera *Pelléas et Mélisande* ▪ For piano: Preludes and Études, *Children's Corner* Suite, and *Suite bergamasque*, including "Clair de lune" ▪ Songs to poems by Baudelaire, Verlaine, and Mallarmé ▪ A string quartet and other chamber music ▪ *Syrinx* for solo flute

Encore: After *Clouds*, listen to *Fêtes* (Festivals), *Prelude to "The Afternoon of a Faun,"* "Clair de lune."

Image credit: Musée d'Art et d'Histoire, Saint-Germain-en-Laye, France/Giraudon/The Bridgeman Art Library.

---

puppet, encouraged him to put a hard, satirical edge on his folk material. Then in *The Rite of Spring* (1913), Stravinsky boldly and brutally imagined the fertility cults of prehistoric Slavic tribes. Here Russian folk music, broken down into repeated, fragmentary motives, is treated as the source of primitive rhythmic and sexual energy, rather than picture-postcard charm.

The musical style that Stravinsky brought to a head in *The Rite* has many features that struck listeners of the time as barbaric, apart from its use of deliberately crude folk-tune fragments. The music is abstract in the sense that it sounds utterly unemotional, by Romantic standards. It is grindingly dissonant. It emphasizes meter in a very heavy, exciting way, and the rhythms themselves are dazzling and unpredictable. Finally, the score is enormously loud: It demands a colossal orchestra, as though the composer wanted to show how he could control—and transform—the chief powerhouse of musical Romanticism.

Igor Stravinsky, *The Rite of Spring*, Part I, "The Adoration of the Earth" (1913)

The first performance of *The Rite of Spring* caused a riot; the audience was shocked and infuriated by the violent, dissonant sounds in the pit and the provocative choreography on the stage, suggesting rape and ritual murder.

The ballet has no real story, and Stravinsky even said that he preferred to think of the music as an abstract concert piece. However, inscriptions on the score specify a series of ancient fertility rites of various kinds, culminating in the ceremonial choice of a virgin for sacrifice. After this she is evidently danced to death in the ballet's second part, entitled "The Sacrifice."

Introduction The halting opening theme is played by a bassoon at the very top of its normal register. Avant-garde composers strained all the elements of music, including the ordinary capabilities of instruments. The bleating bassoon is joined by odd hootings on other woodwinds, gradually building up an extraordinary polyphony that is highly dissonant. The whole section sounds rather like a static series of preliminary fanfares—or, as Stravinsky later suggested, like the calls of prehistoric wildlife.

"Omens of Spring" and "Dance of the Adolescents" After a brief introduction, in which the dancers presumably register an awareness of spring's awakening, the "Dance of the Adolescents" commences with a famous instance of Stravinskian rhythmic irregularity. (Probably the original audience started their catcalls at this point.) A single very dissonant chord is repeated thirty-two times in even eighth notes—but with heavy accents reinforced by short, fat chords played by eight(!) French horns on the most unexpected beats:

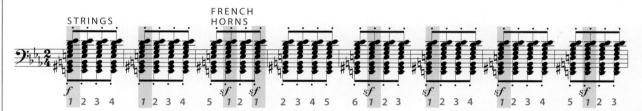

These accents completely upset ordinary meter. Instead of eight standard measures of four eighth notes—1 2 3 4, 1 2 3 4, etc.—Stravinsky makes us hear 1 2 3 4, 1 2 3 4 5, 1 2, 1 2 3 4 5 6, 1 2 3, 1 2 3 4, 1 2 3 4 5, 1 2 3. (For a truly bewildering experience, try beating time to this passage.) Yet these irregular rhythms are also exhilarating, and they certainly drive the music forward in a unique way.

The repeating chords are now overlaid with new motives, derived from Russian folk song. The motives are repeated with slightly different rhythms and at slightly different lengths. This is Stravinsky's distinctive type of ostinato, a technique we have met with in many other kinds of music (see pages 88, 94, and 119); the ostinato is indicated by brackets in the example on page 318. Like Debussy, Stravinsky tends to concentrate on small melodic fragments, but whereas Debussy soon abandons his fragments, Stravinsky keeps repeating his in this irregular, almost obsessive way.

"My idea was that the Prelude should represent the awakening of nature, the scratching, gnawing, wiggling of birds and beasts."

Igor Stravinsky, reminiscing in 1960 about The Rite of Spring

Igor Stravinsky, The Rite of Spring. *Copyright © 1912, 1921 by Hawkes & Son (London) Ltd. Reprinted by permission of Boosey & Hawkes, Inc.*

Folk-song fragment no. 1

BASSOONS

Fragment no. 2

FRENCH HORN

Fragment no. 3

TRUMPETS

mp cantabile

"The Game of Abduction" New violence is introduced with this section, a whirlwind of brilliant rhythms, with much frantic pounding on the timpani.

"Round Dances of Spring" After a moment of respite, a short, quiet introduction conveys a remarkably desolate, empty feeling, partly as a result of its novel orchestration: a high (E♭) clarinet and low (alto) flute playing two octaves apart. Then a slow dragging dance emerges, built out of the third folk-tune fragment from the "Dance of the Adolescents."

The strong downbeat makes the meter hypnotic—but one or two added or skipped beats have a powerful animating effect. The dance reaches a relentless climax with glissando (sliding) trombones, gong, cymbals, and big drum. After a sudden fast coda, the wildlife fanfares of the introduction return to conclude the section.

Four more sections follow our selection in Part I of *The Rite of Spring.* The dynamic "Games of the Rival Tribes" introduces two more folk-tune fragments. A huge masked figure is borne aloft by the male dancers in a slower section, the "Procession of the Sage"; the Sage then performs a brief ceremony,

The climax of *The Rite of Spring. Robbie Jack/Corbis.*

LISTENING CHART 20

Stravinsky, *The Rite of Spring,* from Part I, "The Adoration of the Earth"

Ballet score. 10 min., 45 sec.

5 | 7–13   71   37

7	0:00	**Introduction**	Bassoon "fanfare," *p*, twice interrupted by English horn
	1:04		Fanfares in oboe, high (E♭) clarinet, bass clarinet
	1:40		Buildup
8	2:04		New motive in the oboe and E♭ clarinet
0:29	2:33		Stop; return of the bassoon fanfare, *p*
0:37	2:41	**Omens of Spring**	"Dance of the Adolescents" is foreshadowed; trill; the music stops and starts, ending with a high violin chord.
0:58	3:02		Tempo is established; ♩♩♩♩ rhythm introduced.
9	3:08	**Dance of the Adolescents**	Loud rhythmic passage with irregular accents (French horns); various motives are introduced.
0:36	3:44		Rhythmic passage again
10	3:53		Folk-song fragment no. 1 — bassoons and contrabassoon, etc.
0:28	4:21		Abrupt interruption of the regular rhythm
0:37	4:30		Return of the introductory "Omens" music
0:53	4:46		Folk-song fragment no. 2 — French horn, flutes
1:27	5:20		Folk-song fragment no. 3 — trumpets (triangle)
1:50	5:44		Folk-song fragment no. 2 — piccolos; big buildup
11	6:16	**The Game of Abduction**	Faster; frantic rhythms. Brass is prominent; sliding horn calls.
0:56	7:12		Ending passage: alternation between scurrying figures in the winds and heavy booms in the drums
12	7:33	**Round Dances of Spring**	Slower; introduction: flute trills, clarinet melody
0:34	8:08		The main slow dance rhythm is introduced; woodwind motive.
13	8:45		Folk-song fragment no. 3 (slower than before) — violas, *mf*
0:54	9:39		Folk-song fragment no. 3, *ff*, with cymbals
1:16	10:01		Climactic passage — brass
1:34	10:19		Short coda: faster, with violent rhythmic interjections
1:50	10:34		Brief return of the slow introduction, *p*

no. 1

no. 2

no. 3

Very fast

ff

Slow

mf

"Adoration of the Earth." The concluding orgiastic "Dance of the Earth" is built on a fast and furious ostinato.

What is conspicuously absent from any of this is emotionality. Tough, precise, and barbaric, it is as far from old-line Romantic sentiment as it is from the delicate, shadowy vision of Debussy. In Stravinsky's later works the barbarism was tamed, but the dry, precise quality remained, and so did the exhilarating irregular rhythms. Throughout his long career they provided him with a powerful strategy for movement, unlike that of any other composer. It was the primacy of rhythm that produced Stravinsky's "new language" for music.

Biography

Igor Stravinsky (1882–1971)

The son of an important opera singer, Igor Stravinsky studied law and did not turn seriously to music until he was nineteen. He was fortunate to be able to study with Nikolai Rimsky-Korsakov, a survivor of the nationalist *kuchka* (see page 284) who was still composing actively.

Rimsky's brand of nationalism served young Stravinsky well in the famous (and still outstandingly popular) ballet scores *The Firebird, Petrushka,* and *The Rite of Spring,* which he wrote for the Ballets Russes, a Russian company centered in Paris. This enormously dynamic organization, run by a brilliant producer and man-about-the-arts named Sergei Diaghilev, astonished the blasé Parisian public with its exotic spectacles combining the newest and the most sensational in dance, music, scenery, and costume design. Among Diaghilev's dancers were Vaslav Nijinsky, also choreographer of *The Rite,* and Anna Pavlova; among his designers were Pablo Picasso and Henri Matisse.

After World War I Stravinsky composed more ballets for Diaghilev, as well as other works in a dazzling variety of styles, forms, and genres. One of his most impressive scores, *The Wedding,* was choreographed by Bronislava Nijinska, Nijinsky's sister, who was less famous as a dancer than her brother but much better as a choreographer. Among the first classical composers to be interested in jazz, Stravinsky wrote *Piano Ragtime* in 1917 (and, much later, *Ebony Concerto* for clarinetist Woody Herman's jazz band; clarinets are made of ebony). He became an outspoken advocate of "objectivity" in music, the rejection of Romantic emotionality. For many years after World War I he modeled his music on pre-Romantic composers such as Bach, Handel, and Mozart, transforming the music by his own unique rhythmic and harmonic style. This style is sometimes called Neoclassicism.

His final work in this vein was an opera, *The Rake's Progress,* which is a kind of modern transformation of Mozart's *Don Giovanni.* This was written in America (to English words), where Stravinsky had moved in 1939. After World War II his music grew more abstract and formal in style.

For a quarter of a century people had regarded Stravinsky (and he regarded himself) as the leading Neoclassical composer in the French orbit, at the opposite pole from Schoenberg and the Viennese serialists (see page 327). So he created yet another sensation when, in his seventies, he produced a remarkable group of late compositions employing serial technique. One of the first of these, *Agon,* was written for the great choreographer George Balanchine of the New York City Ballet, who had worked on Stravinsky's Neoclassical *Apollo* twenty-five years earlier with the Ballets Russes.

After some scary stays in American hospitals, on which the composer's comments were particularly caustic, Stravinsky died at his home in New York in 1971. He is buried in Venice, near the grave of Diaghilev.

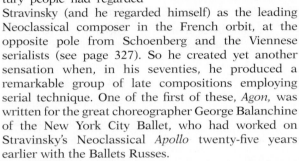

Chief Works: Ballet scores, including *The Firebird, Petrushka, The Rite of Spring, The Wedding, Orpheus, Agon* ■ *The Soldier's Tale,* an unusual chamber-music piece with narrator ■ An "opera-oratorio," *Oedipus the King; The Rake's Progress,* an opera in English (words by the poet W. H. Auden) ■ Two symphonies; concertos; *Symphony of Psalms* for orchestra and chorus ■ Other religious works: a Mass, *Requiem Canticles*

Encore: After *The Rite of Spring,* listen to *Petrushka* and *Symphony of Psalms.* Read *Conversations with Stravinsky* by Robert Craft, a protégé of Stravinsky for many years.

Image credit: Sanford Roth/Science Source.

3 | Expressionism

Even as Stravinsky was rejecting Romantic sentiment, in Austria and Germany composers pressed forward with music that was increasingly emotional and complex. As though intent on taking Romantic fervor to its ultimate conclusion, they found themselves exploiting extreme states, extending all the way to hysteria, nightmare, even insanity. This movement, known as *expressionism,* shares its name with important parallel movements in art and literature (see page 308).

These years before World War I also saw the publication of the first works of Sigmund Freud, with their new analysis of the power of unconscious drives, the significance of dreams, and the central role of sexuality. Psychoanalytic theory had a clear impact on German expressionism; a vivid example is *Erwartung* (Anticipation), a monologue for soprano and orchestra written by Arnold Schoenberg in 1909. In it, a woman comes to meet her lover in a dark wood and spills out all her terrors, shrieking as she stumbles upon a dead body she believes to be his. One cannot tell whether *Erwartung* represents an actual scene of hysteria, an allegory, or a Freudian dream fantasy.

Schoenberg was the leading expressionist in music. He pioneered in the "emancipation of dissonance" and the breakdown of tonality, and shortly after World War I he developed the revolutionary technique of serialism (see page 327). Even before the war, Schoenberg attracted two brilliant Viennese students who were only about ten years his junior and who shared almost equally in his innovations. Schoenberg, Anton Webern, and Alban Berg are often referred to as the Second Viennese School, by analogy with the earlier Viennese trio of Haydn, Mozart, and Beethoven.

Nightmarish images recur in expressionist art. Perhaps the most famous expressionist image is *The Scream,* by the Norwegian artist Edvard Munch (1863–1944). *Album/Art Resource. © 2014 The Munch Museum/The Munch-Ellingsen Group/Artists Rights Society (ARS) New York.*

Arnold Schoenberg, *Pierrot lunaire* (Moonstruck Pierrot) (1912)

5 | 14–15   72–73   38

We met the song cycle in the hands of the Romantic composers Franz Schubert and Robert Schumann (see page 237). *Pierrot lunaire* is the most famous and influential twentieth-century song cycle, but it is a far cry from Schumann's *Dichterliebe*. It sets poems by a minor symbolist poet, Albert Giraud. Like many artists of the time—poets as well as composers—Giraud is not easy to figure out at once. Pierrot is the eternal sad clown, and perhaps represents also the alienated artist; but why is he called "moonstruck" or "lunar"? In poems that are dotted with Freudian imagery, we hear about his obsession with the moon, his amorous frustrations, his nightmarish hallucinations, his pranks, and his adventures.

To match all this, Schoenberg wrote music that utterly lacks the tunes one might expect to find in a set of songs. The soprano does not exactly sing or exactly speak, but performs in an in-between style of Schoenberg's invention called *Sprechstimme* (speech-song). **Sprechstimme** is an extreme example of the avant-garde composers' search for new expressive means—here, sound that is not even fully organized into pitches. Through *Sprechstimme,* Giraud's

"On the two occasions I heard *Pierrot lunaire* I was conscious of the most profound impression I have ever experienced from a work of art. . . . But when I look at the score it still remains completely mysterious."

Letter to Schoenberg from student Alban Berg, 1914

strange moonstruck poems are somehow magnified, distorted, parodied, and haunted all at the same time.

In addition to the soprano, *Pierrot lunaire* calls for five instrumentalists. Altogether they play eight instruments, since three of the players switch between two: flute and piccolo, clarinet and bass clarinet, violin and viola, cello, and piano. Not all the songs involve all the players, so nearly every song has its own unique accompaniment, ranging from flute alone in No. 7 to all eight instruments in No. 21 (the players switch instruments in the middle of this song). Schoenberg's dazzling variety of instrumental effects enhances the inherent strangeness of *Sprechstimme,* and it is clear in the two songs we will examine, which are vastly different in sound and expressive tone.

No. 8: "Night" (voice, piano, bass clarinet, cello)   The poem presents the nightmarish aspect of expressionism; we could easily imagine the screaming figure of Edvard Munch's famous painting (see page 321) responding to a vision of this sort. Schoenberg used the lowest instruments of his ensemble to depict ominous insects, weighty and so utterly unlike real butterflies. Through the last section of the poem we can hear the swarm settling heavily downward, blotting out the light of day.

Schoenberg called this song a *passacaglia,* recalling a type of ostinato piece from the Baroque period. In fact, his music is dominated by the three-note ostinato shown in the margin.

The ostinato is announced at the very beginning by the piano, then taken up by the cello and bass clarinet; it also ends the song. Throughout, the instrumental accompaniment is largely constructed from overlapping versions of it, moved freely to various pitch levels. The soprano is even asked to sing it, at the eerie bottom of her range, on the word *verschwiegen* (secretly)—the only moment in the entire song cycle when Schoenberg has her abandon *Sprechstimme* for conventional singing.

Note, however, that the ostinato is chromatic in essence, its last pitch set a half step below its first. From such simple materials, Schoenberg can both unsettle conventional tonality and match the scary tone of Giraud's words.

No. 18: "The Moonfleck" (voice, piano, piccolo, clarinet, violin, cello)   The piano plays a short introduction, or transition from the previous number. Listen to this piano passage several times. Dense, dissonant, atonal, and alarmingly intense in its motivic insistence, this passage sums up Schoenberg's uncompromising version of musical modernism. It also seems devised to recall the loudest, scariest moments of "Night," one of many such musical connections across Schoenberg's cycle.

In the song itself, the tone shifts abruptly from this intensity; now it is not horror but the nagging bother of an obsession. Pierrot can neither forget nor bear the moonfleck that has soiled his tuxedo. In his setting Schoenberg explores timbres completely different from those of "Night." He uses high-pitched, quicksilver motives, scattered through the whole ensemble, to depict flickering moonlight. Simultaneous fugues and canons are at work, but what the listener perceives is a fantastic lacework of sounds, with hardly a hint of tonality, as Pierrot frantically but in vain brushes at himself. "The Moonfleck" uses extremely complicated technical means to achieve a unique sonorous effect.

Pierrot (on the right) and his fellow prankster Harlequin as musicians, by French artist André Derain. The anxieties of Schoenberg's Pierrot seem to beleaguer these clowns also. *Erich Lessing/Art Resource, NY.*

 **LISTEN**

Schoenberg, *Pierrot lunaire*

5 | 14–15 | 72–73 | 38 | e

No. 8: "Night"

14

0:22
Finstre, schwarze Riesenfalter
Töteten der Sonne Glanz.
Ein geschlossnes Zauberbuch,
Ruht der Horizont — verschwiegen.

Sinister giant black butterflies
Eclipse the blazing disk of sun.
Like a sealed-up book of wizard's spells
The horizon sleeps — secretly.

1:02
Aus dem Qualm verlorner Tiefen
Steigt ein Duft, Erinnrung mordend!
Finstre, schwarze Riesenfalter
Töteten der Sonne Glanz.

From dank forgotten depths
A scent floats up, to murder memory.
Sinister giant black butterflies
Eclipse the blazing disk of sun.

1:29
Und vom Himmel erdenwarts
Senken sich mit schweren Schwingen
Unsichtbar die Ungetüme
Auf die Menschenherzen nieder . . .
Finstre, schwarze Riesenfalter.

And from heaven downward dropping
To the earth in leaden circles,
Invisible, the monstrous swarm
Descends upon the hearts of men,
Sinister giant black butterflies.

No. 18: "The Moonfleck"

15

0:15
Einen weissen Fleck des hellen Mondes
Auf dem Rücken seines schwarzen Rockes,
So spaziert Pierrot im lauen Abend,
Aufzusuchen Glück und Abenteuer.

With a fleck of white — bright patch of moonlight —
On the back of his black jacket,
Pierrot strolls about in the mild evening air
On his night-time hunt for fun and good pickings.

0:33
Plötzlich stört ihn was an seinem Anzug,
Er beschaut sich rings und findet richtig —
Einen weissen Fleck des hellen Mondes
Auf dem Rücken seines schwarzen Rockes.

Suddenly something strikes him as wrong,
He checks his clothes over and sure enough finds
A fleck of white — bright patch of moonlight —
On the back of his black jacket.

0:48
Warte! denkt er: das ist so ein Gipsfleck!
Wischt und wischt, doch — bringt ihn
nicht herunter!
Und so geht er, giftgeschwollen, weiter,
Reibt und reibt bis an den frühen Morgen —
Einen weissen Fleck des hellen Mondes.

Damn! he thinks, There's a spot of plaster!
Rubs and rubs, but can't get rid of it.

So goes on his way, his pleasure poisoned,
Rubbing and rubbing till dawn comes up —
At a fleck of white — bright patch of moonlight!

Biography
Arnold Schoenberg (1874–1951)

Arnold Schoenberg grew up in Europe's most intense musical environment, the Vienna of Johannes Brahms and Gustav Mahler. He was largely self-taught in music, though he found a mentor in the conductor and composer Alexander von Zemlinsky, whose sister became Schoenberg's first wife. (His second wife also had a musical brother, the leader of an important string quartet that featured Schoenberg's music.) A man of unusual versatility, Schoenberg produced important books on music theory, painted (and gave exhibitions of) pictures in expressionist style, and wrote the literary texts for many of his compositions.

His early music—notably *Transfigured Night* of 1899, still his best-known work—extended the late Romantic tradition of Brahms and Mahler. But Schoenberg soon came to feel that he was destined to carry this tradition through to its logical modern development, by way of increasing chromaticism and atonality. Listeners felt otherwise, and Schoenberg's revolutionary compositions of the 1900s probably met with more hostility than any other works in the entire history of music. At the same time, they attracted the sympathetic interest of Mahler and Richard Strauss (see page 335), and drew a coterie of brilliant young students to Schoenberg.

Schoenberg's music grew progressively more and more atonal, but he was nearly fifty before he developed the twelve-tone (or serial) system (see page 327). Of all the "new languages" for music attempted by the early avant-garde composers, serialism was the most radical and also the most fruitful. After World War II, even though some leading radicals rejected Schoenberg's music, they still used his fundamental idea of a serial language for music.

As a Jew, Schoenberg was forced to leave Germany when the Nazis came to power, and he spent the rest of his life in Los Angeles, becoming a U.S. citizen in 1941. His unfinished opera *Moses and Aaron* of 1933 is both a Judaic epic and an allegory of the problem of modernist communication with the public. *A Survivor from Warsaw* was written in memory of the slaughter that occurred in the Warsaw Jewish quarter when the Nazis crushed the uprising there in 1943.

Arnold Schoenberg was a strange personality: gloomy, uncompromising, inordinately proud, and also highly superstitious. Of all the major composers, he was the first great teacher since Bach; besides his close associates of the Second Viennese School, he strongly influenced many other musicians who sought him out as a teacher. Near the end of his life he taught at UCLA.

Chief Works: An early "symphonic poem" for string sextet, *Transfigured Night*; Five Orchestral Pieces; two chamber symphonies, a piano concerto and a violin concerto; five string quartets ▪ *Erwartung* (Anticipation), an expressionist monologue for singer and orchestra; the unfinished opera *Moses and Aaron* ▪ *A Survivor from Warsaw* ▪ Songs, including *The Book of the Hanging Gardens*, to texts by the German symbolist poet Stefan George; *Pierrot lunaire* (Moonstruck Pierrot)

Encore: After *Pierrot lunaire*, listen to *Verklärte Nacht* (Transfigured Night) and Five Orchestral Pieces.

Image credit: Hulton Archive/Getty Images.

Alban Berg (1885–1935), *Wozzeck* (1923)

5 | 16–20   74–75

After Schoenberg, the most powerful exponent of expressionism in music was his student Alban Berg. Berg's opera *Wozzeck*, first conceived during World War I, was completed in 1923. In general plan, this opera can be described as Wagnerian, in that it depends on musical continuity carried by the orchestra. It uses leitmotivs and contains no arias. In more specific matters, its musical style owes much to Schoenberg's *Pierrot lunaire*.

Berg set a remarkable fragmentary play by the German dramatist Georg Büchner, a half-legible draft that was discovered after his death in 1837. In a series of brief, savage scenes spoken in the plainest vernacular, Büchner presents an almost paranoid vision of the helpless poor oppressed by society.

Berg's music for the play's dialogue is all highly intense, and he kept the tension up by writing continuous orchestral interludes during the blackouts between one scene and the next.

Franz Wozzeck is an inarticulate and impoverished soldier, the lowest cog in the military machine. He is troubled by visions and tormented for no apparent reason by his captain and by the regimental doctor. Wozzeck's lover, Marie, sleeps with a drum major, who beats Wozzeck up when he objects. Finally Wozzeck murders Marie, goes mad, and drowns himself. Büchner's play provided the perfect material for an expressionist opera.

Act III; Interlude after scene ii   Scene ii is the murder scene. When Wozzeck stabs Marie, she screams, and all the leitmotivs associated with her blare away in the orchestra, as if all the events of her lifetime were flashing before her eyes.

A blackout follows, and the stark interlude between the scenes consists of a single pitch played by the orchestra in two gut-bursting crescendos—another example of avant-garde stretching of musical effects to the limit.

Scene iii   The lights snap on again. In a sordid tavern, Wozzeck gulps a drink and seeks consolation with Marie's friend Margret. Berg's idea of a ragtime piano opens the scene—one of many signs that European music of the 1920s had woken up to American influences. But it is a distorted, dissonant ragtime, heard through the ears of someone on the verge of a breakdown.

The music is disjointed, confused, shocking. When Margret gets up on the piano and sings a song, her song is distorted, too:

Suddenly she notices blood on Wozzeck's hand. It smells like human blood, she says. In a dreadful climax to the scene, the apprentices and street girls in the inn come out of the shadows and close in on Wozzeck. He manages to escape during another blackout, as a new orchestral interlude surges frantically and furiously.

The whole of scene iii is built on a single short rhythm, repeated over and over again with only slight modifications—*but presented in many different tempos.* This twitching "master rhythm" is marked above the two previous examples, first at a fast tempo, then at a slow one; we first heard it in the timpani in the interlude between scenes ii and iii. Another obvious instance comes when Margret first notices the blood:

Here is yet another kind of ostinato—very different from Stravinsky's (see page 317) or Schoenberg's in the song "Night" (see page 322). Even though this master rhythm may elude the listener in a good many of its appearances, its hypnotic effect contributes powerfully to the sense of nightmare and fixation.

Scene iv Fatefully, Wozzeck returns to the pond where he murdered Marie. The orchestra engages in some nature illustration; we can even hear frogs croaking around the pond. Wozzeck's mind has quite cracked. He shrieks for the knife (in powerful *Sprechstimme* reminiscent of *Pierrot lunaire:* see page 321), discovers the corpse, and sees the blood-red moon and the pond, too, seemingly filled with blood. He falls into the water to wash himself.

At this point, his principal tormenters walk by. The captain and the doctor hear the macabre orchestral gurgles and understand that someone is drowning, but like people watching a mugging on a crowded city street, they make no move to help. "Let's get away! Come quickly!" says the terrified captain—in plain, naturalistic speech, rather than the *Sprechstimme* used by Wozzeck.

In the blackout after this scene, emotional music wells up in the orchestra, mourning for Wozzeck, Marie, and humanity at large. Here Berg adopts and even surpasses the late Romantic style of Gustav Mahler. Anguished leitmotivs from earlier in the opera, mainly in the brass, surge into a great climax, then subside.

Scene v Berg (following Büchner) has yet another turn of the knife waiting for us in the opera's final scene. Some children who are playing with Wozzeck's little son run off to view his mother's newly discovered corpse. Uncomprehending, he follows them. The icy sweetness of the music here is as stunning as the violent music of the tavern scene and the weird pond music. In turning Büchner's visionary play fragment into an expressionist opera, Berg created one of the great modernist theater pieces of the twentieth century.

Wozzeck, London, 2006. *Robbie Jack/Corbis.*

SCHOENBERG AND SERIALISM

Of all early twentieth-century composers, Arnold Schoenberg (1874–1951) was the most keenly aware of the problem caused by ever-broadening dissonance and atonality. The problem, to put it simply, was the clear and present danger of chaos. In the early 1920s Schoenberg found a way that he felt would impose order or control over the newly "emancipated" elements of music.

This resulted in the **twelve-tone system**, defined by Schoenberg as a "method of composing with the twelve tones solely in relation to one another"—that is, *not* in relation to a central pitch, or tonic, which was no longer to act as a point of reference for the music. This method became known as **serialism**. Serialism can be regarded as the ultimate systematizing of the chromaticism developed by Romantic composers, especially Richard Wagner (see page 226).

The Twelve-Tone System

Schoenberg's method of composing with the twelve pitches of the chromatic scale held them to a *fixed order*. An ordered sequence of the twelve pitches is called a **twelve-tone row**, or **series**: hence the term *serialism*. For any composition, he would determine a series ahead of time and maintain it (the next piece would have a different series).

What does "maintain" mean in this context? It means that *Schoenberg composed by writing notes only in the order of the work's series,* or of certain carefully prescribed other versions of the series (see below). As a general rule, he went through the entire series without any repetitions or backtracking before starting over again. However, the pitches can appear in any octave, high or low. They can stand out as melody notes or blend into the harmony. They can assume any rhythm: In the example below, pitch 10 lasts sixteen times as long as pitch 7.

And what are those other "versions" of the series? The series can be used not only in its original form but also be *transposed*, that is, the same note ordering can start from any note in the chromatic scale. The composer can also present the series *backward* (called "retrograde") or *inverted*, that is, with the intervals between notes turned upside down. The basic idea of serialism may seem to impose order with a vengeance by putting severe limits

on what a composer can do. But once the versions are taken into consideration, an enormous number of options becomes available.

Serialism and Unity

Part of the point of twelve-tone composition is that each piece has its own special "sound world" determined by its series. This permeates the whole piece. The next piece has a new series and a new sound world.

Serialism can be regarded as the end result of an important tendency in nineteenth-century music, the search for ever stronger means of unity within individual compositions. We have traced the "principle of thematic unity" in music by Berlioz, Wagner, and others (see page 231). A serial composition is, in a sense, totally unified, since every measure of it shares the same unique sound world. On its own special terms, Schoenberg's serialism seemed to realize the Romantic composers' ideal of unity.

The Second Viennese School

The two composers after Schoenberg quickest to adopt his serialism, Anton Webern and Alban Berg, had both studied with him in Vienna before World War I. Together the three make up the Second Viennese School. They were very different in musical personality, and serialism did not really draw them together; rather it seems to have accentuated the unique qualities of each composer.

Anton Webern (1883–1945) was an unspectacular individual whose life revolved around his strangely fragile artistic accomplishment. Despite his aristocratic background, he became a devoted conductor of the Vienna Workers' Chorus, as well as holding other, rather low-profile conducting positions.

From the start, Webern reacted against the grandiose side of Romanticism, as represented by the works of Richard Wagner and Gustav Mahler. He turned his music about-face, toward abstraction, atomization, and quiet: so quiet that listening to his music, one listens to the rests almost as much as to the notes themselves. His compositions are all extremely brief and concentrated (we discuss one of the briefest on page 362). Webern's entire musical output can fit on three CDs.

Phrase of a Schoenberg melody using a twelve-tone series. *Arnold Schoenberg, Concerto for Piano and Orchestra (1942). Used by permission of Belmont Music Publishers.*

But both Webern's vision of musical abstraction and his brilliant use of serialism made him a natural link between the first avant-garde phase of modernism, around World War I, and the second. Though he was killed in 1945, shot in error by a member of the American occupying forces in Austria, his forward-looking compositions caught the imagination of an entire generation of composers after World War II.

Alban Berg (1885–1935), in contrast, looked back; more than Schoenberg and certainly more than Webern, he kept lines of communication open to the Romantic tradition by way of Mahler. Berg's first opera, *Wozzeck*, was an immediate success on a scale never enjoyed by the other Second Viennese composers. His second opera, *Lulu* (1935), is now also a classic, though it made its way slowly—Berg had only partly orchestrated Act III when he died, and both operas were banned by the Nazis.

Like Webern, Berg met a bizarre end: He died at the age of fifty as a result of an infected insect bite. After his death, it came out that he had been secretly in love with a married woman, and had employed a musical code to refer to her and even to address her in his compositions—among them a very moving Violin Concerto (1935), his last work.

For once, a composer picture that's different: Alban Berg looks out over a life-sized portrait of himself painted by Arnold Schoenberg. *Bettmann/CORBIS.*

 **LISTEN**

Berg, *Wozzeck*, Act III, scenes iii and iv

5 | 16–20   74–75

SCENE iii: A tavern

16	0:28	**Wozzeck:**	**Tanzt Alle; tanzt nur zu, springt, schwitzt und stinkt, es holt Euch doch noch einmal der Teufel!**	Dance, everyone! Go on, dance, sweat and stink, the devil will get you in the end.

(Gulps down a glass of wine)
(Shouts above the pianist:)

			Es ritten drei Reiter wohl an den Rhein, Bei einer Frau Wirtin da kehrten sie ein. Mein Wein ist gut, mein Bier ist klar, Mein Töchterlein liegt auf der . . .	*Three horsemen rode along the Rhine, They came to an inn and they asked for wine. The wine was fine, the beer was clear, The innkeeper's daughter . . .*
	0:58	**Wozzeck:**	**Verdammt! Komm, Margret! Komm, setzt dich her, Margret! Margret, Du bist so heiss. . . . Wart' nur, wirst auch kalt werden! Kannst nicht singen?**	Hell! Come on, Margret! *(Dances with her)* Come and sit down, Margret! Margret, you're hot! Wait, you too will be cold! Can't you sing? *(She sings:)*
	1:36	**Margret:**	***In's Schwabenland, da mag ich nit, Und lange Kleider trag ich nit. Denn lange Kleider, spitze Schuh, Die kommen keiner Dienstmagd zu.***	*But Swabia will never be The land that I shall want to choose, For silken dresses, spike-heeled shoes, Are not for servant girls like me.*
		Wozzeck:	**Nein! keine Schuh, man kann auch blossfüssig in die Höll' geh'n! Ich möcht heut raufen, raufen. . . .**	No shoes! You can go to hell just as well barefoot! I'm feeling like a fight today!

17	2:22	**Margret:**	Aber was hast Du an der Hand?	But what's that on your hand?
		Wozzeck:	Ich? Ich?	Me? My hand?
		Margret:	Rot! Blut!	Red! Blood!
		Wozzeck:	Blut? Blut?	Blood? Blood? *(People gather around.)*
		Margret:	Freilich . . . Blut!	Yes, it is blood!
		Wozzeck:	Ich glaub', ich hab' mich geschnitten, da an der rechten Hand. . . .	I think I cut myself, on my hand. . . .
		Margret:	Wie kommt's denn zum Ellenbogen?	How'd it get right up to the elbow, then?
		Wozzeck:	Ich hab's daran abgewischt.	I wiped it off there. . . .
		Apprentices:	Mit der rechten Hand am rechten Arm?	Your right hand on your right arm?
		Wozzeck:	Was wollt Ihr? Was geht's Euch an?	What do you want? What's it to you?
		Margret:	Puh! Puh! Da stinkt's nach Menschenblut!	Gross! It stinks of human blood! *(curtain)*

Confusion. The people in the tavern crowd around Wozzeck, accusing him. Wozzeck shouts back at them and escapes.

SCENE iv: A pond in a wood

18	0:00	**Wozzeck:**	Das Messer? Wo ist das Messer? Ich hab's dagelassen . . . Näher, noch näher. Mir graut's! Da regt sich was. Still! Alles still und tod . . . Mörder! Mörder! Ha! Da ruft's! Nein, ich selbst.	The knife! Where is the knife? I left it there, around here somewhere. I'm scared! Something's moving. Silence. Everything silent and dead . . . Murderer! Murderer! Ah, someone called! No, it was just me.
			Marie! Marie! Was hast Du für eine rote Schnur um den Hals? Hast Dir das rote Halsband verdient, wie die Ohrringlein, mit Deiner Sünde? Was hangen Dir die schwartzen Haare so wild?	Marie, Marie! What's that red cord around your neck? A red necklace, payment for your sins, like the earrings? Why is your dark hair so wild?
	1:12		Mörder! Mörder! Sie werden nach mir suchen. . . . Das Messer verrät mich! Da, da ist's!	Murderer! Murderer! They will come look for me. . . . The knife will betray me! Here, here it is.
			So! da hinunter! Es taucht ins dunkle Wasser wie ein Stein. Aber der Mond verrät mich . . . der Mond ist blutig. Will denn die ganze Welt es ausplaudern?! — Das Messer, es liegt zu weit vorn, sie finden's beim Baden oder wenn sie nach Muscheln tauchen.	There! Sink to the bottom! It plunges into the dark water like a stone. But the moon will betray me. . . . The moon is bloody. Is the whole world going to betray me? The knife is too near the edge — they'll find it when they're swimming or gathering mussels.
			Ich find's nicht . . . Aber ich muss mich waschen. Ich bin blutig. Da ein Fleck . . . und noch einer.	I can't find it. But I have to get washed. There's blood on me. Here's one spot . . . here's another. . . .
			Weh! Weh! Ich wasche mich mit Blut! Das Wasser ist Blut . . . Blut. . . .	Oh, woe! I am washing myself in blood! The water *is* blood . . . blood. . . . *(drowns)*
19	3:01	**Captain:**	Halt!	Wait!
		Doctor:	Hören Sie? Dort!	Don't you hear? There!
		Captain:	Jesus! Das war ein Ton!	Jesus! What a sound!
		Doctor:	Ja, dort.	Yes, there.
		Captain:	Es ist das Wasser im Teich. Das Wasser ruft. Es ist schon lange Niemand entrunken. Kommen Sie, Doktor! Es ist nicht gut zu hören.	It's the water in the pond, the water is calling. It's been a long time since anyone drowned. Come away, Doctor! This is not good to hear.

Doctor:	Das stöhnt . . . als stürbe ein Mensch. Da ertrinkt Jemand!	There's a groan, as though someone were dying. Somebody's drowning!
Captain:	Unheimlich! Der Mond rot und die Nebel grau. Hören Sie? . . . Jetzt wieder das Ächzen.	It's weird! the red moon, the gray mist. Now do you hear? . . . That moaning again.
Doctor:	Stiller, . . . jetzt ganz still.	It's getting quieter — now it's stopped.
Captain:	Kommen Sie! Kommen Sie schnell!	Let's get away! Come quickly! (curtain)

20   4:30   **ORCHESTRAL MUSIC (Lament)**

4 | The First American Modernist: Ives

As we have seen, Paris and Vienna, centers of intense activity in all the arts, were also the first centers of modernist music. Echoes of modernism, some loud, some soft, were heard elsewhere in Europe: in Italy, where there was a short-lived movement called Futurism, and in Germany, Russia, Hungary, and England.

America, meanwhile, had no rich tradition of classical music, and what we did have was resolutely conservative. So it is amazing that a major modernist composer should have emerged in the United States as early as 1900. *Emerged* is not quite the word, for what also amazes is that Charles Ives worked in isolation, composing in his spare time. His music was little performed until the 1950s.

Many of Ives's compositions have American subjects, such as *Central Park in the Dark* and *Some Southpaw Pitching*. His *Holidays* Symphony includes movements titled "The Fourth of July," "Thanksgiving," and so on. These pieces regularly employ American music from outside the classical tradition: Folk songs, popular songs by Stephen Foster, gospel hymns, and ragtime are all quoted, sometimes in great profusion. Ives especially favored the hymns he remembered from his youth.

Ives was our first important nationalist composer. But he was also more than that: a true American original, a man with amazingly radical ideas about music, and a bold experimenter with musical materials. Ives anticipated many of the most talked-about musical innovations of the early part of the twentieth century — and of the later part, too.

Writing highly dissonant music was the least of it. He also wrote music for pianos tuned to quarter tones (rather than conventional half steps) and several works in which certain elements can be played, or not played, or played differently, depending on the performer's choice. For the whole length of his *Psalm 90*, for chorus, organ, and bells, low C sounds continuously in the organ pedals — for nearly eleven minutes. In one of his major works, the *Concord Sonata* of 1915, the pianist has to use his elbow and a special wooden block that holds sixteen notes down at a time.

To get an idea of the extraordinary range of Ives's work, we examine two works — one of them little known, the other very famous.

Biography

Charles Ives (1874–1954)

Charles Ives was the son of a Civil War military bandmaster and music teacher from Danbury, Connecticut, near New York City. Ives senior was an extraordinary character who enjoyed musical games such as playing two tunes simultaneously in different keys. His father's unconventionality—and his association with popular music—left a lasting impression on Charles.

Ives was a church organist as a teenager, and then went on to Yale, where he was a popular undergraduate (with a D+ average). He absorbed everything that his professor, the eminent composer Horatio Parker, had to teach him. But the American musical climate in the 1890s was basically hostile to modern trends; Parker wrote in a tame, traditional style. For Ives, this was not only dull but somehow also unmasculine. His vision was of a much more vigorous, rough-grained, enthusiastic, experimental kind of music.

When he got his B.A. he hedged his bets and took a job in insurance as well as another church organist position. After a few years he relegated music entirely to his spare time, while pursuing a very successful and innovative business career during the day. He seldom mixed with musicians and for years made little effort to get his works performed or published.

All the while Ives was developing his unique mystical notions about music, which have been linked to nineteenth-century New England transcendentalists, such as Ralph Waldo Emerson. To Ives, the actual sound of music seems to have counted less than the idea of music making as a natural human activity. All kinds of music were equally valid, then, whether popular or sophisticated, harmonious or wildly dissonant, played in or out of tune. What mattered was people's communal joy in music making. Believing that all musical experiments have equal validity, Ives launched into visionary projects that no other composer of the time would have considered.

Ives's late years were clouded by pathos, for after 1920 he gave up music almost entirely due to discouragement and bad health. He also sometimes tinkered with his old music to make it appear even more revolutionary than it was—though the music as he originally wrote it still amazes music historians. For his last thirty years Ives lived in quiet affluence with his wife, Harmony, the sister of a college friend—he had taken her to his junior prom. Harmony seems to have had a strong influence on her husband's ideas about music and life. They lived long enough to see his music admired first by a growing number of American musicians and then by the public at large.

Chief Works: For orchestra, four symphonies and the *Holidays* Symphony, several "Orchestral Sets," *Central Park in the Dark* and *The Unanswered Question* ▪ *Concord* Sonata for piano (movements entitled "Emerson," "Hawthorne," "The Alcotts," "Thoreau") ▪ *Variations on "America"* for organ (written at age seventeen; best known in its arrangement for orchestra) ▪ Chamber music, much of it programmatic ▪ Church music, choral music, and important solo songs, among them "General William Booth enters into Heaven"

Encore: After Orchestral Set No. 2 and *The Unanswered Question*, listen to *Putnam's Camp, The Fourth of July*.

Image credit: Bettmann/CORBIS.

Charles Ives, Second Orchestral Set, second movement, "The Rockstrewn Hills Join in the People's Outdoor Meeting" (1909)

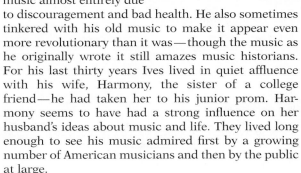 5 | 21–22 | 76 | 39

This orchestral piece is the second of three that make up Ives's Second Orchestral Set. Ives wrote four symphonies; if his orchestral sets are thought of as (very) informal examples of the same genre, this movement would count as the scherzo. For all its obscurity, the title has a true Ivesian ring: The grandeur of nature joins a human festival, apparently some sort of revival meeting.

The piece begins with several false starts, as though any effort to formulate a melody is bound to be defeated by other sounds, rhythms, and bits of tunes coming from this way and that. A dance fragment, first in the strings, then in the woodwinds, is interrupted by snatches of brass band music and piano ragtime. The hubbub gets more and more dissonant and atonal.

Gradually this array of "sound bites" builds up to a passage of forceful irregular rhythms. We catch a fragment of a cakewalk, a ragtime dance of the 1890s. At the climax, the confused juxtaposition of various ideas gives way for just a moment to homophony; the irregular pounding rhythms here remind us of Stravinsky's *The Rite of Spring*—a work written four years after Ives wrote this one. There is a slowdown and a quiet pause.

A new section begins with a fragmentary march in the trombones. Then at last a phrase of a hymn tune begins to crystallize. Only at the fourth try does the melody become clear. "I am coming, Lord!," the rousing chorus from one of Ives's favorite hymns, is orchestrated like a march:

Hymn, "I Hear Thy Welcome Voice"

I am coming, Lord!   Com-ing now to Thee!   Wash me, cleanse me, in the blood That flowed on Calva - ry.

Ives

Slow, swinging tempo

rit.   4

(tune fades)

After this collapses, the piano can be heard playing four-note segments of the whole-tone scale (a hallmark of Debussy—but Ives probably learned it from his inquisitive father). The outdoor meeting ends on an intense but quiet dissonance that is strangely serious, even spiritual—a characteristic Ivesian gesture.

Whole-tone scale

A gospel hymnbook of the time, open at the hymn used in Ives's Second Orchestral Set.

A revival meeting. *Bettmann/CORBIS.*

21	0:00	Introductory
	0:17	Dance fragment, strings; interrupted
	0:29	Dance fragment, woodwinds; interrupted
	0:49	Ragtime fragment, piano
		Kaleidoscopic array of fragmentary ideas; buildup
	1:27	Brass becomes prominent.
	1:58	Cakewalk fragment
	2:07	Climax: homophony
	2:34	Slowdown and pause (solo stringed instruments)
	2:44	March fragment, trombones
	3:00	The hymn is prefigured.
22	3:14	Dance fragment from beginning, brass — collapse
0:13	3:27	Hymn, clearer
0:43	3:57	At last the hymn emerges clearly: "I am coming, Lord!"
0:54	4:08	Fades: a fragmentary whole-tone scale in the piano

"I remember, when I was a boy — at the outdoor Camp Meeting services in Redding (Conn.), all the farmers, their families and field hands, for miles around, would come afoot or in their farm wagons. I remember how the great waves of sound used to come through the trees. . . . There was power and exaltation in those great conclaves of sound from humanity."

Charles Ives

Charles Ives, *The Unanswered Question* (1906)

This famous work—utterly quiet, serene, and solemn—is as different as could be from the cheerful clatter of "The Rockstrewn Hills." It requires two conductors. Ives himself described it best:

> The strings play *ppp* throughout, with no change in tempo. They repre-sent "The Silences of the Druids" who know, see, and hear nothing. The trumpet intones "The Unanswered Question of Existence" and states it in the same tone of voice each time. But the hunt for "The Invisible Answer" undertaken by the flutes and other human beings [Ives is personifying the other woodwind instruments] gradually becomes more active and louder. The "Fighting Answerers" seem to realize a futility, and begin to mock "The Question"—the strife is over. . . . After they disappear, "The Ques-tion" is asked for the last time, and the "Silences" are heard beyond in "Undisturbed Solitude."

What is so novel here—what rivals in innovativeness any of the experiments of the European modernists of the time—is the concept of three distinct, independent levels of music. The smooth string choir, playing consonant harmonies, is one. Another is provided by the dissonant woodwinds, a more and more taunting modernist challenge to the strings. Then there is the single trumpet, sounding like a voice, all the more solemn and haunting for asking its Question only about half a dozen times in the whole composition.

These simultaneous levels do not fit together in the least, in terms of traditional polyphony. Their precise rhythmic or contrapuntal relationship is left to chance. Yet this unusual nondialogue between "Silences," "Questioner," and

"Answerers" proves to be both coherent and poignant: a foretaste, perhaps, of our own age, an age marked by the quiet desperation of noncommunication.

Listen to one or two of the many performances of this extraordinary work available on YouTube.

GOALS FOR REVIEW

► to appreciate the wide stylistic variety of early avant-garde music

► to understand Claude Debussy's distance from the sounds and styles of late Romanticism

► to follow the rhythmic, melodic, and harmonic novelties of Igor Stravinsky's *The Rite of Spring*

► to hear the breakdown of tonality in Arnold Schoenberg's hallucinatory songs

► to appreciate the power of post-Romantic, expressionist opera in Alban Berg's *Wozzeck*

► to track the course of an American avant-garde original, Charles Ives

 macmillanhighered.com/listen8e
Interactive Listening Charts 19–21
Listening Quiz for Chapter 21
Reading Quiz for Chapter 21

Modernism between the Wars

CHAPTER 22

In music, as in all the arts, radical modernism was a primary source of creative energy in the period from before World War I until after World War II. The vision of new "languages" to express the new conditions of modern life was a powerful one, even if the public at large often found those languages hard to understand. The success of some avant-garde works of art—Alban Berg's opera *Wozzeck,* for one—shows that they met with a deep response from minds and hearts battered by the events of the early twentieth century.

Not everyone was as successful as Berg, however; most avant-garde music played to a small, esoteric audience. A figure like Schoenberg, convinced that music's progress depended on his leadership, could accept this and hold uncompromisingly to his principles. Many others, too, never blinked—including, after Ives, several modernists in America, chief among them Carl Ruggles (1876–1971), Roger Sessions (1896–1985), and Edgard Varèse (1883–1965; Varèse came to America from France).

Other composers, both here and abroad, took a more ambivalent view of avant-garde innovation. The force of Romantic tradition was still strong. Some famous twentieth-century names never joined the avant-garde at all and kept on mining the reliable quarries of Romanticism for their own private veins of (they hoped) musical gold. One area where this tendency is particularly clear, as we will see, is early film music.

Other composers worked with the ideas of Schoenberg or Stravinsky, selectively adopting no more than they needed to fulfill their own creative visions. Still others started out wholeheartedly in the avant-garde, only to turn back to more traditional styles. American figures who fall somewhere in this spectrum are Charles Griffes (1884–1920), Samuel Barber (1910–1981), and William Schuman (1910–1992), as well as William Grant Still (1895–1978) and Aaron Copland (1900–1990), whom we come to at the end of this chapter. Both Still, the first important African American composer in the concert music tradition, and Copland also recall nineteenth-century nationalism in their use of American musical idioms.

Of the many impressive composers active in the first half of the twentieth century, several have maintained and even increased their hold on audiences up to the present day—including the opera composers Puccini (see page 274) and Richard Strauss (1864–1949). Strauss started out as a composer of sensational symphonic poems, and then in 1905 created a furor with the modernist opera

The formality of concert life grew in the early twentieth century. Here it is captured in a magnificent, full-dress portrait of the Portuguese cellist Guilhermina Suggia (1885–1950), one of the first women to pursue her instrument professionally. *Tate, London/Art Resource, NY.*

Salome. But soon he retreated to a more Romantic style. It is evident in his opera *Der Rosenkavalier* (The Knight of the Rose, 1911), a dizzying mixture of Wagner, Mozart, and Johann Strauss, the Waltz King (no relation).

Two more major composers who had little to do with avant-garde experiment were Russians who (like Stravinsky) fled the Russian Revolution of 1917: Sergei Prokofiev, who is discussed on page 355, and Sergei Rachmaninov (1873–1943). Rachmaninov was one of the greatest pianists of his time, and his Piano Concertos Nos. 2 and 3 are among the most popular works in the concert repertory. Listen to a section from Rachmaninov's *Rhapsody on a Theme by Paganini,* a concerto-like work for piano and orchestra, in Listening Exercise 2 (page 8).

Unit I

1 | Mixing Classical Form and Jazz: Maurice Ravel

Maurice Ravel, born in 1875 in the south of France, was later attracted to Paris. From the very start, his music was marked by refinement, hyperelegance, and a certain crispness; musicians admire him for his superb workmanship and high style. As Debussy occupied the middle ground between Romanticism and modernism, Ravel carved out a place for himself between impressionism and Neoclassicism (see page 320). While his harmonies and chord progressions often remind us of Debussy, he favored clarity, precision, and instant communication, qualities he found in earlier musical forms and styles—especially, in the case of the piano concerto we study, those of Mozart.

Musical exoticism (see page 283) found a modernist voice in Ravel, and few composers have ranged as widely in imagination as he did. His music visited Spain, Madagascar, Asia, ancient Greece, and America. He even evoked Vienna, in a bitter anti-German parody of waltz music, *La Valse,* composed right after World War I (1919).

Maurice Ravel, Piano Concerto in G (1931)

5 | 23–27   77

A lighthearted piece for piano and small orchestra, the Piano Concerto in G is Ravel's tribute to jazz (his most outspoken tribute, but not his first; like Debussy and Stravinsky, Ravel was fascinated by jazz long before he came to the United States in 1928 and haunted music clubs in Harlem). Americans like George Gershwin and Aaron Copland incorporate jazz accents in their compositions in a fairly direct way (see page 349). With Ravel everything is slightly skewed, as if through a special filter, with a delicacy and elegance that we think of as characteristically French, perhaps, and that Ravel projects more clearly than any other composer.

First Movement (Allegramente)   The first theme is *not* jazzy. A long, lively, folklike tune is presented in the sort of fabulous orchestration that is this composer's hallmark: After a whiplash—literally—a piccolo plays the tune with syncopated *pizzicato* (plucked) string chords and the piano shimmering in the background. But the tune really belongs to a special high trumpet (trumpet in C), which takes it over from the piccolo, with the syncopated chords barked out by the other brass.

The piano now introduces a second theme that recalls the blues—not directly, but clearly enough. A third theme suggests romantic popular songs of the 1930s. Typical of early jazz is Ravel's use of short *breaks,* instrumental interludes between lines of a song lasting just one or two measures (see page 386). He catches this device perfectly with the high clarinet (E-flat clarinet) and a muted trumpet cutting into theme 2, with swishing sounds from the piano and the harp.

At a later point, the harp plays theme 2 itself, in a dreamlike episode that brings this busy movement to a state of near suspension.

After the piano and orchestra have presented themes 2 and 3, the piano engages in vigorous, propulsive music of the sort that often leads to cadences in concertos (see page 185). A new syncopated motive strongly implies that a cadence is coming, though the actual resolution is disguised.

Ravel, Piano Concerto in G, first movement

Free sonata form. 8 min., 15 sec.

5 | 23–27 | 77

23		**EXPOSITION**	
	0:00	**Theme 1**, piccolo, syncopated strings pizzicato
	0:24	**Theme 1**, trumpet, syncopated brass
	0:36	Sudden modulation
		Second group
	0:44	**Theme 2**, piano: slower; interrupted by the "break"
24	1:40	**Theme 3**, piano
0:37	2:17	**Theme 3**, orchestra—bassoon, trumpet
0:55	2:35	Vigorous, driving music for the piano
1:14	2:54	Break, soon repeated
1:47	3:27	Approach to a cadence
25	3:36	**Retransition**: upward scales in the piano
		RECAPITULATION
0:09	3:45	**Theme 1**, piano, **ff**; returns to the tonic key
0:20	3:57	Sudden modulation
		Second group
0:29	4:05	**Theme 2**, piano—with gong
26	4:30	Dreamlike episode: **theme 2**, harp
0:38	5:08	Break; melody continues in the French horn
1:14	5:44	"Cadenza": **theme 3**, with extensive trills
2:04	6:34	**theme 3**, piano and orchestra
2:34	7:04	Piano: vigorous, brilliant; **Theme 1** reemerges
3:07	7:37	Approach to a cadence
		CODA
27	7:42	Orchestra (trumpet), **f**, in the original tonic key, with motives derived from **theme 1**
0:17	7:59	**ff**

> In my own compositions I judge a long period of conscious gestation necessary. During this interval I come progressively, and with growing precision, to see the form and the evolution that the final work will take. . . . But one must spend much time in eliminating all that could be regarded as superfluous in order to realize as completely as possible the definitive clarity so much desired.
>
> *Maurice Ravel, a meticulous musician and man*

In this clear presentation of first theme, second theme group, and music announcing a cadence, Ravel harks back to the sonata form of earlier composers (see page 162). But he does so in the freest possible way. In fact, there is no development section at all, but only a quick move to scales in the piano that prepare the way for the recapitulation of theme 1. Ravel drew on classical tradition but at the same time invented his own super-clear and listener-friendly form for the Piano Concerto in G.

At the very end of the first movement, Ravel borrows a favorite device invented by Debussy, a long series of parallel chords. The effect could hardly be more different: Debussy's chords—in *Clouds,* for example (see page 313)—are *piano,* legato, silky, vague, and atmospheric; Ravel's are *fortissimo* and staccato, crisp and clear.

Ravel (right) with the legendary dancer Vaslav Nijinsky, the star of his ballet *Daphnis and Chloé* in 1912. A year later Nijinsky was responsible for the riot-inducing choreography of Stravinsky's *The Rite of Spring. Bettmann/CORBIS.*

Biography
Maurice Ravel (1875–1937)

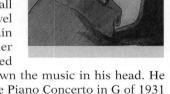

Maurice Ravel was born in a little town in the south of France, two miles from the Spanish border, and was brought to Paris at an early age. His mother came from the Basque region of Spain, and many of his compositions have exotic Spanish resonances—*Boléro,* most famously; also *Habanera, The Spanish Hour,* and others.

Ravel spent no fewer than sixteen lackluster years at the Paris Conservatory, the gateway to French musical life in those days, while his older contemporary Claude Debussy emerged as a leader in the music of modernism. When Debussy died in 1918, Ravel was acknowledged as the leading composer of war-ravaged France. Ravel hated Germany and German music, and he was young enough to volunteer for military service against the Germans in World War I, despite his frail body and retiring personality.

From the time of his first major success, with the impressionistic piano piece *Jeux d'eau* (Fountains; 1901), it was clear Ravel had an amazing ear for sonority, and the magical sound of his music for piano or orchestra is unmatched. He was the most meticulous and exquisite of composers, and his aim was for clarity above all. Some of his most famous compositions make use of classical forms, such as the *Sonatine* for Piano and the Piano Concerto in G.

Ravel never married, seems to have had no close relationships, and lived an uneventful life at his home in Paris. His one big trip, in 1928, was to America; here he met George Gershwin (and Charlie Chaplin) and came back with a small fortune. In 1932, Ravel contracted a rare brain disease; among other symptoms, it rendered him unable to write down the music in his head. He died five years later. The Piano Concerto in G of 1931 was his last work but one.

Chief Works: Orchestral works: *Mother Goose Suite, La Valse,* the ballet scores *Boléro* and *Daphnis and Chloé* ■ One-act operas: *L'Heure espagnole* (The Spanish Hour) and *L'Enfant et les sortilèges* (The Child Bewitched), a delightful childhood fantasy ■ Piano concertos; *Gaspard de la nuit,* one of the hardest pieces ever written for piano; *Jeux d'eau;* and a charming piano *Sonatine* ■ Songs; a string quartet ■ Many arrangements for orchestra, including Musorgsky's *Pictures at an Exhibition* (see page 284)

Encore: After the first movement of the Piano Concerto in G, listen to the second movement; *Boléro; Sonatine* for Piano.

Image credit: Bibliothèque Nationale, Paris, France/Trela/The Bridgeman Art Library.

2 | Folk Music, Nationalism, and Modernism: Béla Bartók

Growing up in Hungary in the 1890s, the young Béla Bartók was first swept away by the international avant-garde leaders Debussy and especially Richard Strauss. Later in his career he was also influenced by his close contemporary Stravinsky. Bartók was, however, a man of multiple careers—pianist, educator, and musicologist as well as composer. His deep commitment to folk music—much deeper than Stravinsky's—and his professional involvement with it as a collector had a decisive impact on his music. Many would say that Bartók was more successful than any other composer in integrating folk music into classical music.

Folk music, especially that of his native Hungary, ensured that Bartók's music would rarely become as abstract as much modernist music was. There is an earthy feel to it; even at its most dissonant, there is an infectious folk-dance swing or a touch of peasant melody. This is true even in works of his most avant-garde period, about 1925–35. The austere String Quartet No. 4 of 1928 is often regarded as Bartók's masterpiece.

> "The right type of peasant music is most perfect and varied in its forms. Its expressive power is amazing, and at the same time it is devoid of all sentimentality and superfluous ornaments. It is simple, sometimes primitive, but never silly. . . . A composer in search of new ways cannot be led by a better master."
>
> *Béla Bartók*

Biography
Béla Bartók (1881–1945)

Béla Bartók showed unusual talent as a pianist and composer at an early age. Music was the avocation of his father, who was principal of an agricultural school in Hungary; after his death Bartók's mother worked as a piano teacher, tirelessly promoting her son's career.

Few musicians have ever had as varied a career as Bartók. He was a prolific composer and a fine pianist, as was his second wife; they appeared as a two-piano team. (Both of his wives had been his students.) In conjunction with another important Hungarian composer, Zoltán Kodály, he directed the Budapest Academy of Music, where the two men tried out new ideas in music teaching. An outcome of this side of Bartók's career is his *Mikrokosmos*, a series of 153 graded piano pieces starting with the very easiest. Well known to most piano students today, the *Mikrokosmos* has probably done more than any other work to introduce modernism to large numbers of musicians in their impressionable years.

Also with Kodály, Bartók undertook a large-scale investigation of Hungarian (and other) folk music, writing several standard books on the topic. He published many folk-song and folk-dance arrangements, and his other compositions are saturated with folk rhythms, modes, and melodic turns. The outstanding nationalist composer of the twentieth century, Bartók left a body of work that equals or surpasses that of any of the nineteenth-century nationalists.

Bartók was strongly opposed to the Nazis. After they came to power in Germany, he refused to concertize there and broke ties with his German publisher. And his liberal views caused him a good deal of trouble from right-wingers in Hungary. In 1940, after the outbreak of World War II, Bartók came to America, but he was not well known here and there was little interest in his music. His last years were a struggle to complete his Third Piano Concerto and the Viola Concerto. His important works earned a wide, enthusiastic audience only after his death.

Chief Works: Concerto for Orchestra, three piano concertos, Violin Concerto, Music for Strings, Percussion, and Celesta (for small orchestra) ▪ Six string quartets; a fascinating Sonata for Two Pianos and Percussion ▪ An opera, *Bluebeard's Castle*, and a ballet, *The Miraculous Mandarin* ▪ *Mikrokosmos* and other works for piano ▪ Many folk-song arrangements for various ensembles, including Six Rumanian Dances

Encore: After Music for Strings, Percussion, and Celesta, listen to the Violin Concerto and Quartet No. 6.

Image credit: Bettmann/CORBIS.

Bartók collecting folk songs: He was using recording equipment just a few years after commercial recordings began coming out. Around 1906, these rural Hungarians seem less amazed by the primitive phonograph than by the camera. *Apic/Getty Images.*

After that time Bartók's music gradually became more accessible, and the references to folk songs in it became more mellow and, often, more poignant. He now used—in his own fashion—established forms such as sonata form and rondo; this made his music easier to follow for listeners already accustomed to these forms from eighteenth- and nineteenth-century music. And many of his last works include passages reminiscent of Romanticism: Violin Concerto No. 2, the popular Concerto for Orchestra, and Quartet No. 6 of 1939.

Béla Bartók, Music for Strings, Percussion, and Celesta (1936)

5 | 28–34   78

This work can be thought of as an informal symphony in the usual four substantial movements, composed for a specially constituted small orchestra. Much of the time the instruments are divided into two sections that answer each other back and forth.* Besides strings, Bartók includes piano, harp, celesta (see page 17), timpani—very important—and other percussion. We do not learn this all at once, however. The celesta makes its first entrance with an exquisite effect halfway through the first movement. The piano, harp, and xylophone arrive only in the second.

Second Movement (Allegro)   The music bubbles over with variety, an exhilarating rush of melodic fragments, striking rhythms, folk-dance fragments, and novel percussion sounds. It is all held together by sonata form.

---

*This is a principle that goes back at least as far as Giovanni Gabrieli in the early Baroque era (see page 81).

A "preface" played by *pizzicato* (plucked) strings precedes theme 1:

The preface, theme 1, and the contrapuntal bridge passage are all energized by motive **a**. One thinks of the motivic single-mindedness of Beethoven's Fifth Symphony (see page 209). Bartók's motive works especially well in the timpani, which play a powerful role in this movement.

There is a full stop after the bridge, so self-conscious that one wonders if Bartók is making fun of sonata-form conventions. The second theme group contains at least three very short themes. Theme 3 has a folk-dance lilt about it:

Suddenly the piano enters with a theme containing odd note repetitions. Since the pianist has hardly played at all up to this point, this new theme feels more like a beginning than a conclusion. Still, it functions as a cadence theme; very soon the *exposition* ends with another exaggerated cadence.

The timpani introduce the *development section*. Motive **b**, played pizzicato, comes in for an extensive workout. After a moment the strings drop down into an accompaniment for an amazing passage for piano, snare drum, and xylophone, punching out syncopated notes. This must have been inspired by the riot-producing "Dance of the Adolescents" in Stravinsky's *The Rite of Spring* (see page 317).

Next, pizzicato string scales in imitative polyphony weave endless new knots and tangles. The scales blend into another folklike tune, similar to theme 3, which is repeated very freely. Introduced by the timpani, a fugue starts up in the lowest register, preparing for the recapitulation. The fugue subject is derived from theme 1, with the meter askew.

And when the *recapitulation* comes, after much signaling from the timpani, and after an expectant slowdown, the meter is changed throughout. Theme 1 vacillates between duple and triple meter, and the second group tips the balance: themes 2 and 4 each return in swinging triple meter.

Béla Bartók, Music for Strings, Percussion, and Celesta. Copyright © 1937 by Boosey & Hawkes, Inc. for the U.S.A., Copyright renewed. Reprinted by permission of Boosey & Hawkes, Inc.

LISTENING CHART 23

Bartók, Music for Strings, Percussion, and Celesta, second movement (Allegro)

Sonata form. 7 min.

5 | 28–34   78

		EXPOSITION		
28	0:00	**Theme 1**	With pizzicato "preface"	
	0:22		Held note, drum	
	0:25	**Bridge**		
			CADENCE Big stop, after drumbeat	
29		**Second group**		
	0:56	**Theme 2**		
0:13	1:10	**Theme 3**	Folklike tune, strong beat	
			Developmental	
0:36	1:32	**Theme 4**	Over a string trill	
1:08	2:04	**Cadence theme**	Piano	
30	2:24		CADENCE Exaggerated cadence; drumbeat	
		DEVELOPMENT		
0:04	2:28	**Section 1**	Irregular rhythms: piano and percussion, leading to the Stravinskian passage	
0:49	3:14	**Section 2**	Pizzicato scales, from the "preface"	
31	3:34		New folklike tune	
			Drum prepares:	
0:30	4:04	**Section 3**	Crescendo	
1:20	4:54	**(retransition)**	Drum grows insistent; slowdown ———————→	
		RECAPITULATION		
32	5:10	**Theme 1**	With timpani; meter change	
0:18	5:28	**Bridge**		
33		**Second group**		
	5:40	**Theme 2**	Transformation: triple meter	
0:11	5:51		New continuations	
0:24	6:04	**Theme 4**	Transformation: triple meter	
0:44	6:24	**Cadence theme**	Piano, as before	
		CODA		
34	6:32		New fast dialogue on theme 1	

Theme 3 returns more freely. It takes the piano's odd "cadence theme" to bring us back to the solid duple meter of the start. As a coda, Bartók stages a fast, intense dialogue on theme 1.

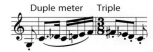

3 | Varieties of American Modernism

Though it had been anticipated by Charles Ives, American musical modernism did not really take off until the 1920s. Then a new generation of composers, born around 1900, came of age. They found many more opportunities open to them than Ives had before World War I. The musical climate was more favorable to new ideas, partly because the war had brought greater awareness of all things European, including European new music. Like important American writers who lived abroad—Gertrude Stein, T. S. Eliot, Edith Wharton, Ernest Hemingway—composers now associated themselves with European modernism in ways their predecessors never had. Many new works of European composers such as Schoenberg and Stravinsky saw their first American performances at this time. Innovative musical styles began to appear, some more and some less experimental, and some incorporating American jazz, blues, and other popular idioms.

In New York City, San Francisco, and elsewhere, musical societies arose to encourage the composition and performance of new music. The International Composers' Guild was created in New York in 1921; it set out to perform only previously unheard works at its concerts. Avant-gardist Edgard Varèse (see page 363), lately emigrated from France, was one of its founders.

The New Music Society of San Francisco, formed by the young American composer Henry Cowell (1897–1965), issued a quarterly pamphlet making available the music of new works. Its guidelines read, in part: "There is little demand for the very new in music . . . NEW MUSIC [the name of their pamphlet] affords a means for the publication of ultra-modern compositions and insures their distribution. . . . NEW MUSIC specializes in the works of Americans . . . but publishes occasional foreign works." Both aggressive modernism and proud nationalism can be sensed in this proclamation.

All three composers discussed here—Ruth Crawford, William Grant Still, and Aaron Copland—would take part in and benefit from these new energies and efforts to promote American modernist music.

Ruth Crawford with the American poet and writer Carl Sandburg, mid-1920s; she would later set to music a number of his poems. *Kim Seeger for the family of Ruth Crawford Seeger.*

Ruth Crawford

Ruth Crawford, also known as Ruth Crawford Seeger, ranks as one of the earliest of American avant-garde modernists. This is all the more extraordinary because she was a woman working in a male-dominated field. She devoted less than a decade of her life, the years from about 1925 to 1933, to full-time composition, and so her musical output is relatively small. It features works for various chamber ensembles, piano music (Crawford was a skilled pianist), and songs for both solo voice and chorus.

Crawford's music is uncompromisingly dissonant in harmony; many works are atonal in the manner of Schoenberg (see page 324). She shows a mastery of clear, transparent counterpoint and relishes the layered textures it can create. Though she would devote herself to collecting and transcribing American folk songs during the 1930s and 1940s, her own earlier music manifests little interest in incorporating this tradition; instead she looked to European modernist predecessors.

Ruth Crawford, Prelude for Piano No. 6 (Andante Mystico; 1928)

5 | 35   79

This work, published in Cowell's quarterly, *New Music*, stands in the tradition of piano miniatures reaching back to the early nineteenth century. Chopin had published a volume of piano preludes—preludes not introducing anything else, a characteristic Romantic gesture—and Debussy had continued the tradition around 1900. So had the Russian composer and mystic Alexander Scriabin (1872–1915), a particularly potent influence on Crawford's expressive approach in this "Mystical Andante."

The work presents a contrapuntal texture of three layers, clearly distinct in pitch. At the beginning we hear, high up, a repeating figure for two parts; this is an **ostinato**, a repeating pattern that will recur through most of the prelude, if with variation. Soon the second and third layers appear: Rolling chords are heard in the piano's low register, and a yearning, chromatic melody emerges in the middle range. The harmonies involved are dissonant, offering little sense of tonal center, or *tonic*.

 LISTENING CHART 24

Crawford, Prelude for Piano No. 6

2 min., 44 sec.

5 | 35   79

0:00	Ostinato in high pitches
0:10	Rolling chords in low pitches
	Melody in middle range emerges.
0:27	Crescendo; ostinato descends.
0:45	First CADENCE
1:03	Ostinato resumes at original pitch.
1:34	Second CADENCE
1:43	Coda: ostinato in bass, rolling chords above
2:16	Final, slow rolling chord

"Damn you."

Ruth Crawford (1930) as she passed a room where a group of men, excluding women, discussed musical matters

The music grows louder and gathers intensity, and the ostinato descends to lower pitch levels, converging on the melody below it, to approach a central climax—and a central cadence in the prelude. Then the ostinato resumes at its original high pitch, and the three layers are restored, only to move more quickly than before to another cadence. After this there is a coda, with a twist: Now the ostinato is heard in the low register, with the rolling chords, slower now, high up above.

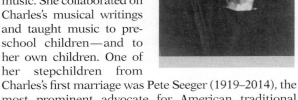

Born into a minister's family in a small town in eastern Ohio, Ruth Crawford showed early musical talent as a pianist. She entered the American Conservatory in Chicago in 1921 but soon sought out private study with the Canadian pianist Djane Lavoie-Herz, whose Chicago studio was something of a hotbed for modernist music, and musical mysticism as well. The young Crawford eagerly imbibed both.

There she met composer Henry Cowell. He had been a student of the musicologist, composer, and new music advocate Charles Seeger (1886–1979), now living in New York. Through Cowell's intervention, Crawford found her way there to study with Seeger. In 1931 she became the first woman to win a Guggenheim Fellowship in composition; she used the fellowship to spend a year studying in Berlin and Paris, where she met Béla Bartók and Alban Berg.

On returning from Europe, Crawford and Seeger were married; they had four children. Crawford took her husband's name and is often referred to as Ruth Crawford Seeger. In 1933, just as her career was taking flight, Crawford the modernist composer fell silent. She had earlier wondered whether a career in composition and raising a family were compatible; her husband seems to have thought that they were not.

Over the next two decades Crawford was not inactive in music, however. After the family moved to Washington, D.C., in 1935, she worked tirelessly in government-sponsored projects to collect, transcribe, arrange, and publish American folk music. She collaborated on Charles's musical writings and taught music to preschool children—and to her own children. One of her stepchildren from Charles's first marriage was Pete Seeger (1919–2014), the most prominent advocate for American traditional music of the second half of the twentieth century.

Crawford had just returned to her own composition, producing the award-winning *Suite for Wind Quintet* in 1952, when she was diagnosed with cancer. She died the next year.

Chief Works: Orchestral music: *Music for Small Orchestra* ■ Piano works: nine preludes; *Study in Mixed Accents* ■ Vocal works: songs for voice and piano setting poems of her friend Carl Sandburg; three *Chants* for chorus ■ Chamber works: String Quartet; *Suite for Wind Quintet* ■ Many arrangements of folk songs for adults and children, including the collection *American Folk Songs for Children*, still in print.

Encore: After Prelude for Piano No. 6, listen to String Quartet, third and fourth movements, and *Music for Small Orchestra*, second movement.

Image credit: Kim Seeger for the family of Ruth Crawford Seeger.

William Grant Still

If carving out a place as a modernist composer was hard for a woman in 1920s America, it was all but impossible for an African American, man or woman. Nevertheless, William Grant Still set his sights early in life on becoming a composer of concert music and opera. By 1919 he had found his way to New York City; in the 1920s he studied with Edgard Varèse and had works performed by the International Composers' Guild.

In New York's Harlem district, a new and vital movement in African American arts and letters formed at this time. It has come to be known as the Harlem

Renaissance, and its luminaries included poet Langston Hughes, novelist Zora Neale Hurston, and jazz musician Duke Ellington (see page 392). Still also took part in this cultural movement, both with his modernist compositions and as an arranger of jazz musicals and early radio music.

From his earliest works, Still strove to capture a distinctive African American identity and sound in his music, and this took him down a different path from many other musical modernists. (His approach was very different from Ruth Crawford's abstract, Europe-derived modernism, for example.) Still's music incorporates styles derived from blues and jazz, and his songs, operas, ballets, and symphonic works return again and again to African American subjects and stories.

We can think of Still's music as a strain of musical nationalism in modernist guise, akin to Bartók's incorporation of his native Hungarian folk music—with the important difference that Still spoke from a minority position in an America dominated by whites.

Biography
William Grant Still (1895–1978)

William Grant Still was born in Mississippi to middle-class parents, his mother a schoolteacher and his father a teacher and local bandleader. Still's father died while he was an infant, but in the following years his mother and stepfather encouraged his musical interests, taking him to concerts and buying him early recordings of classical music.

Still studied science at Wilberforce University in Ohio but left before graduating. He was awarded scholarships to pursue music at Oberlin College and the New England Conservatory. In later years he would win many awards and commissions for his compositions, including two Guggenheim Fellowships.

In 1919 Still settled in New York City and took a position as an arranger for the famous blues bandleader W. C. Handy. Through the 1920s and early 1930s Still arranged music for dance bands, musicals, recordings, and radio shows. His talents for orchestrating and arranging music and for conducting served him throughout his career. After moving to Los Angeles in 1934, he worked as an occasional arranger and composer of music for Hollywood films.

It is as a composer concert music, opera, and ballet, however, that Still is chiefly remembered. His output was large, ranging from solo songs with piano to many orchestral works, ballets, and operas. His work was repeatedly pathbreaking. His *Afro-American* Symphony, premiered by the Rochester Philharmonic in 1931, was the first symphony by a black composer

to be played by a major orchestra. His *Lenox Avenue*, a series of "Choreographic Street Scenes" for announcer, orchestra, and chorus named after the "main street" of Harlem, was broadcast on CBS Radio in 1937.

Still's opera *Troubled Island* became the first opera by a black composer to be staged by a major company when it premiered at the New York City Opera in 1949. It had begun many years before as a collaboration with the Harlem Renaissance poet Langston Hughes; the libretto was completed by Still's second wife, Verna Arvey.

Chief Works: Orchestral music: five symphonies; numerous symphonic poems and orchestral suites ■ Eight operas and four ballets, including *Troubled Island* and *Lenox Avenue* ■ Chamber works for various ensembles ■ Songs for solo voice and various accompaniments, including the cycle *Songs of Separation* ■ Several choral works, including *And They Lynched Him on a Tree*

Encore: After *Afro-American* Symphony, movement 4, listen to movement 1; *Lenox Avenue*; and *Songs of Separation*, final two songs.

Image credit: Used by permission, William Grant Still Music, williamgrantstill.com, all rights reserved.

William Grant Still, *Afro-American* Symphony (1930)

Still's first symphony—he had already composed two symphonic poems and several suites of orchestral movements—proclaims loudly his black musical roots even in its title. But it also stakes his claim to participation in the European symphonic heritage.

On the one hand, it employs a fairly conventional Romantic orchestra, if one augmented with a few unexpected instruments—including a tenor banjo. Also in line with European tradition, it falls into four movements with mostly conventional tempos and forms. A fast first movement in a modified sonata form leads to a slow, melodic second movement and a quick, dancelike third—just as we might expect in symphonies from the nineteenth century. The music usually gives a clear sense of key and tonic; this is not atonal music in the manner of Schoenberg or Crawford.

On the other hand, the melodies, harmonies, and rhythms throughout the symphony have the flavor of jazz and blues. In rhythm, this involves particularly syncopation, or accented notes off the beat of the meter (see page 7). The melodies and harmonies, meanwhile, tend to be built not from the diatonic scale of European classical music (see page 23), but rather from the scale used by blues and jazz musicians. This blues scale differs at several points from the diatonic scale, as can be seen in the comparison of the two in the margin.

Throughout the symphony, Still shows one of his trademarks: a skillful use of orchestral colors achieved especially through alternating choirs of string, woodwind, and brass instruments.

Diatonic scale

Blues scale

Fourth Movement (Lento, con risoluzione)   The fourth and last movement of the symphony shows particularly clearly the impact of Still's mixing of European and African American styles. It is cast in something close to the traditional rondo form we might expect in a symphonic finale. But it takes a slow tempo and offers, as its main **A** theme, a blues-derived hymn to black dignity and freedom. This hymn appears three times in the movement: at the beginning, in yearning strings with low brass accompaniment; in the middle, with the melody given over to the cellos; and at the end, where it wells up into a mighty outcry for trumpets, trombones, and tuba.

The contrasting **B** theme is more lively; it is a version of a blues melody that dominates the first movement of the symphony. In the finale it is at first developed in several variations. It returns in an even quicker episode toward the end of the movement, where Still contrives to merge it with the gradual reappearance of **A**.

In one of his notebooks, Still titled this movement "Aspiration." He also associated each of his movements with verses from the black poet Paul Laurence Dunbar (1872–1906). The stirring verses connected to the finale are given in the margin in Listening Chart 25.

Still, *Afro-American* Symphony, fourth movement (Lento, con risoluzione)

Free rondo. 8 min., 32 sec.

5 | 36–40   80

36		**A** Long, hymnlike melody in strings, accompanied by low brasses and other winds
37	1:43	**B (Episode 1)** New blues theme presented by woodwinds, alternating with horns and trumpets
0:24	2:07	Strings take over blues theme, with more chromaticism, alternating with woodwinds.
0:54	2:37	Buildup to brief climax; subsides to leave only horns and woodwinds
1:26	3:09	Slowed-down version of blues theme; strings with bassoon, later flute
2:48	4:32	Cadence of string melody; woodwind transition back to **A**
38	4:59	**A** Hymn melody returns in cellos; harp is prominent; cut off by **B**.
39	6:16	**B (Episode 2) Vivace:** Blues theme returns in quick, staccato version; woodwinds.
0:16	6:32	Chromatic slides in strings and woodwinds
0:26	6:42	Hymn theme (**A**), varied, begins to reappear, in fast staccato version; timpani and brasses.
0:48	7:04	Chromatic slides in strings; quick blues theme in woodwinds
0:57	7:13	**A** theme emerges again; timpani and brasses.
1:16	7:32	Expectant harmonies
40	7:37	**A** Climactic, partial restatement of hymn theme in brasses; blues figures in strings

Be proud, my Race, in mind and
  soul;
Thy name is writ on Glory's scroll In
  characters of fire.
High 'mid the clouds of Fame's
  bright sky
Thy banner's blazoned folds now fly,
  And truth shall lift them higher.

Paul Laurence Dunbar

Aaron Copland

By the middle of the 1930s the reputation of another American modernist, Aaron Copland, was growing. He would soon rank as America's leading composer. Copland's music passed through several stylistic phases, including a period of avant-garde modernism early in his career. The chief influence on him at this time was Igor Stravinsky, and one of Copland's most impressive works is a strenuous set of twenty Variations for piano (1930), which reflects Stravinsky's dry rhythmic style and his "objective," anti-Romantic bent.

After this, Copland's music grew more traditional. Like Richard Strauss, Bartók, Still, and many others of the time, he held back from the most extreme versions of modernism and forged his own style using the modernist elements he needed. Again like Bartók and Still, Copland adopted a nationalist agenda. From the start he felt that as an American, he should write music that would speak to his fellow Americans. Copland reached out for American music of all kinds, regions, and ages.

He first turned to jazz, in orchestral pieces called *Music for the Theater* and *El salón México*. Later he incorporated cowboy songs in the ballets *Rodeo* and *Billy the Kid*, an old Shaker melody in *Appalachian Spring*, and square dancing in *The Tender Land*, an opera about growing up in the corn belt. Old hymns make an appearance in his song cycle *Twelve Poems of Emily Dickinson*. In this eclectic attitude we can perhaps again trace the influence of Stravinsky, who over his long career also tapped many musical sources, from Russian folk song to Bach, Tchaikovsky, and Schoenberg.

Aaron Copland, *Appalachian Spring* (1945)

5 | 41–44 | 81–84 | 40–42

The ballet *Appalachian Spring* was choreographed and danced by Martha Graham, a towering figure in American modern dance. She conceived of "a pioneer celebration in spring around a newly built farmhouse in the Pennsylvania hills," set in the early nineteenth century. Copland composed the ballet music, and later arranged from it a concert suite in six continuous sections. Our recording is conducted by the composer.

41   **Section 1**   The ballet begins with a very still, clear, static passage of a kind that Copland made very much his own. It seems to catch the spirit of a vast silent landscape at dawn, perhaps, or just before dawn. Solo instruments play meditative figures in counterpoint; an occasional solemn pulse is heard in the harp.

42   **Section 2**   Here "the bride-to-be and the young farmer husband enact the emotions, joyful and apprehensive, their new domestic partnership invited." The celebration of their new house starts with a lively square dance. Soon a slower melody—something like a hymn—rises up in counterpoint to the dance figures, in the wind instruments:

'Tis the gift to be simple, 'tis the gift
  to be free,
'Tis the gift to come down where
  you ought to be,
And when we find ourselves in the
  place just right
'Twill be in the valley of love and
  delight. . . .
When true simplicity is gained
To bow and to bend we shan't be
  ashamed,
Turn, turn will be our delight,
Till by turning, turning we come
  round right.

"Simple Gifts"

After a section of irregular rhythm, reminiscent of Stravinsky, the music dies down into a prayerful version of the hymn. We also hear little fragments of the dance.

Sections 3 and 4   The next two sections pick up the tempo: Section 3 evokes another whirling square dance, and section 4 is a danced sermon by a revivalist and his followers. Both sections include quiet statements of the hymn.

43   **Section 5**   The next dance is choreographed to a set of variations on a Shaker song, "Simple Gifts." (The beginning words of the song are given in the margin above.) The Shakers, a religious sect adhering to celibacy and common ownership of property, founded scattered communities from Massachusetts to Kentucky in the late eighteenth century.

 **LISTEN**

Appalachian Spring

SECTION 5	
0:00	Theme
0:33	Variation 1
1:02	Variation 2
1:51	Variation 3
2:34	Variation 4

CLARINET

p simply expressive

f *mf*

The four variations are extremely simple—little more, really, than playings of the tune or part of the tune by different instruments, in different keys, and in different tempos. Sometimes melodic phrases are heard in imitation.

Section 6   Finally, after some music that the program says is "like a prayer," the hymn and the landscape music return once again. We realize that Copland has ingeniously made one grow out of the other. The ballet concludes very quietly. Perhaps the housewarming celebrations have gone on all night, and we are now experiencing another clear gray dawn, a reminder of the many lonely dawns the pioneer couple will face together in the years to come.

Martha Graham (1894–1991) was one of the legendary group of women who created modern dance—with jazz, one of the great American art forms. She is shown here, with some pioneer women, dancing *Appalachian Spring,* which she commissioned. *Jerry Cooke/Corbis.*

Aaron Copland (1900–1990)

Aaron Copland was the son of Russian-Jewish immigrants living in Brooklyn. After a solid musical education at home, he went abroad to study in Paris. Like many other overseas students, Copland was fortunate to be able to work with a remarkable musician named Nadia Boulanger (1887–1979). For fifty years Boulanger was a revered teacher and mentor of composers, even though she gave up composition herself in deference to the talent of her sister Lili, also a composer, when Lili died tragically at the age of twenty-four. Boulanger encouraged Copland's interest in Stravinsky, whose avant-garde style influenced him greatly.

Back in America, Copland tirelessly promoted American music. He organized an important series of concerts (with another composer, Roger Sessions) to showcase new American scores, wrote articles and books, and formed the Composers' Alliance. In this period, around 1930, his music took on an avant-garde edge, but this direction would not last long.

Later in the 1930s Copland was attracted, like many artists and writers of the period, by leftist ideology and the idea that art should serve the people. From this time through the 1940s his style became more accessible and populist. His most well-known works, many drawing on American folk materials, stem from these years. During World War II he wrote *A Lincoln Portrait* and *Fanfare for the Common Man*, both patriotic works, and *Appalachian Spring*, a celebration of traditional American values.

After 1940 Copland headed up the composition faculty at the important summer school at Tanglewood, Massachusetts, in association with the Boston Symphony Orchestra, but his output as a composer decreased. Among his students was Leonard Bernstein. Devoid of the egoism characteristic of so many artists, Copland was one of the most beloved figures of modern American music.

Chief Works: For orchestra: three symphonies, *A Lincoln Portrait* (with a speaker), *El salón México* (incorporating Latin American jazz), a favorite Clarinet Concerto, written for jazzman Benny Goodman ▪ Film scores: *Of Mice and Men* and *Our Town* ▪ Operas: *The Second Hurricane* and *The Tender Land*; ballet scores *Billy the Kid*, *Rodeo*, *Appalachian Spring* ▪ For piano: Variations (Copland's outstanding modernist work; 1930), a sonata, Piano Fantasy (a fine late work; 1957) ▪ A song cycle to poems by Emily Dickinson

Encore: After *Appalachian Spring*, listen to *El salón México*, Clarinet Concerto, and *Fanfare for the Common Man*.

Image credit: National Portrait Gallery, Smithsonian Institution/ Art Resource, NY.

4 | The Rise of Film Music

At the beginning of this unit we cited some of the new technologies that developed alongside modernism in the arts. One of them, film or cinema, had an immense impact on all the arts of the twentieth century. Almost from its beginnings it offered an exciting new arena for musical composition—comparable, we might say, to the beginnings of public concerts in the eighteenth century (see page 154), but reaching an incomparably larger audience. Film music has come in a bewildering variety of styles. Avant-garde modernism, minimalism, jazz, pop music, rock, and rap have all found a place on soundtracks. Most prevalent of all, however, have been soundtracks employing the symphony orchestra in styles reminiscent of late Romanticism.

This connection was natural, given the Romantics' interest both in opera and in program music. It began with the earliest history of cinema—when some late Romantic styles were still new. In the era of silent film (especially the 1910s and 1920s), live musicians were hired by theaters to provide music to accompany films as they were projected. Pianists or organists would improvise, responding moment by moment to the images on-screen; but their improvisations were often based on published catalogues of favorite themes from Romantic symphonies and operas. In matching these themes to the situations on-screen, the musicians produced something akin to Wagner's leitmotiv technique (see page 268), and indeed some of the melodies in their catalogues were drawn from Wagner's operas.

When new technologies in the late 1920s allowed for soundtracks to be recorded on the filmstrip itself, this leitmotivic procedure evolved. Now composers wrote more-or-less-continuous scores for full orchestra, employing leitmotivs synchronized precisely to the filmed action. An early monument to this new relation of music and film is the horror classic *King Kong* of 1933, with a soundtrack by the most important of early Hollywood composers, the Viennese émigré Max Steiner. This leitmotivic style has remained prominent in cinema composition ever since. (Many films you might see at the movie theater today use it in some form, but it is particularly apparent in recent mythic blockbusters such as the *Lord of the Rings* or *Harry Potter* series.)

Composers for Film

Composers who lavish attention on film music tend not to turn up in textbooks such as this one, yet they represent an important strain of twentieth-century orchestral composition. Along with Max Steiner, who composed the score for *Gone with the Wind* in addition to *King Kong,* we might point to the Italian Nino Rota, who collaborated with Federico Fellini on many films and with Francis Ford Coppola on *The Godfather;* to Tōru Takemitsu, collaborator with the giant of Japanese cinema, Akira Kurosawa (*Ran*); and to John Williams, whose scores for the *Star Wars* films have been fashioned into a regular repertory piece for pops orchestras across the United States.

A composer who devoted himself almost exclusively to music for film, radio, and television is Bernard Herrmann (1911–1975). His most famous scores came in collaboration with Alfred Hitchcock, in films such as *Vertigo* (1958) and *Psycho* (1960). The screeching violins in the shower-murder scene from *Psycho* are an icon of horror-movie music, repeated and caricatured everywhere from cell phone ringtones to *The Simpsons*.

Meanwhile, many twentieth-century concert or classical composers have turned occasionally to film as a creative outlet. We have already seen that William Grant Still composed and arranged film music after he moved to Los Angeles. Aaron Copland and his student Leonard Bernstein (see page 399) also wrote soundtracks. Copland's film music, for example *Our Town* (1940), strongly evokes the American heartland; in this it is related to his ballet *Appalachian Spring*. Bernstein brought a touch of avant-garde modernism to his soundtrack for *On the Waterfront* (1954).

A more recent composer of concert music who has come to particular prominence for his film music is the Chinese-born Tan Dun (b. 1957). His score for *Crouching Tiger, Hidden Dragon* (2000) adroitly mixes instruments from the Western orchestra with those from the orchestra of Beijing opera (see page 297), in which Tan himself performed early in his career. These mixed forces play music styled after traditional Chinese melodies.

Our example of early film music comes from the Soviet Union, where cinema thrived from the 1920s on. Both of the USSR's early leaders, Vladimir Lenin and Joseph Stalin, recognized the power of film as a mass medium of socialist propaganda, so cinema was supported by the Soviet state. The two leading concert composers of the USSR, Sergei Prokofiev and Dmitri Shostakovich, devoted much energy to the new medium. Shostakovich, in fact, had started his career as a silent-film pianist, while Prokofiev fell into a rewarding collaboration with the greatest of Soviet filmmakers, Sergei Eisenstein (1898–1948).

Sergei Prokofiev, *Alexander Nevsky* Cantata (1938)

6 | 1–2   85–86

Sergei Eisenstein's *Alexander Nevsky* ranks among the most monumental and innovative of early sound films. It is also propaganda. The title names a Russian hero from the thirteenth century who, having already defeated marauding Vikings, was called upon to unite Russian forces against invading Germans. The film was produced at a moment when tensions between Germany and the Soviet Union were on the rise. In case its allegory was not clear, the last words of the film are Nevsky's proclamation, "He who comes to Russia with a sword, shall die by the sword."

A year after *Alexander Nevsky* was made, Prokofiev refashioned his soundtrack music as a cantata so that it could be performed in concert. Our excerpts (which stay especially close to the original soundtrack) come from the beginning of the climactic scene in the film, when the Russians and the Germans meet in battle on the frozen surface of Lake Chudskoe. The reenactment is the most astonishing battle scene anywhere in early cinema. At its end the Germans, fleeing in disarray, crash through the ice and perish, to harrowing music for percussion only—which Prokofiev omitted, however, from his cantata.

From the music we get a series of vivid sound-pictures of the action, interspersed with moments when the orchestra stops entirely in favor of the noise of battle itself. Prokofiev begins with the frozen lake and apprehensive Russians watching in silence for the German army (compare the frigid scene with the still morning landscape of Copland's *Appalachian Spring*). Sustained, minor-mode string chords, ominous drumrolls, a rising tremolo melody in the cellos, and strange, scraping noises from the violas set the shivering tone.

The mood is broken by a battle call in the distance—the signal for the Germans to advance; Prokofiev specifies a muted trombone, played backstage. The last six notes of this call will be heard again and again in the brass, sometimes in long note values and sometimes in quicker ones, as the Germans move forward. The energy picks up with the introduction of steady eighth notes in the strings and percussion, while the brass—tuba and horns, later trumpets and trombones also—present the call motive and alternate it with another, ominous chromatic motive.

Gradually the dynamics swell and the texture grows. A chorus is heard singing over and over a homophonic phrase; it is the Germans, intoning a liturgical hymn associated with their cruelty earlier in the film. At the climax, finally, the armies meet. Prokofiev's music abruptly breaks off, and only the noise of battle is heard.

After more than three minutes of cinematic sword-to-sword combat, the Russian trick is revealed: They have lured the Germans onto the lake while keeping much of their force in reserve on the flanks. Now Nevsky gives the order for the flanks to close in ("For Russia! For Russia!"). Prokofiev's music strikes up again, with none of the threatening German sounds from before but now with several new, rousing melodies of victory, alternating helter-skelter in violins, brasses, and other instruments.

		FIRST EXCERPT
1	0:00	The frozen lake; the Russians wait.
	1:19	The German battle call: muted, offstage trombone
	1:45	Staccato eighth notes in strings, drum: rising activity
	1:53	Tuba and saxophones state battle call, overlapping.
	2:14	Trumpet and tuba state three-note threat motive; then descending chromatic melody for trumpet and violins.
	2:55	German chant
	3:58	Climactic statements of battle call; brass and timpani
	4:08	The armies meet.
		SECOND EXCERPT
2	0:00	The Russians close in.

Biography

Sergei Prokofiev (1891–1953)

Sergei Prokofiev was a child prodigy who became a concert pianist, a conductor, and an enormously versatile, productive, and popular composer.

Born in present-day Ukraine, he spent many years at the St. Petersburg Conservatory (like Debussy and Ravel in Paris). His early reputation was as a radical, and one ambitious work was written under the direct influence of Stravinsky's *The Rite of Spring*. But he made an about-face a year later with his *Classical Symphony*, a gentle parody of a Haydn symphony. Easy to hear in Prokofiev's music is a sound that's hard to describe—within a clear ("Haydnish") tonal framework, the use of very simple chords placed in an unexpected way. The *Classical Symphony* was a forerunner of Neoclassicism, which Stravinsky also embraced after World War I, when both Russian composers lived in Paris (keeping their distance from each other).

Prokofiev moved away from modernist extremes and toward clear tonality, tunefulness, and the use of Russian folk themes. But the good-humored parody of *Classical Symphony* turned into a sharper satirical style that could become positively grotesque in scherzos—another Prokofiev characteristic ("scherzo," remember, means joke).

By the 1930s Prokofiev was a recognized star worldwide, but his thoughts turned back to his Soviet homeland, which had been tempting him with many commissions. He returned to live in Russia in 1936, to much acclaim. He must have known that his freedom of expression would be limited, but he could not have anticipated how much. Even pieces he wrote to exalt Stalin and the Soviet Union ran into trouble, increasingly so with the approach of World War II. Time and again the ever-fluent Prokofiev rewrote his works, but only too often they were never approved or performed. Twelve years after his welcome back to Russia, his music was publicly denounced by a Soviet arts commissar and performances were banned.

After years of ill health, Prokofiev died on the same day as Stalin—within the hour. His impressive opera based on Tolstoy's *War and Peace*, begun with official support in 1941, was still in limbo at his death.

A slight but much-loved work by Prokofiev is *Peter and the Wolf*, a narrated children's story with orchestral interludes; each of the characters is represented by his or her own instrument and leitmotiv. The hero, needless to say, is a sturdy little Russian boy.

Chief Works: Operas *The Love of Three Oranges* and *War and Peace* ▪ Ballet scores *Romeo and Juliet* and *Cinderella* ▪ Film scores for *Alexander Nevsky, Lieutenant Kije,* and others ▪ Seven symphonies, including the *Classical Symphony;* piano sonatas and concertos; a beautiful violin concerto (No. 2) ▪ *Peter and the Wolf* for children (of all ages)

Encore: Listen to *Lieutenant Kije* and *Classical Symphony.*

Image credit: Lebrecht/The Image Works.

MUSIC AND TOTALITARIANISM

European composers of the early twentieth century, like everyone else, found their lives profoundly affected by the economic, political, and military upheavals of the time. Besides the sheer threat of annihilation in a time of war, other, less dramatic difficulties loomed. Many institutions that composers' careers depended on—orchestras, opera companies, and the like—disappeared or fell into disarray. Some were victims of changing governments with new priorities. Others did not survive staggering inflation in parts of Europe in the 1920s, worldwide depression in the 1930s, or war in the 1940s.

Modernist composers in the avant-garde in particular faced threats that were not only physical and social but also *ideological*—that is, threats made not on their lives or livelihoods but on their ideas, including musical ideas. This was most evident in (though not restricted to) the two most powerful repressive totalitarian regimes of the era. In Nazi Germany and Stalin's Soviet Union, radical modernism in most of its guises was rejected and banned.

In each country the rationale for repression was the same distorted outgrowth of nineteenth-century nationalism: Art ought to speak straightforwardly to the national "folk" and give voice to its aspirations and history. This was foreign to modernist art's emphasis on originality and individualism, its formal intricacies, and its experimentation—its elitism, as the culture czars in Russia and Germany saw it. For Nazis and Stalinists alike, modernist art had no reason to exist.

Nazi Germany

Hitler's regime promoted music of the great German masters; Beethoven and Wagner were special favorites. But it banned explicitly modernist music, supporting instead the latter-day Romanticism of the aging Richard Strauss, for example (see page 335). Meanwhile Jewish composers and other musicians faced extermination. Those who could fled to countries all over the world, many of them to the United States. Arnold Schoenberg is the best known of these refugees (see page 325), but there were many others, including Kurt Weill, composer of "Mack the Knife," who established a second career on Broadway. Béla Bartók, who was not Jewish but also decided to emigrate when his native Hungary finally joined with Hitler, had a harder time (see page 340).

The Soviet Union

Perhaps the most famous victim of ideological muzzling was one of Russia's greatest composers, Dmitri Shostakovich (1906–1975; Shos-ta-kó-vich). Growing up under Communism, he originally followed the dictates of

German invaders and Russians square off in the battle on ice from Eisenstein's *Alexander Nevsky*—a spectacular sequence that set a high standard for later cinematic war scenes. *Bettmann/CORBIS.*

the state without question. Shostakovich was certainly no radical modernist of the Schoenberg sort; but his music did show novel tendencies, including strongly dissonant harmonies. A darling of the regime in the early 1930s, he nevertheless walked a dangerous path.

With his opera *Lady Macbeth of the Mtsensky Region* of 1934, when he was twenty-eight, he went over the edge. Subject matter and music were equally shocking. The worldwide clamorous success of this work brought Stalin himself to see it. Two days later the official Communist Party newspaper condemned the work and issued a scarcely veiled threat to the composer: "The power of good music to affect the masses has been sacrificed to a petty-bourgeois, formalist attempt to create originality through cheap clowning. It is a game of clever ingenuity *that may end very badly.*"

In fact, Shostakovich was back in favor a year afterward. But his troubles were not over; he was condemned again ten years later—only to be rehabilitated once more when Stalin died. To what extent Shostakovich accommodated the regime, or criticized it by means of half-secret musical signals in his later compositions—signals recognized by his audiences—is a fascinating question still debated.

Dmitri Shostakovich (left), on one of his rare trips to the West (1962). Looming over him is the Communist Party functionary who came along. *Bettmann/CORBIS.*

GOALS FOR REVIEW

▶ to hear the consolidation of modernist styles in works of the 1930s by Maurice Ravel and Béla Bartók

▶ to discern several distinct varieties of American modernism in instrumental works by Ruth Crawford, William Grant Still, and Aaron Copland

▶ to survey the development of film music and listen to an early example by Sergei Prokofiev

macmillanhighered.com/listen8e
Interactive Listening Charts 22–26
Listening Quiz for Chapter 22
Reading Quiz for Chapter 22

The Late Twentieth Century

Only twenty-one years, from 1918 to 1939, separated the two cataclysmic wars of the twentieth century. It was an uneasy period. The devastation of World War I had stunned artists as well as everybody else, and the freewheeling, avant-garde experimentation that had marked the prewar period now played a smaller role. It gave way to the trends we examined in Chapter 22: a turn back to more accessible music, including the use of popular styles, and attempts to reestablish solid standards and norms. Even Schoenberg's serialism of the 1920s (see page 327) can be seen in this light as a kind of stylistic consolidation.

These efforts were undercut by a new round of devastating events. First came the economic depression, long and worldwide, that began in the late 1920s. Then, in the 1930s, the ominous rise of Hitler and the unbelievable (and, by many, disbelieved) tyranny of Stalin led to a second world war. With the Japanese attack on Pearl Harbor at the end of 1941, the United States was thrown into this war to an extent that made our involvement in World War I seem minor. The occupation of France, the siege of Leningrad, the bombings of London, Dresden, and Tokyo, the mass murders in the concentration camps, and the detonation of atom bombs over Hiroshima and Nagasaki—these events were virtually impossible for human beings (including artists) to take in. History seemed to be showing that all human conceptions of the world were inadequate.

In music, these events and uncertainties helped to prompt a new phase of experimental modernism in the 1950s and 1960s. In some respects this phase was even more radical and searching than the avant-garde before World War I. Just as with that earlier avant-garde, however, the challenge of new ideas stimulated a consolidating, consoling reaction. By the 1970s yet another set of styles had begun to appear, turning away from the most extreme implications of the second phase of radical modernism. Today the avant-garde of the 1950s is a somewhat distant memory, and concert music composition is dominated by the styles that arose in reaction to it. In this chapter we sample both of these stylistic waves.

1 | The Postwar Avant-Garde

Experiment and innovation reemerged as the driving forces in music during the third quarter of the twentieth century. It was a fascinating phase—and no less so because two of its main tendencies seem almost contradictory.

First of all, highly intellectual constructive tendencies came to the fore, inspired by Schoenberg's serialism but going far beyond it. There were

Of all the conflicts in the war-ridden twentieth century, World War II was the most terrible. Here the crew of an aircraft carrier in the Pacific takes time out for a jazz concert. *Bettmann/CORBIS*.

even efforts to "serialize" rhythm, dynamics, and timbre—that is, to set up predetermined series of note durations or tone colors or dynamic levels and compose with them in a fixed order. Never before had such complex mathematical theories been advanced to compose and explain music.

Meanwhile, other composers moved in the opposite direction, relinquishing control over some elements of musical construction and leaving them to chance. (We have already discussed an early anticipation of this move, *The Unanswered Question* by the ever-original Ives.) Some of these same composers also worked toward an extreme simplification of musical materials, offering a stark alternative to the cerebral complexities of post–World War II "total serialism."

It may seem strange to find composers who followed such different paths grouped together under the same general rubric of avant-garde modernism. However, both groups, the complex constructivists and the chance composers, pursued the same goal: They all wanted to question the most fundamental premises that had guided music composition before them. Debussy might have blurred the identity of melodic themes, Stravinsky might have undermined the regularity of musical meter, and Schoenberg might have dispensed altogether with tonality. But mainstream modernism after 1945 questioned every one of these features of the musical tradition at once and others as well—to the point of even questioning the composer's role in structuring a work at all.

New Sound Materials

In this light another general tendency of composers after World War II is not at all surprising: their demand for new sound materials. The ordinary orchestra, even as expanded by Debussy, Stravinsky, and others, now struck them as stiff and antiquated. They explored new sonorities—noises, unexpected new sounds squeezed out of old instruments, and an infinite range of musical materials produced not by instruments at all, but by electronics.

It began with composers making new demands on the standard sources of music. Singers were instructed to lace their singing with hisses, grunts, clicks, and other "nonmusical" noises. Pianists had to stand up, lean over the piano, and pluck the strings or hit them with mallets. Using a special kind of breath pressure, clarinetists learned to play chords called *multiphonics*—weird-sounding chords by conventional standards but fascinating to those attuned to the new sound universe.

Western orchestras and chamber music groups had always been weak in percussion, as compared to their counterparts in many non-Western cultures and to jazz. But in the postwar era marimbas, xylophones, gongs, bells, and cymbals of many kinds—percussion instruments that had been used only occasionally in the classical music of earlier times—became standard.

However, the truly exciting prospect for new sonorities in music emerged out of technology developed during the war: the production of music by electronic means.

Electronic Music

Recording equipment can *reproduce* sounds of any sort—music, speech, and all the sounds and noises of life. Electronic sound generators can do something else: They can *generate* sounds from scratch—in principle, any sounds that can be imagined, or calculated using formulas derived from the science of acoustics.

A technological breakthrough during World War II, the development of magnetic tape, made the storing and handling of sound much easier than before. It also opened up exciting possibilities for modifying it by manipulating the tape: making tape loops, changing speed, cutting and splicing, and so on. Across the second half of the twentieth century, we can discern three stages in the evolution of electronic music, each of them defined by new technological possibilities:

• *Musique concrète* Shortly after World War II composers began incorporating the sounds of life into their compositions. This they called "concrete" music because it used actual sound, as contrasted with the "abstract" products of electronic sound generators. Sounds (traffic street noise was a favorite) were recorded on tape, painstakingly manipulated, and then (usually) put on phonograph discs.

Musique concrète lives on, in a sense, in **sampling**, now that technology has made it easy for anything that is recorded—traffic noise, commercial records, special effects—to be put under keyboard control for easy combination.

> "I need an entirely new medium of expression: a sound-producing machine (not a sound-reproducing one)."
>
> *Edgard Varèse, 1939*

Electronic music, then and now: Milton Babbitt, avant-gardist of the 1950s, needed a room full of equipment to create his works; for Tod Machover, a composer at the forefront of music/technology mixes today, a desktop and keyboard might suffice. Top: *William Gedney Photographs and Writings, Duke University David M. Rubenstein Rare Book & Manuscript Library, http://library.duke.edu/digitalcollections/gedney/.* Bottom: *Boston Globe via Getty Images.*

• *Synthesizers* In the first years after World War II, electronic sound generation was unbelievably clumsy, requiring whole rooms full of radio equipment and complicated machinery to carry out tape manipulations—see the photograph above. Only after the advent of transistors (silicon chips were still in the future) could viable equipment be envisaged. In the 1960s various **synthesizers** appeared, designed specifically for music, with arrays of sound-producing modules connected by "patch cords" to create complex sounds.

At first synthesizers worked one note at a time. Still, they allowed many composers to produce taped music and also to combine music on tape with performed live music. It was still difficult to produce customized sound in real time.

• *Computer music* The amazing evolution of personal computers over the last thirty-five years has allowed for an equally amazing evolution in music. Today electronic music can be produced on a laptop, using sequencer software to record, edit, and reproduce digital sounds in patterns and sequences at will. Synthesizers can interact via computer with live musicians as they perform to produce today's cutting-edge interactive computer music.

On the Boundaries of Time

Sonority is one of two areas in which avant-garde music in its post–World War II phase made its greatest breakthroughs. The other area was time and rhythm.

To understand one aspect of this development, let us try to contrast two radically different pieces of music. One is a tiny piece by Schoenberg's student and friend Anton Webern (see page 327), the fourth of his Five Orchestral Pieces of 1913.

Anton Webern (1883–1945), Five Orchestral Pieces (1913)

The whole piece—it is all of six measures long—can be shown on one line of music:

Listen to it several times: The music feels exceptionally concentrated because the relationship between the notes is so strained by the "atomized" orchestration and the complex network of pitches and rhythms. Each note somehow becomes a separate little source of tremendous energy. This might be described as a *very short* time segment of *very high* intensity.

Contrast Webern's tiny orchestral piece with *In C*, a famous avant-garde work from the 1960s by the American composer Terry Riley. *In C* lasts for about forty-five minutes. During this time the instruments freely repeat over and over again a set of fifty-three tiny melodic figures that spell out only three harmonies—three harmonies drawn out over the music's total span. The pitches and rhythms are simple, indeed deliberately soothing. This might be described as a *very long* time segment of *very low* intensity.

With both Webern and Riley, we measure time in the same units: minutes and seconds. Yet the *feeling* of time is very different in the two. It is like the difference between one minute at the end of a tied basketball game and one minute in the middle of an all-night truck run across South Dakota.

Such contrasting perceptions of time now came to be widely explored by musicians of the avant-garde. Webern's intense experience of time made him a major influence in the postwar years, even though he died at the end of World War II. Riley's *In C* and works like it became prophetic of a later development in music which gathered force in the 1970s and 1980s, *minimalism* (see page 369).

Chance Music

In playing his motives, the instrumentalists in Riley's *In C* interact with each other in ways largely unspecified by the composer. One might linger over a particular motive, repeating it while another moves on to other motives. *In C* thus exemplifies the **chance music** we mentioned earlier. This term covers a great variety of music in which certain elements specified by the composer in more conventional music are left to chance. Another element of *In C* that is left up to the performer is its instrumentation—who plays what. Riley says only that it can be played by "any number of any kind of instruments."

In an extreme case, a chance composer might work out a way of throwing dice so as to determine which instruments, which pitches, and so on were to be used. In a less extreme case, a performer getting to a certain place in a piece would be told to play anything at all, so long as it was (for example) loud and fast. Strictly speaking, what would be heard would be determined by chance, but the composer could count on a type of controlled chaos for a limited span of time, a span situated between two passages of fully written-out music.

Whereas earlier modernists had questioned traditional assumptions about melody, dissonance, and meter, chance composers questioned even more basic assumptions about musical time. The musical forms we have studied throughout this book tend to mark off time as a clear linear progress and even make it goal-directed: Think of the move from development to recapitulation in a Beethoven sonata form. Is time always (chance composers would ask: is it *ever*) actually experienced in this way? Even *In C* is felt to be goal-directed in a certain sense, for as the snippets in the margin on page 362 show, the pitches get a little higher and the rhythmic activity intensifies as the piece proceeds.

But must music convey such an experience? Could it instead mark time as a random sequence of events, or even as timeless, like the suspended consciousness we experience in certain kinds of meditation? Such questions, and a passive sense of time that cuts against our goal-directed culture, lie at the root of chance music.

2 | The New Generation

After World War II, promising composers seemed to appear like magic from almost every corner of the globe. Among the leaders from France, Germany, and Italy were Olivier Messiaen (1908–1994), Pierre Boulez (b. 1925), Karlheinz Stockhausen (1928–2007), and Luciano Berio (1925–2003). They were joined by the Poles Witold Lutosławski (1913–1994) and Krzysztof Penderecki (b. 1933), the Hungarian György Ligeti (1923–2006), the Greek Iannis Xenakis (1922–2001), the Americans Milton Babbitt (1916–2011), John Cage (1912–1992), and Elliott Carter (1908–2012), and the Japanese Tōru Takemitsu (1930–1996).

The history of music in the second half of the twentieth century is saturated with the works of these composers. Their music resonates with the anxiety and turmoil of the era, celebrating its triumphs and mourning its tragedies; it would be impossible to maintain that the music of Boulez, Ligeti, and Takemitsu is any less varied, intense, moving, or magnificent than that of any other like period of music history. Yet as the twenty-first century gets under way, by and large the music of these composers has not found its way into the experience of most ordinary listeners. There are many reasons for this, both sociological and aesthetic, which we cannot take up here. As we have seen, modernism's first phase—the phase just before World War I—produced works that now count as "classics": Berg's *Wozzeck*, a fixture in the opera house; Bartók's six string quartets, played by every professional string quartet; and Stravinsky's *The Rite of Spring*, an all-time favorite on recordings. For acknowledged masterpieces written after World War II, however—such as Boulez's song cycle *Le Marteau sans maître* (The Hammer without a Master) or Berio's *Sinfonia*—similar acceptance has been slow in coming.

Edgard Varèse (1883–1965)

All of the composers listed were born in the twentieth century, and most of them after World War I. Edgard Varèse, the first composer we take up, was a generation older—and a fascinating case of a visionary who bridged both avant-garde phases of musical modernism. Though he started his career in Paris and Berlin before World War I, most of his early scores were destroyed in a fire. One of them had caused a scandal at its 1911 premiere. He emigrated to America in 1915, and it was here that he truly found his voice (late in life, like Haydn).

The music Varèse wrote in the 1920s was some of the most radical anywhere at that time. He developed an approach to rhythm and sonority that surpassed anything the other early avant-garde composers had attempted. He thought not so much of music in a conventional sense as of "organized sound" and its "liberation" from scales and the like. *Hyperprism* is scored for seven wind instruments and as many percussion, and *Ionisation* is for percussion alone—thirteen players on forty-five instruments, including a police siren. The manipulation of what others considered "noise" into coherent musical patterns was a heady forecast of things to come after World War II.

Indeed, it was after World War II that this veteran of many a modernist battle came into his own. About 1930, Varèse had tried unsuccessfully to persuade the Bell Telephone Company to set up a research center for electrically produced music. Now the introduction of electronic composing equipment was a vindication of his vision. His *Déserts* (1950–54), for instruments and tape, was one of the most ambitious early essays in electronic music. And his *Poème électronique*—entirely electronic, with only tape and no live performers—is recognized as one of the masterpieces of the genre.

Edgard Varèse, composer of "noise." © *Condé Nast Archive/Corbis.*

Edgard Varèse, *Poème électronique* (1958)

6|4   88

Varèse's *Poème électronique* was just one part of an extraordinary multimedia experience. The piece was written for an exhibit sponsored by the Philips Radio Corporation at the 1958 Brussels World's Fair. The exhibit was housed in a pavilion designed by the famous modernist architect Le Corbusier (1887–1965). "Corbu," as he was called, also designed a sequence of colored lights and images to be projected while Varèse's three-track tape was played from 425 speakers. The exhibit offers a brilliant example of modernist artists of various kinds working in tandem.

As visitors entered the pavilion and walked around, the music came at them from various angles. Likewise, as they kept turning corners, they kept seeing different parts of the superb building and of the light show. All this seems tame to us today, but it was arresting, even stunning, at the time.

There was obviously an element of chance in the way one got to experience *Poème électronique*—an element that the composer of course encouraged. John Cage (see page 367) would have concurred enthusiastically. So it is quite in Varèse's spirit for us to take a quick tour of the pavilion, as it were, and happen to hear just the last few minutes of this music, rather than the entire work.

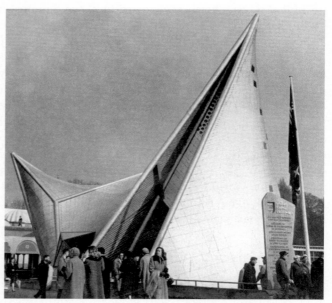

Le Corbusier's pavilion. *The Granger Collection.*

As we stroll within earshot of *Poème électronique*, an electronic crash is followed by various seemingly random rustles. Then a brilliant section displays a variety of electronic effects: low sliding groans, rattles, bell-like noises, and watery sounds. Suddenly something human joins these space-age sounds—a short vocal hum. This tells us that Varèse makes use of *musique concrète* in *Poème:* that is, he uses prerecorded sounds from real life, such as humming, singing, bells, and train noises, as well as material that is generated electronically from scratch.

The rhythm has been highly irregular. Now it slows down, and a sustained chord appears quietly, grows almost unbearably loud, and then fades. Varèse introduces isolated pitches that appear to be arbitrary, though in fact they merge into another sustained chord. We hear drum rhythms, too, and a *musique concrète* snare drum (remember Varèse's affection for percussion instruments in his earlier compositions).

Humanity seems to reassert itself in the form of a soprano solo—but this is manipulated electronically so as to shriek its way out of hearing in the high register. Sharp punctuations decimate the men's voices that follow. A mournful three-note motive (also heard earlier in *Poème*) is played twice with the pitches sliding into one another. Then a momentous-sounding siren moves up, falters, and moves up again until it becomes a violent noise, which ceases abruptly and mechanically.

So ends the *Poème électronique:* for some, on a strange note of unspecified disquiet.

György Ligeti (1923–2006)

György Ligeti studied at the Budapest Academy of Music and as a young man was appointed professor there. Unable to pursue his unique sound visions under the Communist restrictions prevailing in Hungary, he left for the West in 1956. Ligeti was past thirty before his advanced music became known.

Ligeti exemplifies both the search for new sonorities that occupied the postwar avant-garde and their new attitudes toward time. Some of his music uses no clear pitches or chords; or, more accurately, while he may start with pitches and chords, he soon adds so many more pitches that all sense of consonance, dissonance, and even the quality of pitch itself is lost. What remain are "sound complexes" that slowly change with time, blocks of sound that can be experienced better than they can be described.

Violet, Black, Orange, Yellow on White and Red, by the American painter Mark Rothko (1903–1970). The overwhelming yet placid sheets of color merging into one another recall the musical technique in compositions such as Ligeti's *Lux aeterna. Mark Rothko,* Untitled (Violet, Black, Orange, Yellow on White and Red), *1949, Oil on canvas, 81 1/2 × 66 inches (207 × 167.6 cm), Solomon R. Guggenheim Museum, New York, Gift, Elaine and Werner Dannheisser and The Dannheisser Foundation, 78.2461. © 1998 Kath Rothko Prizel & Christopher Rothko/Artists Rights Society (ARS) New York.*

In the time dimension, there is no discernible meter or distinct rhythm. Rather, there is a sense of gradual, almost glacial surging of the sound complexes, followed by a sense of receding—all the while revealing diverse new tone colors.

György Ligeti, *Lux aeterna* (1966)

6 | 5–8 | 89

Ligeti's *Lux aeterna* is written for sixteen solo singers and chorus; often they sing chords that include all twelve pitches of the chromatic scale. We need a new vocabulary even to talk about music such as this, and some new diagrams—our pitch-time graph on page 24, which indicated melodies by lines, doesn't work for Ligeti's sound complexes. To represent them and show how they develop over time, we can use nonmusical figures:

Lux aeterna luceat eis, Domine, cum sanctis tuis in aeternum, quia pius es. . . .

May everlasting radiance shine upon them, O Lord, with thy saints in eternity: for you are merciful. . . .

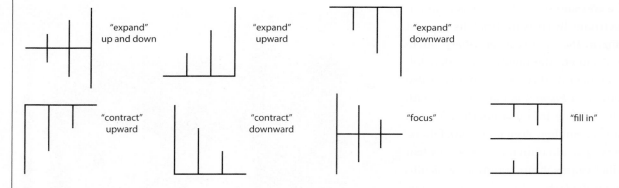

"expand" up and down

"expand" upward

"expand" downward

"contract" upward

"contract" downward

"focus"

"fill in"

Lux aeterna starts with a single pitch, which Ligeti "expands" both upward and downward by slowly adding a dense mix of pitches above and below it. At other times he starts with a single pitch and expands it upward (adding mainly higher pitches) or downward (adding lower ones). Starting with a full-range sound, Ligeti can "contract" it: either downward (by removing notes till only a single low pitch remains), or upward, or to some pitch in the middle—an effect that can be called "focusing," by analogy to a camera lens.

Once we have accustomed our ears to the astonishing rich sonorities that are revealed by the slow ebbing and flowing of Ligeti's sound complexes, we can appreciate that the musical form of *Lux aeterna* is simplicity itself. Four slow sound surges make up the piece (see the separate tracks in Listening Chart 27). The first, for women, expands out to a big sound complex and then fouses *upward* to a high single pitch in octaves. It is balanced by the second surge, for men, and the fourth, for men and women, both of which expand and then focus *downward*. In between comes the climax of the piece, the explosion of men's and women's voices that begins the third surge.

György Ligeti. *Photograph by Peter Anderson. All rights Reserved. Used by permissions of European American Music Distributors Company, sole U.S. and Canadian agent for Schott Music GbmH & Co. KG, copyright owner.*

The words of *Lux aeterna* are taken from the Requiem Mass, but they can scarcely be heard and understood; the piece is a study in sheer vocal sonority. Ligeti wrote other sound-complex pieces employing other forces, such as *Atmosphères* for full orchestra. *Lux aeterna* is his most famous work, thanks to its use in the 1968 Stanley Kubrick film classic *2001: A Space Odyssey*.

Ligeti, *Lux aeterna*

7 min., 54 sec.

6 | 5–8   89

5	0:00	WOMEN'S VOICES	Single pitch, high voices (*Lu*) The sound expands, *up and down*.	
	1:39		A high pitch is added softly: SOPRANO.	
	2:02		The sound contracts *upward*, ending in . . .	
	2:22		a single pitch (octave).	
6	2:28	MEN'S VOICES	The high pitch stops, replaced by a chord (*Domine*) in the high men's voices.	
0:08	2:36		The sound expands *downward*.	
0:36	3:04		More lower voices; higher men's voices drop out; the sound slowly "focuses" to . . .	
1:30	3:58		a held, dissonant chord.	
7	4:03	MEN AND WOMEN	Complex sound, **f** (with a clear high, low, middle)	
			The sound contracts *downward* to a lengthy focus,	
1:30	5:33		ultimately to a single pitch.	
8	5:45		Complex sound — low voices (*Domine*) Sound expands, *up*.	
0:28	6:13		A high note is added: SOPRANO.	
0:58	6:43		The high note is dropped, replaced by a very low note: BASS. Sound contracts *downward* to . . .	
1:45	7:30		a two-note dissonant chord.	

John Cage (1912–1992)

The most consistent radical figure of postwar music was John Cage, the father of chance music. (Charles Ives has to count as the grandfather.) He studied with Schoenberg, among others—when Schoenberg was teaching in California, Cage's home state—and early developed an almost bewildering variety of interests. Cage exhibited specially prepared prints, toured as music director of avant-garde dancer Merce Cunningham's dance company, and was a recognized mycologist (mushroom authority). In the 1950s, his study of Zen Buddhism led him to a fresh attitude toward music, time, and indeed all experience.

Cage posed questions that challenge all the assumptions on which traditional music rests. Why should music be different from the sounds of life? Why compose with "musical" sounds, rather than noises? Why work out music according to melodies, climaxes, twelve-tone series, or anything else that gives the impression of one thing following another in a purposeful order? Why not leave it to chance? The basic message that Cage conveyed is that we should open our ears to every possible kind of sound and every possible sound conjunction. In this, too, he was following in the footsteps of Ives.

John Cage. © *Jack Vartoogian/ FrontRowPhotos.*

John Cage, *4' 33"* (1952)

Often, indeed, the actual sounds Cage produced were less crucial than the "statement" he was making about sound by means of his music. This is the case with *4' 33"*, perhaps his most celebrated work (or statement). Any number of players can perform it. They sit silently on the stage for 4 minutes and 33 seconds.

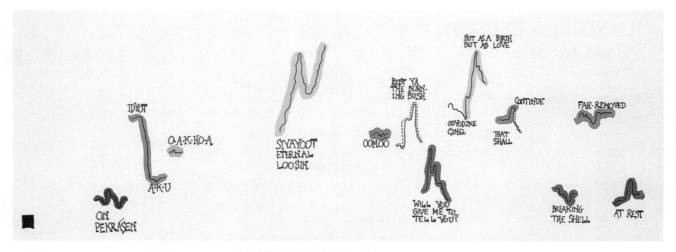

Score for a multilingual solo vocal work by John Cage, *Aria* (1958). The lines represent general melodic contours, the colors different styles of vocal delivery; both are left to be specified by the performer, not the composer. Much is left to the singer's imagination! *John Cage, Aria by John Cage. Copyright © 1960, renewed 1988 by Henmar Press, Inc. Used by permission C.F. Peters Corporation. All rights reserved.*

Is this just an exasperating hoax? What Cage is saying is that silence is an entity, too, as well as sound. When did you last really concentrate on silence? (Try it.) In fact, *4' 33"* consists not of silence but of little bits of random audience noise, sounds from outside the hall, perhaps the thump of the irate listener's heartbeat. And how does the experience of concentrating on near silence for exactly 4 minutes and 33 seconds compare with concentrating for exactly three minutes, or exactly five?

We seldom really analyze our experience freshly. Life is unpredictable and full of surprises; music should be, too. This is the philosophy represented by Cage and his music. It had a major impact on avant-garde composers all over the world, and also on some innovators in popular music.

> "When you get right down to it, a composer is simply someone who tells other people what to do. I find this an unattractive way of getting things done."
>
> *John Cage*

3 | Music at the End of the Millennium

The second wave of avant-garde composers after World War II questioned the traditional features of music in more basic ways than any other generation in European history. But they did not, on the whole, succeed in convincing concert-going audiences to explore these questions with them.

By the 1950s, the concert hall and opera house resounded with a familiar series of established works from the eighteenth and nineteenth centuries, with a healthy dose of twentieth-century works of traditional cast and a few early avant-garde classics (such as *The Rite of Spring* and *Wozzeck*) added into the mix. The works of the second avant-garde wave, instead, tended to be performed in small university halls and at occasional new-music festivals. One arch-modernist composer of the 1950s, Milton Babbitt, wrote an essay about the situation. He proclaimed that the new music could thrive only in the university, and he patiently explained why no listener without specialized musical training should hope to understand it. Babbitt's publisher gave the essay the inflammatory title "Who Cares If You Listen?"

But by the late 1960s many composers began to tire of the difficulty and elitism, as some said, of avant-garde music. New styles emerged that communicated more directly and openly with listeners and renounced the complications of some avant-garde styles.

In a way, composers forging these styles (like the non-avant-gardists of the 1930s) enjoyed the best of both worlds. They could freely exploit whatever musical resources they wanted to, all the while referring back to earlier, more accessible modes of expression.

Steve Reich (b. 1936) and Minimalism

The earliest and most famous of the new styles, emerging in the mid-1960s, is called minimalism. A sharp reaction to the complexities of modernist composition, minimalist music uses very simple melodies, motives, and harmonies repeated many, many times. Terry Riley's *In C,* described on page 360, is an ancestor of minimalism (some say the first great example of it). As this example suggests, minimalist composers carried on at least one aspect of modernist experimentation: its presentation of long, slowly changing blocks of musical time.

Minimalism has worked wonders for American opera, which has become the success story of modern music since *Einstein on the Beach* (1976), by a leading minimalist composer, Philip Glass (b. 1937). Later works such as *Satyagraha* and *Akhnaten,* by Glass, and *Nixon in China* and *The Death of Klinghoffer,* by John Adams (b. 1947), have been performed again and again in this country and abroad, all of them in spectacular productions.

Steve Reich, a philosophy major at Cornell, studied music subsequently and has become, alongside Glass, an acknowledged old master of the minimalist style. A keyboardist, he has performed his work with his own special group—a practice that a number of other contemporary composers follow. His early music explores issues of rhythm and timing in a rather abstract fashion, experimenting with simple, repeated gestures that gradually shift out of and into phase with one another. This can be achieved in various ways, with one performer gradually changing tempo while another stays constant, for example, or by lengthening certain aspects of the initial pattern while keeping others the same. The most famous of Reich's early works are *Piano Phase* (1967), *Four Organs* (1970), and *Clapping Music* (1972).

Reich's later music has broadened from these abstract processes. One of his most impressive pieces, *Different Trains* (1988), included recorded speech and personal memories, and Reich went on to write operas—*The Cave* (1998) and *Three Tales* (2002)—with his wife, video artist Beryl Korot.

Steve Reich, *Music for 18 Musicians* (1974–1976)

6 | 9–10   90–91   44–45

Music for 18 Musicians is one of the early classics of the minimalist style. The eighteen performers include four singers (they sing no words, but only syllables like "doo" and "ah"), a cellist, a violinist, two clarinetists (who sometimes switch to bass clarinets), and a large percussion group: four pianos, three marimbas, two xylophones, and a vibraphone (see page 17). This ensemble produces a timbre favored by the early minimalists—a percussive sound variously ringing and dry and brittle, reminiscent of the gamelans of Indonesia (see page 198). Reich was much influenced by their music; *Music for 18 Musicians* is directed not by a conductor but by the resonant vibraphone, and Reich likened this procedure to the role of the drummers who direct gamelans. Throughout

Reich, *Music for 18 Musicians,* opening

8 min., 38 sec.

6 | 9–10   **90–91**   **44–45**

9	**INTRODUCTION**		
	0:00	Neutral pulse	
	0:14	First harmony	
	0:33	Second harmony	
	0:53	Third harmony	
	1:14	Fourth harmony	
		etc.	
	4:08	Neutral pulse	
10	**SECTION 1**		
0:00	4:20	Theme begins to emerge.	
0:32	4:52	Vibraphone cue: Theme extended, cello prominent	
0:53	5:13	Vibraphone cue: Theme extended again, voices prominent	
1:25	5:45	Vibraphone cue: Cello shifts harmony slightly; later, pulsing clarinets.	

MIDPOINT

2:30	6:50	Clarinets resume theme (with voices).
2:50	7:10	Vibraphone cue: Disassembly of theme begins.
		etc.
4:14	8:34	Vibraphone cue begins Section 2.

Steve Reich. © *Jack Vartoogian/FrontRowPhotos.*

Music, each time the vibraphone plays, it cues changes in the melodies and harmonies.

The piece is rigorously, almost schematically, organized. It falls into an introduction, twelve connected sections lasting about four minutes each, and a conclusion mirroring the introduction—all adding up to almost an hour of music. Our excerpt includes the introduction and first section.

Introduction   *Music for 18 Musicians* begins with another feature beloved by minimalist composers: a regular, repeating pulse, objective and cool—a pulse that will continue for the whole work. Over this pulse, the introduction presents a set of rich harmonies on which the later sections of the work are based. But it does not present them in a conventional manner, as a harmonic progression that might accompany a melody. Instead the musicians linger over each harmony, repeating it over the even pulse for fifteen or twenty seconds or more before shifting to the next one. This is our first hint that musical time for the minimalists moves differently than for conventional composers. The most notable event in the midst of each harmony is contributed by the bass clarinets, which fade in and out twice with their own quick pulses.

Section 1   This four-minute section is based on a single harmony, the first harmony of the introduction, repeated by the pulsing instruments throughout the section. As the pulsing of the percussion instruments smoothly continues, the clarinets, joined later by the voices, begin to present the section's melodic material.

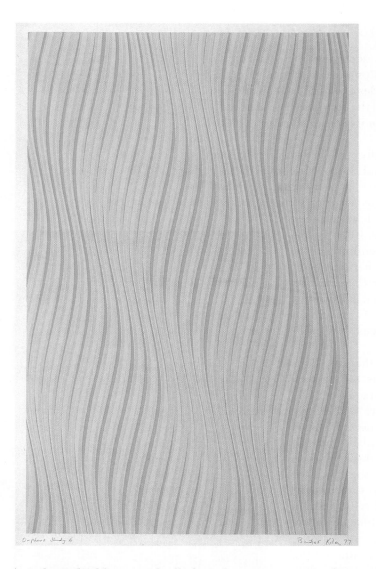

A theme builds up gradually from fragments to something much more continuous; it also rises gradually to higher and higher pitch levels. Each change to greater continuity and higher pitch is cued by the vibraphone.

When the theme, which has a lively, syncopated feel, is completely assembled, the clarinets give it over entirely to the voices and play even pulses, fading in and out, as they did in the introduction. This is the midpoint of the section.

Soon the clarinets take up the main theme again, with the voices. Now the process of assembly we heard before is reversed; at each cue from the vibraphone the theme moves lower in pitch and grows more fragmentary, until little is left. Finally it drops out altogether. All that remains is the endless background pulse, before another cue from the vibraphone signals the beginning of the second section.

Noteworthy here—and a general feature of much minimalist music—is the composer's ability to make us hear *musical process* in a new way, or at least with a new concentration. The incessant repetition of musical materials focuses our attention on the gradual changes they undergo; we hear this music as ordered gestures of slow building and unbuilding.

New Expressionism and Connecting to the Past

The accessibility that marks minimalist music separated it from much avant-garde experiment of the 1950s and 1960s. Composers sought to make their music approachable in other styles as well, styles avoiding both the objective, machinelike repetitiveness of minimalism and the complexities that made avant-garde styles so difficult for listeners. These composers worked to achieve a more direct emotional expression.

Their styles sometimes turned dramatically away from the second wave of the avant-garde, recalling instead late Romantic music. George Rochberg (1918–2005) started out as a forbidding serialist composer in the 1950s, but by the 1970s he was writing string quartets that at one moment sounded like Brahms and at another quoted whole passages from Wagner's *The Valkyrie*. Ellen Taaffe Zwilich (b. 1939) combines yearning melodies reminiscent of Brahms or Mahler with non-Romantic, dissonant harmonies in her Symphony No. 1 (1982). By the time of her *Concerto for Violin and Orchestra* of 1998, late Romantic tonal harmonies are prominent. The moving second movement is based on a rhythmic ostinato; in it we can hear faint echoes of Vivaldi (see page 119).

New music like this that refers to styles older than modernism is sometimes called *postmodern*. The term is taken from analogous trends in the visual arts and especially in architecture. Like these other artists postmodern composers are not exactly *anti*modernist; rather, they pick and choose from modernist and many other styles—from the whole of music history before them, even—to achieve their expressive ends. We might think of these postmodernists as *avant-garde* in the true sense of the term; for hadn't avant-garde composers like Ives, Varèse, and Cage sought above all else the expansion of choice and possibility in musical creativity? If the composer today can choose anything, why *not* choose to sound like Brahms or Vivaldi?

Still other composers, neither postmodernists nor minimalists, found ways to achieve the new, direct-speaking expression while maintaining a clearer connection to the experimental music of the decades after World War II. Some incorporated musical elements from nonclassical traditions, in the manner of William Grant Still or Aaron Copland, but did so with the expanded musical means of the experimenters. All strove to carve out their own individual styles, often highly dissonant, atonal, and venturesome in the use of new performing resources. Indeed *eclecticism* and *stylistic variety* have been watchwords of concert music composition since the 1970s, making it difficult to categorize individual works. In the following pages we examine three compositions of late modernism in very different styles.

Postmodern architecture: the Sony building in Manhattan (1984), designed by Philip Johnson. Unlike modernist skyscrapers, this building looks back knowingly on history. Its alternating wide and thin stripes recall early skyscrapers like the Empire State Building, and its topmost ornaments gesture toward antique furniture—a highboy or a grandfather clock. *Alan Schein Photography/Corbis.*

George Crumb (b. 1929)

George Crumb grew up in West Virginia and spent most of his career as a professor at the University of Pennsylvania. Around 1970 he shot into a wide popularity accorded few modernist composers, as the result of works

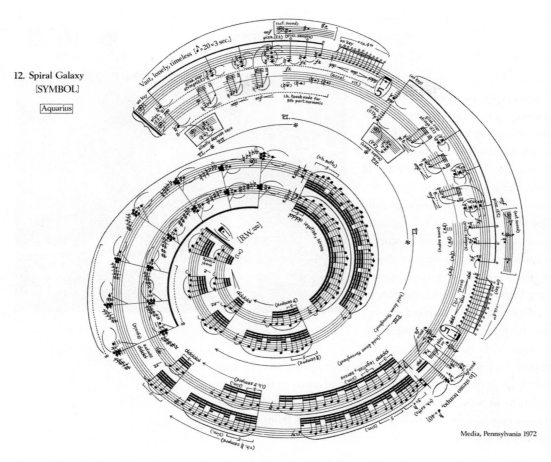

12. Spiral Galaxy
[SYMBOL]

Aquarius

Media, Pennsylvania 1972

George Crumb writes his own scores, often with a distinctive appearance. This picture score for the piano piece "Spiral Galaxy" has become an icon of late modernist music. *Copyright © 1974 by C. F. Peters Corp. All rights reserved. Used by permission.*

that became instant avant-garde classics. Foremost among these was *Ancient Voices of Children*, a song cycle exploring the disturbing, surreal poetry of the Spaniard Federico García Lorca (1898–1936) and calling for amplified voices, amplified piano, and a rich mix of percussion instruments. At one point Crumb calls for a toy piano to play a fragment of a Bach chorale (see page 147), and he often coaxes screams, shouts, and wordless vocal arabesques from performers, as well as more traditional singing. *Ancient Voices* inhabits a space Crumb preferred at this time, halfway between concert and theatrical ritual, and it does so with a distinctive sensitivity to novel timbres and sound combinations.

Other impressive and much-performed works Crumb composed in the same period include *Black Angels* for electric string quartet (it calls on the players to chant and click their tongues in addition to playing their instruments in unconventional ways) and *Vox balaenae* (Voice of the Whale), an evocation of humpback whale songs for electric flute, electric cello, and amplified piano. In the early 1970s Crumb produced two volumes of piano miniatures that remain staples of the avant-garde piano repertory. He called them *Makrokosmos* in homage to the *Mikrokosmos* of Bartók (see page 340).

George Crumb, *Voices from a Forgotten World* (*American Songbook,* Volume 5) (2006)

Around 2000, as he entered his eighth decade, Crumb embarked on a new project of sweeping scope. He began setting traditional American songs of all sorts—ballads, hymns, black spirituals, Civil War songs, popular tunes, and more—in collections he entitled the *American Songbook*. "Setting," however, is too tame a word for what Crumb achieves. These are transformations and re-visionings of the songs, usually retaining their melodies and words intact but framing them in a halo of staccato percussion and haunting resonances. Each volume of the *American Songbook*—to date Crumb has produced seven—is scored for amplified voices, amplified piano, and a quartet of percussionists with almost one hundred instruments at the ready. This percussion orchestra, combining traditional Western instruments with others from around

George Crumb. *Copyright Becky Starobin www.BridgeRecords.com.*

the world, allows Crumb to explore new combinations and timbres with each new song. His *American Songbook* forms a powerful testament at once to the vitality of the avant-garde tradition in which he grew up and to the huge expressive compass of American song repertories. We have chosen two songs from the fifth volume of the *American Songbook*.

"The House of the Rising Sun" is a folk lament set in New Orleans. Its origins are unclear; the earliest recorded performances come from the 1930s, though the song reaches farther back. As is usual in such cases, there are differing sets of words. The most famous version, a number one hit for the Animals in 1964, tells of a man's life gone awry; but the older versions, including the one Crumb sets, are sung instead in the person of a woman seduced and ruined by a "rambler."

The tone of despair evokes from Crumb the ghostly, resonant timbres for which he is famous. The song begins with a barely audible pair of Caribbean steel drums—turn up the volume and listen for this electronic-sounding hum—with soft additions from cymbals, maracas, and more. As the sad, bluesy tune closes its first stanza ("And me, oh God, for one"), a vibraphone plays an atonal interlude; Chinese temple gongs and a blown jug quietly mark the moment. The sustained accompaniment for stanza 2 switches from steel drums to louder vibraphones, punctuated with bongo drums. Again comes the vibraphone interlude. Finally, for stanza 3, the steel drums return, but now the vibraphone continues its mournful melody through the stanza. Fade to silence, with the soprano humming her final phrase.

"Hallelujah, I'm a Bum" dates back to the first decade of the 1900s, when new, comical words were put to the tune of an older religious revival song. (We encountered revival meetings in discussing Ives; see page 331.) Whereas the original refrain ended "Hallelujah, Thine the glory! Revive us again!," the new refrain, in this hymn to idleness and alcohol ("hooch"), ends "Hallelujah, give us a handout, and revive us again!" The new version had a long afterlife, especially during the Great Depression of the 1930s; there was even a spin-off film musical in 1933 featuring Al Jolson, one of the biggest stars of early sound films.

Crumb's rendition retains the form of the song—it is strophic, with a refrain at the end of each stanza—as well as its melody and words. Each stanza begins (listen at 0:00, 0:33, 1:06, and 1:40) with an aggressive, bumptious introduction for piano, marimba, and xylophone; cymbals, tambourine, and several other percussion sounds are also heard. Dissonant, static chords on piano support the first stanza with, at the refrain "Hallelujah . . .," glockenspiel and vibraphone—a jarring combination of shrill bell tones and electric resonance. But the accompaniment grows more active with each succeeding stanza. At the end of the fourth stanza (2:14) the tenor tries to repeat the refrain, but his inebriation gets the better of him and he loses his place. The big bass drum, used earlier in moderation, runs amok, and the music ends in drunken disarray.

Tania León (b. 1943)

Tania León came to the United States in 1967 as a refugee from Cuba, where she had studied at the National Conservatory of Havana. She traces her truly global heritage to France, Spain, Africa, Cuba, and China. Her first position was as musical director of the Dance Theatre of Harlem, the pioneering African American ballet company founded by Arthur Mitchell. (Mitchell was a protégé of George Balanchine's, a collaborator of Stravinsky's at the Ballets Russes.) Today León teaches composition and conducting at Brooklyn College.

León's works, like those of many composers at the end of the twentieth century, unite several musical and cultural traditions under a broad, avant-garde umbrella. Her Latin American and African roots are especially prominent, both in her choices of themes for her works and in many of their musical aspects. She employs a wide range of different performing forces, from solo piano to large orchestra, but various kinds of chamber ensembles, usually including ample percussion, are perhaps her favorite medium. Her harmonies tend to the dissonant and atonal side, but tonality can reassert itself in striking and unexpected ways. Her melodies are angular and modernist, but can break out in jazzy, Latin tunes. Most striking in her music is its enormously dynamic rhythm, a merging of African and Latin drumming with modernist masters of rhythm such as Stravinsky and Bartók that gives León's music a distinct individual sound.

Tania León. *Michael Provost.*

Tania León, *Indígena* (1991)

6 | 13–16 | 94

The title of this work for chamber orchestra can mean "indigenous," describing a native inhabitant of a place, or "an indigenous woman"; more particularly, in Latin American Spanish it refers to the Indians native to the continent. In all these meanings it captures the sense of place and Latin cultural heritage that is a central element in León's expressive world.

The music requires thirteen players on conventional instruments—five strings, four woodwinds, two brass, piano, and percussion. From these forces León conjures a musical depiction of a Latin American Carnival celebration—like a parade at Mardi Gras in Rio de Janeiro. The effect is of joyous cacophony, with individual outcries and hints of organized drumming in complex, overlapping rhythms called polyrhythms (see page 397). At the beginning, free, fanciful solos for wind instruments contrast with moments of more regular rhythms in piano and percussion. Clear beat and meter are asserted and maintained for a time, only to collapse; and León interjects a quiet passage, perhaps evoking the nighttime humming and buzzing of insects.

Finally—announced by surprising, repeated G-major chords in the strings—we seem to hear the approach of a Carnival band and dancers, wandering the streets in costumes and masks. Such groups are called *comparsas*. In their music, León has said, "there's always a winner, and the king of the *comparsas* is the trumpeter. . . . You hear the trumpet from a great distance, and then you hear the polyrhythms getting closer and closer."

In this piece the trumpet wins out, eloquently taking over about halfway through and playing smooth, jazzy tunes as well as jagged modernist melodies. The other instruments, individuals before, step in line with their leader, and

LISTENING CHART 29

Tania León, *Indígena*
8 min., 18 sec.

6 | 13–16 | 94

13	**SECTION 1 (Sustained chords in strings; free solos for winds)**	
	0:03	Flute
	0:22	Brief piano and percussion outburst
	0:31	Clarinet
	0:47	Piano and percussion outburst
	0:51	Bassoon
14	**SECTION 2 (Regular beat; clear meter emerges.)**	
	1:10	Piano ostinato
0:17	1:27	Ensemble begins to come together.
0:29	1:39	Cello solo, regular beat maintained
0:47	1:57	More solos, with regular beat: clarinet, horn, cello
1:24	2:34	Crescendo, drum stroke, silence; regular beat resumes.
1:51	3:01	Collapse: Beat disappears; quiet chords and buzzing sounds in strings.
	TRANSITION	
2:22	3:32	Crescendo; instruments added to sustained chord; oboe solo
15	**SECTION 3 (*Comparsa* band approaches.)**	
	3:57	G-major chords, repeated, in strings
0:21	4:18	Trumpet takes over: long solo.
0:51	4:48	Percussion; others join in.
1:01	4:58	G-major chords reappear.
1:05	5:02	Trumpet resumes: long solo.
1:46	5:43	Ensemble joins in again.
16	5:58	**"La Jardinera,"** trumpet; others respond.
0:24	6:22	Full ensemble
0:45	6:43	**"La Jardinera"** for full ensemble
0:55	6:53	Repeated notes in strings recall G-major chords.
1:13	7:11	**"La Jardinera,"** trumpet
1:27	7:25	Trumpet's final high note marks cadence; fade-out to nighttime buzzing.

La Jardinera

ultimately the trumpet guides them in a famous Carnival melody, "La Jardinera." This quoted melody emerges in bits and pieces. It is offered by the trumpet and answered by the other instruments, then played by the whole band, and finally sounded once more by the trumpet. Its fragmentary appearances are exactly analogous to the emergence of the hymn tune in Ives's "The Rockstrewn Hills" (see page 331), and they show a continuity of modernist technique from one end of the twentieth century to the other.

At the end, the music of the *comparsa* dies away—perhaps it has moved off to another part of town—and we hear again the quiet hum of the night.

John Adams (b. 1947)

John Adams ranks at the forefront of opera and concert music composers today, a true American original in the spirit of Ives and Copland. Raised (like Ives) in New England, he attended Harvard and then moved west to San Francisco in 1971. At first he was strongly influenced by Steve Reich's minimalism; we have already mentioned two of Adams's operas, *Nixon in China* and *The Death of Klinghoffer*, as important works in the minimalist camp. These operas also, in the newsworthy events they portray, helped start a trend of taking stories "plucked from the headlines" as the subject matter for operas. (The trend is sometimes called "CNN opera.") Many of Adams's other works also have American themes, including *On the Transmigration of Souls*, a powerful memorial for September 11, 2001, and *El Niño*, an oratorio about multicultural (especially Latino) inclusiveness in American society.

John Adams. *Lebrecht/The Image Works.*

As the mention of an oratorio (a genre we have heard little of since Handel's *Messiah*, page 140) suggests, there is a strong postmodern strain in Adams's recent output, one witnessed also in the opera we take up here, *Doctor Atomic*. In general, Adams has ranged widely in his musical tastes, more so than most minimalists. He (again like Ives) is inspired by popular as well as highbrow musical styles and genres. In his music we hear echoes of the classical tradition, from Bach through Schoenberg and Stravinsky, brushing up against marches, dance-band music, rock, rap, and even cartoon music.

John Adams, *Doctor Atomic* (2005)

The opera *Doctor Atomic* is set in the days leading up to the first explosion of an atomic bomb in the New Mexican desert in July 1945—a month before atomic bombs were dropped on the Japanese cities of Hiroshima and Nagasaki. The opera offers, through the conventional ingredients of opera—arias, recitatives, choruses—a meditation on the ethics of unleashing such weapons

In a scene from *Doctor Atomic*, workers stare up at the bomb being readied for the first test explosion. *Terrence McCarthy.*

in the world. The meditation comes from the viewpoints of several characters, but especially from "Doctor Atomic," physicist J. Robert Oppenheimer, a leading figure in the top-secret Manhattan Project to build the bomb.

The end of the first act, and its moving climax, takes the form of an aria for Oppenheimer, in which he expresses all his doubts and fears about the awesome new weapon he is creating. For the words of this aria, Adams and his librettist, Peter Sellars, had the brilliant notion of using a sonnet by the early seventeenth-century poet John Donne (1572–1631), "Batter my heart, three-person'd God." Donne's three "persons" are the Trinity—in Christian belief, the threefold presentation of God as Father, Son, and Holy Spirit. "Trinity," however, was also the code name given to the first test detonation of the bomb. Listen to a performance of the aria "Batter my heart" at your campus library or on YouTube.

Donne's sonnet (see the Listen box) is a meditation on the difficulties the poet experienced within himself in his own Christian belief. He is "betroth'd" (promised in marriage) to an "enemy"; like citizens of a captured town, he labors in vain to admit a rescuing force—that is, God. In the opera, instead, it is the bomb itself that Oppenheimer is captured by and betrothed to, and that tears him away from all that is holy.

A sonnet is a lyric poem of fourteen lines, usually falling into two four-line *quatrains* and two three-line *tercets* or, as here, three quatrains and a final couplet. Adams lingers over the words of Donne's first quatrain, unfurling a long, anguished melody for Oppenheimer, supported quietly by lush, tonal harmonies in the low brasses, winds, and strings. Here Donne implores God to put aside mild measures ("you / as yet but knock, breathe, shine, and seek to mend") and remake him through more aggressive means ("bend / Your force to break, blow, burn, and make me new"). Donne's stacking up of verbs in these two lines suggested to Adams more extensive repetitions in his melody: Oppenheimer sings "knock, breathe, knock, breathe, knock, breathe" and "break, blow, break, blow, break, blow." These repetitions of words recall the manner of the Baroque da capo aria (see page 138).

Underscoring this postmodern evocation of an earlier style is the form of this aria. It opens with an orchestral ritornello (see page 116)—an almost violent passage in which brasses and timpani are prominent, reflecting Oppenheimer's torment. After the **A** section, presenting the first quatrain of the poem, the ritornello reappears, and the quatrain is repeated. Only then does Adams move on to the remaining ten lines of the poem. Finally the ritornello recurs once more to end the aria, and with it Act I of *Doctor Atomic*. It is not an **A B A** form like a da capo aria, then, but an **A A B** form. Nevertheless, in its repeating sections clearly marked off by orchestral ritornellos it plainly evokes the earlier aria style.

In the ritornello, the repeating notes and motives for woodwinds and brass and the static, almost unchanging harmonies mark the persistence of minimalism in Adams's style; they sound similar to certain moments in Reich's *Music for 18 Musicians*. On the other hand, the frank emotionality of the melodic line for solo singer, supported by warm harmonies, carries into the twenty-first century an essential feature of opera through most of its history: the focusing of characters' emotional portrayal in arias.

Adams, *Doctor Atomic,* Aria "Batter my heart"

RITORNELLO
Batter my heart, three-person'd God, for you
    As yet but knock, breathe, shine, and seek to mend;
    That I may rise and stand, o'erthrow me, and bend
    Your force to break, blow, burn, and make me new.

RITORNELLO

Repeat music and words above, then:
    I, like an usurp'd town to another due,
    Labor to admit you, but oh, to no end;
    Reason, your viceroy in me, me should defend,
    But is captiv'd, and proves weak or untrue.
Yet dearly I love you, and would be lov'd fain,
    But am betroth'd unto your enemy;
    Divorce me, untie or break that knot again,
    Take me to you, imprison me, for I,
Except you enthrall me, never shall be free,
    Nor ever chaste, except you ravish me.

RITORNELLO (end of Act I)

GOALS FOR REVIEW

▶ to distinguish the second phase of avant-garde modernism, after World War II, from the first

▶ to understand late modernists' radical experimentation with time, chance music, and new electronic media

▶ to sample modernist styles in the 1950s and 1960s: Edgard Varèse, György Ligeti, and John Cage

▶ to listen carefully to a minimalist classic by Steve Reich

▶ to explore varieties of late modernism and postmodernism c. 2000: George Crumb, Tania León, and John Adams

macmillanhighered.com/listen8e
Interactive Listening Charts 27–29
Listening Quiz for Chapter 23
Reading Quiz for Chapter 23

Music in America: Jazz and Beyond

CHAPTER
24

As we have observed a number of times in this book, in the nineteenth century a rift opened between popular music and the music we now call classical. Nowhere has this rift been more apparent than in the United States of America, the most populist of all nations. And nowhere else have such strenuous efforts been made to close the rift. Think back to the various American composers discussed in the last few chapters, from the unlikely modernist Charles Ives, who quoted marches, ragtime, and hymns in his symphonic music, through William Grant Still, down to George Crumb and Tania León. It is not accidental that we have seen each of these composers working with popular as well as "classical" music sources.

Classical and *popular* are fuzzy words, however, especially when applied to music in American history. The terms *cultivated* and *vernacular* can be more illuminating. To cultivate means to nurture and consciously foster. *Vernacular*, on the other hand, refers to one's native language. **Cultivated music**, then, is music that has been brought to this country and consciously developed, fostered at concerts, and taught in conservatories. **Vernacular music** is music we sing and hear as naturally as we speak our native tongue.

There is a bitter twist to this terminology as applied to American music. The word *vernacular* comes from the Latin word *vernaculus,* which is itself derived from *verna:* and *verna* meant a family slave. The heritage of African American music was and is central to the story of American music.

1 | Early American Music: An Overview

Long before European settlers and African slaves arrived here, Native Americans had their own musical styles. (We touched on one of these in discussing sacred chant; see page 59.) As Native Americans were pushed farther and farther west, however, their music played little role in the development of European American and African American music.

The history of music among the early European settlers and their descendants is not a rich one. The Puritans disapproved of music; they thought it was frivolous, except for its supporting role in religion. In Puritan church services, rhyming versions of the psalms were sung like hymns, but when the words of the psalms were printed in the *Bay Psalm Book* of 1640—the first book ever printed in North America—the music was not included, because just a few tunes, known to everyone, were used for all 150 psalms. In succeeding years, much of the energy

of early American musicians was devoted to the composition of new psalm and hymn tunes, and to the teaching and improvement of church singing.

William Billings (1746–1800) of Boston is often mentioned as our first composer. He wrote hymns and **fuging tunes**, which are simple pieces based on hymns, with a little counterpoint added in. When sung with spirit, fuging tunes sound enthusiastic, rough, and gutsy.

Billings's more secular-minded contemporaries enjoyed the Classical music of the era. Benjamin Franklin, who tried his hand at most everything, also tried composing. But without well-established musical institutions, there was not much support for native composers outside the church. The problem in those years is hardly that of distinguishing between cultivated and vernacular music. The problem is finding written music to listen to and talk about at all.

The Cultivated Tradition

As cities grew, first on the East Coast and then farther west, more and more concerts appeared, and with them faithful concertgoers. One such was a New York lawyer and civic leader named George Templeton Strong, who left a four-and-a-half-million-word diary discussing (among other things) all the symphonies, oratorios, and organ music he heard, in unending enthusiastic detail.* By the mid-1800s, all our major cities had their concert halls and opera organizations and amateur choral societies. The 1860s saw the foundation of our first conservatories of music, in Boston, Cincinnati, and elsewhere.

Americans eagerly bought tickets to hear traveling celebrities from Europe, and skilled native composers and performers began to appear. The first American musicians to gain worldwide reputations were the immigrant German

- Vivaldi's concertos in parts
- Bach's songs 2nd collection
- Handel's Coronation anthems
- Heck's art of playing the harpsichord
- Hayden's [*sic*] cantatas

In 1783 Thomas Jefferson's music library contained these and a hundred other items.

---

*Bits of Strong's diary are cited on pages 210–11.

The Concert Singer, by Thomas Eakins. Cultivated music in America: a scene from Philadelphia society of the 1890s. *Philadelphia Museum of Art/CORBIS.*

composer Anthony Philip Heinrich (1781–1861), a quirky early Romantic, and the Louisiana piano virtuoso Louis Moreau Gottschalk (1829–1869).

On the whole, however, Americans were content to look to Italy for opera and to Germany for instrumental music. It is not surprising that the cultivated tradition in American music was essentially German in orientation. Ever since the time of Mozart and Beethoven, German music had earned enormous prestige all over Europe. The mid-nineteenth-century immigration from Germany brought us many musicians who labored for the cause of music in this country.

There were significant native composers at the end of the nineteenth century: John Knowles Paine, Arthur Foote, and Henry Chadwick of the so-called Boston School, and Edward MacDowell of New York. They wrote symphonies, piano miniatures, and so on, in a competent but conservative German Romantic style. Time has not been kind to their work, despite recent efforts to revive it.

The music of Amy Beach (1867–1944), in particular, has stirred interest in recent years. Active as both a composer and a pianist, she made her debut with the Boston Symphony Orchestra at the age of seventeen. "Mrs. H. H. A. Beach" (as she always signed her works) contributed to many established genres, such as the piano concerto, the piano quintet, and the symphony. Her *Gaelic* Symphony of 1896 was the first symphonic work ever composed by an American woman.

The emergence of Charles Ives in the midst of this conservative tradition seems like a miracle of music history (see page 331). Yet Ives profited more than he sometimes cared to admit from the grounding in European concert music he received from his German-trained professor at Yale, Horatio Parker.

Music in the Vernacular

We might well count the psalms and hymns mentioned above as vernacular music, for in colonial days everybody who could carry a tune sang them at church and in the home, and later they were widely sung at revival meetings and the like. Nineteenth-century America was also rich in secular popular music. Two of our most famous composers wrote timeless tunes and ever-popular marches, respectively: Stephen Collins Foster (1826–1864) and John Philip Sousa (1854–1932).

Foster led a dispiriting life. Even in those days, songwriting was closely tied to the music business; Foster was dependent on Christie's Minstrels, the leading traveling theater troupe of the time. They had exclusive rights to his songs and helped popularize them—so much so that some of them soon achieved the status of folk songs. But Foster could never seem to make ends meet. His marriage broke up. He turned to drink and died at the age of thirty-eight.

John Philip Sousa, son of Spanish and German immigrant parents, was a Marine Corps bandmaster who later formed a wildly successful touring band of his own. All Americans know his masterpiece *The Stars and Stripes Forever* (even if they don't all know its name). Leonard Bernstein once said that his greatest regret as a musician was that he hadn't composed that march.

Amy Beach. *Lebrecht/The Image Works.*

Original illustration accompanying a song by Stephen Foster (1862).

A concert at New York's Castle Garden in 1850, in a print issued by Currier & Ives. Their hand-colored lithographs are famous for vividly illustrating nineteenth-century America. *SuperStock/SuperStock.*

African American Music

Foster excelled in sentimental ballads, such as "Jeanie with the Light Brown Hair" and "Beautiful Dreamer." But his most notable songs have to do with the black slaves of his time. There are sentimental "plantation songs" such as "Swanee River" ("The Old Folks at Home") and "Old Black Joe," and comic minstrel songs such as "Oh, Susanna!" and "Camptown Races." The **minstrel show**, performed by white actors in blackface, was very popular at midcentury; it consisted of comedy routines, "Ethiopian" songs, dances, and solos on the banjo (an instrument with African roots). Today this kind of entertainment strikes us as an ugly parody of black speech and character. Yet it can also be seen as an acknowledgment, almost in spite of itself, of the vitality of the slaves' music. From at least the time of Foster, African American music has had a profound effect on the music of America at large, and from there on the music of the world.

What was the slaves' music like? This is hard to say, for there were no devoted folk-song collectors to write it down. Nevertheless, by studying somewhat later black American music and comparing it with today's African music, scholars have been able to show how much the slaves preserved of their native musical traditions.

For example, a musical procedure known as **call and response** is common in West Africa. Phrases sung by a leader—a soloist—are answered or echoed again and again by a chorus. This procedure is preserved in black American church music, when the congregation answers the preacher's "call," as well as in spirituals, work songs, and "field hollers," by which the slaves tried to lighten their labors. It is also an important feature in blues and in jazz, as we shall see.

"The singing was accompanied by a certain ecstasy of motion, clapping of hands, tossing of heads, which would continue without cessation for about half an hour. One would lead off in a kind of recitative style, others joining in the chorus."

James L. Smith, a former slave, recalls call-and-response singing, 1881.

Negro spirituals were first popularized after the Civil War by groups like the Fisk Singers. In 1871, this group of former slaves toured to raise funds for Fisk, one of the earliest African American colleges. *Moorland-Spingarn Research Center, Howard University.*

Spiritual is a term for a religious folk song that came into being outside an established church (white or black). Moving "Negro spirituals," such as "Nobody Knows the Trouble I've Seen" and "Go Down, Moses," were the first black American music to gain the admiration of the white world. After Emancipation, black colleges formed touring choirs. To be sure, spirituals in their concert versions were considerably removed from folk music.

2 | Jazz: The First Fifty Years

Jazz is a performance style that grew up among black musicians around 1910 and has since gone through a series of extraordinary developments. Its first key feature is *improvisation*. When jazz musicians play a song, they do not stick to a written score or duplicate the way they have heard it before. Instead they freely elaborate *around* a song. They add ornaments and newly contrived interludes, called **breaks**. In effect, they are always making up variations on the tunes they are using—variations sometimes of such complexity that the original song almost disappears.

The second key feature of jazz is a special rhythmic style involving highly developed *syncopation*. Syncopation occurs when some of the accents in music are moved away from the main beats, the beats that are normally accented (see page 7). For example, in **2/2** meter, instead of the normal ONE *two* ONE *two*, the accent can be displaced from beat 1 to beat 2—*one* TWO *one* TWO. This is called a "backbeat" in jazz parlance.

In addition, jazz developed syncopation of a more subtle kind, sometimes called **beat syncopation**. Derived from African drumming (see page 397),

RAGTIME: SCOTT JOPLIN (1868–1917)

Unit I

Ragtime, a precursor of jazz, was a style of piano playing developed by black musicians playing in bars, dives, and brothels. In the early 1900s, when phonographs were still new, ragtime became enormously popular throughout America by means of sheet music and piano rolls for mechanical ("player") pianos. The music resembled march music, but while the left hand played strictly on the beat, the right hand syncopated the rhythm in a crisp, cheerful way. "To rag" meant to play in a syncopated style; "ragging" evolved into jazz syncopation.

Scott Joplin was the leading rag composer. The son of an ex-slave, he grew up in Texarkana and worked as a pianist and band musician in many midwestern towns. "Maple Leaf Rag," named after the Maple Leaf Club in Sedalia, Missouri, where Joplin played, was published in 1899. It quickly sold a million copies. You can hear this famous rag in Listening Exercise 1 on page 7.

"Maple Leaf" was followed by "The Entertainer" and many other rags. They stand out for an elegance that might not have been expected in this simple and commercial genre. Joplin even published a small treatise on ragtime, warning those who would race through his pieces: "Never

play ragtime fast at any time." And to those who saw ragtime as a style too lowbrow for their tastes, he wrote: "Syncopations are no indication of light or trashy music, and to shy [i.e., throw] bricks at 'hateful ragtime' no longer passes for musical culture."

Joplin's evident desire to break into cultivated musical circles was not realized. After he moved to New York in 1907 he gradually faded from the limelight. He wrote two operas, the second of which, *Treemonisha*, received a single unstaged performance in 1915. His death in 1917 was noted by few, but at last, in 1972, *Treemonisha* was fully staged and recorded.

Image credit: Bettmann/Corbis.

this technique can also be traced in earlier black American music. In beat syncopation, accents are moved *just a fraction of a beat* ahead of the metrical points. When this happens in just the right way, the music is said to "swing."

Notice that jazz is not so much a kind of music—the music it is based on usually consists of popular songs, blues, or abstract chord series called "changes"—but a special, highly charged way of performing that music.

The Blues

The **blues** is a special category of black folk song whose subject is loneliness, trouble, and unhappiness of every shade. Indeed, the blues is more than song, more than music: It is an essential expression of the African American experience. Though gloom and dejection are at the heart of the blues, not infrequently blues lyrics also convey humor, banter, and especially hope and resilience.

Emerging around 1900, the blues was a major influence on early jazz—and has remained a major force in American music ever since.

Like most folk songs, blues are strophic songs, with many stanzas sung to the same melody, as the singer develops his or her thought, often on the spur of the moment. A blues melody consists typically of three four-measure phrases—hence the expression *twelve-bar blues*—while the matching stanza is in a poetic *a a b* form (line 1 repeated before line 3, which is a miniature punch line). Here are stanzas 1 and 4 of "If You Ever Been Down" Blues:

> STANZA 1   ***a*** If you ever been down, you know just how I feel,
>   ***a*** *If you ever been down, you know just how I feel,*
>   ***b*** Like a tramp on the railroad ain't got a decent meal.

> STANZA 4   ***a*** Yes, one thing, papa, I've decided to do,
>   ***a*** *Oh pretty daddy, I've decided to do,*
>   ***b*** I'm going to find another papa, then I can't use you.

Composed blues—for example, W. C. Handy's famous "St. Louis Blues"—can be more complicated than this one, but the *a a b* poetic scheme is basic for the blues.

Blues melodies (and the bass lines and harmonies under blues melodies) provided jazz musicians with powerfully emotional patterns for improvisation. But more than that, blues also provided jazz with a sonorous model. Jazz instrumental playing has an astonishing vocal quality, as though in imitation of the blues. The trumpet, saxophone, and trombone sound infinitely more flexible and "human" played in jazz style than when played in military band or symphonic style. Jazz instruments seem to have absorbed the vibrant accents of black singing. (This is a feature that jazz passed on to rock music, where the electric guitar is the instrument that powerfully imitates the voice.)

"I'd like to think that when I sing a song, I can let you know all about the heartbreak, struggle, lies, and kicks in the ass I've gotten over the years for being black and everything else, without actually saying a word about it."

Blues, gospel, and soul singer Ray Charles, 1970

Sippie Wallace (1898–1986), "If You Ever Been Down" Blues (1927) (Composed by G. W. Thomas)

6 | 17   95 46

Sippie Wallace was one of several legendary women blues singers who dominated the earliest recordings. She is not as renowned as Ma Rainey or the great Bessie Smith, but she poured her heart out with the best of them in response to the eternal themes of the blues:

STANZA 2

I'm a real good woman but my man don't treat me right
I'm a real good woman but my man don't treat me right.
He takes all my money and stays out all night.

STANZA 3

I'm down today but I won't be down always,
I'm down today but I won't be down always.
'Cause the sun's going to shine in my back door some day.

Wallace accompanies herself on the piano. The recording adds two jazz musicians, but she would have sung just about the same way if she had been performing alone. We've chosen this recording because, modest as it may seem, one of the musicians is the outstanding genius of early jazz, trumpeter Louis Armstrong.

After a brief instrumental introduction, Wallace sings two blues stanzas from the piano bench. The instruments play short breaks in between her lines—the trumpet (Armstrong) in stanza 1, the clarinet (the little-known Artie Starks) in stanza 2. Sympathetic respondents to her "call," they deepen the melancholy of her song and nuance it:

If you ev-er been down you know__ just how I feel,   If you ev-er . . .

Then Armstrong plays a solo section—an entire twelve-bar blues stanza. He does not play the blues melody note by note, but improvises around the melody and its bass. Armstrong has a wonderful way of speeding up the dragging blues rhythm, and his rich, almost vocal tone quality echoes and complements the singer's bleak sound. The clarinet joins him; short as it may be, this is a real example of improvised jazz polyphony.

Wallace, too, joins in quietly during this instrumental chorus; she, too, no doubt, was singing on impulse. She then sings two more stanzas, with instrumental breaks as before.

It's necessary to listen to this recording in a different spirit from that in which we approach the other recordings of Western music accompanying this book. The scratchy sound on these old discs cannot be helped by digital remastering, and the music itself is not "composed," of course. It lies somewhere in between true folk music and jazz, a fascinating juxtaposition of the direct, powerful simplicity of Sippie Wallace and the artistry of Armstrong. With a little imagination, one can virtually hear history happening in this recording: Jazz is evolving from the blues.

 LISTEN

"If You Ever Been Down" Blues

0:10	**Stanza 1**
0:45	**Stanza 2**
1:19	**Trumpet**
1:51	**Stanza 3**
2:24	**Stanza 4**

Sippie Wallace—her name is said to derive from a childhood lisp—was equally known for gospel singing and the blues. African American **gospel music**—ecstatic choral singing in evangelical church services, with high-flying sopranos over the background rhythms of the congregation—grew up at the same time as the blues and ragtime. Wallace was also a pianist and songwriter, who usually sang her own compositions, and published a good many of them. Her performing career began at little churches in Houston and ended with a concert at Lincoln Center, the sprawling New York music facility that houses the New York Philharmonic Orchestra and the Metropolitan Opera.

A publicity photograph of Sippie Wallace from her early recording days. *Pictorial Press Ltd / Alamy.*

New Orleans Jazz

Early jazz was local entertainment for black audiences, an informal, low-budget, and even somewhat casual art. Small bands, usually of six to eight players, typically featured three melody instruments to do the "swinging"—trumpet, clarinet, and trombone. The rhythm section could include piano, banjo, string bass, or even tuba, along with drums and other percussion.

Early jazz players developed the art of collective improvisation, or "jamming." They learned to improvise simultaneously, each developing the special resources of his instrument—bright melodic spurts for the trumpet, fast running passages from low register to high for the clarinet, forceful slides for the trombone. They also acquired a sort of sixth sense for fitting in with the other improvisers. The non-imitative polyphony (see page 30) produced this way is the hallmark of early jazz.

The first important center of jazz was New Orleans, home of the greatest early jazzman, Louis Armstrong, who played cornet and trumpet. Armstrong and his colleagues developed wonderfully imaginative and individual performance styles; aficionados can recognize any player after hearing just a few measures of a jazz record. With players of this quality, it is not surprising that solo sections soon became a regular feature in early jazz, along with collective improvisation.

Recording technology was already crucial in the spread of jazz. As popular records in those days were all just three minutes long, the jazz that has survived from that era is all slimmed down into three-minute segments. Originally issued on labels that appealed to black audiences—coldly categorized as "race records" by the music business—Armstrong's discs of the late 1920s and 1930s not only attracted white listeners but also excited the admiration of a new breed of jazz musicologists and critics.

Jazz in the early 1920s: Louis Armstrong (center front) in his first important band, Joe ("King") Oliver's Creole Jazz Band. Armstrong plays a slide trumpet, his cornet on the floor in front of him. The pianist, Lil Hardin—also a bandleader and songwriter—later married Armstrong and is credited with directing his early career. © JazzSign/Lebrecht Music & Arts/Corbis.

Biography
Louis Armstrong (1901–1971)

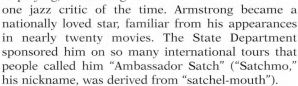

Louis Armstrong was born into abject poverty in New Orleans. He learned to play the cornet in the Colored Waifs' Home, where he had been placed as a juvenile delinquent. Armstrong played in seedy clubs and on riverboats, which were floating dance halls that traveled from town to town on the Mississippi every summer. Riverboats became a cradle of early jazz, importing it up the river from New Orleans to Kansas City and other centers.

Soon Armstrong was playing in pioneering jazz bands led by King Oliver (see page 389) and Fletcher Henderson. He rapidly emerged as a more exciting artist than any of his colleagues. His sophisticated, flowing rhythms, his imaginative breaks and variations, and the beauty and sheer power of his trumpet tone—all these were unique at the time. A famous series of records he made in the 1920s, playing with small New Orleans–style bands, drew jazz to the serious attention of musicians all over the world.

In the 1930s the popularity of jazz led to a great deal of commercialization, and to the cheapening and stereotyping that always seem to result from this process. Armstrong went right along, while often contributing moments of breathtaking beauty to records that were "listenable virtually only when Louis is playing," according to one jazz critic of the time. Armstrong became a nationally loved star, familiar from his appearances in nearly twenty movies. The State Department sponsored him on so many international tours that people called him "Ambassador Satch" ("Satchmo," his nickname, was derived from "satchel-mouth").

However, the more successful Armstrong became in the world of popular music, the more he drifted away from true jazz, to the distress of jazz enthusiasts. His last hit record was *Hello, Dolly!*, the title song of a 1964 Broadway musical; in this number he sang (with his famous raspy delivery) more than he played the trumpet.

Encore: Listen to "West End Blues," "Heebie Jeebies," "Hotter Than That," "St. Louis Blues" (with Bessie Smith).

Image credit: Bettmann/Corbis.

Big-Band Jazz: Swing

Around 1930, jazz gained significantly in popularity, thanks in part to Armstrong's recordings. With popularity came changes, not all of them for the good. Jazz now had to reach bigger audiences in ballrooms and roadhouses. This meant **big bands**, with ten to twenty-five players—and such large numbers required carefully written-out arrangements of the songs played. Improvisation, which was the essence of jazz, was necessarily limited under these conditions.

However, big-band jazz—called **swing**—compensated for some of its lost spontaneity by variety of tone color and instrumental effects. A novel style of band orchestration was developed, based on the contrast between brass (trumpets and trombones) and "reed" (mainly saxophone) groups. Soloists cut in and out of the full-band sounds. Jazz "arrangers," who arranged current songs for the bands, treated this style with the greatest technical ingenuity and verve; they deserve the name of composers. Sometimes they contrived to allow for some improvisation within their arrangements.

With popularity, too, came white musicians and managers, who moved in on what had previously been a relatively small black operation. Not only were black jazz musicians marginalized in the mass market, but their art was watered down to suit the growing audience. The big swing bands that were commercial successes were white, and their leaders—Benny Goodman, Glenn Miller, Artie Shaw—were household names in the 1930s and 1940s. But the best of the big bands were black: those led by Count Basie (1904–1984), Jimmie Lunceford (1902–1947), Chick Webb (1909–1939), and Duke Ellington.

Swing in the late 1930s: one of the most famous of the "big bands" (Glenn Miller's) — brass to the left, reeds to the right. © *Underwood & Underwood/Corbis.*

Duke Ellington, "Conga Brava" (1940)

6 | 18   96   47

The tune used in "Conga Brava" was written by Ellington together with his Puerto Rican sideman Juan Tizol. (A conga is a dance of Afro-Cuban origin, named after the *conga* drum.) In it, the characteristic beat of Latin American music is appropriated by jazz, though only the beginning of this unusual tune—the **a a** section of the **a a b** form—has a Latin beat. Played by trombonist Tizol, the first **a** is presented with a minimal and mysterious accompaniment; but after this ends with a fancy clarinet break (Barney Bigard), the second **a** includes brilliant interjections from the muted brass (an Ellington specialty).

Section **b** is played by the brass choir, with a speedy low clarinet cutting in. The rhythm section switches from a Latin beat to a typical jazz backbeat duple meter. The music begins to swing hard, as the trumpets remove their mutes.

Next, Ben Webster on tenor sax gets his turn with the tune. He sounds genuinely spontaneous; he probably never again improvised around this melody in just this way. After he has gone through **a** and **a**, the muted brass come in again with a lively variation of **b**.

Webster has strayed far from the tune, so it is good to hear the third appearance of the tune in its original form (more or less), now on the reed choir (saxophones). This time the interpolations are by sideman Rex Stewart on trumpet. And this time, after a single **a**, there comes an extraordinary brass-choir version of **b**, with wildly syncopated rhythms. The

LISTEN

"Conga Brava"

0:04	**a a**	Trombone
0:45	**b**	Brass and clarinet
0:59	**a′ a′**	Sax
1:39	**b**	Muted brass
1:47	**a**	Reed choir (with trumpet)
2:07	**b′**	Brass choir
2:32	**a**	Trombone

"My band is my instrument."

Duke Ellington — though he was a first-rate pianist, too

coordination of the brass instruments is breathtaking, and the sheer verve of their variation makes this the high point of the composition.

At the piano, Duke gives a quiet signal for this brass episode before it starts; he also plays a single, hardly audible note in the middle of the episode, as though to remind us who is in charge. The piece ends as it started, with the tune played by Tizol, but it fades halfway through.

How strange to be back to the rather still and mournful conga melody, with its Latin beat! All that exhilarating jazz activity that blew up so suddenly and has now been cut off—was it some kind of dream? Only a master of musical form like Ellington could make you think of such questions after a mere three minutes of music.

Jazzmen as listeners: Duke Ellington and (behind him to the right) Benny Goodman listen to Ella Fitzgerald, one of the great vocalists of the jazz era. You can hear Fitzgerald sing "Who Cares?" in Listening Exercise 5 (page 27).
© *Herman Leonard Photography LLC.*

Unit I

Biography
Duke Ellington (1899–1974)

Edward Kennedy Ellington was born in Washington, D.C., son of a butler who occasionally worked at the White House. The young Ellington considered a career as an artist, but he started playing the piano in jazz bands—ragtime was a major influence—and soon organized his own. He learned arranging, too, and became an almost unique phenomenon: a major bandleader who was also its composer and its arranger.

He was called "Duke" because of a certain aristocratic bearing—and he was fastidious about his music, too. Ellington held fast to his own high standards of innovation and stylishness. And although his band never "went commercial," it did as well as any black band could in the 1930s and 1940s. "Duke Ellington and His Famous Orchestra" were renowned as the backup to sumptuous revues put on at the Cotton Club, an upscale Harlem nightspot that catered to white audiences. Their recordings from around 1930 to 1940 constitute Ellington's major legacy.

After World War II, Ellington went his own imperturbable way, keeping his big band at a time when such organizations were regarded as jazz dinosaurs. He had experimented with long, symphonic-style jazz compositions as a young man, and now he wrote more of these, as well as movie scores, a ballet, and an opera. The Ellington band, which had toured Europe twice in the 1930s, now toured all over the world, including the Soviet Union.

Ellington was finally recognized for what he was, just about America's most eminent composer, and he received the Presidential Medal of Freedom and other tributes. His last creative phase found him writing lengthy religious pieces, called *Sacred Concerts,* for the Ellington band with a Swedish soprano, Alice Babs, who was not really a jazz singer at all.

Ellington's *Sacred Concerts* would have been impossible without Babs—but the same is true of his earlier, better-known music and the musicians of his early bands. These individual soloists, or *sidemen,* as they are called, were vital to Ellington's art in a way singers or instrumentalists very rarely are in classical music. He molded his music so closely to their sometimes eccentric styles of playing that we can hardly conceive of his music without them. (So we give them credit in our write-up on "Conga Brava," page 391.)

Chief Works: Very many songs—one estimate is two thousand—and jazz arrangements ■ Large-scale jazz compositions, including *Creole Fantasy* and *Black, Brown, and Beige* ■ Musical comedies, ballets, an incomplete opera (*Boola*), and other stage music ■ Five film scores; *Sacred Concerts*

Encore: Listen to "Mood Indigo," "Caravan," "Take the 'A' Train," "Ko-ko," "It Don't Mean a Thing (If It Ain't Got That Swing)," "Sophisticated Lady."

Image credit: Corbis/Bettmann.

Popular Song

At the beginning of our discussion of jazz we stressed that it is not a genre of music, but a performance style that went through many developments. As we trace these developments—from New Orleans jazz to swing, bebop, and the rest—we should pause for a moment to consider the material for jazz in its various styles. Blues are iconic, but blues underpin only a small minority of jazz performances. Mostly jazz musicians work their magic on popular songs, and American popular song of the twentieth century is a major vernacular repertory, in a way as important as jazz itself. It flourished in the first half of the century at the hands of a cadre of composers who are household names: Irving Berlin (1888–1989), Jerome Kern (1885–1945), Cole Porter (1891–1964), George Gershwin (1898–1937), and many others.

Early jazz is associated with New Orleans because the players came from there. Popular song is associated with Tin Pan Alley, a district in New York (which relocated a couple of times) where music publishers had their shops and offices. The songs they bought for a pittance they sold as sheet music in as many as a million copies, sometimes, meanwhile collecting royalties on radio and stage performances. It's been said that popular songs are the songs you forgot you knew but remember when you hear the chorus, songs sung in kindergarten as well as in the retirement home: "Blue Skies," "White Christmas," and "God Bless America" (Berlin); "Smoke Gets In Your Eyes" and "The Way You Look Tonight" (Kern); "Lady Be Good," "Somebody Loves Me," and "The Man I Love" (Gershwin)—we could go on and on.

Tin Pan Alley songs were usually simple in construction, easy to hum: a chorus, typically in a form such as **a a b a** or **a b a b**, and a couple of verses—which tend to be forgotten; it's just the chorus that, once you recall it, you can't get out of your head. Not only were jazz and popular song simultaneous developments, one can see that they fed on each other. Jazz musicians needed material for their improvisations and arrangements. Popular songs needed the artistry and expansion of jazz to become impressive listening experiences.

Songs that were favored by jazzmen were called "standards." To *become* a standard, however, such songs needed to catch on with the public through versions by the best-loved singers of the day. Vocalists like Bing Crosby and Frank Sinatra sang the sentimental, jazzy tunes to dance-hall audiences, to the ever-growing radio audience, in the movies, and—most important by the end of the 1940s—on records.

3 | Later Jazz

After World War II the popularity of the big bands collapsed suddenly. They were too expensive to run; furthermore, styles in entertainment had changed, and the smooth, high-powered band sound struck people as cold and slick. The mass market turned to rock'n'roll, itself the outcome of a vital new genre of African American music, rhythm and blues (see page 403). Within jazz itself, the collapse of the big bands had been foreshadowed during the war by a revolutionary new movement called *bebop*.

Bebop

During the early 1940s, young black jazz musicians found it harder to get work than white players in big bands. When they did get jobs, the setup discouraged free improvisation, the life and soul of jazz; the big bands seemed to have co-opted

"Irving just loves hits. He has no sophistication about it—he just loves hits."

Said of Irving Berlin, author of "Alexander's Ragtime Band," "Always," "Easter Parade," and "White Christmas," among other hits

In a recording studio, Charlie Parker listens to a playback as the other musicians wait for his reaction. Will he approve this take of the standard they are recording, or will they have to do another? © *Herman Leonard Photography LLC.*

and distorted a style grown out of black experience. These musicians got together in small groups after work for jam sessions at clubs in Harlem, in New York City. There they developed a new style that would later be called **bebop**. Contrasting sharply with the big bands, the typical bebop combo (combination) was just trumpet and saxophone, with a rhythm section including piano.

Bebop was a determined return to improvisation, then—but improvisation at a new level of technical virtuosity. "That horn ain't supposed to sound that fast," an elder musician is said to have complained to bebop saxophonist Charlie Parker. In addition to unprecedented velocity, Parker and leading bebop trumpeter Dizzy Gillespie (1917–1993) cultivated hard, percussive sounds and sharp, snap rhythms (one derivation of the term *bebop*). The smooth swing of the big bands was transformed into something more aggressive and exciting.

Equally radical was the treatment of harmony in bebop. New Orleans jazz used simple, in fact naïve, harmonies. The big-band, swing arrangers used much more sophisticated ones. Bebop musicians took these complex harmonies and improvised around them in a more and more "far-out" fashion. In some stretches of their playing, even the tonality of the music was obscured. Bebop melodies grew truly fantastic; the chord changes became harder and harder to follow.

"Playing [be]bop is like playing Scrabble with all the vowels missing."

Duke Ellington, 1954

Charlie Parker (1920–1955) and Miles Davis (1926–1991), "Out of Nowhere" (1948)

6 | 19   97   48

The life of Charlie ("Bird") Parker, bebop's greatest genius, reads like a modern-day version of a persistent Romantic myth—the myth of the artist who is driven by the demon of his creativity, finding fulfillment only in his art. Parker was on drugs from the age of fifteen, and in later years could not control his immoderate drinking and eating. A legend in his own lifetime, Parker died at the age of thirty-four after a suicide attempt and a period of hospitalization in a California mental institution.

"Out of Nowhere" is one of the many popular standards of the 1930s that were used as the basis for swing and bebop. Our version of the number was recorded live in a New York nightclub, so it can give us an idea of what an improvised bebop number actually sounded like. Notice the informal opening—no arranged introduction as in Ellington's "Conga Brava." Parker plays the attractive song fairly "straight" to begin with, but he inserts a sudden skittering passage just before the **A′** section (the song is in **A A′** form). This is a preview of things to come.

The trumpet solo by Miles Davis has the characteristic tense, bright bebop sound, some very rapid passage work, and one or two piercing high notes. Then Parker's improvisation shows his impressive powers of melodic development. He builds a whole series of phrases of different lengths, increasingly elaborate, that seem to leave the song in the dust—except that now and then he recalls ever so clearly a melodic turn from it (especially in **A′**). This is a Parker trademark: Again and again his solos strike this balance between fantastic elaboration and return to a more modest starting point.

The irregular, almost discontinuous-sounding rests between Parker's phrases have their own special fascination. You may recognize an Irish jig, which seems to have popped into Parker's head right in the middle of the solo, as the outgrowth of a short melody figure he had come to. He plays the jig at a dizzying rate for just a moment, before inventing something else; amazingly, it fits right in.

At the end of his solo the nightclub audience applauds, and the pianist plays his own improvised solo on the tune's **A** section. The number ends with the **A′** section of "Out of Nowhere" played once again quite simply, except for new trumpet breaks and a new, comical ending.

LISTEN

"Out of Nowhere"

0:00	Tune **A**
0:24	**A′**
0:48	Trumpet **A**
1:12	**A′**
1:36	Sax **A**
2:00	**A′**
2:24	Piano **A**
2:49	Tune **A′**
3:11	Coda

Jazz after Bebop

Melody, harmony, and tonality—these were the very elements in music that had been "emancipated" by Schoenberg, Stravinsky, and other avant-gardists in the early 1900s. With the bebop movement, the avant-garde came to jazz.

Many new jazz styles followed after the bebop emancipation, from the 1950s to the present day. Jazz fans distinguish between cool jazz, free jazz, modal jazz, fusion jazz, Latin jazz, and more. Among the early leaders in this diverse, exciting music were pianist Thelonious Monk (1917–1982), trumpeter Miles Davis (1926–1991), keyboardist Sun Ra (1928–1994), and saxophonists John Coltrane (1926–1967) and Ornette Coleman (b. 1930). They were the first to improvise *really* freely—that is, without even a song or blues as a basis.

Miles Davis (1926–1991), *Bitches Brew* (1969)

Trumpeter Miles Davis, one of the most innovative figures in the whole history of jazz, started out playing with Charlie Parker and other bebop musicians, as we heard in "Out of Nowhere." Soon, however, he realized that his own aptitude (or at least one of his aptitudes) was for a more relaxed and tuneful kind of melody. Davis's style went through many stages—from bebop to cool jazz to modal jazz and beyond—as he worked in various groups with a veritable who's who of modern jazz artists.

Bitches Brew, one of his biggest hits, was also one of his most original. A conscious (and controversial) attempt to blend jazz with rock—*fusion jazz,* as it came to be called—the album used a rhythm section with electric guitar, bass, and two electric keyboards in addition to regular jazz drums, acoustic bass, and augmented percussion. Instead of the traditional chord changes of jazz, this group produced repetitive, rocklike rhythms of great variety and, often, delicacy. This backdrop provides an unlikely but also unforgettable setting for Davis's haunting improvisations.

Our selection covers a solo from the title track of *Bitches Brew.* Before Davis begins, the electric piano and guitar pick out rhythmic patterns against a quiet jazz drum background; mostly the electric guitar has isolated single notes and the electric piano has syncopated, dissonant chords. From the beginning a rocklike ostinato sounds quietly on the electric bass guitar.

The trumpet solo starts with short patterns of relatively long notes, a Davis signature. The mood is meditative, almost melancholy: an evocation of the blues. The backdrop tapestry of sounds grows thicker. Soon Davis is employing more elaborate patterns—a string of repeated notes, scalelike passages up and down—but the effect is, in its own way, as repetitive as the backdrop. Then he explodes into a series of little snaps, a recollection of bebop. As the whole group drives harder and harder, we realize that Davis has now arrived at a wild, free ostinato in the high register. The solo sinks down again after a climactic high trumpet squeal, another Davis hallmark.

6 | 20   98

)) **LISTEN**

Bitches Brew
(excerpt)

0:00	Backdrop
0:42	Dies down
1:05	**Trumpet solo**
2:41	**Trumpet ostinato**
3:20	Climax

Miles Davis. *Amalie Rothschild/ Anomaly Films.*

African Drumming

The syncopated rhythms of ragtime, blues, and jazz derived from traditional African music, particularly drumming. Listen now to a recording of a drum ensemble from Benin, a small West African nation situated

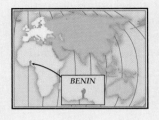

between Ghana and Nigeria. The drummers play music used in the worship of ancestral spirits among the Yoruba people—one of a wide variety of religious and nonreligious uses of drumming in the region.

Syncopation and Polyrhythms

6 | 23   110   51

The rhythms of this music cannot be said to *swing* precisely in the manner of jazz, but they show a complexity and vitality related to jazz rhythms and not native to the European classical music tradition.

These rhythms are related to what we have termed *beat syncopation* in jazz (see page 386). A single drum lays down a basic, fast, four-plus-four pulse; each group of four feels like a beat, and two groups of four take about a second. (This quick pulse is heard all the way through the recording, except for three brief moments: This drummer speeds up momentarily at 1:09, 1:46, and 2:33, with stunning, energizing effect, fitting six strokes into the space otherwise taken up by four.)

Against the main drum's consistent pulse, the other drums play a variety of different rhythms. Sometimes they underscore the main drum's even pulse, or even

duplicate it. Often, however, they play off it with more complicated and varied rhythms, including extensive syncopation within the groups of four (or beats), and occasionally they boldly contradict it.

Such overlapping of varied patterns with the main pulse is essential in West African drumming. Since several rhythmic formulas can be heard at once, it is sometimes called *polyrhythm*. Here are the details of a few clear polyrhythmic interactions:

● One drummer aligns a regular syncopated formula against the main pulse, in this manner:

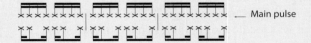

Listen for this four times in the recording, at 0:23–0:29, 0:50–0:53, 1:23–1:28, and 2:13–2:20.

● Another drummer plays an even three-plus-three pulse against the main four-plus-four, seeming to contradict its duple meter with a triple orientation. This occurs prominently twice, at 0:41–0:44 and again at 2:22–2:26.

● One drummer in particular departs freely from the main pulse all the way through this recording. He is the soloist, so to speak, improvising against the more regular and predictable playing of his ensemble mates. His drum is recognizable by its wooden, clickety-clack timbre and by the fact that it plays two distinct pitches (the higher pitch is more wooden-sounding than the lower).

A drumming club in another West African country, Ghana.
Jack Kilby/ArenaPal Images.

With jazz-rock or fusion, Davis and others reached out for vernacular roots in American music. Still, jazz after bebop is usually complex and often difficult to follow. Formerly America's dominant form of truly popular music, this music today can really only be described as "popular" with loyal fans who crowd to jazz festivals from Newport, Rhode Island, to Monterey, California. These fans view with mixed emotions efforts by Washington's Smithsonian Institution and New York's Lincoln Center to cultivate jazz in a classical-concert format, led especially by the latest great jazz trumpet virtuoso, Wynton Marsalis (b. 1961), who is also a great entrepreneur and a great publicist. The life and soul of jazz is its spontaneity. Will spontaneity survive institutionalization and "classic" status?

4 | The American Musical

Throughout the ages and throughout the world, the theater has provided fertile soil for the growth of popular music. America, once the Puritan spirit had subsided somewhat, proved no exception. One of the main sources of modern American popular music can be located in the thriving New York theatrical scene in the decades around 1900. Then as now, the New York City theater district was located at, and known as, Broadway.

Broadway was first of all the home of **operetta**, a very popular European genre of light opera in the nineteenth and early twentieth centuries. Operettas employ spoken dialogue (rather than recitative) between the musical numbers—light, attractive tunes with plenty of dances. Their plots are amusing and far-fetched. Typically they are set in some mythical eastern European country, where amorous, fun-loving aristocrats rub shoulders with merry, contented peasants.

Among the best European composers of operettas were Johann Strauss Jr., "the Waltz King" (*Die Fledermaus* [The Bat], 1874), and Arthur Sullivan (*The Mikado, HMS Pinafore,* and others; these are called "Gilbert and Sullivan" operettas as a tribute to the very witty librettist, W. S. Gilbert). The most important American composer in this tradition was Victor Herbert (1859–1924). Born in Ireland and educated in Germany, Herbert produced more than forty operettas from the 1890s on.

Musical Comedy

It was around 1910 that the American popular theater picked up its characteristic accent. It was a musical accent, and it came from jazz. Although Broadway did not employ actual jazz, it swiftly assimilated jazz syncopation and swing. As projected by white theater bands and carried over into popular songs, this jazz accent contributed more than anything else to the appeal of a new kind of musical show.

Theatergoers had also begun to demand stories that were American and up-to-date, and so the writers of the song lyrics learned to make up smart, catchy verses full of American locutions. To distinguish them from operettas—with their Old World ambience, aristocrats, and waltzes—these new shows were called **musical comedies**, or **musicals**.

The rise of the musical in the 1920s and 1930s was closely tied to the great outpouring of popular songs in this era. It was truly a golden age for song. Not all of them were written for musicals, of course. (Ellington, for example, wrote many songs that had no link to the theater.) But the theater provided songwriters with an extra fee and gave songs invaluable exposure, magnified after 1926 by "talking pictures." Theater songs were popularized by the very successful movie musicals of the 1930s, as well as by radio and 78 rpm recordings.

The two principal composers of early American musical comedy were also composers of many favorite tunes: Jerome Kern and George Gershwin. Kern's masterpiece, *Show Boat* (1927), has returned to the stage again and again, and Gershwin's *Porgy and Bess* (1935), which is more like a jazz opera than a musical, occupies a solid place in the operatic repertory.

Gershwin's actual musicals are seldom heard because most of the plots now seem so silly—but there are exceptions, notably *Of Thee I Sing* (1931), a hilarious spoof of the presidential election process. There is a song from this show in Listening Exercise 5, page 27.

Unit I

The Musical after 1940

Show Boat and *Of Thee I Sing* both look forward to a new sophistication of the musical that came about in the 1940s. Now the plots of musicals were worked out with more care. Instead of being a mere pretext for songs and dances in the manner of a revue, the plot had interest in its own right, and musical numbers grew logically out of it.

Richard Rodgers (1902–1979) and his lyricist Oscar Hammerstein (1895–1960) dominated this period. Their works, such as *Oklahoma!* (1943) and *The King and I* (1951), ran for thousands of performances on Broadway. To this day they define the golden age of the musical—perhaps especially because they offered a sentimental and innocent vision of the world as America in the postwar era wished to see it. It is a vision similar to Aaron Copland's in *Appalachian Spring* (see page 349).

Other musicals tackled more challenging subjects—racism, trade unionism, gangs—but these rarely rivaled the megahits of Rodgers and Hammerstein. One exception to this rule is *West Side Story,* with music by the classical composer and symphony conductor Leonard Bernstein. Here we see the cultivated tradition reaching out to the vernacular—but in a genre defined by the vernacular.

Leonard Bernstein (1918–1990), *West Side Story* (1957)

6 | 21–22   99–100

Leonard Bernstein was one of the most brilliant and versatile musicians ever to come out of America, the consummate crossover artist before the term was invented. Composer of classical symphonies and hit musicals, internationally acclaimed conductor, pianist, author, and mastermind of wonderful shows in the early days of television, he won Grammys, Emmys, and a Tony.

West Side Story (1957) boasts three exceptional features—its moving story, its sophisticated score, and its superb dances, created by the great American choreographer Jerome Robbins. The musical, by turns funny, smart, tender, and enormously dynamic, gave us song classics such as "Maria" and "Tonight." Our recording of *West Side Story* is from the soundtrack to the 1961 movie version of the show.

Background Shakespeare's play *Romeo and Juliet* tells of young lovers frustrated and driven to their deaths by a meaningless feud between their families, the Montagues and the Capulets of Verona.

Leonard Bernstein. *Library of Congress Prints and Photographs Division.*

West Side Story: trouble at the gym. *Photofest, Inc.*

West Side Story transplants this plot to a turf war between teenage gangs on the West Side of Manhattan.

In Shakespeare, the feud is a legacy from the older generation, but in *West Side Story* the bitter enmity belongs to the kids themselves, though it has ethnic overtones. The Jets are whites, the Sharks Puerto Ricans.

Bernardo, leader of the Sharks, is livid when he learns that his sister Maria is in love with Jet Tony. As in Shakespeare, one Jet (Capulet) and one Shark (Montague) die tragically onstage, in a street fight. Tony is shot in revenge, and Maria is left distraught.

Some of the transpositions into the modern world are ingenious. Shakespeare's famous soliloquy "Romeo, Romeo, wherefore art thou Romeo?" shows the lovestruck Juliet fondly repeating her lover's name; Tony cries "Maria" over and over again in his famous song of that title. (An aria in an opera or a song in a musical is, in fact, often equivalent to a soliloquy in a play.) And whereas Shakespeare's young lovers fall in love at a Capulet masked ball, which Romeo has crashed, Bernstein's meet at a gym dance organized by a clueless teacher who hopes to make peace between the gangs.

21 | **Cha-cha** This is the music danced to by the Puerto Rican girls—the Sharks' girlfriends—at the gym where Tony and Maria first meet. The cha-cha, a Cuban dance, was new to the United States when *West Side Story* was written.

"The great thing about conducting is that you don't smoke and you breathe in great gobs of oxygen."

Chain-smoker Leonard Bernstein

The charm of the fragile cha-cha melody owes a good deal to Bernstein's skillful accompaniment. The melody and accompaniment seem nervously aware of each other, but they keep slipping out of sync:

Meeting Scene   Tony and Maria catch sight of one another. The cha-cha may be continuing, but they don't hear it, so neither do we. Or at most they hear fragments of the cha-cha slowed down and made unexpectedly tender, as background for their voice-over.

Ma-ri-a! __ I've just met a

girl named Ma-ri-a! __

And when Tony gets to sing the big romantic number, "Maria," the music is yet another transformation of the cha-cha melody, now sounding rich and enthusiastic. Thematic transformation technique, which Bernstein knew from Wagner and other Romantic composers, allowed him to show Tony's love emerging and blossoming out of that one heart-stopping moment in the gym.

22   **"Cool"**   Later in the action, the Jet Ice tries to persuade his troops to stay calm after the death of their leader, Riff, in the rumble with the Sharks. The main production number of Act I, it consists of an introduction, again with a voice-over; a short song by Ice; a dazzling dance; and then Ice's song again.

The song's introduction uses the motive of the cha-cha melody—the same motive that turns into "Maria"—in a highly charged, syncopated form:

Boy, boy, crazy boy,
Get cool, boy!
Got a rocket in your pocket,
Keep coolly cool, boy!
Don't get hot 'cause, man, you got
Some high times ahead.
Take it slow, and, Daddy-o,
You can live it up and die in bed!

Boy,   boy   crazy   boy, __   Get cool, boy! __   Got a   rocket in your   pocket   Keep coolly cool, __ boy!

After the introduction, Ice sings two stanzas of his song, in 1950s "hip" street language. There is a steady jazz percussion accompaniment.

The dance that follows, subtitled "Fugue," is accompanied throughout by the soft jazz drumbeat. First played by muted trumpet, the fugue subject consists of four slow notes, with an ominous snap at the end of the last of them (see page 402). Soon another theme—the fugue countersubject—comes in, played by flute and vibraphone, featured instruments of 1950s "cool jazz." The two themes combine in counterpoint, along with fragments of the introduction, getting louder and more intricate as the dance proceeds. Bernstein must have thought that fugue, about the most controlled of musical forms, would depict perfectly the Jets' effort to stay cool.

"Cool"

0:14	**Ice**: "Cool"
1:12	**Fugue** begins.
2:40	Fugue breaks down.
3:10	Band version of "Cool"
3:39	**Jets**: "Cool"
4:09	**Countersubject**

But things appear to get out of hand toward the end of the dance. The music stomps angrily and breaks into electrifying improvised drum solos. The Jets yell various words taken from the song, and the song's melody returns, orchestrated in the exuberant, brash style of a big swing band. While the brasses blare away on the tune, breaks (see page 386) are played by the reeds at the end of each line.

To conclude, the Jets sing parts of "Cool" quietly, prior to its atmospheric conclusion. The vibraphone recollects the fugue countersubject.

Fugue subject:

The Later Musical

Stephen Sondheim (b. 1930), who wrote the lyrics for *West Side Story*, was himself an aspiring composer. He has gone on to write words and music for a string of successful musicals with an intellectual bent, such as *A Little Night Music* (1972), *Sweeney Todd* (1979), and *Into the Woods* (1987). *Sweeney Todd* in particular pushed at the border between musical and opera, as Gershwin had done forty years earlier in *Porgy and Bess.*

Meanwhile the musical in the 1960s began to acknowledge the rock revolution. Prominent rock musicals were *Hair* (1967; the latest revival was in 2009), *Grease* (1972), and *Rent* (1996). Rock musicals have had to share space on Broadway with more conventional fare, often from abroad, such as *Les Misérables* (*Les Mis*, 1980), *Cats* (1981), and *The Phantom of the Opera* (1986). Some of these are still running.

Written for the stage, musicals have often been filmed with great success, from *Show Boat* to *Rent*, not to forget *West Side Story*. Back in the early days of movie musicals, Walt Disney had the idea of creating musicals directly for animated full-length films, including *Snow White and the Seven Dwarfs* (1937) and *Pinocchio* (1940). In the 1990s this tradition was revived by the Disney studio with films such as *Beauty and the Beast* (1991) and *The Lion King* (1994). Again we see musical theater reinventing itself—from opera to operetta, from operetta to musical, from musical to filmed musical. Such reinventions will surely continue in the future.

Beyond Broadway and Hollywood, throughout all this time, musical comedy has thrived in the annual student revivals of Broadway hits at thousands of colleges, high schools, junior highs, and summer camps around the country. Take part in one of these, and it will expand your whole idea of music.

5 | Rock

World War II made for massive changes not only in global politics and population but also in all aspects of culture throughout the world. To speak only of music, we have traced the radical developments of avant-garde music in its second phase, and noted the dissolution of the big jazz bands in America as well as the increasing complexity of our musical theater. And while popular song continued to flourish after World War II, it was a new kind of popular song, with less emphasis on melody and more on rhythm—or, more exactly, with a heavy emphasis on music's meter. By the middle of the 1950s the new style took a name that captured this compelling rhythm: *rock'n'roll*. Later, in the 1960s, the name of choice was shortened to **rock**. Teenagers went wild. Their parents, reacting much as parents had thirty years earlier in the face of jazz, bemoaned the demise of civil culture and decent society.

Nevertheless, rock endured and evolved—in fact, it positively burgeoned. Its explosive development from 1955 to 1970 and its reinvention in the following

The final painting by Thomas Hart Benton (1889–1975), *The Sources of Country Music.* Pictured are hymnody, Appalachian fiddle and dulcimer, black banjo and song, cowboy guitar—as well as less direct inspirations: church, train, Mississippi riverboat, and moonshine. Benton painted it for the Country Music Hall of Fame in Nashville. *Courtesy of Country Music Hall of Fame and Museum.*

decades have put rock on a historical par with jazz. If jazz can claim to be America's most distinctive contribution to world art from the first half of the twentieth century, rock can make similar claims for the second half. Today the development of global pop, discussed in Global Perspectives on page 410, depends on various styles of American-derived rock more than on any other musical idiom.

Early Rock'n'Roll

The origins and subsequent history of rock conform to a pattern in American vernacular music we have seen as early as the minstrel show and then in 1930s swing: the mixing of African American and white American styles. Sometimes in rock history this mix was a relatively balanced meeting of differing styles; at other times it looks more like the appropriation of African American idioms for commercial gain by white musicians.

The very earliest rock'n'roll shows this pattern, emerging after World War II from the blending of *hillbilly* or *country* music with **rhythm and blues**. Country music was a white rural style derived from southern and southwestern folk song and emphasizing acoustic guitar, fiddle, and voice. Rhythm and blues was a black urban updating of earlier blues, marked by more pronounced, driving rhythms and electric guitar accompaniment.

Together they created the first rock'n'roll style, *rockabilly,* and the first superstar of rock'n'roll, Elvis Presley. His amazing string of hits in the late 1950s ("Heartbreak Hotel," "Love Me Tender," and many others) combined a lyrical style derived from white popular singers with the strong beat and passionate, throaty vocal delivery of rockabilly. Many of these hits (for example, "Hound Dog") were Elvis's versions of songs originally recorded by black artists.

Across the late 1950s a string of musicians, both white (Jerry Lee Lewis, Buddy Holly) and black (Fats Domino, Little Richard, Chuck Berry), followed Elvis up the charts—and soon it was "Rock around the Clock," as Bill Haley had declared in his 1955 hit. Radio stations and record companies alike realized there was a lasting market for the new sound.

The 1960s: Rock Comes of Age

The blending of black and white styles that resulted in early rock'n'roll lasted into the 1960s and has reappeared in various forms down to this day. At the same time, the early and mid-1960s witnessed the emergence of new styles, many of them clearly black or white in their origin and target audience. There was an explosion of new sounds, distinct from one another and gaining the allegiance of different groups of fans.

Motown, Soul, and Funk

As the civil rights movement of the 1950s evolved into the Black Power movement of the late 1960s, a succession of black styles asserted their independence from white rock. These grew out of several sources: the remnants of black rhythm and

With his sultry voice and sexual stage presence, Elvis Presley had a gripping effect on audiences of the 1950s. *Hulton Archive/Getty Images.*

blues in the late 1950s, most notably represented by singer-pianist Ray Charles; urban doo-wop groups that spawned such hit-makers as the Drifters ("Under the Boardwalk"); and "girl groups" such as the Shirelles ("Will You Love Me Tomorrow?").

The first in this line was the *Motown* style, created by the part-time songwriter and record producer Berry Gordy Jr. of Detroit—"Motorcity" or "Motown." Gordy was the most important black entrepreneur in early rock history. The groups he sponsored, among them the Supremes ("Where Did Our Love Go?") and the Temptations ("My Girl"), evolved polished, lyrical styles and performances featuring dance steps and sequins.

A more visceral style that emerged around the same time was *soul*. Soul derived especially from southern gospel singing combined with the rhythm and blues of Ray Charles. Its leading lights were the powerful Aretha Franklin ("Respect") and James Brown, self-styled as "the hardest working man in show business"—and certainly one of the hardest singing ("I Got You (I Feel Good)").

By the end of the 1960s, soul was evolving into *funk*, a style in which the large bands with wind instruments typical of soul gave way to a sparer, hip sound (fuzz-tone bass guitar ostinatos, syncopated guitar scratching). One of the early groups pointing in this direction was the Bay Area–based Sly and the Family Stone ("Thank You (Falettinme Be Mice Elf Agin)"). A decade later funk, as performed by

"Stop in the name of love!" The Supremes in concert, 1965: Florence Ballard, lead singer Diana Ross, and Mary Wilson. *Bettmann/Corbis.*

George Clinton and his band Funkadelic, was the style early DJs sampled to accompany the first rappers.

The British Invasion

On February 7, 1964, the Beatles landed in New York for their first American tour. The resulting Beatlemania changed the face of rock'n'roll and has never really ended.

Dozens of other British rock bands followed in the wake of the Beatles' arrival, some good, some not. The best of them, cast from the first as a kind of evil-twin mirroring of the Beatles, was the Rolling Stones. What British groups had in common at the start was their emulation of American rhythm and blues and the styles of black American rockers like Chuck Berry and Little Richard.

The difference between the Beatles and the Rolling Stones was not merely the good/bad contrast of their carefully groomed market images. It was musical as well. The Stones specialized in a hard-rocking style led by Mick Jagger's manic vocal presence. The Beatles, in contrast, seemed to blossom in all musical directions, reflecting the differing musical personalities of John Lennon, Paul McCartney, and George Harrison—differences that would tear the group apart by 1970. From covers of Chuck Berry ("Roll Over, Beethoven") and sneakily insightful pop/rock numbers ("She Loves You," "Help!"), they moved on to lyrical ballads ("Yesterday," "Blackbird"), hymnlike anthems ("Hey Jude," "Let It Be"), visionary and psychedelic rock ("A Day in the Life," "Strawberry Fields Forever"), straight-ahead, blues-derived rock ("Revolution"), and irresistible

January 1969: the Beatles in their final concert, an impromptu affair soon broken up by the police, on the roof of the Apple Records building in London. From left: Ringo, Paul, John, and George. *RBO/Camera Press/Redux.*

pop songs harking back to the 1930s ("When I'm Sixty-Four," "Maxwell's Silver Hammer"—surely the sweetest tune imaginable about a serial killer).

American Counteroffensives

The irony of the British groups' interest in American rhythm and blues is that their massive popularity chased dozens of American groups, especially black ones, off the charts and out of business. About the only American music that swam well during the highest tide of the British invasion was the surfing sound out of southern California, led by the Beach Boys ("I Get Around," "Good Vibrations").

Meanwhile another movement looking back to the hillbilly side of rock's ancestry was gaining steam. *Folk rock* was led by Bob Dylan, whose evocative, often socially conscious lyrics ("Blowin' in the Wind," "The Times They Are A-Changin'") rivaled his music in importance. Dylan's resuscitation of white country and folk styles, building on "folkies" such as Woody Guthrie and Pete Seeger, had long-lasting consequences.

The most important of these was creating a place, at the edge of the rock tradition, for the singer-songwriter using acoustic accompaniment. Dylan and the folkies inspired later musicians as different as Bruce Springsteen and Elvis Costello. Women musicians in particular have found the singer-songwriter niche congenial. Their line extends from Joan Baez and Joni Mitchell in the 1960s to Joanna Newsom and Norah Jones today.

Joan Baez and Bob Dylan, 1975. *AP Photo.*

In the late 1960s a broad, mainly white stratum of American youth, espousing free love, free drugs, and ever-louder opposition to the U.S. war in Vietnam, embraced new styles. From San Francisco, a center of this counterculture, came *acid rock,* named after a mind-altering new drug, LSD, or "acid." In the hands of groups like the Grateful Dead, the style joined long, jazzlike improvisations on electric guitar to hallucinatory images in the words; the Dead was the first great "jam band."

Other guitar virtuosos embraced the new, improvisational style and linked it back to rhythm-and-blues guitar playing. The most famous of them were Jimi Hendrix, a rare black musician in the midst of psychedelic acid rock ("Purple Haze"), and the Latin-influenced Carlos Santana ("Black Magic Woman"). This powerful new style of guitar playing would infect groups on both sides of the Atlantic, such as the Who (creators of the rock opera *Tommy*), Cream (led by the blues-influenced guitarist Eric Clapton; "Sunshine of Your Love"), and Led Zeppelin ("Whole Lotta Love"). The guitar work of such groups formed the roots of *heavy metal.*

After the 1960s

By 1970, many of the trends that evolved over the following decades were in place. Self-conscious *art rock* (for example, Pink Floyd's album *Dark Side of the Moon*), singer-songwriter rock, heavy metal, and funk can all be seen as outgrowths of music at the end of the 1960s.

The decade of the 1970s was perhaps most influential, however, in its consolidation of the global *business* of rock. Tendencies under way in the 1960s came to exert ever-greater control over the music people heard: high-tech mass marketing; play-listed, repetitive radio stations; and aggressive promotion of

Jimi Hendrix performing at the Woodstock Festival, August 18, 1969. His psychedelic performance there, on solo electric guitar, of the "Star Spangled Banner" came to represent the festival and youth culture in general, inspiring many and outraging many more. Listen to it on YouTube. *Dick Cunningham.*

"superstars" (the word itself came into common usage at this time, alongside "supertanker" and "superpower"). In 1981 a powerful new outlet emerged to promote a small and carefully selected sample of rock music: MTV began broadcasting music videos nonstop on cable.

These developments repeat, in a general way, what happened to jazz in the years around 1940. A freewheeling array of earlier musical developments came to be channeled and constrained, almost as a result of their own success.

Trends 1980–2000: Punk, Rap, and Post-Rock

Despite—or perhaps because of—this commercialization, rock survived. There were strong new currents countering commercialization and corporate control. Indeed the last decades of the twentieth century brought something of a rejuvenation. Three trends in particular can be pointed to:

• The youthful disaffection that set in by the end of the 1960s, as the idealistic counterculture began to sense its impotence, hardened in the next decade. Its most influential expression was the nihilistic alienation of *punk rock*. In New York City and Britain, groups like the Patti Smith Group ("Gloria"), the Ramones ("Blitzkrieg Bop"), and the Sex Pistols ("Anarchy in the UK") reacted against the commercial flashiness of much rock with what we might call an anti-aesthetic: All expression was possible, including no expression. All musical expertise was acceptable, including none. (Some of the punks were fully aware that in this move they were following the lead of avant-garde modernists like John Cage; see page 367.)

The punk approach gave strong impetus to a kind of populist movement in rock, encouraging the formation of countless "garage bands" and the 1990s' *indie rock,* distributed on small, independent labels. Some punk singers also pioneered an alienated, flat vocal delivery that contrasts both with the impassioned singing of earlier rock and with the streetwise cool of rap. In these features punk looked forward to the unpolished, moving, but somehow distant style of *grunge rock,* led by Kurt Cobain (until his death in 1994) and his band Nirvana.

- First emerging about the same time as punk, *hip-hop* or **rap** has compiled a substantial history as a primary black rhetorical and musical mode. Early on, its influence was transmitted, with stunning postmodern quickness, around the globe. Already by 2000 rap had become a strong current in world pop-music traditions, its influence heard in the vocal delivery of countless rock and pop groups.

Kurt Cobain. *Gie Knaeps/LFI/Photoshot.*

The early 1990s marked rap's moment of highest notoriety in the American mass media. One strain of rap—the violent, misogynist variety known as *gangsta rap*—figured centrally in the public debate, which was marked not only by justifiable distaste at the vision of these rappers but also by unmistakable racist undertones. However, the debate tended to miss two important points: First, while rap originated as a pointed expression of black urban concerns, it was marketed successfully to affluent whites, especially suburban teens. Second, the clamor against gangsta rap ignored the wider expressive vistas of rap as a whole. Already in 1980 rap was broad enough to embrace the hip-hop dance numbers of the Sugarhill Gang ("Rapper's Delight") and the trenchant social commentary of Grandmaster Flash ("The Message"). By the 1990s, rap could range from the black empowerment messages of Public Enemy ("Don't Believe the Hype") to Queen Latifah's assertions of women's dignity and strength ("Latifah's Had It Up 2 Here").

- Around 1990 a new, experimental rock movement began to take shape; soon it was dubbed *post-rock.* Early post-rock groups (for example, Slint; "Good Morning Captain") emerged from the indie rock movement. They typically employed rock instrumentation and technology in a style that features hypnotically repeated gestures (especially bass ostinatos), juxtaposition of contrasting plateaus of sound, slow transitions and buildups, free improvisation, and emphasis of instruments rather than voice. (When a voice is present, it often doesn't so much *sing* as recite fragments of poetry in front of the instrumental backdrop.) This thumbnail sketch alone is enough to reveal post-rock's relation to two other musical movements we have encountered: minimalism (see page 369) and fusion jazz (see page 396).

And just as classic jazz appeared by the 1970s, so today we have classic rock; and the same question might again arise: Can creative freshness survive the prepackaged recycling of rock styles and gestures?

But perhaps, in the end, this is the wrong way to think of rock in the twenty-first century. Perhaps we need to broaden our view now, understanding rock altogether as a spectacularly energetic strain in the popular song tradition that took off with Tin Pan Alley, was fed by blues and jazz, and will be carried forward by the next winner of *American Idol, The Voice,* or another reality-show talent search that replaces them. Whatever songs you download onto your iPhone, it is clear that fussy distinctions of rock from rap, rap from pop, and pop from country can be a limiting way of hearing this broad, rich tradition as it lives on in the new century.

Global Music

We have seen in Global Perspectives on page 77 that European efforts to colonize foreign lands never resulted in the simple substitution of European cultures for native ones, but rather in new, complex mixed cultures. Such is the way of all meetings of distinct cultures and distinct musics.

But a funny thing happened to mixed musical cultures on their way through the twentieth century: recorded sound. Around the globe, the impact on music of technologies that store and play back sound has been revolutionary. Combined with radio and TV broadcasts, and with the modern ease of travel and commerce, it has given musicians and listeners from all parts of the world access to a much wider variety of music than ever before.

Complexities of Globalism

Two opposing tendencies have arisen from this situation. The first works toward the worldwide *homogenization* of musics. Huge stretches of the sonic landscape are now inhabited by styles that are similar in certain basic features: electrified instruments, especially guitars; strong percussive presence; extensive syncopation; and relatively brief song-form presentation.

These features spread out from the American and especially African American pop-music revolution that occurred in the decades after World War II. Since the 1960s the dispersion of styles such as rhythm and blues, rock, soul, and rap has been powerful. Musical currents have, to be sure, flowed in both directions. *Reggae*, to take one example, was formed in the 1960s from a merger of native Jamaican styles with American rhythm and blues and soul, but by the late 1970s it had crossed back over to exert a great influence on American rock itself. The global dispersion has been enabled by a recording industry that has grown increasingly rich, increasingly multinational, and increasingly influential in determining musical tastes. It is enough to make one observer of these developments worry about a "universal pop aesthetic."

A community choir sings in front of stark Soweto Township, Johannesburg, South Africa, 1995. *Louise Gubb/The Image Works.*

There is another tendency, however, opposing this move toward sameness, a move to *localize* music making. People never simply take on foreign things without in some way making them their own. Even as musicians around the world have felt the influence of American pop styles, they have combined these styles in their local musics to forge new, distinct styles. Reggae is one example of this process.

South African Choral Song: Isicathamiya

A South African musical tradition with a difficult name, *isicathamiya* (ees-ee-caht-ah-mée-ah), provides an example of this mix of local and global ingredients reaching back many decades. In the 1990s it became familiar to listeners worldwide through the recordings of the singing group Ladysmith Black Mambazo. Isicathamiya is an all-male, *a cappella* song style that arose among an impoverished class of black, mostly Zulu-speaking migrant laborers. A chief diversion in the laborers' camps was Saturday-night contests among singing groups, and for the musical styles the performers looked back to earlier, complex international roots.

Standing behind isicathamiya are traditions of choral polyphony native to the Zulus and other groups of the region. In the nineteenth century, these traditions merged readily with the four-part harmony of Christian hymn singing brought to the area by European and American missionaries. Then another ingredient was added to the mix: American vaudeville or minstrel shows, with their syncopated, ragtime songs (see page 386 and the picture on page 398). An enormously influential African American minstrel—not a white minstrel in blackface—named Orpheus McAdoo toured South Africa extensively in the 1890s, to the great acclaim of black audiences.

By the 1930s, these musical influences were put together by the first recording stars of the local Zulu singing scene, Solomon Linda and the Evening Birds. Their greatest hit, "Mbube" or "Lion," known to most of us today as "The Lion Sleeps Tonight," was originally recorded about 1939. Then it was re-recorded by pop singers and became a hit in the 1960s. Most recently it was featured in Disney's film and musical *The Lion King*.

"Anoku Gonda"

6|24 111

Solomon Linda's song "Anoku Gonda" (You Must Understand This), from the same period as "Mbube,"

Isicathamiya praktisa: a rehearsal at the Beatrice St. YMCA, Durban, South Africa, 1996. *Carol Muller.*

combines two distinct styles that are still heard today in isicathamiya. The first is a richly harmonized, homophonic style that recites the text freely and shows no clear or consistent sense of meter—**choral declamation**, we can call it. We hear two phrases of choral declamation, stated and repeated in the pattern **a a b b a a**. Notable here, and frequent in isicathamiya, is the slide in all voices from high to lower pitches.

Then, after about a minute, the music takes on a clear meter. This is the second style common in isicathamiya. It is still organized in repeating phrases, but now the texture departs from the simple homophony of the recitational opening section. It uses call-and-response techniques (see page 385), pitting Linda against the rest of the group at first; later the basses in the chorus sing against the group as a whole. The call-and-response phrases alternate with a falling cadential phrase sung by the whole chorus.

 **LISTEN**

"Anoku Gonda"

6 | 24   111

0:00	Unmetered choral declamation
0:00	**a**
0:13	**a**
0:25	**b**
0:30	**b**
0:35	**a**
0:47	**a**
0:57	Metrical call and response: Solomon Linda against the full chorus
1:27	Metrical call and response: Basses against the full chorus

Hill Street Studios/Blend Images/Corbis.

6 | Conclusion

A few thoughts in conclusion: not so much a conclusion to this chapter, but rather to our total effort in this book as a whole.

In the introduction to Unit I, on page 2, we observed that the love and understanding of music is best nurtured by listening again and again to particular pieces. Some musical terminology has been introduced that should help clarify listening, and we have led a guided tour through the history of Western music, from Hildegard of Bingen in her convent to Tania León in her recording studio, by way of Bach, Mozart, Beethoven, Wagner, and Stravinsky. There have been a number of detours beyond Europe, and a fairly long side trip to popular music—but on all routes, the most important thing we've done is *listen*.

Surveys show that many students hang on to the recordings that come with *Listen*, even while they dispose of the book itself. Anyone who keeps the music, we reason, expects or half expects to play it again sometime, and so long as that happens we are more than happy to see the book—which is only here to introduce and explain the music and put it in context—fall away. Teachers are great hopers. We hope, though we'll never know, that sometime in the future you will find yourself listening again to some of the music you were introduced to in *Listen*.

"All music is what awakes from you when you are reminded by the instruments,
It is not the violins and the cornets, it is not the oboe nor the beating drums, nor the score of the baritone singer singing his sweet romanza, nor that of the men's chorus, nor that of the women's chorus,
It is nearer and farther than they."

For Walt Whitman, music was always both mystical and precise.

GOALS FOR REVIEW

▶ to differentiate cultivated and vernacular (or popular) musical traditions

▶ to understand the importance of African American music in American popular traditions

▶ to analyze blues form and follow an example of it

▶ to listen to examples from major styles of jazz history: New Orleans jazz, big-band swing, bebop, and fusion jazz

▶ to explore the history of the American musical

▶ to survey some shifting currents in the history of rock music

---

macmillanhighered.com/listen8e
Listening Quizzes for Chapter 24, Global Perspectives: African Drumming, and Global Perspectives: Global Music
Reading Quizzes for Chapter 24, Global Perspectives: African Drumming, and Global Perspectives: Global Music

Time Lines

The Middle Ages

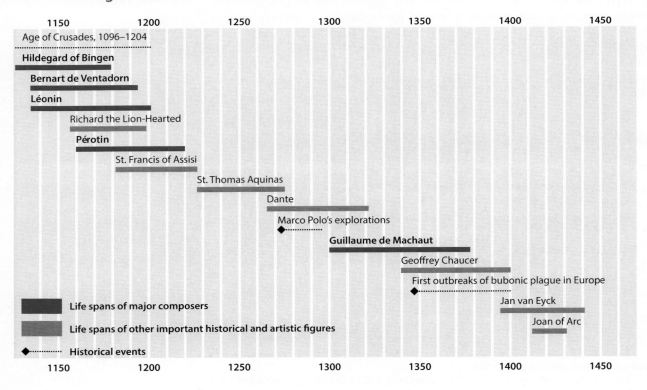

The Renaissance and Early Baroque

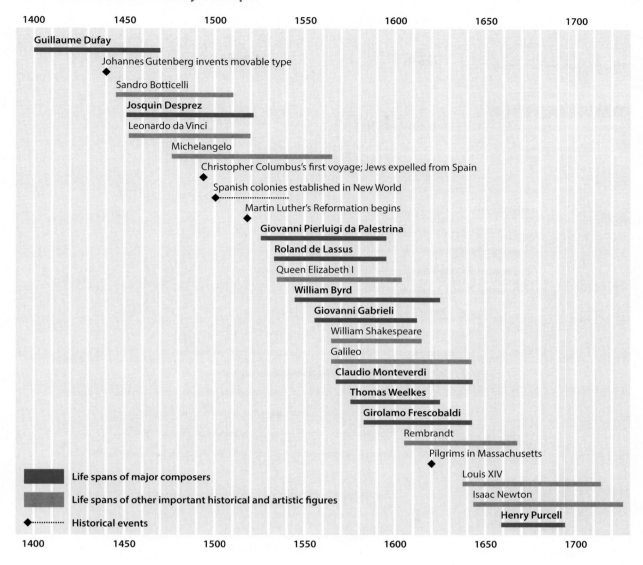

1400   1450   1500   1550   1600   1650   1700

Guillaume Dufay

Johannes Gutenberg invents movable type ◆

Sandro Botticelli

Josquin Desprez

Leonardo da Vinci

Michelangelo

Christopher Columbus's first voyage; Jews expelled from Spain ◆

Spanish colonies established in New World ◆

Martin Luther's Reformation begins ◆

Giovanni Pierluigi da Palestrina

Roland de Lassus

Queen Elizabeth I

William Byrd

Giovanni Gabrieli

William Shakespeare

Galileo

Claudio Monteverdi

Thomas Weelkes

Girolamo Frescobaldi

Rembrandt

Pilgrims in Massachusetts ◆

Louis XIV

Isaac Newton

Henry Purcell

▬ Life spans of major composers

▬ Life spans of other important historical and artistic figures

◆···· Historical events

1400   1450   1500   1550   1600   1650   1700

The Eighteenth Century

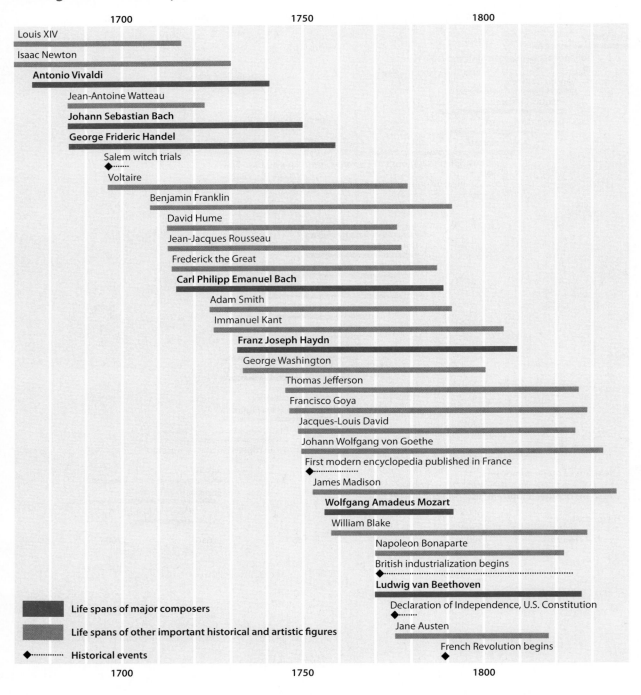

	1700	1750	1800

Louis XIV

Isaac Newton

Antonio Vivaldi

Jean-Antoine Watteau

Johann Sebastian Bach

George Frideric Handel

Salem witch trials

Voltaire

Benjamin Franklin

David Hume

Jean-Jacques Rousseau

Frederick the Great

Carl Philipp Emanuel Bach

Adam Smith

Immanuel Kant

Franz Joseph Haydn

George Washington

Thomas Jefferson

Francisco Goya

Jacques-Louis David

Johann Wolfgang von Goethe

First modern encyclopedia published in France

James Madison

Wolfgang Amadeus Mozart

William Blake

Napoleon Bonaparte

British industrialization begins

Ludwig van Beethoven

Declaration of Independence, U.S. Constitution

Jane Austen

French Revolution begins

Life spans of major composers

Life spans of other important historical and artistic figures

◆········· Historical events

	1700	1750	1800

The Nineteenth Century

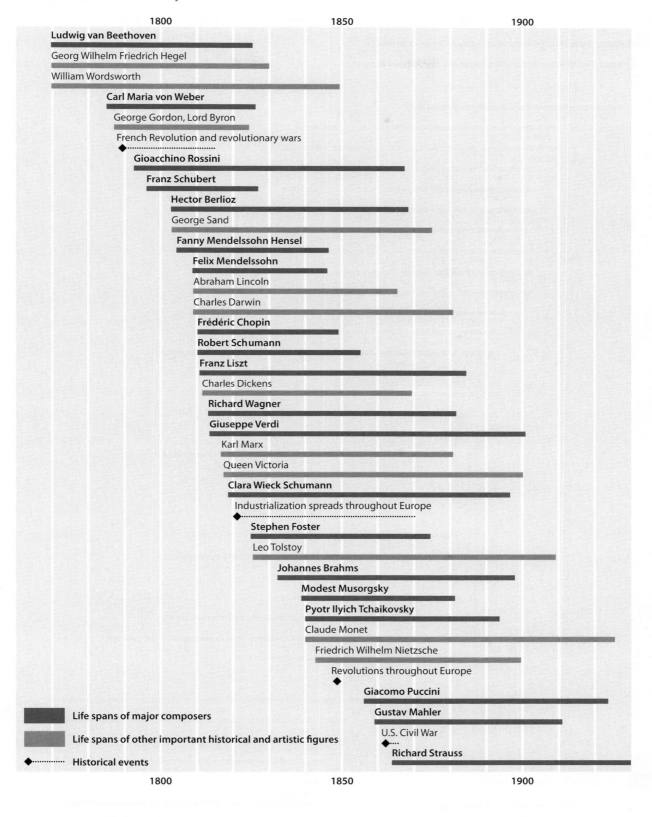

1800   1850   1900

Ludwig van Beethoven
Georg Wilhelm Friedrich Hegel
William Wordsworth
Carl Maria von Weber
George Gordon, Lord Byron
French Revolution and revolutionary wars
Gioacchino Rossini
Franz Schubert
Hector Berlioz
George Sand
Fanny Mendelssohn Hensel
Felix Mendelssohn
Abraham Lincoln
Charles Darwin
Frédéric Chopin
Robert Schumann
Franz Liszt
Charles Dickens
Richard Wagner
Giuseppe Verdi
Karl Marx
Queen Victoria
Clara Wieck Schumann
Industrialization spreads throughout Europe
Stephen Foster
Leo Tolstoy
Johannes Brahms
Modest Musorgsky
Pyotr Ilyich Tchaikovsky
Claude Monet
Friedrich Wilhelm Nietzsche
Revolutions throughout Europe
Giacomo Puccini
Gustav Mahler
U.S. Civil War
Richard Strauss

▬▬▬ Life spans of major composers

▬▬▬ Life spans of other important historical and artistic figures

◆·········· Historical events

1800   1850   1900

The Twentieth Century and Beyond

Thomas Edison
Sigmund Freud
U.S. Civil War
Claude Debussy
Arnold Schoenberg
Charles Ives
Maurice Ravel
Albert Einstein
Pablo Picasso
Béla Bartók
Igor Stravinsky
James Joyce
Virginia Woolf
Alban Berg
Sergei Prokofiev
Martha Graham
William Grant Still
George Gershwin
Ernest Hemingway
Duke Ellington
Aaron Copland
Louis Armstrong
Ruth Crawford
Women's suffrage movement
Frida Kahlo
John Cage
World War I
Charlie Parker
Leonard Bernstein
György Ligeti
Martin Luther King Jr.
Worldwide economic depression
George Crumb
Steve Reich
World War II; Holocaust
Tania León
Cold War
John Adams
Internet revolution

Life spans of major composers

Life spans of other important historical and artistic figures

Historical events

Musical Notation

Many traditions around the world employ different notations for writing their music down. It is never necessary, obviously, to read these notations in order to understand the music or to love it; indeed, many traditions have no notation at all. However, written music examples can help clarify many points about musical style—even ones not written down by their creators—and it will help if you can learn to follow the music examples in this book in an approximate way. The following brief survey of Western musical notation can be used for study or review or reference.

As we have seen in our discussion of musical elements, *time* and *pitch* are really the only ones that can be specified (and therefore notated) with any precision. Think of pitch and time as coordinates of a graph on which music is going to be plotted. The resulting pitch/time grid is quite close to actual musical notation, as shown in the diagrams below.

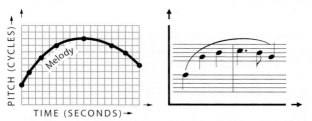

Notes and Rests

The longest note in common use is the *whole note* (o). A half note (♩) lasts for half the time of a whole note, a quarter note (♩) lasts for a quarter of the time, an eighth note (♪) for an eighth, a sixteenth note (♬) for a sixteenth, and so on. (We are dealing here with proportional lengths; how long any note lasts in absolute time depends on the tempo: see page 7).

One whole note

= 2 half notes

= 4 quarter notes

= 8 eighth notes

= 16 sixteenth notes

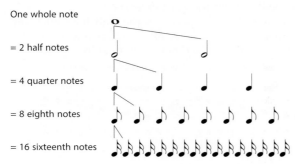

When the short notes come in groups, they can also be notated as shown at the top of the next column.

The *flags*—they look more like pennants—at the sides of the note *stems* have been connected into horizontal *beams* for easier reading:

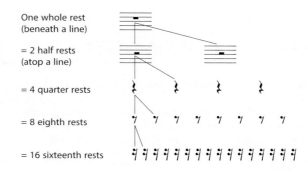

Composers use not only sounds but also short silences called *rests*.

One whole rest
(beneath a line)

= 2 half rests
(atop a line)

= 4 quarter rests

= 8 eighth rests

= 16 sixteenth rests

Compare the whole- and half-note rests, which are slugs beneath or atop one of the lines of the staff.

The shorter rests have their own sort of flags. As with notes, more flags can be added to rests, with each flag cutting the time value in half. Thus, three flags on a rest (𝄿) make it a thirty-second rest.

Rhythmic Notation

Beyond the notation of basic notes and rests, a number of other conventions are necessary to indicate the combining of notes and rests into actual rhythms.

Dotted Notes and Dotted Rhythms A dot placed after a note or rest lengthens its duration by 50 percent. Thus a dotted half note lasts as long as a half note plus a quarter note: ♩. = ♩ + ♩ And a dotted quarter-note rest equals a quarter plus an eighth: 𝄽. = 𝄽 + 𝄾 Even simple tunes, such as "Yankee Doodle," make use of the dot convention.

A *dotted rhythm* is one consisting of dotted (long) notes alternating with short ones:

Ties Two notes of the same pitch can be connected by means of a curved line called a *tie*. This means they are played continuously, as though they were one note of the combined duration. Any number of notes of the same pitch can be tied together.

Ties

Beware: The same sort of curved line is also used to connect notes that are *not* of the same pitch. In this case it means that they are to be played smoothly, one following the next without the slightest break (*legato* or "bound" playing). These curved lines are called *slurs*.

Slurs: legato

To indicate that notes are to be played in an especially detached fashion (*staccato*), dots are placed above or below them.

Staccato dots

Triplets Three notes bracketed together and marked with a 3 (♩♩♩) are called a *triplet*. The three notes take exactly the same time that would normally be taken by two. A quarter-note triplet has the same duration as two ordinary quarter notes: ♩♩♩ = ♩♩

The convention is occasionally extended to groups of five notes, seven notes, etc. For an example, see page 244.

Meter: Measures and Bar Lines A *measure* (or *bar*) is the basic time unit chosen for a piece of music, corresponding to the meter of the piece (see page 5). Measures are marked in musical notation by vertical *bar lines*. Each measure covers the same time span.

In the following example, the time span covered by each measure is one whole note, equivalent to two half notes (measure 1), or four quarter notes (measure 2), or eight eighth notes (measures 3, 4).

Time signature

Measures

Bar lines

Time Signatures In the example above, the meter is indicated by means of a *time signature*. Time signatures are printed on the staffs at the beginning of pieces of music (they are not repeated on later staffs).

In spite of appearances, time signatures are not fractions. The top digit shows *how many beats* are in each measure, and the bottom digit shows *what kind of note* represents a beat. If the bottom digit is 2, the beat is represented by a half note; if 4, by a quarter note, and so on.

In our example, the 2 at the top indicates there are two beats in each measure (duple meter), and the 2 at the bottom indicates that the beats are half-note beats. This time signature can also be indicated by the sign ₵.

Pitch Notation

The letter names A B C D E F G are assigned to the original seven pitches of the diatonic scale. Then the letters are used over and over again for pitches in the duplicating octaves. Octaves are distinguished by numbers (c¹, c²) or prime marks (A′, A″); so-called middle C (c¹) is the comfortable note that virtually any man, woman, or child can sing and that can be played by the great majority of instruments. On a keyboard, middle C sits in the middle, right under the maker's name—Casio, Yamaha, Steinway.

The Staff: Ledger Lines For the notation of pitch, notes are placed on a set of five parallel lines called a *staff*. The notes can be put on the lines of the staff, in the spaces between them, or right at the top or bottom of the staff:

Above and below the regular five lines of the staff, short extra lines can be added to accommodate a few higher and lower notes. These are called *ledger lines*.

Clefs Nothing has been said so far about which pitch each position on the staff represents. To clue us in to precise pitches, signs called *clefs* (French for "key" or "clue") are placed at the beginning of each staff. Clefs calibrate the staff; that is, they connect one of the five lines of the staff to a specific pitch.

Thus in the treble clef, or G clef (𝄞), the spiral in the middle of this antique capital G curls around line 2, counting up from the bottom of the staff. Line 2, then, is the line for the pitch G—the first G above middle C. In the bass clef, or F clef (𝄢), the two dots straddle the fourth line up. The pitch F goes on this line—the first F below middle C. Complicated! But not too hard to learn.

Adjacent lines and spaces on the staff have adjacent letter names, so we can place all the other pitches on the staff in relation to the fixed points marked by the clefs:

There are other clefs, but these two are the most common. Used in conjunction, they accommodate the maximum span of pitches without overlapping. The treble and bass clef staffs fit together as shown in Figure 1 below.

The notation of six A's, covering five octaves, requires two staffs and seven ledger lines (see Figure 2).

Sharps and Flats; Naturals The pitches produced by the black keys on the piano are not given letter names of their own. (This is a consequence of the way they arose in history; see page 23.) Nor do they get their own individual lines or spaces on the staffs. The pitch in between A and B is called A sharp (or A♯, using the conventional sign for a sharp), meaning "higher than A." It can also be called B flat (B♭), meaning "lower than B." In musical notation, the signs ♯ and ♭ are placed on the staff just *before* the note that is to be sharped or flatted.

Which of these two terms is used depends partly on convenience, partly on convention, and partly on theoretical considerations that do not concern us here. In the example below, the third note, A♯, sounds just like the B♭ later in the measure, but for technical reasons the composer (Béla Bartók) notated it differently.

The original pitches of the diatonic scale, played on the white keys of the piano, are called "natural." If it is necessary to cancel a sharp or a flat within a measure and to indicate that the natural note should be played instead, the natural sign is placed before a note (♮♩) or after a letter (A♮) to show this. The following example shows A sharp and G sharp being canceled by natural signs:

Key Signatures In musical notation, it is a convention that a sharp or flat placed before a note will also

affect any later appearance of that same note *in the same measure*—but not in the next measure.

There is also a way of specifying that certain sharps or flats are to be applied throughout an entire piece, in every measure, and in every octave. Such sharps and flats appear on the staffs at the very beginning of the piece, even prior to the time signature, and at the beginning of each staff thereafter. They constitute the *key signature:*

is equivalent to:

Scores

Music for a melody instrument such as a violin or a trumpet is written on one staff; keyboard instruments require two—one staff for the right hand, another for the left hand. Music for two or more voices or instruments, choirs, bands, and orchestras is written in *scores*. In scores, each instrument and voice that has its own independent music gets its own staff. Simultaneously sounding notes and measure lines are aligned vertically. In general, high-sounding instruments go on top, the low ones on the bottom.

Shown on page 424 is a page from Mozart's "Jupiter" Symphony, with arrows pointing to the various details of notation that have been explained above.

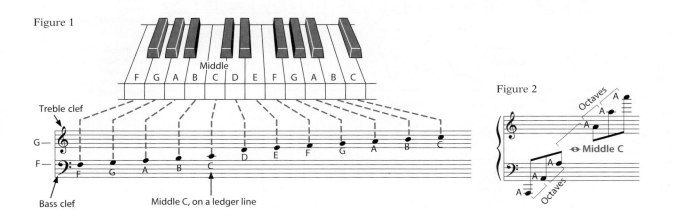

Figure 1

Figure 2

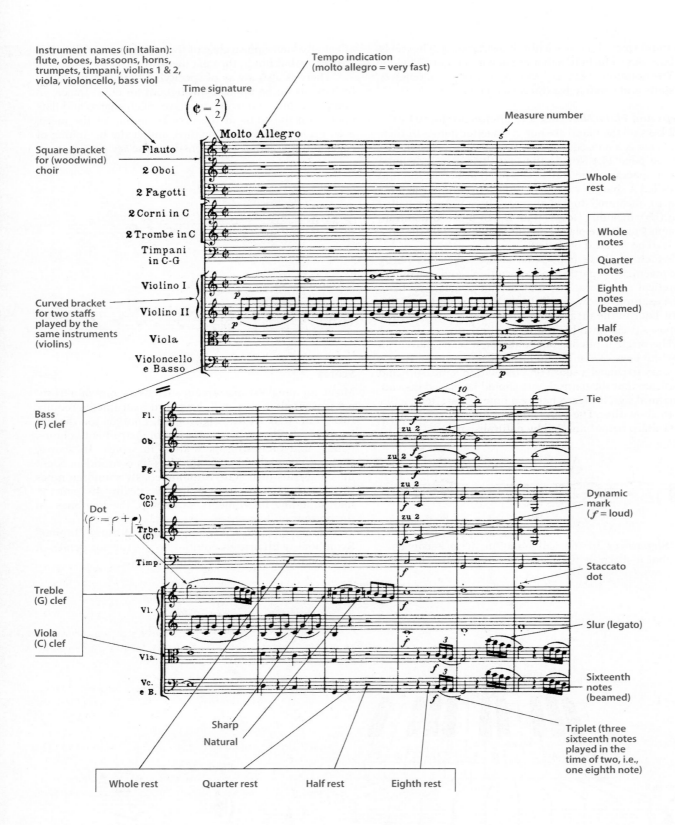

Glossary of Musical Terms

The italicized words refer to other definitions in the glossary, which you can look up if necessary. The page numbers refer to fuller explanations in the text.

A cappella (ah kah-pél-la): Choral music for voices alone, without instruments *(65)*

Accelerando (a-chel-er-áhn-do): Getting faster

Accent: The stressing of a note—for example, by playing it somewhat louder than the surrounding notes *(5)*

Accidentals: In musical notation, signs indicating that a note is to be played *sharp, flat,* or *natural*

Accompanied recitative: See *recitative (138)*

Adagio: Slow tempo *(8)*

Alba: *Troubadour* song about a knight leaving his lady at dawn *(50)*

Allegro; allegretto: Fast; moderately fast *(8)*

Alto, contralto: The low female voice

Andante: A fairly slow tempo, but not too slow *(8)*

Andantino: A little faster than *andante (8)*

Antiphon: A genre of plainchant usually in a simple melodic style with very few melismas *(47)*

Aria: A vocal number for solo singer and orchestra, generally in an opera, cantata, or oratorio *(84, 138)*

Arioso: A singing style between *recitative* and *aria (86)*

Arpeggio: A chord "broken" so that its pitches are played in quick succession rather than simultaneously *(130)*

Ars antiqua, ars nova: Contemporary terms for the "old technique" of thirteenth-century *organum* and the new *polyphonic* music of the fourteenth century *(55)*

A tempo: At the original tempo

Atonality, atonal: The absence of any feeling of *tonality (311)*

Avant-garde: In the most advanced style *(302)*

Azan: An Islamic call to worship, issued five times daily by a muezzin *(58)*

Bar: See *measure (5)*

Baritone: A type of adult male voice similar to the *bass,* but a little higher

Bar line: In musical notation, a vertical line through the staffs to mark the measure *(422)*

Bass (not spelled "base"): (1) The low adult male voice; (2) the lowest vocal or instrumental line in a piece of music

Basso continuo: See *continuo (82)*

Basso ostinato: An *ostinato* in the bass *(83, 119)*

Beam: In musical notation, the heavy stroke connecting eighth notes (two beams connect sixteenth notes, etc.) *(421)*

Beat: The regular pulse underlying most music; the lowest unit of *meter (4)*

Beat syncopation: In jazz, the fractional shifting of accents away from the beats *(386)*

Bebop: A jazz style of the 1940s *(394)*

Bel canto: A style of singing that brings out the sensuous beauty of the voice *(257)*

Bel canto opera: Term for early Romantic opera, which featured *bel canto* singing *(258)*

Big bands: The big jazz bands (10 to 20 players) of the 1930s and 1940s *(390)*

Binary form: A musical form having two different sections; **AB** form *(132)*

Biwa: A Japanese four-stringed lute; heard in *gagaku (198)*

Blues: A type of African American *vernacular music,* used in jazz, rhythm and blues, rock, and other styles of popular music *(387)*

Blues scale: A scale used in blues, jazz, and related styles that differs in several pitches from the diatonic scale customary in classical music *(348)*

Break: In jazz, a brief solo improvisation between song phrases *(386)*

Bridge: In *sonata form,* the section of music that comes between the first theme and the second group and makes the *modulation;* also called *transition (163)*

Cadence: The notes or chords (or the whole short passage) ending a section of music with a feeling of conclusiveness. The term *cadence* can be applied to phrases, sections of works, or complete works or movements *(26).*

Cadence theme: In *sonata form,* the final conclusive theme in the *exposition (164)*

Cadenza: An improvised passage for the soloist in a concerto, or sometimes in other works. Concerto cadenzas usually come near the ends of movements *(124).*

Call and response: In African and early African American music, a style in which a phrase by a leading singer or soloist is answered by a larger group or chorus, and the process is repeated again and again *(385)*

Cantata: A composition in several movements for solo voice(s), instruments, and perhaps also chorus. Depending on the text, cantatas are categorized as secular or *church cantatas (145).*

Canzona: A lively, fuguelike composition, one of several 16th- and 17th-century genres of instrumental music *(92)*

Chaconne (cha-kón): Similar to *passacaglia (119)*

Chamber music: Music played by small groups, such as a string quartet or a piano trio *(188)*

Chance music: A type of contemporary music in which certain elements, such as the order of the notes or their pitches, are not specified by the composer but are left to chance *(362)*

Chanson (shahn-sohn): French for song; a genre of French secular vocal music *(55)*

Chant: A way of reciting words to music, generally in *monophony* and generally for liturgical purposes, as in *Gregorian chant (45, 57)*

Character piece: A short Romantic piano piece that portrays a particular mood *(243)*

Choir: (1) A group of singers singing together, with more than one person singing each voice part; (2) a section of the orchestra comprising instruments of a certain type, such as the string, woodwind, or brass choir

Choral declamation: Chordal recitation by a chorus with free, speechlike rhythms *(412)*

Chorale (co-ráhl): German for hymn; also used for a four-part harmonization of a Lutheran hymn, such as Bach composed in his Cantata No. 4 and other works *(146)*

Chord: A grouping of pitches played and heard simultaneously *(28)*

Chromaticism: A musical style employing all or many of the twelve notes of the *chromatic scale* much of the time *(226)*

Chromatic scale: The set of twelve pitches represented by all the white and black notes on the piano, within one *octave (23)*

Church cantata: A *cantata* with religious words *(145)*

Clef: In musical notation, a sign at the beginning of the *staff* indicating the pitches of the lines and spaces. The main clefs are the treble (or G) clef (𝄞) and the bass (or F) clef (𝄢) *(422)*.

Climax: The high point of a melody or of a section of music *(26)*

Closing theme: Same as *cadence theme (164)*

Coda: The concluding section of a piece or a movement, after the main elements of the form have been presented. Codas are common in *sonata form (164)*.

Coloratura: An ornate style of singing, with many notes for each syllable of the text *(136)*

Compound meter: A meter in which the main beats are subdivided into three, e.g., **6/8**—*one* two three *four* five six *(5)*

Con brio: Brilliantly, with spirit

Concerto, solo concerto: A large composition for orchestra and solo instrument *(115, 183)*

Concerto grosso: The main early Baroque type of concerto, for a group of solo instruments and a small orchestra *(115)*

Concert overture: An early nineteenth-century genre resembling an opera overture—but without any following opera *(248)*

Con moto: Moving, with motion

Consonance: Intervals or chords that sound relatively stable and free of tension, as opposed to *dissonance (28)*

Continuo (basso continuo): (1) A set of chords continuously underlying the melody in a piece of Baroque music; (2) the instrument(s) playing the continuo, usually cello plus harpsichord or organ *(83, 110)*

Contralto, alto: The low female voice

Counterpoint, contrapuntal: (1) *Polyphony;* strictly speaking, the technique of writing *polyphonic* music; (2) the term *a counterpoint* is used for a melodic line that forms polyphony when played along with other lines; (3) *in counterpoint* means "forming polyphony" *(29)*

Countersubject: In a *fugue*, a subsidiary melodic line that appears regularly in *counterpoint* with the *subject (129)*

Crescendo (kreh-shén-do): Getting louder *(156)*

Cultivated music: In America, genres and styles of music that were brought from Europe and subsequently nurtured here through formal training and education *(381)*

Da capo: Literally, "from the beginning"; a direction to the performer to repeat music from the beginning of the piece up to a later point *(138)*

Da capo aria: An aria in **ABA** form, i.e., one in which the **A** section is sung *da capo* at the end *(138)*

Dance suite: See *suite (91, 132)*

Declamation: The way words are set to music, in terms of rhythm, accent, etc. *(68)*

Decrescendo (dee-kreh-shén-do): Getting softer *(12)*

Development: (1) The process of expanding themes and short motives into larger sections of music; (2) the second section of a *sonata-form* movement, which features the development process *(164)*

Diatonic scale: The set of seven pitches represented by the white notes of the piano, within one *octave (23)*

Dies irae: "Day of wrath": a section of the *Requiem Mass (253)*

Diminuendo: Getting softer *(12, 156)*

Dissonance: Intervals or chords that sound relatively tense and unstable, in opposition to *consonance (28)*

Divertimento: An 18th-century genre of light instrumental music, designed for entertainment *(153)*

Dotted note: In musical notation, a note followed by a dot has its normal duration increased by a half *(421)*

Dotted rhythm: A rhythm of long, dotted notes alternating with short ones *(421)*

Double-exposition form: A type of *sonata form* developed for use in concertos *(183)*

Downbeat: A strong or accented *beat*

Duet, duo: A composition for two singers or instrumentalists *(192)*

Duple meter: A meter consisting of one accented beat alternating with one unaccented beat: *one* two *one* two *(5)*

Duration: The length of time that a sound is heard *(4, 7)*

Dynamics: The volume of sound, the loudness or softness of a musical passage *(11)*

Eighth note: A note one-eighth the length of a whole note *(421)*

Electronic music: Music in which some or all of the sounds are produced by electronic generators or other apparatus *(360)*

Ensemble: A musical number in an opera, cantata, or oratorio that is sung by two or more people *(189)*

Episode: In a *fugue*, a passage that does not contain any complete appearances of the fugue *subject (129)*

Erhu (ár-hoo): A Chinese low-pitched fiddle; heard in Beijing opera *(299)*

Espressivo: Expressively

Estampie (ess-tom-pée): An instrumental dance of the Middle Ages *(51)*

Étude (áy-tewd): A piece of music designed to aid technical study of a particular instrument *(243)*

Exposition: (1) The first section of a *fugue (128)*; (2) the first section of a *sonata-form* movement *(163)*

Expressionism: An early twentieth-century movement in art, music, and literature in Germany and Austria *(320)*

Fermata: A hold of indefinite length on a note; the sign for such a hold in musical notation *(210)*

Festive orchestra: A brilliant-sounding Baroque orchestra with drums, trumpets, and/or French horns, used for gala occasions *(101, 109)*

Figured bass: A system of notating the *continuo* chords in Baroque music, by means of figures; sometimes also used to mean continuo *(111)*

Finale (fih-náh-lay): The last movement of a work, or the *ensemble* that concludes an act of an *opera buffa* or other opera

First theme: In *sonata form,* a *motive* or tune (or a series of them) in the *tonic* key that opens the *exposition* section *(163)*

Flag: In musical notation, a "pennant" attached to a note indicating that the length is halved (two flags indicate that it is quartered, etc.) *(421)*

Flat: In musical notation, a sign (♭) indicating that the note to which it is attached is to be played a *semitone* lower. A double flat (♭♭) is sometimes used to indicate that a note is played two semitones lower *(23)*.

Form: The "shape" of a piece of music *(35)*

Forte (fór-teh); fortissimo: Loud; very loud *(f; ff) (12)*

Fragmentation: The technique of reducing a theme to fragmentary *motives (166, 210)*

Frequency: Scientific term for the rate of sound vibration, measured in cycles per second *(10)*

Fuging tune: A simple anthem based on a hymn, with a little *counterpoint (382)*

Fugue (fewg): A composition written systematically in *imitative polyphony*, usually with a single main theme, the fugue *subject (91, 128)*

Functional harmony, functional tonality: From the Baroque period on, the system whereby all chords have a specific interrelation and function in relation to the *tonic (83)*

Gagaku (gáh-gáh-koo): A group of Japanese orchestral styles, named for the Chinese characters meaning "elegant music," which were performed in traditional court ceremonies and rituals; includes togaku (tó-gáh-koo) and komagaku (ko-má-gáh-koo) *(196)*

Gakuso: A Japanese zither with thirteen strings; heard in *gagaku (198)*

Galliard: A Renaissance court dance in *triple meter (74)*

Gamelan: A traditional Indonesian orchestra consisting of gongs, *metallophones,* and other instruments *(198)*

Gapped chorale: A setting of a *chorale* melody in which the tune is presented in phrases with "gaps" between them, during which other music continues in other voices or instruments *(146)*

Genre (jáhn-ruh): A general category of music determined partly by the number and kind of instruments or voices involved, and partly by its form, style, or purpose. "Opera," "symphonic poem," and "sonata" are examples of genres *(38)*.

Gesamtkunstwerk (geh-záhmt-kuhnst-vairk): "Total work of art"— Wagner's term for his music dramas *(266)*

Gigue (zheeg), jig: A Baroque dance in a lively *compound meter (132)*

Glissando: Sliding from one note to another on an instrument such as a trombone or violin *(318)*

Gospel music: Genre of African American choral church music, associated with the *blues (388)*

Grave (grahv): Slow *(8)*

Gregorian chant: The type of *chant* used in the early Roman Catholic Church *(45)*

Ground bass: An *ostinato* in the bass *(83, 119)*

Half note: A note half the length of a whole note *(421)*

Half step: The *interval* between any two successive notes of the *chromatic scale;* also called a *semitone (24)*

Harmonize: To provide each note of a melody with a *chord (28)*

Harmony: The simultaneous sounding of different pitches, or *chords (28)*

Heterophony: *Monophonic* texture in which subtly different versions of a single melody are presented simultaneously *(197)*

Hichiriki (hée-chee-ree-kée): A Japanese double-reed wind instrument; heard in *gagaku (197)*

Homophony, homophonic: A musical texture that involves only one melody of real interest, combined with chords or other subsidiary sounds *(29)*

Hymn: A simple religious song in several stanzas, for congregational singing in church *(61)*

Idée fixe (ee-day feex): A fixed idea, an obsession; the term used by Berlioz for a recurring theme used in all the movements of one of his program symphonies *(250)*

Imitation, imitative polyphony, imitative counterpoint: A *polyphonic* musical texture in which the various melodic lines use approximately the same themes; as opposed to *non-imitative polyphony (30)*. See also *point of imitation.*

Impressionism: A French artistic movement of the late 19th and early 20th centuries *(306)*

Interval: The difference or distance between two pitches, measured by the number of *diatonic scale* notes between them *(22)*

Introduction: An introductory passage: the "slow introduction" before the *exposition* in a symphony, etc.; in an opera, the first number after the overture

Inversion: Reading or playing a melody or a *twelve-tone series* upside down, i.e., playing all its upward intervals downward and vice versa *(129, 327)*

Isicathamiya (ees-ee-caht-ah-mée-ah): An *a cappella* song style that is part of the South African choral song tradition *(411)*

Isorhythm: In fourteenth-century music, the technique of repeating the identical rhythm for each section of a composition, while the pitches are altered *(55)*

Jazz: A major African American performance style that has influenced all twentieth-century popular music *(386)*

Jing (cheeng): A male role in *jingju*, or Beijing opera, enacting a warrior, a bandit, or a god *(298)*

Jinghu (chéeng-hoo): A Chinese high-pitched, two-stringed fiddle; heard in Beijing opera *(299)*

Jingju (chéeng-chu): The most famous variety of Chinese musical drama; meaning "theater of the capital," it is known in English as Beijing (or Peking) opera *(297)*

Jongleur (jawn-glér): A medieval secular musician *(44)*

Kabuki (kah-bóo-kee): A Japanese tradition of musical drama involving singing actors, chorus, and orchestra *(297)*

Kakko: A Japanese two-headed barrel drum; heard in *gagaku* *(197)*

Key: One of the twelve positions for the *major-* and *minor-mode* scales made possible by using all the notes of the *chromatic scale* *(32)*

Key signature: Sharps or flats placed at the beginning of the staffs to indicate the *key*, and applied throughout an entire piece, in every measure and in every octave *(423)*

K numbers: The numbers assigned to works by Mozart in the Köchel catalogue; used instead of *opus* numbers to catalogue Mozart's works *(165)*

Largo; larghetto: Very slow; somewhat less slow than largo *(8)*

Ledger lines: In music notation, short lines above or below the staff to allow for pitches that go higher or lower *(422)*

Legato (leh-gáh-toe): Playing in a smooth, connected manner; as opposed to *staccato* *(422)*

Leitmotiv (líte-moh-teef): Guiding, or leading, motive in Wagner's operas *(268)*

Lento: Very slow *(8)*

Libretto: The complete book of words for an opera, oratorio, cantata, etc. *(137)*

Lied (leed; pl. *lieder*): German for "song"; a special genre of Romantic songs with piano *(233)*

Line: Used as a term to mean a *melody*, or melodic line *(24)*

Liturgy: The system of prayers and worship of a particular religion *(45)*

Madrigal: The main secular vocal genre of the Renaissance *(72)*

Major mode: One of the modes of the *diatonic scale*, oriented around C as the *tonic*; characterized by the interval between the first and third notes containing four *semitones*, as opposed to three in the *minor mode* *(32)*

Mass: The main Roman Catholic service; or the music written for it. The musical Mass consists of five large sections: Kyrie, Gloria, Credo, Sanctus, and Agnus Dei *(63)*.

Mazurka: A Polish dance in lively *triple meter* *(229)*

Measure (bar): In music, the unit of *meter*, consisting of a principal strong beat and one or more weaker ones *(5)*

Medieval modes: See *mode* *(46)*

Mele pule (mél-eh póol-eh): Hawai'ian prayer song *(58)*

Melisma: In vocal music, a passage of many notes sung to a single syllable *(48)*

Melody: The aspect of music having to do with the succession of pitches; also applied ("a melody") to any particular succession of pitches *(24)*

Metallophone: An instrument like a xylophone, but with keys of metal, not wood *(199)*

Meter: A background of stressed and unstressed beats in a simple, regular, repeating pattern *(5)*

Metronome: A mechanical or electrical device that ticks out beats at any desired tempo *(8)*

Mezzo (mét-so): Italian for half, halfway, medium (as in *mezzo forte* or *mezzo piano*—**mf, mp**) *(12)*

Mezzo-soprano: "Halfway to soprano": a type of female voice between *contralto* and *soprano*

Miniature: A short, evocative composition for piano or for piano and voice, composed in the Romantic period *(229)*

Minimalism: A late twentieth-century style involving many repetitions of simple musical fragments *(369)*

Minnesingers: Poet-composers of the Middle Ages in Germany *(49)*

Minor mode: One of the modes of the *diatonic scale*, oriented around A as the *tonic*; characterized by the interval between the first and third notes containing three *semitones*, as opposed to four in the *major mode* *(32)*

Minstrel show: A type of variety show popular in nineteenth-century America, performed in blackface *(385)*

Minuet: (1) A popular seventeenth- and eighteenth-century dance in moderate *triple meter*; (2) a movement in a sonata, symphony, etc., based on this dance *(132, 173)*

Mode, modality: In music since the Renaissance, one of the two types of *tonality: major mode* or *minor mode*; also, in earlier times, one of several orientations of the *diatonic scale* with D, E, F, and G as tonics *(32)*

Moderato: Moderate tempo *(8)*

Modulation: Changing key within a piece *(34)*

Molto allegro: Faster than *allegro* *(8)*

Monophony, monophonic: A musical texture involving a single melodic line, as in *Gregorian chant*; as opposed to *polyphony* *(29)*

Motet: Usually a sacred vocal composition *(54, 72)*. Early motets were based on fragments of Gregorian chant.

Motive: A short fragment of melody or rhythm used in constructing a long section of music *(25)*

Movement: A self-contained section of a larger piece, such as a symphony or concerto grosso *(116)*

Musical comedy, musical: American development of *operetta,* involving American subjects and music influenced by jazz or rock *(398)*

Music drama: Wagner's name for his distinctive type of opera *(266)*

Musicology: The scholarly study of music history and literature

Music video: Video "dramatization" of a popular song, rock number, or rap number

Musique concrète (moo-zeek kohn-krét): Music composed with natural sounds recorded electronically *(360)*

Mute: A device put on or in an instrument to muffle the tone

Nationalism: A nineteenth-century movement promoting music built on national folk songs and dances, or associated with national subjects *(283)*

Natural: In musical notation, a sign (♮) indicating that a sharp or flat previously attached to a note is to be removed *(423)*

Neoclassicism: A twentieth-century movement involving a return to the style and form of older music, particularly 18th-century music *(320)*

Nocturne: "Night piece": title for Romantic *miniature* compositions for piano, etc. *(245)*

Non-imitative polyphony: A *polyphonic* musical texture in which the melodic lines are essentially different from one another; as opposed to *imitative polyphony (30)*

Non troppo: Not too much (as in *allegro non troppo,* not too fast)

Note: (1) A sound of a certain definite pitch and duration; (2) the written sign for such a sound in musical notation; (3) a key pressed with the finger on a piano or organ

Octatonic scale: An eight-note scale (used by Stravinsky and others) consisting of half and whole steps in alternation *(310)*

Octave: The *interval* between a pair of "duplicating" notes, eight notes apart in the *diatonic scale (22)*

Opera: Drama presented in music, with the characters singing instead of speaking *(83, 135)*

Opera buffa (bóo-fa): Italian comic opera *(189)*

Opera seria: A term for the serious, heroic opera of the Baroque period in Italy *(137)*

Operetta: A nineteenth-century type of light (often comic) opera, employing spoken dialogue in between musical numbers *(398)*

Opus: Work; opus numbers provide a means of cataloguing a composer's compositions *(117)*

Oratorio: Long semidramatic piece on a religious subject for soloists, chorus, and orchestra *(141)*

Orchestra: A large group of instruments playing together *(18);* it has been configured differently at different periods of Western music *(108, 156, 227);* see *festive orchestra, gagaku, gamelan*

Orchestra exposition: In Classical concerto form, the first of two *expositions,* played by the orchestra without the soloist *(184)*

Orchestration: The technique of writing for various instruments to produce an effective total orchestral sound

Organum: The earliest genre of medieval *polyphonic* music *(52)*

Ornamentation: Addition of fast notes and vocal effects (such as *trills*) to a melody, making it more florid and expressive. Ornamentation is typically improvised in the music of all cultures, and in Western music is often written out *(109).*

Ostinato: A motive, phrase, or theme repeated over and over again *(83, 94, 119, 317)*

Overtone: In acoustics, a secondary vibration in a sound-producing body, which contributes to the tone color *(12)*

Overture: An orchestral piece at the start of an opera, oratorio, etc. (but see *concert overture*)

Paraphrase: The modification and decoration of *plainchant* melodies in early Renaissance music *(60)*

Part: Used as a term for (1) a section of a piece; (2) one of the *voices* in contrapuntal music; (3) the written music for a single player in an orchestra, band, etc. (as opposed to the *score*)

Passacaglia (pah-sa-cáhl-ya): A set of variations on a short theme in the bass *(119, 322)*

Passion: A long, oratorio-like composition telling the story of Jesus' last days, according to one of the New Testament gospels

Pavan (pa-váhn): A slow, sixteenth-century court dance in *duple meter (74)*

Pentatonic scale: A five-note *scale* (familiar from folk music) playable on the black notes of a keyboard *(310)*

Phrase: A section of a melody or a tune *(26)*

Piano; pianissimo: Soft; very soft *(p; pp) (12)*

Piano trio: An instrumental group usually consisting of violin, cello, and piano; or a piece composed for this group; or the three players themselves

Pitch: The quality of "highness" or "lowness" of sound; also applied ("a pitch") to any particular pitch level, such as middle C *(10)*

Pizzicato (pit-tzih-cáh-toe): Playing a stringed instrument that is normally bowed by plucking the strings with the finger *(13)*

Plainchant, plainsong: Unaccompanied, *monophonic* music, without fixed rhythm or meter, such as *Gregorian chant (45)*

Poco: Somewhat (as in *poco adagio* or *poco forte,* somewhat slow, somewhat loud)

Point of imitation: A short passage of *imitative polyphony* based on a single theme, or on two used together *(66)*

Polonaise: A Polish court dance in a moderate *triple meter (246)*

Polyphony, polyphonic: Musical texture in which two or more melodic lines are played or sung simultaneously; as opposed to *homophony* or *monophony (29)*

Polyrhythm: The simultaneous presentation of distinct or conflicting rhythmic patterns, especially in African music *(397)*

Prelude: An introductory piece, leading to another, such as a fugue or an opera (however, Chopin's Preludes were not intended to lead to anything else) *(129)*

Premiere: The first performance ever of a piece of music, opera, etc.

Presto; prestissimo: Very fast; very fast indeed *(8)*

Program music: A piece of instrumental music associated with a story or other extramusical idea *(228, 247)*

Program symphony: A symphony with a program, as by Berlioz *(249)*

Quarter note: A note one-quarter the length of a whole note *(421)*

Quartet: A piece for four singers or players; often used to mean *string quartet*

Quintet: A piece for five singers or players

Qur'anic recitation: An Islamic tradition in which the revelations of the prophet Muhammad gathered in the Qur'an (or Koran) are chanted or sung in Arabic *(57)*

Ragtime: A style of American popular music around 1900, usually for piano, which led to *jazz (386)*

Range: Used in music to mean "pitch range," i.e., the total span from the lowest to the highest pitch in a piece, a part, or a passage

Rap: Genre of African American popular music of the 1980s and 1990s, featuring rapid recitation in rhyme *(409)*

Recapitulation: The third section of a *sonata-form* movement *(164)*

Recitative (reh-sih-ta-téev): A half-singing, half-reciting style of presenting words in opera, cantata, oratorio, etc., following speech accents and speech rhythms closely. Secco recitative is accompanied only by *continuo;* accompanied recitative is accompanied by orchestra *(84, 138)*.

Reciting tone: Especially in *chant*, the single note used for musical "recitation," with brief melodic formulas for beginning and ending *(47)*

Reed: In certain wind instruments (oboe, clarinet), a small vibrating element made of cane or metal *(15)*

Requiem Mass, Requiem: The special *Mass* celebrated when someone dies

Resolve: To proceed from *dissonant* harmony to *consonance (29)*

Rest: A momentary silence in music; in musical notation, a sign indicating a momentary silence *(421)*

Retransition: In *sonata form*, the passage leading from the end of the *development* section into the beginning of the *recapitulation (164)*

Retrograde: Reading or playing a melody or *twelve-tone series* backward *(327)*

Rhythm: The aspect of music having to do with the duration of the notes in time; also applied ("a rhythm") to any particular durational pattern *(4, 6)*

Rhythm and blues: Genre of African American music of the early 1950s, forerunner of *rock (403)*

Rhythm section: In jazz, the instrumental group used to emphasize and invigorate the meter (drums, bass, and piano)

Ritardando: Slowing down

Ritenuto: Held back in tempo

Ritornello: The orchestral material at the beginning of a concerto grosso, etc., which always returns later in the piece *(116)*

Ritornello form: A Baroque musical form based on recurrences of a *ritornello (116)*

Rock: The dominant popular-music style of the late 20th century *(402)*

Rondo: A musical form consisting of one main theme or tune alternating with other themes or sections (**ABACA, ABACABA,** etc.) *(177)*

Round: A simple type of *imitative polyphony*, with all voices entering with the same melody *(54)*

Row: Same as *series (327)*

Rubato: "Robbed" time; the free treatment of meter in performance *(227)*

Ryuteki (ree-óo-tay-kée): A Japanese side-blown flute; heard in *gagaku (197)*

Sampling: Especially in rap, the extraction, repetition, and manipulation of short excerpts from other popular songs, etc. *(360)*

Sarabande: A Baroque dance in slow *triple meter*, with a secondary accent on the second beat *(132)*

Scale: A selection of ordered pitches that provides the pitch material for music *(22)*

Scherzo (scáir-tzo): A form developed by Beethoven from the *minuet* to use for movements in larger compositions; later sometimes used alone, as by Chopin *(209)*

Score: The full musical notation for a piece involving several or many performers *(423)*

Secco recitative: See *recitative (138)*

Second group: In *sonata form*, the group of themes following the *bridge*, in the second key *(164)*

Second theme: In *sonata form*, one theme that is the most prominent among the second group of themes in the *exposition (164)*

Semitone: Same as *half step (24)*

Sequence: (1) In a melody, a series of fragments identical except for their placement at successively higher or lower pitch levels *(26)*; (2) in the Middle Ages, a type of *plainchant* in which successive phrases of text receive nearly identical melodic treatment *(48)*

Serialism, serial: The technique of composing with a *series*, generally a *twelve-tone series (310, 327)*

Series: A fixed arrangement of pitches (or rhythms) held to throughout a serial composition *(327)*

Sforzando: An especially strong accent; the mark indicating this in musical notation (**sf** or **>**) *(11)*

Sharp: In musical notation, a sign (♯) indicating that the note it precedes is to be played a *half step* higher. A double sharp (✕) is occasionally used to indicate that a note is played two semitones higher *(23)*.

Sho: A Japanese mouth reed organ with seventeen pipes; heard in *gagaku (197)*

Simple meter: A meter in which the main beats are not subdivided, or are subdivided into two, e.g., **2/4, 3/4, 4/4** *(5)*

Sixteenth note: A note one-sixteenth the length of a whole note *(421)*

Slur: In musical notation, a curved line over several notes, indicating that they are to be played smoothly, or *legato (422)*

Solo exposition: In Classical concerto form, the second of two *expositions*, played by the soloist and the orchestra *(184)*

Sonata: A chamber-music piece in several movements, typically for three main instruments plus *continuo* in the Baroque period, and for only one or two instruments since then *(181)*

Sonata form (sonata-allegro form): A form developed by the Classical composers and used in almost all the first movements of their symphonies, sonatas, etc. *(162)*

Song cycle: A group of songs connected by a general idea or story, and sometimes also by musical unifying devices *(237)*

Sonority: A general term for sound quality, either of a momentary chord, or of a whole piece or style *(61)*

Soprano: The high female (or boy's) voice

Spiritual: Religious folk song, usually among African Americans (called "Negro spiritual" in the 19th century) *(386)*

Sprechstimme: A vocal style developed by Schoenberg, in between singing and speaking *(321)*

Staccato: Played in a detached manner; as opposed to *legato (422)*

Staff (or stave): In musical notation, the group of five horizontal lines on which music is written *(422)*

Stanza: In songs or ballads, one of several similar poetic units, which are usually sung to the same tune; also called verse

Stop: An organ stop is a single set of pipes, covering the entire pitch range in a particular tone color *(20)*

Stretto: In a *fugue*, overlapping entrances of the fugue *subject* in several voices simultaneously *(129)*

String quartet: An instrumental group consisting of two violins, viola, and cello; or a piece composed for this group; or the four players themselves *(187)*

Strophic song: A song in several *stanzas*, with the same music sung for each stanza; as opposed to *through-composed song (235)*

Structure: A term often used to mean *form*

Style: The combination of qualities that makes a period of art, a composer, a group of works, or an individual work distinctive *(38)*

Subito: Suddenly (as in *subito forte* or *subito piano*, suddenly loud, suddenly soft) *(12)*

Subject: The term for the principal theme of a *fugue (128)*

Subject entries: In a *fugue*, appearances of the entire fugue *subject* after the opening *exposition (128)*

Suite: A piece consisting of a series of dances *(91, 132)*

Swing: A type of big-band jazz of the late 1930s and 1940s *(390)*

Symbolism: A late nineteenth-century movement in the arts that emphasized suggestion rather than precise reference *(306)*

Symphonic poem: A piece of orchestral *program music* in one long movement *(279)*

Symphony: A large orchestral piece in several movements *(161)*

Syncopation: The accenting of certain beats of the meter that are ordinarily unaccented *(7, 386, 397)*

Synthesizer: An electronic apparatus that generates sounds for electronic music *(21, 361)*

Tempo: The speed of music, i.e., the rate at which the accented and unaccented beats of the meter follow one another *(7)*

Tenor: The high adult male voice

Ternary form: A three-part musical form in which the last section repeats the first; **ABA** form *(175)*

Texture: The blend of the various sounds and melodic lines occurring simultaneously in a piece of music *(29)*

Thematic transformation: A variation-like procedure applied to short themes in the various sections of Romantic *symphonic poems* and other works *(232)*

Theme: The basic subject matter of a piece of music. A theme can be a phrase, a short *motive*, a full tune, etc. *(25)*

Theme and variations: A form consisting of a tune (the theme) plus a number of variations on it *(169)*

Through-composed song: A song with new music for each stanza of the poem; as opposed to *strophic song (235)*

Tie: In musical notation, a curved line joining two notes of the same pitch into a continuous sound *(421)*

Timbre (tám-br): Another term for *tone color (12)*

Time signature: In musical notation, the numbers on the staff at the beginning of a piece that indicate the meter *(422)*

Toccata: Especially in Baroque music, a written-out composition in improvisational style, generally for organ or harpsichord *(92)*

Tonality, tonal: The feeling of centrality of one note (and its chord) to a passage of music; as opposed to *atonality (31)*

Tone: A sound of a certain definite pitch and duration; same as *note*

Tone color: The sonorous quality of a particular instrument, voice, or combination of instruments or voices *(12)*

Tone poem: Same as *symphonic poem (279)*

Tonic (noun): In *tonal* music, the central-sounding note *(31)*

Transition: A passage whose function is to connect one section of a piece with another; see *bridge*

Transpose: To move a whole piece, or a section of a piece, or a *twelve-tone series*, from one pitch level to another *(327)*

Trill: Two adjacent notes played very rapidly in alternation

Trio: (1) A piece for three instruments or singers; (2) the second, or **B**, section of a *minuet* movement, *scherzo*, etc. *(132, 173)*

Trio sonata: A Baroque sonata for three main instruments plus the *continuo* chord instrument

Triple meter: Meter consisting of one accented beat alternating with two unaccented beats: *one* two three *one* two three *(5)*

Triplet: A group of three notes performed in the time normally taken by two *(422)*

Troubadours, trouvères: Aristocratic poet-musicians of the Middle Ages *(49)*

Tsuridaiko (tzóo-ree-díe-koh): A large Japanese barrel drum; heard in *gagaku (197)*

Tune: A simple, easily singable melody that is coherent and complete *(25)*

Twelve-tone row (or twelve-tone series): An ordering of all twelve notes of the *chromatic scale*, used in composing *serial* music *(327)*

Twelve-tone system: Method of composition devised by Arnold Schoenberg in which the twelve pitches of the octave are ordered and strictly manipulated *(327)*

Upbeat: A weak or unaccented beat leading to a *downbeat*

Variation form: A form in which a single melodic unit is repeated with harmonic, rhythmic, dynamic, or timbral changes *(91, 119)*

Variations: Sectional pieces in which each section repeats certain musical elements while others change around them *(91)*

Vernacular music: Music that was developed in America outside the European concert music tradition *(381)*

Vivace, vivo: Lively *(8)*

Vocables: Sung syllables that have no precise meaning, e.g., "tra-la-la" *(59)*

Voice: (1) Soprano, alto, tenor, bass; (2) a contrapuntal line—whether sung or played by instruments—in a *polyphonic* piece such as a *fugue*

Waltz: A nineteenth-century dance in *triple meter*

Whole note: The longest note in normal use, and the basis of the duration of shorter notes (half notes, quarter notes, etc.) *(421)*

Whole step, whole tone: The interval equal to two half steps (semitones) *(24)*

Whole-tone scale: A scale, used sometimes by Debussy, comprising only six notes to the octave, each a whole tone apart (i.e., two semitones) *(310)*

Word painting: Musical illustration of the meaning of a word or a short verbal phrase *(69)*

Yueqin (yuéh-chin): A Chinese lute; heard in Beijing opera *(299)*

Index

Unit I CD Contents

This free CD contains the music for the Listening Exercises in Unit I of this book, which will help you practice listening for fundamental elements of music.

1 **Scott Joplin, "Maple Leaf Rag"**
Scott Joplin, piano
Courtesy of Shout! Entertainment a division of Retropolis LLC.

2 **Sergei Rachmaninov, *Rhapsody on a Theme by Paganini* (excerpt)**
Vladimir Ashkenazy, piano; Philharmonia Orchestra; Bernard Haitink, conductor
℗1972 The Decca Music Group Limited. Courtesy of Decca Music Group Limited under license from Universal Music Enterprises.

3 **Franz Schubert, Symphony No. 8 ("Unfinished"), I (excerpt)**
San Francisco Symphony; Herbert Blomstedt, conductor
℗1992 The Decca Music Group Limited. Courtesy of Decca Music Group Limited under license from Universal Music Enterprises.

4 **George and Ira Gershwin, arranged by Nelson Riddle, "Who Cares?"**
Ella Fitzgerald with the Nelson Riddle Orchestra
Courtesy of The Verve Music Group, under license from Universal Music Enterprises.

5 **Ludwig van Beethoven, "Joy Theme" from Symphony No. 9, IV**
New York Philharmonic; Leonard Bernstein, conductor
Originally Released 1969 SONY BMG MUSIC ENTERTAINMENT.

6 **Igor Stravinsky, *Symphony of Psalms*, II (excerpt)**
London Symphony Orchestra; Michael Tilson Thomas, conductor
℗1993 SONY BMG MUSIC ENTERTAINMENT.

7 **Franz Schubert, String Quartet in A Minor, No. 13, D.804, I (excerpt)**
Tokyo String Quartet
℗1990 BMG Music.

8 **Ludwig van Beethoven, Piano Concerto No. 5 ("Emperor"), III (excerpt)**
Murray Perahia, piano; Concertgebouw Orchestra; Bernard Haitink, conductor
℗1987 SONY BMG MUSIC ENTERTAINMENT.

9 **Pyotr Ilyich Tchaikovsky, *The Nutcracker*, "Dance of the Sugar Plum Fairy"**
New York Philharmonic; Leonard Bernstein, conductor
Originally Released 1968 SONY BMG MUSIC ENTERTAINMENT.

10–15 **Benjamin Britten, *The Young Person's Guide to the Orchestra***
New York Philharmonic; Leonard Bernstein, conductor
Originally released 1961. All rights reserved by Sony Music Entertainment.